ESSAYS ON RELIGION AND HUMAN RIGHTS

This collection of seminal essays by David Little addresses the subject of human rights in relation to the historical settings in which its language was drafted and adopted. In this book, which features five original essays, Little articulates his long-standing view that fascist practices before and during World War II vivified the wrongfulness of deliberately inflicting severe pain, injury, and destruction for self-serving purposes and that the human rights corpus, developed in response, was designed to outlaw all practices of arbitrary force.

Drawing on the natural rights tradition, the book contends that, although there must be an accountable human rights standard, it should nevertheless guarantee wide latitude for the expression and practice of religious and other conscientious beliefs, consistent with outlawing arbitrary force. This book further details the theoretical grounds of the relationship between religion and human rights, and it concludes with essays on U.S. policy and the restraint of force in regard to terrorism and to cases such as Vietnam, Afghanistan, and Pakistan. With a foreword by John Kelsay, this book stands as a capstone of the work of this influential writer on religion, philosophy, and law.

David Little is a Research Fellow at the Berkley Center of Religion, Peace, and International Affairs, Georgetown University. He retired in 2009 as Professor of the Practice in Religion, Ethnicity, and International Conflict at Harvard Divinity School and as an associate at the Weatherhead Center for International Affairs at Harvard University. He was a member of the U.S. State Department Advisory Committee on Religious Freedom Abroad from 1996 to 1998.

Essays on Religion and Human Rights

GROUND TO STAND ON

DAVID LITTLE
Berkley Center of Religion, Peace, and
International Affairs, Georgetown University

CAMBRIDGE
UNIVERSITY PRESS

32 Avenue of the Americas, New York, NY 10013-2473, USA

Cambridge University Press is part of the University of Cambridge.

It furthers the University's mission by disseminating knowledge in the pursuit of education, learning, and research at the highest international levels of excellence.

www.cambridge.org
Information on this title: www.cambridge.org/9781107072626

© David Little 2015

This publication is in copyright. Subject to statutory exception and to the provisions of relevant collective licensing agreements, no reproduction of any part may take place without the written permission of Cambridge University Press.

First published 2015

A catalog record for this publication is available from the British Library.

Library of Congress Cataloging in Publication Data
Little, David, 1933–
Essays on religion and human rights : ground to stand on / David Little.
   pages   cm
Includes bibliographical references and index.
ISBN 978-1-107-07262-6 (hardback)
1. Human rights – Religious aspects.   2. Human rights – Moral and ethical aspects.   I. Title.
BL65.H78L56   2014
201'.723–dc23   2014021612

ISBN 978-1-107-07262-6 Hardback

Cambridge University Press has no responsibility for the persistence or accuracy of URLs for external or third-party Internet Web sites referred to in this publication and does not guarantee that any content on such Web sites is, or will remain, accurate or appropriate.

Contents

Acknowledgments		*page* vii
Foreword by John Kelsay		xiii
Introduction		1

PART I. IN DEFENSE OF RIGHTS

1	Ground to Stand On: A Philosophical Reappraisal of Human Rights Language	25
2	Critical Reflections on *The Last Utopia: Human Rights in History* by Samuel Moyn	57

PART II. RELIGION AND RIGHTS

3	Religion, Human Rights, and the Secular State: Clarifications and Some Islamic, Jewish, and Christian Responses	83
4	Religion, Human Rights, and Public Reason: Protecting the Freedom of Religion or Belief	112
5	Rethinking Religious Tolerance: A Human Rights Approach	143
6	A Bang or a Whimper? Assessing Some Recent Challenges to Special Protection for Religion in the United States	170
7	Religion and Human Rights: A Personal Testament	177

PART III. RELIGION AND THE HISTORY OF RIGHTS

8 Religion, Peace, and the Origins of Nationalism — 201

9 Roger Williams and the Puritan Background of the Establishment Clause — 243

PART IV. PUBLIC POLICY AND THE RESTRAINT OF FORCE

10 Terrorism, Public Emergency, and International Order: The U.S. Example, 2001–2014 — 275

11 The Role of the Academic in Times of War — 332

12 Obama and Niebuhr: Religion and American Foreign Policy — 346

Afterword: Ethics, Religion, and Human Consciousness — 363

Appendix: Ethics and Scholarship — 389

Index — 399

Acknowledgments

Because the ideas expressed in these essays have been germinating over a fairly long career and because they cover several areas of scholarship, there is an unusually large number of people to thank. In mentioning the host of people who have aided in producing this volume, I, of course, bear exclusive responsibility for whatever deficiencies and shortcomings there are.

I must begin by paying tribute to my "doktorvater," Jim Adams, who, along with other luminaries at Harvard University in the early sixties, such as Hal Berman, Talcott Parsons, Bob Bellah, and Perry Miller, introduced me to the social significance of religion and, in particular, to the critical connections between religion and law. It was thanks to Adams that I began to take seriously the ideas of natural law and natural rights, including the right to freedom of conscience, as manifested especially in sixteenth- and seventeenth-century Anglo-Saxon Puritanism.

The interest in Puritanism developed further after assuming my first teaching post at Yale Divinity School in 1963, as the result of lively encounters with David D. Hall, then a burgeoning Puritan scholar at Yale, as well as exposure to the work of Edmund S. Morgan, also at Yale at the time. David Hall and I renewed our relationship when I joined him at Harvard Divinity School in 1999, and he continues to shape my thinking about Puritanism, particularly through his important recent book, *A Reforming People*, mentioned several times in these pages.

My years at Yale Divinity School, 1963–1971, were the setting for my reflections in Chapter 11 on the Vietnam War, and I wish to commend several colleagues for their respect and thoughtful counsel during that tumultuous time even while, in most cases, they disagreed with my position on Indochina policy. They are Jim Gustafson, Sydney Ahlstrom, Julian Hartt, Bob Johnston, Chuck Forman, Bill Muehl, and Bill Coffin. It was during that period that I also began to refine my thinking about the just-war tradition, presented in Chapters 11 and 12, usually as the result of conversations and sometimes debates with one or more of them. Their arguments had a good deal to do with me eventually changing my mind on the position I had taken.

Some of the graduate students present at Yale during the 1960s would become important academics and continue to influence the thinking that lies behind the essays in this volume, namely, Gene Outka, Jock Reeder, Jim Childress, Jim Laney, and Barney Twiss. In particular, Reeder and Twiss took the trouble to read and comment insightfully on different drafts of Chapter 1 (and other of my writings), as well as to provide ongoing friendship and stimulation in countless conversations and interactions ever since. In Twiss's case, we collaborated in writing a book on comparative religious ethics. Reeder and I co-taught a seminar on rights and virtues at Harvard Divinity School in the early 2000s in which we discussed early versions of Chapter 1, and I am deeply grateful to him and the students in those classes for their challenging reactions. I owe a special debt of gratitude to one of the students, David Golumbowski, who first raised the question of why a case of necessity – causing the death of another to save one's own life – did not undermine my central argument concerning the wrongfulness of hurting others to one's advantage. We shall have to see if he and others are satisfied with my answer.

During the seventies and eighties I taught at the University of Virginia with cherished colleagues Jim Childress and Julian Hartt, and there had the pleasure of working with several graduate students who would also have a continuing influence on my thinking: Ed Santurri, James Calvin Davis, John Feldman, and John Kelsay. Santurri and I have for a long time discussed, and sometimes debated, the ethics of politics and war in a way that has been highly instructive for me. What became Chapter 12 was first delivered as a lecture at St. Olaf College where Santurri teaches. Davis explored Roger Williams very insightfully and went on to become a leading Williams scholar. Feldman wrote an important dissertation on the Puritans, Locke, and economic policy, interests he continues to develop in a most impressive way. He read and commented on several of the chapters in this book. Beginning at Virginia, Kelsay and I have worked closely together over the years. He and I, along with our colleague at the time, Abdulaziz Sachedina, collaborated on a project close to the central concerns of this volume: the idea of human rights and, especially, freedom of conscience, which we looked at comparatively between Western Christianity and Islam. That project culminated in a book on the subject, co-authored by the three of us. I wish to thank Sachedina and Kelsay for that collaboration, on the basis of which I rethought my approach to the comparative study of ethics by connecting it to the human rights movement. I am also indebted to Kelsay for his sustained counsel and friendship and for the repeated exchanges of ideas we have shared over the years. I am, of course, especially grateful for his assistance in compiling, editing, and producing this volume. Without him and his good offices, this book would not have come about. In that connection, I want to express my profoundest gratitude to James Broucek and Kirk Essary, graduate students in religion at Florida State University, for editing and readying the manuscript for publication. They have done invaluable service. During the years I taught at the University of Virginia, I spent time visiting several times at Amherst College, co-teaching with David Wills and Susan Niditch in the areas of human rights and war and peace. These were memorable occasions, and I owe a debt of gratitude to both of them for thoughtful and instructive conversations about some of the ideas in this book.

Chapter 10, on terrorism, public emergency, and the protection of rights, is the fruit of work begun when I was senior scholar at the U.S. Institute of Peace (USIP) during the 1990s. I have produced a manuscript, as yet unfinished and unpublished, on public emergencies and human rights, which provides the framework of analysis for Chapter 10 and thus can be considered (I hope) partial fulfillment of my obligation to USIP for supporting my work. I wish to thank four extremely able assistants who worked with me on various stages of the project (and on much more): Barry Seltser, Tim Sisk, Darrin McMahon, and Scott Hibbard. They have all gone on, in their various ways, to distinguished careers in academia or public service. Recently, Seltser read parts of the manuscript and made some very helpful suggestions. In particular, I am grateful to Ambassador Samuel W. Lewis, president of the USIP in my early years there and a strong supporter of the project. It was an honor and a delight to work for Sam, who died recently, and I dedicate Chapter 10 to him. I would also like to thank Sabine von Schorlemer, then of the Technical University of Dresden, Germany, for the invitation to deliver a lecture in 2006 updating my study of terrorism and public emergencies. She provided a very thoughtful response to the lecture. In addition, I wish to thank Geoffrey Stone for kindly reading part of Chapter 10 and giving me invaluable advice and counsel on it.

While I was at USIP, I also conducted an extensive study on the problem of nationalism and religion, with a focus on the role of human rights, including freedom of conscience, religion, and belief. The research and publications associated with that project lie behind Chapter 8, on religion, peace, and the origins of nationalism. The four assistants mentioned earlier were again of great assistance in organizing conferences and conducting research in regard to the project. Scott Hibbard was especially involved in that work, and therefore I owe him a special debt of gratitude. Scott and I collaborated on several publications at USIP, and I have continued to profit greatly from his own subsequent work on religious nationalism. I also want to thank the then-president of USIP, Dick Solomon, for his continuing encouragement and support.

Because the field of law and religion is so central to the concerns of this volume, a number of the chapters touch on that subject, and thus there are several experts in the field to whom I owe special thanks. Cole Durham has been a longtime friend and associate from whom I have learned much about the relation of religion to human rights. I thank him in particular for inviting me to deliver a lecture in the fall of 2013 at a conference on international law and religion at the Brigham Young University Law School, where he teaches. The event was extremely stimulating and inspired me to turn the lecture, duly revised, into Section I of the Introduction to this volume. Versions of one or another of Chapters 3–5, all on aspects of religion and human rights, have been commented on by Durham and by Jeremy Gunn, John Witte, Jr., and Abdullahi An-Naʿim to all of whom I am deeply grateful. I am also keenly thankful to Gunn for his careful editorial advice regarding Chapter 9, on Roger Williams and the Puritan background of American ideas of church and state. Witte has been a close friend and colleague for a long time, and I owe much to his writings and continuing conversations.

I especially appreciate the help of Doug Laycock regarding Chapter 6, which criticizes the positions of three authors on the role of freedom of conscience in American law. I also wish to acknowledge Tim Shah and Tom Farr of the Religious Freedom Project at the Berkley Center for Religion, Peace, and International Affairs at Georgetown University for commissioning the original essay and for the continuing stimulation and support for the study of freedom of conscience that their program provides. As to Chapter 7, which contains personal reflections on the subject of religion and human rights, I thank Azizah al-Hibri for inviting me to give the lecture in 1998 at the T. C. Williams School of Law, University of Richmond, which formed the basis for the chapter. In addition, I wish to thank her colleague, Scott Davis, for a stimulating response to the lecture (and to other writings of mine). John Norton Moore is one other legal colleague from whom I have benefited greatly over the years. Our association covers the periods at Yale, Virginia, and USIP, and for eight years, more recently, we co-taught a week-long seminar on ethics, law, and American foreign policy at the Virginia Law School, which helped me much better understand international humanitarian law and the laws of armed combat.

I need to express my gratitude to several esteemed faculty members and graduate students who were at Harvard University during the first decade of the new century when I taught there. I benefited greatly from recurring conversations on topics directly pertinent to the themes of this volume with several members of the Divinity School faculty: Fr. Bryan Hehir, Bill Hutchison, Francis Fiorenza, Don Swearer, Arthur Dyck, and Ron Thiemann. Sam Huntington and I joined together, in different combinations, with Michael Ignatieff and Jessica Stern to teach a graduate lecture course on global politics and religion, which was enormously important for my thinking in regard to the themes of this book. We instructors by no means always saw eye to eye, but the exchanges, particularly on the subjects of religion and human rights and of religion and nationalism, were memorable.

The group of graduate students whom I had the good fortune to encounter in my ten years at Harvard were all eagerly engaged in one or another of the central topics of this book. Christian Rice, Melanie Adrian, Peter Chang, and Bronwyn Roantree all touched in their doctoral projects on the subjects of natural rights, religion and human rights, or freedom of conscience, whereas David Kim focused on the Reformation background, and Atalia Omer and Tatta Yukie on religion and nationalism. Jonas Clark was of great help in drafting an early version of Chapter 10. All of them contributed greatly to sharpening my understanding of the central themes of this volume. I owe a special debt of gratitude to Atalia Omer for her thoughtful editorial suggestions in regard to Chapter 8 on religion and nationalism. I also wish to acknowledge two of her colleagues at the Kroc Institute where she now teaches: Scott Appleby and Jason Springs. They are all three a continuing source of stimulation and insight. Karen Tse, a graduate of Harvard Divinity School and my advisee, has gone on to make an inspiring contribution to the practice of human rights by founding and directing International Bridges to Justice, an organization committed to the training of public defenders and to reducing torture as an investigative technique. Buddy Karelis and Kevin Jung have both very kindly looked at several of the chapters in this book and commented on them most insightfully. They have been good friends and instructive conversation partners. David Hollinger has been a faithful and stimulating correspondent, prompting me to take up the work of Samuel Moyn and responding to earlier versions of Chapter 2 where I examine Moyn's book on the history of human rights.

Finally, I sing the praises of my long-suffering wife, Priscilla, who has endured the ardors of completing this manuscript with limitless patience and goodwill. It is a source of great encouragement to know that, although she does not wish to accompany me in every twist and turn of argument that appears in this book, she shares with me the same underlying passion and conviction that the subjects dealt with in the book are of urgent importance.

Foreword

It is a pleasure to offer these brief remarks on this collection of David Little's essays on human rights. Although the scope of Little's work over his long career makes him a contributor to a number of disparate conversations, the current volume points to interests he has been developing since the 1980s. In some ways, one might even see this work as the point on which all his earlier publications converge.

Commenting on an earlier version of this manuscript, an anonymous reviewer wrote of Little's distinctive voice. He or she suggested this distinctiveness in particular with respect to studies in Christian ethics. And it is true: David Little's way of relating the sources of Christian practical reason to contemporary issues in public life is very different from that of Stanley Hauerwas, James Gustafson, the late John Howard Yoder, or any number of other scholars one might identify with Christian ethics as a field. But then, Little's voice is also distinctive when it comes to discussions of religion and law, domestic and international politics, and the comparative study of ethics. Readers of the current volume will quickly see this. I am confident they will also appreciate the alternative that Little presents.

As an example, consider the discussion of the place of religion in the development of notions of human rights. For some, the idea that this history is a matter of marginalizing religion is regarded as a commonplace, hardly in need of examination. This is so for people at both ends of a spectrum – that is, those who judge that a gradual removal of notions of deity, invocations of scripture, or of the voices of ecclesiastical authorities from public life constitutes a positive phenomenon provide such an account. So do those who judge such removal as a matter worthy of regret. In the essays collected here, Little provides evidence that calls into question the common assumption of both groups. Referring readers to Brian Tierney's important work on the place of rights in late medieval Europe, Little then proceeds to develop a detailed and persuasive account of the role of left-leaning Protestants in the elaboration and institutionalization of the language of rights in England, the United States, and elsewhere.¹ Certainly the contributions of those to whom Little draws attention do not stand alone. The religious voice of Roger Williams, for example, must be joined to the voices of others who, if they were not entirely secular, were certainly more critics than developers of Christian or other forms of faith. Little's point is well taken, however. In the development of modern notions of human rights, religious and secular voices alike played a role. At times competitors, at other points in complementary relation, the creative interaction between religious and secular views remains important to the present-day progress of human rights, particularly in the international arena.

In one sense, the development of human rights as an aspect of international politics constitutes the greatest chapter in the history of this vocabulary. It also points to a number of very great challenges. And as it turns out, many of these are related to the question of religion. Little has always emphasized the importance of religion in matters related to legitimation. In this he follows Max Weber, who taught us that, of all the varied sorts of work for which human beings invoke religion, the most characteristic have to do with distinguishing forms of order. Whether and how a given set of social-political realities reflects "the way things ought to be" is, as a matter of historical fact, typically worked out with reference to notions we would classify as religious. In this regard, the important contributions of Little regarding the methods and purposes of comparative studies of ethics are worth noting; they set the table for his discussions of Islam and human rights in this volume and elsewhere.² In some sense, the proposal here is relatively simple and straightforward. In the historic development of the human rights idea, those left-leaning Protestants mentioned earlier focused on (1) a distinctive notion of faith as a work of God, and thus not susceptible of compulsion by human beings; (2) an account of conscience as both the arena of God's work of enabling individuals in the matter of faith and also as a personal or "private monitor" by which one evaluates courses of action one has or contemplates undertaking; and

---

[1] For Tierney's work on the medieval background, see *The Idea of Natural Rights* (Grand Rapids, MI: Wm. B. Eerdmans, 2001), as well as *Religion, Law, and the Growth of Constitutional Thought 1150–1650* (Cambridge: Cambridge University Press, 1982).

[2] Among others, see David Little, "Max Weber and the Comparative Study of Religious Ethics," *Journal of Religious Ethics* 2/2 (1974): 5–40; David Little and Sumner B. Twiss, *Comparative Religious Ethics* (San Francisco: Harper & Row, 1978); and David Little, John Kelsay, and Abdulaziz Sachedina, *Human Rights and the Conflict of Cultures* (Columbia, SC: University of South Carolina, 1988). The last most closely approximates the approach Little takes in this volume.

(3) a concept of natural law, by which all human beings know of and are accountable to a few, very basic moral notions – do not murder, do not steal, and the other directives identified with the "second table" of the Decalogue. Taken together, these notions suggested the rightness or legitimacy of a form of order in which the power of governments to enforce religious or other forms of belief should be restricted; as well, those articulating these ideas pointed to the possibility of what we would now describe as a religiously pluralistic society.

With respect to the global possibilities of human rights norms, Little begins by investigating whether or not the set of notions developed by the left-leaning Protestants might be present in other traditions – at least, by way of analogy. In the case of Islam, for example, one should consider a number of Qur'anic verses in which God instructs the Prophet regarding matters of faith. "Had your Lord willed, all the people on earth would have believed." Faith is a work of God, not of human beings. As such, "there is no compulsion in religion." Unwilling faith is an impossibility.[3]

Then, too, the Qur'an speaks frequently of the "heart" or the "self" in ways that remind one of the discourse on conscience. God is the one who "created the self [al-nafs] and inspired it with knowledge of right and wrong."[4] Such knowledge, while confirmed through revelation, is available on "reflection," that is, through the use of ordinary capacities. In particular, when the text mentions adherence to the "well known," the reference is to a set of proprieties tied to the coordination of social life. As with the notion of natural law, these properties involve prohibitions of murder, theft, and wrongful sexual activity. They also prescribe truthful speech and care for parents.[5]

On Little's count, these aspects of Islam suggest the possibility of a pro–human rights position. In this he is joined by a number of contemporary Muslim scholars, and his discussions of work by Abulaziz Sachedina and Abdullahi an Na'im have an important place in this collection of essays. Nor is Islam the only case discussed. Here, as elsewhere, Little takes up material from Judaism, Buddhism, and other traditions. In this he is able to draw usefully on material developed in slightly different ways in the various publications associated with his direction of the Project on Religion, Nationalism, and Intolerance at the United States Institute of Peace.[6]

---

[3] Qur'an 10: 99; 2: 256.
[4] Qur'an 91: 7–8.
[5] Cf., among others, Qur'an 2: 83, 110, 195, 197, 215.
[6] Cf., for example, David Little, *Sri Lanka: The Invention of Enmity* (Washington, DC: United States Institute of Peace, 1994); idem, *Ukraine: The Legacy of Intolerance* (Washington, DC: United States Institute of Peace, 1991).

Throughout these essays, Little explores the prospects for the international regime of human rights outlined in the various UN declarations and conventions produced in the aftermath of World War II. As an historical matter, these texts represent an attempt to name the wrongs done during that conflict and to promote a kind of social order by which these wrongs might be avoided. Little makes much of this. He believes one can say more, however. As he has it, agreement on the wrongs of National Socialism on the part of those drafting the Universal Declaration of Human Rights invites us to consider the possibility that the vocabulary of human rights is not only a matter of historical construction but also points to something about the nature of human beings. This leads to the argument developed in "Ground to Stand On," the essay that opens this collection. As well, various criticisms of this argument, which in some sense counts as Little's development of the historic notion of natural law, are addressed in an epilogue.

Some will be convinced by this argument regarding the foundations of human rights claims. Other readers will prefer to stay with history, and thus to focus on the many ways by which Little's essays clarify and extend the project of international human rights. I think that all will find here that distinctive voice already mentioned. Speaking as one of the many people who count David Little as teacher, colleague, and friend, I am very pleased by the publication of this book and commend the clear and passionate vision of its author.

John Kelsay
Florida State University
May 19, 2014

Introduction

The Introduction is divided into three parts. The first section constitutes, it is hoped, a perspicuous summary of the arguments regarding the justification of human rights and the relation of human rights to religion that underlie the essays in this book.[1] The second section provides some background and elucidation of key ideas. The third section provides a brief description of the relevance of the central themes introduced in the first two sections to the various essays in the book.

I

The position defended here follows from an effort to recover and rehabilitate the natural rights tradition. The idea of natural rights is taken not to depend on religious belief, though religious belief is certainly to be protected and accommodated. Rather, the idea of natural rights rests on an understanding of human nature as "rational, self-aware, and morally responsible."[2]

---

[1] A version of this summary, entitled "The Justification of Human Rights," was delivered at the Twentieth Annual Symposium on International Law and Religion, J. Reuben Clark Law School, Brigham Young University, October 7, 2013.

[2] Brian Tierney, *The Idea of Natural Rights: Studies on Natural Rights, Natural Law and Church Law, 1150–1625* (Atlanta: Scholars Press, 1997), 76. "A 'right' is an entitlement, a due liberty and power to do or not to do certain things; 'natural' means what is neither of human devising (by law or by agreement) nor conferred by a special command of God [or other supernatural warrant]. Natural rights are thus entitlements belonging to human nature as such, in virtue of the superanimal sensibilities and capacities, and therefore to every human being." T. E. Jessop, "Natural Rights," *Dictionary of Christian Ethics*, ed. by John MacQuarrie (Philadelphia: Westminster Press, 1967), 225. The phrase, "superanimal sensibilities and capabilities," is important. Given that the capacity for sentiency is common to human beings and animals, some rights, such as a right against cruelty, also apply to animals and may be claimed on their behalf. But the full range of human rights, including equal protection of rights to "freedom of conscience, religion, or belief," legal due process, freedoms of speech, assembly,

This understanding supports a primary notion of subjective rights, which means that all individuals, simply as individuals, possess an entitlement to demand (or have demanded for them) a certain performance or forbearance under threat of sanction for noncompliance. The understanding also entails certain correlative duties and obligations owed by every individual in respect to protecting the rights of others.

Though moral and legal rights may converge, they are distinguishable in regard to the character of the applicable sanction: *legal rights* are physically enforceable within a system of laws whose officials possess effective authority over a monopoly of legitimate force; *moral rights* are otherwise enforceable, for example, by verbal censure.

The range of subjective rights under consideration is focused especially on the protection of certain requirements for survival taken to be common to every human being. Among other things, natural rights protect against *arbitrary force*, which, minimally, is the infliction of death, physical impairment, severe pain/suffering, destruction of property, and involuntary confinement for entirely self-serving and/or knowingly mistaken reasons. To refer only to self-interest or knowingly to deceive in the act of inflicting death, severe pain, and so on, is "morally incomprehensible" because the reasons given are no reasons at all.[3] That is because the natural aversion to force gives everyone a very good reason to avoid or resist it, and appealing purely to self-interest as a basis for inflicting force does not even address, let alone override, such a strong reason. As an attempt at justification, such an appeal is simply irrelevant. The same is true where unfounded or mistaken reasons are offered. This is not an observation about what human beings happen to believe or not. It is an observation about what, as rational and moral agents, human beings *are able*

---

participation in government, and so on, are, of course, unique to human beings. They make sense only if there is what Locke called the capacity for "abstract rationality" or what Calvin designated the ability "to comprehend the principles of the law." As natural rights developed in the Western Christian tradition, they have been considered "minimal" or "vestigial" in that they are "left over" after "the fall," or the willful defection of human beings from divinely appointed standards of human fulfillment. Implied is that human perversity and limitation are, as it were, "baked into" the idea of natural rights. As such, natural rights provide imperatives of moral restraint and guidance that are necessary but by no means sufficient for human fulfillment.

[3] A case of "necessity," in which an innocent party is killed in order for someone else to survive, is not an exception to this statement because the reasons excusing the act must also include strong proof that there was no alternative course of action. Such a defense is based *not only* on a reference to the self-interest of the one doing the killing. It therefore does not utterly disregard the interests of the victim, as in a "pure" case of arbitrary force. Still, cases of necessity so described *are* inescapably perplexing from a moral point of view precisely because of the gravity of the prohibition against hurting others to one's advantage. As an exhibit of the unavoidable perplexity, see, for example, Hugo Grotius's somewhat tortuous discussion of the issue in *Rights of War and Peace* (Westport, CT: Hyperion Reprint, 1979), 92–94.

to believe or not, *are able* to make sense of or not. It is about the meaning of moral reason as regards the justification of action pertaining to critical aspects of human survival. Thus, the random slaughter of some twenty-six school children and teachers in Newtown, Connecticut, in December 2012, perpetrated by a gunman acting as he pleased, is necessarily regarded as an instance of "senseless violence."

On this understanding, force (as sanction) may be used in response to arbitrary force so long as it is demonstrably aimed at combating and restraining arbitrary force and does that consistent with three "rules of reason": necessity, proportionality, and effectiveness.

Accordingly, it is held that human rights language, consisting of rights regarded as both moral and legal, rests on such an understanding. Six points may help clarify this understanding of human rights language.

1. Such language was drafted and codified in direct response to a paradigmatic case of arbitrary force, namely, the record, particularly, of German fascist practices before and during World War II.
2. It enshrines a basic set of rights, referred to in Article 4 of the International Covenant on Civil and Political Rights (ICCPR) as "nonderogable" (nonabridgeable) rights, which protect everyone against the worst forms of arbitrary force: extrajudicial killing; torture, "cruel, inhuman, or degrading treatment or punishment"; enslavement; denials of certain forms of due process; and violations of freedom of conscience, religion, or belief. Protection against discrimination "solely on the ground of race, colour, sex, language, religion or social origin" is also required.[4] This list should include what are called, "atrocity crimes," as codified in the Statute of Rome, the Charter of the International Criminal Court. Genocide, crimes against humanity, war crimes, and aggression, as defined in the Charter,[5] are all egregious examples of arbitrary force. In addition, there is an important connection between human rights law and the law of armed combat or "humanitarian law," as exemplified in the Geneva Conventions of 1949 and, particularly in Article 3, common to all four conventions. That article enshrines nonderogable human rights protections against such things as "violence to life and person, murder of all kinds, mutilation, cruel treatment or torture," and so on.

---

[4] Articles 6, 7, 8.1 and 2, 11, 15, 16, and 18 explicitly identified as nonderogable, appear in Article 4.2 of the ICCPR. The prohibition against discrimination is mentioned in Article 4.1 and in the context may also be assumed to be nonderogable.

[5] Statute of Rome, Articles 5, 6, 7, and 8. The crime of aggression is not defined in the Charter, but left to further negotiation and agreement. Still, endeavoring to prohibit aggression is, at the least, an effort to outlaw "wars of conquest" that regularly exemplified self-serving uses of force.

Beyond these provisions, there is no comparable list of nonderogable rights in the International Covenant on Economic, Social, and Cultural Rights, but there are some interesting developments in that direction. In General Comment 14, the Committee on Economic, Social, and Cultural Rights has enumerated a set of "core obligations" requisite for guaranteeing Article 12 of the ICESCR, which guarantees "the right of everyone to the enjoyment of the highest attainable standard of physical and mental health," and it has ruled that "a State party cannot, under any circumstances whatsoever, justify its non-compliance with the core obligations ... which are non-derogable."[6] Failure to enforce these obligations, where feasible, would constitute *arbitrary neglect*, a close relative of arbitrary force.[7]

3. It adds a set of "derogable" rights (abridgeable under only the most extreme circumstances, such as emergencies), as, for example, freedom of speech, assembly, and participation in government, that are designed to assure maximum protection against the violation of nonderogable rights.

4. Though human rights language explicitly obligates individuals, it also obligates states,[8] meaning that states exercise force legitimately insofar

---

[6] The core obligations, which every state party is bound to comply with, are such things as "ensuring the right to access to health facilities, goods and services on a non-discriminatory basis, especially for vulnerable or marginalized groups"; "ensuring access to minimum essential food which is nutritionally adequate and safe, and to ensure freedom from hunger for everyone"; "ensuring access to basic shelter, housing, and sanitation, and an adequate supply of safe and potable water"; and "ensuring equitable distribution of all health facilities, goods and services." Committee on Economic, Social, and Cultural Rights, General Comment 14, The right to the highest standard of health (Twenty-second Session, 2000), reprinted in a compilation of General Comments and General Recommendations adopted by Human Rights Treaty Bodies, UN Doc. HRI/GEN/1/Rev/6 at 85 (2003).

[7] Although the subject of "arbitrary neglect" is referred to in a number of the essays in this volume, it is by no means developed to the degree it needs to be. The arguments worked out in Chapter 1 and elsewhere focus primarily on the "civil and political rights" aspect of human rights language. I believe, as I hint here and there, and as I think representatives of the natural rights tradition clearly held, that the same basic arguments employed in Chapter 1 can, with some adjustment, be applied to the question of economic, social, and cultural rights. However, I readily concede that those of us who advocate such arguments bear the burden of proof. It is the new thinking by the Committee on Economic, Social, and Cultural Rights in respect to the "nonderogability" of certain basic economic and social rights that has prompted me to appreciate the need to expand the arguments in this book to include more explicitly economic and social rights. To be sure, there already exist some good general studies on the subject; for example, William F. Felice, *The Global New Deal: Economic and Social Human Rights in World Politics* (New York: Rowman & Littlefield, 2003), and George Kent, *Freedom from Want: The Human Right to Adequate Food* (Washington, DC: Georgetown University Press, 2006).

[8] The Preamble of the UDHR states, "The General Assembly proclaims this [document] as a common standard of achievement for all peoples and nations, *to the end that every individual*

as they enforce human rights; otherwise, they administer force illegitimately, which is to say, arbitrarily.
5. With the development of the modern state, the technology of repression has outstripped the organs of restraint, making all the more urgent the protection of human rights.
6. Violations of nonderogable rights and prohibitions against atrocity crimes are "wrong in themselves" – "outrages," that is, against the "conscience of humankind," in the updated language of the Preamble to the Universal Declaration of Human Rights (UDHR), and they are also a severe threat to "peace in the world," as the Preamble also says.

Thus, the moral foundation of human rights language consists of "natural" rather than "extranatural" or "supernatural" assumptions concerning the absolute inviolability of prohibitions against arbitrary force. The idea of natural rights also pertains to the protection of public goods – health, safety, order, and morals[9] – that are assumed to be of common natural concern as vital requirements for human survival. The natural grounding in both cases is "secular" in the sense that it is accessible to and obligatory on all human beings, regardless of distinctions "such as religion," in the words of Article 2 of the UDHR.

Where, then, does religion come in? A key feature of arbitrary force as practiced by the German fascists was the relentless imposition by force of a specific set of beliefs on everyone under their control. That meant the systematic persecution of all religious and other forms of dissent. Such actions were a serious violation, according to a natural rights understanding, because coercion is not a justification for believing the truth or rightness of anything. When someone says, "Believe what I tell you or I'll punish you," that is a clear case of arbitrary force – of using force without justification. Expressions of belief can, of course, be curtailed by coercion, but that just begs the question whether such coercion is justified.

In human rights language, therefore, such reasoning protects "conscience, religion, or belief" against "being subject to coercion which would

---

and every organ of society, ... shall strive by teaching and education to promote respect for these rights and freedoms and by progressive measures, national and international, to secure their universal and effective recognition and observance" (italics added). Similarly, the Preambles of the ICCPR and the ICESCR state, "*Realizing* that the individual, having duties to other individuals and to the community to which [the individual] belongs, is under responsibility to strive for the promotion and observance of the rights recognized in the present Covenant, ..." *Considering* the obligations of States under the Charter of the United Nations to promote universal respect for, and observance of, human rights and freedoms" (italics in original).

[9] See Article 18.3, ICCPR. It is not clear that the term "public morals" has any determined meaning in human rights jurisprudence.

impair... freedom to adopt a religion or belief of [one's] choice" (Art. 18.2, ICCPR).

When held up alongside the "natural" justification of human rights language, the special protection of "conscience, religion, or belief" (and the practices associated with them), assured by Article 18 of the UDHR and ICCPR, introduces what I call a "two-tiered" system of justification.

The first tier lays down a "natural" (secular) justification that serves to hold people everywhere accountable to the terms of the language, backed by a provision for universally legitimate enforceability (subject to the three "rules of reason"), as well as to provide standards of protection to which everyone may appeal, regardless of religious or other identity.

The second tier permits and secures a wide, highly pluralistic range of "extranatural" justifications for human rights language and, of course, for much else related to the broad expanse of human social life and experience. Second-tier matters are irreducibly pluralistic because, among other things, they involve intimate, subjective experience in regard to social attachment, loyalty, and identity, as well as ultimate sacred commitments not readily given up. Learning to tolerate and respect without violence these inescapable differences by upholding the right to freedom of conscience, religion, or belief appears to be both "right in itself" and critical to achieving peace, as is conclusively shown in the recent book by Grim and Finke on the connection between violence and violations of religious freedom.[10]

Religious and other forms of second-tier justification are undoubtedly indispensable for mobilizing adherents to the cause of human rights. It is also clear that whether it supports or challenges human rights language, sustained attention to that language by different communities of conscience, religious or not, can help identify lacunae or blind spots in the human rights instruments; can assist in finding, where necessary, colloquially acceptable substitutes for human rights language; and can even bring about significant change, for example, in interpreting and applying religious freedom, as has happened as the result of litigation by minority religions in the United States and elsewhere.

Engagement with human rights matters in these ways illustrates the importance of the second tier in the ongoing, often complicated, and sometimes testy negotiations between the two tiers. One additional function of particular significance, performed by the second tier, is the process of appealing for conscientious exemptions from general and neutral laws permitted by human

---

[10] Brian J. Grim and Roger Finke, *The Price of Freedom Denied: Religious Persecution and Conflict in the Twenty-First Century* (New York: Cambridge University Press, 2011).

rights jurisprudence.[11] Of special note is the requirement that, in imposing restrictions on conscientious belief and practice, the state bears the burden of proof in demonstrating both that there is a compelling state interest at stake and that the restriction is as unintrusive as possible.[12] In that way tier two serves to limit the reach of tier one and to be a reminder of its obligation of special deference to tier two.

At the same time, all these second-tier undertakings are themselves constrained by the first tier, in accord with the underlying assumptions of human rights language. Tier-two justifications must yield to the inviolability of the "natural" prohibitions against arbitrary force and arbitrary neglect, as well as of the state's responsibility – "as prescribed by law" and as is "necessary" – for protecting the public goods of safety, health, order, and morals and the "fundamental rights and freedoms of others" (Art. 18.3, ICCPR).

The proposal, in sum, is that human rights language rests on a natural rights understanding that prescribes a two-tiered theory of justification. Accordingly, the first tier protects, encourages, and is limited by the second tier, but it also constrains the second tier in very important ways.

II

I started attending seriously to the subject of human rights in the 1980s, sparked initially by the election of President Ronald Reagan at the beginning of the decade. Reagan's predecessor, Jimmy Carter, together with an active cohort of members of Congress, had given human rights a central place in the conduct of U.S. foreign policy, but when Reagan came to office he made clear his strong opposition to Carter's emphasis and his determination to reconfigure radically the role of human rights in foreign affairs. At first, it appeared that his administration would ignore human rights altogether. But gradually it turned to enlisting human rights in the fight against communism, with especially controversial effects in Central America, where Reagan's policies were perceived by critics as much more attentive to the abuses of the communists than of their anticommunist opponents.

The intense and continuing debates between Carter and Reagan supporters at the time peaked my interest in human rights on the level of law and policy, as well as of theory. It was not, it seemed, simply a question of how the state and

---

[11] Human Rights Committee, General Comment No. 22, para. 11 in Tad Stahnke and Paul Martin, eds., *Religion and Human Rights: Basic Documents* (New York: Center for the Study of Human Rights, Columbia University, 1998), 94.
[12] Ibid., para. 8, 93–94.

others might interpret and apply human rights but also of how, if at all, they could be justified. That is where the idea of natural rights came in. Whatever other influences there are, human rights language is undeniably rooted in the natural rights tradition, associated as it is with Western philosophical and theological thought. The problem was that, at the time, controversies over the status of natural rights theory were as acute and seemingly intractable as the controversies over law and policy. The idea of natural rights is not the only conceivable basis for supporting human rights, but to refute it successfully removes human rights' most venerable foundation.

The idea of natural rights – that human beings "are entitled to make certain claims by virtue simply of their common humanity"[13] – has long been under assault, going back to the well-known attacks in the eighteenth and nineteenth centuries by David Hume, Jeremy Bentham, and Karl Marx. Related attacks continued into the twentieth century, gaining momentum around the time of the adoption of the UDHR by the UN General Assembly in December 1948. Anticipating that event, the American Anthropological Association, for example, submitted a widely noted statement on human rights to the UN Human Rights Commission in 1947, denouncing the very idea of universally binding moral claims, and that conclusion was supported by an influential essay on natural rights written in the same year by Margaret Macdonald.[14] Subsequently, similarly skeptical statements appeared up into the 1980s, advanced by figures such as Alasdair MacIntyre[15] and Richard Rorty.[16]

In the midst of all the controversy, I, however, remained unconvinced by the opposition to the idea of natural rights. In 1986, I published an essay on natural rights and human rights,[17] reexamining the ideas of John Locke (1632–1704) in some detail and arguing that Locke's natural rights theory did not fit the fashionable Marxist model, according to which rights talk expresses nothing more than bourgeois interests that are essentially egoistic in character. On the contrary, the whole point of natural rights for Locke was to protect everyone everywhere *against* self-serving rule, something that permitted anyone in command to "do to all his subjects whatever he pleases,

---

[13] Margaret Macdonald, "Natural Rights," in A. I. Melden, ed., *Human Rights* (Belmont, CA: Wadsworth Publishing Co., 1970), 40.
[14] Ibid.
[15] Alasdair MacIntyre, *After Virtue: A Study in Moral Theory* (Notre Dame, IN: University of Notre Dame Press, 1981), 67.
[16] Richard Rorty, *The Consequences of Pragmatism* (Minneapolis: University of Minnesota Press, 1982), xlii–xliii.
[17] David Little, "Natural Rights and Human Rights: The International Imperative," in Robert Davidoff, ed., *Natural Rights and Natural Law: The Legacy of George Mason* (Fairfax, VA: George Mason University Press, 1986), 67–122.

without the least liberty to anyone to question or control those who execute his pleasure[,] . . . and . . . whatsoever he does, whether led by reason, mistake, or passion, must be submitted to." Such an arrangement also allowed individuals to stand as judges in their own case, where "he who was so unjust as to do his brother an injury, will scarce be so just as to condemn himself for it."[18] Nor did Locke exempt economic life from these strictures: Everyone everywhere possesses "a right to the surplusage of [another's] goods . . . as will [prevent] extreme want, where [there is] no means to subsist otherwise." Moreover, no one may "justly make use of another's necessity, to force him to become his vassal, by withholding that relief God requires him to afford to the wants of his brother, than he that has more strength can seize upon a weaker [person], master him . . . , and with a dagger at his throat offer him death or slavery."[19]

Having endeavored to set the record straight, I proceeded in my article to mount a constructive case in favor of a natural rights approach. The line of argument was stimulated by a passing comment of Locke's and by some perceptive insights of Gregory Vlastos[20] and Thomas Nagel[21] about the nature of the conditions under which pain may or may not be inflicted or relieved. Commenting on the education of youth, Locke denounced the high esteem bestowed on military conquerors "who for the most part are but the great butchers of mankind." Their typical exploits, he says, tend to encourage an "unnatural cruelty," "especially the pleasure [taken] to put anything in pain that is capable of it."[22] The implication, supported by the suggestions of Vlastos and Nagel, is that giving self-serving reasons for inflicting pain or for taking advantage of someone in pain by withholding relief is the essence of cruelty, something morally unthinkable or indisputably "wrong in itself."

In this way the idea of a natural right can, I contended, be justified. The argument provides warrant for the notion of a subjective entitlement possessed by all individuals, simply as individuals, to demand (or have demanded for them) that no one of them shall be subjected to arbitrary force or arbitrary neglect under threat of sanction for noncompliance. Given that a claim of this sort is meant to be respected universally, certain correlative duties and

---

[18] John Locke, *Two Treatises of Government* (New York: New American Library, 1965), Second Treatise, ch. II, sect. 13, 316–317.
[19] Locke, ibid., First Treatise, ch. 4, sect. 42, 205–206.
[20] Gregory Vlastos, "Justice and Equality," in Richard B. Brandt, ed., *Social Justice* (Engelwood Cliffs, NJ: Prentice-Hall, Inc., 1962), esp. 51.
[21] Thomas Nagel, "Limits of Objectivity," in Sterling M. McMurrin, ed., *Tanner Lectures on Human Values* (Salt Lake City: University of Utah Press, 1980), esp. 108.
[22] James L. Axtell, *The Educational Writings of John Locke* (Cambridge: Cambridge University Press, 1968), 226–227.

obligations to respect the right are, by implication, owed by every individual to every other individual.

The right is "natural" because *any* mature, competent human being, "without [that is] distinction of any kind, such as race, colour, sex, language, religion, political or other opinion, national or social origin, property birth or other status,"[23] is expected to recognize the blatant incongruity and, hence, patent unjustifiability of inflicting pain or taking advantage of those in pain for self-serving motives, and consequently is obligated to refrain from acting in that way. Anyone reliably suspected of so acting is therefore liable to sanction – subject, of course, to the three "rules of reason": necessity, proportionality, and effectiveness. That is true whether, as Locke implies, the motives are disguised by reason[24] or are the result of a knowing or negligent mistake or simply of passion. Indeed, Locke's whole theory of government, including the design for administering legal sanctions, is grounded in this understanding. "I easily grant," he says, "that civil government is the proper remedy for the inconveniences of the state of nature" where "self-love will make men partial to themselves and to their friends, . . . and that ill-nature, passion, and revenge will carry them too far in punishing others[.]"[25] In short, the ultimate objective of government is that everyone "may be restrained from invading others' rights and from doing hurt to one another, and [that] the law of nature be observed, which wills the peace and preservation of all mankind."[26]

Around the time this article supporting natural rights appeared, I published a related essay on the Puritan dissident and founder of the Rhode Island colony, Roger Williams (1603–1683), in which I analyzed and promoted his defense of freedom of conscience and the separation of church and state.[27] I believed the effort was important not only because Williams's arguments were intrinsically appealing, as well as anticipating some of Locke's ideas, but also because Williams had, for the most part, been so badly misunderstood by those who should know better. In particular, there was (and continues to be) the widespread failure to understand the Calvinist roots of Williams's thinking, a

---

[23] UDHR, Article 2.
[24] By implication, any appeal to reason under a system in which "whatsoever [a person in command] does . . . must be submitted to" is illicit. An appeal to reason is in principle subject to correction and need not be submitted to unless it passes certain common standards of "good reasons" shared by commander and commandee.
[25] Locke, *Two Treatises of Government*, Second Treatise, ch. II, sect. 13, 316.
[26] Ibid., ch. II, sect. 7, 312.
[27] David Little, "Roger Williams and the Separation of Church and State," in James E. Wood, Jr., ed., *Religion and State: Essays in Honor of Leo Pfeffer* (Waco: Baylor University Press, 1985), 3–23.

point I introduced in the essay, but went on to develop more extensively in subsequent writings.[28]

The key idea is the distinction between the two tables of the Decalogue, or Ten Commandments, which has been the focus of a deep and abiding tension in Reformed Christianity, beginning with Calvin himself. Early in his career, Calvin taught that it was not the state's job to enforce the first table – matters of religious belief or conscience – but only the second table – moral and civic matters – whose principle is that "all individuals should preserve their rights" in regard to life, liberty, and property, or what Calvin often called natural rights. This teaching assumed a distinction between the "inward forum" or conscience that should not be subject to coercion, and the "outward forum" or affairs of state that should. Later in his career, Calvin sharply altered his position, authorizing the state to regulate the first as well as the second table.

Williams's position on freedom of conscience and church-state relations was, in large part, simply an elaboration of the early Calvin, whereas his opponents, the authorities of the Massachusetts Bay colony who expelled him, sided with the later Calvin. In defending himself, Williams provided extensive commentary on the two tables of the Decalogue, on the distinction between the jurisdictions of the "inward" and "outward" forums, and, like Calvin and other members of the Reformed tradition, on the importance of constitutional government, including protection of "natural and civil rights and liberties" that make up the "natural freedom of the people." Noteworthy was his ability to advance his views in the Rhode Island colony by successfully excluding any reference to religious privilege in the Charter of 1644 and the Civil Code 1647 and by explicitly codifying an expansive right to freedom of conscience in the Charter of 1663. His mode of discourse in defending such provisions – intermixing extensive biblical exposition with "free-standing" appeals to reason, nature, and experience – is very much in the Calvinist tradition, starting with Calvin himself.[29]

Although for Williams the idea of temporal government is divinely ordained, he leaves no doubt that the "power, might or authority" of particular governments "is not religious, Christian, etc., but natural, humane, and civil."[30]

---

[28] See Chapter 9 of this volume. The essay was originally published as David Little, "Roger Williams and the Puritan Background of the Establishment Clause," in T. Jeremy Gunn and John Witte, Jr., eds., *No Establishment of Religion: America's Original Contribution to Religious Liberty* (New York: Oxford University Press, 2012), 100–124.
[29] See David Little, "Calvin and Natural Rights," *Political Theology* 10, 3 (2009), 411–430.
[30] *The Complete Writings of Roger Williams* (New York: Russell & Russell, Inc., 1963), III, 398.

Clearly implied is a notion of "secular" or "public reason," according to which any well-ordered government should be conducted. The notion rests on "natural" rather than "extranatural" or "supernatural" assumptions concerning the protection of public goods, such as health, safety, and order, which are taken to be of universal concern as vital requirements of human survival.

It also rests on the idea that any attempt by an earthly government to regulate coercively matters of conscience or belief, except those that incite to a violation of public safety or order, constitutes an act of arbitrary or unjustified force – of "soul rape," as Williams repeatedly calls it. "The binding and rebinding of conscience [by force], contrary [to] or without its own persuasion, so weakens and defiles it that it... loseth its strength and the very nature of a common honest conscience."[31] The essence of conscience is inward consent based on a conviction of truth and right. Physical force, in and of itself, cannot produce that. Belief depends on reasons consisting of argument and evidence, and the threat of force, as in a case of robbery or rape, is not a reason in the proper sense because it lacks justification. Thus, the only "weapons" suitably employed in the inward forum are "spiritual," namely appeals and arguments subject to rational standards, whose object is consensual or heartfelt agreement. Accordingly, "forcing the conscience of any person" is action that deforms conscience by inducing hypocrisy, narrow-mindedness, or self-betrayal.

Consequently, Williams favored a broadly pluralistic society including all manner of Protestants, Catholics,[32] Jews, "Mohammedans," and "pagans" or native Americans, and even those "who turn atheistical and irreligious." By no means did he support protection only for those groups manifesting a "hyperindividualistic," strongly "protestant" religious outlook, as has been alleged. On the contrary, Williams advocated accommodating as diverse a range as possible in matters of religion and conscience, urging only that the rights and duties, benefits and burdens, of citizenship be kept scrupulously separate from such considerations. As with Locke, the overriding objective of such an arrangement is "keeping the peace." "Among those that profess the same God and Christ as Papists and Protestants, or the same Muhammed as the Turks and Persians,... civil peace would [not] be broken (notwithstanding their differences in religion) were it not for the bloody doctrine of persecution, which

---

[31] Ibid., IV, 209.
[32] Williams does flirt at one point with the acceptability of requiring the display of special insignia on members of religious groups such as the Catholics as a means of protecting national security – though he does that in the context of a discussion of reasons for trusting and respecting Catholics and, in fact, for considering some extremist Protestant sectarians as a greater threat to national security than Catholics. Ibid., IV, 313–315.

alone breaks the bonds of civil peace, and makes spiritual causes the causes of their bloody dissensions."[33]

It is true that throughout his lifetime and well into the eighteenth century, Williams's ideas had little impact outside Rhode Island.[34] However, as I argued in the article, all that changed around the time of the American Revolution and the founding of the Republic by way of Williams's influence on Locke, Isaac Backus (1724–1806), and John Leland (1754–1841). Backus was an intrepid lobbyist for religious liberty at the time of the Constitutional Convention and as such was directly influenced by Williams. He wrote an early biography of Williams and regularly cited him, even though he was not as radical as Williams. Backus sought to remove established religion such as existed in many of the colonies at the time, but he still advocated support for a form of civil religion requiring a religious test for public office. Leland, like Backus, a Baptist advocate for religious freedom, also stood in the shadow of Williams. He struck a critical bargain with James Madison, agreeing to support the Constitution if Madison would introduce a bill of rights, including a provision for freedom of conscience.[35]

Williams's influence on Locke is a more uncertain matter, although there is significant scholarly support for it,[36] and the similarities of argument in regard to natural rights, freedom of conscience, and the separation of church and state are striking. Nevertheless, whatever Williams's impact on Locke, Locke, like Backus, was not as liberal as Williams, arguing that atheists, Catholics, and Muslims should not be accorded freedom of conscience.

Since I wrote those two essays in the 1980s, the literature on natural rights, including the connection to freedom of conscience, has grown substantially, often in strong support of certain lines of argument in the tradition. Brian

---

[33] Williams, "Bloody Tenent Yet More Bloody," cited in *On Religious Liberty: Selections from the Works of Roger Williams*, James Calvin Davis, ed. (Cambridge, MA: Harvard University Press, 2008), 183.
[34] As a possible, very important exception to that statement, the expansive provision for religious freedom contained in the West New Jersey Concessions and Agreements of 1664, adopted under Quaker influence, recapitulates word for word, with some additions, the language of the Rhode Island Charter of 1663.
[35] William Lee Miller, *The First Liberty: America's Foundation in Religious Freedom* (Washington, DC: Georgetown University Press, 2003), 177.
[36] See Martha C. Nussbaum, *Liberty of Conscience: In Defense of America's Tradition of Religious Equality* (New York: Basic Books, 2008), citing confirmation from Quentin Skinner who points out that "Williams [was] a prominent part of the literature . . . with which Locke was certainly familiar." Fn. 18, 371; cf. 41; cf. Edwin Gaustad, *Liberty of Conscience: Roger Williams in America* (Grand Rapids: Eerdmans Publishing Co., 1991), 196; Miller, *First Liberty: America's Foundation in Religious Liberty*, 176.

Tierney's book, *The Idea of Natural Rights*,[37] published in 1997, revolutionized study of the topic by refuting the popular belief that natural rights represent a "deformed version of Christian ideas," glorifying egoistic individualism, as Marx claimed, and emphasizing an antireligious bias derived from the Enlightenment, as is still widely held. Rather, the idea of natural rights is to be understood as the product of a "great age of creative jurisprudence" in twelfth- and thirteenth-century medieval Europe at the hands of inventive canon lawyers and monastic theologians whose moral and legal theories "may still prove of value in our political discourse."[38] Of special importance in anticipating Locke's arguments against arbitrary force is Tierney's description of the right of self-defense – considered in the tradition as "the greatest of rights" – namely, "a natural inalienable right [inhering] in individuals and communities... that could be exercised by subjects against a tyrannical ruler."[39]

Judith Shklar's influential essay, "The Liberalism of Fear," appearing in 1989,[40] strongly reinforced the approach I was developing. Her central claim – that the critical feature of a liberal theory of government is the prevention of "arbitrary, unexpected, unnecessary, and unlicensed acts of force [including] habitual and pervasive acts of cruelty and torture performed by military, paramilitary, and police agents in any regime"[41] – eloquently rephrased and updated Locke's view that I had highlighted in my 1986 essay. The same is true of her contention that the liberalism of fear "certainly does begin with a *summum malum*, which all of us know and would avoid if only we could" – namely, the deliberate infliction of physical and emotional pain on the weak in order to satisfy the interests of the strong.[42]

Shklar did caution against too readily drawing moral conclusions from the fact that "the fear of systematic cruelty is so universal," because stating facts about beliefs does not prove they are morally right or wrong.[43] However, that difficulty is avoided, as it seemed to me, because the implication of Locke's theory is not, finally, about what human beings do believe but about what they are capable of believing; not about reporting facts but about what makes sense and about what can be believed, in taking a position on right and wrong.

---

[37] Ibid. See fn. 2, above.
[38] Ibid., 27, 42.
[39] Ibid., 314.
[40] Judith Shklar, "The Liberalism of Fear," in Nancy L. Rosenblum, ed., *Liberalism and the Moral Life* (Cambridge, MA: Harvard University Press, 1989), 21–38.
[41] Ibid., 29.
[42] Ibid.
[43] Ibid., 30.

The Realm of Rights by Judith Jarvis Thomson, published in 1990,[44] gave new energy to the philosophical defense of natural rights, arguing in a way consistent with the tradition that "there is no possible world in which an act's being an instance of 'causes a person pain' is irrelevant to the question of whether it is wrongful."[45] Going further, she advances a proposition very close to the conclusion drawn from our earlier discussion of Locke: that nontrivial necessary moral truths exist such as "one ought not torture babies to death for fun."[46]

A. John Simmons's *The Lockean Theory of Rights*,[47] appearing in 1992, goes a long way toward showing both that Locke had "a developed and consistent theory of rights" that deserves to be taken seriously and that his theory serves not only "as a viable foundation for *his* political philosophy" but also "may serve as a viable foundation for *ours*."[48] Simmons convincingly shores up the proposition that, alongside a distinctly theocentric grounding of Locke's philosophy, there exists an self-standing "secular strain" of thought, summarized by Locke's reference to a "law of nature" "which obliges everyone" and "reason which is that law," teaching that human beings "are not made for one another's uses."[49]

John Witte's book, *The Reformation of Rights: Law, Religion, and Human Rights in Early Modern Calvinism* (2007), illuminates the way the Calvinist tradition carried forward the natural rights narrative, more or less picking up where Tierney left off. More than Tierney, Witte also shows the relevance of the natural rights tradition to questions of freedom of conscience and religious pluralism, both the more restrictive approach of the later Calvin, as well as of Theodore Beza and Johannes Althusius, and the more inclusive approach of John Milton, a friend and ally, personally and intellectually, of Roger Williams.

Martha Nussbaum's impressive study, *Liberty of Conscience: In Defense of America's Tradition of Religious Equality* (2008), compellingly commends

---

[44] Judith Jarvis Thomson, *The Realm of Rights* (Cambridge, MA: Harvard University Press, 1990).
[45] Ibid., 15.
[46] Ibid., 18–19.
[47] A. John Simmons, *A Lockean Theory of Rights* (Princeton, NJ: Princeton University Press, 1992).
[48] Ibid., 353–354.
[49] Ibid., 36–46. The reference is to Locke, *Two Treatises of Government*, Second Treatise, ch. II, sect. 6, 311. If one agrees with Simmons, section 6 exhibits the two sorts of appeal – the theocentric and the secular rational – side by side. It is unfortunate that Jeremy Waldron, in *God, Locke, and Equality: Christian Foundations of Locke's Political Thought* (Cambridge: University of Cambridge Press, 2002), arguing in favor of an exclusively theocentric basis of Locke's thought, does not mention or treat Simmons's claims. They raise serious questions about Waldron's case.

Williams for his distinctive contribution to guaranteeing equal freedom of conscience in the American experience. To her credit, she correctly emphasizes Williams's appeals to natural or "secular" reason, which are certainly there. Unfortunately, she ignores the importance of his supplementary appeals to scripture and doctrine, as well as the central place in his thought of natural rights thinking, impressed on him by the Calvinist tradition in which he stood. Her failure to appreciate the role of natural rights is especially surprising because she highlighted it in an earlier book[50] and has proceeded, revisionistically, to be sure, to appropriate it in developing her "capabilities" approach to social reform and development.

But most important in the effort to bring natural rights and human rights together – my overall objective in the 1986 article – was a book published in 1999 by Johannes Morsink, *The Universal Declaration of Human Rights: Origins, Drafting, and Intent*.[51] Morsink indicates that, at the very start of the process of drafting the UDHR, one delegation proposed to begin the document with the following words, "Recognizing that the United Nations has been established for the specific purpose of enthroning the natural rights of man."[52]

Although this wording was not adopted, Morsink thinks it supports the presumption that there is "some kind of connection" between "natural rights philosophies," which Morsink identifies with the Enlightenment, and the language adopted in the UDHR. It is not that the drafters self-consciously and intentionally attempted to enshrine natural rights theory. For the most part, they were not interested in philosophical questions, and they wanted to minimize as much as possible what they took to be loaded terms.[53] Rather, they shared, usually unreflectively, three critical assumptions with the natural rights tradition.

One essential assumption was that "by nature" everyone everywhere possesses an "inalienable" set of moral rights that are independent of and prior to any legal rights temporal governments may bestow, thereby constituting a standard for judging the conduct of government, and especially the administration of force.[54] The drafters resolutely rejected the heart of fascism: absolute subjection of the individual to the collective good defined by the state. In

---

[50] Martha C. Nussbaum, *Frontiers of Justice: Disability, Nationality, and Species Membership* (Cambridge, MA: Harvard University Press, 2006), ch. 1.
[51] Johannes Morsink, *The Universal Declaration of Human Rights: Origins, Drafting, and Intent* (Philadelphia: University of Pennsylvania Press, 1999).
[52] Ibid., cited at 282.
[53] Ibid., 294.
[54] Ibid., 295.

the words of the Chilean delegate, the UDHR is based on the belief that "the state should not be allowed to deprive the individual of . . . dignity and . . . basic rights."[55] This point is memorably inscribed in the drafting process. At first, the delegates from the eight communist countries tried aggressively to modify that proposition beyond recognition in the interest of preserving as much governmental discretion as possible. However, in the end they effectively acquiesced to it by abstaining, rather than directly opposing the final document and its central message. They did so, apparently, to be able to hold the Nazis to account.[56]

Another assumption was the expectation of standard moral reactions to events of a certain kind. Drafters heartily endorsed the language of the Preamble, "Whereas disregard and contempt for human rights have resulted in barbarous acts which have outraged the conscience of mankind," because they all shared the view that any other way of assessing the practices of the Nazis before and during World War II was unthinkable. More than anything else, it was their common "outrage," prompted by the "horrors of the war," and dramatized particularly by the Holocaust, that energized and guided the drafting of the UDHR.[57] In his careful analysis of some of the articles of the UDHR, Morsink shows how the final wording was consciously and specifically formulated in reaction to what were considered egregious violations in regard to taking life, inflicting pain and suffering, enslaving, and so on.[58] Morsink states that one reason the drafters did not draw on "Enlightenment precedents" is that they "had no need of examples from the Enlightenment . . . The horrors of World War II gave them all . . . they needed to be justified" in producing the UDHR.[59]

Part of the underlying expectation in face of the "outrages" under consideration was an assumption concerning the twofold foundation of rights language. In the first place, "the drafters surely thought that proclaiming [the] Declaration would serve the cause of world peace," a sentiment strictly in line with the thinking of Williams and Locke. However, Morsink continues, "they did not think of the human rights they proclaimed as only or merely a means to that end." They also thought "these rights have an independent grounding [for] the members of the human family to whom they belong and who possess them as birthrights. If this were not so, a government could torture people

---

[55] Cited at ibid., 38.
[56] Ibid., 23–24.
[57] Ibid., 27, 91, 300.
[58] Ibid., ch. 2.
[59] Ibid., 320.

(or violate any other right) as long as it was thought to serve the cause of peace."[60]

Morsink does not call attention to a third assumption concerning a connection between natural rights and human rights relating to the question of freedom of conscience, but such a connection would be hard to miss in light of what he says about the understanding underlying the provisions in the UDHR: "There is no presumption in the Declaration that the morality of human rights requires any kind of religious foundation.... [T]he drafters went out of their way to avoid having the Declaration make a reference to God or to man's divine origin.... [I]t gives everyone total freedom of religion, including the right not to have one."[61]

As indispensable as Morsink's discussion is for connecting natural rights and human rights, it is seriously deficient in that he unduly limits the natural rights tradition to the Enlightenment. Thanks to Tierney, we now know how mistaken that view is, as are beliefs that natural rights are to be understood as invariably egoistic and antireligious.

Morsink also causes confusion when he states that the drafters paid no heed to natural rights thinking because all they needed was their impression of "the horrors of World War II" to feel justified in producing the UDHR. The point is that the drafters' reaction to the horrors of World War II was a prime example of natural rights thinking. The practices designed and implemented by Hitler and the German Nazi regime exemplified paradigmatically "disregard and contempt" for the fundamental moral prohibitions aimed at punishing and preventing arbitrary force (and its relative, arbitrary neglect). Those prohibitions underlie all three of the common assumptions just laid out connecting natural rights and human rights: the priority of moral rights over legal rights; the expectation of standard moral reactions to events of a certain kind, including fundamental convictions about promoting world peace and about the violation of basic rights as "wrong in itself"; and the "natural" (secular) grounding of basic rights.

In keeping with this summary of a proposed way of justifying human rights and the relation of human rights to religion, I have argued that a common theme of great importance brings the natural rights tradition and human rights language together. That is a fundamental commitment to a set of moral and legal rights designed to combat and restrain arbitrary force (and arbitrary neglect), whether manifested as inflicting death, suffering, or pain; or failing to prevent or relieve them for purely self-serving or misleading reasons; or

---

[60] Ibid., 320.
[61] Ibid., 263.

coercively regulating expressions of conscience, religion, or belief that pose no threat to public order, safety, or health. In regard to the subject of religion and human rights, I hope, in short, to have provided some firm "ground to stand on."

III

The chapters of this volume are divided into four parts, each one of which expands in different ways on the themes identified earlier.[62] The first part, "In Defense of Rights," consists of two chapters that, respectively, develop and defend the theory of human rights language and the reconstructed account of natural rights that lies behind it, as sketched out in Sections I and II of this Introduction. The first chapter, "Ground to Stand On," elaborates the basic argument of the book, followed in Chapter 2 by a critical examination of what amounts to a wholesale rejection of that argument – in respect both to human rights and natural rights – by historian Samuel Moyn in his influential book, *The Last Utopia: Human Rights in History*.

The second part, "Religion and Rights," contains five chapters designed to spell out in greater detail the two-tier theory of justification introduced in Sections I and II. This is done in Chapter 3, "Religion, Human Rights, and the Secular State," by a critical examination and comparison of the thought of the Muslim legal scholar, Abdullah An-Na'im, and of Talal Asad, an influential anthropologist specializing in the comparative study of Middle Eastern and Western culture. Chapter 4, "Religion, Human Rights, and Public Reason: Protecting the Freedom of Religion or Belief," responds to the call at the end of Chapter 3 for more detailed legal analysis of the way the two tiers interact by taking up decisions and judgments by the European Court of Human Rights, as well as by quasi-legal bodies such as the Human Rights Committee and the Special Rapporteur on Religious Freedom. In the process, John Rawls's idea of "public reason" is reconstructed for better effect, and some criticisms of the present drift of human rights law made by legal scholar, Malcolm Evans, are assessed. Chapter 5, "Rethinking Tolerance: A Human Rights Approach," is an attempt to clarify the ill-defined meaning of "tolerance" in the human rights instruments by means both of textual and linguistic analysis and a consideration of proposals for clarification by scholars from different religious

---

[62] Four of the thirteen essays in this volume (counting the Afterword) have been published elsewhere: Chapters 5, 7, 8, and 9. Versions of two others have been published elsewhere, though they have all been substantially reworked: Chapters 3 and 10. Part of Chapter 4 has been published elsewhere as part of another essay.

traditions. Chapter 6, "A Bang or a Whimper: Assessing Some Recent Challenges to Religious Freedom in the United States," examines critically certain purported attacks on conventional American ideas of freedom of religion by the legal scholars Winifred Sullivan, Marci Hamilton, and Brian Leiter, on the assumption that controversies over religious freedom within the United States are of comparative interest, at least to the broader international discussion. Chapter 7, "Religion and Human Rights: A Personal Testament," is an autobiographical and apologetic statement of my way of connecting the study of religion and human rights to personal conviction.

The third part, "Religion and the History of Rights," contains two chapters that address the development of constitutionalism and natural rights in Western Europe and colonial America as important antecedents to modern human rights language. Chapter 8, "Religion, Peace, and the Origins of Nationalism," sets the discussion in the context of current debates concerning the meaning of nationalism, its beginnings, and its relation to the conditions of national and international peace. Chapter 9, "Roger Williams and the Puritan Background of the Establishment Clause," examines Williams's contribution to the rise of modern constitutionalism and natural rights, again on the assumption that the American experience is of comparative interest (at least) to understanding the background of natural rights thinking.

The fourth part, "Public Policy and the Restraint of Force," contains three chapters addressed to questions involving limits on the international use of force – questions of importance for the subject of religion and the enforcement of rights. Inhibiting arbitrary force is of central and consistent concern. Chapter 10, "Terrorism, Public Emergency, and the International Order: The U.S. Example, 2001–2014," describes and evaluates the responses of the administrations of George W. Bush and Barack Obama to the threat of international terrorism in regard to the degree of their compliance with international norms. The analysis concentrates on the success or failure of efforts to enforce human rights in reaction to acts of terror justified religiously by al Quaeda and others. I regret that I did not have the time necessary to develop my thoughts on the Obama administration's decision in September 2014 to use military force against the advances of the Islamic State in northern Iraq and Syria. My tentative conclusion to date is that the case is very complicated, morally and legally. Chapter 11, "The Role of Academic in Times of War," continues the examination of just-war thinking, this time as a point of reference for evaluating U.S. policies in Indochina in the 1960s and early 1970s. My own changes of mind and heart in that regard are a particular focus of attention. Chapter 12, "Obama and Niebuhr: Religion and American Foreign Policy," analyzes the points of agreement and disagreement between President Obama and an avowed influence, the Protestant theologian Reinhold Niebuhr, attending in particular to the place of just-war thinking as a guide to the licit use of force in Obama's policies in Afghanistan and Pakistan. The role of religion in policy making is of special interest.

Finally, the subject of the Afterword, "Ethics, Religion, and Human Consciousness: Further Reflections on a "'Two-Tiered' Approach to Justification," was prompted by some comments of John Kelsay, author of the Foreword and a wise counselor in the creation of this volume. He suggested that the essays by themselves lack an explicit, sufficiently systematic, account of how religious justifications might go together with the philosophical underpinnings of the whole enterprise. I attempt a response to Kelsay's challenge in this closing essay, drawing particularly on recent work in the philosophy of mind, which, it is argued, complements and illuminates the underlying arguments of the book.

In the Appendix, "Ethics and Scholarship," I elaborate on some of the themes taken up in Chapter 11 and in the Afterword.

PART I

In Defense of Rights

1

Ground to Stand On

A Philosophical Reappraisal of Human Rights Language*

HUMAN RIGHTS LANGUAGE AND ITS DISCONTENTS

Too frequently modern philosophers, theologians, and scholars have failed to think carefully about the "human rights revolution" that occurred after World War II in reaction to German, Japanese, and other versions of fascism. That revolution, marked by the adoption of the Universal Declaration of Human Rights (UDHR) on December 10, 1948, represented not only extensive international political and legal transformation but also something of enormous philosophical importance. The best way to honor that importance, more than six decades later, is by subjecting human rights language to the critical reflection it deserves.

The major reason for the failure is that philosophers, theologians, and scholars have not grasped or directly confronted the central purposes of human rights language or the basis on which the drafters of the UDHR believed that language to rest. Its central purposes are to hold people everywhere accountable to the terms of that language, backed by a provision for universally legitimate enforceability, and to provide standards of protection to which everyone may appeal. The basis invoked in the Preamble to the UDHR is unapologetically universalistic. It is something called the "conscience of mankind" which was assumed to have been "outraged" by the "barbarous acts" committed across the globe before and during World War II.

---

* I would like to express my appreciation to the students in successive seminars on "Rights and Virtues" and to Professor John R. Reeder with whom I co-taught the seminar at Harvard Divinity School during the spring and fall semesters of 2008. The discussions were highly challenging and illuminating and helped me clarify my arguments in this essay. I appreciate, too, the responses of Charles Karelis, Kevin Jung, David Golumbowski, John Kelsay, John Reeder, and Sumner Twiss.

Rather than considering seriously the provenance, character, and underlying rationale of human rights language, philosophers, theologians, and scholars have been distracted too often by at least five questionable lines of argument:[1]

(1) Some have argued that it is impossible to provide a universal philosophical justification for human rights language, whether on the basis of presumably vague notions such as the "conscience of mankind" or, for that matter, on any basis. While accepting the impossibility of a universal justification, adherents divide over the importance of this conclusion. Some are inclined to set aside human rights language altogether; others believe most of its benefits can be preserved on a more modest basis.

As examples of the dismissive view, we may begin with Alasdair MacIntyre's familiar words: "[T]he truth is plain: there are no such rights [as human rights], and the belief in them is one with belief in witches and unicorns.... Human rights are fictions."[2] Stanley Hauerwas is similarly disparaging: "America is the only country that has the misfortune of being founded on a philosophical mistake – namely, the notion of inalienable rights [something human rights are claimed to be]. Christians do not believe that we have inalienable rights."[3] Nor can we forget the late Richard Rorty's resounding challenge: The urge to find "some universal common truth in morality or anything else," is an "urge," wrote Rorty, "that should be repressed." Despite the contrary claims

[1] By no means have all philosophers failed to attend to or to support human rights language in a thoughtful way. See, for example, Alan Gewirth, *Human Rights: Essays on Justification and Application* (Chicago: University of Chicago Press, 1982); James W. Nickel, *Making Sense of Human Rights: Philosophical Reflections on the Universal Declaration of Human Rights* (Berkeley: University of California Press, 1987); and Carlos Santiago Nino, *The Ethics of Human Rights* (Oxford: Clarendon Press, 1991). Although these are all perceptive and significant contributions to the philosophy of human rights, none of them addresses the subject as I do in this chapter. For that reason, I do not find their arguments persuasive, as I have indicated in other publications. The position developed in what follows clearly distinguishes me from the approaches of figures such as these.
  Three authors with whom I am in deep sympathy and who have influenced my thinking are Judith Jarvis Thomson, *The Realm of Rights* (Cambridge, MA: Harvard University Press, 1990), along with other writings of hers; Christian Rice, "For the Common Moral Benefit: Thinking through the Conditions Necessary to Secure the Moral Priority and Fixity of Individual Rights" (Th.D. thesis, Harvard University, 2008); and Sumner B. Twiss, especially his excellent essay, "Torture, Justification, and Human Rights: Toward an Absolute Proscription," *Human Rights Quarterly* 29, 2 (May 2007), 346–367. It is not the first time that Twiss's outlook and mine have converged in an important way.
[2] Alasdaire MacIntyre, *After Virtue: A Study in Moral Theory* (South Bend, IN: Notre Dame Press, 1981), 67.
[3] Stanley Hauerwas, *Hauerwas Reader*, eds. John Berkman and Michael Cartwright (Durham, NC: Duke University Press, 2005), 608.

of human rights advocates, we cannot, he said, accuse torturers of violating some inherent standard of proper action because for Rorty no such standard exists.[4]

More recently, members of a group of scholars from anthropology, international relations, and law – identifying themselves by their blog, "The Immanent Frame"[5] – have been following their mentor, Talal Asad, in their disdain for "liberal rights discourse," as they call it. For Asad, human rights language not only does not represent a transnational system of moral and legal accountability but, in reality, constitutes little more than a self-serving cover for ulterior national interests, particularly on the part of dominant countries such as the United States. Human rights are, he says, but "floating signifiers that can be attached to or detached from various subjects and classes constituted by the market principle and by the most powerful nation-states."[6]

Peter Danchin, a legal scholar and member of the group, takes a similar position.[7] Danchin's thesis is that the standard liberal attempt to discover "a convincing argument or theoretical basis" for certain "fundamental" or "basic" human rights is impossible, since any such claim is historically contingent and invariably partial.[8] It fails to understand the "indeterminacy of rights discourse,"[9] which is, in reality, a "non-foundational, and hence perpetually self-(re)creating, attempt to find an overlapping consensus on a plurality of equally ultimate, equally sacred – but intrinsically incommensurable – values."[10] In fact, any attempt "to seek to posit an objective foundation for rights... risks only catastrophe – the possibility of a single, ruthless, and

---

[4] Richard Rorty, *Consequences of Pragmatism* (Minneapolis: University of Minnesota Press, 1982), xlii–xliii.
[5] The group consists of Peter Danchin, Elizabeth Shakeman Hurd, Saba Mahmood, and Winifred Sullivan, whose blog is dedicated to criticizing various aspects of the "liberal hegemony," in a phrase of Sullivan's. They all exhibit, often explicitly, the influence of Talal Asad, who has made a career of "problematizing" the liberal interpretation of human rights language. See, for example, *Formations of the Secular: Christianity, Islam, and Modernity* (Stanford: Stanford University Press, 2003). Chapter 3 of this volume contains, in part, an extended critique of Asad's criticisms of human rights language. See Chapter 6 for a critique of Sullivan's book, *The Impossibility of Religious Freedom*.
[6] Asad, *Formations of the Secular*, 158.
[7] Peter Danchin, "Of Prophets and Proselytes: Freedom of Religion and the Conflict of Rights in International Law," *Harvard International Law Journal* 49, 2 (Summer 2008), 316. Cf. Danchin, "Who is the 'Human' in Human Rights? Claims of Culture and Religion," *Maryland Journal of International Law* 24, 94 (2009).
[8] Danchin, "Of Prophets and Proselytes," 316.
[9] Ibid.
[10] Ibid., 313.

fanatically pursued 'final solution' on the one hand; the possibility of a blind, obscurantist irrationalism, on the other."[11]

Although Jeffrey Stout is less grandly dismissive in believing that the benefits of human rights language may be retained without depending on universalistic philosophical claims, he is no less skeptical of the ideas of "inherence" and "inalienability" that are constitutive of human rights language. He refers to rights conceived of in the "usual, highly theoretical, metaphysical way" as "just-so stories."[12]

(2) Historian Samuel Moyn attempts to provide a radical deconstruction, if not total demolition, of human rights language in his book, *The Last Utopia: Human Rights in History*.[13] His argument is that such language is essentially utopian or illusory in that it has no integrity or practical significance of its own. It is the language of visions and dreams. It was formulated without regard to the real-world atrocities of the World War II period and, contrary to widespread assumptions, is not part of a long-standing lineage of ideas. Mainly because of its indeterminacy and impotence, it was essentially ignored throughout the 1950s and 1960s and did not gain currency until the middle 1970s, after another and very different utopian idiom – anticolonialism – had exhausted itself. As a matter of fact, the present understanding of human rights language – as a universal system of moral and legal protection of basic individual rights – was not invented until then, and that understanding, on Moyn's account, is itself no less "utopian," no less unrealistic, for promoting standards that have no chance of being realized.

(3) Others believe the "rights" part of human rights language to be inadequate and claim that the important assurances enshrined in the UDHR and other instruments can be better justified in another way. An example is the work of Martha Nussbaum. Even though she is far more sympathetic to "rights talk" than most of the dissenters already mentioned, she too displays important reservations at critical points. In *Frontiers of Justice*, Nussbaum does express appreciation for human rights theories – associated, for example, with Hugo Grotius – as an antidote to the lack of due provision for the disabled

---

[11] Ibid., 317. Because, to an important extent, Danchin's view overlaps with Asad's, the criticisms of Asad in Chapter 3 also apply to Danchin. Apart from that, the arguments developed in subsequent portions of this chapter are intended to refute claims such as Danchin's regarding the impossibility of providing "a convincing argument or theoretical basis for certain 'fundamental' or 'basic' human rights."
[12] Jeffrey Stout, *Democracy and Tradition* (Princeton, NJ: Princeton University Press, 2004), 204ff.
[13] Samuel Moyn, *The Last Utopia: Human Rights in History* (Cambridge, MA: Harvard University Press, 2010). See Chapter 2 of this volume for an extended critique of Moyn's arguments.

and vulnerable that she convincingly argues is the consequence of Rawlsian contractualism.[14] Nevertheless, when all is said and done, she too casts aspersions on rights language as vague and confusing, having been the subject of conflicting interpretations and "deep philosophical disagreement."[15] For these reasons she famously prefers the language of "capabilities," although without, in my view, entirely coming clear on the ambiguities surrounding her use of that language.[16]

(4) Some commentators have maintained that philosophical reflection on human rights language is unimportant. One example, going back to 1946, is that of the earliest reactions to human rights language by a UNESCO committee made up of "many of the leading thinkers of the day."[17] Having assembled a remarkably uniform list of basic human rights solicited from leaders in government, religion, philosophy, and scholarship around the world, the committee emphasized that agreement extended *only* to the list of rights and *not* to the grounds on which they are justified. In a famous comment, Jacques Maritain, a member of the committee, remarked, "We agree about the rights on the condition no one asks us why."[18] Whether intended or not, this sentiment is commonly interpreted to mean that the justification of human rights is a secondary question in the sense that support for human rights rests on a coincidental consensus regarding "what" human rights are, not "why" we affirm them, and that such consensus is the most we can or ought to hope for.

---

[14] Martha Nussbaum, *Frontiers of Justice: Disability, Nationality, and Species Membership* (Cambridge, MA: Belknap Press, 2006), 19–20; 29ff.

[15] Ibid., 284–5.

[16] I have two main objections to Nussbaum's position. First, to show that language (such as rights language) is abused or subject to controversy does not invalidate that language; it simply calls for correction and for a defense of proper usage. Second, rights language is "ought" language, whereas capabilities language is "can" language. Given that "ought implies can" and that "can does *not* imply ought," rights (or entitlement) language is logically prior. On occasion, Nussbaum appreciates this point, but, in my view, does not see it through: "To say people have a right to something is to say that they have an urgent entitlement to it. The idea of capability all on its own does not yet express the idea of an urgent entitlement based on justice. However, the capabilities approach makes this idea of a fundamental entitlement clear, by arguing that the central human capabilities are not simply desirable social goals, but urgent entitlements of justice" (*Frontiers of Justice*, 290). She seems here to be admitting that "capabilities" in her sense do, after all, *presuppose* a notion of right, namely, "an urgent entitlement," and thus, by implication, will require an independent defense of rights language.

[17] Mary Ann Glendon, *A World Made New: Eleanor Roosevelt and the Universal Declaration of Human Rights* (New York: Random House, 2001), 57.

[18] Cited at ibid., 77.

An array of human rights advocates, some legal scholars, some not, provide other examples. Paul Sieghart, in a definitive legal study, remarks that if there was ever a need to worry about the philosophical or theological grounds of human rights, those days are over, because all we need to do now is to "refer to the rules of international human rights law as defined in the relevant instruments which have been brought into existence since 1945."[19] Political scientist Jack Donnelly argues that we may be satisfied with a purely "analytic or descriptive" theory of human rights, rather than a "normative or prescriptive" one because "there is [now] a remarkable international consensus on the list of rights."[20] And Michael Ignatieff recommends that we seriously scale back our expectations. The idiom of human rights is not intended to serve, he says, as "an ultimate trump card in moral argument" or "for the proclamation and enactment of eternal verities." It is rather "a discourse for the adjudication of conflict," a much more prosaic, down-to-earth language of political "trade-offs and compromises."[21]

(5) Some theologians believe that secular justifications of human rights language are insufficient and so argue that one or another religious justification is necessary. They take the fact that the UDHR and subsequent documents exclude religious warrants as a basis for justification as a serious shortcoming. One example of that reaction is *Justice: Rights and Wrongs*, by Nicholas Wolterstorff.[22] In supporting the moral potency of rights language in general and of human rights language in particular, Wolterstorff advances a theological argument as the only satisfactory justification for "inherent rights," as he calls them.[23] He contends that rights language, including human rights, assures vital protection against arbitrary abuse, resting on a conviction of the irreducible, equal worth of every human being. Secular theories, such as those of Ronald Dworkin,[24] Alan Gewirth,[25] or John Rawls,[26] do not succeed in grounding the idea of equal inherent human worth nor is there much likelihood, in his opinion, that other such theories can ever do so. The only defensible alternative, on his view, is a theistic conviction, namely, that the God of Hebrew and Christian Scriptures "bestows worth" on all human beings

---

[19] Paul Sieghart, *The International Law of Human Rights* (Oxford: Clarendon Press, 1983), 15.
[20] Jack Donnelly, *Universal Human Rights in Theory and Practice* (Ithaca, NY: Cornell University Press, 1989), 21–23.
[21] Michael Ignatieff, *Human Rights as Politics and Idolatry* (Princeton, NJ: Princeton University Press, 2001), 20, 84.
[22] (Princeton, NJ: Princeton University Press, 2008).
[23] Wolterstorff, *Justice: Rights and Wrongs*, chs. 13, 14, and 15.
[24] Ibid., 333–334.
[25] Ibid., 335–340.
[26] Ibid., 15–17.

"equally and permanently."[27] Michael Perry provides another version of a religious argument for the justification of human rights.[28] This claim is that key human rights terms such as "the inherent dignity" of "all members of the human family" necessarily presuppose a religious or sacred ground and therefore that "the idea of human rights is ineliminably religious."[29] Although Perry does not share Wolterstorff's belief in one preferred theological position, he does agree that "there is, finally, no intelligible secular version of... human rights."[30] Accordingly, determining the grounds of human rights "is, finally [and unavoidably], a theological project."[31]

David Novak takes a comparable position from the perspective of Judaism.[32] Concentrating on "the question of the religious foundation of human rights," Novak claims that "the task of the religious believer – Jewish, Christian, or Muslim – is to provide a better foundation for the [human rights] claims of the secular realm where the vast majority of... citizens profess religious belief and, indeed, see their very allegiance to that secular realm as itself being religious."[33] He defends this claim by arguing that for Judaism religion can only be seen "as the source of *all* other rights,"[34] whether understood as the rights among human beings or between them and God. The major problem with secularist views of human rights, such as the social contract theory, is that society "must be seen as an artificial construct"[35] created by a collection of unattached individuals. Such a view makes the offensive assumption "that the human individual is sovereign rather than God."[36]

From a Muslim point of view, Abdulaziz Sachedina is more equivocal concerning the question of the religious grounds of human rights, though, in the last analysis, he also embraces the need for a theological justification.[37] On the one hand, there exists deep in Islamic scripture and theology, he says, a

---

[27] Ibid., 360.
[28] Michael J. Perry, *The Idea of Human Rights. Four Inquiries* (New York: Oxford University Press, 1998).
[29] Ibid., 39.
[30] Ibid., 35.
[31] Ibid., 39.
[32] David Novak, "Religious Human Rights in Judaic Texts," in John Witte, Jr. and Johan D. van der Vyver, eds., *Religious Human Rights in Global Perspective: Religious Perspectives* (The Hague: Martinus Nihoff Publishers, 1996), 175–201.
[33] Ibid., 200–201.
[34] Ibid., 177, original italics.
[35] Ibid., 179.
[36] Ibid., 180.
[37] Sachedina, *Islam and the Challenge of Human Rights* (New York: Oxford University Press, 2009). See David Little, "Foreword," for a brief discussion of the ambiguity in the book regarding the need for a religious justification of human rights, vii–xii.

notion of "universal ethical cognition," close to the concept of conscience, that "does not require any justification independent of the naturally endowed innate [moral standards]."[38] It is on this basis that the language of human rights can be defended as equally available to and binding on all human beings, regardless of religious identity. This is also the basis for guaranteeing religious pluralism and freedom of conscience in line with the concept of "functional secularity." According to that idea, religious and political authorities are legally separated, and laws and policies are determined independently of any controlling religious point of view.

On the other hand, Sachedina is not entirely comfortable with this proposal. He is particularly bothered by the "secular moral foundationalism" that he believes underlies standard Western-oriented interpretations of human rights.[39] In eliminating any religious references from the UDHR, the drafters "pursued a thorough-going secularism" that distorted the understanding and implementation of human rights by ignoring the need for a religious basis for "life's sacredness and human beings' possession of inherent dignity and rights."[40] For Sachedina, it is a reconstructed theory of Islam that ultimately provides a convincing remedy for these deficiencies by picturing "the equivalence and equal rights of human beings as a divinely ordained system."[41]

To consider seriously the provenance, character, and underlying rationale of human rights language is to feel the force of that language. It is to find reasons for reassessing claims about the impossibility of universal justifications, about the inadequacy and impracticality of rights language, about the unimportance of philosophical reflection, and about the insufficiency of secular justifications and the need for religious ones. In short, it is to appreciate the importance of the purposes of human rights language and the inseparability of those purposes from the underlying rationale.

THE NATURE AND ASSUMPTIONS OF HUMAN RIGHTS LANGUAGE

In this chapter, I shall be referring primarily to the so-called International Bill of Rights, composed of the UDHR and two supplementary international covenants: one on Civil and Political Rights (ICCPR) and the other on Economic, Social, and Cultural Rights (ICESCR). It should be borne in mind

[38] Ibid., 50.
[39] Ibid., 170.
[40] Ibid., 10, 24.
[41] Ibid., 201.

that, as treaties,[42] the two covenants have legal force that a declaration, such as the UDHR, does not typically have, even though the UDHR is now widely regarded as having taken on the special status of customary international law.[43] It should also be recognized that the common belief in three "generations" of human rights – civil-political, economic, and collective – all supposedly conceived of and adopted sequentially, is mistaken. The first two sets of rights are explicitly included alongside each other in the UDHR; the collective rights of peoples have their origin in the minority treaties of the League of Nations and in various articles of the UN Charter (e.g., Art. 55), are implied in Article 28 of the UDHR, and are specified in common Article 1 (the right of the self-determination of peoples) of the ICCPR and the ICESCR.[44]

Drawing in part – here and there critically – on the indispensable work of Johannes Morsink[45] and Mary Ann Glendon,[46] I summarize the basic features of human rights language in the following way:

- Human rights language presupposes an understanding of "a right" *simpliciter* as an individual or subjective entitlement to demand (or have demanded on one's behalf) a certain performance or forbearance under threat of sanction for noncompliance. It also includes related terms, such as "duty" and "obligation."
- As such, it has a strongly *deontic* tone, whose chief defining characteristic is *requiredness* or *bindingness*, implying *legitimate enforceability* of either a legal or nonlegal sort. Legal enforcement rests on the authorized regulation of physical force/coercion, whereas nonlegal enforcement is the justified application of sanctions short of physical force/coercion (e.g., verbal censure or condemnation).
- It is legal language, both authorizing and enjoining states to enforce human rights. As legal entities, states are "obligated" "to promote *universal respect for, and observance of*, human rights and freedoms," as prescribed in the Preambles to the ICCPR and the IESCR (emphasis added). The

---

[42] Both covenants became binding international treaties in 1976, when the requisite number of States Parties had ratified each one. At present, 168 states have ratified the ICCPR (plus 74 signatories), and 162 have ratified the ICESCR (plus 7 signatories).
[43] Dennis J. Driscoll, "The Development of Human Rights in International Law," in Walter Laquer and Barry Rubin, eds., *The Human Rights Reader* (New York: New American Library, 1979), 46.
[44] Philip Alston, "The Commission on Human Rights," in Philip Alston, ed., *The United Nations and Human Rights: A Critical Appraisal* (Oxford: Clarendon Press, 1992), 188.
[45] *The Universal Declaration of Rights: Origins, Drafting, and Intent* (Philadelphia: University of Pennsylvania Press, 1999).
[46] Ibid.

obligation of the States Parties committed to the two covenants rests not only on their act of agreement but also on another basis of state obligation that transcends statutory or treaty agreements and is grounded in universal peremptory principles known as *jus cogens*.[47]

- It is *moral* language that is *universal* in character. "Moral" means language that addresses matters of fundamental human welfare in a way that is taken to be justified and to be of great importance. "Universal" means language believed to apply justifiably to all human beings everywhere in that everyone may both appeal and be held accountable to it. Both the moral and universal valence are illustrated by statements such as these from the UDHR Preamble and from Articles 1 and 2: "[R]ecognition of the inherent dignity and of the equal and inalienable rights of all members of the human family is the foundation of freedom, justice and peace in the world." "[D]isregard and contempt for human rights have resulted in barbarous acts which have outraged the conscience of humankind."[48] "All human beings are born free and equal in dignity and rights. They are endowed with reason and conscience and should act toward one another in a spirit of brotherhood." "Everyone is entitled to all the rights and freedoms set forth in this Declaration, without distinction of any kind, such as race, color, sex, language, religion,... national or social origin,... birth or other status."

- It is moral language that is *noncomprehensive*.[49] The assumed moral grounds apply exclusively to the rights and freedoms enumerated in the instruments and are otherwise deferent to and respectful of "freedom of

---

[47] *Jus cogens* principles protect individuals everywhere against practices such as genocide, slavery, torture, and apartheid, and they are taken to rest ultimately on principles with strong moral content such as the one invoked in the Preamble to the UDHR. In describing the idea of *jus cogens*, Martti Koskenniemi states, "It is inherently difficult to accept the notion that states are legally bound not to engage in genocide, for example, only if they have ratified and not formally denounced the 1948 Genocide Convention. Some norms seem so basic, so important, that it is more than slightly artificial to argue that states are legally bound to comply with them simply because there exists an agreement between them to that effect, rather than because, in the words of the International Court of Justice (ICJ), noncompliance would 'shock the conscience of mankind' and be contrary to 'elementary considerations of humanity'." Koskenniemi, "The Pull of the Mainstream," cited in Henry J. Steiner and Philip Alston, eds., *International Human Rights in Context: Law, Politics, Morals* (Oxford: Oxford University Press, 2000), 78.

[48] "Humankind" is an appropriate updating of the original word, "mankind."

[49] According to John Rawls, a "comprehensive doctrine" is a religious or philosophical system of belief intended to apply to a large, possibly unlimited, number of adherents; that includes "conceptions of what is of value in human life, and ideals of human character, as well as ideals of friendship and associational relationships, and much else that is to inform our conduct"; and that applies potentially, to life as a whole. See, John Rawls, *Political Liberalism* (New York: Columbia University Press, 1996), 13. The point here is that the understanding of moral

thought, conscience, religion, or belief" (Art. 18 UDHR, ICCPR). The documents take no position on philosophical or theological controversies regarding the ultimate grounds and nature of moral life and responsibility, let alone metaphysical and cosmological ideas related to them; rather, they leave such questions up to individual conscientious deliberation under the right to freedom of religion or belief. Moreover, the documents adopt a "thin approach" to the government's role in dealing with comprehensive doctrines. In contrast to a "thick approach," in which a government takes "responsibility for the delivery and maintenance of a special cultural, religious, or linguistic tradition," in a thin approach the government sets up "a fair (legal) framework within which its people can, singly or in groups, pursue their own notions of... human good, as long as [other enumerated rights and freedoms] are not violated."[50]

- Accordingly, the language is *religiously neutral or "secular" in a narrow sense*. This is true in two ways:
  - Proposals for declaring that human rights depend on a belief in "divine origin" and "immortal destiny" were deliberately excluded during the drafting process consistent with the underlying commitment to universal accessibility and accountability, regardless of "language, religion,... national or social origin,... birth or other status."[51] To have included religious references in the Declaration as the preferred basis of human rights would obviously have violated that commitment. If "secular" is taken to mean *not requiring religious warrants*, then the Declaration is, it is true, "a secular document by intent."[52] It assumes a secular or nonreligious warrant sufficient to justify the rights enumerated in the document.

At the same time, the Declaration is not an example of "outright secularism,"[53] if that phrase implies, as it ordinarily does, opposition to

---

justification is self-consciously limited in its application to the practice of the enumerated rights and freedoms and expressly does not pretend to regulate beliefs and practices beyond that.

Professor John Reeder has pointed out that a position may be noncomprehensive in a second sense as well. It may reject, as Rawls and Nussbaum do, *any* foundational metaphysic or epistemology, at least so far as the grounds of "political liberalism" go (see Rawls, *Political Liberalism*, 97; Nussbaum, *Frontiers of Justice*, 163). My position is noncomprehensive in the first, but not in the second, sense, as will become clear. I admit, of course, that any noncomprehensive grounds that may be supplied as a basis for human rights would have to be compatible with a broader theological or philosophical position.

[50] Morsink, *Universal Declaration of Human Rights*, 259.
[51] Ibid., 284–290.
[52] Ibid., 289.
[53] Ibid.

and disrespect of religious belief. The very idea of a "thin approach" to the relation between the government and religion, guaranteed by Article 18 of the UDHR and the ICCPR, entails that religious (and, equally, nonreligious) beliefs are fully "respected" in the sense of being permitted and protected by the state. Nor is there any prohibition against offering religious (or other) justifications for human rights as enumerated in the documents, or against discussing and advocating them in public. It is simply that there is no provision for such beliefs to be legally required or enforced.[54]

Thus, the Declaration contains a "two-tiered" approach to justification. The first level provides "secular" or religiously neutral grounds sufficient for considering the rights enumerated in the document as obligatory upon and accessible to everyone everywhere, regardless of religious identity. The second level, guaranteed by Article 18, invites and protects the right of religious (and equally nonreligious) people to avow whatever comprehensive doctrine they may embrace.

- States may limit religious or other conscientious practices in respect to public safety, order, health, or morals, but only so long as the limitations respect the "rights and freedoms of others," are "prescribed by law" "in a democratic society" (Art. 29.2 of the UDHR and Art. 4 of the ICCPR), and are administered on the basis of "the right to equality and nondiscrimination."[55] That means that the grounds on which the state applies the limitations "must be based on principles not deriving exclusively from a single tradition," but "from many social, philosophical and religious traditions."[56]

---

[54] The point here is that any reference to religious warrants in the UDHR was intentionally eliminated by the drafters. It is true that the Human Rights Committee, an eighteen-member supervisory agency mandated by the ICCPR (Pt. IV) for the purpose of monitoring State Party compliance and issuing General Comments on the meaning of the Covenant, has held that art. 18 of the ICCPR does not prohibit the recognition of a "state religion" or one that is "established as official or traditional." However, the committee concomitantly imposes rigorous conditions that in effect threaten the standard prerogatives of a state or established religion; it declares that under a state or established religion there shall be no "impairment of the enjoyment of any of the rights under the Covenant . . . nor any discrimination against adherents of other religions or non-believers." See United Nations Human Rights Committee, General Comment No. 22 (48), Article 18, in *Religion and Human Rights: Basic Documents*, eds. Tad Stahnke and Paul Martin (Columbia University: Center for the Study of Human Rights, 1998), 94.

[55] United Nations Human Rights Committee, General Comment No. 22 (48), Article 18, in *Religion and Human Rights: Basic Documents*, eds. Tad Stahnke and Paul Martin (Columbia University: Center for the Study of Human Rights, 1998), 93–94.

[56] See fn. 54, above.

- Thus, the authority of the language extends *only* to the regulation of practice in regard to the enumerated rights and freedoms, and *not* to beliefs (presumably, even beliefs critical of existing human rights), except for such beliefs as "incite to discrimination or violence" (ICCPR, Art. 20.2).[57]
- The language applies not merely to nations. It constitutes, rather, "'a common standard of achievement for all peoples and nations' toward which 'every individual and every organ of society' should 'strive' and by which the conduct of nations and peoples can be measured."[58]
- Morally grounded human rights provide the standard for formulating and enforcing the law, which explains the meaning of the statement in the UDHR Preamble, "human rights should be protected by the rule of law," lest human beings, the Preamble goes on, "be compelled to have recourse, as a last resort, to rebellion against tyranny and oppression."
- The "rule of law," in turn, implies two subsidiary requirements:
  - Certain rights are "nonderogable," or not subject to suspension, even under extreme circumstances like public emergencies. These include protections against racial, gender, ethnic, linguistic, religious, and other forms of discrimination, as well as against arbitrary killing, torture, involuntary medical experimentation, and against slavery. They also include protections against violations of certain due process rights, and the denial of the freedom of conscience, religion or belief.
  - Civil and political rights, like freedom of opinion, expression, assembly, association, and participation in government, including the freedom to vote, while derogable – albeit under carefully circumscribed conditions – are understood to be indispensable guarantees against the violation of nonderogable rights.
- In addition to "rule of law" provisions, other provisions guaranteeing economic, social, and cultural rights are also required in order to assure "freedom from fear and want," as is stated in the Preambles to the UDHR, ICCPR, and the ICESCR.[59]

---

[57] ICCPR art. 20.2 also includes "hostility" as an indication of prohibited incitement. However, widespread legal opinion (including that of the present UN Special Rapporteur on Freedom of Religion or Belief) excludes it for being an "inward" emotion or attitude, and as such effectively impossible to police. In that respect, it is unlike violence or discrimination, which refer to legally identifiable forms of overt behavior. Thus, religious hate speech would be legally liable if and only if it "incited" to discrimination or violence.

[58] Comments by Eleanor Roosevelt, chair of the drafting committee of the UDHR. Cited in Glendon, *A World Made New*, 177.

[59] See Introduction, 4, above, concerning the mention of nonderogable economic and social rights as an elaboration of this point.

As Morsink shows, language of this sort is best understood in light of the consequences of mid-twentieth-century fascism. The essence of fascism was the absolute subjection of the individual to the will of the community.[60] In the name of collective ideals, as interpreted by "der Fuehrer," anything might be done. As Hitler put it, "National Socialism takes as the starting point... neither the individual nor humanity... [but] *das Volk*... [and] desires to safeguard [it], even at the expense of the individual."[61]

The response to such malevolence by those who drafted the UDHR was a feeling of "shared moral revulsion" toward "the absolutely crucial factor of the Holocaust" and the relentless subversion of any and all individual civil, cultural, religious, legal, political, or economic protections. Without that common feeling of revulsion, "the Declaration would never have been written."[62] Embracing the words from the Preamble, cited earlier, that "disregard and contempt for human rights have resulted in barbarous acts which have outraged the conscience of mankind," the drafters "generalized their own feelings over the rest of humanity." They believed that any morally healthy human being would be similarly outraged when confronted with such occurrences and would naturally welcome protections against the recurrence of any comparable event. According to Morsink, it is that reaction that explains "why the Declaration has found such widespread support."[63]

Both the diagnosis of the worldwide catastrophe and the prescription for cure and prevention seemed to the drafters immediately obvious and compelling: "The majority of [them] saw no need to go beyond what they considered to be the obvious and self-evident moral facts about inherent [and inalienable] rights."[64] That meant that the rights enumerated in the UDHR were understood in effect as "morally self-justifying" and *for that reason* were not in need of justifications for "comprehensive" religious or philosophical doctrines.[65] Regardless of differences of culture, ethnic or national identity, religion, "or

---

[60] According to Robert O. Paxton, *The Anatomy of Fascism* (New York: Alfred A. Knopf, 2004), "Fascism may be defined as a form of political behavior marked by obsessive preoccupation with community decline, humiliation, or victimhood and by compensatory cults of unity, energy, and purity, in which a mass-based party of committed nationalist militants, working in uneasy but effective collaboration with traditional elites, abandons democratic liberties and pursues with redemptive violence and without ethical or legal restraints goals of internal cleansing and external expansion" (218).
[61] Allan Bullock, *Hitler: A Study in Tyranny* (New York: Harper & Row, 1962), 401.
[62] Morsink, *Universal Declaration of Human Rights*, xiii–xiv.
[63] Ibid., 91, 300.
[64] Ibid., 293–294. Cf. Glendon, *A World Made New*, 232: All the framers could do "was to state the truths they believed to be self-evident."
[65] See fn. 49.

other opinion," etc., all human beings – simply as human – are entitled to appeal to human rights and are legitimately held accountable to them. Similarly, human rights are taken to be superior to the structure, laws, and policies of governments and to constitute a prior standard of governmental legitimacy and accountability.

A PROPOSED DEFENSE OF THE DRAFTERS' RATIONALE

At one point, Morsink refers to the reaction of the drafters as exemplifying "the classical theory of moral intuitionism," which "supposes that people everywhere have a moral sense or faculty that – unless... blocked [thereby rendering them incompetent] – gives them unaided access to the basic truths of morality."[66] Although he denies that the drafters consciously held such a theory, he attributes to them some of the theory's assumptions – in particular an epistemological belief, as opposed to a metaphysical one, that all morally competent human beings have the capacity to comprehend immediately certain basic moral truths. Indeed, he interprets the reference in Article 1 of the UDHR to all human beings as "endowed with reason and conscience" in that way. It is not, in the drafters' minds, a metaphysical claim, which might lead to the conclusion that infants and seriously incompetent adults, who lack reason and/or conscience, have no human rights. It is, instead, that reflecting on the notions of "reason and conscience" might suggest ways in which human beings *come to apprehend* moral truths of the sort assumed by human rights language. Rather than applying to matters of "being," as Morsink puts it, the terms apply to matters of "knowing."[67]

It is difficult to be sure whether Morsink is right about this interpretation, because he mentions that the drafters "came to see [the] phrase ['endowed with reason and conscience'] as quite problematic [because of the unwelcome metaphysical implications just mentioned] and only kept it in out of respect for [Charles] Malik," a Lebanese Christian Thomist, who was one of the principal drafters.[68] On the other hand, as Morsink himself admits, the interpretation does help make sense of the words, "conscience of mankind," words that the drafters certainly regarded to be of central importance and that were emphatically affirmed by non-Western drafters such as the Chinese scholar, P. C. Chang, on the basis of his own Confucian tradition.[69] The words assert

---

[66] Morsink, *Universal Declaration of Human Rights*, 300.
[67] Ibid., 296.
[68] Ibid., 297.
[69] Ibid., 299. It is of considerable interest that a recent Harvard doctoral dissertation by Peter Chang demonstrates compellingly important similarities concerning the idea of conscience

the capacity, assumed to be universal among competent human beings, to apprehend certain basic moral truths noninferentially, a capacity that the language of the UDHR and subsequent instruments clearly presupposes and that helps clarify in what sense the drafters might have thought of the language as "morally self-justifying." It is also likely that this epistemological approach serves to make sense of the reference to "reason" in Article 1, or so I suggest later.

However, I must add that the "metaphysical problem" – exactly to whom the human rights apply – cannot so easily be set aside as the drafters thought. Although it is obviously incorrect, on any proper understanding of human rights language, to hold that human rights apply only to individuals who are fully competent rationally, it is not incorrect to apply them to beings who *ideally may be expected* to exhibit rational competence, namely beings born of *homo sapiens*. It is only such beings who, ideally at least, are capable of taking advantage of the full range of human rights, including civil and political rights, such as freedom of religion, speech, assembly, political participation, cultural opportunity, and the like, just as it is only such beings who may be held accountable for respecting and complying with human rights standards. Infant human beings, as well as human beings suffering from serious impairments or disablements of various kinds, are regarded as "deficient" or "incompetent" to the degree they cannot themselves appeal to rights provisions (though others may appeal on their behalf) or be held fully accountable to them. Appropriate adjustments for "diminished responsibility" are entailed, as are remedial provisions to assist such persons to achieve competence to the degree possible. In addition, some human rights, of course, continue to apply to infants and incompetent people (and conceivably by extension to higher animals as well[70]), such as nonderogable rights prohibiting discrimination, arbitrary

---

between the eighteenth-century British philosopher, Joseph Butler, and the seventeenth-century Neo-Confucian Chinese scholar, Wang Yang Ming. Peter Chang, "A Comparative Study of Bishop Joseph Butler's and Wang Yang Ming's Conception of Conscience," thesis presented for the degree of Doctor of Theology in Comparative Religion, Harvard University, 2008.

[70] Prohibitions against torture of and cruelty to higher animals have wide moral appeal, whereas prohibitions against arbitrary life-taking, medical experimentation, and "enslavement" (coercive confinement in zoos or as pets) are much more controversial. Even so, it is interesting that these subjects *are* morally controversial in many societies. Obviously, other nonderogable rights, such as freedom of religion or prohibitions of being imprisoned "merely on the ground of the inability to fulfill a contractual obligation" (ICCPR, Art. 11) or being held guilty of violating retroactive laws (ICCPR, Art. 15), would not be applicable. It also makes no sense to speak of holding higher animals accountable to human rights standards of any kind, as though they might be thought liable to legal proceedings and punishment for violations. The

life-taking, torture, cruel treatment, medical experimentation, enslavement, and the suspension of certain legal protections.

Given that the theory of moral intuitionism remains controversial[71] and that it has encountered well-known objections, one of which is that all talk of self-evidence or self-justification is in fact an abdication of reason, an exhortation to believe in moral truth "for no reason at all," what might be said in support of a position that seems in some ways reminiscent of that theory?

To begin with, four firmly held propositions[72] would appear to underlie the outraged reaction of the drafters, both as a basis for their diagnosis of the problem and for their prescription regarding the cure and future prevention:

(1) The use of force – defined as the infliction of death, impairment, disablement, deprivation, severe pain and/or involuntary confinement – begs strong moral justification wherever it occurs, both because of the obvious adverse consequences that result from using force and of the powerful temptation in human affairs to use force arbitrarily (i.e., without "strong moral justification").[73]

---

latter considerations, which distinguish human beings, ideally understood, from higher animals indicate why from a human rights point of view higher animals are in a different moral category and are not properly the subjects of *human* rights as such. Whatever points of moral overlap there may be are not determined by a simple extension of the conditions of the proper moral treatment of human beings, because morality as applied to human beings presupposes a capacity for responsibility and "understanding what one is doing" that does not apply to higher animals. See Thomson, *Realm of Rights*, 292–293, and Part I, "Rights What They Are."

[71] Though it is not without its ardent defenders (e.g., Robert Audi, *Moral Knowledge and Ethical Character* (New York: Oxford University Press, 1997)).

[72] I am grateful to Scott Davis for properly prompting me to think through what I hope is a more satisfactory defense of my position than I had previously provided. See his interesting "Comment," *Journal of Religious Ethics* 35.1 (March 2007), 165–170, on my "On Behalf of Rights: A Critique of *Democracy and Tradition*," *Journal of Religious Ethics* 34.2 (June 2006), and my response to him in "The Author Replies...," *Journal of Religious Ethics* 35.1 (March 2007), 171–175. In that response I suggest a version of the four following propositions, and I make a promise that "much more must (sometime) be said" (173), a promise I am herewith attempting to make good on. In doing that, I have seen fit to reconsider and redeploy an earlier article of mine, "Natural Rights and Human Rights: The International Imperative," in Robert P. Davidow, ed., *Natural Rights and Natural Law: The Legacy of George Mason* (Fairfax, VA: George Mason University Press, 1986), 67–122.

[73] This definition is intentionally stated in a way that is morally neutral. All of the references denote things that are *highly unfavorable or unwanted, but not (yet) wrong*. Moral wrongness is determined in regard to whether or not the reasons given for causing death, impairment, disablement, etc., justify those consequences. That is the force of the phrase, "begs strong moral justification," implying that death, impairment, disablement, etc., may or may not be judged to be morally wrongful. The required justification must be "strong" precisely because the consequences are commonly regarded as highly unfavorable or unwanted and thus demand an especially powerful defense. Accordingly, "adverse," which can mean either "unfavorable"

(2) No human being could reasonably doubt that Hitler's grounds for the kind and amount of force used at his command were grossly self-serving and manifestly unfounded and led to forms of arbitrary abuse that *must* be labeled "atrocities" (i.e., strongly condemnable). That should be plain to everyone; those who fail to recognize it are themselves under moral suspicion.

(3) Hitler's atrocities rested on a belief in total domination, namely, the right of a government to treat citizens in any way it sees fit.

(4) An indispensable means of inhibiting the recurrence of such practices and of avoiding "as a last resort" "rebellion against tyranny and oppression" (Preamble, UDHR) is the affirmation and enforcement of human rights as enumerated in the international instruments.

The rest of our defense consists in adducing certain rational considerations conducive to embracing these four propositions.

Let me first suggest that the consequences of fascism, and particularly the Holocaust and all it symbolized, vivified powerfully and indelibly constituent features of human rationality. Wherever the infliction of death, impairment, disablement, deprivation, severe pain, and/or involuntary confinement occurs, certain reasons must fail, and fail in a special way, as efforts at justification. At a minimum, those would be reasons that are *self-serving* or *unfounded*. To offer personal pleasure or the simple fact that one wills it as a reason for torturing a baby,[74] or to state that an act of inflicting death and other harms is undertaken for some reason that is manifestly untrue or self-contradictory, is not only morally irrational as a justification, but morally condemnable as well. The "condemnability" of such reasons lies in part how they "fail in a special way." But their special failure also implies something else: The infliction of death and other harms for such "reasons" itself provides justifying grounds

---

or "harmful" (*Concise Oxford English Dictionary*), is understood here to mean "unfavorable" but *not* "harmful," because again, the second meaning would predispose a judgment of the moral wrongness of acts causing one or all of the unfavorable consequences. Because of this explanation, the words "injury" and "harm" do not appear in our definition. The Latin root, *iniuria*, means "injustice" or "wrong," thus disqualifying "injury" as a morally neutral word. The first meaning of "harm" is "physical *injury*," understood, I am assuming, as "wrong" or "unjust" behavior (*Concise Oxford English Dictionary*, italics added). The "powerful temptation" to arbitrariness in respect to using force adds a second layer of gravity to the need for a particularly strong justification. For these clarifications, I am indebted to a conversation with John Kelsay.

[74] The example is borrowed from Thomson, *The Realm of Rights*, 13ff. The example is at the center of an important discussion by Thomson of the broader proposition: "Other things being equal, one ought not cause others pain" "is surely a necessary truth[.] [I]t not merely is but could not have failed to be the case that an act's being an instance of 'causes a person pain' is favorably relevant to its being wrongful" (15).

for taking forceful action in response, thereby constituting a warrant for self-defense.

Though the same argument works for the ideas of death, impairment, disablement, deprivation, and involuntary confinement – and in a complete treatment would be so defended – consider, as one example of the recommended argument, the relation of reason-giving to the experience of severe physical pain.[75] As Hume reminded us, it would be senseless to ask for reasons why human beings seek to avoid (or relieve) pain.[76] Resisting its occurrence or seeking relief from it constitutes, noninferentially, a prima facie good and a justifying reason for evasive or compensatory action, whatever limitations there may be as to how one goes about it. It would be as absurd to inquire why someone acted to deflect a blow to the head by an assailant as it would be to want to know why someone with a bad headache reached for an aspirin.

Given this necessary connection between reason and pain, it follows that anyone engaged in inflicting pain or depriving others of relief would bear a very heavy burden of proof. Only certain kinds of reason may pass muster: (1) those that support actions designed to help the recipient avoid or relieve overall pain, such as an excruciating surgery; (2) those that support actions intended to achieve some other compelling benefit from the recipient's point of view, such as survival; or (3) those that support actions undertaken to deter or restrain the recipient from, say, overreacting to mistreatment by excessively (unjustifiably) inflicting pain or failing to relieve it.[77]

Please note: The critical reference point of the reasons justifying the infliction of pain or the failure to relieve it is the benefit or discipline of *the recipient* who is, of course, the primary locus of the pain-related reasoning process I am describing. Obviously, the reasons apply under only the most compelling

---

[75] Defined for our purposes as "a strongly unpleasant bodily sensation," *Concise Oxford English Dictionary* (Oxford: Oxford University Press, 2002), 1024. We have in mind incontestably "unpleasant bodily sensations," in whatever culture they occur, such as a stick in the eye, a needle under the fingernail, or a metal drill penetrating the root of a tooth.

[76] David Hume, *Enquiry Concerning the Principles of Morals*, P. Niditch, ed. (Oxford: Oxford University Press, 1975), 293.

[77] I leave out of this account the question of the justifiability of inflicting pain as punishment because of certain complications, especially the problem of appropriate limits, once an offender has been detained and rendered harmless. It is the problem, in human rights terms, of how precisely to interpret the part of UDHR, Art. 5 that prohibits the subjection of detainees to "cruel, inhuman or degrading treatment or punishment." Although there is more to be said, the reasons for opposing the death penalty put forward by Justice William J. Brennan in the U.S. Supreme Court's ruling in *Furman v. Georgia* appear to me very convincing. Among others, they are that a punishment is "cruel and unusual" if there is a less severe means available for achieving the same purpose (life imprisonment) and if there is a high probability of arbitrary application. See Peter Irons, *Brennan vs. Rehnquist: The Battle for the Constitution* (New York: Alfred A. Knopf, 1994), ch. 10.

and extraordinary circumstances, implying an additional set of what we might call standards of due caution, or "rules of reason," such as the tests of *necessity* (unavoidability), *proportionality* (efficiency), and *effectiveness*.[78] Thus, someone engaged in applying pain or failing to relieve it might allege in good faith an intention of serving the well-being or the restraint of the recipient, while still executing the act negligently (and possibly culpably) with respect to one or more standards of due caution.

There are, it is true, certain exceptional conditions that to a degree modify this schema of reasons. Those are conditions constituting the so-called necessity excuse, according to which the deliberate infliction of extreme pain on one person might save the life or prevent the severe disablement of someone else. An example is painfully knocking an individual unconscious who might otherwise unintentionally divulge the whereabouts, and thereby occasion the death, of an innocent fugitive. A necessity excuse typically presupposes a sharp clash of practical prescriptions, involving a decision knowingly, if regretfully, to violate a standard expectation – in this context, the expectation that decisions concerning the infliction of pain or the failure to relieve it will attend primarily to what benefits or disciplines the recipient.[79] The example before us clearly violates that expectation and thereby causes harm,[80] because pain is inflicted not for the benefit of the recipient but of someone else.

Even if the excuse were accepted in a given case, it is important to remember that such an excuse covers only a very exceptional, and thus very narrow, set of conditions, namely a direct, imminent threat to the life or limb of one person or persons that is preventable with high probability by inflicting pain on someone else. Also, if anything, necessity appeals raise the level of stringency required in

---

[78] Importantly, if a given act meets all these standards, as in the case of a surgeon who successfully and with due caution amputates the limb of a patient otherwise likely to die, *no harm is done to the patient* (where "harm" = "wrong"). That is true despite the fact that the patient is disabled by the operation.

[79] Appeals to "necessity" work differently in the case of a recipient who is directly benefited or disciplined by the infliction of pain and that of an innocent bystander who is caused pain for the benefit of someone else. "Having to do" an unfavorable or unwanted thing to a recipient (amputate a limb for the sake of survival), so long as it is done for the recipient's own good and with due caution, *causes no harm* to the recipient (where "harm" = "wrong"). The inflictor of pain does not have to be excused of anything. However, "having to do" an unfavorable or unwanted thing to an innocent bystander, even with due caution (efficiently knocking unconscious an unsuspecting individual who will otherwise unintentionally divulge the whereabouts of an innocent fugitive) *does cause harm* to the bystander (again, where "harm" = "wrong"). It is that harm that must be *excused* by reference to "necessitous circumstances."

I am indebted to Sumner Twiss and David Golumbowski for prompting me to take account of circumstances of necessity as they apply to an innocent but implicated bystander.

[80] See fns. 73 and 79.

meeting the standards of due caution. What is more, a necessity appeal is to be understood as an *excuse* in a strict and particular sense: An appeal to necessity mitigates the responsibility of the inflictor of pain; it does not set aside the fact that a bona fide act of necessity is at best "weakly justified" because of the harm caused to an innocent bystander.[81]

Beyond these reasons, decisions to bear pain at high cost for the sake of others must be regarded as discretionary acts, as acts of "self-giving," but even there they must still conform to an adjusted version of the schema just presented. That is, reasons justifying altruistic pain-bearing must support actions designed to avoid or relieve the overall pain of relevant others, must support actions intended to achieve some other significant benefit for relevant others, or must support actions of "substitutionary pain-bearing" where the recipient "stands in" for others in cases of the therapeutic or disciplinary application of pain. Notice, too, that reasons in support of acts of this kind are aimed either at the overall relief of pain or at the achievement of some greater good – an example, in other words, of "purposeful pain."

It should be added that there must be clear and demanding evidentiary standards for determining whether one or more of these justifying or excusing reasons are *in fact* operative in a given case. Of course, evidentiary standards and procedures for verifying them vary from culture to culture, and it remains to be seen how we might go about resolving differences among them. Here the key consideration is that societies as a rule develop some form of institutionalized procedure with exacting standards of verification for adjudicating the reasons for action wherever the infliction of pain is concerned and for certifying whether or not they conform to one or another of the justifying or excusing reasons. This common feature would appear to underlie legal, medical, religious, and military institutions, wherever they arise, whose responsibility it is to enforce, in one way or another, a burden of proof that is required where the application of pain is in question.

It should now be plain why self-serving or manifestly unfounded reasons for causing pain or withholding relief must fail. That is because they disregard what is required when it comes to justifying actions bearing on the experience of pain. "Grossly self-serving reasons," typically identified as "gratuitous" (or "totally uncalled for") – as, for example, acts undertaken primarily for the pleasure or self-gratification of the perpetrator or acts of a "willful" sort, where

---

[81] To be sure, a third-party act of necessity is justified, but the justification is not as "strong" as is ideal because of the accompanying harm to the innocent bystander. Although such an act can, under extreme circumstances, be acceptable, designating it as "weakly" justified conveys its morally ambiguous character. Accordingly, those engaged in acts of necessity are described paradigmatically as persons with "dirty hands."

the perpetrator's interest is the only thing that counts – obviously defy the prescribed calculus, according to which inflicting pain is justified if and only if it convincingly serves to benefit or discipline the recipient, or is altruistically assumed by the recipient according to an adjusted version of the same schema, or else is "excused" by the exceptional circumstances pertinent to a necessity appeal.

The same is true of "manifestly unfounded reasons." They purport to justify or excuse inflicting pain for one or another of the required reasons, but in plain fact do not do that and thus stand in violation in the same way as self-serving reasons do. It needs to be added that reasons for inflicting pain or failing to relieve it might be unfounded not only because the reasons given do not in fact reduce the recipient's overall pain, or otherwise benefit or discipline the recipient, or else excuse disregarding these considerations by means of an appeal to necessity but also because they violate one or more "standards of due caution" that, as we saw, are required when it comes to applying pain. Obviously, the most egregious form of action would be willful or knowing misrepresentation and comprehensive negligence, although a variety of lesser mistakes, with varying degrees of liability based on proving the selective violation of one or another of the standards, could be committed as well.

It should also now be plain why reasons of this kind are not only "morally irrational" but also "morally condemnable." Assuming "moral language" to mean, as we have, language that addresses matters of fundamental human welfare in a way that is taken to be justified and to be of great importance, the structure of pain-related reasons clearly qualifies. Considerations of avoiding or relieving pain are a constitutive part of "fundamental human welfare"; justifying or excusing reasons for action causing pain are primarily keyed to a reduction of the recipient's overall pain or to benefiting or disciplining the recipient. Justifying or excusing reasons concerning avoiding or relieving pain are indisputably of "great importance," anywhere and anytime. Consequently, self-serving or mistaken reasons offered in justification of actions that inflict pain must be taken as severe *moral* violations. In the words of Judith Jarvis Thomson, "there is no possible world in which an act's being an instance of 'causes a person pain' is irrelevant to the question whether it is wrongful."[82]

The connection of all this to the idea of a right and, accordingly, to questions of "legitimate enforceability" of a legal or extralegal sort also falls into place. Understanding a right *simpliciter*, as I do, to be "an individual entitlement to demand a certain performance or forbearance under threat of sanction for noncompliance," inflicting pain for self-serving or manifestly mistaken reasons establishes for the victim an entitlement to censure that act and, within

[82] Thomson, *Realm of Rights*, 15. See fn. 74.

limits, to inflict pain in response, in order to deter or curtail the action of the perpetrator. This response would be an example of "legitimate enforceability." It applies to all individuals equally because, as we have seen, each individual human being is the primary locus of the pain-related reasoning process.

The problem, of course, is that legitimating defensive acts for everyone that involve the infliction of pain, even under prescribed limits, opens the door to "state of nature" conditions. The key consideration here is my reference in the first of the propositions, mentioned earlier, that underlay the reactions of the drafters of the UDHR – namely, fear of the strong human temptation to apply force arbitrarily, which includes the infliction of pain. Because human beings appear to have a strong interest in gaining advantage by inflicting pain for self-serving or mistaken reasons, there arises a need for carefully circumscribed institutional control in these matters, as I have just pointed out. That is an important explanation for the emergence of legal institutions and, more specifically, of criminal law, one of whose primary objectives is to identify and restrain actions involving the infliction of pain undertaken for self-serving or mistaken reasons.[83]

Although legal systems attend in one way or another to the problem of arbitrary pain infliction, they obviously vary as to how much and what kind of attention they give to protecting individual rights as a way of achieving that objective. It is true that, as the result of the "human rights revolution," constitutional provision for rights protection has spread to many countries of the world, as has ratification of the international human rights code. At the same time, by no means is every country included, and even in countries that have adopted rights-oriented constitutions, there remains considerable debate over the understanding and implementation of rights provisions. Beyond that, there is still the broader normative question of whether individual-rights-oriented legal systems are superior to others. For that reason, it is necessary to continue to reflect on the justifiability of legal rights.

IMPLICATIONS OF THE "LOGIC OF PAIN"

We are now in a better position to see the appeal of my central argument: The experience of fascism in the mid-twentieth century produced a "human rights revolution" in philosophical terms, as well as in legal and other ways, because

---

[83] H. L. A. Hart's general comment about criminal law (as well as morality) "in all societies" can be applied specifically to the strong interest that human beings have in inflicting pain to their own advantage: "[O]bligations and duties are thought of as characteristically involving sacrifice or renunciation, and the standing possibility of conflict between obligation or duty and interest is, in all societies, among the truisms of both the lawyer and the moralist." *Concept of Law* (Oxford: Oxford University Press, 1961), 85.

it made transparently clear the moral power of the "logic of pain." In short, my argument provides grounds for at least one "moral a priori": the necessary moral irrationality and condemnability of inflicting pain or failing to relieve it for self-serving or unfounded reasons. It also provides a basis for deriving a concept of individual moral right with important legal implications.

As such, the account enables us to begin to understand and appreciate how it is the drafters of the UDHR could have embraced the four propositions introduced earlier. Still, my comments so far have applied most directly only to propositions (1) and (4), about the requirement of "strong moral justification" – as well as the temptation to violate it, in respect to one feature of the use of force, the infliction of pain – and about the derivation of a concept of individual rights. I must now go on to say something more about propositions (2) and (3), making sure to connect them to the other propositions and to my broader argument.

Propositions (2) and (3) rest both on "normative" and "descriptive" or "empirical" claims. The normative claims concern the belief that using force for "grossly self-serving" or "manifestly unfounded" reasons equals "forms of arbitrary abuse that *must* be labeled 'atrocities' (i.e., strongly condemnable)" (2) and the implicit judgment that the effects of Hitler's use of force did amount to "atrocities" (3). The descriptive claims are that "Hitler's grounds for the kind and amount of force used at his command were [in fact] grossly self-serving and manifestly mistaken" (2) and that Hitler had "a belief in total domination, namely the right of a government to treat citizens in any way it sees fit" (3).

Assuming that the infliction of pain and the failure to relieve it was a constitutive and systematic feature of Hitler's use of force, enough has been said to indicate how a justification of the normative claims works. As to the descriptive features, it is not difficult to supply compelling evidence. The following passages make clear the self-serving character of Hitler's rule, as well as his fundamental conviction regarding his right to treat citizens in any way he saw fit.

[Hitler's] twelve years' dictatorship was barren of all ideas save one – the further extension of his own power and that of the nation with which he had identified himself.... [T]he sole theme of the Nazi revolution was domination, dressed up as the doctrine of race.... [The Nazi Constitution was] "the will of the Fuehrer." This was in fact literally true. The Weimar Constitution was never replaced, it was simply suspended by the Enabling Law, which was renewed periodically and placed all power in Hitler's hands. Hitler thus enjoyed a more complete measure of power than Napoleon or Stalin or Mussolini, since he had been careful not to allow the growth of any institution which might... be used to check him.... What Hitler aimed at was arbitrary power.[84]

In regard to arbitrary abuse undertaken for manifestly unfounded reasons, the evidence, again, is overwhelming. To provide a pretext for Hitler's invasion of Poland in the fall of 1939, Nazi agents staged a fake Polish attack on a German radio station by having a dozen or so prisoners killed and left on the premises dressed as Polish soldiers.[85] The circumstances surrounding subsequent German invasions of other European countries were no different.

On the 10th May, 1940, the German forces invaded the Netherlands, Belgium, and Luxembourg. On the same day the German Ambassadors handed to the Netherlands and Belgian Governments a memorandum alleging that the British and French Armies, with the consent of Belgium and Holland, were planning to march through those countries to attack the Ruhr, and justifying the invasion on these grounds. Germany, however, assured the Netherlands and Belgium that their integrity and their possessions would be respected. A similar memorandum was delivered to Luxembourg on the same date.

There is no evidence... to justify the contention that the Netherlands, Belgium, and Luxembourg were invaded by Germany because their occupation had been planned by England and France. British and French staffs had been cooperating in making certain plans for military operations in the Low Countries, but the purpose of this planning was to defend these countries in the event of a German attack. The invasion of Belgium, Holland, and Luxembourg was entirely without justification. It was carried out in pursuance of policies long considered and prepared, and was plainly an act of aggressive war. The resolve to invade was made without any other consideration than the advancement of the aggressive policies of Germany.[86]

The same, again, is true in the case of the simultaneous invasion of Norway and Denmark on April 9, 1940. Hitler claimed that his occupation of those countries was undertaken to protect their neutrality against the aggressive designs of the Allied forces. However, judging from the policies subsequently instituted under occupation regarding the treatment of Jews, forced labor, diversion of natural resources, and suppression of civil liberties, together with evidence of growing resistance movements in both countries, such a reason for using force was unquestionably unfounded.

---

[84] Bullock, *Hitler: A Study in Tyranny*, combining citations, respectively, from 806, 403, and 266.
[85] Ibid., 546.
[86] Judgment of the International Military Tribunal for the Trial of German Major War Criminals. London: His Majesty's Stationery Office, 1951. Shofar FTP Archive File: imt/tgmwc/judgment/j-invasion-belgiumLast-Modified: 1997/09/12.

Indeed, the obvious flimsiness of Hitler's reasons for using force is completely consistent with his general theory of propaganda, clearly delineated in *Mein Kampf*. Hitler deliberately had little interest in working hard to create a valid justification for his policies. Although propaganda ought always, he said, contain "a certain factor of credibility," propagandists need not worry overly about its truth or validity, because such things are never of primary concern to the "broad masses." Rather, the masses "love a commander more than a petitioner and feel inwardly more satisfied by a doctrine, tolerating no other beside it..., than by [enjoying] liberalistic freedom...." "They are equally unaware of the shameless spiritual terrorization and the hideous abuse of their human freedom, for they absolutely fail to suspect *the inner insanity of the whole doctrine*. All they see is the ruthless force and brutality of its calculated manifestations, to which they always submit in the end."[87]

I need hardly add that not only did Hitler's "justifications" for the massive amounts of pain inflicted by his multiple invasions constitute "willful or knowing misrepresentation" but they also were meant to disguise a pattern of "comprehensive negligence" in regard to what we called the standards of due caution.

Assuming, again, that Hitler's use of force at home and abroad inflicted enormous pain on countless human beings, along, of course, with unimaginable numbers of deaths and forms of impairment, disablement, deprivation, and involuntary confinement, the critical point is that Hitler's policies violated in the extreme the two indications of the unjustified infliction of pain I have adduced: self-serving and mistaken reasons. My basic argument is that the close conjunction of our "moral a priori" about reason and pain and the strong evidence that Hitler in fact violated in the extreme its conditions warrants the conclusion that people, whoever and wherever they might be, had an inherent right to condemn and, if possible, to resist such action (with proportionate means). It also substantiates the claim in Proposition (2) that such a realization "should be plain to everyone; those who fail to recognize it are themselves under moral suspicion."

Even supposing for the moment that I am right about the "normative" side of my argument – about the moral a priori, that is – someone may nevertheless still object that the "empirical certainty" I claim in the Hitler case is never possible, because descriptive or empirical claims are always probabilistic, are always open to further investigation and correction. Is it not possible that new evidence might appear in the future disconfirming my

---

[87] Adolf Hitler, "The Bigger the Lie, the Better," in William Ebenstein ed., *Man and the State: Modern Political Ideas* (New York: Rinehart and Co., 1947), 302 (emphasis added).

picture of Hitler as an egregious and systematic violator of the conditions of the moral a priori? Frankly, the challenge is highly implausible. The evidence is so overwhelming, so conclusive in this case that I am moved to invoke a relevant comment by Ludwig Wittgenstein regarding empirical certainty. According to Wittgenstein, it would not be correct to doubt that I have a brain inside my head even though "so far no one has opened my skull in order to see whether there is a brain inside." That is so because, as he puts it, "everything speaks for, and nothing against its being the case that that is what one would find there."[88] A similar conclusion regarding the relevant facts surrounding Hitler's actions seems equally certain.

But I want to go further than Wittgenstein. Something crucial is added by tying empirical and moral certainty together. That combination is especially compelling. Because of the logic of pain, affected individuals faced with an "open-and-shut case" are strongly entitled to condemn and resist. Moreover, we can better understand how the drafters of the UDHR could have come to regard the fascist experience in the way they did and how they could have drawn the conclusions they did about how to prevent a recurrence. Human rights language is fully in order. In the face of the compelling convergence of "normative" and "descriptive" characteristics evident in the fascist case, a "deontic" code of "inherent" and "inalienable" rights and correlative "duties" and "obligations," with both moral and legal features, is very much warranted.

In the first place, it is the particular moral grounding that provides the basis for universal accountability, including legitimate legal enforceability, that is an intrinsic feature of human rights language. Without some such grounding, people are only hypothetically accountable, depending on whether they happen in one way or another to have committed themselves to human rights standards. Lacking such a commitment, an exercise of enforcement is illegitimate. So long as there is no binding basis for accountability, individuals or governments that consistently refrain from accepting such standards, as did Hitler, are morally and legally exempt from their jurisdiction.

In the second place, nonderogable rights, so essential to the whole human rights code, may be seen, among other things, as fundamental protections against violations of the logic of pain. Consider the phenomenon of torture:

> [T]orture terrorizes. The body in pain winces; it trembles. The muscles themselves register fear. This is rooted in pain's biological function of impelling us in the most urgent way possible to escape from the source of pain – for that impulse is indistinguishable from panic. U.S. interrogators have reportedly

---

[88] Ludwig Wittgenstein, *On Certainty*, G. E. M. Anscombe and G. H. von Wright, eds. (New York: Harper & Row, 1969), 18e (I have altered the translation slightly).

used the technique of "waterboarding" to break the will of detainees.... As anyone who has ever come close to drowning or suffocating knows, the oxygen-starved brain sends panic signals that overwhelm everything else....

And torture humiliates. It makes the victim scream and beg; the terror makes him lose control of his bowels and bladder. The essence of cruelty is inflicting pain for the purpose of lording it over someone – we sometimes say "breaking" them – and the mechanism of cruelty is making the victim the audience of your own mastery. Cruelty always aims at humiliation.... Underneath whatever religious significance that attaches to torturing the vanquished, the victor tortures captives for the simplest of motives: to relive the victory, to demonstrate the absoluteness of his mastery, to rub the loser's face in it, and to humiliate the loser by making him scream and beg. For the victorious warrior, it's fun; it's entertainment. It prolongs the rush of victory.[89]

As the Abu Ghraib scandal made clear, torture is the perfect tool for arbitrary domination. In its nature, it readily strips the application of pain of all moral and legal restraint. That is true even in cases of interrogational torture in face of a looming threat:

The authorities know there may be a bomb plot in the offing, and they have captured a man who may know something about it, but may not. Torture him? How much? For weeks? For months? The chances are considerable that you are torturing a man with nothing to tell you. If he doesn't talk, does that mean it's time to stop, or time to ramp up the level of torture? How likely does it have to be that he knows something important? Will one out of a hundred suffice to land him on the waterboard?... Do you really want to make the torture decision by running the numbers? A one-percent chance of saving a thousand lives yields ten statistical lives. Does that mean that you can torture up to nine people on a one-percent chance of finding crucial information?[90]

This passage shows why torture is necessarily morally questionable, even against the specter of a looming threat. It is because of the uncertainty or indeterminacy under which pain is inflicted, both as to effectiveness and to limits. Arguments permitting torture in extreme circumstances, as in ticking bomb scenarios, invariably posit a high probability that the suspect possesses reliable actionable information regarding the impending catastrophe. As such, even these arguments presuppose the importance of avoiding arbitrary pain, and it is arguable that the existence of such conditions might reasonably serve

---

[89] David Luban, "Liberalism, Torture, and the Ticking Bomb," *Virginia Law Review* 91, 6 (October 2005), 1431–1432. This is, by my reckoning, a brilliant essay on the problem of torture.
[90] Ibid., 1442–1443.

to excuse the use of torture in a very narrow range of circumstances. Nevertheless, it should also be unmistakably clear why a strong general presumption against torture is properly prescribed in the human rights instruments. That is because of the irreducible difficulty of knowing *whether or not* such circumstances apply in a given case, as well as *how* to determine the amount and character of pain allowable in those circumstances. In short, torture is inherently liable to arbitrary use.[91]

It should also be clear why the drafters considered the derogable rights – legal and political safeguards – to be so important in protecting against violations of the nonderogable rights, such as the prohibition against torture. "The experience of the war had reinforced the belief [of the drafters] that the cluster of rights spelled out in articles . . . 19, 20, and 21 [freedom of opinion and expression, of association, and participation in government] are universally the first ones dictators will seek to deny and destroy."[92] In the light of the fascist experience, the importance of ensuring basic economic and social entitlements should also be mentioned. One of the chief instruments of suppression used by Hitler and other dictators is the withholding or diverting of the means of survival. It is not a stretch to suggest that willfully inflicting or permitting starvation, malnutrition, and disabling sickness is as much a violation of the logic of pain as is resort to torture or to cruel and inhuman treatment or punishment.[93]

I am arguing then that the drafters were correct to identify the consequences of fascism as a paradigm of cruel treatment, treatment that necessarily triggered the system of individual entitlements enumerated in the human rights code.

---

[91] Add to that the overwhelming temptation, once torture is permitted, to employ it "for a wider range of purposes against an increasing proportion of the population." *Torture in the Eighties*, Amnesty International (London, 1984), 7. Karen Tse, founder and CEO of International Bridges to Justice, an organization devoted to training public defenders and raising human rights awareness in a number of countries in Asia and Africa, reports that torture has become a routine investigative technique in all the countries where her organization works.

[92] Morsink, *The Universal Declaration of Human Rights*, 69.

[93] I strongly disagree with Nicholas Wolterstorff's disparagement of most "positive rights," such as "the right to rest and leisure, including reasonable limitation of working hours and period holidays with pay" (Art. 24, UDHR) or the right to education (Art. 26, UDHR). The importance of limitations on working hours and provision for paid leisure should be understood against the appalling "legacy of the company town" in the United States and elsewhere during the nineteenth and early twentieth centuries. Talk about conditions of exploitation! Moreover, his assertion that a right to education cannot be a "human" right (meant for all human beings) because not every human being is capable of being educated ignores the fact that many of the "negative rights" (rights of noninterference) he does espouse are also subject to a similar provision. The right of free speech cannot be said to apply meaningfully to someone who cannot speak or otherwise find a means of expression. The same applies in the case of limitations on working hours or time off with pay. Such rights apply only to people capable of exercising them. Those general limitations do not invalidate the rights for those who are capable of exercising them. See Wolterstorff, *Justice: Rights and Wrongs*, 314ff.

With respect to the logic of pain, civil and political rights are particularly essential for ferreting out self-serving and mistaken reasons. There will, of course, be areas of uncertainty over which interpretation and combination of rights are best suited for maximum protection against arbitrary pain. Those are subjects for continuing dialogue and comparative reflection. There will also be areas of uncertainty over whether in one society or another different forms of legal and political arrangement may exist alongside of or as supplements to rights guarantees, but which provide worthy layers of added protection. That, too, is a subject for ongoing cross-cultural investigation and interaction. Nevertheless, the fascist model stands as the ultimate reference point for assessing all such proposals. How close to or far from the kinds of discrimination, the elimination of restraints on legal, political, and economic life, the violation of standards of decency concerning the use of torture, cruel and unusual treatment or punishment, enslavement, and so on, a given government or other group is becomes the final index of moral and legal legitimacy.

Finally, my proposed defense supports a noncomprehensive moral and legal position. That means, as I said earlier, that the assumed moral grounds apply exclusively to the rights and freedoms enumerated in the instruments and, within limits, are otherwise deferent to and respectful of "freedom of thought, conscience, religion or belief" (Art. 18 UDHR, ICCPR). The proposed position does not pass judgment on philosophical or theological controversies regarding the ultimate grounds and nature of moral life and responsibility, or the practical conclusions drawn from them, or the metaphysical and cosmological ideas related to them, but leaves such questions open to individual conscientious deliberation under the right to freedom of religion or belief.

The position would, of course, constitute "outer limits" on matters of conscientious belief in that it would enjoin the inhibition of actions deduced from particular theological or philosophical comprehensive doctrines that in practice violate the human rights code. However, it would not prohibit inter- and intracultural debate over the contents of the code or over efforts to amend the code according to due process.

CONCLUSION

I have endeavored to give an account of why the drafters composed human rights language in the way they did by suggesting a theoretical defense of that language. My underlying conviction is that without some such defense the language cannot fulfill its intended purposes: to hold people everywhere accountable to the terms of the language, backed up by a provision for universally legitimate enforceability, as well as to provide standards of protection to which everyone may appeal.

My approach is preliminary in several ways. I did not elaborate on the sort of (limited) epistemological or metaphysical argument I made here: More will, of course, eventually need to be said. Epistemologically, the appeal is, in a nutshell, an invitation to reflect on what I called "the logic of pain," by which I mean the way reason works in regard to the infliction or relief of pain. The idea is that one cannot correctly understand the concept of pain without simultaneously grasping its rational structure or logic in the justification of action.

I did concede that certain metaphysical beliefs are implied by my account, though those, too, will need much more attention than is provided here. There is no denying that an idea of "rational competence" is presupposed, as I pointed out, by human rights language. By definition, human rights only fully apply to people capable of being held accountable, of taking responsibility for their actions, such as respecting freedom of religion and cultural expression, as well as freedom of speech, assembly, and participation in government; such actions only make sense in respect to competent adult human beings. My conviction – and here the arguments of Martha Nussbaum are helpful – is that the capabilities necessary for appealing and being held accountable to human rights language have a special status as necessary presuppositions for acting in accord with human rights standards. Perhaps more than Martha Nussbaum, I do not flinch at making requisite metaphysical claims insofar as they are entailed by the epistemological argument I am advancing. This is, I concede, only a beginning, but it perhaps succeeds in sketching out how a fuller discussion might proceed.

Nor did I say nearly enough about how to assess reasons for inflicting or failing to relieve pain beyond the necessary unacceptability of two minimal indications: self-serving and manifestly unfounded reasons. This is a very important challenge, but I may soften its impact by making two points:

(1) I believe that these two indications, however minimal, are nevertheless analytically highly potent, as their application to the Hitler case demonstrates. They are all I really needed to make my case, and they are similarly illuminating, I submit, in my ongoing assessment of the practices of governments and others around the world. It is not hard to show that the recent cases of "mass atrocity crimes," identified with Rwanda, Srebrenica, Kurdish Iraq, Somalia, Darfur, and Burma, are obvious violations of one or both of these indications. And, surely, it is cases like these that ought above all to command the most urgent and sustained international attention and reaction.

I may add that another reason for favoring my approach is the increasing effectiveness, under conditions of globalization and the growing availability of advanced instruments of military and political domination, of inflicting pain and other aversive experiences on defenseless citizens. As Albert Speer pointed out in testimony at the Nuremberg trials, "Hitler's dictatorship differed in one fundamental point from all its predecessors in history. His was the first dictatorship in the present period of modern technical development, a dictatorship which made complete use of all technical means for the domination of its own country.... [One] result was the far-reaching supervision of the citizens of the state and the maintenance of a high degree of secrecy for criminal acts."[94] Things have only gotten more ominous in this respect since Hitler's time.

(2) I also suggest that these two indications are an important beginning place, at least, for applying the approach historically. That is, I assume that the basic wrongness of inflicting pain or failing to relieve it for self-serving or manifestly unfounded reasons is an indispensable reference point for what we might call a comparative study of tyranny. An important component of such a study would be to investigate the adequacy or inadequacy of the "institutions of restraint," according to which the reasons for applying pain by rulers or others were or were not subject to effective public scrutiny and evaluation.

Furthermore, the strong temptation to inflict pain or to fail to relieve it for self-serving or unfounded reasons, to which I alluded throughout this chapter, together with what appears to be an infinite capacity of human beings to create and sustain political systems weighted against public scrutiny, evaluation, and restraint, provides an important explanation for the prominence of tyranny in human history and of the phlegmatic pace at which effective resistance to it has proceeded.

---

[94] Bullock, *Hitler: A Study in Tyranny*, 380.

2

Critical Reflections on *The Last Utopia*
Human Rights in History *by Samuel Moyn*

Moyn's book, published in 2010,[1] provides an influential account of the history and status of human rights language that is in many ways diametrically opposed to the underlying arguments in this book. It therefore deserves an extended response.

Moyn argues that human rights language has, for the most part, been badly misunderstood, both in common usage and by historians and experts. The idea that it has a long-standing pedigree, possibly going back to ancient Western civilization, then developed during the Middle Ages, gathered momentum in association with premodern natural rights challenges to state supremacy, culminated in the post–World-War II period in reaction to fascist atrocities, and, in accord with its universalist principles, expanded its international influence and efficacy up to the present – all very smoothly and inexorably – is largely an illusion.

In fact, "when 'human rights' entered the English language in the 1940s, it [did so] unceremoniously, ever accidentally,"[2] employing notions that "were the victims of their own vagueness."[3] The term was "as a throwaway line, not a well-considered idea," "an empty vessel that could be filled by a wide variety of different conceptions."[4] It involved "stillborn" language,[5] language that remained "peripheral at its time," with only "marginal power."[6] Above all, it is a "myth that human rights were a direct response to the worst crimes

---

[1] Samuel Moyn, *The Last Utopia: Human Rights in History* (Cambridge, MA: Harvard University Press, 2010).
[2] Ibid., 44.
[3] Ibid., 64.
[4] Ibid., 51.
[5] Ibid., 89.
[6] Ibid., 68, 86.

of the century."⁷ "They were not a response to the Holocaust, and [were] not indeed focused on the prevention of catastrophic slaughter,"⁸ because "in the debate around the Universal Declaration in the UN General Assembly," "the genocide of the Jews went unmentioned." "Only decades later" did the "commitment to human rights crystallize [around the] Holocaust memory."⁹

The original indeterminacy and impotence of human rights language, rather, were underscored by its lack of historical antecedents, by some early opposition and indifference coupled with feeble support, and then by its ready susceptibility in the 1960s and later to radical reformulation based on the fads of the times.

As to its history, believing that natural rights anticipate human rights is, for Moyn, indefensible. That is because natural rights depended directly on political order: They were inseparable from the state, not only for guaranteeing rights but also for defining them. Thomas Hobbes and Hugo Grotius, the principal architects of natural rights, argued as much,¹⁰ and they were supported by developments in both France and England. The French Declaration of the Rights of Man and Citizen applied only to French citizens as the title indicates,¹¹ and English and early American charters of rights were, "in their origin, stipulations between kings and their subjects," Alexander Hamilton is quoted as saying. "Were [there] no prince," Moyn concludes, "no enumeration of rights would be necessary."¹²

Natural rights language was "from the beginning," then, "part of the authority of the state, not invoked to transcend it."¹³ Because people had rights only as members of a given state, rights did not meaningfully extend beyond its borders. Rights, Moyn says, were not "natural" or "human" in a universal, transnational sense, but strictly "political" and "civil" within a given jurisdiction. One reason, in short, that Moyn doubts that human rights language as ratified had a consistently universalist, transnational meaning is that there are

---

⁷ Ibid., 82–83.
⁸ Ibid., 47.
⁹ Ibid., 83.
¹⁰ Ibid., 18ff.
¹¹ On p. 27, Moyn quotes Article 3 of the French Declaration: "the principle of all sovereignty resides essentially in the nation; no group, no individual may exercise authority that does not emanate from it."
¹² Ibid., 24. Moyns cites approvingly Emmanuel Joseph Sieyes's criticism of the "American commitment to rights" as being "too dependent on an antique tradition of aristocratic rights talk stretching back to the Magna Carta."
¹³ Ibid., 7.

no precedents for interpreting rights that way. Therefore, any such construction amounted to a decided afterthought, a subsequent invention, which needs explanation. "If human rights now so thoroughly define cosmopolitanism as to seem the only possible form, it is precisely not because of their ancient vintage."[14]

As to what happened to human rights language once adopted, it was at first either disregarded or it became the instrument of Cold War rhetoric and, eventually, of utopian visions. The prevalent spirit of political realism, whether expressed by Americans, such as Hans Morgenthau, Stanley Hoffmann, and Reinhold Niebuhr, or Europeans like Raymond Aron and E. H. Carr, disparaged human rights as naïve or a cause of hypocrisy and favored a balance-of-power strategy between East and West, based on the priority of state sovereignty.[15] The only conceivable reason why human rights language might be useful was as a tool for marketing the UN, "a far cry from utopian multilateralism based on human rights."[16]

With similar effect, the large majority of the legal community, led by the American Bar Association, successfully opposed all efforts by the U.S. Senate to ratify human rights instruments, exalting state sovereignty and "vilify[ing] internationalism in all of its forms as global communism in disguise."[17] The campaign, so supported, "proved [to be] effective partisan rhetoric in appeals to the American way."[18] Moyn gives modest credit to mainline American Protestants, working through national and international councils of churches and cooperating with like-minded representatives of other faiths, for elevating the image of human rights, especially the right of religious freedom.[19] However, they did not, after all, achieve very impressive results. Their efforts were widely dismissed as the preoccupation of those in "a suitably feminine field."[20]

The most influential advocates of human rights during the 1950s were a "global diplomatic elite, often schooled in Western locales, who helped tinker with the Declaration at a moment of symbolic unity."[21] Of special importance were non-Anglo-European Christians, such as Charles Malik of Lebanon and Carlos Romulo of the Philippines, both of whom were active in the drafting

---

[14] Ibid., 41.
[15] Ibid., 59, 73, 188, 189.
[16] Ibid., 59.
[17] Ibid., 73.
[18] Ibid., 73–74.
[19] Ibid., 53.
[20] Ibid., 62.
[21] Ibid., 66.

of the UDHR; this group was strongly aided by European Catholics, such as Jacques Maritain and Gerhard Ritter. Particularly the Catholics twisted the wax nose that was human rights language into the shape of a "third-way, personalist, communitarian alternative to liberal atomism and materialist communism alike," with a "continuing antisecularist agenda," aimed, above all, at defending Christianity against the rising tide of communism.[22]

Like American Ecumenical Protestants, the Catholics placed special emphasis on the right to religious freedom, presumably to bolster their numbers in the worldwide contest with the communists.[23] Moyn concedes the European Christians had an impact on the postwar Christian democratic movement throughout Western Europe. They succeeded in defining human rights in exclusively civil and political terms – "social and economic rights were dropped"[24] – and they thereby contributed to the establishment of an anticommunist European Convention of Human Rights, along with a court

---

[22] Ibid., 74. See p. 109 for a reference to the commitment of Malik and Romulo, shared with European Catholics, such as Maritain, to Christian Personalism. In his book, *The Rights of Man and Natural Law* (London: Geoffrey Bless, 1945), Jacques Maritain, the French Catholic philosopher and influential member of the postwar human rights movement, advances a form of antisecularism that is utterly mystifying as to how far he believes the state should go in supporting "the true religion, once known" (17). On the one hand, he explicitly favors a pluralist state rather than a Christian state, as well as the right of non-Christians to express themselves in public and to be represented "in the councils of the nation," and he rejects any common religious creed for citizens, along with all attempts to impose political or legal disadvantages on non-Christians (17). On the other hand, "States," after World War II, he says, "will be obliged," "willingly or unwillingly," "to make a choice for or against the Gospel. They will be shaped either by the totalitarian spirit or by the Christian spirit" (16). "It is by virtue of institutions, manners, and customs, that such a political society might be called Christian, not in its appearance, but in its substance" (17). Such a society "would be conscious of its doctrine and its morality. It would be conscious of the faith that inspires it and it would express it publicly" (17); it would be *theist* or *Christian*, not in the sense that it would require every member of society to believe in God and to be Christian, but in the sense that it recognizes that in the reality of things" (15; original italics). In a lengthy footnote, he recommends "the recent Concordat [in 1943] concluded between the Holy See and Portugal." "The Portuguese State allows freedom of religion and does not grant to any Church the privilege of State Church – this without itself assuming an attitude of neutrality. 'Put in a few words, the Portuguese State, which permits all cults and does not support an official Church, is not neutral as regards doctrine and morals. The State adopts the principles of Catholic Christian doctrine and morals,'" a statement by one Cardinal Cerejeira expressly commended by Maritain. Maritain's endorsement of the cardinal's statement is especially confounding, because he goes on to admit that the Portuguese state, at that time, "is an example not to be followed (a systematic dictatorship which, moreover, although indeed not totalitarian, but friendly to Spanish totalitarianism which is itself friendly to fascism and nazism, constitutes an ideal bait to lure onto the hook of totalitarianism minds lacking in political experience)" (fn. 1, 19).

[23] Moyn, *The Last Utopia*, 72.
[24] Ibid., 79.

designed to apply it.[25] The problem was their understanding of the language turned out to be but a function of the Cold War. In the end, the movement proved to be ephemeral, based as it was on a belief in "a utopia too vague [and] then too conservative to matter."[26]

A crucial turning point in Moyn's account takes place in the 1960s in the form of an accelerated anticolonialist campaign throughout the "third world." That campaign introduced a new utopian vision concerning the rights of peoples in rebellion against colonial domination. In particular, it caused a "conceptual revolution"[27] in human rights language: "[T]he utopia" that "mattered most was postcolonial, collective liberation from empire, not individual rights canonized in international law."[28] The rhetoric was closely tied to "the promise of self-determination"[29] and "anticolonial nationalism"[30] and to rejecting "any supervening concept of international rights."[31]

With the emphasis on collective as opposed to individual rights, the new rhetoric gravitated away from Western interpretations of rights, illustrating the "fateful connection" between anticolonialism and Marxist thought that was so evident among the leaders of the "nonaligned nations" (e.g., Sukarno and Nehru in Asia, Nasser in the Middle East, and Nkrumah and Kaunda in Africa).[32] To the extent these leaders had any transnational interests, they favored "alternative internationalisms, in a spirit very different from that of contemporary human rights."[33] Schemes such as "Pan-Africanism" and "Pan-Arabism" were "focused not on classical liberties, or even 'social [and economic] rights,' but [on] collective economic development"[34] and were accordingly devoted to state control and central management.

Moyn stresses that "postwar anticolonialists rarely invoked the phrase 'human rights,' or appealed to the [UDHR]."[35] At the same time, he holds that anticolonialism was, after all, "*a rights of man* movement, with all the dependence on the state that concept implied in modern history,"[36] recalling his description of the natural rights tradition discussed earlier. This point

---

[25] Ibid., 78–79.
[26] Ibid., 47–48.
[27] Ibid., 108.
[28] Ibid., 85.
[29] Ibid.
[30] Ibid., 173.
[31] Ibid., 85.
[32] Ibid., 91ff.
[33] Ibid., 86.
[34] Ibid.
[35] Ibid., 85.
[36] Ibid.

might suggest that he thinks the anticolonial movement "betrayed or 'captured' human rights, destroying their original meaning." However, he makes clear that is not what he intends: "Given the uncertainty of the meaning and the marginal power of the idea of human rights in the 1940s, it is better to regard the eventual force of anticolonialism at the UN as its own distinctive tradition – one that the rise of human rights in their more contemporary sense would have to replace."[37] In short, in the 1960s and early 1970s, human rights language was effectively displaced by a utopian vision of "collective liberation," which, in turn, eventually gave way to an utterly novel ideal, "the last utopia" – namely, our present universalist, suprastate understanding, with its unprecedented elevation of the equal protection of individual rights.

How this conflict between "competing utopias" took place is described in the last chapter in Moyn's account. The transition from the ideals embodied in anticolonialism to those associated with a modern human rights outlook resulted from a convergence of reactions to the excesses of centralized collective control and unrestricted state sovereignty. "Socialism with a human face died in 1968," beginning with the dismantling of the Prague Spring by means of the Soviet invasion of Czechoslovakia and followed by its cascading collapse across the region, which "left new ideological space for the human rights strategy of dissidence to become central to the Soviet Union in the early 1970s and thereafter many other places as well."[38] The adoption of the Helsinki Final Act of 1975 by the Conference on Security and Cooperation in Europe, with its provisions for individual protections, together with the highly publicized Charter 77 movement and its campaign to hold states to their previous rights commitments, gave further credence to new transnational standards of governmental accountability in Eastern Europe.[39]

Similar reactions in Latin America to the abuses caused by centralized national control added momentum. A military coup in Uruguay in 1973, closely followed by the assassination of the Chilean president, Salvador Allende, at the hands of a military junta and then, beginning in 1976, the "dirty war" in Argentina, a product of a highly repressive police state, all called into question the principle of unregulated state supremacy.[40] Moreover, the ill effects of detaching collective rights from individual rights, as abundantly exemplified in the experience of anticolonialism in Africa and elsewhere,

---

[37] Ibid., 86.
[38] Ibid., 136.
[39] Ibid., 148ff.
[40] Ibid., 140.

also made more compelling a new approach to human rights. The anticolonial experience had apparently replicated the "disastrous consequences" of the passion for self-determination in Europe between the wars, when countless individuals and groups suffered grievously "as contiguous ethnonational groups sought collective redemption."[41]

These and similar reactions elsewhere to events in the 1960s and early 1970s, such as U.S policies in Indochina and the Watergate scandal, paved the way for the election of President Jimmy Carter in 1976 and his commitment to elevate human rights – now understood as universal, transnational norms of equal individual protection – as the final standard to which governments should be held to account. It was in the late 1970s that human rights "were reclaimed from anticolonialism, and made a central part for the first time of the foreign policy of American liberalism."[42] For Moyn, Carter was elected as the result of "a campaign suffused with promises of moral transcendence of politics" or "the primacy of moralism," something that "opened the way for the astonishing explosion of 'human rights' across the American landscape."[43] He was elected because of a "widespread desire" on the part of the American public to substitute "morality for failed politics," "to drop utopia and have one anyway."[44]

The problem was that Carter's brand of moralized politics left him and his supporters "with a heavy burden later."

> First, the moment that favored pure moral visions passed, not least in American party and electoral politics, as Jimmy Carter's brief presidential career illustrates so vividly. Second, and more important, partisans of the human rights idea were forced to confront the need for [a] political agenda and programmatic vision – the very things whose absence allowed for their utopia to emerge so spectacularly and discontinuously in the first place. If human rights were born in antipolitics, they could not remain wholly noncommittal toward programmatic endeavors, especially as time passed.[45]

One highly unfortunate outcome, in Moyn's opinion, was that such utopian language could so easily be redefined by Carter's successor, Ronald Reagan, to combine "unrelenting opposition to communist regimes who would never reform" with "a friendly attitude toward rightist dictators supposedly on a path to liberalism," thereby making the language of human rights "a potent

---

[41] Ibid., 197.
[42] Ibid., 209.
[43] Ibid., 154.
[44] Ibid., 175.
[45] Ibid., 213.

antitotalitarian weapon for the first time."[46] It was an interpretation, Moyn concludes, that would "have many tragic consequences at the time and since."[47] Such are the wages of utopianism.

Among the many claims Moyn makes in his complicated narrative, one of them is certainly correct: "The astonishing explosion" of human rights in the late 1970s meant that for the first time that the subject was of urgent concern in the United States and elsewhere. Human rights were not quite so neglected after the adoption of the UDHR as Moyn makes out. Still, they did not command anywhere near the attention in those intervening years as they did from around 1976 on, and that fact, as Moyn sees, demands explanation. The only problem is that Moyn's explanation is in large measure incorrect, partly because it is based on a seriously flawed account of both the nature and background of human rights language.

Moyn is not altogether forthcoming about his own interpretive framework. It is not until page 214, thirteen pages from the end of the book, that he reveals it. If human rights, he says,

> had been forged in a moment of post-Holocaust wisdom, they would have had a completely different historical bearing, both focused on genocide prevention from the beginning and restricted to that incontestable cause without having to shoulder the burden of addressing all global ills and diverse political agendas. But they did neither of these things.

These are the utterances of a follower of Raphael Lemkin, a Polish Jew and jurist, and the intrepid champion after World War II of outlawing genocide. Through his indefatigable efforts, Lemkin almost single-handedly brought about the adoption of the Genocide Convention by the UN General Assembly two days before it adopted the UDHR on December 10, 1948. For Lemkin, however, the proximity of those two votes was not a happy occurrence. While ardently favoring the prohibition of genocide, he sharply opposed the codification of human rights: "Instead of seeing or seeking common ground, Lemkin chided human rights advocates *for the very utopianism* that his opponents ascribed to him."[48] For example, he regarded the attempt to outlaw discrimination "by fiat of law," rather than by a gradual "historical process," as "laughably unrealistic." It is, he said, "merely a description of Utopia, but Utopia belongs to fiction and poetry, not to law."[49] Unfortunately, Lemkin became

---

[46] Ibid., 217.
[47] Ibid.
[48] Samantha Power, *"A Problem from Hell": America and the Age of Genocide* (New York: Basic Books, 2002), 76 (italics added).
[49] Cited at ibid.

obsessive about his cause and, consequently, "found himself mouthing the same arguments as notorious human rights abusers. In his fury, he ignored all he had in common with his human rights rivals."[50]

By waiting until the end of the book to acknowledge his Lemkinian convictions (and by mentioning Lemkin only once in passing[51]), Moyn buries the lead and, as a result, fails to take responsibility for disclosing his own orientation and defending it carefully. Moyn's commitment to Lemkin's outlook undoubtedly explains his disparaging attitude toward human rights and his readiness to identify them as mere utopianism ("a throwaway line, not a well-considered idea," "an empty vessel," "stillborn," "peripheral at its time," having only "marginal power"). It also explains his astounding penchant for denying that human rights had anything to do with Nazi atrocities ("the myth that human rights were a direct response to the worst crimes of the century"; "they were not a response to the Holocaust, and [were] not indeed focused on the prevention of catastrophic slaughter"; "only decades later" did the "commitment to human rights crystallize [around the] Holocaust memory").

The serious difficulty is that all these statements betray some of the same obsessive characteristics as Lemkin does in his attack on human rights. They are expressed with similar passion and similar dogmatic assurance, and are in the same way "not well-considered"; they are simply asserted without any support whatsoever. Furthermore, as with Lemkin in his fury, uttering such statements risks, inadvertently to be sure, aiding and abetting the opponents of human rights.

To begin with, Moyn supplies almost no analysis of the text of the international human rights instruments, nor does he examine any of the extensive jurisprudence that has developed in response to them. It is therefore impossible to tell what the evidence is for drawing such self-confident conclusions about the original indeterminacy and impotence of human rights language. Unless I am mistaken, there are only two references in the entire book to the actual text of the instruments. The first is this: "[T]he Universal Declaration retains, rather than supersedes, the sanctity of nationhood, as its text makes clear."[52] However, even here it is unclear what exactly Moyn is alluding to. There are two possibilities. The Preamble to the UDHR mentions "all peoples and nations," but only in connection with their obligations to consider the Declaration "as a common standard of achievement"; "to promote respect for" the "rights and freedoms" contained in it "by progressive measures, national

---

[50] Ibid.
[51] Moyn, *Last Utopia*, 82.
[52] Ibid., 81.

and international"; and "to secure their universal and effective recognition and observance."

In addition, Article 29.2 does authorize the state to limit "the exercise of... rights and freedoms" in regard to "meeting the just requirements of morality, public order and the general welfare," but only insofar as it is the general welfare "in a democratic society" and the limits "are determined by law solely for the purpose of securing due recognition and respect for the rights and freedoms of others." Obviously, neither one of these references provides unqualified support for the "sanctity of nationhood."

The second reference appears in his discussion of the anticolonial movement in the 1960s and early 1970s. In that context, he says, "the utopia that still mattered most was postcolonial, collective liberation from empire, not individual rights canonized in international law."[53] To a certain extent, this is an important concession on Moyn's part because it runs against his recurring claim that original human rights language was incoherent, empty, stillborn, and so on. It suggests instead that the language had a fixed focus and coherence around the notion of individual rights. At the same time, he leaves in doubt how seriously he takes the reference by trivializing it as the less important of two kinds of utopian speech.

Another problem is that Moyn simply ignores without defense overwhelming evidence against his assertions about the irrelevance of Nazi atrocities and the Holocaust to the drafting of the UDHR. In a bibliographical essay, he calls Johannes Morsink's book, *The Universal Declaration of Human Rights: Origins, Drafting, and Intent*,[54] a "fine drafting history," but never refers to it in the text, and only once, without comment, in a footnote.[55] As demonstrated in the Introduction and chapter 1 of that volume, Morsink supplies extensive and compelling evidence supporting the indispensability of Nazi atrocities, including "the absolutely crucial factor of the Holocaust,"[56] to the drafting and adoption of the UDHR. In chapter 2, titled, "World War II as Catalyst," Morsink makes a particularly powerful case by showing in painstaking detail how the final wording of many of the articles in the UDHR was drafted in deliberate response to Nazi practices.[57] Because Moyn nowhere takes up or endeavors to refute Morsink's arguments and evidence – particularly having praised the book! – there is no reason to accept his claims concerning the lack of connection between human rights language and World War II.

[53] Ibid., 85.
[54] See Introduction, fn. 49.
[55] Moyn, *Last Utopia*, 255, fn. 31.
[56] Morsink, *Universal Declaration of Human Rights*, xiii–xiv.
[57] Ibid., 37–52.

The same is true of his claims concerning the relation of the natural rights tradition to human rights. The assertions that natural rights language was "from the beginning" "part of the authority of the state, not invoked to transcend it," and that rights were not "natural" or "human" in a universal, transnational sense, but were strictly "political" and "civil" within a given jurisdiction, are flatly mistaken, as I argue in the Introduction to this volume.

As with key literature regarding the World War II provenance of human rights language, Moyn again mentions, but nowhere seriously engages, studies that are now indispensable to the understanding of the natural rights tradition. In his bibliographical essay, he divides the positions of the relevant authors into four categories, two of which emphasize the medieval background, and the other two, the importance of Renaissance humanists and seventeenth-century premodern thinkers.[58] In his brief commentary, Moyn takes no position himself among the different schools, but only makes the following remark: "No matter who is correct, of course, the results for the history of human rights are a matter of background preconditions, not immediate causation."[59] What is baffling about this is that in his own description of the history of natural rights in chapter 1, Moyn shows no sign of neutrality. There he discards all impartiality, clearly siding against the work of Brian Tierney, a member of the second category of scholars who stress "continuity in Christian natural law, . . . [and] then [trace it] it forward into early modern developments."[60]

Evincing Hobbes as one of the chief architects of the natural rights tradition, as Moyn does, is completely contrary to Tierney's conclusions:

> Hobbes's work is best seen as an aberration from the mainstream of natural rights thinking that flowed from the medieval jurists through Ockham, Gerson, Grotius to Pufendorf and Locke. . . . It is at least clear that, in Hobbes's theory, the natural state of humankind was one of "war of all against all," that everyone had a right to everything, "even to another's body," and that no one had a duty to respect the rights of others. But how can this conceivably be regarded as the origin of modern rights theories?[61]

> Some authors, most famously Hobbes, tried to use a theory of absolute natural rights to sustain a doctrine of absolute sovereign power; but the argument . . . was, I think, ultimately incoherent. In the final outcome, modern constitutional thought evolved in the way it did partly because the practice of

---

[58] Moyn, *Last Utopia*, 312, 313.
[59] Ibid., 313.
[60] Ibid.
[61] Tierney, *Idea of Natural Rights*, 341.

monarchical absolutism could not easily be reconciled with a theory of the state expressed in the language of natural rights.[62]

There are strong reasons for judging Tierney right about Hobbes, and if Moyn has evidence to the contrary, he is bound to present it. Obviously, if Hobbes is a bona fide natural rights thinker, then Moyn's picture of natural rights as completely dependent on the state gains support. But if Hobbes is, in fact, an "aberration," the support disappears.

Grotius, the second of Moyn's natural rights architects, is a more complicated case. Tierney thinks of him as a legitimate natural rights thinker who, as such, is given to defending a right of resistance "against tyranny that we often encounter in medieval and early modern sources," a response understood as "a form of just warfare based on the right of self-defense."[63] However, for Grotius the right to resist authority is for the most part inoperative once a state is established, lest anarchy occur. Grotius does allow some exceptions in the most extreme circumstances, though he displays considerable reluctance on the subject, leading Tierney to conclude that, on balance, Grotius did not favor absolutism, though he was so horrified by the consequences of overzealous resistance that he came close to supporting it.[64] In any case, the only issue here concerns the degree to which Grotius was a consistent natural rights advocate, namely, one who seeks to impose natural rights limits on the exercise of sovereignty. As with his analysis of Hobbes, Tierney's conclusion is of no help to Moyn. Once again, if Moyn has reasonable objections to Tierney's conclusions, he should supply them or modify his description.

Why Moyn would ignore Locke in these matters is incomprehensible.[65] By now, there can be no dispute that Locke is a central figure in the tradition, and anyone undertaking to speak for the tradition will have to take a position on what Locke meant by natural rights. If Moyn disagrees with accounts similar to the one given in the Introduction to this volume, and such accounts are not hard to come by, then, as elsewhere, he is obliged to state and defend his case. Such accounts, of course, see Locke as the resolute enemy of arbitrary political

---

[62] Ibid., 289.
[63] Ibid., 337.
[64] Ibid., 337–338. See Richard Tuck, *Natural Rights Theories*, for a more unqualified statement of the deep ambivalence of Grotius's thought. Tuck describes Grotius's book, *The Right of War and Peace*, as "Janus-faced, and its two mouths speak the language of both absolutism and liberty" (79).
[65] Moyn mentions Locke only once in passing (23), and then only in reference to a right to property.

Critical Reflections on The Last Utopia

power. Richard Tuck, another author Moyn mentions but does not engage, provides what, in my view, is a perspicuous summary of Locke's thought:

> [For Locke] it is enough to rule out absolutism that the sovereign ought under no circumstances to act in an arbitrary or unjust way towards his subjects, given a general theory of sovereignty as created by agreement. For if there is such a restriction on possible actions by a sovereign, men cannot put themselves under a sovereign who might break it: that would be to consent to another man's acting in an immoral way and would thus go against the fundamental principles of the law of nature. All that was needed to establish the constraint on absolutism was thus a clear statement of what kind of rights men may possess over each other in a pre-civil society, that is, a clear statement of the right which both he and Grotius believed in, to execute offenders against the law of nature.[66]

There are several other serious shortcomings to Moyn's account of the natural rights tradition. Locke's view that precivil natural rights imposed limitations on government were anticipated by Puritan groups active in the English Civil War (1642–1649) in a way that calls into question Moyn's characterization of the English rights tradition. One such group was the Levellers, leftish members of Cromwell's New Model Army, who joined enthusiastically in the successful overthrow of the monarchy and sought to replace it with a constitutional democracy.[67] From 1647 to 1649, they proposed three "Agreements of the People" – one a year – revising and making some concessions to opponents as they went. But they were consistent on essential features, such as an expanded view of freedom of conscience and no religious tests for public office; equality before the law; universal male suffrage (with a few exceptions); annual parliamentary elections; due process of law, including protection against self-incrimination; trial by jury and the right to call witnesses; no imprisonment for debt; and the abolition of the death penalty except for murder.

There is evidence, it is true, that the arguments of Leveller leaders, such as John Lilburne, William Walwyn, and Richard Overton, conformed to a degree to Moyn's characterization of the English rights tradition as derived from ancient national sources. They all, on occasion, emphasized the radical implications of the English legal tradition going back to Magna Carta and, before that, to the laws laid down by Edward the Confessor in the eleventh century, which, they claimed, were only partially deviated from by William the Conqueror in the Norman Conquest of 1066. They all understood the

---

[66] Tuck, *Natural Rights Theories*, 173.
[67] See Richard Ashcroft, *Revolutionary Politics and Locke's Two Treatises* (Princeton, NJ: Princeton University Press, 1986), 155–166.

tradition as uninterrupted in warranting "a mutual contract between king and people, which Lilburne tellingly identified with the Agreement of the People."[68]

At the same time, there were differences among Leveller leaders regarding the grounds on which the constitution should rest. John Lilburne, founder of the movement, started out invoking the "ancient rights of Englishmen" symbolized by Magna Carta as the sacred precedent, thereby conforming to Moyn's description. However, Lilburne eventually changed his mind and came to agree with fellow Levellers, such as Richard Overton and William Walwyn. Walwyn told him that "Magna Carta hath been more precious in your esteeme that it deserveth," precisely because its authority is too narrow, too bound to the outmoded tradition of a single state. Rather, it is natural reason and an appeal to natural rights, universally understood, that is finally the only authentic grounds for the newly proposed constitution.[69]

Overton elaborated on the point with a characteristic flourish: "Reason hath no precedent; for reason is the foundation of all just precedents." The "natural radical principle of reason," which undergirds all "natural human rights and freedoms," "is conveyed to all men in general, and to every man in particular," that "by all rational and just ways and means," all human beings may "save, defend, and deliver [themselves] from all oppression, violence, and cruelty whatsoever."[70] Natural rights included freedom of conscience against governmental intrusion: "Where a conversion is not and cannot be obtained," "there no human compulsive power or force is to be used."[71] Nor did he limit the scope of natural rights to civil and political matters, "it being against the radical law of nature and reason that any man" "that is not any enemy thereto" "should be deprived of human subsistence."[72]

No matter how much Overton, Walwyn, and Lilburne talked about England's venerable past, "they no longer viewed history as imbued with 'prescriptive force.' They saved it instead for purposes of illustration."[73] For them

---

[68] See R. B. Seaberg, "The Norman Conquest and the Common Law: The Levellers and the Argument from Continuity," *Historical Journal* 24 (1981), 791–806, cited in Janelle Greenberg, *The Radical Face of the Ancient Constitution: St. Edward's "Laws" in Early Modern Political Thought* (Cambridge: Cambridge University Press, 2001), 227.

[69] Perez Zagorin, *A History of Political Thought of the English Revolution* (London: Routledge & Kegan Paul, 1954), 16, 22, 27, 29.

[70] A. S. P. Woodhouse, ed., *Puritanism and Liberty* (Chicago: University of Chicago Press, 1974), 323, 325, 333.

[71] Ibid., 332.

[72] Ibid., 333.

[73] Greenberg, *The Radical Face of the Ancient Constitution*, citing a comment by Quentin Skinner, 137.

natural rights, grounded in reason, ultimately guaranteed the civil, political, and economic rights of individuals everywhere, thereby constituting a universal standard for the legitimacy of the state. In that, Locke and the Levellers were of one mind.

One final difficulty with Moyn's account of the natural rights tradition concerns his puzzling treatment of Georg Jellinek's important study of the Puritan sources of natural rights, a subject related to the preceding discussion.[74] Moyn focuses on French reactions to Jellinek's claim that the French Declaration was not an indigenous document but was derived from American colonial sources, commenting that the French "were predictably unhappy with [Jellinek's] attempt to steal their birthrights."[75] Although hinting that Americans may have had the better argument, he nevertheless concludes that the sources of both traditions "remained hard to isolate"[76] and that, in any case, disputes over such questions are, after all, "tawdry" and only illustrate "how deeply nationalism has defined, not simply the rights of man, but partisan interpretations of their trajectory in an age of revolution."[77] In short, Moyn thinks the whole debate only reconfirms his thesis about the state-centered character of natural rights, and he reinforces the point by proceeding to link "the American commitment to rights" to the British tradition, "stretching back to the Magna Carta, which merely reserved prerogatives 'negatively' from the king rather than actually founding the polity 'positively' on rights principles."[78]

But Moyn's summary of this matter ignores something very important. He mentions in passing that Jellinek roots American rights talk in the Reformation, but lets the point drop, possibly because, if proven, it would further undermine his central argument. To be sure, Jellinek does think that, by means of a careful word-by-word comparison, he is able to show that the French Declaration is largely derived from colonial American charters of rights that were drafted and ratified before it.[79]

---

[74] Moyn, *Last Utopia*, 24–25. Georg Jellinek, The *Declaration of the Rights of Man and of Citizens: A Contribution to Constitutional History* (Westport, CT: Hyperion Press, 1979), first published in German in 1895.
[75] Moyn, *Last Utopia*, 24.
[76] Ibid.
[77] Ibid.
[78] Ibid., 24–25.
[79] See Jelllinek, *Declaration of Man and of Citizens*, chs. 2 and 5. The derivation would, of course, exclude Article 3 of the French Declaration, which refers to the principle that "all sovereignty resides essentially in the nation; no group, no individual may exercise authority that does not emanate from it." There is no such reference in the colonial charters, and it represents a serious, peculiarly French, deviation from the natural rights tradition.

However, Jellinek argues for more than that. A major conclusion is that "the idea of establishing inalienable, inherent and sacred rights of the individual is not of political but religious origin," and "its first apostle was not Lafayette but Roger Williams,"[80] the dissident Puritan founder of the Rhode Island colony in 1636. It was Williams who first established "as a recognized principle of the state" "the right of liberty of conscience," and with it "the conception of a universal right of man."[81] Jellinek leaves no doubt that by "universal right" he means a standard distinct from and prior to any particular national heritage or tradition. "American declarations of rights... enumerate a much larger number of rights than the English declarations, and look upon these rights as innate and inalienable. Whence comes this conception of American law? "[N]ot," says Jellinek, "from the English law."[82] Here, as previously, Moyn is obligated to face up to the full range of argument and evidence supplied by the scholars he mentions and, then, if he has objections, to defend them.

We come, finally, to Moyn's explanation for the delayed reaction to human rights. By now, we have established strong reasons for doubting one part of his explanation – that human rights language as first formulated and ratified in 1948 was impotent because it was "utopian," "vague," "empty," "stillborn," unrelated to World War II, and lacked historical antecedents and, as a result, was supposed to be susceptible to whatever interpretation came along later. If, on the contrary, the language can be shown to be generally coherent and cogent, and to be deeply connected to contemporaneous events and to a long-standing lineage of ideas in favor of universal standards of individual protection to which all governments are accountable, then the picture changes significantly.

Having just emphasized the successful campaign of the American Bar Association against ratifying any human rights instruments, with its "effective partisan rhetoric" and "populist appeals to the American way," Moyn then draws a curious conclusion: "Nevertheless," he says, "the emphasis on American conservatism in the end skews the picture as a whole."[83] He explains the statement by referring to what he thinks is of much greater importance for the fate of human rights in the postwar period: the influence of European Christian conservatism, which first co-opted human rights language and "later mummif[ied] it as the Cold War began."[84]

---

[80] Ibid., 77. See Chapter 9 in this volume.
[81] Ibid., 75–76.
[82] Ibid., 56. See David Little, "Differences Over the Foundation of Law in Seventeenth and Eighteenth Century America," in R. Griffin-Jones and M. Hill, eds., *Magna Carta, Religion and the Rule of Law* (Cambridge: Cambridge University Press, 2015).
[83] Moyn, *Last Utopia*, 74.
[84] Ibid.

But whatever the significance of European Christianity in defining and directing human rights in the 1950s, it is highly peculiar to reckon it as more important than what happened in the United States. Without question, the United States became the ideological as well as strategic center of the Western side of the Cold War, with Western Europe as its lieutenant. For good or ill, what occurred in the United States set the pace for the rest of the "free world." That was certainly true for the subject of human rights.

What took place in the United States at the time was the mobilization of American conservatism as we know it today, manifesting itself not only in economic and legal thinking but also religiously and politically. Of special interest is the religious aspect of the new movement, because from this period forward American political culture would be profoundly colored by the emergence of Evangelical Protestantism. Led by figures such as Billy Graham, his father-in-law, L. Nelson Bell, and Carl F. H. Henry, American Evangelicals reconstituted themselves in calculated reaction to much that their rivals, the then-dominant Ecumenical Protestants, represented.[85] The Evangelicals opposed not only the liberal attitudes of the Ecumenicals toward scripture and doctrine but also their interest in religious cooperation, as expressed in the National Council of Churches, and their ideals of internationalism as manifested in the World Council of Churches and the United Nations. Evangelicals were particularly incensed at the relentless attacks by the Ecumenicals on the idea that America is an "exceptional" nation, especially chosen of God to reform the world, and because of its special rights and privileges properly free of all international legal and political limitations. For Evangelicals, America was just such a nation, particularly so during the Cold War with the growing threat of "godless" communism. Accordingly, Evangelicals eagerly embraced the powerful anticommunist impulses sweeping the country in the form of McCarthyism and McCarranism and helped create a "new American national religion," focused on public expressions of religious loyalty, military superiority, and a free-market economy, that would strongly influence American political culture thereafter.[86]

Singularly objectionable to the Evangelicals was the keen support for human rights found among many Ecumenicals.

---

[85] See David A. Hollinger, "After Cloven Tongues of Fire: Ecumenical Protestantism and the Modern American Encounter with Diversity," published in the *Journal American History* (June 2011) and reprinted along with much interesting additional material in Hollinger, *After Cloven Tongues of Fire: Protestant Liberalism in Modern American History* (Princeton, NJ: Princeton University Press, 2013).

[86] T. Jeremy Gunn, *Spiritual Weapons: The Cold War and the Forging of a New American National Religion* (Westport, CT: Praeger, 2009).

Disagreements between [Ecumenicals] and [E]vangelicals about the place of Christianity in America paralleled disagreements about the relation of Christianity to human rights globally. While [Ecumenicals] were proud of having played a role in advancing a human rights agenda within the UN and had no trouble recognizing that the diversity of the UN's constituencies made predicating human rights on a narrowly Christian foundation inappropriate, [E]vangelicals castigated the UN's Universal Declaration of Human Rights because, in the words of the *Christianity Today* editor, Carl F. H. Henry in 1957, the declaration "incorporates no references to a supernatural Creator, nor does it anywhere assert that God endows mankind with specific 'rights' and 'duties.'"[87]

The contribution of one Ecumenical Protestant leader, O. Frederick Nolde, represented in particular what Evangelicals detested about human rights. Nolde had played a significant role in getting human rights accepted as part of the UN Charter and in drafting the final language of Article 18 of the UDHR, guaranteeing freedom of conscience, religion, or belief.[88] He stated explicitly that "freedom demands a broader base than can be offered by religion alone" and that ideas about extending religious liberty needed to be placed in a "secular context,"[89] by which he apparently meant "a common, religiously impartial moral space shared by people of very different fundamental commitments and identities."[90] As Evangelicals, to their horror, could well understand, Nolde's thinking conformed closely to the assumptions underlying the UDHR.

For Evangelicals, the problem was not that human rights were "utopian" or illusory or the language "vague," "empty," or "stillborn"; they had no difficulty understanding what human rights generally stood for, how they were grounded, or the nature of the restrictions they would impose on America's international behavior. They understood all that quite well and *for that very reason* opposed human rights with everything they had. Moreover, it is this clear, if thoroughly antagonistic, understanding that consolidated their relationship with conservatism and with the "partisan rhetoric" and "populist appeals to the American way" characteristic of the American Bar Association and a growing number of political figures, particularly in the South.

[87] Hollinger, "Cloven Tongues of Fire," *Journal of American History*, 25.
[88] John S. Nurser, *For All Peoples and All Nations: The Ecumenical Church and Human Rights* (Washington, DC: Georgetown University Press, 2005), ch. 2: "The Man: Fred Nolde." Cf. David Little, "The Legacy of Ecumenical Protestantism: Nolde's Contribution," The Nolde Lecture, Lutheran Seminary of Philadelphia, October 1, 2013. Forthcoming in *Soundings*, 98.1 (February 2015).
[89] Nurser, *For All Peoples and All Nations*, 99.
[90] The sentence is drawn from David Little, Foreword to Nurser, *For All Peoples and All Nations*, xi.

In fact, despite the antipathy to international jurisdiction that exercised the ABA in its campaign against the UN Genocide Convention in 1950, "the main opposition to the treaty was rooted in states' rights,"[91] something of special concern in the South. Escalating objections to racial discrimination intensified southern apprehensions "that human rights treaties in general and the Genocide Treaty in particular would be used to dismantle southern segregation." Support for states' rights and rejection of federal encroachment had strong appeal, and connecting those issues to the Genocide Convention produced lasting consequences.[92]

Opposition to human rights instruments as a way of protecting southern segregation was related to growing national disagreement over civil rights and to the fears of conservatives that these instruments, if ratified, would significantly advance the cause of civil rights. Conservative apprehensions were not without foundation. One month before the UN Charter was adopted and human rights had yet to be incorporated, W. E. B. Du Bois, a member of the NAACP, denounced the Charter for ignoring hundreds of millions of people of color who were, in his words, "clamoring for human rights."[93] Two years later, he was party to an NAACP petition to the UN Human Rights Commission that protested U.S. human rights violations of racial equality. Sensing the issue placed the United States in an embarrassing position, the Soviet delegate to the Commission demanded an immediate investigation of the NAACP charges. In response, the Commission chair, Eleanor Roosevelt, called the delegate's bluff by expressing a willingness to allow access for Soviet examiners if Americans were granted similar access to the Soviet Union. The Soviets, of course, refused, and the issue was dropped, but it further intensified conservative perceptions that internationalism in any form was Soviet domination in disguise.[94]

For Evangelicals, national sovereignty was not the only issue; southern racial patterns should be respected, too, or if they were to be changed, it was no affair of the federal government. L. Nelson Bell, Billy Graham's father-in-law, called attention "to those barriers of race which have been established by God," and he stood behind people opposed to forcing change.[95] He and Graham, along with other Evangelicals, denounced extreme racism, but only as an individual sin, and at least until 1963, Graham, like other Evangelicals,

---

[91] Natalie Hevener Kaufman, *Human Rights Treaties and the Senate: A History of Opposition* (Chapel Hill, NC: University of North Carolina Press, 1990), 52.
[92] Ibid.
[93] Moyn, *Last Utopia*, 93, fn. 23.
[94] Joseph P. Lash, *Eleanor: The Years Alone* (New York: W. W. Norton & Co., 1972), 66–69.
[95] Hollinger, "After Cloven Tongues of Fire," 35.

opposed as ineffective efforts to change government policy by demonstrations such as Martin Luther King's March on Washington.[96]

In rehearsing the incident concerning the NAACP and the UN Human Rights Commission, Moyn emphasizes the failure of the intitiative and Du Bois's resulting dismissal, predictably taking it as yet another example of how inconsequential any appeal to human rights was in the late 1940s and 1950s.[97] But the incident was not inconsequential. It reinforced an intense, widespread, and very effective campaign in the United States against clear and straightforward standards including racial equality, which, if ratified, portended serious social disruption. There could be no doubt just how volatile the issue was, given what happened in the years following the passage of the Civil Rights Act in 1964, an act that took significant steps toward complying with nondiscrimination provisions in the human rights instruments.

Moyn's mistakes in explaining why human rights language was disparaged or ignored in the late 1940s and 1950s are similar to his errors in explaining why the same thing happened in the 1960s and early 1970s. After 1948, Realists, it is true, dismissed human rights as utopian, but they were but supplementary players. The principal cause of the early eclipse of human rights in American politics and popular culture was the combined effort of American conservatives, legal, religious, and political. None of them were troubled by human rights language because it was utopian, vague, or incoherent. Rather, they were troubled because of the very clarity and coherence of the challenges it posed for existing American law and policy, both domestically and internationally – challenges all the more potent because of their long-standing support from the natural rights tradition.

Similarly, Moyn misses key elements in his description of the history of human rights in the 1960s and 1970s, in part for the same reason. The primary mistake, as in the earlier period, is to assume that the language of the UDHR is utopian or illusory for being disconnected from the world – in particular, from events surrounding World War II – as well as incoherent, empty, stillborn, and the like. The fact that it is arguably not any of those things leads us, once again, to question Moyn's basic arguments, this time concerning the fortunes of human rights in the 1960s and 1970s.

As we know, Moyn's view is that the utopian ideology of "collective liberation," associated with the anticolonial movement in the 1960s and early 1970s, succeeded in eclipsing human right language by replacing it. The ideology did not destroy its original meaning or revise it by co-opting it, because then the

---

[96] Ibid., 35–36.
[97] Moyn, *Last Utopia*, 101–104.

language would have had some clarity and integrity in the first place. Rather, the original meaning was simply set aside until the utopian visions of anti-colonialism had run their course, and thereafter it was thoroughly and novelly reconstituted in the form of the "last utopia." For Moyn, that is a code word for our present universalist, suprastate understanding, with its unprecedented elevation of the equal protection of individual rights that came into being with the election of Jimmy Carter in 1976. It is, Moyn thinks, a perspective that lay at the heart of Jimmy Carter's own version of utopianism, his "antipolitical moralism."

What Moyn misses, at bottom, is this: Not only is original human rights language generally coherent and cogent for having been drafted in response to Nazi atrocities in the World War II period, as well as grounded in a long-standing natural rights tradition, but it also contained, just because of these things, a particular message of deep relevance for the anticolonial movement and its ideology of collective liberation. The message is that all forms of collective life, including states, are ultimately called to account according to what we might stipulate as *the test of basic individual protection*. By that is meant the following:

> Each and every individual, no matter what ethnicity, nationality, religion, culture, gender, or location, has the enforceable right to condemn and to resist the sort of arbitrary injury perpetrated in the name of National Socialism. This applies, especially, to "nonderogable rights," as specified in Art. 4 of the International Covenant on Civil and Political Rights (ICCPR). They are protections against extrajudicial killing, torture, cruel and unusual punishment and treatment, enslavement, denials of due process, and violations of the freedom of conscience, religion or belief. It also applies to "derogable rights" (rights abridgeable under emergency conditions) such as freedom of speech, assembly, press, and participation in government, which, if operational, constitute a critical bulwark against the occurrence of Nazi-like atrocities. Finally, it includes protections against other "atrocity crimes," such as genocide and ethnic cleansing. These, too, are crimes against individuals who, as members of a victimized group, may be singled out for mistreatment simply because they are such.

> These rights are best understood as comprising outside moral and legal constraints on the behavior of all forms of collective life. The purpose is not to enfeeble or defeat collective life, but to provide conditions under which it can become healthy, constructive, and edifying. Observing these rights is necessary, if not sufficient, to that end. To be sure, provisions will need to be made to guarantee the independence and integrity of minority and other communities, and that undertaking will require the most delicate

balancing of individual and group rights. What is not allowed is for any form of collective life, in the name of self-defined purposes or values, to violate or disregard fundamental individual rights, no matter how "traditional" or otherwise authorized the purposes and values may be deemed to be.[98]

It is true that the due protection of group rights, and particularly of minorities, was not adequately provided for in the UDHR, and that deficiency may well have had some effect on the discrediting of human rights language in the anticolonial period. This does not prove that original human rights language as a whole was vacuous or incoherent, but it does show that there existed some serious blind spots and lacunae that needed urgent correction.

Article 27, para. 1 reads, "Everyone has the right freely to participate in the cultural life of the [dominant] community, to enjoy the arts and to share in scientific advancement and its benefits." This clearly assimilationist formulation was the result of a deliberate decision by the drafting committee to reject a proposed article guaranteeing more robust minority protection. The rejected proposal assured the right of members of racial, linguistic, or religious minorities "to establish and maintain schools and cultural and religious institutions and to use their own language in the press, in public assembly and before the courts and other authorities of the State."[99] However, Eleanor Roosevelt, speaking for representatives from predominantly immigrant societies, opposed the proposal, arguing that if it were adopted "immigrant groups might want to avail themselves of the rights spelled out in such an article and so threaten the unity of their countries and their respective policies of amalgamation."[100]

Contentious from the beginning, the provision for cultural "amalgamation" would lead to continuing disputes and recurring revision and amendment. Thirty years later, the article covering minority protection in the ICCPR assured the rights of persons belonging to ethnic, religious, or linguistic minorities to participate in and practice their own customs and traditions, and the UN Declaration of the Rights of Indigenous Peoples, adopted by the UN General Assembly in 2007 and "lent support" by the United States in 2010, goes considerably further in guaranteeing expansive minority rights in regard not only to culture, religion, and language but also to land, governance, and economic development. That Declaration, of course, remains essentially aspirational and undoubtedly covers a multitude of unresolved

---

[98] David Little, "On Behalf of Rights," *Journal of Religious Ethics* 34.2 (June 2006), 307. The citation is somewhat revised.
[99] Cited in Morsink, *Universal Declaration of Human Rights*, 272.
[100] Cited at ibid., 276.

issues between minorities and host governments. Still, it clearly marks growing international sensitivity to the question of collective rights and the need to accommodate them, and it marks a huge change in outlook in fifty-five years.

At the same time, one interesting aspect of evolving thinking about collective rights is the resolute reaffirmation of the importance of individual protection. Article 7 of the Declaration of the Rights of Indigenous Peoples guarantees the "rights to life, physical and mental integrity, liberty and security of person" to "indigenous individuals"; Article 44 declares that "all the rights and privileges herein are equally guaranteed to male and female individuals"; and Article 46.2 states, "In the exercise of the rights enunciated in the present Declaration, human rights and fundamental freedoms of all shall be respected."

It is exactly the right to basic individual protection, enshrined in the UDHR – despite deficiencies and the selective need for revision – that was lost sight of and then rediscovered as the anticolonial movement worked itself out. Moyn's description of the course of colonialism and all of his examples, from Eastern Europe, Latin America, and Africa, lead to the conclusion that, as I put it above, "the transition from the ideals embodied in anticolonialism to those associated with a modern human rights outlook resulted from a convergence of reactions against the excesses of centralized collective control and unrestricted state sovereignty." His own summary tells the whole story: "[I]t was hard to forget the interwar politics of self-determination in Europe, with the disastrous consequences for individuals and groups victimized as contiguous ethnonational groups sought collective redemption."[101]

Accordingly, the appearance in the late 1970s of the view of human rights as a set of universalist, suprastate standards given particularly to the equal protection of individual rights is not, on this account, a completely novel formulation, an utterly new invention, but rather a belated recovery of the original intention of human rights language. Indeed, part of the reason for doubting that such language is "mere utopianism" is the very fact that it came to make sense, to capture imaginations, as the result of real-world experience. It is consequently hard to see how the test of basic individual protection can ever again completely be ignored or put aside.

Moyn is partially correct that the Carter human rights policies suffered from inconsistency between rhetoric and accomplishment. "At the verbal

---

[101] See Roland Burke, *Decolonialization and the Evolution of International Human Rights* (Philadelphia: University of Pennsylvania Press, 2010), for an argument supporting the relevance of human rights norms to the anticolonial movement. See fn. 41.

level, the official position of the United States was loud and clear. The victims of those who trampled on human rights were acknowledged and their plight publicized,... [even though] the immediate costs to the violators varied and were usually slight." On the other hand, "the victims who survived and who had enough freedom to speak out applauded the [Carter] policy and believed that conditions would have been far worse had the United States remained silent."[102]

Certainly, Moyn is right about some of the mistakes of the Reagan human rights policies. The idea, central to the Reagan administration, that human rights criticism should be reserved for communist countries because authoritarian regimes in Central America and elsewhere were readily democratizing at the time was for the most part based on a cruel illusion.[103]

In any case, however, the shortcomings of either administration do not detract from the importance of human rights standards. They only illustrate the complexities and challenges of applying the standards conscientiously.

---

[102] Gaddis Smith, *Morality, Reason and Power: American Diplomacy in the Carter Years* (New York: Hill & Wang, 1986), 55.
[103] David Little, "Natural Rights and Human Rights: The International Imperative," in Robert Davidoff, ed., *Natural Rights and Natural Law: The Legacy of George Mason* (Fairfax, VA: George Mason University Press, 1986), 76–79, esp. fn. 27.

PART II

Religion and Rights

3

Religion, Human Rights, and the Secular State

Clarifications and Some Islamic, Jewish, and Christian Responses

AN-NA'IM'S PROPOSAL

Abdullahi An-Na'im, Sudanese legal scholar, human rights expert, and the Charles Howard Candler Professor of Law at Emory University, recently published a book entitled *Islam and the Secular State: Negotiating the Future of Shari'a*, which favors thinking of the ideas of religion, human rights, and the secular state as interdependent and mutually supportive and applies this approach to Islam in general, as well as to three countries where Islam is highly influential: India, Turkey, and Indonesia.[1] The approach is supplemented by an earlier comparative study of constitutional government in Africa.[2]

The central argument – that each of the key notions, correctly considered, entails and depends on the others – may be stated in its broadest outlines before addressing its relevance to Islam. Religion, capable of inspiring intense, if strongly particularistic loyalties, may well become overbearing toward both adherents and outsiders if it is not disciplined by the principles of the secular state and human rights. The secular state, understood as a modern, religiously neutral territorial state regulated by a commitment to constitutionalism and equal citizenship, restrains such domineering tendencies by "deregulating" religion. It thereby encourages a healthy diversity and pluralism and a spirit of tolerance within and among religious communities. Human rights, as enshrined in the growing collection of post–World War II international documents, constrains religions by imposing basic, universal individual and group protections, including provisions for especially vulnerable groups such as women and minorities.

---

[1] (Cambridge, MA: Harvard University Press, 2008).
[2] *African Constitutionalism and the Role of Islam* (Philadelphia: University of Pennsylvania Press, 2006).

At the same time, the acceptance of a secular state is likely to be enfeebled and severely beleaguered without religious support, especially in those parts of the world where initial antipathy on the part of religious groups toward the whole idea of secularism might be deep and widespread. Accordingly, room must be made for the robust public expression of religion as part of the broader exercise of politics, all, to be sure, in accord with duly authorized constitutional limits and other civic obligations to be mentioned shortly. Importantly for An-Na'im, a religiously neutral state does not require religiously neutral politics.

Furthermore, the idea of a secular state, properly understood, is historically and culturally contingent and variable. Although the European and American models have achieved considerable influence throughout the world, they are not by any means all the same, nor should they be considered impervious to adaptation and revision, as determined by different conditions and circumstances. If, in Europe and elsewhere, adherence to a secular state has come to mean the complete privatization of religion or a belief in human earthly well-being that excludes religion, those beliefs are not the last word. They should be challenged and contested.

For An-Na'im, what a secular state means will have to be negotiated in different legal, political, and cultural settings, including Islamic settings. Consequently, local religious dispositions in belief and practice will, among other things, have both to be considered and, up to a point, accommodated. This process will and should color the shape and character of particular secular states in distinctly different ways.

Essentially, the same points apply to human rights. The idea that human rights, as formulated, remain abstract, remote, and uninspiring, absent the fervency and commitment religion can generate, is a familiar point of An-Na'im's.[3] Given the influence of religion, especially in certain places, these limitations, as he writes elsewhere, "are unlikely to be overcome without solidarity and cooperation among different religious communities."[4] Without drawing a vital connection between human rights and indigenous religious predispositions, different peoples around the world will not feel that they themselves "own" human rights and, accordingly, will not be motivated to do much about them.

But human rights standards are also abstract in another sense: They are not self-applying. Like all general codes, they require contextual interpretation and

---

[3] See, for example, Abullahi An-Na'im, "Islamic Foundations of Religious Human Rights," in John Witte, Jr. and Johan D. van der Vyver, eds., *Religious Human Rights in Global Perspective: Religious Perspectives* (The Hague: Martinus Nijhoff Publishers, 1996), 337–359.

[4] An-Na'im, "Synergy and Interdependence of Human Rights, Religion, and Secularism," unpublished ms., 6.

adjustment, and consequently various provisions will have to be negotiated in reference to diverse cultural and religious settings. Moreover, human rights documents, as they stand, contain a rich complexity of different protections – from bodily and psychological integrity to civil, political, economic, social, and cultural freedoms and opportunities – all of which, given local variations, cannot help being coordinated and implemented in different ways. Again, acute cultural and religious sensitivity is called for.

Finally, the secular state and human rights, on An-Na'im's account, cannot get along without each other either. Unchecked, the secular state, based on the principle of sovereignty and on the right to a monopoly of legitimate force over the inhabitants of a given territory, can incline, An-Na'im implies, toward a pattern of arbitrary control over the ideals and practices of citizens. Here, an international human rights regime can represent an effective system of transnational accountability. Conversely, human rights are ineffective and unproductive unless they are implemented by actual governments, operating according to the principles of constitutionalism and equal citizenship that characterize the modern secular state.

If religion, human rights, and the secular state are all interdependent notions that mutually modify one another and that are conditioned by local culture and experience, the same is true of the constitutive features of the secular state – namely, constitutionalism and equal citizenship – together with an added feature of the greatest importance, something An-Na'im calls "civic reason." By limiting and dispersing legal and political power and by protecting human rights, constitutional government defines and upholds the privileges, duties, and rights of citizenship, which, in turn, ensure that the ideals and interests of citizens can, in a fair and equitable manner, influence the laws and policies of government.

Accordingly, citizens are at liberty, among other things, to express their religious interests publicly and to try to advance them politically, though only so long as that is done in accord with the requirements of civic reason. Civic reason – a variation on John Rawls's idea of "public reason"[5] – dictates that, in passing laws or adopting policies that have the force of law, the reasons given and the way they are presented presuppose a common language of deliberation that most citizens may be expected to share. Such a language cannot rest on religious warrants because not all the citizens of a duly constituted secular state can be expected to agree to those warrants. For example, Muslim citizens would be free to advocate a law prohibiting the sale of alcohol, but they would

---

[5] See Chapter 4 for an extended discussion of Rawls's idea of public reason and its connection to human rights language.

be required to justify such a proposal on the basis of public health or safety, or some other commonly accessible principle, rather than on the basis of the Qur'an or Islamic tradition. In addition, they would be required to abide by an unfavorable outcome, assuming it is arrived at by due process.

An-Na'im devotes most of his book to applying this analytical framework to Islam, both as tradition and as manifested in three present-day societies: India, Turkey, and Indonesia. The key argument is that, accurately interpreted, Islam is fully compatible with human rights and the idea of the secular state. It simultaneously benefits from that relationship, and contributes to it. Precisely by means of embracing and engaging these ideas, Islam, misguided for too long, can recover the essentials of its faith.

Two essential principles are of special importance. One is *the principle of tolerance* – namely, the legitimacy of tolerating competing interpretations of Islam, rather than endeavoring, in accord with the mistaken idea of an "Islamic state," to enforce one interpretation over others. "The religious neutrality of the state [is] a necessary condition for Muslims to comply with their religious obligations. Religious compliance must be completely voluntary according to personal pious intention, which is necessarily invalidated by coercive enforcement of those obligations."[6]

The second might be called *the principle of adaptation* – namely, the legitimacy (and unavoidability) of adjusting Islamic teachings to variable historical circumstances. In An-Na'im's words, "the meaning and implementation of the Qur'an and Sunna in everyday life are always the product of human interpretation and action in a specific historical context. It is simply impossible to know and apply Shari'a in this life except through the agency of human beings."[7] The implication is that, because interpreting Islamic scripture is invariably subject to the limitations of human judgment, there is no way to correct for error except by means of ongoing, untrammeled deliberation and consent. Obstructing that process through coercive interference by the state only perverts the process.

On An-Na'im's reading, the Islamic tradition exhibits a deep tension between religious authority, determined and exercised by a process of deliberation and consent, and state authority, characterized by the use of force. In a word, the history of Islam is the story of oscillation between two models relating religious and state authority. One is of "complete conflation or convergence, based on the prototype of the Prophet in Medina, [which] assumes that political

---

[6] An-Na'im, *Islam and the Secular State*, 4.
[7] Ibid., 20.

and military leadership must necessarily accompany religious leadership."[8] The other is of "complete separation." It "may have been the dominant view in practice, although it was rarely, if ever, openly acknowledged because of the perceived need for rulers to enjoy Islamic legitimacy." According to An-Na'im, "most political regimes in Islamic history [have fallen] in between these two polar models."[9]

He argues that with the death of the Prophet, the conflation model is forever after inapplicable because "Muslims do not accept the possibility of prophets after the Prophet Muhammad"; therefore, no merely human successor could possess the measure of divine wisdom required for successfully combining religious and state authority.[10] "All rulers since Abu Bakr, the first caliph (632–634), have had to negotiate or mediate the permanent tension between religious and political authority, because none of those rulers has been accepted by all Muslims as capable of holding the supreme position of the Prophet, who defined Islam and determined how it could be implemented."[11]

The three case studies of India, Turkey, and Indonesia exemplify the way An-Na'im goes about evaluating variable patterns of relationship between religion and the state, mainly as regards Islam, though, to a lesser extent, other religions, too. Consistent with his central thesis, he assesses the records of these three countries in the light of the balance they achieve between religion, human rights, and the secular state.

For example, he charges the British colonial authorities in India with failing to get the balance right by arbitrarily enforcing a certain understanding of Shari'a that had the effect of "freezing" or "fossilizing" the status of Muslim women. The authorities thereby impeded the process of deliberation and negotiation according to which Muslims (and other religious believers), operating under a secular state duly regulated by human rights and the principles of constitutionalism and equal citizenship, should be allowed to proceed.[12]

And he criticizes "Nehru's legacy" whereby the postcolonial Indian government, in the name of equal treatment, addressed more insistently the ill effects of caste-based discrimination sanctioned by orthodox Hinduism than the damage done to Muslim women by unfair marriage or inheritance laws. Moreover, in matters involving public benefits and burdens, the state regularly favored the opinions of conservative members of the Muslim (as

[8] Ibid., 53.
[9] Ibid., 53.
[10] Ibid., 53.
[11] Ibid., 53–54.
[12] Ibid., 289.

well as Hindu, Sikh, and Christian) communities as representative of those communities, thereby denying the rights of equal citizenship. Such indulgence also wound up pandering to communalist politics and led to the rise of Hindu nationalism, characteristic of the 1980s and 1990s, with all of the regressive social and political consequences that resulted from those developments.[13]

As regards Turkey, An-Na-im calls to account the tradition of "authoritarian secularism" associated with Kemal Ataturk. It is, he says, "based on the complete state control of religion. It regulates religious education and religious practice, controls the finances of mosques, puts imams on the government payroll, and dictates men's and especially women's dress codes at school and work." Such a policy, he concludes, "necessarily undermines constitutionalism and human rights in the name of upholding these principles."[14]

In the case of Indonesia, An-Naʻim delivers a mixed judgment concerning the Pancasila system, according to which the state officially recognizes six religions: Islam, Catholicism, Protestantism, Hinduism, Buddhism, and Confucianism. On the one hand, Pancasila "embodies and promotes commitments to social and religious pluralism and tolerance, all of which contribute to an ethos of inclusive citizenship." On the other hand, however, it has been unduly subject to Islamic influence, as exemplified by changing one of the principles of Pancasila, "belief in God," to "belief in one supreme God," in deference to Muslim sentiments. Such a reformulation both tilts too much in favor of one of the official religions and discriminates against nontheistic as well as nonreligious citizens. Also, "Pancasila attempts to impose artificial and narrow uniformity among highly diverse Indonesian identities, seeking to force some four hundred ethnic and language groups into the [six prescribed] categories of religion. This clearly violates the equal citizenship of Indonesians who wish to be identified in different terms." The system was further compromised by being imposed in 1983 by an authoritarian government.[15]

The idea that there exists a constructive, mutually enriching relationship between the concepts of religion, human rights, and the secular state, as described by An-Naʻim, is, on its face, very appealing. It is, of course, of obvious significance for current and often heated discussions about the political interpretation and application of Islam. As such, the thesis is consonant with similar stimulating recommendations put forward by other contemporary liberal Muslim thinkers such as Abdulaziz Sachedina (*The Islamic Roots of*

---

[13] Ibid., 171–173.
[14] Ibid., 219.
[15] Ibid., 259–260.

Democratic Pluralism[16] and *Islam and the Challenge of Human Rights*[17]) and Abdolkarim Soroush (*Reason, Freedom, and Democracy in Islam*[18]).

As does An-Naʻim, both of these authors explicitly endorse the indispensable role of duly secular governments, largely compliant with human rights standards and the principles of constitutionalism and equal citizenship, in encouraging authentic Islam. That is an actively tolerant Islam, open to the free and equal expression of many voices, both Islamic and non-Islamic, within the same political community. Also, as does An-Naʻim, both authors believe that a properly chastened Islam can make a helpful contribution to a richer and fuller understanding of both the secular state and human rights, an understanding that would make things truly intercultural, rather than being the product of just the Western tradition.

But it is appealing beyond that. The proposal resonates with key assumptions underlying human rights language and with related conceptions of the secular state – as regulated by human rights and by the principles of constitutionalism and equal citizenship – and by the idea of "civic" or "public reason." Moreover, as An-Naʻim himself hints, the proposal extends beyond Islam and can be shown to find support in segments of other religions, such as Judaism and Christianity.

First, however, there is some confusion at the heart of An-Naʻim's proposal that needs to be exposed and clarified, and more needs to be said by way of defending his general approach.

To claim, as he does repeatedly, that all aspects of the relations between religion, human rights, and the secular state, including its constituent parts, are properly "historical and contextual," "contested and contingent," and therefore infinitely susceptible to open-ended negotiation, appears, ultimately, to leave everything up in the air. If there are finally no reliable "fixed points," no "outside constraints," as to what shall be meant by "human rights" or "the secular state," including the meaning of constitutionalism, equal citizenship, and civic or public reason, or what the implications of these things are for religion, then it is not clear in what way the terms may be said to condition or limit one another, and thereby comprise a productive *inter*relationship. On An-Naʻim's proposal, the meaning of each of the terms would appear to remain perennially up for grabs in an unending and inconclusive process of interactive redefinition.

---

[16] (New York: Oxford University Press, 2001).
[17] (New York: Oxford University Press, 2009).
[18] (New York: Oxford University Press, 2000).

As a matter of fact, An-Na'im himself fudges on this point. On the one hand, he asserts that human rights are not absolute, because among other reasons,[19] they are "the product of a consensus-building process" that is presumably authorized by consensual agreement among different cultures and societies on the basis of their local experience. "Since all societies adhere to their own normative systems, which are necessarily shaped by their own context and experience, any universal concept cannot simply be proclaimed or taken for granted."[20]

On the other hand, he declares that unless human rights are regarded as a standard of universal accountability resting on the "essential foundations of civilized humanity," the obligation to obey human rights would be based exclusively on a given government's "willingness or ability to uphold them," thereby letting human rights offenders off the hook.[21] Used this way, his conviction about "the essential foundations of civilized humanity" looks suspiciously like a "universal concept" with strong moral content that is either "proclaimed or taken for granted" (it is nowhere defended by him). Otherwise, individual states could choose to comply or not, depending on circumstances as they see them, because consent alone would be the ultimate basis of obligation.

An-Na'im's discussion leads to further confusion. He "does not," he says, "uphold human rights as the standard by which Islam itself should be judged, but only proposes that these rights constitute an appropriate framework for the *human* understanding of Islam and interpretation of Shari'a."[22] As he puts it, "I need a secular state to be a Muslim. I am neither suggesting that Shari'a is inherently incompatible with constitutionalism, human rights, or democracy nor calling for it to be subordinated to these principles."[23]

---

[19] An-Na'im gives another reason for rejecting the absoluteness of human rights, namely, that "many of them are qualified in various ways, and some can be suspended in times of emergency" (*Islam and the Secular State*, 113). That "many" or "some" rights are qualified or may be suspended in times of emergency does not include all rights, as is stated, for example, in Article 4 of the International Covenant on Civil and Political Rights (ICCPR). That article alludes to a set of "nonderogable" rights, such as discrimination based solely on race, language, religion, etc., extrajudicial killing, enslavement, torture, and so on. There is certainly a presumption that these rights have "strong stringency" on a universal basis. Most of them, it is true, are not fully absolute because States Parties have the right to modify them on the basis of particular "reservations" and "understandings," and "necessity excuses" are conceivably applicable to some of them, such as extrajudicial killing and torture. On the other hand, it is hard to imagine that particular modifications or necessity excuses would be allowed in regard to crimes like discrimination (as defined) or genocide (as defined). Such crimes *would* appear to be absolute in the sense of being absolutely prohibited everywhere and always.

[20] Ibid., 113–114.
[21] Ibid., 115.
[22] Ibid., 112, original italics.
[23] Ibid., 282.

An-Naʻim does not mean there are no points of divergence between traditional Shariʻa legislation and human rights standards or the standards of consititutional government and equal citizenship. On the contrary, he admits sharp discrepancies in respect to the treatment of women, minorities, and the right to religious freedom, and in these cases he calls for inherited Shariʻa norms to be radically reformed in line with the human rights and the norms of the secular state.[24] His argument is that "the principles of constitutionalism, human rights, and citizenship are in fact more appropriate for realizing the ideal of the Prophet's community of Medina in the concrete context of present Islamic societies than unrealistic adherence to earlier models that are no longer workable."[25]

The problem here is that the standards of equal treatment regarding gender, minorities, and religion prescribed by the principles of human rights and the secular state are themselves at the mercy of what Islam is believed to teach. We must wait on the outcome of debates between An-Naʻim and his fellow Muslims to decide whether the equal treatment of women, minorities, and religious believers ought to be enforced as a human right. Human rights and the principles of constitutional government and equal citizenship have no independent status according to which the teachings of the Shariʻa might be held to account.

It is perfectly possible, of course, to envision a setting in which religious believers might experience a conflict between religious obligations and obligations to human rights or constitutional principles. In such circumstances, hard choices would have to be made. But that sort of conflict presupposes *different* claims resting on *different* principles. Human rights and constitutional standards, accordingly, have an autonomous standing alongside, and possibly over against, religious standards. By reducing the grounds of obligation exclusively to religious commitments, An-Naʻim runs the risk of forfeiting any independent status according to which the standards of human rights and the secular state might be understood to constrain and possibly to conflict with religious belief and practice.

Nor do An-Naʻim's comments on the grounds of human rights do very much to straighten out the difficulties:

> The framers of the Universal Declaration of Human Rights avoided identifying religious justifications for [human rights] in an effort to find common ground among believers and nonbelievers. However, this does not mean that human rights can only be founded on secular justifications, because that

[24] Ibid., 109.
[25] Ibid., 110.

does not address the question of how to make human rights equally valid and legitimate from the perspectives of the wide variety of believers around the world. The underlying rationale for the human rights doctrine itself entitles believers to seek to base their commitment to these norms on their own religious beliefs, in the same way that others may seek to affirm them on the basis of secular philosophy. All human beings are entitled to require equal commitment to the human rights doctrine by others, but they cannot prescribe the grounds on which others may wish to found their commitment.[26]

These observations misunderstand the rationale that undergirds human rights language in the Declaration and elsewhere, as mentioned in the Introduction and developed in Chapter 1. I described there a "two-tiered" approach to justification. One level involves a secular (or religiously neutral) appeal taken to be moral and universal in character and that is limited to the specific rights enumerated in the Declaration and its progeny. It entitles every human being "to all the rights and freedoms set forth in the Declaration, without distinction of any kind, such as... religion." The second level of justification is provided for by Article 18 of the Declaration, guaranteeing the right to freedom of conscience and religion or belief. That right invites individuals and groups, as desired, to develop and embrace, according to conscience, their own religious or secular justifications for human rights and much else.

To assume, as a "first-level justification," a universal and religiously neutral moral ground for human rights language, as the drafters did, was required to make sense of the language and to fulfill its intended purposes: holding everyone everywhere accountable to the terms of the language, regardless of religion or belief, and, under the same condition, providing standards of protection to which everyone everywhere might appeal.

That justification is, I argued, illustrated by the "logic of pain," as manifested in the Hitler experience and his reliance on self-serving and unfounded reasons for inflicting massively unfavorable, unwanted consequences on millions of people. Because human rights language was both formulated and justified against that background and the array of specific violations perceived to have occurred, there exist fixed reference points for interpreting and applying that language.

Tensions and conflicts between the two levels of justification are, of course, to be expected. Debates over such matters are an irrepressible and interminable feature of human rights discourse. But the key point is that on this account human rights language possesses an autonomous status, resting, so to speak, on its own bottom. In interactions with religion and the secular state, including

[26] Ibid., 115–116.

ideas of constitutional government, equal citizenship, and civic or public reason, it has a basis on which to exert independent leverage.

As a matter of fact, An-Na'im in a few places contends for a kind of religiously neutral "first-level justification" himself, intermittently disregarding his usual opposition to such appeals. At one point, he rejects the right of Muslims favoring an Islamic state to implement such a preference, declaring that "belief in Islam, or any other religion, logically requires the possibility of disbelief, because belief has no value if it is coerced."[27] The separation of religion and state, he says elsewhere, "is necessary for the very possibility of religious belief."[28] This line of argument is especially interesting because it grounds the right to religious freedom *not*, after all, in Islamic belief, but in a prior logical or rational condition of *all* belief – namely, in the conceptual incompatibility of belief and coercion. In this instance, whether or not a human rights claim is justified does not rest on scriptural or theological interpretation, but on a universal, religiously neutral appeal. As An-Na'im's own reference makes clear, it can be used to override a particular, religiously warranted prescription.

THE CONTRARY VIEW OF TALAL ASAD

To help advance the process of clarification, I take up an approach to religion, human rights, and the secular state that is very nearly antithetical to An-Na'im's proposal. The approach is developed by Talal Asad, Distinguished Professor of Anthropology at the City University of New York, in a book titled *Formations of the Secular: Christianity, Islam, Modernity*.[29] Its central argument needs to be addressed and answered if claims by An-Na'im and others in favor of a constructive interdependence between the ideas of religion, human rights, and the secular state are to be sustained. In fact, it is a fair assumption that Asad's position on these matters encapsulates a widespread suspicion, if not antagonism, inside and outside scholarly circles, toward proposals such as An-Na'im's that take a generally favorable attitude toward "modernity" and associated ideas of the secular state and human rights as they bear on religion.

For Asad, "the unprecedented powers and ambitions of the modern state and the forces of the capitalist economy have been central to the great transformation of our time."[30] Even though he occasionally disclaims any intention to

---

[27] Ibid., 268.
[28] Ibid., 94–95.
[29] See Chapter 1, fn. 5. See also Chapter 8 for a more complex and nuanced understanding of the origins and character of nationalism. See Talal Asad, *Formations of the Secular: Christianity, Islam, Modernity* (Stanford: Stanford University Press, 2003).
[30] Ibid., 253.

ascribe blame or make moral judgments about this "great transformation," his analysis is by no means value-free. The profound interconnection of nationalism, the modern nation-state, and the idea of secularism can only be characterized, from his point of view, as morally and religiously ominous. "Nationalism," he writes, "with its vision of a universe of national *societies* (the state being thought of as necessary to their full articulation) in which individuals live their worldly existence requires the concept of the secular to make sense. The loyalty that the individual nationalist owes is directly and exclusively to the nation."[31]

This view of the "centralizing state,"[32] which is oriented toward "worldly existence" and rests "on coercion," or what Asad also calls "the exercise of violence,"[33] and which is regarded as the ultimate, exclusive, and all-determining authority not only over politics and economic affairs but also over the place and character of morality and religion, suggests the very "totalizing" and dominating image of the secular state that An-Na'im himself fears, absent appropriate checks and balances. As Asad puts it, "the nation-state is not a generous agent and its law does not deal in persuasion."[34]

On Asad's view, the doctrine of "secular nationalism" arose in Europe and was closely connected to colonialism. The process of investing the modern state with supreme authority required, first, the experience of "disenchantment," according to which modern techniques of production, political organization, education, warfare, travel, entertainment, medicine, and so on, imply "direct access to reality" – without recourse, that is, to supernatural assumptions.[35] Traditionally understood ideas of religion, myth, magic, and the sacred become radically redefined and recategorized so as to be subject to secular political regulation. Such an arrangement does not necessarily mean rejecting or dispensing with religious or "sacred" symbols altogether, but simply controlling and reshaping them for secularly defined purposes. The second step on the part of the Europeans was to try to "globalize" this system of understanding and practice by transplanting it among colonized peoples: "In their attempt to outlaw customs the European rulers considered cruel it was not the concern with indigenous suffering that *dominated* their thinking, but the desire to impose what they considered civilized standards of justice and humanity on a subject population – that is, the desire to create new human subjects."[36]

---

[31] Ibid., 193. Emphasis in the original.
[32] Ibid., 227.
[33] Ibid., 256.
[34] Ibid., 6.
[35] Ibid., 13.
[36] Ibid., 110. Original italics.

At present, it is the American model of secular nationalism, with its universal hegemonic aspirations and its now unrivaled military, political, and economic capabilities, that is regnant and therefore, to Asad's mind, particularly threatening. Asad's description of this model is not complimentary. American secular nationalism has, in effect, expanded the European pattern of hegemonic domination, although, in keeping with its traditions, it has cast its mission of spreading secular political and economic values in a distinctly religious and therefore particularly high-handed mode: "Americans are likely to see enemies not just as opponents but as evil." And because of the same domineering inclinations, "the repeated explosions of intolerance in American history... are entirely compatible (indeed intertwined) with secularism in a highly modern society."[37]

In the same spirit, Asad believes that the "myth of liberalism," together with the constitutive idea of "universalizing reason" that underlies this Euro-American secularist construct, actually "go[es] against the grain of human and social nature" and, consequently, must be violently imposed and maintained. He invokes the image of a garden constantly threatened by a surrounding jungle that may only be held back by policies of perpetual violence and destruction: "For to make an enlightened space, the liberal must continually attack the darkness of the outside world that threatens to overwhelm that space."[38]

Of special interest for our concerns is Asad's treatment of "a secular system like human rights,"[39] as he calls it. Rather than representing a transnational system of accountability, à la An-Na'im, Asad concludes that international human rights are little more than biased instruments in the service of the existing nation-state system. Human rights are, he says, "floating signifiers that can be attached to or detached from various subjects and classes constituted by the market principle and by the most powerful nation-states."[40] Asad is very explicit on this point.

> The American secular language of redemption, for all its particularity, now works as a force in the field of foreign relations to globalize human rights. For that language does, after all, draw on the idea that "freedom" and "America" are virtually interchangeable – that American political culture is (as the Bible says of the Chosen People) "a light unto the nations." Hence, "democracy," "human rights," and "being free" are integral to the universalizing moral

---

[37] Ibid., 7. The first citation is a quotation from the historian, Eric Foner.
[38] Ibid., 59.
[39] Ibid., 129.
[40] Ibid., 158.

project of the American nation-state – the project of humanizing the world – and an important part of the way very many Americans see themselves in contrast to their "evil" opponents.[41]

The basic argument appears to be that because international human rights documents address themselves to Member States or States Parties,[42] we may conclude that the only licit and effective authorities for interpreting and enforcing human rights are independent sovereign nation-states themselves. It is states alone, according to Asad, that have "exclusive jurisdiction" to "decide the fate" of individual citizens.[43] Furthermore, he claims that human rights are not concerned with the "civil status" of citizens, but only with what he calls their "natural being,"[44] something he takes to be entirely independent of citizenship. Consequently, "the identification and application of human rights law has no meaning independent of the judicial institutions that belong to individual nation-states . . . and the remedies that these institutions supply."[45]

Commenting on the statement in the Preamble to the Universal Declaration that unless human rights are "protected by the rule of law," human beings will be "compelled to have recourse, as a last resort, to rebellion against tyranny and oppression," Asad repeats the same point. He argues in part[46] that this reference is circular because whether or not human rights are in given cases protected by the "rule of law" is itself determined by the judicial institutions of the individual nation-states. There is also the further problem, he seems to suggest, that because human rights standards are definitively interpreted by national courts, there is no possibility in practice of distinguishing human rights standards from particular court rulings concerning what is lawful.

Asad slightly qualifies his arguments about the supremacy of national courts by mentioning transnational human rights institutions, such as the European Court. However, he contends that such institutions do not do much, in the

---

[41] Ibid., 147.
[42] The Universal Declaration (UDHR) (which technically is not a treaty or convention) uses the term, Member States, whereas documents, such as the ICCPR, that are treaties or conventions use the term, States Parties. However, it should be noted that both these documents (and others) refer, in addition, to "the peoples of the United Nations" (Preamble, UDHR) or to "all peoples" (ICCPR Art. 1). Very significantly, *peoples as well as states* are directly addressed by international human rights documents. This point should be borne in mind in the light of my later critique of Asad's view.
[43] Asad, *Formations of the Secular*, 137.
[44] Ibid., 129.
[45] Ibid., 129.
[46] In addition, on 138 Asad makes another point about a convergence between the idea of the "rule of law" and a doctrine of "social justice" that excludes rights, which is, frankly, not easy to understand.

final analysis, to alter the domineering status of the nation-state. Either the transnational institutions simply "act as larger proto-states" (presumably with the same "totalizing" effects as individual nation-states have), or they do not require that member states give up much of their authority after all.[47]

Let me begin by affirming some of what Asad argues for, particularly in regard to the importance of the modern nation-state system in influencing the terms of contemporary understanding and practice, including religious understanding and practice. He does touch on some problems in the formulation and administration of human rights and humanitarian law. And he is especially insightful when it comes to identifying the capacity for arbitrary domination on the part of the more powerful nations, such as the United States, and for arranging things, often unfairly and high-handedly, in their own interest. During much of the presidency of George W. Bush, the country was indeed governed by an administration officially committed to preemptive unilateralism at home and abroad, and of ignoring or disdaining international initiatives and institutions in favor of promoting and extending "our values" around the world. It is another matter, of course, whether Bush policies can be said to constitute the norm for all of American foreign policy.

Still, even the willingness to concede that the United States is at times capable of exemplifying the kind of domineering tendencies Asad associates with the modern secular nation-state system gives reason to conclude that Asad's claims can only be partly right and that An-Na'im's proposal, properly understood, has merit after all.

For we cannot have it both ways. We cannot, on the one hand, criticize Bush policies, as Asad does, for high-handedness and the unilateral pursuit of "secular" economic, military, and strategic interests under a self-serving banner of religion, and simultaneously embrace Asad's view that *all* national and international standards codifying the ideas of human rights and the secular state are nothing but the tools of self-serving nation-states. The reason is that this criticism itself rests on holding delinquent behavior, on the part of the United States or anyone else, accountable to those very national and international standards.

For example, most of the objections to American policy in Iraq were based on the assumption that the United States had violated or was in danger of violating the rule of law, as well as its obligations to human rights and humanitarian law and to the United Nations Charter.[48] Moreover, most critics have not considered the capacity of the American government to enforce its

---

[47] Ibid., 129 and 139.
[48] See Chapter 10 for an extended evaluation of U.S. compliance with the international rule of law.

policies, either through the national courts at home or by the use of military might abroad, to end the debate over those policies. Critics contend either that national courts have frequently failed in their responsibility to uphold the constitution, or that the U.S. government has, in critical instances, violated its international obligations. Asad therefore goes too far in contending that beliefs about right understanding and practice are determined finally by the "exercise of violence" on the part of a nation-state. It is, in fact, such "exercises of violence" arguably performed outside the law, that often trigger the loudest objections.

Against Asad, then, it can be argued that objections and criticisms of this sort rest on firm ground and that, even with all the possibilities for misunderstanding and manipulation, the ideas of human rights and the secular state nevertheless offer some potent standards of transnational accountability, including certain "fixed features" and "outside constraints." I now consider the ideas of human rights and the secular state in that light, sketching as I go some thoughts on the role of religion, in particular of Christianity, Judaism, and Islam.

HUMAN RIGHTS

Although Asad notes briefly the effects of German fascism and the record of atrocities committed during World War II as the basis for drafting and adopting the Declaration and its progeny,[49] he does not grasp the full significance of those events. Nor does he understand the true character and implications of the human rights system that was inaugurated in 1948.

Above all, human rights were formulated in direct and self-conscious response to a version of "modern secular nationalism" of a highly pathological kind. Fascist Germany is the paradigmatic case of Asad's image of the modern secular nation-state. Under Hitler, the state asserted supreme authority both to define the "true interests" and "true ideals" of all citizens, including what is an acceptable understanding of religion and morality, and to impose that "totalizing vision" by means of relentless "exercises of violence" that depended completely on the state's "exclusive jurisdiction."

As mentioned earlier (and further developed in Chapter 1), the Declaration was drafted and justified against the background of the Hitler experience and Hitler's reliance on self-serving and unfounded reasons for inflicting massively unfavorable, unwanted consequences on millions of people. The first level of the "two-tiered" approach to justification assumed by the drafters provides "secular" or religiously neutral grounds for moral and legal limits

[49] Asad, *Formations of the Secular*, 57, 138–139.

on the exercise of governmental power that are universally obligatory and accessible.

As mentioned, the fact that the provisions of the Declaration and its progeny were composed against the background of particular violations means that the provisions are not purely abstract or formal, but prohibit specifiable kinds of behavior. For example, the provision in Article 2 against discrimination based on race, language, gender, religion, and so on, should be understood to ban the kinds of discrimination actually practiced by the Nazis. Similarly, the protections in Articles 19, 20, and 21 of opinion and expression, peaceful assembly and association, and participation in government, respectively, are framed as constitutional safeguards in response to the specific pattern of behavior exhibited by the German government.[50] Preventing similar behavior such as that practiced before and during World War II was understood by the drafters to be absolutely indispensable in thwarting future forms of "pathological nationalism."

The second level of justification, guaranteed by Article 18 of the Declaration, protects something else persistently subverted by the German government: the rights of conscience and the freedom of religion or belief. Fascism constituted a direct, comprehensive, and systematic assault on five categories of the right to freedom of religion or belief that came to be safeguarded by the Declaration and its progeny: free exercise, nondiscrimination, special protection for minorities, protection against "religious hatred that incites to discrimination, hostility, or violence,"[51] and the liberty of parents or guardians to select the religious education of their children or wards. It thereby denied all opportunity for embracing and expressing thoughts, ideals and commitments not subject to governmental regulation.[52] Accordingly, part of the drafters' underlying rationale for supporting the freedom of "thought, conscience, and religion [or belief],"[53] or the provision that "no one shall be subject to coercion which would impair his freedom to have or to adopt a religion or belief of his choice," as it came to be expressed,[54] was a conviction concerning the conceptual incompatibility of belief and coercion, already alluded to by An-Na'im. The record of the Nazis in enforcing their doctrines and punishing dissent provided the drafters with all the confirmation they needed.[55]

---

[50] See Chapter 1 for a discussion of Morsink's account of the provenance of human rights language.
[51] ICCPR Article 20.2.
[52] See Chapter 4 for an enumeration of, and further commentary on, the five belief rights.
[53] The phrase, "or belief," appears in the second clause of Article 18 and thus may be taken to be assumed in the wording of the first clause.
[54] ICCPR, Article 18.2, or UN Declaration on the Elimination of All Forms of Intolerance and Discrimination (DEID), Article 1.2.
[55] Morsink, *Universal Declaration of Human Rights*, 261.

Five additional remarks may be made by way of refuting Asad's critique and further strengthening An-Naʻim's proposal.

First, again contrary to Asad, human rights protections are in fact crucially aimed at the "civil status" of individual citizens. Nearly one-fourth of the articles of the Declaration concern legal rights because, as Morsink points out, "the drafters were aware of how far the nazification of the German legal system had gone" and of how important it was to make sure such conditions were not allowed to repeat themselves.[56] Nor is it the case, as Asad argues, that the determination of the civil rights of citizens in legal and other respects depends on the "exclusive jurisdiction" of the sovereign nation-state. "The cumulative effect of the legal provisions of the Charter, of the Universal Declaration and other instruments, and of subsequent state practice, is that human rights are no longer matters of domestic jurisdiction alone. They have become internationalized both politically and in law."[57]

Second, when it comes to the legal ratification of human rights conventions, it is true, as Asad claims, that States Parties do retain a certain amount of discretion by, for example, registering special "reservations" and "understandings" on the act of adherence, thereby qualifying their obligations to uphold certain human rights provisions. But although such action does weaken universal compliance, state discretion is by no means unlimited. An-Naʻim rightly points out that "even when a state refuses to commit to a positive international law obligation, as embodied in a treaty, the nation-state may still be bound to uphold the law if it is believed to be *jus cogens* [namely, part of a set of overriding peremptory legal principles]. These principles of international law, which may not be derogated from, include proscriptions [against] slavery, genocide, torture, and apartheid. Claims of state sovereignty are [in this respect subordinated] to *jus cogens* [principles]."[58] Furthermore, even during conditions of emergency, when derogation from certain (though not all) rights is permitted, states are nevertheless held accountable to the United Nations to prove the existence of an emergency, as well as the need for and the extent and duration of a "state of exception."[59]

Third, Asad is mistaken about the reference in the Preamble of the Declaration to the need for the protection of human rights by the rule of law, lest people be "compelled to have recourse, as a last resort, to rebellion against

---

[56] Ibid., 43.
[57] Dennis J. Driscoll, "The Development of Human Rights in International Law," in Walter Laquer and Barry Rubin, eds., *Human Rights Reader* (New York: New American Library, 1979), 44.
[58] An-Naʻim, "The Interdependence of Human Rights, Religion, and Secularism."
[59] See Article 4 of the ICCPR.

tyranny and oppression." In the light of the legislative history, the meaning is clear. To avoid "understandable rebellion," which could result should states fail to enforce human rights, states are obligated to implement human rights by means of national laws in such a way that those laws comply with human rights standards.[60] Given the point I have been making, that human rights represent an independent standard in respect to national laws, there is nothing circular here, as Asad claims.

Fourth, although, as conceded, various nations, including the United States, do at times gravely violate human rights, charges concerning such violations are only possible because human rights exist as a set of standards independent of the rulings of national courts and legislatures. Nor, by any means, are charges of human rights violation by this or that state utterly inoperative or ineffective under present conditions. In fact, there exists a multiplicity of international and national governmental and nongovernmental institutions and organizations that, together with the media, act to monitor the human rights performance of states around the world, and to do that with considerable, if variable, success.[61] That success can be verified, among other things, by observing the lengths to which states frequently go to avoid public scrutiny and criticism. Although the monitoring system is far from perfect, it is certainly incorrect to describe it as nonexistent or without effect.[62]

Of special importance in this regard is the formation of the International Criminal Court. The key element, as President Clinton emphasized when he signed the founding document in December 2000, is the importance of "international accountability for bringing to justice perpetrators of genocide, war crimes and crimes against humanity."[63] Such a court was part of the vision born of the horrors of the Nazi experience and was consequently anticipated in the Genocide Treaty, which came into force in 1951.[64] There can be little

---

[60] Morsink, *Universal Declaration of Human Rights*, 307–312.
[61] See Todd Landman, *Protecting Human Rights: A Comparative Study* (Washington, DC: Georgetown University Press, 2005) and Samantha Power and Graham Allison, eds., *Realizing Human Rights: Moving from Inspiration to Impact* (New York: St. Martin's Press, 2000).
[62] Because Asad does not mention the range of human rights problems attending transnational corporations and others, I have not taken up that problem here. Still, this area of concern, which is receiving increasing attention, shows further that, although the nation-state is not disappearing or is by any means of small significance in regard to human rights difficulties, it is by no means the end-all of such difficulties.
[63] Cited by David J. Scheffer, "Staying the Course with the International Criminal Court," *Cornell International Law Journal* vol. 35 (Nov. 2001–Feb. 2002), 63.
[64] See Convention on the Punishment of the Crime of Genocide, Article VI: "Persons charged with genocide ... shall be tried by a competent tribunal in the State of the territory of which the act was committed, or by such international penal tribunal as may have jurisdiction with respect to those Contracting Parties which shall have accepted its jurisdiction."

doubt that, in the long run, "the new permanent court... is going to exist"[65] and is going irreversibly to advance the ideal of universal legality, despite the efforts of the Bush administration to disable it. What remains unclear is exactly when the United States is going to recover "the tradition of moral leadership" that is committed to these ideals.[66]

Finally, Asad's claim that religious and moral understanding and practice are totally at the mercy of the modern nation-state is greatly overstated. However much in need of further clarification, proposals such as An-Na'im's to establish positive connections between Islam and the principles of human rights and the secular state – and to use those connections as a basis for holding to account the performance of Muslim and non-Muslim governments around the world – give promise that points of reference independent of state control do exist. And An-Na'im has general support from other Muslim scholars, such as Sachedina and Soroush. Beyond that, active reform efforts in places such as Turkey and Iran are mainly compatible with such proposals. How likely they are to succeed is uncertain, but their long-term chances should not be underrated.

The same point can be applied to Christianity. Thanks to the definitive work of Brian Tierney, we now have abundant historical evidence regarding the constructive connection between Christianity and the modern development of human rights.[67] The key ideas, born of theological and legal disputes beginning in twelfth-century Roman Catholicism, were of a fundamental "subjective right" to self-defense naturally and inalienably claimable by every human being simply by virtue of being human. "In the last resort one could exercise [this] inherent natural right... [,]that no human law could take away[,] against any oppressive authority, even an oppressive pope."[68] By elaborating certain notions of conscience found in the Pauline epistles and combining them by the seventeenth century with this doctrine of a natural right to self-defense, freedom of conscience and religion came, according to Tierney, "to be seen as one of the natural [human] rights."[69]

---

[65] David J. Scheffer, "A Treaty Bush Shouldn't Unsign," *New York Times* (April 6, 2002), A27.
[66] Part of Clinton's comment on signing the Rome Treaty, cited in Scheffer, "Staying the Course with the International Court," 63. In 2010, the Obama administration took up an exploratory, working relationship with the International Criminal Court.
[67] See Brian Tierney, *The Idea of Natural Rights: Studies on Natural Rights, Natural Law and Church Law, 1150–1625* (Atlanta: Scholars Press, 1997).
[68] Brian Tierney, "Religious Rights: An Historical Perspective," in John Witte, Jr. and Johann D. van der Vyver, eds., *Religious Human Rights in Global Perspective: Religious Perspectives* (The Hague: Martinus Nijhoff Publishers, 1996), 29.
[69] Ibid., 42.

That these rights were considered "natural" means more than that they were believed to be equally and universally available to all human beings. It also means that they are considered to be justified independent of religious conviction. The whole idea (as with the drafters of the Declaration) is that there exists a universal, indubitable, and unavoidable standard of moral appraisal of the behavior of state and other authorities. In short, here is a powerful example of the way a religious tradition such as Christianity comes to embrace and affirm a set of independent "outside constraints" on religious understanding and practice that are fully compatible with the concept of human rights.[70]

Incidentally, these points should cause An-Na'im to revise the widely affirmed, but mistaken, assertion that the concept of human rights was "premised on the Enlightenment" and that Christianity simply "reconciled itself" to the idea over time.[71] Tierney's exhaustive work renders that view out of date.

Although the writings of the Jewish religious thinker, Yeshayahu Leibowitz, in his compelling volume, *Judaism, Human Values, and the Jewish State*,[72] deal more with the secular state than human rights, his passing remarks on human rights are nevertheless interesting as an example of Jewish religious reflection on the question. Some of Leibowitz's strongest theological apprehensions arise in response to the policies of the state of Israel in regard to the occupied territories:

> As for the "religious" arguments for the annexation of the territories, these are only an expression, subconsciously or perhaps overtly hypocritical, of the transformation of the Jewish religion into a camouflage for Israeli nationalism. Counterfeit religion identifies national interests with the service of God and

---

[70] Asad's claim, in an obscure excursus on natural rights (130ff.), that the ideas of natural and human rights "depend on" "national rights" (135), and thus on the prior existence of "a strong, secular state" capable of enforcing its will by violent means, is completely insupportable, if he means by that claim that a state's interpretations of rights are accepted as ultimately determinative.

[71] An-Na'im, "Synergy and Interdependence of Human Rights, Religion, and Secularism," 5. This is not, of course, to suggest that the Enlightenment (along with other intellectual movements) did not contribute to the evolution of human rights thinking. But it is to suggest – most emphatically – that the process of development did not *begin* in the eighteenth century. Incidentally, it is also to suggest that the Enlightenment itself is a much more complex historical movement than is typically acknowledged, with therefore quite variable implications for human rights thinking, variations that still obtain today. One has in mind the fact that the Enlightenment had British, French and German versions and that they did not all come to the same conclusions about the nature, basis, and scope of rights or about religion and state, or about other subjects as well. It is time that simplistic references to "the Enlightenment project" are called into question or, as they say, "problematized."

[72] (Cambridge: Harvard University Press, 1992).

imputes to the state – which is only an instrument serving human needs – supreme value from a religious standpoint.[73]

Leibowitz claims that the State of Israel was dramatically transformed by the occupation of the West Bank and Gaza after the 1967 War:

> The change was not simply of quantity but of substance. Its significance consists not in the increase of the number of Arabs subject to Jewish rule . . . , but in the denial of the right of independence to the Palestinian people. Israel ceased to be the state of the Jewish people and became an apparatus of coercive control of Jews over another people. What many call "the undivided Land of Israel" is not, and never can be, the state of the Jewish people, but only a Jewish regime of force. *The state of Israel today is neither a democracy nor a state abiding by the rule of law, since it rules over a million and a half people deprived of civil and political rights.*[74]

> [W]e are able to maintain our rule over the rebellious people only by actions regarded the world-over as criminal. We refer to this as "policy" rather than "terror" because it is conducted by a duly constituted government and its regular army. The "aberrant cases" of necessity became the rule, since they are not incidental to a conquering regime but essential to it.[75]

Here, in short, is a suggestion from a Jewish theological perspective that basic, universal standards of proper treatment – fundamental human rights, it would seem – constitute an appropriate "outside constraint" on religious understanding and practice.

THE SECULAR STATE

The human rights documents help clarify the notion of the secular state. According to the Preamble and Article 2 of the Declaration, Member States are obligated to promote "universal respect for and observance of human rights and

---

[73] Ibid., 226.
[74] Ibid., 243. Emphasis added. Elsewhere, Leibowitz dismisses the relevance of "rights talk" to the question of land allocation between Israel and the Palestinians (see 241–242). However, one has the impression that he has something different in mind here from what he thinks are the valid rights claims Palestinians may properly make as victims of Israeli rule, which he mentions in this quotation.
[75] Ibid., 244. Of some relevance to Leibowitz's discussion is a point Asad makes. It is that the idea of "military necessity," permitted by the laws of armed combat, "can be extended indefinitely" in the interests of achieving victory (or protecting national security). Therefore, he says, any measure whatsoever can, in the end, be justified (Asad, *Formations of the Secular*, 118), and, consequently, the idea of effective restraints on force and suffering in time of war are for all practical purposes undermined. Although this is certainly going too far, it must be admitted that this is a very worrying point, particularly because of the difficulties at present with the international enforcement of humanitarian law against offending states.

fundamental freedoms" by guaranteeing all the rights and freedoms contained in the Declaration "without distinction of any kind, such as... religion." The requirement is strengthened and further specified in Article 2 of the ICCPR: "Each State Party to the present Covenant undertakes to respect and to ensure to all individuals within its territory and subject to its jurisdiction the rights recognized in the present Covenant, without distinction of any kind, such as... religion." The unmistakable implication is that participating states must be "secular" or religiously neutral in the sense of not allowing fundamental commitments – matters of religion or belief – to affect the protection of human rights and freedoms.

There is one complication in human rights jurisprudence that must be addressed: That is a statement apparently tolerating the legitimacy of established religions made by the Human Rights Committee, an eighteen-member supervisory agency mandated by the ICCPR (Pt. IV) to monitor State Party compliance and to issue General Comments on the meaning of the Covenant. Interpreting Article 18 of the ICCPR, the Committee declares the following:

> The fact that a religion is recognized as a state religion or that it is established as official or traditional or that its followers comprise a majority of the population, shall not result in any impairment of the enjoyment of any of the rights under the Covenant, including articles 18 and 27 [minority protection], nor in any discrimination against adherents of other religions or non-believers. In particular, certain measures discriminating against the latter, such as measures restricting eligibility for government service to members of the predominant religion or giving economic privileges to them or imposing special restrictions on the practice of other faiths, are not in accordance with the prohibition of discrimination based on religion or belief and the guarantee of equal protection under article 26.[76]

Without revoking "recognition" of state religions or of religions established as official or traditional or as occupying majority status, the Committee explicitly and extensively imposes a set of conditions or "outside constraints" on such bodies that radically challenge their conventional legal prerogatives. Adopting laws or policies that result in "any" impairment or discrimination on the basis of religion or belief would be impermissible. That specifically rules out discriminating against individuals or groups because of their religion or belief. In addition, it presumably raises serious questions about invoking religious or other fundamental belief as the exclusive basis for adopting laws or policies

---

[76] UN Human Rights Committee General Comment No. 22 (48) (Article 18) para. 9 in *Religion and Human Rights Documents*, ed. by Tad Stahnke and J. Paul Martin (New York: Center for the Study of Human Rights, Columbia University, 1998), 94.

because of the obvious potential for discrimination. At the very least, such an action would assure the right of challenge under the equal protection article. In short, the Committee's comment leaves established or majority religions but a shadow of their former selves.

Further clarification follows from an examination of Article 18.3 of the ICCPR. It states that "freedom to manifest one's religion or beliefs may be subject only to such limitations as are prescribed by law and are necessary to protect public safety, order, health, or morals or the fundamental rights and freedoms of others."

Five elements are notable about this paragraph.

1. First, that the use of the word "manifest" refers to public expression or practice and not simply to the holding of a belief;
2. Second, that "belief" as in the phrase, "religion or belief," refers to a philosophical belief that has the same fundamental or "conscientious" status that a religious belief has for a believer;
3. Third, that the reference to "safety, order, health, or morals" is modified by the word "public," suggesting that these terms refer to "goods" to which all citizens of a given state share a common claim and in which they all share a common interest;
4. Fourth, that because appropriate measures to protect these "public goods" are regarded as possible "limitations" (or "outside constraints") on the public expression or practice of religion or belief, the basis for understanding and interpretation must not be necessarily attached to or dependent on particular religions or beliefs. In other words, there is implied here the idea of what is called, "public reason" – a set of norms and procedures of justification that are publicly available or assumed to be held in common;
5. Fifth, that the phrase, "prescribed by law," implies that the state's "legal function" – namely, the formulation and enforcement of law backed by coercion – applies authoritatively to this sphere of public goods, something we might call, *the domain of the secular*. In cases of conflict between religion or belief and the domain of the secular, the state has the right to enforce its determinations, but always and only, be it noted, so long as it does not exceed the boundaries of its domain and it acts in accord with the "fundamental rights and freedoms of others," as required.

These five observations sharpen understanding of the secular state. The central idea of "deregulating religion," mentioned earlier in relation to An-Na'im's account, falls into place. State and religious authority are *differentiated*,[77] particularly in respect to the coercive or enforcement function of the state, and all religions (or beliefs) are given a free and equal chance to manifest their convictions within the "limitations" or "outside constraints" imposed by the domain of the secular.

In keeping with the human rights requirements of nondiscrimination, benefits and burdens in the public sphere may not be apportioned simply on the basis of race, gender, religion, national or social origin, or birth, and so on. That is precisely because such indications are not what all citizens of a given society hold in common. They do not all have the same religious beliefs, nor the same race or gender. Yet, they all do share a common material interest in public health, safety, order, and morals, and it is therefore acceptable on the part of the state, acting in the service of that common interest, to impose restrictions in regard to protecting it.

When it comes, for example, to the meaning of the elusive term "public morals," the Human Rights Committee emphasizes that it must be understood in a *pluralistic* fashion: "The Committee observes that the concept of morals derives from many social, philosophical, and religious traditions." Consequently, it concludes that "limitations on the freedom to manifest a religion or belief for the purpose of protecting morals must be based on principles not deriving exclusively from a single tradition."[78] The implication is that the same would apply to the other public goods as well. In implementing limitations for the purpose of protecting public health, safety, and order, as well as morals, the state would be obliged to search, where possible, for the common denominator among the various traditions of religion or belief represented among the citizenry. Where no common denominator exists, the state, through its duly constituted legal and political procedures, must make the best judgment it can, based on what are assumed to be publicly shared and accessible standards of reason.

Accordingly, the principle of pluralism, which was, I noted, so important in An-Na'im's proposal, can be seen to apply to our subject in two ways. As I just pointed out, one way is in understanding and applying the limitations or outside constraints on the manifestations of religion or belief that are associated with the domain of the secular. Judgments in that regard must be plural and public in the appropriate sense. The other is aimed at An-Na'im's chief concern: the free play of many divergent beliefs and practices present within and among different religious and other traditions that may be manifested inside the limits imposed by the domain of the secular.

---

[77] Jose Casanova, *Public Religions in the Modern World* (Chicago: University of Chicago Press, 1994), 20–39.
[78] General Comment Adopted by the Human Rights Committee under Article 40, Paragraph 4, of the International Covenant on Civil and Political Rights, UN Doc. CCPR/c/21/Rev.1/Add.4, September 27, 1993, para. 8, 3.

For one thing, such pluralism is fully endorsed by the human rights documents. I have argued elsewhere that, far from being indifferent to or having no interest in religion and similar beliefs, human rights law is in fact *deferent* to such concerns.[79] Part of that deference is guaranteeing free, equal, and open expression and practice consistent with the authorized limits discussed here. In addition, the authorized limits would decidedly not exclude religious or philosophical commentary on public affairs, including the domain of the secular. A good example is Casanova's fascinating discussion of the prominent and generally permissible role of Roman Catholic social and economic advocacy within the public arena.[80] The only proviso is that, when it comes to passing laws or rendering judicial decisions in the public arena, the actions must rest on "public reason" rather than on particular religions or beliefs.[81]

The next step is to consider examples of religious support from the three traditions for this outline of the idea of the secular state. The underlying argument, again contrary to Asad, is that insofar as respectable exemplars of the three religions can be shown to embrace this outline, it is not correct to claim that religious interests as such are totally and inalterably opposed to the "modern secular nation-state."

We already know of An-Na'im's support for something close to this interpretation. Along similar lines, Sachedina says,

> The thesis that Islam does not make a distinction between the religious and the political requires revision in the light of what has been argued in this volume. Even the all-comprehensive sacred law of Islam, the Shari'a, presupposes the distinction between spiritual and temporal, as it categorized God-human and interhuman relationships respectively. God-human relations are founded upon individual autonomy and moral agency regulated by a sense of accountability to God alone for any acts of omission or commission. Interhuman relations, in contrast, are founded on an individual and collective social-political life.... This latter category... has customarily provided Muslim governments with the principle of functional secularity that allows them to regulate all matters pertaining to interpersonal justice. The same principle rules out the authority of Muslim governments to regulate religious matters except when the free exercise of religion for any individual is in danger.... The foundation of a civil society in Islam is based on the equality

---

[79] David Little, "Studying 'Religious Human Rights': Methodological Foundations," in Johann van der Vyver and John Witte, Jr., eds., *Religious Human Rights in Global Perspective: Legal Perspectives* (The Hague: Martinus Nijhoff, 1996), 52.

[80] Casanova, *Public Religions in the Modern World*, ch. 7: "Catholicism in the United States: From Private to Public Denomination."

[81] I take up the subject of public reason more extensively in Chapter 4.

in creation in which the privilege in citizenry attaches equally to Muslim and non-Muslim, entailing inclusive political, civil, and social membership in the community.[82]

From the perspective of Judaism, Leibowitz comes to comparable conclusions. His conclusions are couched in terms that are highly critical of the existing Israeli state for not being secular enough and consequently for corrupting both religion and state:

> The demand for separation of religion from the existing secular state derives from the vital religious need to prevent religion from becoming a political tool, a function of the governmental bureaucracy, which "keeps" religion and religious institutions not for religious reasons but as a concession to pressure groups in the interest of ephemeral power-considerations. Religion as an adjunct of secular authority is the antithesis of true religion. It hinders religious education of the community at large and constricts the religious influence on its way of life. From a religious standpoint, there is no greater abomination than an atheistic-clerical regime. At present we have a state – secular in essence and most of its manifestations – which recognizes religious institutions as state agencies, supports them with its funds, and, by administrative means, imposes, not religion, but certain religious provisions chosen arbitrarily by political negotiation.... The secular state and society should be stripped of their false religious veneer.[83]

> The function of the state is essentially secular. It is not service of God.... Religion, that is man's recognition of his duty to serve God, cannot be integrated with the machinery of government. The political organization, necessary as a condition of survival, merely sets the ground for the struggle for religion, which is by its very nature an eternal struggle that will never end in victory. The state of Israel of our day has no religious significance, because no such struggle is being conducted in it.... The state, as such, has no religious value. No state ever had.[84]

Lastly, a Christian example. One of the most interesting illustrations of this pro-secularist perspective in the history of Christianity is the seventeenth-century New England Puritan, Roger Williams.[85] Williams was a fervent and in many

---

[82] Sachedina, *Islamic Roots of Democratic Pluralism*, 137. I am not assuming that there are no significant differences between An-Na'im and Sachedina (or Soroush, either). I simply emphasize the obvious and important overlap of views regarding the affirmation of "secular space" from several explicitly Islamic points of view.
[83] Leibowitz, Judaism, *Human Values and the Jewish State*, 176–177.
[84] Ibid., 215–216.
[85] Although Williams is not a contemporary representative of his religion, as are the other figures I have cited, he nevertheless does have, it can be argued, profound "contemporary significance." See Chapter 9 of this volume for a fuller account of Williams's thought.

ways orthodox Calvinist. As one of the founders of the Rhode Island colony, he is particularly well known for participating in the establishment of "the first commonwealth in modern history to make religious liberty... a cardinal principle of its corporate existence and to maintain the separation of church and state on these grounds."[86] A crucial feature of his resolute support for freedom of conscience and separation of political and religious authority was his unflinchingly "secularist" attitude toward the state. He could hardly have been clearer on this point.

Although, he says that the general institution of earthly government is authorized by God "for the preservation of mankind in civil order and peace," particular governments derive their legitimacy exclusively from the human constituents who make up "the commonwealth, the body of people and the civil state" and who "communicate" authority "unto [the magistrates], and [en]trust them with it." Accordingly, governments "can have no more power than fundamentally lies in the bodies or [constituencies] themselves, *which power, might, or authority is not religious, Christian, etc., but natural, humane, and civil.*"[87] Williams supports this interpretation by arguing that when St. Paul speaks of the lawful functions of government in the thirteenth chapter of the Epistle to the Romans, he mentions only the "second table" of the Decalogue, which applies to interhuman relations, and not the "first table," which concerns divine-human relations.[88]

There is a recurring emphasis in these examples on what looks like a commitment to or a belief in the propriety of an independent sphere of secular jurisdiction, a "domain of the secular," that is, in each of the three cases, encouraged from a religious point of view. And even though religious believers recommend such a doctrine, the doctrine itself is understood as publicly or commonly accessible and thus need not be "necessarily attached to or dependent upon particular religions or beliefs," as I put it earlier.

CONCLUSION

It is important, I have contended, to establish a set of limits or outside constraints with regard to human rights and the secular state in order that various public manifestations of religious thought and practice be effectively restrained. This effort to identify a set of constraints may be thought of as an

---

[86] Sydney E. Ahlstrom, *A Religious History of the American People* (New Haven: Yale University Press, 1972), 172.

[87] Roger Williams, *Complete Writings* (New York: Russell & Russell, 1963), vol. 3, 398 (emphasis added). I have here and there modernized Williams's prose to make it more readable.

[88] Ibid., 151.

elaboration and clarification of Abdullahi An-Na'im's important suggestion about the interdependence of religion, human rights, and the secular state. In keeping with the spirit of An-Na'im's proposal, it should now be clear that a commitment to a set of constraints is by no means foreign to religious traditions like Judaism, Christianity, and Islam, but, in fact, finds eloquent resonance and support in at least some parts of such traditions. To demonstrate that fact greatly strengthens An-Na'im's proposal, because it proves that significant common ground does indeed exist for promoting the objectives that he seeks.

However, what I have attempted here is only a first step. It remains to look comparatively and in detail at what we might call the "sore points" of confrontation between religion and the "domain of the secular." How are courts and legislatures in different countries, respectively influenced by Judaism, Christianity, and Islam (to begin with), undertaking to adjudicate competing claims between the right to "freedom of religion or belief" and the prescribed "limitations" imposed by the universal need to protect "public health, order, safety, and morals"?

It is only when we begin systematically to examine decisions and laws in that context that we can begin to see how the relations among "religion, human rights, and the secular state" are being negotiated in practice. And it is, in turn, only when we have that information, based on comparative legal investigation carried out in the light of the set of constraints we have proposed, that we may begin to construct some general and intercultural guidelines regarding how, in practical terms, religion, human rights, and secularism *ought to be* related to each other. I take up such an examination in the next chapter.

4

Religion, Human Rights, and Public Reason

Protecting the Freedom of Religion or Belief*

INTRODUCTION

According to Malcolm Evans,[1] the international protection of religion or belief does not at present stand on very firm ground: "The last fifty years of the twentieth century have seen a diminution in the importance attached to the achievement of freedom of religion or belief, both by its incorporation *into* the human rights canon and by the manner in which it has fared *as* a human right".[2] He expands on this depressing assessment in several arresting comments:

> The importance – indeed, centrality – of the freedom of thought, conscience and religion is understood by the international community and firmly embedded within the system of human rights protection. The capacity of international human rights instruments and mechanisms to add definition to the concept and grant it a place commensurate with the nature of the beliefs and the opinions of [religious] believers is, as has been seen, a matter of some doubt. The freedom of thought, conscience and religion may be protected as a human right: but this does not mean that the relationship between a secularist concept of human rights and religious perspectives of the rights and duties of the individual can, or should, be determined exclusively from and through its perspectives.[3]

---

* I wish to express my thanks to Jonas Clark, a student at Harvard Divinity School, for his invaluable assistance in composing this chapter.
[1] Malcolm D. Evans, *Religious Liberty and International Law in Europe* (Cambridge: Cambridge University Press, 1997).
[2] Malcolm D. Evans, "Historical Analysis of Freedom of Religion or Belief as a Technique for Resolving Religious Conflict," in Tore Lindholm, W. Cole Durham, Jr., and Bahia G. Tahzib-Lie, eds., *Facilitating Freedom of Religion or Belief: A Deskbook* (Leiden: Martinus Nijhoff, 2004), 14; original italics.
[3] Evans, *Religious Liberty and International Law*, 375–376.

There are important lessons to be drawn from the way in which the discussions [surrounding the drafting of the 1981 UN Declaration against Intolerance and Discrimination] evolved, the most important of which concerns the way [they] veered away from the central problems posed by the definition of religion or belief and the content of the freedom of manifestation. This demonstrates the extreme difficulty – some might say impossibility – of setting the power of religious and other life-defining concepts within the framework of a system of human rights which is premised upon universalist presuppositions with which they are not necessarily in harmony.[4]

[Statements by the Special Rapporteur for Freedom of Religion or Belief concerning the need for everyone, including religious people, to commit to a culture of tolerance and nondiscrimination by avoiding "categorical, inflexible attitudes," "blind obstinacy" and "gratuitous accusations," as well as "impulsive, and ineffectual initiatives"] means that freedom of religion does not include the right of others to adhere to a religion which is intolerant of the beliefs of others. On this view, "Human Rights" has itself become a "religion or belief" which is itself intolerant of other forms of value systems which may stand in opposition to its own central tenets as any of those it seeks to address.

In seeking to assert itself in this fashion, the international community risks becoming the oppressor of the believer, rather than the protector of the persecuted. [It must learn] to accept that in the religious beliefs of others the dogmas of human rights are met with an equally powerful force which must be respected, not overcome.[5]

In his book, *Religious Liberty and International Law in Europe*, Evans provides a careful and illuminating analysis of some of the conceptual confusions and other deficiencies characteristic of the drafting discussions and final formulations of the key documents pertinent to the international protection of religion or belief: the Universal Declaration of Human Rights (UDHR) (especially Articles 2, 7, 16, 18, 19, 26, and 29), the International Covenant of Political and Civil Rights (ICCPR) (especially Articles 2, 4, 8, 17, 18, 19, 20, 21, 22, 23, 26, and 27), the UN Declaration on the Elimination of All Forms of Intolerance and Discrimination (DEID), and the European Convention for the Protection of Human Rights and Fundamental Freedoms (ECHR) (especially Articles 8, 9, 10, 11, 12, 14, 15), and the First Protocol to the Convention, Article 2. In addition, he has some very revealing and, in places, dispiriting things to say about the results of the work of the bodies designated to implement the various

---

[4] Ibid., 245.
[5] Ibid., 260–261.

instruments: the Human Rights Committee, established to review and transmit reports from Member States regarding compliance with the ICCPR and to issue "such general comments as it may consider appropriate," including interpreting the meaning of relevant articles; and the European institutions designated to implement the European Human Rights Convention. Finally, he reflects interestingly and sometimes critically on the work of the Special Rapporteur for the Freedom of Religion or Belief, mandated in 1986 to examine and report on incidents and governmental actions inconsistent with the provisions of the DEID and to recommend remedial measures.

Still, Evans's reservations concerning the structure and foundations of the provisions and mechanisms designed and developed since the end of World War II to protect and promote the freedom of religious and other similar beliefs are unsettling. Of course, the claim that the human rights system, with its "secularist" and "universalist" presuppositions, has itself become an intolerant and domineering form of religion or belief, potentially more persecutor than protector, is hardly new. But such views are, to say the least, unexpected from specialists such as Evans. Legal and other experts in the field tend to engage in intramural or in-house debates and critiques, calling this or that legal judgment to account, pointing to this or that unclarity or shortcoming in the law or its interpretation, or advocating one change or another in the way things are done or understood. They do not typically assault the foundations of the "house" itself. And although they, echoing the former UN Special Rapporteur, Asma Jahangir, regularly decry the serious failure around the world to match performance with standards, they do not normally lay most of the blame, as Evans appears to do, at the feet of the system itself. On the contrary, specialists seem widely to share a fervent commitment to the basic provisions and framework of human rights law as it bears on freedom of religion or belief, and although they energetically debate its proper meaning and application, they seem to believe that its basic premises are secure and that recent developments in the administration of the law are promising.

I share this outlook and feel the need to defend it against Evans's challenges, even if there are specific areas of weakness. This defense is important for four reasons: The challenges come from an eminent and influential specialist, they are the product of painstaking work, they match fashionable complaints against the human rights system as a whole and rights to freedom religion or belief in particular, and any thoughts on "a way forward" require taking a stand against such objections.

Because the attack is foundational, it is necessary to think comprehensively about the human rights framework, including provisions for the international protection of religion or belief. That means looking both at the underlying premises of the framework as a whole, including its key language and provisions, and at the practice of the implementing institutions, such as the Human Rights Committee of the ICCPR, the UN Special Rapporteur, and the Human Rights Commission and Court of the European Convention, reconstituted, as of 1998, into a single court.[6] I also sample some of the recent expert commentary,[7] at least selectively and somewhat conjecturally.

HUMAN RIGHTS AND PUBLIC REASON

A helpful way to make sense of human rights language as the drafters understood it is to see it in relation to John Rawls's idea of public reason.[8] The fit is by no means perfect, and some important adjustments must be made. Still, when viewed that way, it is possible to appreciate the basic strengths of the language, including the way it both accommodates and delimits references to the secular. Five parallels are worth noting.

First, Rawls describes the notion of public reason as the appropriate idiom of communication among the citizens of a democratic order, "of those sharing the status of equal citizenship," who, "as a collective body, exercise final political and coercive power over one another in enacting laws and amending their constitution." "The subject of their reason," he says, "is the good of the public," of what is required of "society's basic structure of institutions, and of the purposes and ends they are to serve." That good refers primarily to "constitutional essentials," namely, the character and ranking of "certain basic

---

[6] Protocol 11 to the European Convention on Human Rights, opened for signature on May 11, 1994, and effected on October 31, 1998. "Until 31 October 1998 the European Commission was able to make a determination that a claim was inadmissible (under Articles 25 and 26 of the European Convention) or, as a means of eliminating claims with no merit, determine the claim to be manifestly ill-founded or an abuse of the right of petition even if technically admissible (Article 27). After that date, the European Commission was effectively replaced by a new Court," Paul M. Taylor, *Freedom of Religion: UN and European Human Rights Law and Practice* (Cambridge: Cambridge University Press, 2005), 17; see also 16 and fn. 44. The new Court has taken over the previous functions of the Commission by means of three-member committees selected from the entire body of justices (forty-seven, at present, in accord with the number of Contracting States).

[7] Drawn, for the most part, from Carolyn Evans, *Freedom of Religion under the European Convention on Human Rights* (New York: Oxford University Press, 2001); Tore Lindholm, Cole Durham, and Bahia Tahzip-Lie, *Facilitating Freedom of Religion or Belief*, Paul Taylor, *Freedom of Religion*; and *Emory International Law Review* 19. 2 (Summer 2005).

[8] John Rawls, *Political Liberalism* (New York: Columbia University Press, 1996), Lecture IV. I am grateful to Christian Rice for stimulating my thinking regarding the connection between human rights and the notion of public reason.

rights, liberties, and opportunities (of the kind familiar from constitutional democratic regimes)."[9]

Second, public reason, Rawls emphasizes, has a distinctly limited reach. It provides common terms of discourse in a society assumed to be made up of citizens espousing a variety of divergent "general and comprehensive doctrines." These doctrines are religious or philosophical systems of belief intended to apply to a large, possibly unlimited, number of adherents and that include "conceptions of what is of value in human life, and ideals of human character, as well as ideals of friendship and associational relationships, and much else that is to inform our conduct," and, potentially, to life as a whole.[10] In face of an array of such doctrines that invariably compete with each other, public reason "is framed solely to apply to the basic structure of society, its main political, social, and economic institutions," and "it is presented independently of any wider comprehensive religious or philosophical doctrine";[11] as such, it is considered to be a "freestanding view."[12]

There is presumed to be, he goes on, "no reason why any citizen, or association of citizens, should have the right to use state power to decide constitutional essentials as that person's, or that association's, comprehensive doctrine directs. When equally represented, no citizen could grant to another person or association that political authority. Any such authority, therefore, is without grounds in public reason."[13] In short, public reason provides a common, religiously neutral language of last resort in regard to the regulation of force.

The fact that public reason is conceived of as freestanding by being independent of any comprehensive religious or other doctrine implies that the idea is *secular in a limited sense*. Officially, it neither authorizes nor is authorized by any religious position, yet it espouses a notion of "reasonable pluralism" and a commitment to tolerance of diverse religious and other convictions so long as adherents to those convictions agree to live in accord with the constitutional essentials presupposed by the idea of public reason.[14]

Third, Rawls mentions that "reasonable comprehensive doctrines recognize [these values]," leading to his notion of "overlapping consensus."[15] For reasons based on an interpretation of their own respective traditions, proponents of "reasonable comprehensive doctrines" consensually embrace as

---

[9] Ibid., 213, 214, and 217.
[10] Ibid., 13.
[11] Ibid., 223.
[12] Ibid., 144.
[13] Ibid., 226.
[14] Ibid., 170, 194–195.
[15] Ibid., 133–172.

freestanding the values associated with public reason. As such, the values accepted by the overlapping consensus imply their own independent, non-comprehensive grounding, arrived at, for Rawls, on the basis of what he calls "political constructivism."[16]

Rawls makes very clear that, in his view, an overlapping consensus is not the same as a "modus vivendi" based on a coincidental and temporary convergence of convictions and interests. It is, rather, a "moral conception" based on "moral grounds."[17] It supports a notion of public reason involving a deliberate and self-conscious commitment to a "principle of legitimacy," according to which each citizen accepts a *moral duty* – "the duty of civility" – "to be able to explain to one another on those fundamental questions how the principles and policies they advocate and vote for can be supported by the political values of public reason."[18] In other words, public reason is a common framework of communication based on values that each citizen can reasonably expect others to endorse.[19]

Fourth, Rawls considers public reason to apply in general to the conduct of official forums, such as the proceedings of the legislature and the official communications and actions of the executive. Interestingly, however, it applies especially to the judiciary and, above all, to the highest court in a constitutional democracy with judicial review: "This is because the justices have to explain and justify their decisions as based on their understanding of the constitution and relevant statutes and precedents." Because that is sometimes not the orientation of legislators and executives, "the court's special role makes it the exemplar of public reason."[20]

---

[16] "Political constructivism," as contrasted with moral realism or "moral constructivism," à la Kant, consists of four features that supply the basis on which political values for citizens of a liberal society are agreed on: an *impartial procedure*; an emphasis on *practical reason* – thinking about subjects like a just constitutional regime as the object of political endeavor; a *complex conception of person and society*, according to which persons belong "to a political society understood as a fair system of social cooperation from one generation to the next; and a commitment to *the idea of the reasonable*, rather than the idea of truth (*Political Liberalism*, 91–95, and, generally, Lecture III).

[17] Ibid., 147.

[18] Ibid., 217.

[19] Ibid.

[20] Ibid., 216. Although Kent Greenawalt takes up the relation of public reason to judicial determinations somewhat inconclusively in Chapters 22 and 23 of *Religion and the Constitution: Establishment and Fairness* (Princeton: Princeton University Press, 2008), he makes some suggestions in those chapters and elsewhere that are relevant to Rawls's position here. When judges issue formal opinions, Greenawalt says, they are in effect speaking "for the government" thus disallowing "a judge from asserting the truth of any doctrinal religious proposition as if it should carry direct weight in a case" (62). Judges are free to invoke their religious views in other contexts, but when, for example, Supreme Court justices are rendering an official

Fifth, Rawls stresses that the idea of public reason is *an ideal*, consisting of an understanding and a set of rational norms to be aspired to, and not something that is necessarily operational in complete form in the real world.[21]

In comparison, human rights language reveals significant similarities at all five points: First, it is a language fitted to the ideal of democratic citizenship where the "good of the public" or "general welfare" is understood to encompass a "society's basic structure of institutions," and particularly its "constitutional essentials," including "certain basic rights, liberties, and opportunities," as well as specific public goods. In the words of UDHR, Article 29.2: "Everyone shall be subject only to such limitations as are determined by law solely for the purpose of securing due recognition and respect for the rights and freedoms of others and of meeting the requirements of morality, public order, and the general welfare in a democratic society."[22] Similarly, rights to freedom of expression, peaceful assembly, and association may be limited only where "the rights and freedoms of others"; or public, safety, order, health, or morals; or national security must be protected (ICCPR, Arts. 19, 21, and 22). The same is largely true for the right to the freedom of religion or belief,[23] except that states are explicitly required to punish, among other things, expressions of "religious hatred" "that constitute ... incitement to discrimination ... or violence" (Art. 20.2, ICCPR).[24] Presumably, by violating basic protections against discrimination and violence, such incitements are seen as a direct threat to "the good of the public."

As to the grounds on which the state protects public goods, it has been authoritatively determined that they must be truly public or broadly inclusive. They must, that is, "be based on principles not deriving exclusively from a

---

opinion, they "must rely on justifications, such as the avoidance of civil strife" that "do not take a stand on religious matters" (493).

[21] Ibid., 213.

[22] ICCPR, Article 18.3 does not mention democracy as such, though Article 25 prescribes several of the conditions of democratic participation in government. Cf. ECHR, Article 9.2 "Freedom to manifest one's religion or beliefs shall be subject only to such limitations as are prescribed by law and are necessary in a democratic society in the interests of public safety, for the protection of public order, health or morals, or for the protection of the rights and freedoms of others."

[23] Unlike ICCPR Article 19, 21, and 22, Article 18 does not include "national security" as a basis for imposing limitations, because the right to freedom of religion or belief is considered nonderogable (Art. 4).

[24] ICCPR Article 20.2 also includes "hostility" as an indication of prohibited incitement. However, widespread legal opinion (including that of the present UN Special Rapporteur on Freedom of Religion or Belief) excludes it for being an "inward" emotion or attitude, and as such effectively impossible to police. In that respect, it is unlike violence or discrimination, both of which refer to legally identifiable forms of overt behavior. Thus, religious hate speech would be legally liable if and only if it "incited" to discrimination or violence.

single tradition," but "from many social, philosophical and religious traditions."[25] Beyond these provisions, Articles 3 through 21 of the UDHR (Arts. 6–27 of the ICCPR) further enumerate the basic rights of "equal citizenship" under the rule of law.[26]

Second, human rights language is designed to provide guidance in the face of a large array of divergent and competing comprehensive views. As a way of finding minimal common ground with many different belief systems, it is a language "presented independently of any wider comprehensive religious or philosophical doctrine" and is, as such, presupposed to be the language of last resort in regard to the regulation of force. No individual or group, as Rawls says, "should have the right to use state power to decide constitutional essentials [as the comprehensive doctrine of that individual or group dictates]."

This orientation explains why, after a series of contentious deliberations over proposals – eventually rejected – to include in the Preamble references to "divine origin" and "immortal destiny," the drafters reached consensus that "the Universal Declaration is a secular document by intent."[27] "Secular" is meant here to include, in the spirit of Rawls, a notion of public good that is assumed to be held in common by all citizens and that does not directly depend on any religious or other comprehensive view. This orientation also explains why the drafters ultimately concluded that the document should take no position "on the nature of man and of society" and that all "metaphysical controversies, notably conflicting doctrines of spiritualists, rationalists, and materialists regarding the origins of [human rights]" should be avoided.[28] Rather, these matters should be left to individual conscientious deliberation under the protection of the freedom of religion or belief.

That means more than that religious (and, equally, nonreligious) beliefs are fully respected by being provided for and protected by the state, subject of course to the limitations mentioned. There is also no prohibition against offering religious (or other) justifications for human rights as enumerated in the documents or against discussing and advocating them in public. It is simply that no provision exists for legally requiring or enforcing such beliefs.

---

[25] United Nations Human Rights Committee, General Comment No. 22 (48), Article 18, in *Religion and Human Rights: Basic Documents*, eds. Tad Stahnke and Paul Martin (Columbia University: Center for the Study of Human Rights, 1998). Though the General Comment applies specifically to the term "public morals" in Article 18.3, it may be assumed to apply similarly to "public order, safety, and health" wherever the terms appear in the covenant.

[26] According to the Preamble of the UDHR, "human rights should be protected by the rule of law."

[27] Johannes Morsink, *The Universal Declaration of Human Rights: Origins, Drafting, and Intent* (Philadelphia: University of Pennsylvania Press, 1999), 289.

[28] Ibid., 287.

Furthermore, it explains why the document adopts a "thin approach" to the government's role in dealing with comprehensive views. In contrast to a "thick approach," in which a government takes "responsibility for the delivery and maintenance of a special cultural, religious, or linguistic tradition," in a thin approach the government sets up "a fair (legal) framework within which its people can, singly or in groups, pursue their own notions of... human good, as long as [the rights, freedoms, and public goods] mentioned in Article 29 are not violated."[29]

Third, the authoritative ruling that the grounds on which the state protects public goods must be "be based on principles not deriving exclusively from a single tradition," but "from many social, philosophical and religious traditions," hints at Rawls's idea of an overlapping consensus, though more must be said. As we saw, an overlapping consensus on Rawls's understanding is not simply the acceptance of a set of values resulting from a coincidental and temporary convergence of convictions and interests. It is rather a common consensual commitment on the part of the adherents of many different comprehensive doctrines to values associated with public reason regarded as freestanding or as having their own independent, noncomprehensive grounding.

The drafters held such a view, even though the particular grounds they came to embrace are by no means the same as Rawls's. They were not "political constructivists," as we see later. For now, let me highlight the points of similarity between Rawls's position and theirs.

In particular, a careful review of the legislative history of the UDHR confirms the conclusion that it was the result of serious and extensive interaction among a large number of people from around the world, many of whom were representatives of what Rawls calls "reasonable comprehensive doctrines." For reasons based on an interpretation of their own respective traditions, they eventually reached consensus on the provisions of the UDHR:

> Before the whole two-year process from drafting and deliberation to adoption reached its end, literally hundreds of individuals from diverse backgrounds had participated. Thus [Charles] Malik, [a Lebanese Christian Thomist who was one of the principal drafters] could fairly say, "The genesis of each article, and each part of each article, was a dynamic process in which many minds, interests, backgrounds, legal systems and ideological persuasions played their respective determining roles."[30]

Moreover, as with Rawls, the values embodied in the Declaration and subsequent documents involve "moral conceptions" and assumed "moral grounds,"

---

[29] Morsink, *Universal Declaration of Human Rights*, 259.
[30] Cited in Mary Ann Glendon, *A World Made New: Eleanor Roosevelt and the Universal Declaration of Human Rights* (New York: Random House, 2001), 225.

illustrated by the following passage from the Preamble: "Disregard and contempt for human rights have resulted in barbarous acts which have outraged the conscience of mankind." The underlying moral convictions include a "principle of legitimacy," according to which each citizen accepts a *moral duty* – along the lines of Rawls's "duty of civility" – to operate in accord with the system, as well as to extend and promote it. In its Preamble, the UDHR is declared to be

> a common standard of achievement for all peoples and nations, to the end that every individual and every organ of society, keeping this Declaration in mind, shall strive by teaching and education to promote respect for these rights and freedoms and by progressive measures, national and international, to secure their universal and effective recognition and observance, both among the peoples of the Member States and among peoples and territories under their jurisdiction.

Above all, the values agreed to as the result of an overlapping consensus are considered freestanding. To have included in the Preamble references to the central ideas of religious or other comprehensive doctrines, as was proposed, would have contradicted the principle of nondiscrimination, according to which human rights are attributed "without distinction of any kind, such as ... religion ... or other opinion."[31] In addition, the values are noncomprehensive in the sense that they apply only to the rights, freedoms, and public goods enumerated in the UDHR and other documents, leaving the elaboration and defense of comprehensive doctrines to individual conscience.

Fourth, human rights language is legal in character, which means it is intended to be submitted to the interpretation and administration of judicial and quasi-judicial bodies such as the European Commission and Court of Human Rights, the ICCPR Human Rights Committee, and the UN Special Rapporteur on Freedom of Religion or Belief. These bodies and officials, in line with Rawls's comments about the highest court of a well-ordered democracy, may be understood to be special "exemplars of public reason," meaning that their judgments and patterns of reasoning, together with reactions to them, should be the particular focus of efforts to understand and apply public reason in its human rights form.

Fifth, considering the UDHR "as a common standard of achievement for all peoples and all nations" suggests that human rights language is "ideal" in Rawls's sense. That means that human rights language enshrines values to be aspired to and that they are not necessarily operational in complete form in the real world. But it also means that the language is ideal in that it

---

[31] Article 2, UDHR.

stands as a proposal or hortation offered for conscientious consideration. The language may punish only violations in practice of the enumerated rights, freedoms, and public goods; it may not regulate beliefs as such, presumably even beliefs that support or criticize existing human rights. In other words, human rights language constitutes "outer limits" on matters of conscientious belief by authorizing the legal inhibition of actions deduced from particular theological or philosophical comprehensive doctrines that in practice violate the human rights code. It does not prohibit deliberation and debate over the contents of the code or over efforts to amend it according to due process.

Despite these five instructive parallels between Rawls's idea of public reason and human rights language, there is, as I have hinted along the way, one critical point of divergence. That concerns the way in which the "constitutional essentials" – namely, "certain basic rights, liberties, and opportunities" – are justified.

As a "political constructivist," Rawls regards basic rights as derivative, as the result of a political agreement, not the precondition for one, whether the agreement is arrived at among nations or among members of a single state. Internationally, Rawls's approach is tailored to established, sovereign nation-states that already understand themselves to be constitutional democracies. He starts with the idea of "sovereign peoples" and their representatives, rather than with individuals, and a reasonable international agreement concerning basic rights would, on Rawls's account, permit significant deviations from fundamental human rights norms.[32]

Similarly, provisions for basic rights in any well-ordered constitutional democracy only *come after* the founding agreements of the society have been accepted. Strictly speaking, basic rights are the result of a "political construction." Moreover, the founding agreements – the fundamental "fair terms of cooperation" – are determined by the "reciprocal advantage" they represent to contracting parties, a notion that explicitly does not rest on any prior "moral

---

[32] In *The Law of Peoples* (Cambridge: Harvard University Press, 2001), 30ff., Rawls envisions his famous notion of the "original position" as applying in two stages: The first stage relates to individuals faced with the task of agreeing to a system of common benefit where, it is understood, no one's comprehensive doctrine may take precedence over others. The second stage relates to a set of "sovereign peoples" faced with the task of agreeing to an international arrangement between liberal and less liberal peoples ("decent hierarchical peoples," 59ff.). In the second stage the critical actors are not individual citizens but the representatives of the national interests of the various peoples concerned. On Rawls's description, the agreement allows substantial deviations from international human rights norms, especially discrimination based on religion or belief. According to the ICCPR, Article 4.1, the right of nondiscrimination may under no circumstances be abridged.

authority" or "order of moral values."³³ The contractors' reason for entering into the social contract in the first place is that "they are prudential seekers of their own advantage . . . imagined as concerned to advance their own conception of the good . . . [with] no stipulation that such a conception need include any altruistic elements."³⁴ It is only after the contractors have agreed to cooperate on the basis of mutual advantage that the terms of Rawls's famous image of the Veil of Ignorance apply, according to which they accept as reasonable the principles of justice, including the "constitutional essentials."

The assumptions underlying human rights language are very different. According to the words of the Preamble to the UDHR, "All human beings are born free and equal in dignity and rights." Basic rights are, *to begin with*, "inalienable" and the property of "all members of the human family" and "should be protected by the rule of law." Some rights, such as protections against racial, religious, gender, and other forms of discrimination, as well as extrajudicial killing, torture and cruel, inhuman, or degrading treatment or punishment, involuntary medical or scientific experimentation, or violations of the freedom of religion or belief, are under no circumstances to be subject to political or legal abridgement. In the terms of international law, such basic rights comprise a set of obligations that transcend statutory or treaty agreements and are grounded in universal peremptory principles, at once legal and moral in character.³⁵ Certainly, genocide and other "crimes against humanity" enumerated in the Rome Statute must be understood in the same way.³⁶

Accordingly, human rights are understood to *precede* or *predate* all international agreements and covenants, including human rights covenants, as well as all national constitutions, rather than to derive from or depend on them. The UDHR was taken to represent a prior

> common standard of achievement for all peoples and nations, to the end that every individual and every organ of society, keeping this Declaration in mind, shall strive by teaching and education to promote respect for these rights and freedoms.

The "two-tier" approach to justification assumed by the drafters, mentioned in the Introduction and developed in Chapter 1, both incorporates Rawls's fitting commitment to a set of freestanding and (narrowly) secular "constitutional essentials," including robust protection for freedom of religion and belief, and

---

[33] Rawls, *Political Liberalism*, 97.
[34] Martha Nussbaum, *Frontiers of Justice: Disability, Nationality, and Species Membership* (Cambridge: Harvard University Press, 2006), 56.
[35] See Chapter 1, fn. 47.
[36] See Chapter 3, fn. 63.

overcomes the limitations of his "political constructivism." One level involves a secular (or religiously neutral) appeal taken to be moral and universal in character and to be limited to the specific rights enumerated in the Declaration and its progeny. It becomes the ground for a belief in rights that are "prepolitical" in that they provide prior moral standards of political and legal legitimacy. The second level is identified by Article 18 (UDHR and ICCPR) and the other belief rights that guarantee the various facets of the right to freedom of conscience and religion or belief. They protect the ambition of individuals and groups to embrace and manifest, according to conscience, their own religious and/or nonreligious justifications for human rights and much else.

The first level of justification is illustrated, I have argued, by the "logic of pain," as manifested in Hitler's relentless reliance on self-serving and unfounded reasons for inflicting massively unfavorable, unwanted consequences on millions of people. Because human rights language was both formulated and justified against that background and the array of specific violations deemed to have occurred, there exist fixed reference points for interpreting and applying that language.[37]

The second level of justification protects something else persistently subverted by the fascists: the right to freedom of religion or belief. Fascism constituted a direct, comprehensive, and systematic assault on the various rights to freedom of religion or belief that came to be safeguarded by the Declaration and its progeny.

THE PROTECTION OF FREEDOM OF RELIGION OR BELIEF

The principal right to freedom of conscience, religions, or belief, as formulated by Article 18 of the ICCPR, is stated as follows:

> Everyone shall have the right to freedom of thought, conscience and religion. The right shall include freedom to have or to adopt a religion or belief of his choice, and freedom, either individually or in community with others and in public and private, to manifest his religion or belief in worship, observance, practice and teaching. No one shall be subject to coercion which would impair his freedom to have or to adopt a religion or belief of his choice.... [38]
> Freedom to manifest one's religion or belief may be subject only to such

---

[37] See Chapter 1, 54.
[38] Article 18.1 and 2 ICCRR. (For similar wording, cf. Declaration on the Elimination of Intolerance and Discrimination, Art. 1.1).

limitations as are prescribed by law and are necessary to protect public safety, order, health, or morals or the fundamental rights and freedoms of others.[39]

Article 9, the comparable provision in the ECHR, leaves out the reference to coercion, as well as reaffirms the language of the UDHR, which asserts the freedom of a person "to change his religion or belief," and adds to the limitations clause the phrase "necessary in a democratic society."

These provisions, together with four other rights directly relevant to the subject, constitute the basic points of reference for the exercise of public reason – the "constitutional essentials" or "basic rights, liberties, and opportunities" bearing on freedom of religion or belief:

1. "No one shall be subject to discrimination by any State, group of persons or person on the grounds of religion or other beliefs."[40] This right includes provisions against "intolerance based on religion or belief."[41] Discrimination has a clear legal meaning in the documents, namely, "any distinction, exclusion, restriction or preference based on religion or belief and having as its purpose or as its effect nullification or impairment of the recognition, enjoyment or exercise of human rights and fundamental freedoms on an equal basis."[42] Although intolerance is equated with discrimination in certain sections of the documents,[43] elsewhere it is not.[44]
2. "Persons belonging to [ethnic, religious or linguistic] minorities shall not be denied the right, in community with other members of their group, to enjoy their own culture, to profess and practice their own religion, and to use their own language."[45]
3. There is a right to be free of "religious... hatred that incites to discrimination, hostility or violence."[46]
4. "Respect for the liberty of parents and, when applicable, legal guardians to ensure the religious and moral education of their children in conformity with their own convictions."[47]

---

[39] Article 18.2, ICCPR; cf. Article 1.3 of DEID.
[40] Article 2.1, DEID.
[41] See the DEID.
[42] Article 2.2 of DEID. Cf. Articles 2 and 27 of the ICCPR, and Articles 2 and 7 of the UDHR.
[43] Article 2.2.
[44] Article 4.2.
[45] Article 27, ICCPR; cf. Article 27.1, UDHR.
[46] Article 20.1 of the ICCPR. Cf. Article 7 of the UDHR.
[47] Article 18.4, ICCPR.

The key language of relevance to the idea of public reason, and of central importance in deliberations and controversies over the implementation of the rights of freedom of religion or belief, refers to the "two limbs" of the principal right to freedom of thought, conscience, freedom, or belief. The first limb is contained in ICCPR, Article 18.1, 2, and 4 and ECHR, Article 9.1: It does not allow "any limitations whatsoever"[48] in regard to harboring thoughts of any kind or choosing and holding beliefs, either religious or not, that have the same status that a religious belief has for a believer. This broad understanding may be inferred from the fact that the right to freedom of thought, conscience, and religion "protects theistic, nontheistic and atheistic beliefs," as well as "the right not to profess any religion or belief."[49] The second limb is made up of the so-called limitations clauses in ICCPR, Article 18.3, and the ECHR, Article 9.2, which permit the abridgement of the "manifestation" or overt expression or exercise of such freedom in the name of protecting public safety, order, health, or morals or the fundamental rights and freedoms of others.

As Rawls would propose, the provisions guaranteeing both "absolute" freedom of thought, conscience, religion, or belief, and the right to manifest belief within limits, presuppose a distinctly confined (noncomprehensive) realm of common, secular, sometimes "neutral," interest, called the "public good," that rests on "constitutional essentials" or "basic rights" and prescribes certain general standards of rationality for interpreting and applying the limitations. In addition, it is decidedly legal language, thereby giving priority to judicial and quasi-judicial reasoning as the focus of the exercise of public reason. Overall, such language constitutes the basic terms and patterns of reasoning that all citizens, operating in accord with the system, can reasonably expect others to endorse and employ in conducting public business.

As the result of an admittedly unsystematic review of the evidence, I am ready to conclude that, despite some problems, the general drift of interpretation of the right to freedom of religion or belief by quasi-judicial authorities, such as the Human Rights Committee and the Special Rapporteurs and judicial bodies like the European Commission and Court of Human Rights, as well as by notable legal and other specialists working in the field, is, overall, promising. This conclusion is not consistent with Evans's claim that we are witnessing a "diminution in the importance attached to the achievement of freedom of religion or belief." Growing evidence exists of movement, against some impediments to be sure, toward realignment of the protection of

---

[48] United Nations Human Rights Committee General Comment No. 22 (48) (Art. 18), para. 3: Stahnke and Martin, *Religion and Human Rights Documents*, 92.
[49] Ibid., para. 2.

religion or belief with its founding objective: to inhibit the rise of total domination expressed as the enforcement of a particular comprehensive doctrine. I say, "against some impediments," because much of the jurisprudence developed especially by the European Commission and Court of Human Rights has presented obstacles to progress. Still, those obstacles appear to be in the process of modification, partly, no doubt, in response to compelling expert criticism, as well as to countervailing judgments and opinions on the part of transregional bodies and officials. In short, the ingredients of a heartening revisionist jurisprudence begin to emerge.

REVISIONIST JURISPRUDENCE

In *Freedom of Religion*, Paul Taylor summarizes a dissatisfaction, widely shared until recently, regarding the record of the European Commission and Court in protecting the freedom of religion or belief. Mentioning the tendency to indulge states by granting them an overly wide "margin of appreciation," or excessive discretion, Taylor draws what he believes is "the inescapable conclusion" that "the European Court [has been] more willing to accommodate State interference with religious freedom than affirm and uphold the measures of protection that have been entrusted to it."[50] Moreover, the "European institutions have undoubtedly accommodated clear instances of State intolerance (particularly against minority religions)."[51]

But not all the news is bad. Over against this troubling record at the regional level, the Human Rights Committee and the Office of Special Rapporteur have, according to Taylor, performed much better. The Committee "appears to have been far more consistent than the European institutions" "when applying Article 9 of the European Convention and, in particular, has not shown equivalent respect for State restrictions on religious freedom." It has "made a number of critical advances in standards affecting religious freedom in the face of substantial obstacles posed by the demands of the States," which, for Taylor, can provide constructive guidance.[52] This is also true of the work of the Special Rapporteur whose reports have effectively singled out areas of urgent concern and "could be of invaluable help in enabling the European Court to apprehend more fully the right to [freedom of] religion or belief in the global context and in the light of recurring threats to such practices."[53]

---

[50] Taylor, *Freedom of Religion*, 344.
[51] Ibid., 351.
[52] Ibid., 350–351.
[53] Ibid., 338.

Nor is that all. Taylor, and others such as Carolyn Evans, assemble evidence of changing opinion on the part of the European institutions so that there is now some "room for cautious optimism."[54] Taylor speaks of an "increasingly interventionist trend" in favor of advancing religious pluralism and minority protection and away from a "policy of least intervention and of accommodating State intolerance."[55] Some of the areas where these changes are taking place, possibly in response to initiatives by the international human rights organs and to continuing criticism by specialists, suggest crucial subjects for future investigation. Let us sample three of them.

Forum Internum

This idea, understood as "the internal and private realm of the individual against which no State interference is justified in any circumstances"[56] underlies the first limb of the freedom of religion or belief, namely, freedom of thought, conscience, religion, or belief that is protected against all coercion that would impair one's freedom to have or to adopt a religion or belief of one's choice. The central issue is what constitutes a coercive infringement of the right to harbor and avow a religion or belief.

Traditionally, the European Commission and Court have effectively ignored this issue by construing it as a question of the manifestation of belief under the second limb of the freedom of religion or belief. Three cases illustrate the point: In *V. v. The Netherlands*,[57] the Commission denied the applicant's appeal that he be exempted from participation in a compulsory professional pension scheme on religious grounds because "the refusal to participate in such a pension scheme, although motivated by the applicant's particular belief, cannot ... be considered as an actual expression of belief."[58] The Commission's interpretation of the case as a matter of expression or manifestation of belief seems misplaced. A better interpretation is that the applicant objects because he is being coerced by state authority to violate the basic convictions of his *forum internum*. *Valsamis v. Greece*[59] and *Efstatiou v. Greece*[60] are a second example. In both, the Court rejected applications brought by Jehovah's Witness children who were punished for their refusal, because of

---

[54] Carolyn Evans, *Freedom of Religion under the European Convention*, 207.
[55] Taylor, *Freedom of Religion*, 350–351.
[56] Ibid., 115.
[57] *V. v. Netherlands*, App. No. 10678/83 (1984) 39 D&R 267.
[58] Ibid., 126.
[59] *Valsamis v. Greece* (1997) 24 EHRR 294.
[60] *Efstatiou v. Greece* (1997) 24 EHRR 298.

their religious commitment to pacifism, to participate in a military parade. The Court claimed that the children's right to hold and manifest their beliefs free of coercion was still intact. However, as Carolyn Evans remarks, "To be forced to act in a way that the individual considers a serious violation of his or her religious beliefs is arguably equivalent to being forced to recant a religion or belief. The neat distinction between the internal and external realm is difficult to maintain in such a case."[61]

In 1993 the Human Rights Committee broke things open in regard to reconceiving the legal status of the *forum internum* and complicated "the neat distinction between the internal and external realm" by issuing an official comment on the right of conscientious objection to military service:

> The [ICCPR] does not explicitly refer to a right of conscientious objection, but the Committee believes that *such a right can be derived from article 18*, inasmuch as *the obligation to use lethal force may seriously conflict with the freedom of conscience* and the right to manifest one's religion or belief.[62]

Until this comment, the prevailing assumption was that the *forum internum* is duly protected so long as people are not coerced to recant fundamental beliefs or to express beliefs contrary to their basic convictions. Now, by implying that certain actions, such as being forced to use force, are covered not just by the right to manifest one's religion or belief but may also, in fact, reasonably be construed as a direct violation of "the freedom of conscience" – *the forum internum* – is to open the door to an important new range of protections. According to Taylor, the implication is that "all forms of compulsion to act contrary to one's beliefs *prima facie* raise issues for the *forum internum* where the necessary connection is established between a protected form of belief and compulsion contrary to the belief – a principle which could apply equally to the imposition of tax and social security schemes."[63]

Incidentally, the Committee's Comment helps clarify some conceptual confusion created by careless drafting in regard to Article 18 in the UDHR and ICCPR. There was not much rhyme or reason for the way in which "thought" and "conscience" were combined with "religion" and "belief," and therefore the notions may fairly be read as "supporting each other," "rather than as

---

[61] Carolyn Evans, *Freedom of Religion under the European Convention*, 77.
[62] UN Human Rights Committee General Comment No. 22 (48) (Art. 18) UN Doc. CCPR/C/21/Rev.1. Add. 4 (1993). Stahnke and Martin, *Religion and Human Rights Documents*, 94; emphasis added.
[63] Taylor, *Freedom of Religion*, 153.

separate concepts worthy of independent analysis and development."[64] The main objective was to make sure that atheists and other nonbelievers were included along with religious believers under the protection of Article 18,[65] but this left open, of course, the question of what distinguishes a belief protected under Article 18 from one that was not. The European Court has gone some distance in this respect by ruling that, for purposes of Article 18, belief "denotes views that attain a certain level of cogency, seriousness, cohesion, and importance."[66] It might be pointed out that such a description comes close to the traditional understanding of "conscience" and "conscientiousness," which only serves to underscore further the interdependence of the central concepts mentioned in Article 18. Such an observation also reminds us of the traditional significance of the doctrine of "sovereignty of conscience," entailing as it does the deference of the state to claims of conscience and its concurrent obligation to show cause wherever those claims are restricted or penalized.

There is some evidence that the European institutions are ready, within limits, to think anew about the effects of coercion on the *forum internum*. In *Darby* v. *Sweden*,[67] the Commission found for an applicant, a nonresident who requested an exemption from a church tax to the Lutheran Church with which he was not in agreement. It ruled that the failure to grant an exemption was a clear violation of the applicant's "forum internum rights" under Article 9(1):

> The Commission considers that the applicant's payment of church tax, on the basis of the legal obligation upon him, cannot be characterized as a "manifestation" of his religion. What is at issue here is thus the applicant's general right of religion under the first limb of Article 9, para. 1.[68]

It is true, of course, that the Commission refused to apply the *Darby* rationale to *C.* v. *United Kingdom*,[69] a case in which a committed pacifist refused, on grounds of conscience, to pay that portion of his income tax designated for military purposes unless the government assured him that the money would go for nonmilitary activities. The pacifist's application was denied

---

[64] R. B. Lillich, "Civil Rights," in T. Meron, ed., *Human Rights in International Law: Legal and Policy Issues* (Oxford: Clarendon Press, 1984), 159, fn. 243, cited at Taylor, *Freedom of Religion*, 205–206.

[65] Sydney Liskofsky, "The UN Declaration on the Elimination of Religious Intolerance and Discrimination: Historical and Legal Perspectives," in James E. Wood, Jr., ed., *Religion and the State: Essays in Honor of Leo Pfeffer* (Waco, TX: Baylor University Press, 1985), 456.

[66] *Campbell and Cosans* v. *United Kingdom* (Ser. A) No. 48 (1982) ECtHR para. 36, cited at Taylor, *Freedom of Religion*, 208.

[67] *Darby* v. *Sweden* No. 187 (1990) ECtHR, annex to the decision of the Court, 24.

[68] Ibid., 18–19, paras. 50–51, cited in Taylor, *Freedom of Religion*, 156.

[69] App. No. 10358/83, 37 Eur. Comm. HR Dec. & Rep. 142 (1983).

because, according to the Commission, the "obligation to pay taxes is a *general* one which has no specific conscientious implications in itself. Its *neutrality*... is... illustrated by the fact that no taxpayer can influence or determine the purpose for which... tax contributions are applied."[70] The Commission appeared to hold that, although being required to pay a specific tax to a religious organization that one opposed, as in *Darby*, does constitute a violation of the *forum internum*, there can be no similar exemption from neutral and generally applicable laws in matters of taxation or anything else.

However, the reasoning of the Commission and the Court has not been altogether consistent in this respect,[71] and a more recent decision by the Court may betoken a promising "new approach"[72] or a "marked shift in thinking."[73] In *Thlimmenos v. Greece*,[74] a Jehovah's Witness had been discharged from his job because he was convicted of a felony several years earlier as the result of his conscientious objection to military service. Though the Court did not pass judgment on whether the earlier conviction was a violation of Article 9, it did rule that there were grounds for exempting the applicant from what was clearly a neutral and generally applicable employment law. The Court determined that the conviction in this case was no ordinary conviction, and therefore the applicant was being unfairly treated because of a conviction for a prior act of conscience: "The right not to be discriminated against in the enjoyment of the rights guaranteed under the Convention is also violated when States without an objective and reasonable justification fail to treat persons whose situations are significantly different."[75]

Arcot Krishnaswami had emphasized this point in his definitive study of discrimination in religious rights and practices: "Since each religion or belief makes different demands on its followers, a mechanical application of the principle of equality which does not take into account these various demands will often lead to injustice and in some cases even to discrimination."[76] Commenting on *Thlimmenos*, Carolyn Evans concurs:

> The ruling that a general and neutral law may be discriminatory if it does not allow for exemptions for people on the basis of religion [or belief] is unprecedented in the Article 9 case law.... [I]t could revolutionize the approach

---

[70] C. v. *United Kingdom*, cited at Taylor, *Freedom of Religion*, 154, emphasis added.
[71] Carolyn Evans, *Freedom of Religion under the European Convention*, 184ff.
[72] Taylor, *Freedom of Religion*, 189.
[73] Carolyn Evans, *Freedom of Religion under the European Convention*, 199.
[74] *Thlimmenos v. Greece* (2001) 31 EHRR 411.
[75] Taylor, *Freedom of Religion*, cited at 189–190.
[76] Arcot Krishnaswami, "Study of Discrimination in the Matter of Religious Rights and Practices," in Stahnke and Martin, eds., *Religion and Human Rights: Basic Documents*, 14.

of the Court to general and neutral laws.... If the discrimination principle becomes used as a matter of routine in Article 9 cases it is possible that many types of claims that have been rejected routinely by the Court or Commission in the past will now be far more likely to succeed.[77]

The key implication is that this line of reasoning, if pursued and developed in regard to safeguarding the *forum internum*, represents new hope for minorities. It is they of course who are the chief victims of the familiar alliance between religious majorities and the state. The argument that the best hope of minorities is the legislative process by which to change objectionable laws is too often a counsel of despair – they are, after all, minorities! That argument also exhibits a failure to comprehend the critical role of public reason, which is the implicit obligation of judicial authorities to protect the rights of the *forum internum* as a guarantee against the encroachments of domineering comprehensive doctrines.

There are, of course, good reasons for setting high standards for conscientious exemptions from general and neutral laws. The consequences for pubic order of extreme permissiveness are not hard to imagine. Still, up until recently, particularly in the European system, it is not the minorities and their conscientious claims that have been indulged. Rather it is the majorities and their state sponsors who have had the upper hand. The latest trends, although hopeful, have a considerable distance to go to improve the balance. However difficult it may be for judges to be assured that conscientious claims reach an acceptable "level of cogency, seriousness, cohesion, and importance,"[78] there seems no alternative but to continue to try. Otherwise, we surrender the fundamental assumptions of the entire human rights system.

Manifestation of Religion or Belief

If the "first limb" of the protection of religion or belief concerns safeguarding the *internal forum* against coerced submission to what are regarded as objectionable beliefs and practices, the "second limb," regarding the "manifestation" of a religion or belief, concerns what might broadly be called a provisional right of free exercise. That is the right overtly to express or act on a religion or belief "in worship, teaching, practice or observance," "subject only to such limitations as are prescribed by law and are necessary to protect public safety, order, health, or morals or the fundamental rights and freedoms of others" (Art. 18.1 and 3 of the ICCPR; Art. 9.2 of the ECHR adds,

---

[77] Carolyn Evans, *Freedom of Religion under the European Convention*, 199.
[78] A reference to the defining characteristics of religious and nonreligious fundamental conviction in *Campbell and Casans v. UK*, cited in Taylor, *Freedom of Religion*, 208.

as we know, "necessary in a democratic society," words similar to those in Art. 29.2 of the UDHR).

On paper, the burden of proof clearly rests with the government in regard to applying these provisions. It must show that any limitation on the manifestation of religion or belief is both "necessary" and "proportionate"; that is, the limitation must be designed and administered so as to impose the least restrictive burden consistent with addressing a compelling state interest or "pressing social need."[79] However, as with the protection of the *forum internum*, the European Commission and Court have until recently tended rather consistently to favor state interests over the free exercise of religion or belief by individuals or groups.

> While the Commission and Court are prepared to scrutinize State action with some care in cases where there has been overt and intentional discrimination against members of a religious group, they have generally given States a wide margin of appreciation in determining whether or not a restriction on the manifestation of religion or belief is necessary. In most cases it seems to be sufficient in practice for the State to show that it has acted in good faith in order for it to be able to justify limitations on religion or belief under Article 9 (2).[80]

Several cases dealing with the sensitive subject of religious apparel illustrate the point. In *Karaduman v. Turkey*,[81] the Commission upheld a state law requiring that a photograph attached to a degree certificate depict the candidate as bareheaded instead of wearing a Muslim headscarf, as the applicant had done. The Commission placed considerable weight on Turkey's national commitment to the principle of secularity and the resulting need, as it saw it, to limit religious manifestations that "may constitute pressure on students who do not practice that religion or those who adhere to another religion," as well as represent a threat to public order from "fundamentalist religious movements."[82]

Similarly, the Court decided in favor of the state in *Dahlab v. Switzerland*,[83] where, according to the Swiss law supporting religious neutrality, the applicant, a Muslim, could not wear an Islamic headscarf in the state school where she taught. While acknowledging her skill as a teacher and the absence of any disturbance, the Commission nevertheless worried about the possible

---

[79] UNHRC General Comment No. 22, Stahnke and Martin, *Religion and Human Rights: Basic Documents*, para. 8, p. 93.
[80] Carolyn Evans, *Freedom of Religion under the European Convention*, 134.
[81] *Karaduman v. Turkey* App. No. 16278/90 (1993) 74 D & R 93.
[82] Cited by Taylor, *Freedom of Religion*, 254.
[83] *Dahlab v. Switzerland* (App. No. 42393/98), Judgment of Feb. 15, 2001.

"proselytizing effect" of such an exhibition and the message of intolerance and gender inequality represented by the headscarf.

The Court ruled in the same way in *Sahin v. Turkey*.[84] The case concerned a young Muslim female medical student at the University of Istanbul who, as the result of wearing her headscarf in violation of a 1998 law, was refused access to classes and examinations at the university. The Court ruled in favor of the government of Turkey, determining that the law against headscarves was necessary and proportionate in a democratic society and that in such sensitive matters the state should be given a wide margin of appreciation. Particularly when it comes to regulating religious symbols in educational institutions, said the Court, "the role of the national decision-making body must be given special importance."[85] Consequently, there had been no violation of Art. 9 of the ECHR.

Decisions such as *Sahin v. Turkey*, granting states a wide margin of appreciation in limiting manifestations of religion or belief, have been subjected to extensive criticism by specialists.[86] But beyond that, there are a few hopeful signs of more scrupulous concern for protecting free exercise on the part of the European Court and some very promising developments in that regard at the international level.

The Court's recent ruling in *Metropolitan Church of Bessarabia and others v. Moldova*[87] is especially encouraging. The case addressed the highly sensitive problem of the legal registration of religious organizations. The applicants consisted of the Metropolitan Church of Bessarabia and several Moldovan members of the church council who claimed that Moldovan state authorities violated Article 9 by denying official recognition to the church, thereby preventing the practice of their religion. Not only were they prohibited from gathering for religious purposes but there was also no legal protection of the church's physical assets. The Court held that "the refusal by the Moldovan Government to recognize the applicant Church, ... is an interference in the right of that church and of the other applicants to freedom of religion, as safeguarded by Article 9 of the Convention." Of great consequence, the Court decided "that it was not for the State to determine [as it had claimed it had the

---

[84] *Leyla Sahin v. Turkey*. ECHR Grand Chamber, Application No. 44774/98. Nov. 10, 2005). I am grateful for the analysis of this case contained in Melanie Adrian, *Restricting the Republic: France, the Veil, and Religious Freedom*, Ph.D. Dissertation (Harvard University, 2007), 235ff.
[85] Cited in ibid., 236–237.
[86] E.g., ibid., Kevin Boyle, "Human Rights, Religion and Democracy: The Refah Party, projects.essex.ac.uk/her/V1N1/Boyle, pdf.; W. Cole Durham, Jr., "Facilitating Religion or Belief through Religious Association Laws," in Lindholm, Durham, and Tahzib-Lie, *Facilitating Religion or Belief: A Deskbook*, 375–376.
[87] *Metropolitan Church of Bessarabia and others v. Moldova* (2002) 35 EHRR 306.

right to do] whether or not there was a real distinction between these different groups or what beliefs should be considered distinct from others."[88]

Moreover, in *Metropolitan Church*, the Court interpreted in a very significant way the meaning of the words, "necessary in a democratic society," which constitutes one of the general requirements concerning the limitation of free exercise mentioned in Article 9 of the ECHR.

> In order to determine the breadth of the margin of appreciation in this case the Court must take into account what is at stake, namely *the need to maintain true religious pluralism, which is inherent in the notion of a democratic society*. Similarly, great weight should be given to this need where it must be decided, as required by Article 9 (2), whether the interference meets a "pressing social need" and is "proportionate" to the legitimate aim pursued.[89]

In two other recent decisions, *Hasan and Chaush* v. *Bulgaria*[90] and *Serif* v. *Greece*,[91] cases in which the state also interfered in internal differences within a religious community, the Court similarly ruled against the state on the grounds of its commitment to the principle that "the autonomous existence of religious communities is indispensable for pluralism in a democratic society and is thus at the very heart of the protection which Article 9 affords."[92]

Over and above these encouraging trends on the part of the European Court, the work of the Human Rights Committee and the Special Rapporteur is, in general, even more promising. In its General Comments on Article 18 of the ICCPR, the Committee has greatly strengthened the principles of religious pluralism and free exercise, comparable to the expanded protection it provided the *forum internum* by anchoring the right to conscientious objection to military service in the freedom of conscience, as I noted earlier.

Along with affirming the inclusion of nonreligious belief under the protection of Article 18, the Committee asserted that

> Article 18 is not limited in its application to traditional religions or to religions and beliefs with institutional characteristics or practices analogous to those of traditional religions. The Committee therefore views with concern any tendency to discriminate against any religion or belief for any reasons, including the fact that they are newly established, or represent religious minorities that may be the subject of hostility by a predominant religious community.[93]

---

[88] Cited at Taylor, *Freedom of Religion*, 223–224.
[89] Cited at ibid., 308; emphasis added.
[90] *Hasan and Chaush* v. *Bulgaria* (2002) 34 (6) EHRR 1339.
[91] *Serif* v. *Greece* (1999) 31 EHRR 633.
[92] *Hasan and Chaush* v. *Bulgaria* at para. 62, cited at ibid., 310.
[93] Stahnke and Martin, *Religion and Human Rights: Basic Documents*, para. 2, 92.

Moreover, the Committee helpfully clarified the meaning of "the freedom to manifest religion or belief" in the following way:

> The observance and practice of religion or belief may include not only ceremonial acts but also such customs as the observance of dietary regulations, the wearing of distinctive clothing or headcoverings, participation in rituals associated with certain stages of life, and the use of a particular language customarily spoken by a group. In addition, the practice and teaching of religion or belief includes acts integral to the conduct by religious groups of their basic affairs, such as, inter alia the freedom to choose their leaders, priests and teachers, the freedom to establish seminaries or religious schools and the freedom to prepare and distribute religious texts or publications.[94]

And although the Committee admits the permissibility of a "state religion" or a religion "established as official or traditional" or one including "the majority of the population," these conditions

> shall not result in any impairment of the enjoyment of any of the rights under the Covenant... nor in any discrimination against adherents of other religions or non-believers. In particular, certain measure discriminating against the latter, such as measures restricting eligibility for government service to members of the predominant religion or giving economic privileges to them or imposing special restrictions on the practice of other faiths, are not in accordance with the prohibition of discrimination based on religion or belief and the guarantee of equal protection.[95]

These sentiments are all in the direction of implementing the robust protection of the right to manifest religion or belief. According to Taylor, the Human Rights Committee, in carrying out its duties, "appears to have been far more consistent than the European institutions have been when applying Article 9 of the European Convention and, in particular, has not shown equivalent respect for State restrictions on religious freedom."[96]

He also gives high marks to the contribution of the Special Rapporteur "in underscoring the significance of all forms of the manifestation of religion."[97] The attention given to the dangers of discrimination and the mistreatment of minorities and "sects" has been of particular importance in strengthening commitments to the international protection of religion or belief.[98]

---

[94] Ibid., 92–93.
[95] Ibid., 94.
[96] Taylor, *Freedom of Religion*, 350.
[97] Ibid., 338.
[98] Ibid., 319, 336.

Additionally, the Special Rapporteur has thoughtfully suggested that what constitutes a "manifestation" of religion or belief should be left primarily to believers, and not to the state.[99] This is important because it would mean that the state and the human rights bodies would no longer be allowed to make judgments in matters where they have no competence, namely in regard to whether specific actions are compellingly related to a religion or belief and therefore ought to be protected under the right to free exercise.

The Special Rapporteur has also moved creatively in regard to modifying laws in countries such as France that forbid the wearing of Muslim headscarves in school. A recent report cites with approval concerns that laws banning the wearing of religious symbols in public schools "may neglect the principle of the best interests of the child and the right of the child to access to education." It also supports a proposal that states where such prohibitions exist consider "alternative means" to law, such as mediation and student participation in policy making, as a way of balancing state interests with the rights of children to religious liberty.[100]

Tolerance

In his remarks quoted at the beginning of this chapter, Malcolm Evans is particularly troubled by comments of the UN Special Rapporteur for Freedom of Religion or Belief made in the 1990s concerning the subject of religious tolerance. Evans interprets recommendations of the Special Rapporteur, regarding the need to avoid adopting attitudes toward members of other faiths that are "inflexible" or "obstinate" and making charges that are "gratuitous" or "impulsive," as an indication that freedom of religion does not include, as Evans says, the right "to adhere to a religion which is intolerant of the beliefs of others." Evans raises an important question: When human rights officials tell religious believers what attitudes and opinions to have, and how to express them, are they not guilty of the very intolerance they accuse others of having? Evans's worry is that the human rights system is itself taking on the form of a new orthodoxy – a new domineering comprehensive doctrine. It readmits through the back door what it is supposed to bar at the front.

The meaning of tolerance and intolerance in the human rights documents *is* problematic. In one place in the DEID, intolerance appears to mean the same as discrimination.[101] Elsewhere, however, a distinction between tolerance and

---

[99] Report of the Special Rappoteur on Freedom of Religion or Belief, Asma Jahangir, E/CN.4/2006/5 9 January 2006, para. 41, 13.
[100] Report of the Special Rapporteur on Freedom of Religion or Belief, January 2006, para. 46, 14.
[101] Article 2(2) of DEID. Cf. Articles 2 and 27 of the ICCPR, and Articles 2 and 7 of the UDHR.

discrimination is implied. States are instructed to "prohibit" discrimination by means of legislation, whereas they are supposed to "combat" intolerance by taking "all appropriate measures."[102] Nor is intolerance, unlike discrimination, defined anywhere in the documents, leaving the concept open to interpretation.[103]

Nevertheless, Asma Jahangir, the former Special Rapporteur on Freedom of Religion or Belief, has provided some thoughtful guidelines for thinking about this problem in a recent report, "Incitement to Racial and Religious Hatred and the Promotion of Tolerance,"[104] written with Doudou Diene, the Special Rapporteur on Contemporary Forms of Racism, Racial Discrimination, Xenophobia and Related Intolerance. By working out the implications of these guidelines, it is possible to eliminate some of the lack of clarity that are attached to the ideas of tolerance and intolerance, and thereby to reduce Evans's worries about human rights as representing a new intolerant comprehensive doctrine.

Jahangir provides fresh clarity to the ideas of tolerance and intolerance. On her account, to be intolerant in a legally liable sense is to express views or to behave in ways that "constitute incitement to acts of violence or discrimination against individuals on the basis of their religion [or belief]."[105] This is Jahangir's interpretation of Article 20.2 of the ICCPR, which prohibits by law any advocacy of national, racial, or religious hatred that incites to discrimination, violence, or hostility.[106] She clarifies her view with this important comment:

> The Special Rapporteur notes that article 20 of the Covenant was drafted against the background of the horrors committed by the Nazi regime during the Second World War. The threshold of the acts that are referred to in article 20 is *relatively high* because they have to constitute advocacy of national, racial or religious hatred [of the sort exemplified by the Nazis].[107]

She elaborates as follows:

> The right to freedom of religion or belief, as enshrined in the relevant international legal standards, does not include the right to have a religion or belief

---

[102] Ibid., Article 4.2.
[103] See Chapter 5, 145–147.
[104] A/HRC/2/3, 20 September 2006.
[105] Ibid., para. 47, p. 11; cf. para. 37, 10.
[106] See 63 and fn. 57. It is noteworthy that Jahangir narrows the punishable acts to violence and discrimination and leaves out the reference to "hostility" that is included in Article 20.2. Unlike violence and discrimination, hostility, as an attitude or emotion, is notoriously hard to police.
[107] Ibid., para. 47, 11; emphasis added.

that is free from criticism or ridicule.... *Defamation of religions may offend people and hurt their feelings but it does not necessarily or at least directly result in a violation of their rights, including the right to freedom of religion.* Freedom of religion primarily confers a right to act in accordance with one's religion but does not bestow a right for believers to have their religion itself protected from all adverse comment.[108]

In short, outside a narrow range of behavior, namely direct incitement to acts of violence or discrimination, the expression of attitudes and opinions inspired by a religion or belief is not, on a proper human rights understanding, punishable by law.[109] From a legal point of view, people have a wide margin of leniency to criticize the beliefs and practices of others, even including the "defamation of religions." Accordingly, tolerance implies a disposition to "suffer" or bear with beliefs and practices regarded as deviant or objectionable without inciting to violence or discrimination.[110] To violate the stipulation against incitement is to be intolerant in a legally liable way.

Jahangir goes so far as to rule out applying Article 4(a) of the Covenant of the Elimination of All Forms of Discrimination (CERD) to religion or belief. That article makes punishable by law "all dissemination of ideas based on racial superiority or hatred." There is, she says, good reason why there is no such provision regarding religion or belief in any of the human rights documents. "The elements that constitute a racist statement are not the same as those that constitute a statement defaming a religion. To this extent, the legal measures, and in particular criminal measures, adopted by national legal systems to fight racism may not necessarily be applicable to defamation of religion."[111]

---

[108] Ibid., paras. 36 and 37, 10; emphasis added.
[109] Considering all of the relevant portions of the international instruments, we might criticize Ms. Jahangir for narrowing too much the range of legally liable behavior. Article 29 of the UDHR, Article 18.3 of the ICCPR, and Article 9.2 of the ECHR, which provide for limitations of the manifestation of religion or belief on the basis of public order, health, safety, morals or the rights and freedoms of others, are undoubtedly also relevant to the determination of legally liable behavior. Nevertheless, even taking those additional limitations into account, Ms. Jahangir's emphasis on a very high threshold for restricting religious or other fundamental beliefs or practices is welcome as a way of protecting freedom of religion or belief and is distinctly pertinent to the interpretation and application of the limitations provisions.
[110] See Chapter 5, 150–155.
[111] There is warrant for concern about the article even as regards racist ideas; see Karl Josef Partsch, "Racial Speech and Human Rights: Article 4 of the Convention on the Elimination of All Forms of Racial Discrimination," in Sandra Coliver (ed.), *Striking a Balance: Hate Speech, Freedom of Expression and Non-discrimination* (Article 19, International Centre against Censorship, Human Rights Centre, University of Essex, 1992): "When article 4 was adopted, the clause concerning the prohibition of ideas based on racial superiority met with the strongest opposition. *It is indeed hardly possible to define or even imagine the direct effect which the mere*

Whatever the intention of earlier statements on religious tolerance by Special Rapporteurs, it should be clear that the current Special Rapporteur in no way interprets human rights law as imposing a new comprehensive doctrine. She is far from suggesting that human rights officials go around proposing laws that tell religious believers what attitudes and opinions to have and how to express them. She even states explicitly that however the matter is in regard to racist ideas, the mere dissemination of ideas of religious superiority, a practice very hard to disconnect from fervent belief, is *not* punishable by law.

Let me emphasize that this interpretation connects in an important way to my broader argument concerning the grounds of the human rights system. Jahangir's explicit reference to the Nazi background of Article 20 of the ICCPR, and to what counts as legally proscribed behavior, underscores my point that the human rights approach in general and the protection of religion or belief in particular aim at inhibiting all forms of comprehensive doctrine in keeping with a set of minimum, common protections contained in the idea of public reason. So long as the minimum, common protections – the constitutional essentials (basic rights, etc.) – undergirding the idea of public reason are observed, the system itself is expressly *not* comprehensive because it welcomes and allows for a diversity of comprehensive doctrines. In fact, it legally guarantees a wide range for competition among them, even including the expression of strong forms of disapproval and disdain.

There is, it is true, another more expansive and exalted idea of tolerance contained in the human rights documents and alluded to in the report by the two Special Rapporteurs. It is well expressed in Article 26.2 of the UDHR, describing a central purpose of education as the promotion of "understanding, tolerance, and friendship among all nations, racial or religious groups." In the report, the "promotion of tolerance" is articulated as a disposition to support "policies and programmes in the fields of education, social, economic and cultural life, favouring the interactions between communities," as well as "the value of cultural and religious diversity associated with the promotion of unity within society" and "the creation of conditions facilitating encounter, dialogue and joint action for harmony, peace, human rights, development and combat against all forms of racism, discrimination, and xenophobia."[112] On this understanding, intolerance, presumably, would mean opposing these objectives.

There is much more to be said on the relation of the two types of tolerance adduced here than I have space for, the one a disposition to bear with beliefs

---

dissemination of ideas may have on the enjoyment of human rights or freedoms" (26; emphasis added).
[112] A/HRC/2/3, 20 September 2006, para. 63, 15.

and practices regarded as deviant or objectionable without inciting to violence or discrimination; the other a more affirmative attitude that welcomes diversity of belief and practice and encourages encounter and dialogue. The most important point for my purposes is that the two types should always be considered together. The ideals of encouraging "interactions between the communities," of valuing "cultural and religious diversity," and of "facilitating... encounter, dialogue and joint action" ought never be advocated without conscientiously guaranteeing the first type of tolerance, and for protecting expressions of strong disagreement and disapproval, short, of course, of incitement to violence or discrimination.[113] Although Jahangir urges Member States to "avoid stubbornly clinging to free speech in defiance of the sensitivities existing in society with absolute disregard of religious feelings," they should also avoid, she says, "suffocating criticism of a religion by making it punishable by law."[114] It is only by guarding against the preferential treatment of one religion or belief over others that the ideals of diversity and of an equal right to interaction and encounter can be achieved.

CONCLUSION

The future of the international protection of religion or belief depends, I have argued, on two conditions. First, it means embracing and reaffirming the revised notion of public reason rooted in the human rights system as worked out after World War II. That notion presupposes certain "constitutional essentials" – certain basic rights and freedoms – that were formulated in reaction to unmistakable crimes resulting from the coercive imposition of a particular comprehensive doctrine and that were designed to impede or prevent the recurrence of anything like it ever after. Moreover, the recommended notion of public reason is of special pertinence to the protection of religion or belief, because it was these protections that were so systematically and extensively subverted.

It should be emphasized that far from abolishing religious or other fundamental forms of expression from the "public square," as the usual complaint against the idea of public reason goes, sustained and expansive public consideration of such forms of expression is in fact inescapable. Without it, it would be impossible to decide exactly what the limits of public reason are in given circumstances, as the current jurisprudence concerning the meaning of *forum internum*, "manifestation of religion or belief," or "tolerance" indicates.

---

[113] Or the violation of the other limitations stipulated in the instruments, see Chapter 1, fn. 55.
[114] Ibid., para. 66, 15.

Second, it means applying in practice the constitutional essentials so as to thwart any particular comprehensive doctrine from asserting control over a society. Reviewing the performance of the European and international human rights institutions, I have concluded that there is room for both concern and hope. The recently reconstituted European Court of Human Rights shows signs of making some progress in this regard, and the Human Rights Committee and the former UN Special Rapporteur, Asma Jahangir, have been particularly creative in setting and interpreting the constitutional essentials as they apply to freedom of religion or belief. The way forward, I suggest, is to acknowledge these promising developments and to encourage more aggressively their further advancement.

5

Rethinking Religious Tolerance

A Human Rights Approach

The idea of "tolerance," especially as applied to religious and other fundamental beliefs, occupies a prominent place in international human rights documents, as well as in current discussions of those documents and their application around the world. At the same time, the term is neither clearly defined in the documents, nor is it used with much consistency or clarity in recurring efforts at interpretation. Moreover, the concept is frequently disparaged as inadequate, misleading, and needing to be replaced.

The time is therefore ripe to review and reconsider the idea of tolerance in the context of human rights usage so as to determine whether the word has any useful meaning. An additional reason for reexamining the idea of tolerance in relation to human rights is that the language of human rights is by now well established internationally. More than any other idiom, it provides both common norms regarding proper human treatment within and among nations and a basis for at least partial enforcement of those norms. Thus, the potential payoff of refining terminology here is somewhat greater than in normal academic discussions.

BACKGROUND ASSUMPTIONS

All countries that are party to human rights instruments, such as the International Covenant on Civil and Political Rights (ICCPR), and that are therefore bound to promote human rights around the world, have cause to be urgently concerned about violations of what we may call "belief rights."[1]

---

[1] The term "belief rights" is preferable because it is a more inclusive term than "religious rights," which is often used. The legislative history behind the use of "belief" in the documents makes clear that nontheistic and atheistic fundamental beliefs are to be assured equal protection alongside religious beliefs. See Natan Lerner, *Religion, Beliefs, and International Human Rights* (Maryknoll, NY: Orbis Books, 2000), 5.

There are two reasons for this concern. One is that the whole edifice of existing human rights standards is premised on the need to protect individuals against collective domination and the unlimited opportunity for arbitrary abuse that follows from it. Worldwide recognition of that fact constituted a fundamental lesson of fascism in both its German and Japanese versions. That lesson, in turn, gave rise after World War II to the "human rights revolution," which in several important respects did indeed represent "a world made new."[2]

One prominent feature of such domination is abrogating the right to dissent in matters of "conscience, religion or belief," as the international human rights documents put it. In particular, fascism comprised a direct, comprehensive, and systematic assault on the five categories of belief rights that are guaranteed in the human rights documents: tolerance,[3] nondiscrimination,[4] protection of minorities,[5] protection against "religious or racial hatred that incites to discrimination, violence or hostility,"[6] and "respect for the liberty of parents and, when applicable, legal guardians to ensure the religious and moral education of their children in conformity with their own convictions."[7] Awareness of the effects of the kind of wholesale and unrelenting violation of these norms that occurred at the hands of the fascists explains both why protection against such violation is so liberally provided for in the documents and why human rights proponents must be hypervigilant in making sure similar violations do not recur.

A second reason for urgent concern is that all five categories of belief rights are in one way or another threatened by contemporary developments, especially by the intensification in the post–World War II period of what can be called "ethnoreligious nationalism." The term describes a state of affairs in which one ethnoreligious group gains or tries to gain politicolegal control of the inhabitants of a given territory, typically undertaking to assert and preserve its collective identity at the expense of minorities. As recent experience in Bosnia, Kosovo, the Sudan, Sri Lanka,[8] India, Burma, Tibet,[9] Northern Ireland,

---

[2] Mary Ann Glendon, *A World Made New: Eleanor Roosevelt and the Universal Declaration of Human Rights* (New York: Random House, 2001).
[3] Universal Declaration of Human Rights (UDHR), Article 18; International Covenant on Civil and Political Rights (ICCPR), Article 18; and UN Declaration on the Elimination of All Forms of Intolerance and Discrimination. Based on Religion or Belief (DEID), Articles 1, 2.2, 4.2.
[4] UDHR, Articles 2, 7; ICCPR, Articles 2, 26, and DEID, Articles 2, 4.
[5] ICCPR, Article 27.
[6] UDHR, Article 7, ICCPR, Article 20. 2.
[7] ICCPR, Article 18.4.
[8] See David Little, *Sri Lanka: The Invention of Enmity* (Washington, DC: United States Institute of Peace Press, 1994).
[9] Tibet might appear to represent a variation from the general description of ethnoreligious nationalism provided here, in that the nationalist campaign of the majority – the Han Chinese – against the Tibetans, although strongly ethnic in character, has historically had a nonreligious

Iran, and Israel, illustrates, such efforts variously involve intolerance, discrimination, unfair disadvantage, persecution, repression, expulsion, and even liquidation.

Actually, all modern nations are to a greater or lesser extent caught up in struggles between majorities and minorities over ethnic, cultural, and religious identity; at any given time, some expressions of that struggle simply take more destructive and violent forms. It is because ethnoreligious tension is a universal condition that belief rights are universally pertinent. Along with other human rights, they provide a fundamental guarantee against the ill effects of collective domination.

Incidentally, there is some encouraging evidence in a new book by Ted Robert Gurr, *Peoples vs. States: Ethnopolitical Conflict in the New Century*,[10] showing that the spread and influence of belief rights – especially tolerance and nondiscrimination toward minorities – form one important reason for what Gurr describes as a precipitous worldwide decline, since 1995, of ethnonational conflict.

Uncertain Status of the Idea of Tolerance in the Human Rights Documents

Though the concepts of tolerance and its antonym, intolerance, occupy a significant place in the language of human rights, neither term is anywhere defined. It is different with the companion terms, discrimination and nondiscrimination.[11] In the Declaration on the Elimination of All Forms of Intolerance and Discrimination based on Religion or Belief (DEID),

---

or even antireligious Maoist cast to it. For one thing, however, the Tibetan response does exhibit an intensely ethnoreligious element, and, for another, the character of Han nationalist activity is still accurately covered by the phrase, "religion or belief," thus activating the relevance of belief rights in an important way. See David Little and Scott W. Hibbard, *Sino-Tibetan Coexistence: Creating Space for Tibetan Self-Direction*, a Conference Report (Washington, DC: United States Institute of Peace Press, 1994).

[10] (Washington, DC: United States Institute of Peace Press, 2000). Though the book features the importance of tolerance and nondiscrimination in regard to minority cultures, it is not particularly enlightening in regard to the specific place of religion (see David Little, "State Structure and Conflict in Multiethnic Societies: Reflections on Recent Data" (unpublished paper)). Incidentally, this book should be contrasted with a much less optimistic account – *Minorities at Risk*, published by Gurr and associates with the same press in 1993. The 1993 book makes much of the point that ethnopolitical conflict, which was reported to be on the increase at the time, is the result of various kinds of minority discrimination: economic, political, and cultural (including religion).

[11] Lerner, in *Religion, Beliefs and International Human Rights*, says, "*Discrimination*, the term used in all the anti-discrimination treaties and declarations, has a clear legal meaning. This is not the case with *intolerance* which is vague and lacks clear legal meaning. *Intolerance* has been used to describe emotional, psychological, philosophical, and religious attitudes that may

discrimination presumably refers to *overt behavior* that creates "any distinction, exclusion, or preference based on religion or belief, and having as its purpose or as its effect nullification or impairment of the recognition, enjoyment, or exercise of human rights and fundamental freedoms on an equal basis."[12]

Not only is there no definition of tolerance and intolerance but also the relationship between the notions of tolerance and nondiscrimination, or intolerance and discrimination, terms that are frequently paired together, is ambiguous, if not confusing. The article I just cited defining discrimination says, "the expression 'intolerance and discrimination based on religion or belief' means...," and then it goes on to give the definition of discrimination just quoted. This suggests that intolerance and discrimination mean the same thing.

However, in Article 4.2, the language proceeds apparently to *distinguish* between intolerance and discrimination: "All States shall make all efforts to enact or rescind legislation where *necessary to prohibit any such discrimination*, and to take all appropriate measures *to combat intolerance* on the grounds of religion or other beliefs in this matter" [emphasis added]. Countering discrimination is specifically a legislative matter. Intolerance, in contrast, seems to mean something else, because it is to be dealt with in a different way, namely to be "combated." The trouble is that what is meant by the phrase "to combat intolerance" remains vague in part because we are not told in the first place what intolerance is.

One other reference – Article 13 concerning the right to education, in the International Covenant on Economic, Social and Cultural Rights – is no more helpful: It says that "education" shall enable all persons to participate effectively in a free society, to promote understanding, *tolerance*, and friendship among all nations, and all racial, ethnic or *religious* groups" (emphasis added). Again, it is hard to know what it would mean "to promote tolerance" in regard to religious or other groups, without knowing what tolerance is.

There is an additional problem in regard to the specific idea of religious tolerance and intolerance. Article 20.2 of the ICCPR states, "Any advocacy of national, racial, or *religious* hatred that constitutes incitement to discrimination, *hostility* or violence shall be prohibited by law" (emphasis added). Although the phrase is not altogether free of uncertainty and ambiguity, interpreting "incitement to discrimination or violence" is something the law,

---

prompt acts of discrimination or other violations of religious freedoms, as well as manifestations of hate and persecutions of persons of different religion or belief" (22).

[12] DEID, Article 2.2.

including international law, has considerable experience with, partly because standard examples or explicit definitions (as in the case of discrimination) act as determinate points of reference. But although discrimination and violence typically refer to overt behavior, "incitement to hostility" and the "religious hatred" that might lead to it are more "inward," involving matters of feeling, attitude, and belief, which are not as easily identified and regulated by law.

Moreover, the language of Article 4 (a) of the Convention on the Elimination of All Forms of Racial Discrimination (CERD) poses a certain perplexity in regard to the meaning of religious tolerance. It states that "all dissemination of ideas based on racial superiority or hatred," as well as incitement to acts of discrimination or violence toward any race or ethnic group, and "also the provision of any assistance to racist activities, including the financing thereof," shall be "punishable by law." Currently, the relevant documents (UDHR, ICCPR, DEID) do not contain a similar provision in relation to religion or belief. Still, language of that kind might, by extension, be seen to apply to "religious ideas," because it is not unusual for religious groups to claim superiority over others.[13] What is more, one frequently hears that claims of superiority are "intolerant" and ought to be discouraged in a world of many faiths. Should, then, claims to religious superiority be liable to legal punishment in the same way that racial claims are? Does "religious tolerance" entail enforcing the belief that no religion is better than any other? Such a suggestion, were it adopted, would of course have radical and disruptive implications in regard to what is considered permissible religious belief and expression.

There is one final problem concerning the meaning of tolerance in the documents that must be mentioned. Article 18.3 of the ICCPR says, "[F]reedom to manifest one's religion or belief may be subject only to such limitations as are prescribed by law, and are necessary to protect public safety, order, health, or morals or the fundamental rights and freedoms of others." Accordingly, states may coercively restrict or punish "manifestations" of religious belief (understood mainly as actions or practices) in regard to certain "compelling state interests" of the sort enumerated in the article. In other words, states are not required to "tolerate" religious actions or practices that conflict with those interests.

Although these provisions give a state some leverage in controlling the possible excesses of religious action, the provisions are also, as is obvious, elastic and open-ended. They permit considerable discretion on the part of the state that,

---

[13] In *Religion, Beliefs and International Human Rights*, 61, Natan Lerner calls Article 4 of CERD "an ambitious article" "that is applicable to similar texts dealing with religion."

absent clear and commonly understood guidelines, may, and frequently does, lead to serious abuse. Consequently, if a state were to employ the limitations clause as a pretext for mistreating an otherwise harmless religious group, as states have been known to do, such a state would itself be contributing to the very kind of intolerance that the documents prohibit.

It is interesting that the Human Rights Committee, which is responsible for implementing and interpreting the ICCPR, has begun to impose guidelines for applying the limitations clause. For example, in regard to limiting religious activity on the basis of "public morals," it has declared that states must base their judgments "on principles not deriving from a single tradition," because, as it says, "the concept of morals derives from many social, philosophical and religious traditions."[14] In other words, warrants for limiting religious behavior in respect to public morals must be pluralistic in character and represent a consensus of different perspectives, rather than an exclusive commitment to any one religious or philosophical position. It seems obvious that a certain understanding of "tolerance" having an important bearing on religion is implied here, though it is, as usual, nowhere explicated as such.

It should be added that a "state religion" or one "established as official or traditional" is not as such ruled out by the Human Rights Committee in its commentary on Article 18 of the ICCPR. Nevertheless, the ICCPR makes very clear that that kind of arrangement "shall not result in any impairment of... any of the rights under the Covenant, ... or any discrimination against adherents of other religions or non-believers."[15]

UNCERTAIN STATUS OF THE IDEA OF TOLERANCE IN ORDINARY USAGE

Because the human rights documents offer so little guidance in determining a clear and consistent meaning of tolerance (and intolerance), it is reasonable to seek help by consulting commentaries on ordinary usage. The problem is that much of the existing literature yields very little guidance. Among other things, the term is often disparaged and trivialized, deemed inappropriate as a term of political evaluation, enshrouded in mystery, or discussed inconsistently.

Here are some examples:

- In *The Culture of Disbelief*, Stephen Carter asserts that tolerance is an objectionable term because it implies a condescending and patronizing

[14] United Nations Human Rights Committee General Comment No. 22 (48) (Art. 18) in Tad Stankhe and J. Paul Martin, eds., *Religion and Human Rights: Basic Documents* (Center for the Study of Human Rights, Columbia University, 1998), 94.
[15] Ibid., 94.

attitude toward beliefs not shared. The word should be discarded for not conveying the kind of equal respect that ought to be cultivated among people with divergent religious and other fundamental beliefs.[16]
- Stanley Fish mischievously offers what he calls "Fish's first law of tolerance-dynamics" in *There's No Such Thing as Free Speech and It's a Good Thing, Too*. Because, as he claims, tolerance "is exercised in inverse proportion to there being anything at stake," it is merely a synonym for indifference and may accordingly be written off as a trivial notion.[17]
- Richard Rorty defines religious tolerance, in particular, as "the willingness of a religious group to take part in discussion without dragging religion into it."[18] On Rorty's account, religion and tolerance are mutually exclusive, and therefore the very notion of "religious tolerance" is self-contradictory. Rorty's idea is related to Fish's: Tolerance entails religious indifference in the sense of implying a readiness, in the interest of tolerance, to set religion aside altogether.
- Avishai Margalit in part supports Rorty's idea that religion and tolerance do not go together. He defends the fashionable view that monotheistic religions, in particular, are in their nature incapable of embracing tolerance. That is because monotheism rests on an idea of indisputable revelation, which makes it impossible to "live with" those thought to be "in error." The phrase associated with pre–Vatican II Roman Catholicism – "error has no rights" – is supposed to illustrate that claim.[19]
- The book in which Margalit's essay appears is titled *Toleration: An Elusive Virtue*.[20] Few of the essays in the book, some of which are written by distinguished philosophers, do much to offset the title.
- David Heyd, editor of the aforementioned book on toleration, argues that the term cannot be applied to states, but only to persons. If accepted, such a suggestion would, among other things, disqualify normal human rights usage, which regularly classifies states as "tolerant" or "intolerant."[21]
- Martha Minow, in an essay titled, "Putting Up and Putting Down: Tolerance Reconsidered," starts out defining tolerance as the acceptance of

---

[16] Stephen Carter, *The Culture of Unbelief: How American Law and Politics Trivialize Religious Devotion* (Basic Books, 1993), 92–96.
[17] Stanley Fish, *There's No Such Thing as Free Speech and It's a Good Thing, Too* (New York: Oxford University Press, 1994), 217.
[18] Richard Rorty, "Towards a Liberal Utopia: An Interview with Richard Rorty," *The Times Supplement*, June 24, 1944, 14.
[19] Avishai Margalit, "The Ring: On Religious Pluralism," in David Heyd, ed., *Toleration: An Elusive Virtue* (Princeton, NJ: Princeton University Press, 1996), see 155–156.
[20] Ibid.
[21] David Heyd, *Toleration: An Elusive Virtue*, Introduction, 15–16.

different points of view "without interference or disapproval." But, a few pages later, she suggests that tolerating another view may in fact include disapproving of it.[22]

Rehabilitating Tolerance

Despite the fact that the idea of tolerance (and intolerance), including its connection to religion, is in various ways "elusive," both in the language of the human rights documents and in much of the commentary on ordinary usage, there is nevertheless good reason to believe that the drafters of the documents chose just the right term for their purposes. If we proceed more thoughtfully and methodically than is sometimes evident, we can perhaps go some distance toward making sense of the term. If we cannot clear up all the difficulties and objections, we can begin to provide some general guidance.

To begin with, we should remember that it is not uncommon for abstract nouns, such as tolerance, to take on a variety of meanings in ordinary usage. That may be one reason terms such as these appear to be so perplexing. We are not surprised when we are told that words like "love," "justice," "truth," and so on, are subject to contextual variation. That is no doubt true, too, of tolerance, and part of the task of clarification and refinement is to sort out and illuminate the various meanings.[23]

Furthermore, if the meaning of tolerance varies in common usage, and if nothing is done in legal documents, such as the human rights instruments, to stipulate what is to be meant by the term, the unexposed ambiguities may confuse those entrusted with interpreting and enforcing the idea.

Although, as I believe, tolerance does have several meanings, it has, it seems clear, one primary meaning, which happens, as we see later, to be directly

---

[22] Martha Minow, "Putting Up and Putting Down: Tolerance Reconsidered," *Osgood Hall Law Journal* 28, 2 (1990), 92–96.
[23] One account that displays more sensitivity to the complexity of the meaning of tolerance than usual is Michael Walzer's interesting book, *On Toleration* (New Haven: Yale University Press, 1997). Walzer puts forward five possible meanings of tolerance: as resigned acceptance, as indifference, as principled recognition of the rights of others to diverse beliefs, as respect for diversity of a "vive-la-difference" sort, and as an essential expression of moral autonomy that is taken to be a "necessary condition of human flourishing" (10–11). Unfortunately, these various meanings are not systematically applied throughout the book. Another problem with the book, which is of special relevance to my investigation, is that having emphasized the importance of finding and maintaining the limits of tolerance, and having mentioned, in passing, the indispensability of a human rights approach in that connection (5), Walzer fails to elaborate the point or to sustain it in the course of surveying various kinds of tolerant arrangements. To approach his survey from a human rights perspective would, I believe, have altered significantly a number of Walzer's judgments about the arrangements he examines.

relevant to important language in the human rights documents. Drawing on the term's etymology, the dictionary, and the results of sustained attention to common usage, I propose the following as the primary meaning of tolerance, Tolerance 1:

> A response to a set of beliefs, practices, or attributes, initially regarded as deviant or objectionable, with disapproval, but without using force or coercion.[24]

The initial meaning of the Latin word *tolero*, also reflected in the Oxford English Dictionary, is "to endure, bear with or suffer." The same idea is conveyed when the term is associated with inanimate objects. The "tolerance" of a piece of metal is its capacity to bear strain. As applied to human beings, in this primary sense, it refers to an experience of inner strain based on acts of self-denial or renunciation. In the face of beliefs, practices, or attributes taken to be offensive, there is a strong natural temptation to resort to force or coercion to try to restrain or punish those associated with what is regarded as offensive. One feels assaulted and aggrieved by such encounters and is inclined to retaliate accordingly. To endure, bear with, or "suffer" the pain associated with restraining the inclination to retaliate is, I am suggesting, what lies at the core of the primary meaning of tolerance. As such, tolerance appears to be related, though not equivalent, to other moral virtues such as self-sacrificial love, forgiveness, and mercy, which also involve renunciation of strong natural impulses to the contrary in favor of showing consideration or regard for the interests of others.

Interestingly, a second meaning of the Latin word, *tolero*, is "to support, sustain, nourish, or protect." Here to tolerate is to "bear" in a somewhat different way, namely, in the sense of carrying a load. There is the implication that to bear with offensive ideas and behavior on the part of individuals is at the same time to bear or support – in the sense of nourishing and protecting – something of great common benefit.

Highly relevant language from the human rights documents is found in ICCPR, Article 18.2: "No one shall be subject to coercion which would impair [the freedom] to have or to adopt a religion or belief of [one's] choice." We can assume that the understanding of coercion in this passage includes not only the exercise or threat of physical force but also the imposition of unwanted

---

[24] As between the two proposals regarding the meaning of tolerance proposed by Martha Minow, it is the one including the idea of disapproval I take to be correct. On my proposal, an initial reaction of disapproval is logically essential to all of the meanings of tolerance, in one way or another.

or involuntary pressure or restraint. In regard to governmental action toward religion, coercion would include, as one scholar says, "conditioning benefits or burdens on holding or renouncing certain religious beliefs [or practices]."[25] In other words, an example of unacceptable coercion would be government-imposed discrimination against religious individuals or groups, in which the threat of punishment is employed to enforce a discriminatory law or policy.

Let me note that the terms "physical force" and "coercion" are in ordinary discourse frequently regarded as synonymous with "violence." The terms can, of course, be stipulated that way if so desired, but it is more in keeping with human rights usage to take violence to mean "illicit" or "unjustified" force or coercion. On that understanding, force or coercion that is inconsistent with human rights norms would count as "violence," whereas force or coercion that is consistent with the norms would be regarded as "legitimate" or "justified."

Accordingly, a state practices tolerance, in the primary sense, to the extent that it responds to beliefs, practices, or attributes regarded in some quarters as offensive in a way that accords with belief rights.[26] Such a state will, in effect, resist "violence," or the exercise of illicit force and coercion, in two ways: It will itself refrain from administering force/coercion toward individuals or groups identified with the disagreeable beliefs, practices, or attributes so long as those individuals or groups do not themselves violate belief rights (or other human rights). Second, it will protect such individuals or groups from being subjected to illicit force/coercion by others. Conversely, a state is intolerant (in the primary sense) if it employs force/coercion against such individuals or groups or fails to protect them from violent treatment by anyone else.

---

[25] Lerner, *Religion, Beliefs and International Human Rights*, 99.
[26] As mentioned earlier, David Heyd, editor of *Toleration: An Elusive Virtue*, argues in his introduction (15–16) that governments or states cannot be said to be tolerant or intolerant. That is true, he says, for the same reason that they cannot be said to manifest other moral virtues, such as being patient or engaging in self-restraint. The reason is that a state has "no views, no likes and dislikes, which it has to suspend so as to honor people's autonomy or liberty." This is a deeply puzzling claim and one that, as I said, surely flies in the face of standard human rights usage. According to such usage, it is perfectly intelligible to classify regimes as "tolerant" or "intolerant." If we are to be told we must stop talking that way, we will need strong reasons, which he does not, so far as I can see, provide. Indeed, when one contemplates the degree to which state laws and policies in regard to the treatment of religious individuals or groups (as well as much else) are influenced by "special interests" of all kinds, it is frankly hard to comprehend the contention that real-world governments have "no views, no likes and dislikes" that are not, in one way or another, in contention with "people's autonomy or liberty." Until the case is made convincingly to the contrary, there seems no reason to refrain from applying the terms "tolerant" and "intolerant" to governments as well as to other collective bodies, such as religious organizations, educational institutions, etc.

The claim that tolerance has a primary meaning suggests, as I mentioned earlier, that the term has other meanings as well. For example, Fish and Rorty do appear to be right that we sometimes associate the idea of tolerance with indifference, though, even there, the matter is more complex than either seems to understand.[27] A fuller account would need to sort out the different senses of the term in all their complexity. For simplicity's sake, I allude here to only one additional meaning of tolerance, a meaning that also happens to be of special relevance to human rights language.

If the primary definition of tolerance I have given were the exclusive meaning, it would leave us in a strange position. For then we would have to reserve the word "tolerant" *only* for those governments, groups, or individuals who refrain from using violence (as defined) against other individuals or groups regarded as offensive, and the word "intolerant" *only* for those who, in contrast, employ violence against other individuals or groups adhering to what are considered disagreeable views, practices, and so on.

But that is an odd result, because we commonly mean more than that by tolerance/intolerance. Even if they do not treat others violently, people who are readily dismissive of the beliefs or practices of others of whom they disapprove, who do not listen or give others a "fair hearing," and who do not respectfully consider alien views are normally referred to as intolerant. Conversely, people who act in the opposite way are ordinarily referred to as tolerant.

This suggests a second, rather more exalted meaning of tolerance, a meaning that is tied to two specific features. One involves deliberately positing and embracing a larger point or reason – call it a "greater good" – for refraining from

---

[27] If I may quote myself: "To describe modern Americans as tolerant about religion could be interpreted to mean that the theological differences among, say, Episcopalians, Presbyterians, and Baptists are not at present of much real interest to anyone and that these groups get on harmoniously at present in part because they simply ignore what distinguishes them one from the other.

"However, that way of putting it ignores the fact that the differences were not always of such little consequence. During the middle of the eighteenth century in Virginia, people were routinely flogged and imprisoned over the theological differences of those very three Protestant groups. Indeed, the pattern of ferocious intolerance was the background of Thomas Jefferson's Statute for Religious Freedom, passed by the Virginia legislature in 1786 in order to establish the guarantees of free exercise and nondiscrimination in regard to religious affairs, and thereby to end the religious conflict that disrupted life in Virginia until that time" (David Little, "Tolerance, Equal Freedom and Peace," in W. Lawson Taite, ed., *The Essence of Living in a Free Society* (Dallas: University of Dallas Press, 1997), 157).

The point is that the idea of tolerance-as-indifference only makes sense against a background of conflict and hostility that had to be overcome by means of an exercise of tolerance in the primary sense (the adoption of the Statute for Religious Freedom). If there were no such history, we would not employ the word "tolerant" at all, but speak of indifference pure and simple.

using force/coercion against those of whom one disapproves. We may refer to this feature as adopting a *theory of tolerance*. An example would be a belief in the general benefits of open and fair exposure to diverse and conflicting opinions and patterns of behavior, including the opportunity to hear and respond to even passionately held objections, criticisms, and expressions of disapproval, where the setting is free of violence. John Stuart Mill claimed that, without tolerance, the conditions of rational criticism are destroyed, and, he believed that everyone benefits by "supporting, sustaining, nourishing, and protecting" a system of tolerance.

A belief in the general moral and spiritual benefits of a process of self-discipline or self-training associated with the practice of tolerance would be a second example of a theory of tolerance, one that has strong resonance in several religious traditions. In this case, the occasion of learning to endure or bear with explicit expressions of disagreement and disapproval serves to strengthen an individual's ability to conquer the temptation to retaliate violently. A comment by the Dalai Lama illustrates this sort of theory: "Tolerance cannot be learned from your guru. It can only be learned from your enemy."[28] The idea is that welcoming occasions to restrain oneself by exercising tolerance in face of disagreement and antagonism becomes a personal training technique for overcoming the inclination to violence, as well as a contribution, it is further assumed, to a more peaceful and healthy society.

Other religions, such as Christianity, might tie tolerance to a belief in the love of enemy and advocate it alongside "forgiveness" and "mercy" as the best way to treat those whom one regards as offensive. Such behavior might be proposed as an optimal way to promote individual sanctification as well as to help advance the Kingdom of God.

The other feature of this second meaning of tolerance involves a *commitment to a set of virtues* associated with the idea of strong, active respect for those of whom one disapproves. These virtues might be said to comprise the proper "rules of engagement" in regard to the practice of tolerance, such as attentiveness, fairness, honesty, openness, and self-criticism, all of which are to be accompanied by a certain degree of emotional restraint.

We may thus define this second meaning of tolerance, Tolerance 2, as follows:

> A response to a set of beliefs, practices, or attributes that are initially regarded as deviant or objectionable, with *refined* disapproval, but without using force or coercion.

[28] Jeffrey Hopkins, ed. and trans., Tenzin Gyatso, *The Dalai Lama at Harvard* (Snow Lion Publications, 1988), 185.

The phrase "refined disapproval" is intended to convey the idea of tolerance as an intentional, self-conscious attitude and practice characterized by the two features I mentioned – having a theory and being committed to a set of virtues. Accordingly, occasions of disagreement and disapproval are consciously and intentionally to be put to use, or taken advantage of, so as to produce something constructive and beneficial, rather than something destructive and injurious. It is in that way that the experience of disapproval is "refined" or "sublimated" in the sense of "made sublime."

It seems reasonable to conclude that the drafters of the human rights documents meant to go beyond the minimal meaning of Tolerance 1 toward something closer to Tolerance 2 when they declared in the Preamble of DEID "that it is essential to promote understanding, tolerance, and respect in matters relating to freedom of religion or belief," or when they enjoined in Article 13 of ICESC that states shall direct educational institutions "to promote understanding, tolerance and friendship among... all racial, ethnic, or religious groups." It is possible, too, that the encouragement of something similar to Tolerance 2 lies behind the injunction in DEID, Article 4.2, that states must undertake to "combat intolerance" (presumably, by encouraging expressions of Tolerance 2). Finally, but more conjecturally, an understanding of Tolerance 2 may underlie the proscription in Article 20, para. 2 of the ICCPR against "any advocacy of... religious hatred that constitutes incitement to... hostility." It would appear that accepting a theory of tolerance of the sort sketched, as well as practicing a set of virtues such as the ones suggested, would work to mitigate the socially destructive versions of hatred and hostility that the wording of the article undoubtedly intends to prohibit.

Further Thoughts on Tolerance 1 and Tolerance 2

The two definitions I have supplied make clear that there is considerable conceptual overlap between the two types of tolerance. In addition, it must be emphasized that both notions presuppose a condition of equal treatment. As we have seen, the idea of tolerance in the human rights documents is indissolubly linked to the principle of nondiscrimination. It would be impossible to practice tolerance of any sort, according to the documents, if there were any evidence of discrimination against individuals or groups "based on religion or belief."

At the same time, Tolerance 2 goes further than Tolerance 1 in some ways. In particular, it is not enough, from the perspective of Tolerance 2, simply to refrain from acts of violence/discrimination against individuals or groups perceived as offensive: A higher standard of *informed respect* is demanded.

Respect for difference and disagreement would be "informed" because, by embracing a larger rationale for tolerance and undertaking a conscious commitment to a concomitant set of virtues, a person or group would have come self-consciously to "see the point" of difference and disagreement, and thereby to have welcomed it as something positive or worthy of respect, rather than something to be suppressed by force or coercion.[29] Please note: The objects of disapproval are not eliminated; they are just treated in a different way.

This question of respect is central to the idea of Tolerance 2, but it is not itself free of perplexity. It therefore calls for some further elucidation. The following quotation from an essay by Isaiah Berlin on the views of J. S. Mill vividly poses some of the problems with the term.

> Toleration [may well imply] a certain disrespect. I tolerate your absurd beliefs and your foolish acts, though I know them to be absurd and foolish. Mill would, I think, have agreed. He believed that to hold an opinion deeply is to throw our feelings into it. He once declared that when we deeply care, we must dislike those who hold the opposite views.... He asked us not necessarily to respect the view of others – very far from it – only to try to understand and tolerate them; only tolerate; disapprove, think ill of, if need be mock or despise, but tolerate; for without conviction, without some [antipathy], there was, he thought, no deep conviction, and without deep conviction there [are] no ends of life.... But without tolerance the conditions for rational criticism ... are destroyed. He therefore pleads for reason and toleration at all costs. We may argue, attack, reject, condemn with passion and hatred. But we may not suppress or stifle, for that is to destroy the bad and the good, and is tantamount to collective moral and intellectual suicide. *Sceptical respect* for the opinions of our opponents seems to Mill to be preferable to indifference or cynicism (emphasis added).[30]

The fundamental issue here is the meaning of "respect" in relation to tolerance, and it is quite possible that the ambiguities that attend the term are at bottom why, after all, tolerance may remain, an "elusive virtue."

The passage just quoted is itself very ambiguous on the subject. It begins by contending that tolerance may well imply "a certain disrespect" and then goes

---

[29] Incidentally, such conditions suggest a reason for rejecting Stephen Carter's dogmatic claim that tolerance is connected irredeemably and without qualification to an attitude of condescension and disrespect, and therefore that it should be discarded. There is no doubt that tolerance has conveyed such attitudes at certain historical times and places and even that it may, in some contexts, continue to denote such attitudes at present. The mistake, as I have been saying all along, is to think too univocally about the term and to ignore the rich and potent variety of possible meanings and usages that characterize it, some of which distinctly offset the objectionable connotations Carter calls attention to.

[30] Isaiah Berlin, "John Stuart Mill and the Ends of Life," in *Four Essays on Liberty* (Oxford: Oxford University Press, 1979), 184.

on to state that Mill "asked us not necessarily to respect the view of others – very far from it"; however, later the passage reverses course and introduces the idea of "sceptical respect." That notion would not appear to be the same as out-and-out disrespect, and it also seems to be something different from showing *no* respect to the views of others. To understand fully Mill's theory of tolerance, as well as the list of practical virtues he might connect to it, would require, it appears, a complete exposition of the interesting, but hardly transparent, notion of skeptical respect. Then it would be necessary to see how the notion can be made consistent with the other statements made in the passage about respect.[31]

Still, we can surmise from Berlin's discussion that Mill's theory of tolerance would be rather permissive and inclusive compared to other conceivable theories of tolerance. In the face of beliefs, practices, or attributes that are disapproved of, he would not, short of actions taken to "suppress or stifle," disqualify strong feelings of hostility, the use of extremely harsh language or emotional response, or adherence to a fervently held "deep conviction."

What would have to be determined is whether (once it is understood) Mill's theory is finally acceptable and, if so, what the precise and proper limits of respect and tolerance that result from it are. In short, what are the virtues or practices of tolerance that follow from Mill's theory? How will we know when one is "suppressing and stifling" the beliefs, practices, or attributes of others? How will we know when the requisite forms of attentiveness, fairness, and so on, are or are not being exhibited?

Such are the deeper questions entailed in beginning to think through a theory of tolerance and its concomitant virtues. It should be clear from this brief excursus that that task is a very demanding one.

---

[31] As a way of straightening things out, it might be suggested that the subject of tolerance rests on an implicit distinction between attitudes toward persons, on the one hand, and their beliefs and practices, on the other, and that tolerance, properly understood, applies to the first, but not the second. This is the view of David Heyd (Introduction, *Toleration: An Elusive Virtue*, 14). Heyd writes, "We do not tolerate opinions and beliefs, or even actions and practices, only the subjects holding disliked beliefs and the agents of detested actions." It might follow that this same distinction applies also to the idea of respect, and if Mill were to observe it, all the ambiguities would go away. This, however, is a very peculiar proposal, and I am afraid that it will not help. One way of tolerating, or respecting, another person is to "bear with, endure or suffer" that person's views and practices, rather than "suppressing or stifling" them (in Mill's words). Indeed, it is logically impossible to separate the views or practices from the person in regard to applying the concept of respect that is affiliated with tolerance. If it were not for the "disliked beliefs" and the "detested actions," *there would be no cause* to practice tolerance or respect toward the person who holds those beliefs and engages in those actions. Moreover, in suppressing or stifling views or practices, one visits coercive restraint or punishment *on the person*. The real question is, *What are the proper limits of tolerance and respect in regard to persons who hold disliked beliefs and perform detested actions*?

The Special Problem of Enforceability

There is one issue requiring special attention that seems to represent an important dissimilarity between the two meanings of tolerance. That is the question of legal enforceability. Clearly, Tolerance 1 is legally enforceable, with the possible exception of one provision (identified later). To the extent that a state employs force/coercion consistently to restrain or punish acts of intolerance (as defined), it is obviously acting to enforce tolerance. Conversely, to the extent a state fails to enforce tolerance, it is failing in one of its primary responsibilities, according to human rights norms.

More specifically, states are certainly capable – indeed, they are required under the human rights instruments – to enforce the first three of the belief rights: tolerance, nondiscrimination, and protection of minorities. In addition, they undoubtedly have both the responsibility and the capability to enforce part, at least, of the fourth belief right: restriction of expressions of "religious hatred" that incite to "discrimination . . . or violence."

However, whether they can effectively enforce the provision against "incitement to hostility," including, possibly, the mere dissemination of ideas of religious superiority, remains, for reasons already mentioned, a highly difficult and controversial matter. Among other things, this issue raises the extensive debate in human rights circles over the propriety and usefulness of hate speech laws. The issue is too complicated to take up here, though it seems fair to report that the worldwide record of accomplishment of hate speech laws is until now quite inconclusive.[32]

The problem we need to address is whether Tolerance 2 is legally enforceable. Is it, in fact, the state's job to pick out and enforce particular theories of tolerance, such as those espoused by John Stuart Mill or the Dalai Lama, or by Christians or other traditions of religion or belief? Is it, in addition, the state's job to inculcate by force/coercion, if necessary, a set of "tolerance virtues"?

On one level, surely, it is *not* the state's job to do these things. Part of the meaning of the "freedom of conscience, religion, or belief" is that people should be left free to work matters of this kind out for themselves. To be specific, developing and embracing theories of tolerance, and adopting codes of virtue, such as those associated with Tolerance 2, are deeply connected, it would seem, to the central objectives of religious or other belief traditions. As such, they are unmistakably protected against governmental interference by the belief rights. As a matter of fact, to call something a "virtue" in the first place suggests that it is in some important sense freely, rather than coercively, initiated and sustained by individual agents.

---

[32] See David Little, "Tolerance, Equal Freedom, and Peace," esp. 175–186, for a discussion and evaluation of the international controversy over hate speech laws.

This point implies that cultivating or promoting tolerance, as is advocated by the documents, is by no means the exclusive domain of states, and that would seem to be the case especially in regard to Tolerance 2. Theologians, philosophers, and historians, as well as religious bodies, along with other nongovernmental organizations, the media, professional and civic associations, and certain activities of "civil society," have an indispensable role to play, something to which more attention needs to be given. We shall return to this subject shortly.

All the same, the language of the documents is complicated on this point, as we have seen. Not only does it enjoin (however controversially) the punishment of any "advocacy" of religious hatred that incites to hostility but it also (possibly) requires punishing any dissemination of ideas of religious superiority as such. This comes very close to providing a warrant for state regulation of "conscience, religion or belief," *not*, be it noted, in regard to the impact of ideas on overt behavior (such as influence on acts of violence or discrimination), but in regard to the nature of the ideas themselves or of their influence exclusively on inner attitudes and emotions (namely, "hostility").

To pursue this line of thinking is, quite obviously, to open the way to the legal enforcement of Tolerance 2, because, presumably, theories that encourage forbidden ideas would be coercively repressed in favor of theories taken to be acceptable. Such a development could, in turn, introduce a profound conflict into the process of interpreting and applying belief rights because states would be required simultaneously *to regulate and not to regulate* matters of "conscience, religion or belief." Given the difficulty of drawing meaningful limits in this area, pursuing such a line of thinking runs the risk of encouraging the expansion of state-sponsored intolerance.

A similar problem arises in regard to promoting tolerance by means of public education. If, as we suggested, the prescription in Article 13 of the ICESCR, requiring that public education "promote understanding, tolerance and friendship among all nations and all racial, ethnic or religious groups," moves in the direction of Tolerance 2, then such a program unavoidably becomes a matter of state enforcement. Accordingly, the state would again find itself in the business of regulating questions that typically belong to the sphere of "conscience, religion or belief."

Without aiming to resolve these difficulties, all we can do here is to call attention to them in hopes that our analysis of the two meanings of tolerance begins to illuminate critical points of tension.[33] If we are right, these points of

---

[33] One suggestion for coping with the deep tension between the state's obligation, under a human rights understanding, to encourage a belief in and a commitment to tolerance and,

tension constitute a very serious and sensitive area of human rights discussion that demands the highest degree of sustained, clear-headed consideration from scholars and practitioners around the world.

RECENT THEORETICAL REFLECTION ON TOLERANCE

I may try to help the discussion along by briefly examining some examples of theories of tolerance, or parts of theories, that are prompted by the requirements of Tolerance 2. I shall do that in a way that emphasizes why such theories are, as I hinted earlier, so *unsusceptible to coercive regulation* and so in need of protection against it.

To begin with, there is no reason to agree with Avishai Margalit's assertion that monotheistic religions are essentially incompatible with tolerance because they are metaphysically dogmatic and exclusive. Nor, similarly, is there any reason to agree with Richard Rorty's claim that religion and tolerance are mutually exclusive.

To take one from among innumerable possible examples, many among the Christian Anabaptist tradition were unswerving monotheists, fervently committed to what they regarded as the exclusively true faith in Jesus Christ. Nevertheless, they refrained on principle from advocating or using force/coercion against people whose beliefs or practices they (often strongly) disapproved of. Dietrich Philips, the sixteenth-century Dutch Anabaptist, wrote in that spirit:

> Christians [ought to] persecute no one on account of faith. For Christ sends his disciples as sheep in the midst of wolves, but the sheep does not devour the wolf....
>
> No congregation of the Lord may exercise dominion over the consciences of men with the outward sword, to force unbelievers to believe, nor to kill the false prophets with sword and fire.[34]

It is, accordingly, self-evident that an monotheist like Philips qualifies as tolerant, certainly according to the definition of Tolerance 1. Nor is there any

---

simultaneously, to refrain from directly enforcing beliefs and commitments, is to "raise consciousness" about tolerance through education and otherwise by exposing citizens to the *variety* of different religious and other (like Mill's) theories of tolerance, rather than singling out and favoring one over others. Such a policy would rest on the reasonable assumption that fulfilling the state's undisputed obligation to restrain intolerance that incites to violence and discrimination (Tolerance 1), strongly requires the cultivation of a more "refined" understanding of tolerance (Tolerance 2) that itself cannot finally be enforced but *only* encouraged.

[34] Dietrich Philips, "The Church of God," in George Hunston Williams, ed., *Spiritual and Anabaptist Writers* (Philadelphia: Westminster Press, 1957), 252–253.

prima facie reason to doubt that he or countless other religious (or nonreligious) advocates of nonviolence – whether of an absolute or modified sort – could also qualify according to the terms of Tolerance 2.

If, for example, the views of J. S. Mill cited earlier hold any water, there seems no basis for concluding that, so long as it does not "suppress or stifle," a coherent theory of tolerance could not include "metaphysically exclusive" ideas, or a conviction that one holds a superior position to others, or even permits, in certain circumstances, the expression of strong language and passionate emotional outbursts, or the harboring of intensely hostile feelings that typically accompany attitudes of "righteous indignation."

Just what form the limits on these things take finally depends, of course, on one's assessment of the theory, such as Mill's, that serves to define and defend the limits of tolerance. Still, Mill unquestionably puts forward an arresting and engaging description of tolerance, one that will have to be considered in any theorizing about the idea. And one reason for guaranteeing protection of the "freedom of conscience, religion or belief" is precisely to allow proponents of competing theories to ponder and evaluate such proposals in a nonviolent, "tolerant" atmosphere.

I mentioned earlier the important place that the nongovernmental sphere plays in the cultivation of Tolerance 2. I included in that category the work of philosophers, theologians, and historians; religious groups; the media; civic associations; and certain activities undertaken in the name of "civil society." There follow four recent examples of innovative theological and historical work related to theorizing about tolerance, which encourage the belief that quite significant work in the area is beginning take place and suggest models for further reflection.

The examples consist of the recent work of four notable religious analysts: James Carroll, columnist, writer, former Catholic priest, and author of the best-selling book, *Constantine's Sword: The Church and the Jews*;[35] Brian Tierney, historian of Christianity and author of an important article on "Religious Rights: An Historical Perspective";[36] Abdolkarim Soroush, distinguished Iranian Muslim scholar and author of a collection of essays, *Reason, Freedom, and Democracy in Islam*;[37] and Adam Seligman, noted sociologist of religion and editor of *Essays on the Religious Roots of Tolerance*, that includes contributions from Jewish, Muslim, and Christian scholars.[38]

---

[35] (New York: Houghton & Mifflin, 2001).
[36] In John Witte, Jr. and Johan D. van der Vyver, eds., *Religious Human Rights in Global Perspective: Religious Perspectives* (The Hague: Martinus Nijhoff Publishers, 1996).
[37] (New York: Oxford University Press, 2000).
[38] Adam Seligman, ed., *Essays on the Religious Roots of Tolerance*, published in *Journal of Human Rights* vol. 2, no. 1 (March 2003). The volume is the product of a Ford Foundation gathering

The writings of the first three figures, Carroll, Tierney, and Soroush, are thoroughly compatible with the human rights approach developed in this chapter; the work of the fourth, Adam Seligman, is, in general, not. An explicit premise of the Seligman study, which makes it important and challenging and, at the same time, quite controversial, is that, in the first place, "rights-based discourse," including human rights language, is "not a religious [form of discourse]."[39] Because it has by now become thoroughly secularized and cut off from whatever religious roots it may once have had, such language must stand in opposition to a way of thinking that is typically religious. Moreover, the vision of liberalism, on which human rights discourse has historically rested, is itself no longer tenable.[40] For these reasons, new resources for tolerance, other than those associated with human rights and liberalism, must be sought from within the religious traditions themselves.

Compatible Approaches

Each of the first three approaches addresses, in its own way, the problem of religious intolerance by proposing to reexamine one or other religious tradition with the objective of separating out and reappropriating certain key ideas, themes, or ways of thinking that are taken to be inherent in the traditions. Each then undertakes to deploy them so as to "promote tolerance" of the sort that is, generally speaking, consistent with a human rights understanding. Interestingly, the various emphases among them bring out some of the complexities and perplexities in the notion of tolerance I have drawn attention to throughout this chapter.

Of the three, Carroll's approach is the most radical. The fundamental thesis of his book is that the appalling history of Christian attitudes and practices toward the Jews is in an important way traceable to certain intolerant beliefs that lie very deep in the sacred texts and doctrines of Christianity. Though more is involved, the symbol of the cross and the association of the Jews with Jesus's crucifixion in the New Testament accounts epitomize the problem.

Carroll argues that this association, which came strongly to motivate the pervasive spirit of anti-Semitism in Christianity, is, in fact, an inauthentic feature of the early Christian outlook because it is the result of an ulterior and ignoble interest in communal self-protection. In order not to be confused with

of scholars of the three faiths who come from different disciplines and countries. The group met in Vienna in April 1999.
[39] Seligman, Introduction, *Religious Roots of Tolerance*, 8.
[40] See Seligman, ch. 1, "Tradition and Toleration."

the Jews, who were at the time being subjected to a repressive campaign by the Roman authorities, early Christian authors modified the actual responsibility of the Romans for the crucifixion by deliberately slanting the story against the Jews. In reality, says Carroll, such anti-Jewish sentiment is quite out of keeping with the underlying message of Jesus and of the apostle Paul.

Carroll's subsequent narrative describes the unfolding story of how the symbol of the cross has been repeatedly turned against the Jews to work the most grievous forms of intolerance and hostility. The vision of Emperor Constantine, by which he is instructed to turn the cross into a sword of conquest, becomes the guiding motif for much of the violence that is thereafter visited on the Jews (and others).

In the interests of overcoming such intolerance, Carroll advocates a deep renovation of Christian theology and life, starting with the interpretation of the Christian scriptures and especially the idea of the cross, along with any notion that Christianity supersedes and is thus superior to Judaism. He contends that modern calls for tolerance toward Jews that remain, so to speak, theologically unreconstructed do not eliminate the real problem. He quotes one author as follows: "To label a group the most heinous of enemies and then to demand for them tolerance ... is probably to make demands that the human psyche, over the long run, must have difficulty meeting."[41]

Carroll's book is controversial, and the point here is not to try to resolve the controversy. One may wonder whether Carroll should have explored more fully, for example, certain alternatives within the tradition that he himself applauds so as to determine just how "inevitable" anti-Semitism was[42] and whether there do not exist other important resources for religious tolerance in the tradition. However that may be, his approach is important from our point of view because it courageously entertains the possibility of deep and extensive revision and reconstruction of the central tenets of a tradition in the name of ferreting out intolerance.

In particular, there is much compelling material in Carroll's book that bears on a problem we have troubled over earlier – the degree to which the sheer holding and dissemination of hostile ideas itself constitute an incitement to violence/discrimination. Even if he does not settle this complicated matter, he raises it unforgettably. Moreover, Carroll's book vividly and memorably demonstrates the distressing consequences of conflating the critical distinction

---

[41] Carroll, *Constantine's Sword*, 271.
[42] Ibid. See, for example, 369 (and fn. 668), where Carroll affirms the Calvinist side of the Reformation for having "set loose forces that favored Jews and that would contribute to their liberation."

between "religion-and-belief" and force-and-coercion that, as I have argued, underlies both the concept of tolerance and the human rights documents.

Brian Tierney's essay draws on his unparalleled command of the history of rights language in the Christian tradition,[43] combining that with some arresting insights regarding the resources of tolerance within Christianity. He points out, in the spirit of James Carroll, that there is a "potentiality for intolerance" in Christian scriptures and early church history, but also that there is a competing ideal of "spiritual liberty" born of the belief that the human being is a "morally autonomous individual, endowed with reason and conscience and free will."[44]

Tierney emphasizes that the commitment to religious freedom and tolerance that finally develops out of part of the tradition was a combination of historical contingencies and a legacy of ideas associated with the ideal of spiritual liberty. The fusing of the notion of conscience, which appeared in some important ways in Christian scriptures, with the notion of individual right, as it evolved throughout the Middle Ages and Reformation, yielded by the sixteenth century a quite liberal and influential concept of "religious right" and an expanding commitment to religious tolerance. Although, according to Tierney, ideas of skepticism and expediency had their effect, "the most important" argument for tolerance by this time was that "the practice of persecution was radically contrary to the teaching of Jesus himself."[45]

According to Tierney, the idea of "religious rights," emerging as it did from within, rather than from outside, a specific religious tradition, continues to have huge saliency in the modern world. Perhaps, he concludes, the only answer to solving the "grievous effects of religious conflict and religious persecution" throughout the contemporary world "is the one that Christians discovered so painfully when they compared the words of Jesus with all the hatreds and cruelties of their contemporary world; that is, the need for a return to the original sources of religious tradition and a reconsideration of their implications in the light of our accumulated centuries of experience."[46]

In his effort to offset what he regards as widely held misimpressions of Islam, Abdolkarim Soroush provides a strong and rather remarkable defense of tolerance. Such a defense is, he argues, perfectly in accord with the heart of Islamic teaching. "Faith," he says, "is a matter of exclusively personal and private experience. We embrace a faith individually just as we confront our

---

[43] See Brian Tierney, *The Idea of Natural Rights: Studies on Natural Rights, Natural Law and Church Law 1150–1625* (Atlanta: Scholars Press, 1997), which conveniently brings together a number of Tierney's definitive articles on the subject.
[44] Tierney, "Religious Rights," 20.
[45] Ibid., 36.
[46] Ibid., 44.

death individually.... Expressions of faith are public but the essence of faith is mysterious and private. The domain of faith is akin to the arena of the hereafter, ... : 'And everyone of them is brought to the day of judgment individually.'"[47]

Just as faith is individual and personal and thus not subject to public control, so, according to Soroush, it cannot be forced. "True faith is contingent on individuality and liberty.... [T]he hand of tyranny is unable to sow the seed of religiosity in the soil of hearts.... Coercion has no place here."[48] His lyrical elaborations of this point are worth quoting:

> The prophets founded a faithful-spiritual community, not a legal-corporeal society. They started from faiths and hearts, then proceeded to rites and obligations. They were aware that one may base a legal-ritual society upon force and imposition. However, it is not as easy to steer such a society toward faith. One may use coercion in enforcing religious regulations, but how can one inculcate faith? Is action without conviction, body without soul, appearance without essence worth all the torments and sacrifices of the prophets? Their quarry was to attract and acquaint the brisk, free, and impalpable faith with the hearts of the faithful, thus suffusing them with humility and devotion, both spiritually and physically. They radiated, like sunshine, upon hearts and let the inner heat glow through frosted limbs. Their interlocutors were ardent hearts, their method was enchantment, the outcome of their mission was consensual faith, not fearful obedience. They knew themselves and explicitly told their interlocutors: "How can we compel you, while you are reluctant?"[49]

Soroush proceeds to elaborate on the distinction between religion-belief and force-coercion. To compel the confession of belief, he says, to indoctrinate and propagandize by intimidation, to "shut down the gates of criticism, revision, and modification so that everyone would succumb to a single ideology," produces not a society of faith, "but a monolithic and terrified mass of crippled, submissive, and hypocritical subjects."[50] "People may be compelled to act in unison, but they may not be made to understand religion uniformly. They may be compelled to confess a faith, but they may not be forced to accept faith in their hearts."[51] Religious belief, he asserts, "will grow and flourish wherever it wishes and in whatever fragrance and color it pleases. The faithful community is more like a wild grove than a manicured garden."[52]

---

[47] Soroush, *Reason, Freedom, and Democracy in Islam*, 140 (Qur'anic quotation: 19:95).
[48] Ibid., 141.
[49] Ibid., 141.
[50] Ibid., 142.
[51] Ibid., 143.
[52] Ibid.

This line of argument leads Soroush to commend liberal democracy, based on human rights standards and a firm commitment to tolerance, as the most satisfactory environment in which genuine religious faith can prosper.

A Different Voice

Starting, as I mentioned, with the premise that religious grounds for tolerance must typically stand in opposition to a human rights understanding, as well as to the ideas of liberalism with which it is historically associated, Seligman and most of his associates proceed to lay out alternative approaches to religious tolerance.

For example, Seligman's own suggestion, and one in part supported by Menachem Fisch in his essay, "A Modest Proposal: Toward a Religious Politics of Epistemic Humility,"[53] is an argument from religiously based skepticism or epistemological diffidence, as it might be called. Insofar as certain strands in Judaism, and probably also in Christianity and Islam, posit a profound separation between divine ways and thoughts, on the one hand, and those of human beings, on the other, believers are expected to be modest and self-restrained in what they may claim to know about ultimate truth. An attitude of modesty, humility, and even skepticism of a kind would, consequently, seem to be rooted in the very character of a belief in divine sovereignty. It follows, according to this proposal, that if believers are modest about their own religious knowledge, they will also be restrained about trying forcibly or coercively to impose such knowledge on others. The result is a warrant for religious tolerance that is directly and positively authorized by a religious tradition itself, rather than depending on some alien, secular basis, such as human rights liberalism.

Another interesting proposal in a rather different vein is put forward by Sholmo Fischer, in his contribution to the Seligman volume, "Intolerance and Tolerance in the Jewish Tradition and Contemporary Israel."[54] He poses a dilemma for certain proponents of Judaism that present-day practice in Israel attempts to resolve. One horn of the dilemma is that the Jewish tradition makes room for tolerating religious dissenters and outsiders by excusing them, for various reasons, from responsibility for their disbelief or their deviance from halachic ways. The opposing horn, however, is that there is much support in the tradition for favoring as essential to Judaism the public enforcement of communal practices and a distinctive Jewish national ethos.

[53] Seligman, *Essays on the Religious Roots of Tolerance*, 49–64.
[54] Ibid., 65–80.

The tension between these two points has led some religious leaders in Israel to advocate a "new contract" that would "tolerate formal deviation from the Halacha in [certain] new[ly] instituted arrangements in exchange for increased Jewish ... educational and cultural programs in state schools and state-sponsored settings and media." One document, quoted by Fischer, states that even "if there is no room, from a halachic point of view to compel the observance of the commandments, it is appropriate to create a 'public sphere' which will reflect the Jewish character of the state."[55]

Fischer concludes that for the foreseeable future "the state [in Israel] will probably never treat all religions and belief equally, and perhaps certain individual freedoms will remain curtailed in a way not practiced in the United States." If there are some disadvantages to such an arrangement, they are offset in Fischer's mind by securing "republican or communitarian forms of trust and solidarity."

Suggestions such as these that are put forward in Seligman's book are an important part of the discussion of religious tolerance and for that reason are completely welcome. The objections to a human rights approach, with its liberal associations, are frequently and often heatedly registered in many parts of the world, and these ardent objections need to be confronted and discussed in the forthright way many of the essays in Seligman's book discuss them.

Furthermore, a human rights approach is by no means necessarily opposed to theorizing about human rights from different and even rejectionist perspectives. Indeed, the documents themselves clearly permit and encourage diversified and open-ended cogitation of that sort – precisely in the name "freedom of conscience, religion or belief." As we have seen, there is much room within the documents for further clarification and, perhaps, also, for modification – all of which could be aided by serious and expansive theoretical discussion. Nor is there any reason to reject reasons for supporting tolerance, or any other human right, on religiously particularistic grounds. Again, that is thoroughly permissible on the terms of the documents themselves.

Still, there is one point at which the "different voice," represented by Seligman and the essays in his book, will certainly invite energetic response from those committed to a human rights approach. That is the oversimplified and rather narrow account of a human rights approach provided by Seligman in his introduction and first chapter and assumed throughout the book by most of the other contributors.

For one thing, the potency and staying power of the human rights approach, purely as an empirical matter, are rather severely underappreciated by

[55] Ibid., 78.

Seligman's account. The spread of human rights norms in the form of expanding expectations concerning constitutionalism and the rule of law around the world, the growing agitation for international tribunals devoted to the enforcement of those norms, the irreversible reliance on those norms in international fora, such as the Organization of Security and Cooperation in Europe (and Central Asia), the ardent promotion of human rights, particularly by individuals and groups associated with the vulnerable and abused of the world – all this and more attest to the expanding influence and efficacy of human rights.

Nor, again, is it the case that the human rights approach and its interpretation rest exclusively or uniformly on any one philosophical or theological base or interpretation, or that they necessarily commit one to a secularist, rational-choice outlook of the sort Seligman portrays. The sketches of the three preceding theorists of tolerance, Carroll, Tierney, and Soroush – whose views are fully compatible with a human rights understanding – make that obvious, and those examples are just the beginning.

But what is most striking and what will prompt the strongest response from human rights advocates is the failure of Seligman to account for the fundamental reason why the human rights idiom took hold in the first place and why it has endured so remarkably ever since. In particular, Seligman ignores the reasons why the human rights idiom has achieved such widespread normative dominance and why it has come to set the terms of reference within which subjects such as tolerance must now be considered, both by those who support a human rights approach, and those who do not.

That reason is, as I suggested earlier, *the specter of collective domination definitively symbolized by the fascist experience*. Because of that, it is a safe assumption that people who oppose or seek to contain "rights talk" in favor of "republican or communitarian forms of trust and solidarity," or other examples of collective control, will face one ultimate and unavoidable challenge: By now, they will have to address and reassure a much wider audience than just the members of their own tradition that dissidents, minorities, and other "outsiders" in their midst are in fact securely protected, as individuals and as groups, against the threat of collective domination. That will mean demonstrating that adequate provision has been made for expressions of dissent and disagreement, for equal protection under the law, and for the other "rights guarantees" that shield individuals and groups from severe arbitrary injury at the hands of public authorities.

No doubt there is some room for negotiation and accommodation in regard to local conditions. Special provision for majoritarian preferences within limits (national holidays, forms of public symbolic expression, etc.) may be allowable according to human rights standards. As we saw, state religion as such is not prohibited, and that fact may be interpreted to permit certain deviations from absolute equality in the name of accommodating the interests of particular religious and cultural traditions.

Nevertheless, however much room there may be for maneuver in the interest of majority ideals and preferences, there can be little doubt that all objections and proposals must finally pass a fixed and ultimate "human rights test" that continues to command strong and widespread moral, as well as political and legal, authority in the world today. If that is so, then perhaps the human rights idiom, for all its imperfections and incompleteness, is not yet – either theoretically or practically – beside the point.

CONCLUSION

We have argued that though the idea of tolerance is perplexing, both in the human rights documents and in much commentary on ordinary usage, there are compelling reasons for embracing the notion and for undertaking to clarify and refine it in relation to human rights language. On careful analysis, the concept can be seen to do some important work in establishing the conditions of peace. Offensive beliefs, practices, or attributes, which might be and often are the cause of violent conflict, are, so to speak, disarmed when they are no longer met with force or coercion (Tolerance 1). Moreover, when they are conceived of and treated not as something necessarily threatening and destructive, but as a potential source of mutual edification, their existence can actually strengthen social bonds rather than weaken them (Tolerance 2).

It can be that intolerance, understood as the disposition to use force or coercion to punish or suppress people whose views or "ways" are considered objectionable or deviant, was the besetting sin of fascism. The sin was besetting in the sense that it encompassed or comprehended all the other forms of viciousness that have come to be associated with the movement, and it reveals why from the beginning fascism constituted a total and unrelenting assault on the very foundations of social harmony and peace. Trying to stifle dissent, disagreement, and discord by force appears to be the surest way, eventually, to engender dissent, disagreement, and discord. Insofar as the human rights movement has grasped that lesson and has accordingly identified the idea of tolerance as an indispensable condition of worldwide peace, it has made a contribution devoutly to be welcomed and advanced.

6

A Bang or a Whimper? Assessing Some Recent Challenges to Special Protection for Religion in the United States[*]

Three American authors have, in recent years, expressed strong reservations about what they regard as standard American legal attitudes and practice toward protecting the right to religious freedom. Although their arguments are addressed specifically to the American tradition, there are wider implications for the international discussion of the subject. The arguments, therefore, call for a response.

The authors and books in question are Winifred Sullivan, *The Impossibility of Religious Freedom* (2005);[1] Marci Hamilton, *God vs. the Gavel: Religion and the Rule of Law* (2005);[2] and Brian Leiter, *Why Tolerate Religion?* (2013).[3] Sullivan is a legally trained religious studies professor at Indiana University; Hamilton is a chaired professor at the Yeshiva University Law School in New York City; and Leiter is director of the Center for Law, Philosophy, and Human Values and a chaired professor at the University of Chicago Law School.

All three authors begin by announcing either that they see no reason to single out religion for special treatment or that granting exemptions to religious believers does enormous harm to society. At first blush, it does look as though their challenges pose an ominous threat to the protection of religious freedom, at least as we ordinarily understand the idea in the United States.

If religious freedom is, in fact, "impossible," as advertised by Sullivan's title, then our accepted ways of thinking would seem to be in deep trouble. The same appears to be true if Hamilton's opening claim is correct that there should be no exemptions for religious people from general and neutral laws

---

[*] I wish to thank Douglas Laycock for his help – for valuable materials sent, for rapid-fire e-mail responses to my queries, and for saving me from mistakes.
[1] (Princeton, NJ: Princeton University Press, 2005).
[2] (New York: Cambridge University Press, 2005).
[3] (Princeton, NJ: Princeton University Press, 2013).

unless they can prove that "exempting them will cause no harm to others."[4] Again, the conclusion would seem to hold if there is, as Leiter argues, nothing whatsoever about religion itself that warrants special exemption. The three have different axes to grind, but they are one in representing what looks like growing suspicion in American society about bestowing special privileges on religion.

However, there is a problem. On inspection, the arguments of each book are not, in their various ways, altogether consistent. The authors all shout loud, threatening utterances out the front door, while whispering more agreeable, less startling words out the back. Taken together, the shouts and whispers of all three do prompt us to reconsider our tradition concerning religious freedom, but in a way that is not, after all, quite as threatening as it first appeared.

SULLIVAN

Sullivan has two principal objections to providing special legal protection for religion. One is that it results in discrimination against "those who do not self-identify as religious."[5] The last sentence of her book asserts that whatever it is legal protection of religion is intended to do is "not best realized through laws guaranteeing religious freedom but through laws guaranteeing equality," such as, one supposes, freedom of speech or assembly.[6] The second objection is that the category "religion" "can no longer be coherently defined for purposes of American law."[7]

Much of her book attempts to demonstrate the saliency of these two objections by discussing a case involving complaints against an ordinance imposed by the city of Boca Raton, Florida, prohibiting the erection of any but flat gravestones in a public cemetery.[8] The plaintiffs appealed for an exemption on grounds of religious freedom, but were denied it on the basis of a very narrow definition of religion. Sullivan, a witness for the plaintiffs, strongly criticizes the narrowness of the ruling, but then goes on to draw a puzzling inference. She concludes that the real problem was not with the judge's narrow understanding, but with the vagueness of the category of religion itself and with the discriminatory effect such vagueness inevitably has on religiously unconventional individuals such as the plaintiffs.

---

[4] Hamilton, *God vs. the Gavel*, 5.
[5] Sullivan, *Impossibility of Religious Freedom*, 8.
[6] Ibid., 159.
[7] Ibid., 150.
[8] *Warner v. Boca Raton* 64 F. Supp. 2d 1272 (1999); 267 F. 3d 1223 (2001).

Her inference is all the more puzzling because she then proceeds at the end of her book to make statements that wind up undercutting her original objections. She affirms in ringing words "the right of the individual, every individual, to life outside the state – the right to live as a self on which many given, as well as chosen, demands are made";[9] a few pages earlier she declares that "religion is ... arguably different from speech, movement, association and the like" – the legal protection of which presumably guarantees equality. "To be religious is, in some sense," she says, "to be obedient to a rule outside of oneself and one's government, whether that rule is established by God, or otherwise. It is to do what must be done ... and doing so at some personal cost."[10]

Sullivan here is suspiciously close to defending the familiar idea of sovereignty of conscience, closely related to religious belief, and to implying that the right to it is *not*, after all, "best realized by laws guaranteeing equality." In addition, being obedient to a higher rule, "whether established by God, or otherwise," recalls a broad, inclusive view of conscience – applicable to religious and nonreligious people alike – that is readily found in traditional American defenders of religious freedom such as Roger Williams, James Madison, and Thomas Jefferson. In fact, it is curious that Sullivan did not herself see fit to oppose a more inclusive understanding of conscience to the judge's crabbed interpretation in the Boca Raton case.

HAMILTON

In a devastating review of Hamilton's book titled "A Syllabus of Errors,"[11] Douglas Laycock reveals, among other shortcomings, similar kinds of inconsistency in Hamilton's argument. Up until the last chapter, her opposition to all religious exemptions that cause any harm presupposes a highly expansive notion of "harm." Without a careful definition of the term, religious people, seeking to build a house of worship or to institute a feeding program, could be denied exemptions depending on what any neighbor, zoning board, or taxing authority happened to consider harmful, thereby extensively inhibiting religious free exercise.

However, when she comes to the final chapter, "The Path to the Public Good," she abruptly adopts a more nuanced understanding, one that is a good deal closer to conventional approaches to religious exemptions. She

---

[9] Sullivan, *Impossibility of Religious Freedom*, 159.
[10] Ibid., 156.
[11] Douglas Laycock, "A Syllabus of Errors," *Michigan Law Review* vol. 105: 1169 (April 2007).

there speaks of the task "of balancing the value of religious liberty over and against the harm to others if a religious individual or institution is permitted to act contrary to the law," and of "weighing" "the importance of respect and tolerance for a wide panoply of religious faiths" with "whether the harm that the law was intended to prevent can be tolerated in a just society."[12] Suddenly, protecting religious liberty has important value, and to restrict it is itself a harm that must be *balanced* and *weighed* against the harm to "the public good" of granting exemptions to existing laws. It is now a question of competing harms, and Hamilton does favor some exemptions, as in the case of military service or the religious use of peyote, where, one assumes, the threat to the public good is not too great. In the final chapter, she clearly adopts a much less radical position and comes close to, though never quite embraces, standards set by federal and state versions of the Religious Freedom Restoration Act (RFRA), according to which the government may "substantially burden" the exercise of religion only if the burden imposed is "(1) in furtherance of a compelling governmental interest, and (2) is the least restrictive means of furthering that ... interest."

Laycock identifies a second inconsistency, though one Hamilton also does not seem aware of. In the concluding chapter, she argues for the exclusive competence of legislatures to perform the necessary balancing acts. Contrary to RFRA and the state and federal Religious Freedom Restoration Acts and Religious Land Use and Institutionalized Persons Act, she contends that courts have absolutely no place. Only legislatures are capable of adequately "assessing the public good in the light of all circumstances and facts, and weighing social goods and harms."[13] What she forgets is that much of her discussion leading up to these claims consists of an extended and detailed catalog of repeated and egregious failures by legislatures to get the balance right. As Laycock concludes, "her faith in legislatures is incomprehensible, because she has little good to say about them."[14]

LEITER

Leiter introduces his subject by pointing out that, although special protection for religion is widely accepted in America, no one has ever provided a "credible principled argument" exactly why "we ought," as he says, "to accord special legal and moral treatment to religious practices."[15] He does not believe any

---

[12] Hamilton, *God vs. the Gavel*, 297.
[13] Ibid., 297.
[14] Laycock, "Syllabus of Errors," 1173.
[15] Leiter, *Why Tolerate Religion?*, 7.

such argument can be made and spends much of the book telling us why. To be sure, he is willing to tolerate religion, but that has nothing to do with religion as such, nor does it mean that religious practices should enjoy any special exemptions.

Religion should be tolerated because, like all beliefs about what people take to be good and how they should live – whether the beliefs are religious or not – individuals are best left free to decide and, within limits, to act on their decisions. State interference in such matters, except where compelling public interests are at stake, is bad for individuals and for society. Thus, good laws ought to protect equally as much "private space" as possible consistent with public order, and that includes making room for religion. That is true, says Leiter, whether one follows Rawls or Mill, apparently assuming that theirs are the only positions worth considering.

But however favorable Leiter is toward equally tolerating religion as one set of beliefs among many in a pluralistic society, there is cause, on an initial reading, for concern. First, for him the key defining characteristic of religious belief is "insulation from evidence and reasons" as understood by common sense and science,[16] something that is not, in his view, especially laudable. Consequently, although religion is due minimal respect, as are all beliefs about what is good and how life should be lived, it has no right to be considered intrinsically valuable. Some believers are virtuous, others vicious, but the ratio of virtue to vice in any given situation is variable and unpredictable. Leiter does worry that his disparaging view of religion might lead a society, like France, to demean or disadvantage religious groups, but thinks that can be prevented by doing something France ought to do: adopt religiously neutral laws consistent with a commitment to "principled toleration." I must say, in passing, that despite Leiter's reassurances, I continue to worry that the inability to find *anything* of general value in religion might, in fact, lead to demeaning and disadvantaging religion.

Second, he considers whether religion might gain some special protection by being tied to the idea of conscience, though he emphasizes, again and again, that it is *conscience,* inclusively understood, *not* religion as such, that would deserve protection. At one point, he celebrates the fact that nonreligious individuals across the world are now developing belief systems that "do not run any of the risks" associated with a "potentially harmful brew" of claims of conscience that are "insulated from evidence," in a way characteristic, he thinks, of religious believers.[17]

---

[16] Ibid., 34.
[17] Ibid., 62.

But putting aside his invidious reflections on religion, the bigger problem is that he appears, on the surface, to favor a "no exemptions approach" from neutral, generally applicable laws, even for conscience inclusively understood.[18] That is a startling proposal indeed. Among other reasons, it rests for Leiter on the difficulty courts have in figuring out what a claim of conscience amounts to once it is disconnected from religious belief, because religious claims "provide evidential proxies for conscience that are much easier for courts to assess."[19] This consideration troubles him. If conscientious exemptions should be honored, and religious claims are more easily identified than nonreligious claims, then, despite all his efforts, religion would, ironically, wind up getting favored treatment after all!

In fact, however, Leiter, like Sullivan and Hamilton before him, does not consistently follow through. Very much in passing and in what I would call a distinct whisper, Leiter makes a huge concession: "[I]t is possible," he says, "that a scheme of universal exemptions for [inclusive] claims of conscience, with suitable evidential standards, might do well enough to blunt the inequality objection. In that event, the inequality of treatment of claims of conscience is not *necessarily* fatal to a scheme of universal exemptions of conscience."[20]

Notice what is being said: A scheme of universal exemptions for conscience is acceptable so long as "suitable evidential standards" are applied without discrimination to both religious and nonreligious people alike, and as Leiter has told us, we most readily find out what those standards are by considering religious expressions of conscience. Because, on his own account, religious expressions of conscience turn out to be a crucial source of "suitable evidential standards" for conscience, Leiter has given us, quite inadvertently, an additional reason to "tolerate religion" and perhaps even to value it!

For those of us who believe in the validity and importance of granting exemptions from neutral, generally applicable laws for both religious and nonreligious conscience, consistent with protecting compelling public goods, we may conclude from this review of Sullivan, Hamilton, and Leiter that the bark of these three self-styled opponents is worse than their bite.

The results of this examination certainly do not prove once and for all that conscience – profoundly connected, but not limited to religious belief – has, after all, a right to legal deference, because we have hardly canvassed all possible objections. But it is interesting that in these three cases, at least, well-known experts in the field find it very difficult, no matter how hard they try, to escape the grip of these powerful ideas.

---

[18] Ibid., 115, 132.
[19] Ibid., 95.
[20] Ibid., 99; original emphasis.

No doubt we should be troubled by the flashy, ominous-sounding objections with which the three authors open their books. They are the things that will grab the headlines and will likely reinforce growing, if unexamined, suspicion in the United States toward special protection for religion. But in the long run the best antidote – employed here – is to follow scrupulously the arguments of all three books, always holding the authors to account. Far from strengthening the opposition, such a procedure will show, I believe, how resilient our tradition actually is.

Not that the proffered challenges fall completely flat. Working through the challenges forces us to face up to and rethink some remaining problems. One is identifying and developing "suitable evidential standards" for conscience, inclusively understood. It is clear that stretching the defining features of conscience to cover an expanding array of claims is likely to make it hard to be certain that standards are in every case being applied consistently and fairly.

For Leiter a claim of conscience means a moral imperative (above and beyond "crass self-interest") "central to one's integrity as a person, [and] to the meaning of life,"[21] an interesting proposal, but one that obviously calls for further consideration. We may also infer from Sullivan's passing suggestions that conscience might mean being "obedient to a rule outside of oneself and one's government, whether that rule is established by God, or otherwise." However we work out the definition, it will remain highly abstract. All the same, this is hardly the first time the law has faced the difficulty of applying abstract principles to widely different circumstances.

A second problem is raised by Hamilton: whether the courts or the legislatures should be entrusted with the responsibility of balancing harms related to the protection of conscience. I agree with Laycock that one thing Hamilton *does* achieve, however inadvertently, is to provide sufficient reason for doubting that legislatures are exclusively competent in these matters.

---

[21] Ibid., 95.

7

Religion and Human Rights

A Personal Testament*

The subject of religion and human rights is something in which I have more than academic or professional interest. It is true I have invested considerable time and energy to the question throughout my scholarly life. In recent years, I have paid special attention to the more practical aspects – namely, the degree to which states and other actors have actually complied with the standards of religious freedom and equality enshrined in the international human rights documents. At the same time, I have come to see that my efforts in this area are not "value-free"; in fact, they express a deeper worldview that, for better or worse, I hold and am pleased to avow. In this chapter I attempt to lay out the sources and features of that worldview.

As it happens, I am a committed Presbyterian layman and have served at various times as an officer in that church. That means I stand in what is known as the "Reformed" tradition of Protestant Christianity, which stems from

---

* This address was composed and delivered while I was still employed by the United States Institute of Peace, and it reflects only my views and not necessarily those of the institute. It was originally presented at the University of Richmond Law School, November 4, 1998, while I was still a resident of Washington, DC. Though the following prefatory comment no longer obtains, it was included in the original text and conveys my sentiments on the delicate question of publicly discussing religious views while in government service. As such it is, perhaps, of wider interest:

> It is very gratifying to be invited, as I have been on this occasion, to discuss my personal theological perspective on the question of religion and human rights Of course, it is, as a rule, neither seemly nor fitting for employees of the United States government, such as I am, to go around trumpeting their personal religious convictions. In a religiously pluralistic society like ours, it is better for public officials to find, where possible, a language of common cause. At the same time, there is, and ought to be, nothing secret or shameful about the personal religious dispositions of government employees, and, so long as the setting where they are discussed is fair and open (as this one surely is), there ought to be opportunities to exhibit and scrutinize those dispositions publicly.

Originally published in the *Journal of Law and Religion*, vol. xviii, no. 1 (2002).

the sixteenth-century French theologian and religious leader, John Calvin (1509–1564). Calvin's general approach is summarized by the motto, *ecclesia reformata semper reformanda* – "the church reformed, ever reforming." Those words signal Calvin's strong concern for church life and organization, both as an expression of Christian commitment and as a model for social and political life. Moreover, the motto implies Calvin's characteristic emphasis on the obligation of Christians to act out their beliefs in institutional and practical ways.

It was emphases such as these, in addition to some much-disputed doctrines concerning "predestination," the sovereignty of God, supremacy of scripture, and the civil enforcement of Reformed orthodoxy, that set Calvin and his followers at odds with Roman Catholics of the day, as well as with other Protestant reformers, such as Martin Luther. Some of these predilections, including the way he implemented them, were responsible for giving Calvin what may charitably be called a controversial reputation.

During the latter part of the sixteenth century, the Calvinist movement gathered momentum, spreading throughout northern Europe to other parts of Switzerland and to Germany, Holland, France, and Great Britain. Among other things, it had an important impact on seventeenth-century European colonial expansion, reaching far-flung places like the American middle colonies and South Africa (with some notorious consequences) via the Dutch, and the American colonies in New England via the British.

In my own case, the Puritan ancestors on my father's side settled in a town near Boston, Massachusetts, in the 1640s, and their descendants proceeded to fan out across what became the United States and to produce a prodigious number of Calvinist clergy, right up to the present. My father, recently deceased at age 100, was a Presbyterian clergyman, as were his father and four preceding generations before him, and as are several of my father's immediate descendants and near relatives. (When I once declared my own intention to become a Presbyterian minister – a declaration I never made good on – my father remarked that our family is in a rut!)

In Great Britain and eventually in America, Reformed Christians, known unflatteringly as "Puritans," split up into several subgroups over controversies about theology, church order, and the proper relation of the church to the state. As one of those subgroups, Presbyterians took their name from the Greek New Testament word, *presbyteros*, meaning "elder"; thus, Presbyterians are a church "ruled by elders." On the basis of Calvin's preference for a kind of democracy, elders came eventually to be elected by each local church; representatives were then selected from among those officials, and they in turn were delegated to an ascending series of governing bodies. The system of church governance thus came to include a local "presbytery," a regional "synod," and a national "general assembly."

Accordingly, Presbyterians pride themselves on having been early proponents of representative democracy in both church and state, and there is some truth in that belief. At the same time, it should not be forgotten that in seventeenth-century England, Presbyterians were not unfairly regarded as staunch reactionaries who wanted – against the will of many – to force their church on the whole country, as they had already succeeded in doing in Scotland. The campaign to accomplish that end in the 1640s failed because of the resistance of fellow Calvinists (as well as non-Calvinists), some of whom favored a more liberal brand of democracy in church and state and a more pluralistic social order than did the English Presbyterians.

In America, Reformed Christianity, including the Presbyterian Church, has exhibited a similar pattern of internal division and tension. In the American Civil War, for example, Presbyterians, along with other churches, split over the question of slavery. Even today, Presbyterians are deeply divided into "liberal" and "conservative" wings, in part over questions of homosexuality and the role of women in the church, but also over broader theological, scriptural, and political issues.

I mention this contentious background because it provides the context within which my own Christian faith and many of my professional interests, including my devotion to human rights, have been negotiated. "Negotiated" is very much the right word. Ever since I was an adolescent struggling with questions of religious belief, I have been in dialogue with my tradition. I first became acquainted with it, of course, in my home and then at a Presbyterian school from which I graduated – the College of Wooster in Wooster, Ohio. I studied the tradition more closely at Union Theological Seminary in New York City, and more fully still at Harvard University, where I pursued a doctorate in Christian ethics and sociology of religion. At Harvard, I produced a dissertation that modified and partially defended Max Weber's famous essay, *The Protestant Ethic and the Spirit of Capitalism*.[1] Weber's thesis was that Calvinist Puritanism in England and America made a decisive contribution to the rise of modern capitalist society.[2]

In many ways, my entire educational career was an exchange, and sometimes a debate, with the Puritan tradition from which I came. Nor did things change

---

[1] The dissertation was published as David Little, *Religion, Order, and Law: A Study in Pre-Revolutionary England* (Harper & Row 1969), and was republished in 1984 by the University of Chicago Press.
[2] Max Weber, *The Protestant Ethic and the Spirit of Capitalism* (New York: Scribner, 1958).

after I completed my formal education. I have tried ever after to decide which parts of the tradition I could and which parts I could not accept. The process of negotiation is still going on. In what follows, I sketch out how that process has proceeded and draw some conclusions about the subject before us, religion and human rights in relation to my own religious beliefs.

THE AMBIGUITY OF CALVINISM

As I have suggested, Calvinism, throughout its 460-year history, is a deeply equivocal movement. In my view, there is much that is repulsive in the tradition, but also much that is highly appealing. The trick is to separate the one from the other.

Oversimplifying somewhat, I divide Calvinism into reactionary and liberal tendencies, and briefly characterize each of them. Then I indicate where I stand and why. As might be suspected, I favor the "liberal tendencies" and identify myself with them. In fact, they constitute the framework of my own religious faith, as well as the ultimate basis of my commitment to human rights.

I emphasize that this classification *is* oversimplified, primarily because the ideas and actions of the principal figures in the tradition, including John Calvin, do not always stay put. These ideas and actions can be caught shifting back and forth between reactionary and liberal tendencies, both because of the circumstances in which the figures found themselves and because of the nature of the ideas being espoused. Those ideas are open-ended and subject to different and conflicting interpretations, which produces a tradition that is both dynamic and unstable. To distinguish the wheat from the chaff is no easy task. At the same time, I have no doubt that these conflicting tendencies are present and do constitute basic elements in the tradition.

Reactionary Tendencies

Calvin, along with his Puritan descendants, has generally acquired a bad reputation in popular and academic culture. One thinks of Nathaniel Hawthorne's description in the introduction of his book, *Mosses from an Old Manse*, in which he pictures the once gloomy walls of the manse's study "made still blacker," as he puts it, "by the grim prints of Puritan ministers that hung around."[3] Puritans are imagined as a uniformly disagreeable and censorious

---

[3] Nathaniel Hawthorne, *Mosses from an Old Manse* (New York: Hurst & Co., 1850), 7. Hawthorne goes on: "These worthies looked strangely like bad angels – or, at least, like

lot, inconsolably distressed, as the saying goes, by the thought that someone somewhere might be happy.

This image is, alas, not altogether mistaken. Calvin himself presided over a Geneva that was in many ways severely repressive of both thought and action. He created a supervisory body known as the Consistory, whose business it was to snoop around all over town rooting out unorthodox belief and lax moral behavior, and to haul offenders before a magistrate to receive what Calvin and other town leaders believed to be their just (and sometimes quite harsh) deserts.

And who can forget the infamous public burning of Michael Servetus for heresy on October 27, 1553? That verdict was the result of a civil trial in Geneva in which the public prosecutor was none other than John Calvin himself. Moved by a certain amount of pity, Calvin unsuccessfully advocated execution by sword rather than burning, but he entertained no doubts whatsoever about the propriety of capital punishment in this case. Servetus's heretical views concerning the Trinity were taken, among other things, as a severe threat to public order.

It is sometimes claimed that the significance of the burning of Servetus has been exaggerated.[4] The event was, to be sure, something of an exception; there are no other unambiguous examples of heresy executions in Calvin's career. What is more, Calvin did not suppress all forms of what he would regard as heretical or questionable literature. The Qur'an was tolerated during his time, as were various classical Roman writings, which were anything but orthodox in faith or morals.

As a matter of fact, Calvin did, in theory, have a rather robust view of the freedom of conscience and of the separation of what he called the "spiritual power" and the "power of the sword."[5] He sharply distinguished between an "inner forum," or conscience, and an "outer forum," or civil authority, and from time to time emphatically spoke of these as "two worlds, over which different kings and different laws have authority."[6] As a consequence, he asserted, the two spheres must "always be examined separately,"[7] even when, he went on, "the

---

men who had wrestled so continually and so sternly with the devil that somewhat of his sooty fierceness had been imparted to their own visages."

[4] See most recently Marilynne Robinson, *The Death of Adam: Essays on Modern Thought* (Boston: Houghton Mifflin, 1998), 200.

[5] *Calvin: Institutes of the Christian Religion* (2 vols.) bk. 4, ch. XI, § 8, 1220 (John T. McNeill ed., Ford Lewis Battles trans., Library of Christian Classics vols. XX–XXI, Philadelphia: Westminster Press 1960); see ibid., 1220 n. 15.

[6] Ibid., bk. 3, ch. XIX, § 15, 847–848.

[7] Ibid.

whole world was shrouded in the densest darkness of ignorance, this tiny little spark of light remained, that recognized [human] conscience to be higher than all human judgments."[8] As we shall see, this doctrine of the sovereignty of conscience was to have important consequences for later Calvinism and for those societies that were touched by its influence. In fact, this belief may have worked to modify somewhat Calvin's record of persecution, at least as compared with more unrelenting patterns of abuse, such as those associated with the Catholic Inquisition.

Nevertheless, Calvin had an infuriating habit of taking away with one hand what he had given with the other. That was his reactionary side. Having affirmed the centrality and importance of the sovereignty of conscience and of protecting that sovereignty from the interference of the "outward forum," Calvin turned right around and instructed the city of Geneva to enforce coercively "the outward worship of God" and to defend by the same means "sound doctrine of piety and the position of the church."[9] Or, again, having declared unmistakably that the "church does not have the right of the sword to punish or to compel, not the authority to force, not imprisonment, nor the other punishments, which the magistrate commonly inflicts,"[10] he nevertheless conspired with the Genevan authorities to enforce in numerous ways the doctrines and scriptural interpretations of the Reformed church.

And, although the public burning of Servetus may have been the only pure example of a heresy execution in Calvin's career, there were nevertheless other troubling cases, fully supported by Calvin, such as an instance of banishment for heresy[11] and one of beheading for a combination of blasphemy and sedition.[12] Still worse, from 1543 to 1545, more than twenty victims were publicly burned as witches with Calvin's acquiescence.

The same inconsistency concerns Calvin's belief in a universal moral law, which to his mind is applicable to and obligatory on all human beings,

---

[8] Ibid., bk. 4, ch. X, § 5, 1183; cf.: "human laws, whether made by magistrate or by church, even though they have to be observed (I speak of good and just laws), still do not of themselves bind the conscience." Ibid., 1184.

[9] Ibid., bk. 4, ch. XX, § 2, 1487.

[10] Ibid., bk. 4, ch. XI, § 3, 1215.

[11] Jerome Bolsec, an ex-Carmelite monk, was banished in 1551 for denouncing Calvin's doctrine of predestination. See John T. McNeill, *The History and Character of Calvinism* (Oxford: Oxford University Press, 1954), 172.

[12] In 1547 Jacques Gruet, a member of an anti-Calvin Genevan family, was beheaded in part at least for holding what were regarded as blasphemous views, though charges that he was involved in a seditious plot may also have influenced the decision; see Francois Wendel, *Calvin: The Origins and Development of His Religious Thought*, Philip Mairet trans. (New York: Harper & Row, 1963), 87.

regardless of culture or religion. Again, Calvin distinguished between two areas of human experience: the order of "higher things" (strictly religious matters) and the order of the "things of this life" (the moral and civil sphere). This distinction, Calvin thought, corresponds to the two tables of the Decalogue, namely, the "religious" commandments (1–4), and the "moral" commandments (5–10). What he called the "light of reason" or "universal impressions of a certain civic fair dealing and order," to which all human beings had natural access, apply to the moral table, but not to the religious.[13] Human reason was, Calvin believed, more severely corrupted in religious than in moral matters.

Theoretically, at least, the "power of the sword" applies to the moral sphere, but *not* to the religious. Physical force is capable, up to a point, of effectively restraining and punishing violence and arbitrary injury, which represent a persistent and fundamental threat to the universal moral order and recurring evidence of which indelibly marks the "fallen condition" of all humanity. However, applying physical force to the "inner forum," the conscience, and to the "things of the spirit," thereby attempting to compel religious belief, only distorts and deforms the spirit. Such enlightened ideas might – and, in the hands of others, actually did – provide the foundation for a liberal theory of religious freedom and tolerance. But that was not true, for the most part, in Calvin's case.

Again, having emphatically affirmed these ideas in theory, Calvin frequently turned his back on them in practice, disregarding the implications that would have permitted all people freedom to believe and practice as they were disposed so long as they observed the basic requirements of a common moral law. In direct contradiction to such ideas, Calvin proceeded to inspire in many followers in Switzerland, France, Germany, England, Scotland, and colonial America the very impulses to authoritarianism and coercive repression of religious dissent for which the Calvinist legacy is unfortunately famous.

This outcome was no doubt heavily influenced by the strength of Calvin's own personality, which was unmistakably marked by an "authoritarian character."[14] Calvin became increasingly convinced that "he was acting solely by virtue of a divine mission" and therefore "did not admit discussion of his ideas – especially not about dogmatic principles, but not even about matters of personal opinion, sometimes of only the smallest importance."[15]

---

[13] *Calvin: Institutes*, bk. 2. ch. II, § 13, 272–273.
[14] Wendel, *Calvin*, 82.
[15] Ibid.

Liberal Tendencies

In the words of Lord Acton, Calvin's goal "was to create not a new church, but a new world, to remodel not doctrine only, but society,"[16] and one of the most important results of his efforts was to check "the reigning idea that nothing limits the power of the State."[17] Having so eloquently enunciated the two fundamental principles – the sovereignty of conscience and the existence of a universal moral law that is prior to and relatively independent of religious belief – even Calvin could not successfully inoculate all his followers against the radical implications of these principles. Thus, in addition to the reactionary side, there is, as I suggested earlier, an important liberal strand of thought – frequently a minority view, but no less powerful – that began to embrace the revolutionary potential of Calvin's two principles. This liberal strand of thought and action thereby paved the way for many of the human rights ideas we affirm today.

As Max Weber understood so acutely, sometimes in spite of itself Calvinism turned out to be a powerful social, political, and economic influence, especially in England and the United States. In particular, the two principles, sovereignty of conscience and an independent moral law, came to have an important impact in these countries.[18] The story is complicated and so must here be reduced to a brief sketch.[19]

---

[16] Lord Action, *Lectures on Modern History* (New York: Meridian Books, 1961), 132.
[17] Ibid., 136.
[18] In what is otherwise a provocative and original collection of essays, Marilynne Robinson surrenders, unfortunately, to a one-sided and uninformed interpretation of the writings of Max Weber, particularly his essay on the Protestant ethic. See Robinson, *The Death at Adam*, 23–24, 180–181. As I contend in *Religion, Order, and Law*, Weber's treatment of Calvin and the Puritans *is* deficient in some ways, as are some of the details of his attempt to demonstrate the connection between Puritanism and the rise of modern capitalist society. However, with appropriate revision, based on a fuller and more sustained investigation of the theology and social thought of Calvin and the English Puritans, together with a careful analysis of the relevant economic and legal developments of the period, as well as a more nuanced and systematic deployment of Weber's own theoretical proposals, much of what Weber argued for in the essay on the Protestant ethic can after all be vindicated.

For compelling confirmation of Weber's basic insights regarding the connection between "ascetic Protestantism" and modern capitalism, see David Landes's magisterial volume on economic history, *The Wealth and Poverty of Nations: Why Some Are So Rich and Some So Poor* (New York: W.W. Norton & Co. 1998), especially 174–179. Weber's general perspective regarding the connection between culture and economic behavior in fact underlies Landes's whole approach. (Incidentally, there are also fascinating suggestions scattered throughout Landes's book regarding the important connection between religious tolerance and economic development, which demand further reflection and examination and which are related to some of the themes of this chapter.)

[19] For a fuller account, see David Little, *A Christian Perspective on Human Rights*, in Abdullahi Ahmed An-Na'im & Francis M. Deng, eds., *Human Rights in Africa: Cross-Cultural Perspectives* (Washington, DC: Brookings Institution, 1990), 59–103.

While Calvin was still alive, English Calvinists began applying his thought to politics with some important results. Explicating his belief in the inherent "rights of each individual" regarding matters of religion and conscience, as well as property, political participation, and civil resistance, Calvin's English followers began explicitly using the language of "natural rights."[20] These rights were understood to apply equally to each and every human being and, above all, to protect them against arbitrary government. The rights were "natural" in the sense that they were neither earned nor achieved, nor did they depend on any particular religious belief or affiliation. Moreover, they implied a civil order with extensive built-in restraints against abuse that could support the common benefit of all citizens in respect to religion, politics, law, and economic activity. In a word, the theory implied that force might permissibly be used only in keeping with moral constraints as defined by natural rights. Violations of these moral constraints by tyrannical governments justified, in extreme circumstances, duly restrained counterforce against them.

Just such resistance, justified accordingly, was what the Puritan armies led by Oliver Cromwell pitted against the "tyranny" of Charles I in the 1640s. The Puritans claimed that the Stuart monarchy had become grossly arbitrary, and thus thoroughly illegitimate, in part because it had systematically violated the natural rights of its citizens. In the name of restoring those rights, appeals to which had become widespread in the seventeenth century, the government needed first to be restrained by forceful means as necessary and thereafter to be drastically restructured.

To be sure, Cromwell's reforms, which lasted until 1660, did not by any stretch of the imagination amount to a liberal democratic order, though Cromwell himself harbored conflicting views about democracy and freedom of conscience that reflected the ambivalence of the Calvinist tradition.[21]

---

[20] There has been considerable misunderstanding of this usage in the scholarly literature; see ibid. especially 76–97 and, in particular, fns. 40, 41, and 82 for criticisms of Quentin Skinner, *The Foundations of Modern Political Thought* (2 vols.) (Cambridge: Cambridge University Press, 1978), and for criticisms of Richard Tuck, *Natural Rights Theories: Their Origin and Development* (Cambridge: Cambridge University Press, 1979). As I attempt to demonstrate, Skinner and Tuck (along with others like Jeffrey Stout who trade on their ideas) have rather seriously misrepresented the character and range of Calvinism regarding natural rights ideas and religion. See, also, David Little, "Calvin and Natural Rights," in *Political Theology* vol. 10, no. 3 (2009), 411–430, for an updated account of Calvin's connection to natural rights thinking.

[21] In addition to the other black marks attached to Cromwell's name, we may not forget the shameful record of his Irish campaign (1649–1650), which exhibits "his intention to extirpate the Roman Catholic religion, as far as it was practiced openly," as Robert S. Paul states in *The Lord Protector: Religion and Politics in the Life of Oliver Cromwell* (Grand Rapids: Eerdmans Publishing Co., 1964), 216. In justifying the indiscriminate slaughter and destruction, Cromwell, like other Puritans, invoked Old Testament precedents, reportedly saying that there

During and after the revolution, English Puritans fragmented into various parties – ranging from reactionary to very liberal. One of the extreme liberal parties, known as "the Levellers," drew up a series of remarkable draft constitutions in the latter 1640s – called "Agreements of the People" – favoring full-fledged constitutional democracy, with provisions for equality before the law, division of powers, judicial reform, the prohibition of religious tests for public office, and a revolutionary doctrine of the freedom of religion and conscience.

Leveller religious convictions recalled Calvin's distinction between the two tables of the law and between an "inner" and "outer forum." The inner sphere is guided by the spirit and "not by the sword," they declared. "For the sword pierceth the flesh; it toucheth but the outward man; it cannot touch the inward. Therefore, where a conversion is not obtained [by the spirit], there no compulsive power or force is to be used."[22]

And the Levellers significantly expanded on the Calvinist commitment to democratic governance, going beyond what Calvin himself intended. In the words of one member,

> For really I think that the poorest he that is in England hath a life to live, as the greatest he; and therefore truly, sir, I think it's clear, that every man that is to live under a government ought first by his own consent to put himself under that government; and I do think that the poorest man in England is not at all bound in a strict sense to that government that he hath not had a voice to put himself under.[23]

In addition to a commitment to democratic rights, Levellers and other radical Puritan sectarians of the period referred to additional human rights themes of the greatest importance today, such as economic and gender rights. Levellers and their confreres would not have understood the tendency in some circles these days to disparage human rights of an economic and social kind. One writer, having affirmed political and civil rights, including freedom of conscience, went on to declare that "every man of us, in duty to our own natures and to our native country," is justified in seeking

---

were "great occasions in which some men were called to great services, in the doing of which they were excused from the common rules of morality: such as the practices of Ehud and Jael, Samson and David: and by this they fancied they had a privilege from observing standing rules" (cited at ibid., 217).

[22] Richard Overton, *An Appeal from the Commons to the Free People* (1647), in A. S. P. Woodhouse, ed., *Puritanism and Liberty: Being the Army Debates (1647–9) from the Clarke Manuscripts with Supplementary Documents* (Chicago: University of Chicago Press, 1951), 323, 332.

[23] *The Putney Debates*, in Woodhouse, *Puritanism and Liberty*, 53.

the recovery of our natural human rights and freedoms, that all orders, sorts, and societies of the natives of this land may freely and fully enjoy a joint and mutual neighborhood, cohabitation, and human subsistence, it being against the radical law of nature and reason that any man should be deprived of a human subsistence, that is not an enemy thereto.[24]

As to the reform of gender relations, sectarian women of the time attacked "their limited educational opportunities, their confinement to domestic duties, [and] their subjection to their husbands."[25] In line with radical appeals to equal rights in the affairs of church and government, these women and their supporters advocated full equality in marriage:

> During the [Puritan Revolution] and Interregnum the very foundations of the old patriarchal family were challenged. [26]

> [O]nce the religious sanction was taken away or weakened, then the whole society was subject to challenge and re-scrutiny from a new point of view – that of reason, natural right, popular consent and common interest. The Leveller principle that men and women were born free and equal and could only be governed by their own consent had implications for the family as well as for society in general.[27]

One other Puritan who emerged out of "the seed-ground" of Calvinism,[28] was active during and after the Puritan Revolution, and who had a particularly important influence on the liberal tradition in America was Roger Williams. Williams was certainly a Calvinist, though a rather deviant one. He was committed in his way to the doctrines of predestination, supremacy of scripture, and sovereignty of conscience and to the idea of popular participation in church and government, but he interpreted some of these doctrines and ideas in radical ways. For example, Williams argued that if God were indeed the sole author of election, then (contrary, certainly, to Calvin's practice in Geneva) God's authority ought to be allowed to operate freely and thus without any interference from the civil magistrate.

Williams pushed Calvin's ideas of sovereignty of conscience and the separation of civil and ecclesiastical authority to the limit. In his hands, those ideas implied a system of extensive religious freedom, which Williams, at considerable personal cost, openly advocated in colonial Massachusetts in the 1630s.

---

[24] Overton, in Woodhouse, *Puritanism and Liberty*, 333.
[25] Keith Thomas, *Women and the Civil War Sects*, 13 *Past & Present* (April 1958), 42, 55.
[26] Ibid., 55.
[27] Ibid., 54.
[28] "Calvinism [is] itself, the main seed-ground of the Puritan movement," Woodhouse, *Puritanism and Liberty*, 36.

His more reactionary Congregationalist colleagues, John Cotton and John Winthrop, responded by expelling him, and thereby causing him to find his way to what became the colony of Rhode Island where he managed against great odds to establish "the first commonwealth in modern history to make religious liberty a cardinal principle of its corporate existence and to maintain the separation of church and state on these grounds."[29]

How remarkable and groundbreaking an innovation his achievement was cannot be overstated:

> The trouble with welcoming everyone to a haven of religious liberty was that, sooner or later, everyone came. Baptists arrived early....
>
> Anglicans also arrived [later, after Williams's death]. Though [Williams] strongly disagreed with and often denounced them, he would not have prevented their worship. Congregationalists appeared about the same time, too late to permit Williams the irony of a public welcome as opposed to a public trial. Jews emigrated while Williams was still alive, no doubt giving much satisfaction to one who had complained about the 'incivilities and inhumanities' of England against them [and had declared the need] to make way "for their free and peaceable Habitation among us." And many others came to Rhode Island seeking only to escape religion, not to embrace it...
>
> Liberty of conscience brought them all, but in largest numbers it brought the Quakers.[30]

So radical was his commitment to religious liberty that, in the name of tolerance and inclusiveness, Williams resolutely declined to evangelize Native Americans because, among other reasons, "[f]orced coercion was no conversion at all," as one biographer puts it.[31] "To have dominant cultures or powerful nations determine the religion of a powerless people was [in Williams's mind] to learn absolutely nothing from the history of the ancient or the European world."[32]

CONTEMPORARY HUMAN RIGHTS THINKING

There continues to be the dominant belief that modern human rights thinking is the consequence primarily of the European Enlightenment. That is

---

[29] Sydney E. Ahlstrom, *A Religious History of the American People* (New Haven, CT: Yale Univsersity Press, 1972), 182.
[30] Edwin S. Gaustad, *Liberty of Conscience: Roger Williams in America* (Grand Rapids, MI: Eerdmans Publishing Co., 1991), 175–176.
[31] Ibid., 30.
[32] Idid.

supposed to mean that human rights are, among other things, antagonistic to religion. These conclusions are mistaken in three ways.

First, the Enlightenment itself was hardly "one thing." There are important differences, especially between the British and French versions, when it comes to the relation of religion and state.

Second, as I have been hinting, the notion of human rights – namely, *the existence of subjective claims, regarded as inborn and unearned, that are antecedent to and independent of governmental authority and that ascribe to individuals a legitimately enforceable moral title or warrant to constrain the behavior of others as regards inhibiting the exercise of conscience, political participation or the control of property, or inflicting arbitrary injury* – goes back well before the European Enlightenment of the eighteenth century. If my preceding suggestions are correct, the Calvinist tradition, which antedates the Enlightenment by one-and-a-half centuries, is crucial, although it is, of course, but one part of a much older tradition of natural rights.[33]

Third, although a careful reading of John Locke's writings themselves should have dispelled stubborn beliefs that the rights he stood for are militantly secular, the grounds for those convictions collapse completely once Locke's brand of "Enlightenment ideology" is located historically.

Locke, who is properly thought of as one of the central philosophical sources of modern views of human rights, needs to be seen squarely as an heir of the Calvinist tradition. There can be little doubt that "Locke's *Two Treatises of Government* [is] the classic text of radical Calvinist politics."[34] And recent scholarship makes abundantly clear that Locke's influential doctrines of natural rights to conscience and the "separation of church and state," as well as to property, civil resistance, and to political participation and democratic governance, are both inconceivable apart from the Calvinist legacy and are more sympathetic to the integrity of religious commitment than is conventionally understood, precisely when they are read in the light of that legacy.[35]

---

[33] See the writings of Brian Tierney; for example, *Religious Rights: An Historical Perspective*, in John Witte, Jr. & Johan D. van der Vyver, eds., *Religious Human Rights in Global Perspective: Religious Perspectives* (The Hague: Martinus Nijhoff Publishers, 1996), 17.

[34] Skinner, *The Foundations of Modern Political Thoughts*, vol. 2, 239.

[35] See Little, *supra* n. 17. *Cf.* Richard Ashcraft, *Revolutionary Politics & Locke's "Two Treatises of Government"* (Princeton, NJ: Princeton University Press, 1986), for an emphasis, on the connection between the Levellers and Locke (149–165). *See* Ashcraft's important, but partially misguided, essay, "Religion and Lockean Natural Rights," in Irene Bloom, J. Paul Martin, and Wayne L. Proudfoot, eds., *Religious Diversity and Human Rights* (New York: Columbia University Press, 1996), 195, and a brief response that is both appreciative and critical, in David Little. "Rethinking Human Rights: A Review Essay on Religion, Relativism, and Other Matters," 27.1 *Journal of Religious Ethics* 151, 167–168 (Spring 1999).

The very two principles that I have identified and that Locke also believed in – sovereignty of conscience and a universal moral law relatively independent of particular religious and cultural commitments – underlie contemporary human rights thinking and go some distance toward creating a hospitable environment for religion. Unless we see that, we cannot possibly make sense of existing human rights documents and the way they are currently being interpreted.

Both the language and the prevailing interpretation of the provisions for "freedom of conscience, religion or belief" have very little to do with the spirit of anticlericalism and suspicion of religion characteristic of the French Enlightenment and its resulting approach to questions of religion and state that has prevailed in France from the time of the revolution to the present.[36] On the contrary, authoritative interpretation of the right to the freedom of religion implies that religious and other fundamental beliefs represent *an exceptional limitation on the law* that entails special respect and protection. By suggesting, for example, that a right of conscientious objection may legitimately be derived from the provisions for freedom of religion and conscience, human rights jurisprudence can be said to reflect not a spirit of hostility or even indifference toward religion, but, in fact, an attitude of *deference* toward it.[37]

That interpretation illuminates the pervasive provisions in human rights law curtailing all forms of "coercion" that "would impair freedom to have or to adopt a religion or belief"[38] and, accordingly, calls attention to operative assumptions concerning the "separation of sword and spirit" and the "sovereignty of conscience."

As to the relevance of an idea of a common moral law, the Universal Declaration of Human Rights sets the standard by speaking in the Preamble of "the inherent dignity and of the equal and inalienable rights of all members of the human family"[39] and by claiming in Article 1 that "[a]ll human beings

---

[36] On a recent trip to France for the purpose of investigating the strong anti-sect/anti-cult position taken at present by the French government, I was told repeatedly that the persistence of the "laicist" or anticlerical tradition dating back to the French Revolution causes French people, and especially the government, to look with great apprehension on expressions of religious fervency, such as the sects and new religious movements represent, particularly if they seem to be exerting significant public influence.

[37] *See* David Little, "Studying 'Religious Human Rights': Methodological Foundations," in Johan D. van der Vyver & John Witte, Jr., eds., *Religious Human Rights in Global Perspective: Legal Perspectives* (The Hague: Martinus, Nijhoff Publishers, 1996), 45, 50–52.

[38] International Covenant on Civil and Political Rights, Article 18.2 (Dec. 16, 1966), U.N.T.S. 171, 999.

[39] Universal Declaration of Human Rights preamble (Dec. 10, 1948), U.N.G.A. Res. 217 A(III) <http://www.un.org/Overview/rights/html> (accessed on Mar. 23, 2002).

are born free and equal in dignity and rights." When these words are coupled with the statement, again in the Preamble, that "disregard and contempt for human rights have resulted in barbarous acts which have outraged the conscience of mankind,"[40] there can be no doubt that the terminology rests on a moral understanding favoring the universal validity and application of human rights.

Add to that the centrality in human rights literature of the principle of nondiscrimination. According to Article 2 of the Universal Declaration (which is reaffirmed in all subsequent instruments), "*Everyone* is entitled to all the rights and freedoms set forth in this Declaration, *without distinction of any kind*, such as race, colour, sex, language, *religion*, political or other opinion, *national or social origin*, property, *birth or other status.*"[41] This language appears conclusively to exclude any special religious, national, or cultural beliefs or status as a basis for being protected by or having access to human rights. Human beings are held to possess human rights and to be accountable and obligated to live up to them, *not* because they are Muslim, or Christian, or Buddhist, or Jewish, or Hindu, or a member of any particular religious or philosophical tradition. The whole point of human rights is that they are taken to be binding and available, regardless of any particular identity or conviction.[42]

WHERE I STAND

My religious faith is best understood in relation to the two principles I have identified throughout as those underlying human rights thinking: a common moral law and the sovereignty of conscience.

As to the common moral law, the longer one ignores concrete examples, the easier it is to sustain thoroughgoing beliefs in cultural relativism and other forms of particularism and skepticism that cast doubt on moral universals and human rights. But when such examples are considered, it becomes clear that those beliefs are mistaken. If we know anything, we know for sure that the genocidal slaughter or raping or expulsion of the sort witnessed during the Holocaust, or more recently in Bosnia, Kosovo, and Rwanda, is morally abhorrent in itself, no matter who does it, where, or on what pretext. Nor can there be any serious doubt that everyone ought to know that and may

---

[40] Ibid.
[41] Ibid., Article 2 (emphasis added).
[42] The above two paragraphs are taken, in modified form, from Little, "Rethinking Human Rights."

accordingly be held accountable for acting in violation of such knowledge. Nor, finally, can it be doubted that each individual subjected to treatment of that kind – no matter what his or her culture, religion, or ethnicity – possesses an inherent right *not* to be so treated and that, consequently, everyone thereby owns by birth a legitimately enforceable moral title to justify condemning and, if possible, resisting the infliction of that sort of arbitrary injury. In short, we cannot avoid the fact that we implicitly accept what can only be called a taboo or "sacred prohibition" against genocide and other gross forms of arbitrary injury.

Though there is, of course, more to be said about the grounds of human rights, this is for our purposes all we need to confirm St. Paul's conviction that human beings have a law "written on their hearts,"[43] according to which "the whole world may be held accountable."[44] That law is taken to be "inherent" and "inalienable" in the sense that it constitutes a prior and fixed constraint on human life. It is such a conviction, I believe, that undergirds the "human rights revolution" and ultimately disarms all forms of moral skepticism and relativism.

To the objection that, even if true, this conviction does not get us very far, I counter with three points. First, to be satisfied that there exists, after all, some kind of basic universal moral knowledge is in the present philosophical climate not incidental or trivial. Second, a clear lesson of the experience with fascism, state socialism, and ultranationalism is the realization that certain basic individual interests must never be allowed to be sacrificed to the doctrine of communal domination. Whatever concessions need to be made to the independence and integrity of minority and other communities, establishing protections against the abuse of individuals perpetrated in the name of collective ideals, such as was practiced by fascists and others, remains the ineradicable foundation of human rights. Third, experiments with communal domination that have afflicted the twentieth century also leave no doubt that human beings have by no means outgrown their obstinate and perverse proclivity for violating the sacred prohibition against genocide and other forms of arbitrary injury. They have simply expanded their technical aptitude for so doing.

There is a deep problem posed by moral knowledge of this kind that Reformed Christianity, in my opinion, answers commendably. It is that, however unwavering and intense our reaction against genocide and other

---

[43] *Rom* 2:15 (R.S.V.) [hereinafter, all biblical quotes refer to the Revised Standard Version Bible].
[44] Ibid., at 3:19.

intolerable forms of arbitrary injury, and however clearly that reaction seems to confirm our commitment to a taboo against such practices, on reflection, we appear to lack any equally secure understanding as to why we react the way we do or how we might go about explaining and defending the basis of such a reaction. We know something well enough, but we are uncertain why or how we know it.

Perhaps our reaction is, after all, simply the product of our upbringing, simply the result of a cultural bias we just happen to have inherited. There are, to be sure, all sorts of superstitious taboos. What is different about the taboo against genocide? Or, we ask ourselves, even if other cultures and religions have come to agree that genocide and other forms of gross arbitrary injury are morally abhorrent, what exactly does that prove except that several traditions happen to have agreed on something? The mere fact that a group of people (however large or small) concur that certain actions are right or wrong does not itself validate or invalidate those actions.

Or, perhaps thinkers like Freud and Nietzsche are correct that our most elemental moral convictions are the result of a pathological religious heritage – a grand illusion – from which, for the sake of our health, we must liberate ourselves. We may, in other words, begin to wonder whether our attachment to a "taboo" against arbitrary injury is rooted in psychological and social dispositions as unseemly and unflattering as are, according to Freud, our attachments to a taboo against incest.

Or, perhaps the sociobiologists are right that aversive reactions to arbitrary killing are "really" adaptive mechanisms that facilitate the survival of the species in some grand Darwinian sense. Possibly, it is simply a useful fiction for people to believe that they have "certain knowledge" that genocidal behavior is wrong because it keeps them playing their proper evolutionary role. Of course, if this account is true, then our aversive reactions lose their moral force, and we are deprived of our righteous indignation in face of the genocidal behavior of Nazism or ultranationalism. For then genocide is wrong only if perpetuating the human race is a good thing to do, and the question must be answered, why that is so? In other words, if the taboo against genocide depends on a prior belief in the desirability of human survival, the question then becomes what makes *that* belief compelling.

The problem with all such theories and explanations, as well as others we might mention,[45] is that, finally, they "reduce away" the essential character

---

[45] For example, versions of Pragmatism and Hobbesianism, some of which are widely influential these days.

of our primary moral reactions, such as our commitment to the taboo against genocide. A special virtue of religious positions, by contrast, is that they reinforce and undergird in one way or other the "sacredness" of our primary moral reactions – the sense of awe and immutability that accompanies those reactions – rather than undermining or distorting that sacredness. In that way, religious positions provide what is in my estimation a more convincing account of our real moral experience than the reductive approaches I have mentioned.

Reformed Christianity, in particular, gives high priority to the sacredness of the moral law. It might be argued, in fact, that a belief in a universal moral law that is prior or "given" is the linchpin of the entire system. Without "natural" or commonly available knowledge of the basic rights and obligations of human existence, for which human beings are assumed to be responsible, the central emphasis on human disobedience and transgression, which in turn evokes a compensating need for the restoration and rehabilitation of humanity, would not make sense. For it is the belief that human beings are profoundly impaired, spiritually and morally, and that they therefore need assistance to recover their moral and religious competence that lies at the heart of Reformed theology.

Assistance comes in two forms. Political assistance, including the possibility of coercion, is necessary up to a point to help restore competence by guiding and goading human beings to meet their fundamental moral responsibilities. These responsibilities are identified in the "second table" of the Decalogue and are spelled out more specifically as basic "natural" (human) rights, namely, provisions for protecting such things as conscience, property, and political participation and for ensuring freedom from tyranny. These rights certainly focus on political and civil matters and, especially among the liberal Calvinists, on constitutional democracy in state and church. However, the rights are not only civil and political; they also address issues of economic and gender equality. At bottom, the essential function of all these "natural" rights and duties is to prevent or restrain the infliction of arbitrary injury on any and all human beings.

Above and beyond political assistance, however, religious assistance is also required. Particularly for the liberal Calvinists, that form of assistance is distinctly noncoercive. It presupposes a "realm of freedom," a sphere of "sovereign conscience," where every person is at liberty to negotiate fundamental beliefs as it seems fitting to do. It is a place where beliefs and practices (so long as they do not violate the common moral law) are scrutinized and evaluated in accord with the "laws of the spirit," not the "laws of the sword." This way of thinking, of course, lays a foundation for the "freedom of conscience, religion, or belief," which underlies contemporary human rights thinking.

For the (liberal) Reformed Christian, the image of Jesus as a radical political innovator is at the heart of things. Repeatedly defying expectations as to what sort of messiah he was supposed to be, Jesus sets forth the revolutionary notion that his "kingship is not of this world"; if it were, he says, his followers would have fought to protect him.[46] Instead, his mission has no other objective than "to bear witness to the truth" and to perform that witness in a decidedly nonviolent, noncoercive way,[47] though that meant submitting himself to severe abuse – "even death on a cross."[48] The "truth" in question concerns human rehabilitation achieved through divine demonstrations of "mercy," "grace," and "forgiveness," which are intended to dissolve the barriers of hostility, defensiveness, and vengefulness that accompany and further entrench the disposition to violate and disobey the common law of humanity. As "gifts," they are in their nature uncoerced and voluntary; unless they are offered and received willingly, they lose their point.

The essential message of a liberal Calvinist like Roger Williams is thus that everyone should be left free to embrace the claim of truth I have described, or not to embrace it. If they reject the claim, people should be completely at liberty, without threat of violence or coercion, or other civil penalty or disadvantage, to choose any one of a myriad of alternative claims. This approach provides an arresting model of religious communication, one that by implication sharply restricts the coercive functions of the state and liberates a sphere of "religion and belief" where conscience is sovereign.

At the same time, if religion and morality are distinguished in the way this approach suggests, there are nevertheless at least four ways, on Calvin's understanding, in which, religious conviction "reaches out" and instructively supplements moral thought and practice. I myself affirm versions of all four convictions, and they might readily be applied to human rights thinking and practice.

First, even though basic moral knowledge is firmly implanted in the human heart, human beings try to find ways to avoid the imperative force of the moral law. People may claim, for example, that because we cannot on reflection really be sure there are any moral constants, such uncertainty excuses noncompliance with or indifference to the moral law. According to Calvin, the theological conviction that moral knowledge is part of the structure of the universe undergirds and reaffirms the bindingness of primary moral reactions. It dispels doubt and emboldens action "in the paths of righteousness."

---

[46] John 18:36.
[47] Id. at 18:37.
[48] Phil 2:8.

Second, religious conviction overcomes other sorts of doubt that can enfeeble moral commitment. When, Calvin says, we see the righteous

> laden with afflictions stricken with unjust acts, overwhelmed with slanders, wounded with abuses and reproaches; while the wicked on the contrary flourish, are prosperous, obtain repose with dignity and that without punishment, we must straightway conclude that there will be another life in which iniquity is to have its punishment, and righteousness its reward.[49]

Anticipating Kant, Calvin seems to be saying that if the moral law is part of the structure of the universe, and if profiting by victimizing the innocent is a violation of that law, it will be necessary to long for and to believe in a final vindication. If there is no confidence of that kind, then, in the ultimate sense, justice is a delusion and innocent suffering pointless. Whatever the details of a belief in eternal life, there must be some underlying conviction that cruelty and victimization are not the last word in the human story.

Third, religious knowledge for Calvin supplements moral insight in that it helps illuminate the task of applying general principles to specific circumstances. People, as a rule, are well aware of general moral principles (such as the wrongness of arbitrary injury), but things get less clear as one is required to put principles into practice. "The adulterer will condemn adultery in general, but will [forget that principle when it comes to] his own adultery."[50] For Calvin, the Bible and informed preaching can be of great assistance in guiding people in particular circumstances.

Fourth, religious conviction provides motivation for living up to the demands of morality in the face of weakness of will. People may at times know well enough what they are to do, but lack the "perseverance" to carry it out. Religious encouragement and "mutual counsel" in association with committed fellow believers are of great value at that point.

CONCLUSION

This account is one person's way of linking religion and human rights to personal religious commitment. It suggests that the liberal Calvinist tradition provides a particularly strong historical and theological foundation for a belief in human rights. At the same time, it can by its nature be nothing more than a recommendation. In the spirit both of liberal Calvinism and contemporary human rights understanding, fundamental beliefs in things such as

[49] *Calvin: Institutes*, bk. 1, ch. V, § 10, 62.
[50] Ibid., bk. 2, ch. II, § 23, 282.

the "foundations of human rights" or the "theological resources for human rights thinking," however fervently embraced, are nevertheless matters of "conscience, religion or belief" and as such are subject to the conditions of "the sovereignty of conscience" and the "laws of the spirit." Other people are clearly at liberty to propose alternative ideas, and it is hoped that resulting exchanges will contribute to the indispensable process of what Roger Williams called the "chewing and weighing" of fundamental beliefs.

PART III

Religion and the History of Rights

8

Religion, Peace, and the Origins of Nationalism[*]

INTRODUCTION: NATIONALISM AND THE LIBERAL PEACE

Nationalism is a matter of increasing interest to scholars of religion, conflict, and peace. An important reason is that in recent times so many lethal conflicts appear to involve religiously colored disputes over the boundaries and character of nation-states, as in the cases of Northern Ireland, the former Yugoslavia, Sri Lanka, Kashmir, Sudan, Nigeria, Iraq, and Israel-Palestine. Other countries, such as India and Egypt, were subject in the 1970s and 1980s to sectarian strife and executive assassination, with a potential for greater violence generated by appeals to one or another version of "religious nationalism."[1] At issue in all such cases is the make-up of the "nation" or "people" who control the state of a given territory. Religion plays a role by helping define national identity or "peoplehood," thereby influencing the ideals and values according to which the state is organized and legitimated. It turns out that the process by which nation and state coalesce and interact is fraught with political, economic, cultural, and territorial competition, and as a result, too frequently, with violent conflict.

Some students of the subject distinguish between two types of nationalism, "liberal" or "civic" and "illiberal" or "ethnic," as a way of tracking the connection between nationalism and peace.[2] They are advocates of what is known as

---

[*] I wish to thank Professor Atalia Omer for urging fuller attention to some of the criticisms of modern nationalism that exist in the literature, and Professor David Y. Kim for assistance in assembling invaluable source materials, particularly in regard to the discussion of Luther and the Anabaptists.
[1] See Scott W. Hibbard, *Religious Politics and Secular States: Egypt, India, and the United States* (Baltimore: Johns Hopkins University Press, 2010).
[2] Jack Snyder, *From Voting to Violence: Democratization and Nationalist Conflict* (New York: W.W. Norton & Co., 2000), 316–317. Edward D. Mansfield and Jack Snyder, *Electing to Fight: Why Emerging Democracies Go to War* (Cambridge, MA: MIT Press, 2005), and cf. Edward

"the liberal peace." They maintain that the orderly and properly sequenced development of robust liberal political and economic institutions is a critical condition of national and international peace,[3] whereas illiberal or ethnically exclusivist institutions increase the probability of violence.

According to Jack Snyder, violence is restrained by means of "thick versions of liberal or constitutional democracy," consisting "of an ample set of

---

D. Mansfield and Jack Snyder, "Democratic Transitions and War: From Napoleon to the Millennium's End," in Chester A. Crocker, Fen Osler Hampson and Pamela Aall, eds., *Turbulent Peace: The Challenges of Managing International Conflict* (Washington, DC: United States Institute of Peace Press, 2001), ch. 8; David Little, "Religion, Nationalism, and Intolerance," and some of the other essays in Timothy L. Sisk, ed., *Between Terror and Tolerance: Religious Leaders, Conflict, and Peacemaking* (Washington, DC: Georgetown University Press, 2011); David Little and Donald K. Swearer, eds., *Religion and Nationalism in Iraq: A Comparative Perspective* (Cambridge, MA: Harvard University Press, 2006) for a comparison of the dynamics of ethnoreligious nationalism in four postcolonial cases: Bosnia-Herzegovina, Sudan, Sri Lanka, and Iraq; and Scott Hibbard, *Religious Politics and Secular States*. Jurgen Habermas in "The European Nation-State: Its Achievements and Its Limits," in Gopal Balakrishnan, ed., *Mapping the Nation* (London: Verso, 1996), comes to similar conclusions using slightly different terminology.

In addition to studies drawing explicit connections between constitutional democracy, nationalism, and peace, there is a broad literature relating constitutional democracy and peace that is relevant to the literature on nationalism. Of special importance is a new collection of essays on the subject by Michael W. Doyle, *Liberal Peace: Selected Essays* (New York: Routledge, 2012). Doyle emphasizes that "democratic institutions" "promote peace and mutual respect among democratic peoples," "enhance human rights, produce higher levels of political participation, and decrease state repression," "serve to protect the mass of the population from state indifference during a natural disaster," and stimulate economic growth and inclusiveness, and that weak democratic institutions foster violence (202–203). Cf. 214–216, supporting the conclusion that "empirical confirmation of the liberal peace is exceptionally strong" (216) though also admitting both that further theoretical testing continues to be required (216) and that, although liberal states are generally peaceful among themselves, they are also guilty of bellicosity toward nonliberal states, as in the imperialist and colonialist wars of the nineteenth century (67). See, also, R. J. Rummel, *Power Kills: Democracy as a Model of Nonviolence* (New Brunswick, NJ: Transaction, 2004) and Morton H. Halperin, Joseph T. Siegle, and Michael M. Weinstein, *Democracy Advantage: How Democracies Promote Prosperity and Peace* (New York: Routledge, 2005). Examples of special relevance to nationalism are Ted Robert Gurr, *Peoples versus States: Minorities at Risk in the New Century* (Washington, DC: United States Institute of Peace Press, 2000); Gurr and Barbara Harff, *Ethnic Conflict in Global Politics* (Boulder, CO: Westview Press, 2004); Michael W. Doyle and Nicholas Sambanis, *Making War and Building Peace: United Nations Peace Operations* (Princeton, NJ: Princeton University Press, 2006); Larry Diamond, *The Spirit of Democracy: The Struggle to Build Free Societies throughout the World* (New York: Times Books, 2008); and Roland Paris, *At War's End: Building Peace after Civil Conflict* (New York: Cambridge University Press, 2004).

[3] Scholars such as Snyder, Mansfield, Gurr, and Paris, among others, emphasize the importance of "orderly development" or proper sequencing in the creation of liberal institutions. A disorderly transition from authoritarianism to democracy, where, for example, elections precede the creation of stable political, civil, and economic institutions, can greatly increase the likelihood of violence. "The rule seems to be: Go fully democratic, or don't go at all." Edward D. Mansfield and Jack Snyder, "Democratic Transitions and War," in Crocker, Hampson, and Aall, eds., *Turbulent Peace*, 124. Cf. Gurr, *Peoples versus States* and Paris, *At War's End*.

preconditions for a stable, productive, peaceful society": "a certain degree of wealth, the development of a knowledgeable citizenry, the support of powerful elites, and the establishment of a whole panoply of institutions to insure the rule of law and [equal] civic rights."[4] Similarly, Michael Doyle and Nicholas Sambanis, on the basis of their detailed study of conditions for successfully resolving civil war, conclude that "the rule of law and constitutional consent," including "a basic framework of rights and duties of citizens," are crucial foundations for durable peace.[5] By contrast, the presence of illiberal or ethnic nationalism, which "bases its legitimacy on common culture, language, religion, shared historical experience, and/or the myth of shared [ethnicity], and ... use[s] these criteria" as the exclusive basis for citizenship, engenders a high risk of violence of either an institutionalized sort, as in authoritarian systems, or outside institutional control, as in insurgencies and civil wars.[6]

A particularly important recent study highlights the urgency of protecting "a basic framework of rights and duties of citizens," and especially freedom of conscience, for the sake of peace. The study is by Brian J. Grim and Roger Finke and is called *The Price of Freedom Denied: Religious Persecution and Conflict in the Twenty-First Century*.[7] On the strength of a broad and rigorous empirical survey, the book reflects strong support for the liberal peace. It concludes that "to the extent that governments and societies restrict religious freedoms, physical persecution and conflict increase."[8]

To be sure, this typology of "liberal/civic" versus "illiberal/ethnic" nationalism has been challenged. Skeptics point out that national identity, even in the allegedly most "liberal" or "civic" of countries, such as the United States or France, "comes loaded with inherited cultural baggage that is contingent upon their peculiar histories," including a privileged language or religion, or a domineering ethnic group or economic class. In fact, the skeptics continue, "claims about ... authentic or original identity most often represent

---

[4] Snyder, *From Voting to Violence*, 316–317.
[5] Doyle and Sambanis, *Making War and Building Peace*, 340.
[6] Snyder, *From Voting to Violence*, 24 and 352–353. There is controversy among scholars over how important political, economic, and social grievances are in causing civil wars. One dissenter is Paul Collier, "Economic Causes of Civil Conflict and their Implications for Policy," in Crocker, Hampson, and Aall, eds., *Turbulent Peace*, where he defends his now-famous aphorism, "greed not grievance" (see 144ff.). For a critique of Collier's views and the similar views of other social scientists, see comments in the Introduction in David Little and Donald K. Swearer, eds., *Religion and Nationalism in Iraq: A Comparative Perspective* (Cambridge, MA: Harvard University Press, 2006), 5–6.
[7] Brian J. Grim and Roger Finke, *The Price of Freedom Denied: Religious Persecution and Conflict in the Twenty-First Century* (New York: Cambridge University Press, 2011).
[8] Ibid., 222.

ways of silencing debate about the interpretation of...complex and often contradictory cultural legacies."[9] In short, a national image advertised as liberal and civic typically conceals illiberal or ethnically preferential and economically unjust components.

A second criticism is that, if liberal or civic nationalism means a commitment to universal equal freedom, it is questionable how liberal a system of segmented, diversely populated nation-states can be in which each state has as its primary obligation favoring the interests of its own citizens.[10] The problem is both internal and external. Domestically, granting completely equal status to all the diverse cultural and social ideals is not feasible. Some degree of preference and ranking is unavoidable. As to the international aspect, even the most liberal nation-state thwarts the universal spread of equal freedom, politically and economically, to the extent it is called on, as it frequently is, to protect the security and welfare of its own citizens at the expense of others.

A third criticism challenges the coherence of the notion of religious freedom as a purported ingredient of the liberal peace by calling it "impossible" to define and apply without bias[11] and by arguing that legal and other attempts to do so inevitably produce perverse results.[12] The claim is that modern law bearing on religious freedom has typically favored privatized, individualistic, and voluntary, or "protestant," forms of religion, while disfavoring public, communal, and ascribed forms, conditions that are now supposed to be changing to some extent. In the United States, for example, it is asserted that the law increasingly privileges religious groups over nonreligious ones, creating a new kind of discrimination.[13] Beyond such claims, this line of attack calls into question the worth of a liberal order as such, including the rule of law and human rights standards in general.[14]

It needs to be stressed that, however arresting these criticisms are, they do not altogether refute the claims of the advocates of liberal peace. That is because

---

[9] Bernard Yack, "Myth of the Civic Nation," in Ronald Beiner, ed., *Theorizing Nationalism* (Albany: State University of New York Press, 1999), 106. Cf. Samuel P. Huntington, *Who Are We? The Challenges to America's National Identity* (New York: Simon & Schuster, 2004), 30ff.

[10] Judith Lichtenberg, "How Liberal Can Nationalism Be?" in Beiner, *Theorizing Nationalism*, ch. 9.

[11] Winifred Fallers Sullivan, *The Impossibility of Religious Freedom* (Princeton: Princeton University Press, 2005). See Chapter 6 for a critique of Sullivan's book.

[12] Winifred Fallers Sullivan, "Religious Freedom and the Rule of Law: Exporting Modernity in a Postmodern World? (HeinOnline – 22 *Mississippi College Law Review* 173 (2002–2003), 181ff.

[13] Winifred Fallers Sullivan, "The Conscience of Contemporary Man:" Reflections on *U.S. v. Seeger* and *Dignitatis Humanae*," *U.S. Catholic Historian* 24: 107–123 (Winter 2006), 119–123.

[14] See Chapter 1, fn. 5.

those claims rest on extensive evidence showing that *relative* differences in the incidence of liberal or illiberal attributes in given nation-states in fact match important variations in the probability of peace or violence, duly defined and measured. Any successful refutation would have to expose flaws in the procedures and conclusions of such studies.

Still, even if the data generally hold up as claimed (a not unimportant conclusion), there is merit to some of the criticisms. To establish that, as with any ideal type, boundaries distinguishing one type from another are usually more porous, more subject to cross-boundary "slippage" in the real world than is often admitted, could be significant for the study of peace. Acknowledging that nationalism by nature incorporates illiberal or ethnically exclusive and economically unjust elements serves at once to dispel complacency and intensify attentiveness to the lurking sources of antagonism and grievance that provoke violence.

The same is true of efforts to resolve political, economic, cultural, and territorial contests within the nation-state, as well as conflicts between national and international obligations outside it. Acute awareness of the difficulty of finding equitable compromises to the daunting "dilemmas of nationalism" would appear to be the beginning of wisdom. It could inspire new, imaginative ways of negotiating and accommodating peacefully and as justly as possible the congeries of interests and obligations characteristic of modern nation-states. Even the general charges against liberalism, including the rule of law and the right to religious freedom and other human rights, might generate sensitivity to legal and political blind spots and to inadvertent forms of discrimination. Whether the benefits extend beyond that remains to be seen.

JUSTPEACE: AN ALTERNATIVE?

It is such considerations as these that underlie a broader critique of the liberal peace associated with the concept *justpeace*. The concept involves a notion of "strategic peacebuilding" that is "comprehensive," "architectonic," and "sustainable," where all relevant factors are considered in relation to each other in an "interdependent" and "integrative" way.[15] Viewed from that perspective, some proponents regard the liberal peace as "far too narrow"[16] and something

---

[15] John Paul Lederach and R. Scott Appleby, "Strategic Peacebuilding: An Overview," in Daniel Philpott and Gerard F. Powers, eds., *Strategies of Peace: Transforming Conflict in a Violent World* (New York: Oxford University Press, 2010), 40–41.

[16] Daniel Philpott, "Introduction: Searching for Strategy in an Age of Peacebuilding," in Philpott and Powers, *Strategies of Peace*, 4. Cf. Daniel Philpott, *Just and Unjust Peace: An Ethic of Reconciliation* (New York: Oxford University Press, 2012), 2, 9, 70–73, 176–177, 207, 209.

to "move beyond."[17] At issue are not only the shortcomings of overlooking the persistent, subtle, and complex interaction of liberal and illiberal forces constitutive of nationalism or of disregarding the domestic and international "dilemmas of nationalism" alluded to earlier. Also in question, say some just-peace proponents, is the limited range of concerns identified with the liberal peace, namely, "to end armed violence and to establish human rights, democracy, and market economies [premised on] the liberal tradition that arose from the Western Enlightenment."[18]

According to one proponent, peacebuilding "is far wider, deeper, more encompassing and involves a far greater array of actors, activities, levels of society, links between societies, and time horizons than the dominant [liberal peace] thinking realizes."[19] That would mean, for one thing, giving more attention to the role of religion in peacebuilding than secularly oriented descendants of the Enlightenment are inclined to do.[20] As one example, religious resources favoring forgiveness, reconciliation, and restorative justice might be consulted as a way of supplementing, if not replacing, exclusive reliance on retributive justice, which is characteristic of the liberal peace.[21] For another thing, it would imply seriously reevaluating the close association between neoliberal economic policies and the liberal peace. "Marketization strategies that ignore social welfare" and perpetuate inequality and poverty in postconflict settings are exacerbated by a global economic order indifferent to "local culture, customs, institutions and processes."[22] Similarly, it is argued that the liberal peace

---

[17] Oliver P. Richmond, "Conclusion: Strategic Peacebuilding beyond the Liberal Peace," in Philpott and Powers, *Strategies of Peace*, 361.
[18] Philpott, "Introduction," 4.
[19] Ibid.
[20] Ibid., and Gerard F. Powers, "Religion and Peacebuilding," in Philpott and Powers, *Strategies of Peace*, 319–322. Such a complaint applies to Grim and Finke, *The Price of Freedom Denied*. Their "religious economies" approach, holding that deregulated religion is beneficial in the same way as is a deregulated market, relies on three Enlightenment figures: Voltaire, David Hume, and Adam Smith. Grim and Finke take them to believe that every religion characteristically seeks to dominate by repressing competitors, and the best way to prevent that is to increase the number of competitors, making it hard for any one religion to gain a monopoly. On their account, to believe in the superiority of one's religion is necessarily to regard competitors as "dangerous and wrong" and to warrant repression, as exemplified, they think, by the New England Puritans. Such a claim, of course, disregards radical English and American Puritans, not to mention Anabaptists, who helped constitute the "free church" tradition in Western Christianity. Members of that tradition regularly believed in the superiority of their religion and simultaneously favored, often at great cost, the universal protection of the freedom of conscience.
[21] Philpott, "Reconciliation: An Ethic for Peacebuilding," in Philpott and Powers, *Strategies of Peace*, ch. 4.
[22] Richmond, "Conclusion," in Philpott and Powers, *Strategies of Peace*, 360.

is too closely tied to the traditional structure of the nation-state. What the justpeace approach calls for is a substantial expansion of horizons to include peace efforts at the international and transnational level and, simultaneously, at the "subnational" or local and grassroots level.[23]

In sum, without intending to refute the essential conclusions of liberal peace advocates – that liberal or civic nationalism promotes peace of a certain kind, whereas illiberal or ethnic nationalism promotes the opposite – justpeace proponents seek to expand the discussion to include a more comprehensive range of considerations relevant to achieving a truly durable and just peace. What remains unclear among justpeace proponents is whether the liberal peace framework "can be salvaged and improved" or whether "more radical thought is required to go beyond this paradigm of peacebuilding."[24]

One important step toward clarifying that issue is to examine afresh the historical origins of nationalism as background to the idea of liberal peace. The objective is to sharpen understanding of what exactly the idea means, the better to decide what to make of it. That involves determining how pertinent the "liberal/civic//illiberal/ethnic" typology is to the beginnings of nationalism and assessing, from an historical point of view, how accurate the charges are against the typology and related aspects of the notion of liberal peace. In particular, we shall have to sort out the role and significance of religion, as well as characterize the attitudes of early nationalists toward corrective and economic justice and toward negotiating and accommodating both transnational and subnational interests and obligations. We shall also need to begin, at least, to come to terms with the more general assault on liberalism I described, including on the rule of law, the idea of freedom of religion, and other human rights.

THE ORIGINS OF NATIONALISM: THE SCHOLARLY SETTING

Undertaking the task we have set ourselves is especially demanding because we must work against considerable historical neglect and misunderstanding. Claiming as we shall that the Protestant Reformation marks a decisive point of origin, we have to make up for the fact that students of nationalism have either neglected the Reformation altogether[25] or commented on it only in

---

[23] Lederach and Appleby, "Strategic Peacebuilding," in Philpott and Powers, *Strategies of Peace*, 26–27.
[24] Richmond, "Conclusion," in Philpott and Powers, *Strategies of Peace*, 361.
[25] E.g., E. J. Hobsbawm, *Nations and Nationalism: Programme, Myth, Reality* (Cambridge: Cambridge University Press, 1991); Walker Conner, *Ethnonationalism: The Quest for Understanding* (Princeton, NJ: Princeton University Press, 1994); Mark Jurgensmeyer, *The New Cold War? Religious Nationalism Confronts the Secular State* (Berkeley: University of California Press, 1993).

passing.[26] Others have mischaracterized its influence by overlooking or misconstruing the contribution of the Calvinist wing of Reformed Christianity.[27] Historians who have commented on the Reformation and its aftermath have either made the same mistake[28] or written inconsistently on the subject.[29]

[26] E.g., Ernest Gellner, *Nations and Nationalism* (Ithaca: Cornell University Press, 1983); Benedict Anderson, *Imagined Communities* (London: Verson, 1991); Anthony D. Smith, *Chosen Peoples: Sacred Sources of National Identity* (Oxford: Oxford University Press, 2003), William R. Hutchison and Hartmut Lehmann, eds., *Many Are Chosen: Divine Election and Western Nationalism* (Minneapolis: Fortress Press, 1994), and Caspar Hirschi, *Origins of Nationalism: An Alternative History from Ancient Rome to Early Modern Germany* (Cambridge: Cambridge University Press, 2012).

[27] E.g., Liah Greenfeld, *Nationalism: Five Roads to Modernity* (Cambridge, MA: Harvard University Press, 1993); Monica Duffy Toft, Daniel Philpott, and Timothy Samuel Shah, *God's Century: Resurgent Religion and Global Politics* (New York: W.W. Norton & Co., 2011).

[28] E.g., Brad S. Gregory, *The Unintended Reformation: How a Religious Revolution Secularized Society* (Cambridge, MA: Harvard University Press, 2012). Gregory does not say much about nationalism, but he believes the "entire tradition of modern liberal thought" is represented by Thomas Hobbes, who is supposed to have opposed any mixing of religion and politics (162). Gregory's claim is mistaken in two ways. First, as a consummate Erastian, Hobbes did not exclude religion but subordinated it to his ideal of an all-powerful "unitary executive." Second, most Calvinists vigorously rejected Hobbes's ideal, holding out, to one degree or another, for a church independent of the state. Even the most separationist minded of them, such as Roger Williams, did not favor completely divorcing religious belief from political life (see fn. 135).

A second example is Philip Hamburger's book, *Separation of Church and State* (Cambridge, MA: Harvard University Press, 2002), contending that the "separation of church and state" in American legal history is a radical nineteenth-century doctrine, invented by nativist Protestants in reaction to Catholic immigrants, that is sharply distinct from the earlier idea of the disestablishment of religion and that has only the most oblique connection to the Calvinist wing of the Reformation (22ff.). For one thing, Hamburger has seriously overstated the differences between the ideas of disestablishment and separation of church and state in the American legal tradition, as Kent Greenawalt has shown in his telling review (*California Law Review* 93:367 (2005)). For another, Hamburger vastly oversimplifies the nineteenth-century data, as Jeremy Gunn amply demonstrates in "Religion in the Public Square: The Contested History of the Establishment Clause," in T. Jeremy Gunn and John Witte, Jr., eds., *No Establishment of Religion: America's Contribution to Religious Liberty* (New York: Oxford University Press, 2012), esp. 26–38. Lastly, and most important for our purposes, Hamburger's tendentious reading of Roger Williams overlooks extensive supplementary appeals to "reason and experience" that Williams makes that warrant at once a sharp separation between conscience and civil authority and a basis for constructive relations between them. These are themes that lie deep in the Calvinist tradition and that conflict with or significantly modify Hamburger's account. (See my analysis of the Calvinist tradition and of Williams's place in it, esp. fns. 133 and 135, and Chapter 9 in this volume for a fuller account of Williams's views.) Winifred Sullivan expresses strong support for Hamburger's book in "Religious Freedom and the Rule of Law," 181, and her book, *Impossibility of Religious Freedom*, is generously endorsed by Hamburger on the book jacket.

[29] Diarmaid McCullough, *The Reformation: A History* (New York: Viking, 2004). On 42, McCullough dismisses the relevance of the idea of nationalism until the eighteenth century. But on 649 he reverses himself and announces that the Reformation promoted "a common

In addition to three notable exceptions to this general picture,[30] a sophisticated and sustained account of the role of the Reformation in the rise of nationalism is contained in Anthony Marx's *Faith in Nation: Exclusionary Origins of Nationalism*.[31] For Marx, the Reformation decisively affected the ideas of nationhood in sixteenth- and seventeenth-century Protestant England and France under the influence of the Catholic Counter-Reformation, as the result of sometimes violent interactions between the state and the respective religious communities. However, his argument that the idea of national identity was in each case simply the product of a state-manipulated policy of religious uniformity ignores the independent role of religion, as well as the competing conceptions of nation advocated by different segments of the

cultural and religious identity" as the basis for state power, thereby encouraging the evolution of a "state-nation" into a "nation-state."

[30] J. N. Figgis, *From Gerson to Grotius: 1414–1625* (Cambridge: Cambridge University Press, 1956); Philip S. Gorski, *The Disciplinary Revolution: Calvinism and the Rise of the State in Early Modern Europe* (Chicago: University of Chicago Press, 2003); and Ernest Barker, "Book I: State and Society," esp. "The Sixteenth Century and the National State," in *Principles of Social and Political Theory* (Oxford: Clarendon Press, 1956), 13–29. Speaking of the relation of the Protestant Reformation to the "rise of national feeling," Barker says that in the Lutheran and Anglican cases "a return was made to the classical unity of the Greek city-state," "but not, or not to the same extent, in the area of Calvinism" (14–15). Later he says that in some places Calvinism "stood for the cause of the minorities and the rights of the 'gathered' Free Church based upon voluntary compact," leading to "an argument against... absolutism, and a plea for the contracted rights of the people" as the basis for the national state (17). See also "Christianity and Nationality" in Barker, *Church, State, and Education* (Ann Arbor: University of Michigan Press, 1957), 131–150, for a related line of argument concerning the contribution of "Nonconformity" in England to the rise of liberal nationalism.

[31] Anthony Marx, *Faith in Nation: Exclusionary Origins of Nationalism* (New York: Oxford University Press, 2003). Marx defines "nationalism" as "a collective [or mass] sentiment or identity, bounding and binding together those individuals who share a sense of large-scale political solidarity aimed at creating, legitimating, or challenging states." "Nationalism is the potential basis of popular legitimacy or expression of support for state power, and as such the two are tied by definition" (6). Marx's definition of nationalism and his analysis of its development place him somewhere in between two different and competing schools of thought on the subject: the "modernists" and the "primordialists." Modernists (e.g., Ernest Gellner and E. J. Hobsbawm) hold that nationalism does not exist until the appearance of modern states such as France and the United State in the eighteenth century. (The term was coined by Johann Gottfried Herder in the late 1770s.) Critical to this understanding is the capacity of the modern state to consolidate a "people" into a "mass society" by means of new, inclusive techniques of communication, commerce, education, law enforcement, and bureaucratic control. In contrast, primordialists (e.g., Anthony Smith) emphasize the importance of popular or "national" consciousness or identity without reference to the state, a characteristic that may be accentuated and intensified by the modern state, but that, in many cases, antedates the modern state by centuries. I follow Marx's "middle way." The heart of nationalism is the link between "nation" and "state," but the origins of the link and the process of its development significantly precede the eighteenth century. In fact, that process of development is very important in the shaping of the modern state.

Reformation and the diverse effects those conceptions had on subsequent forms of nationalism.[32]

THE REFORMATION AND NEW NOTIONS OF "PEOPLEHOOD"

The Protestant Reformation, appearing just as the medieval Catholic establishment in Europe was dissolving into a collection of separate self-governing territorial states, was all about reimagining the meaning of "nation" or "people" to go along with these new states. Through publications in the vernacular and related means of mobilizing the public, the Reformation elevated in various ways, often in an innovative theological idiom, a "politically oriented popular consciousness," implying a new sense of popular awareness, political empowerment, and national identity or "peoplehood."

Behind this new thinking lay two sources: Renaissance humanism and Catholic conciliarism. Both undoubtedly had an impact on the early nationalist attitudes of the Reformers, though the role of humanism was less direct and less salient, except, perhaps, in the case of England. To be sure, recent scholarship has demonstrated a decided preoccupation with national identity on the part of the humanist movement: "Towards the end of the fifteenth century, German, French, Spanish and English scholars fashioned themselves simultaneously as humanists of [classical] Italian greatness and as champions of a free and authentic nation. In both roles they claimed to contribute to the honor of their nation."[33] Still, the nationalist spirit associated with the humanist movement was not, in general, connected to the new populism that would become so important.[34] There is some debate about the Florentine humanists,[35] but the northern humanists appear to have supported consistently "a traditionally hierarchical picture of political life"[36] and "a durable oligarchic rule" in relation to which they performed "a mainly celebratory function."[37]

By contrast, conciliarism radically challenged existing authority, ecclesiastical and political. Reaching its peak of influence at the Council of Constance in 1414–15 CE, the movement favored rule by church council rather than

---

[32] The same defects can be found in McCullough's second comment (on p. 649 in *Reformation: A History*) mentioned in fn. 29.
[33] Hirshi, *Origins of Nationalism*, 152.
[34] Ibid., 215.
[35] At ibid., 137, Hirshi takes issue with Skinner's characterization of "civic humanists" like Bruni as taking an active part in running the commonwealth (Quentin Skinner, *Foundations of Modern Political Thought*, 2 vols. (Cambridge: Cambridge University Press, 1978), 79–84.
[36] Skinner, *Foundations of Modern Political Thought*, 1:238–239.
[37] Hirshi, *Origins of Nationalism*, 135.

papal monarchy. In various ways and degrees, its advocates introduced constitutionalism as a way to ecclesiastical and political peace, proposing to limit the power of both church and state by distinguishing and carefully defining their respective jurisdictions and functions by means of "definite laws and statutes," as Jean Gerson, one of the leaders, put it.[38] Gerson held that the two societies, "ecclesiastical" and "secular," are each "perfect," or self-sufficient, in their own right. Ecclesiastical authorities have no right or aptitude for interfering in worldly matters, especially in regard to the administration of physical force.[39]

Conciliarists interpreted their key principle, "the people's welfare is the ultimate law," in accord with a doctrine of natural rights that added to the sense of popular empowerment, and they based membership in the councils on representation from what they called "the four *nationes* – the *Gallicana, Italiana, Anglicana,* and *Germanica.*"[40] "Each nation could elect its own president, ... hold its meetings in a proper assembly room, dispatch delegates to the committees, and most importantly, pass a single vote for all its members."[41]

Nicholas of Cusa (1401–1464), one of the more progressive leaders, sought to expand the significance of the "contractual" or "covenantal" relationship between the rulers and the "people" in both church and state. "Since all men are by nature free," he wrote, "it follows that every government, whether it rests its authority on written law or on the voice of the prince, derives solely from the common consent and agreement of the subjects." Officials of the Christian church likewise depend on the voluntary assent of the faithful, and according to Nicholas, "it would be well that this ultimate popular derivation of Church authority should be emphasized in his own day by the revival of the primitive practice of congregational election of bishops and priests."[42]

It should be emphasized that, despite its (variable) emphasis on the freedom of the people and their right to participation, conciliarism nowhere favored anything close to a modern view of freedom of conscience where the doctrines of the church were concerned. The Council of Constance regarded itself as a duly constituted legal institution and, going back on its renunciation of the right of the church to use force, "claimed coercive powers over the entire Christendom."[43]

---

[38] Cited by Matthew Spinka, *John Hus and the Council of Constance* (New York: Columbia University Press, 1965), 19.
[39] See Skinner, *Foundations of Modern Political Thought*, 2:114–123.
[40] Hirshi, *Origins of Nationalism*, 82.
[41] Ibid., 44.
[42] John B. Morrall, *Political Thought in Medieval Times* (New York: Harper & Bros., 1962), 129.
[43] Spinka, *Jan Hus and the Council of Constance*, 69.

However, as to the political order, conciliarists made "deeply influential contributions to the evolution of a radical and constitutionalist view of the sovereign State."[44] For Gerson, wherever a ruler is above the law, there can be no authentic political community. That is because political order is fundamentally grounded in the necessity to restrain arbitrary power, something that can be achieved only by adopting common constitutional standards. In a "strongly anti-Thomist and anti-Aristotelian style," Gerson, like other conciliarists, believed that, because of the fall, human beings were otherwise unable to control bias, partiality, passion, and revenge in pursing their interests.[45] Rulership, unregulated by constitutional standards, simply reverts to the chaotic conditions of what later would be called the state of nature.

Though conciliarism lost out to papalism within the Roman Catholic church, its central tenets had an important impact on some of the Reformation ideas about peoplehood and citizenship, albeit in different ways and degrees. Three quite divergent movements stemming from the Reformation may be singled out: *accommodationism, renovationism,* and *reformism.* Accommodationism is an example of "illiberal" or "ethnic" nationalism, whereby religion accommodates or acquiesces, among other things, to a centralized, territorial state;[46] renovationism, in reaction, represents a radical, utopian version of "liberal" or "transethnic" nationalism; and reformism tries, erratically and with considerable ambivalence, to work out a middle way between the two options. In short, reformism exhibits oscillation between liberal and illiberal nationalism, as well as between national and transnational responsibilities. Much of the instability associated with modern nationalism, including struggles over the two dilemmas – the tension between liberal and illiberal forms, and between national and international obligations – is eloquently foreshadowed in the reformist experience.

Accommodationism

The key feature of accommodationism is the mobilization of popular support for a consolidated, unitary[47] territorial state closely allied with an exclusive

---

[44] Skinner, *Foundations of Modern Political Thought,* 2:115.
[45] Ibid., 2:116.
[46] "Accommodationism" as used in this chapter means something opposite to what it means in the hands of legal scholars like Martha Nussbaum. For her, it defines a policy whereby the state allows for exemptions on grounds of religion to neutral and generally applicable laws. See Nussbaum, *Liberty of Conscience: In Defense of America's Tradition of Religious Equality* (New York: Basic Books, 2008), ch. 4, and *The New Religious Intolerance: Overcoming the Politics of Fear in an Anxious Age* (Cambridge, MA: Harvard University Press, 2012), 68ff.
[47] "Unitary" here means a system of government in which the powers of the constitutent parts of government are vested in a strong central executive authority, sometimes referred to as

national religion and an hereditary, hierarchical system of authority and status. Despite some fits and starts, the German reformer, Martin Luther (1483–1546), eventually encouraged such an arrangement, and two influential leaders of the English Reformation, Archbishop John Whitgift (1530–1604) and Richard Hooker (1554–1600), advocated it consistently and without reservation.

Luther is a complicated case. Although he sometimes adopted the nationalist idiom of the humanists, as when he characterized the French as duplicitous, the Scots as haughty, the Spanish as cruel, and the Italians as insidious, treacherous, and untrustworthy,[48] he refused to follow the humanist custom of singularly elevating his own people.[49] But his influence, if circuitous, was no less important. Unlike the humanists, he helped inspire the "new populism" that eventually transformed the elitist and politically marginal activities of the humanists into a mass movement.[50] The new populism was to a certain extent a function of the rejection of Latin and the astonishing spread of vernacular literature, made possible by the invention of printing in the late fifteenth century[51] and successfully exploited by Luther in making his writings popularly accessible. It was also the result of his anticlericalism, illustrated by his famous slogan, "the priesthood of all believers," and of his conciliarist sympathies, which led him to prefer representative councils over the papacy and occasionally, if inconsistently, to condone political resistance to oppressive rule.

But, preponderantly, Luther's legacy is associated with his conviction that the people are best served by supporting a strong, religiously uniform, unitary government. That conviction rested on his growing fear of anarchy and a certain indifference and passivity regarding the institutional reform of both church and state. At first, Luther wanted to remove icons and images from the churches because of their association with Catholicism. But he changed his mind when he saw people taking things into their own hands. Such practices would create "pretty preliminaries to riot and rebellion" and a loss of respect for

"absolutist," though the term needs to be applied with caution, particularly in the case of Hooker.
[48] Hirshi, *Origins of Nationalism*, 202.
[49] Ibid., 203.
[50] Ibid., 215. The phrases, "new populism" and "mass movement" are Hirshi's. He makes the important point that despite Luther's skepticism about the humanist brand of nationalist language, he eventually accelerated the rise of nationalism by means of effective "religious propaganda." But Hirshi also makes some dubious points, such as labeling Luther a "religious fundamentalist" responsible for the rise of "confessionalization" that temporarily retarded the rise of nationalism. These terms and claims are neither well defended nor consistent with what he says elsewhere.
[51] Anderson, *Imagined Community*, 39.

order and authority.[52] Had not St. Paul counseled a duty of passive obedience to temporal rulers? Luther thought so and said as much in responding to the Peasants' Revolt in Germany of 1524–1525. He reminded the rebels that the wickedness and injustice of rulers do not excuse rebellion and that, in defying their obligations to temporal authority, the peasants "forfeited body and soul" and thereby "abundantly merited death."[53] He displayed no compunctions whatsoever about the methods used by the princes in subduing the peasants or about the appalling costs of such action.[54] Luther even went so far as to say that tyrants exist not because they are scoundrels, but "because of the people's sin."[55]

Luther came to favor an established national church in close alliance with a unitary territorial government as the only secure bulwark against chaos. Despite occasional utterances limiting the authority of state to "life, property, and other external things on earth," and precluding it from regulating religious belief and practice,[56] Luther gravitated not only "to attacking the jurisdictional powers of the Church [of the Medieval period], but also to filling the power-vacuum this created by mounting a corresponding defense of the secular authorities," including the right of the prince "to appoint and dismiss the officers, as well as to control and dispose of Church property."[57]

This is the key to "Luther's nationalist influence."[58] According to the principle, *cuius regio eius religio* – "a territory's religion is that of its ruler," a principle Luther stalwartly supported – the people of a state must take on the faith of the ruler, which, in turn, becomes the primary index of national identity. Uniform religion is the essential link between "nation" and "state." This principle was first officially implemented by the Peace of Augsburg in 1555 as the basis for political sovereignty and order among the Lutheran and Catholic territories that made up Germany at the time. Having embraced the ruler's religion, any believers found out of place were at liberty either to emigrate to the territory where their religion was practiced or to stay put and acquiesce. Proselytism

---

[52] Quoted in Carlos Eire, *War against the Idols: The Reformation of Worship from Erasmus to Calvin* (Cambridge: Cambridge University Press, 1986), 72.
[53] Skinner, *Foundations of Modern Political Thought*, 2:18.
[54] Philip Schaff, *History of the Christian Church*, vol. VI, *Modern Christianity: The German Reformation* (New York: Charles Scribner's Sons, 1888), pp. 447–448; cited in James Turner Johnson, *Just War Tradition and the Restraint of War: A Moral and Historical Inquiry* (Princeton, NJ: Princeton University Press, 1981), 52–53.
[55] Cited by Skinner, *Foundations of Modern Political Thoughts*, 2:19.
[56] John Witte, Jr., *Reformation of Rights: Law, Religion, and Human Rights in Early Modern Calvinism* (Cambridge: Cambridge University Press, 2007), 131.
[57] Skinner, *Foundations of Political Thought*, 2:14–15.
[58] Figgis, *From Gerson to Grotius*, 60.

across or within political borders was strictly prohibited. A century later, the agreement was expanded to include other religious groups and other parts of Europe in the Peace of Westphalia of 1648, a treaty that laid down important legal and political foundations for the modern nation-state system.

When it came to working out the institutional structures of church and state, Luther was more devoted to tearing down than building up. As to the church, he sought to liberate Germany from the domination of the papacy and canon law; as to the state, he was happy to accept whatever powers that were, so long as they, too, were liberated from Catholic control. His indifference to the organization of the state never really changed; there is no evidence he ever reflected on the comparative merits of monarchy, aristocracy, or democracy nor sought to integrate his disparate comments on the restraint of political power into any kind of general theory of government.

On the subject of church order, Luther's policies were the result of inadvertence. Without much reflection, he at first recommended replacing the discredited Catholic tradition with simple New Testament norms. When that failed, as the result of a series of severe social, political, and economic crises in the 1520s and 1530s, he acquiesced to a kind of accidental reappropriation of Catholic canon law, so long as it was shorn of all traces of papal authority. He went along, as Skinner puts it, so as to "fill the power vacuum" that had been created by the removal of the Catholic system. Authority over spiritual and temporal matters once invested in the church in medieval times now became the responsibility of the unitary state.[59] "By the mid-1550s, the medieval canon law had returned to ... German society, but now largely under the control of civil authorities and under the color of civil law."[60]

It should be emphasized that, by encouraging the substantial extension of state authority over church affairs, Luther weakened significantly one tenet of conciliarist thought: the independence of the church. Although conciliarists never succeeded in putting into practice their commitment to the separation of the spiritual and temporal communities, the idea was very much there in theory. By definition, accommodationism minimizes the separation of church and state.

J. N. Figgis's claim that Luther, along with the sixteenth-century Anglican leaders, Whitgift and Hooker, transferred "to the State most of the prerogatives that had belonged in the Middle Ages to the Church,"[61] applies more

---

[59] Ibid., 63.
[60] John Witte, Jr., *Law and Protestantism: The Legal Teachings of the Lutheran Reformation* (New York: Cambridge University Press, 2002), 83–84.
[61] Figgis, *From Gerson to Grotius*, 55.

directly and with less qualification to the Anglicans than to Luther. Whitgift and Hooker were accommodationists *par excellence* because they developed elaborate theological and other warrants for defending a unitary territorial government against the threats of both Catholic recusants and a growing number of Reformed Protestant agitators. For them, national identity consisted in the exclusive alliance of the state with the national – "English" – church, causing them to set aside even the limited space for popular independence and resistance admitted by Luther. Except for the conciliarist emphasis on the national character of the church, they were less indebted to conciliarism than Luther and closer to some aspects of humanist teaching on nationalism, especially its traditionally hierarchical picture of political life.

Archbishop John Whitgift and Richard Hooker were children of and leading apologists for the Henrician and Elizabethan settlements in England. Taken together, these two arrangements – the one occurring in 1532 when Henry VIII (1509–1547) broke with Rome and "nationalized" the English church, and the other in 1559, when Elizabeth I (1558–1603), shortly after ascending the throne, secured passage of the Supremacy and Uniformity Acts – consolidated the English Reformation. According to the Supremacy Act, the English monarch, a layperson, became "Supreme Governor" of the church, and anyone not acknowledging the queen's ultimate religious authority would be ineligible for public office or for a university degree. Later, authorizing still severer punishments, the Uniformity Act established Anglicanism as the only lawful religion of England.

Although Elizabeth, partly by temperament and partly by political instinct, was at first ill disposed to enforce Anglicanism too rigidly, she was, nevertheless, prompted by circumstance to unify state and nation by means of an increasingly exclusionary religious policy.[62] She created thereby a remarkable early example of "religious nationalism," according to which one religion, uniformly imposed by the state on the inhabitants of a given territory, is a key determinant of national identity, and thus of popular political consciousness and loyalty.

The strong current of anti-Catholicism that Elizabeth inherited, inspired by widespread revulsion toward the fervent pro-Catholic policies of her half-sister, Mary Tudor (1553–1559), formed an important part of the strategy by which she would solidify support for her government. It was helped along by a

---

[62] The thesis that "exclusionary religion" inspires early nationalism in sixteenth-century England and elsewhere in Western Europe is the central claim of Marx in his *Faith in Nation*. There are, as we shall see, strengths and weaknesses to this thesis. Although Marx is rather good on what we call "accommodationist" Protestantism, he is considerably weaker on the character and role of the Puritan reformists, to whom we shall turn in a later section.

series of consequential events: a pattern of intimidating efforts undertaken in the early years of her reign by the Roman pontiff; the challenge to the English Crown of the Catholic claimant, Mary Queen of Scots; the ominous designs of Catholic Spain, which were finally terminated in the dramatic defeat of the Armada in 1588; and the continuing military conflicts with Catholic Ireland.

The other part of the strategy – namely, the efforts from the 1550s onward to try to domesticate the growing body of Reformed Protestant opposition to the Elizabethan settlement, the so-called Puritan movement – was less successful, at least in the long run. Thanks to the efforts of Whitgift, Elizabeth weakened the movement temporarily, but it would prove harder over time to contain this group and gain control of its considerable energies. Though the movement was complex and various, many Puritans had religious, national, and political goals deeply at odds with the prevailing system. In a profound sense, the contest between Elizabeth – together with her Stuart successors, James I (1603–1625) and Charles I (1625–1649) – and much of the Puritan movement was over the kind of nationalism that would eventually prevail in England: the Tudor-Stuart version or something quite different.

Though Elizabeth tried to suppress "Catholic sedition" with increasing ardor during the 1580s, and though Whitgift and Hooker supported her efforts, it was especially the Puritan threat that they had in mind in mounting their spirited defense of the Elizabethan order. Whitgift was appointed archbishop in 1583 and immediately declared war on the Puritans whom Hooker disparagingly referred to as "patrons of liberty." It is they who "shaketh universally the fabric of government,... overthroweth kingdomes, churches, and whatsoever now is through the providence of God by authority and power upheld."[63] By means of new authority and newly perfected inquisitorial techniques, Whitgift went about stringently enforcing subscription by the clergy to the Acts of Supremacy and Uniformity. Hooker's *Laws of Ecclesiastical Polity*, dedicated to Whitgift, provided the theory for Whitgift's practices.[64]

At the heart of their position was the idea, familiar to accommodationists, that the temporal commonwealth is best entrusted with the coercive

---

[63] Richard Hooker, *Laws of Ecclesiastical Polity* (London: J.M. Dent & Sons, 1958), 2 vols, I, 362–363.

[64] In *Separation of Church and State*, 32–38, Philip Hamburger makes much of the fact that Hooker mischaracterized the Puritan dissenters as seeking a strong version of separation, rather than a more benign form of disestablishment. But if the distinction between separation and disestablishment is not as sharp as Hamburger claims (see fn. 28), but rather marks considerable overlap with degrees of difference, then it is likely that Hooker's description matched the views of some segments of a complex movement, views that would become more prominent in the seventeenth century, as in the case of Roger Williams (see the later discussion).

supervision of all "outward action." Hooker rejected the claims of Catholics and Puritans to the right of the church to supervise its own affairs, and like Luther, though more consistently, Whitgift and Hooker believed that the effects of the Gospel are but inward or "ghostly." Accordingly, the English Crown does not overstep its authority in regulating outward action, including the faith and life of the church, so long as it respects the traditions of the English Reformation, understood "as a return to the past, a vindication of the rights of the Crown against usurped [papal] jurisdiction."[65]

Recovering and exercising legitimate political and ecclesiastical jurisdiction are the very soul of peace and tranquility. First, monarchy is incomparably better than polyarchy. "Where many rule, there is no order," declares Whitgift, taking issue with a Puritan preference for electoral government.[66] Second, proper order depends on conforming to what is established and traditional. "There are few things known to be good," writes Hooker, "till such time as they grow to be ancient."[67] What was decided in the dim past binds the present because "corporations are immortal," and "we were alive in our predecessors and they in their successors do still live."[68] That is the proper meaning of the adage, "the voice of the people is the voice of God." The age-old "general and perpetual voice of the people" has from time immemorial reaffirmed the inseparable unity of church and state under the guidance of the earthly monarch. "There is not any man of the Church of England but the same man is also a member of the commonwealth, nor any man a member of the commonwealth which is not also of the Church of England," writes Hooker.[69]

Third, national peace and security also depend on maintaining the existing political, social, and religious status system established from ancient times. In the allocation of political power and authority, "hereditary birth giveth right unto sovereign dominion," as Hooker put it, and the same is true of social rank. "The Church of God esteemeth [the nobility to be of] more worth than thousands,"[70] and any proposal "which bringeth equally high and low unto parish churches" or in any way challenges "the majesty and greatness of English nobility" is utterly intolerable.[71]

---

[65] Maurice Powicke, *The Reformation in England* (Oxford: Oxford University Press, 1961), 51.
[66] Cited in David Little, *Religion, Order, and Law* (Chicago: University of Chicago Press, 1984), 143.
[67] Hooker, *Laws of Ecclesiastical Polity*, II, 29.
[68] Ibid., I, 195.
[69] Hooker, *Works*, John Keble ed. (Oxford: Clarendon Press, 1888), 3 vols., III, 330.
[70] Hooker, *Laws of Ecclesiastical Polity*, II, 475.
[71] Ibid.

Even more than Luther, Hooker played down the independence of the church advocated by the conciliarists. Although admitting that church councils have some significance in determining the church's life and thought and that its rulings may have advisory value, he believed that the "just authority" of the established civil government in overseeing the church "is not therefore to be abolished."[72]

Renovationism

The various individuals and groups that made up the "Radical Reformation" represented, in one way or other, a fundamental and widespread repudiation of accommodationism. Most offensive was the close identification of Christianity with the new, postmedieval territorial state, particularly with the emerging patterns of authoritarian control over the church, including the enforcement of religious uniformity and the willingness to accept as the basis for church order the dominant hierarchical, unitary, and territorial forms of political and social organization. Impatient with what they regarded as dishonorable compromises with the world, these people "espoused, rather, a radical rupture with the immediate past and all its institutions, and [were] bent upon either the restoration of the primitive Church or the assembling of a new Church, all in an eschatological mood far more intense than anything to be found in normative Protestantism or Catholicism."[73]

> A new kind of Christian had emerged, . . . not a reformer but a converter, not a parishioner but . . . a sojourner . . . whose true citizenship was in Heaven, ... no longer primarily . . . German or . . . Gentile, . . . husband or . . . wife, . . . nobleman or . . . peasant, but a saint . . . , a fellow of the covenant . . . , a bride of Christ. . . . The Radical Reformation [transformed] the Lutheran doctrine of the priesthood of all believers [into] a universal lay apostolate[, mainly] the common man and woman, [but also] former friars, monks, and nuns, . . . as well as patricians and noblemen.[74]

The term "renovationism" is designed to convey how profound and extensive were the social revolutionary implications of the Radical Reformation. That the radicals themselves declined to advocate social programs, but instead generally withdrew from and were indifferent to worldly institutions, does not obscure the fact that their message bespoke a total and final renovation of the

---

[72] Skinner, *Foundations of Modern Political Thought*, 2:105.
[73] George Hunston Williams, *The Radical Reformation* (Kirksville, MO: Sixteenth Century Journal Publishers, Inc., 1992), 1303.
[74] Ibid., 1277.

world and everything in it. Nor should the implications of their preaching be overlooked because most of their attention was devoted not to the temporal kingdom, but to the heavenly one yet to come. It is hardly surprising that what these renovators said and did struck the authorities as seditious in the extreme.

Some of the radicals, such as Thomas Muentzer (1488?–1525), were standard revolutionaries, inciting armed rebellion, as he did as a leader of the Peasants' Revolt of 1525. Most Anabaptists rejected Muentzer's violent apocalypticism, but they shared his antipathy to the political and religious establishment, as well as his high regard for the common lay people and for those victimized by the existing system.

These predilections seriously challenged the prevailing ideas of "nation" and "state." What it meant to be a "people," and, by implication, what form of government might best accommodate such an understanding were profoundly reconceived. Most of the radicals were Anabaptists, and their central belief in adult baptism epitomized the point. For Anabaptists, the conventional practice of infant baptism subverted an indispensable feature of the Christian life: *mature individual conscientious consent*. In particular, the practice exemplified four objectionable features of accommodationism. It was authoritarian for being forced on the underaged by authorities not consensually appointed. It determined membership on the basis of birth, elevating as key marks of Christian identity accidental, ascribed factors, such as ethnic identity and inherited status. It discouraged a spirit of intentional, responsible participation in favor of passivity and subservience, and given the close connection between church and state, it was, above all, coercive. The prescribed practice was under the supervision of the state, and any defection from the obligations of baptism would be civilly punished.

Though differences existed among the Anabaptists, there were also salient continuities. Basic was the impulse to form a consensual or "free church," as Conrad Grebel, founder of the Swiss Brethren, emphasized. Christians must "[g]o forward with the Word and establish a Christian church" on the basis of "common prayer and decision according to faith and love, without command or compulsion."[75] The true church is a "voluntary association of the faithful" that "on principle administers its own affairs without the aid or the interference of the temporal government," and where "the free will of the individual and liberty from the constraints of the authorities were... the distinct marks."[76]

---

[75] Conrad Grebel and friends, "Letters to Thomas Muntzer," in George Huntson Williams, ed., *Spiritual and Anabaptist Writers* (Philadelphia: Westminister Press, 1958), 79.
[76] Hans-Jurgen Goertz, *The Anabaptists* (London: Routledge, 1996), 86.

In a word, the "individual congregation had no superior; it was independent and democratically organized."[77]

The Anabaptist idea of "participatory lay religion" was combined with the belief that a Christian's primary obligation was to a "universal Church not linked to race or nation," but to "a People... transcending any earthly state and never to be subsumed under one."[78] Most Anabaptists acknowledged that the earthly government is divinely ordained to restrain transgressions in "outward affairs," but there its jurisdiction ended. As an early Mennonite leader put it, "the ruler has received his sword not to sit in judgment... over spiritual matters, but to keep his subjects in good order and peace, and to protect the good and to punish the wicked."[79] Their notion of true people- or nationhood implied a state with drastically limited authority. Only those states were truly legitimate that respected and tolerated freedom of conscience.

Though limited government of that kind is to be respected, Anabaptists generally refused to participate because it would mean complicity in the use of force. In their early statement of faith, the Schleitheim Confession of 1527, they declared that "it is not appropriate for a Christian to serve as a magistrate because... the... magistracy is according to the flesh, but [the discipline of Christians] is according to the spirit: their citizenship is in this world, but the Christians' citizenship is in heaven; the weapons of their conflict and war are carnal and against the flesh only, but the Christians' weapons are spiritual, against the fortification of the devil."[80]

The suggestion that such "apolitical" beliefs were socially irrelevant is misleading. However much Anabaptists may have isolated themselves, the political impact of their views was critical. They contributed to revolutionizing conceptions of nation and state not only by offering a vision of limited government and an expanded role for "civil society" that encouraged increased voluntary political and civil participation and new opportunities for the free exercise of conscience but also by implying that state interests are circumscribed by compelling transnational conditions and obligations. Specifically, their views implied the principle of conscientious objection to military service, a notion that would assume enormous significance in the development

---

[77] Claus Peter Clasen, *Anabaptists: A Social History* (Ithaca: Cornell University Press, 1972), 426.
[78] Williams, *Radical Reformation*, 1286–1287.
[79] Cited by James M. Strayer, *Anabaptists and the Sword* (Lawrence, KS: Coronado Press, 1976), 320.
[80] Cited at ibid., 121. There were related reservations about paying taxes, particularly in support of the use of force, though on that matter some Anabaptists were more willing to compromise than others.

of liberalism. In keeping with their fundamental beliefs, Anabaptists invoked a "higher right," based on conscience, to exemption from participation in a primary function of the state, the use of force. Although commonplace now, the idea that ordinary citizens, in addition to clergy and monastics, had a right to exemption was earthshaking at the time. By their statements and actions – typically viewed in the sixteenth century as desperate and futile – Anabaptists were laying down precedents for transforming life in the West.[81]

Anabaptists introduced other radical ideas, which, to be sure, were not always consistently put into practice. Although the "cultural gap between educated leadership and uneducated clergy and laity characteristic of the Roman church and the Protestant established churches was narrowed drastically among Anabaptists," their ability to overcome "the patriarchal principle of men over women" in regard to marriage and social relations was by no means uniformly successful.[82] There is considerable evidence that what was affirmed in principle was not widely realized in fact.[83] That is also true of the tendency over time of Anabaptist communities to take on the characteristics of ethnic enclaves, which was altogether out of keeping with their original inspiration. Nevertheless, the revolutionary potential of their early message was always there.

That potential was important in two other respects. Except in a few extreme groups, Anabaptists regarded private property as a God-given trust that entailed a stringent obligation to share possessions with those in need, both inside and outside the community. "Extravagance was forbidden, while everything beyond the actual need of the individual member was placed at the disposal of the whole group."[84]

It is also reasonable to attribute to Anabaptists the early practice of what has come to be called "restorative justice." Forsaking retributive, usually coercive, punishment associated with the earthly magistrate, Anabaptists emphasized consensual acts of forgiveness and mercy aimed at overcoming estrangement and restoring right relations between offender, victim, and community. Expelling a resolutely unrepentant offender from the group was the closest they

---

[81] See MacCulloch, *The Reformation: A History*, 682: "Radical thinkers and preachers in the early stages of the Reformation [were at the time] marginalized and rejected by Catholics and Protestants alike. . . . [M]ainstream Christianity is only now reexamining [their] alternative views of the future and recognizing how much value there is in them. A modern Anglican . . . is likely to be more like a sixteenth-century Anabaptist in belief than . . . a sixteenth-century member of the Church of England."
[82] Clasen, *Anabaptists: A Social History*, 426.
[83] Williams, *Radical Reformation*, fn. 15, 763, 762.
[84] Peter James Klassen, *Economics of Anabaptism, 1525–1560* (London: Mouton & Co., 1964), 42.

came to practicing retributive justice, and that act, be it noted, was nonviolent in character.

Reformism

Reformism represents a middle way between accommodationism and renovationism. Its representatives try to mediate and negotiate between the radical differences of the two types. That leads to enormous disruption, innovation, and dynamism in regard to national and international institutions and to considerable tensions and differences of opinion among the individuals and groups who make up this unstable type.

The tensions and differences may be tracked as to whether they tend more toward accommodationism or renovationism. Although reformists are distinguished from either extreme by their efforts to hold features of both sides together, there are still strong variations in emphasis among them. Some incline, with certain reservations, toward a religiously uniformist understanding of the state, thereby endorsing a more expansive role for state authority in religious and other matters than Anabaptists could ever accept. Others incline in the opposite direction, though with a difference. They favor certain renovationist ideas about limiting government, reconceiving citizenship, and protesting social, legal, and economic injustice. At the same time, their commitment to institutional reform, and thus to active involvement in the political and legal order, sets them apart from the renovationists. Anabaptists, adopting a more utopian or eschatological outlook, had little confidence in human efforts to reconstruct society. They did attempt, locally, to put into practice some of their radical views concerning church order and social life, but those efforts were intended more as testimony to the coming kingdom than as a scheme for social reform.

The leading example of reformism is the Calvinist branch of the Reformation, starting with the Genevan reformer, John Calvin (1509–1564).[85] There is clear evidence of the ambiguous effects of the movement's influence on the development of nationalism in premodern Switzerland, France, Holland, England, and colonial New England. With the accommodationists, Calvin pretty much took a "people" or nation where he found it – situated, that is, within the territorially administered boundaries of postmedieval Europe, and he came to favor a close alliance between the state and an exclusive national religion, tolerating up to a point inherited patterns of status and authority. At

---

[85] Parts of what follows are borrowed from a forthcoming essay, "Calvinism, Constitutionalism, and the Ingredients of Peace."

the same time, he sought to reform those "new nations" in accord with key renovationist values, such as the independence of church from state, freedom of conscience, new ideas of citizenship, participatory government, special protection for the deprived and vulnerable, and transnational obligations. His far-flung spiritual offspring reflected much of the same ambivalence.

Calvin interacted extensively with Anabapist refugees in Geneva, even marrying the widow of one of them. Although he sometimes harshly opposed their views, "his assertions that discipline and suffering were characteristic of the true Church were also Anabaptist themes . . . [and] many of Calvin's followers proved over the next century that they could be as . . . politically revolutionary as any Anabaptist."[86] Though modified and reformulated, radical Anabaptist conceptions of peoplehood and citizenship played an important role in reformist thinking.

Calvin encountered both humanism and conciliarism as a student, and he was undoubtedly exposed to early forms of nationalist discourse expressed by both movements. However, the influence of conciliarism was particularly notable in regard to Calvin's commitment to constitutionalism, as applied to both state and church.[87] Consistent with conciliarist theory, constitutional government became for him the vehicle for expressing the voice of "the people" by means of national representation, the separation of ecclesial and civil powers, plural authority, and a provision for the fundamental rights of communities and individuals. All this contributed considerable impetus and shape to the "new populism" associated with the Protestant Reformation.

Drawing on the conciliar tradition, Calvin elaborated a position approximating in various ways the characteristics of modern constitutionalism. As to the state, Calvin held the following:

- "Every commonwealth rests upon laws and agreements," preferably written,[88] that are regarded as fundamental to the protection of the "freedom of the people,"[89] a term he frequently invoked. Written law

---

[86] MacCulloch, *Reformation*, 190.
[87] John Mair, an influential Scottish conciliarist, taught at the College de Montaigu while Calvin was a student there. Calvin scholars are divided over the whether Calvin actually attended his lectures, but whether he did or not, the spirit of conciliarism was certainly in the air during Calvin's student days and "it is likely that [Mair] exercised deeper influence upon the future reformer than is generally admitted," Francois Wendel, *Calvin: Origins and Development of his Religious Thought* (New York: Harper & Row, 1950), 19.
[88] Calvin's *Homilies on I Samuel*, 10, cited in Herbert D. Foster, "Political Theories of Calvinists," *Collected Papers of Herbert D. Foster* (Privately Printed, 1929), 82.
[89] John Calvin, *Institutes of the Christian Religion* 2 vols., John T. McNeill ed., Ford Lewis Battles trans. (Philadelphia: Westminster Press 1960), bk. 4, ch. XX, para. 31, 1519.

is "nothing but an attestation of the [natural law], whereby God brings back to memory what has already been imprinted in our hearts."[90]
- The structure of government should be polyarchic rather than monarchic, "a system compounded of aristocracy and democracy."[91] For "it is very rare for kings so to control themselves that their will never disagrees with what is just and right, or for them to have been endowed with such great keenness and prudence, that each knows how much is enough. Therefore, mens' [sic] fault or failing causes it to be safer and more bearable for a number to exercise government."[92]
- "The best condition of the people [is] when they can choose, by common consent, their own shepherds: for when any one by force usurps the supreme power, it is tyranny."[93]
- "Certain remedies against tyranny are allowable, for example when magistrates and estates have been constituted, to whom has been committed the care of the commonwealth; they shall have power to keep the prince to his duty and even to coerce him if he attempt anything unlawful."[94] Especially toward the end of his life, and facing the Huguenot revolt in France, Calvin welcomed duly authorized redress on the part of "constitutional magistrates," as he called them, countenancing armed rebellion under their authority in extreme cases.[95] Shortly before he died, Calvin even went so far as to condone acts of individual resistance against tyrannical rulers.[96]
- A set of basic rights and freedoms are taken to undergird the founding agreement and to comprise an imprescriptible limit on governmental power. They are a collection of what are best described as the "original natural rights of freedom," "associated with the second table of the Decalogue," and stressing especially the protection of "personal liberty and property," as well as the rights of conscience.[97]

A few comments on the rights of liberty and property, as well as conscience, are in order. Underlying Calvin's commitment to constitutional government,

---

[90] Calvin's *Commentary on the Psalms* ch. 119, cited in Foster, *Collected Papers*, 82.
[91] *Institutes* bk. 4, ch. XX, para. 8, 1493.
[92] Calvin's *Homilies on I Samuel*, 8, cited in Foster, *Collected Papers*, 82.
[93] Calvin's *Commentary on Micah*, 5:5.
[94] Calvin, *Homily on I Samuel*, cited in Foster, "Political Theories of the Calvinists," 82.
[95] *Institutes*, bk. 4, ch XX, para. 31, 1518–1519, and fn. 54.
[96] See Willem Nijenhuis, "The Limits of Civil Disobedience in Calvin's Last-Known Sermons," *Ecclesia Reformata: Studies on the Reformation*, Vol. II (New York, Leiden and Köln: E. J. Brill, 1994), ch. 4, discussing Calvin's *Homilies on I and II Samuel*.
[97] Josef Bohatec, *Calvins Lehre von Staat und Kirche mit besonderer Berücksichtigung des Organismusgedankens* (Scientia Aalen:1961), 94–95 (translations are mine).

as with the conciliarists, was an abhorrence of arbitrary power. Gradually, he came to support constitutionally authorized armed rebellion aimed at resisting "the fierce licentiousness of kings" "who violently fall upon and assault the lowly common folk"[98] or, as he puts it elsewhere, exercise "sheer robbery, plundering houses, raping virgins and matrons, and slaughtering the innocent."[99] To tolerate such atrocities is both to violate the natural "inborn feeling" "to hate and curse tyrants" and to "betray the freedom of the people."

It is, then, the fundamental purpose of constitutions, and of the basic rights they protect, to restrain arbitrary power – defined as taking life, inflicting severe pain and suffering, expropriating property, and inhibiting thought and action basically for self-serving purposes. Such behavior is taken to be both wrong in itself and likely to provoke violent resistance. Accordingly, restraining the impulse to act that way – an impulse believed to be endemic to human experience – is the primary justification for constitutional government.[100]

Although particular constitutions may vary in certain ways, they all have as their ultimate purpose to limit power by "equally press[ing] toward the same goal," namely, what Calvin calls, "equity." It is "equity alone," he says, that "must be the goal and rule of all laws."[101] As the essence of the moral law "God has engraved upon the [human mind]," the idea consists of two rules: first, "that everyone's rights should be safely preserved,"[102] and second, that everyone "be beneficent to neighbors" and "helpful to the necessities of

---

[98] *Institutes* bk. 4, ch. XX, para. 31, 1519.
[99] Ibid., bk. 4, ch. XX, para. 24, 1512.
[100] It is this conviction, central to Calvin's thought, that is an important point of connection to what Judith Shklar has called the "liberalism of fear" in her classic essay by that name (in Nancy L. Rosenblum, ed., *Liberalism and the Moral Life* (Cambridge, MA: Harvard University Press, 1989)). Because of the deep-seated and widespread human disposition toward the exercise of arbitrary power – to inflict, that is, severely aversive consequences for self-serving purposes – plural government and the legal protection of individual rights (against arbitrary killing, torture, enslavement, persecution of "conscience, religion or belief," etc.) are urgently required on a universal basis. This general point is either not addressed or addressed confusingly (see fn. 135), by critics of liberalism, the rule of law, and existing human rights norms, such as Danchin, Hurd, Mahmood, Sullivan, and their mentor, Asad. (See Chapter 1, fn. 5.) Although particular governments, including constitutional democracies, must of course be called to account according to constitutional, rule of law, and human rights standards, it is those very standards that are taken by "liberals of fear" best to protect against the violations resulting from the exercise of arbitrary power and to reduce the related occurrence of violence. Any successful refutation must begin by addressing the extensive evidence that by now supports that position (see fn. 2).
[101] *Institutes*, bk. 4, ch. XX, para. 16, 1504.
[102] Calvin, *Four Last Books of the Pentateuch*, Exodus 20:20, 110–111, m.ccel.org/ccel/calvin/comment3/comm._vol03.rtf.

others," relieving indigence with abundance.[103] The second rule of equity in particular recalls the stringent obligation, assumed by the Anabaptists, to share wealth with those in need.

But the idea of equity had another significance for Calvin, related again to Anabaptist ideals, namely their commitment to "restorative justice." Understood as "voluntary moderation" and "abatement of severity" directly associated with Christian love, equity tempers the strong human impulse "to demand our right with unflinching rigor."[104]

> Almost all are so blinded by a wicked love of themselves, that... they flatter themselves that they are in the right.... Christ reproves that obstinacy... and enjoins his people to cultivate moderation and equity, and to make some abatement of the highest rigor, that, by such an act of justice, they may purchase for themselves peace and friendship.[105]

Perfect justice, Calvin seems to be saying, is justice informed by love. Although never ignored, claims for the meticulous protection of everyone's rights by means of a rigorous application of retributive justice must always be assessed in the light of the higher, overriding claims of "peace and friendship." Although (to my knowledge) Calvin nowhere attempts to institutionalize restorative justice in anything like the forms being proposed these days, he clearly and persistently provides aid and comfort for such ideals.

Civilly and politically, Calvin did labor during his career in Geneva to expand the rules of due process[106] and to enlarge substantially the civil franchise,[107] and eventually, as I have mentioned, he supported armed rebellion abroad aimed at restraining tyrannical power. As to economic justice, he embraced a theory of property rights going back to monastic theologians and developed by the conciliarists.[108] It involved drawing a distinction between "inclusive rights," which naturally entitle all human beings to adequate sustenance and health, and "exclusive rights" that protect private property, but

---

[103] Calvin, *Epistles of Paul the Apostle to the Romans and to the Thessalonians*, Ross Mackenzie trans. (Grand Rapids: Eerdmans Publishing Co., 1976), II Thessalonians 3:12, 420.
[104] Calvin, *Commentary on Matthew* 5:25, cited in David Yoon-Jung Kim, "Law, Equity, and Calvin's Moral Critique of Protestant Faith," Th.D. Dissertation, Harvard Divinity School, 2012, 164, 171. I am indebted to Kim's dissertation for illuminating the central importance of the idea of equity in Calvin's thought, as well as the connection of the idea to a "natural law conception of rights."
[105] Ibid.
[106] John Witte, Jr., *The Reformation of Rights*, 52.
[107] Foster, "Calvin's Programme for a Puritan State," in *Collected Papers*, 65.
[108] Brian Tierney, *Idea of Natural Rights: Studies on Natural Rights, Natural Law and Church Law* (Atlanta: Scholars Press, 1997), chs. IX, X.

only so long as the inclusive rights are provided for. Although Calvin nowhere spelled out specific state obligations, he defined "a just and well-regulated government" as one that upholds "the rights of the poor and afflicted" "who are exposed as easy prey to the cruelty and wrongs of the rich,"[109] and he favored and supported in practice welfare efforts in Geneva, both public and private.[110]

Calvin's ideas on the rights of conscience are tied to his theory of the church and, it turns out, to a deep and pervasive ambivalence concerning constitutional government. On the one hand, he defends a strong doctrine of the sovereignty of conscience, which depends on a critical distinction between the "internal" and "external" forum. The first concerns personal, inward deliberation regarding fundamental belief and practice regulated by "spiritual power," meaning reliance on reasons and argument. The second concerns "external" or public deliberation regarding "outward behavior" – the needs of "the present life," such as food, clothing, and the laws of social cooperation – that are regulated by the "power of the sword," something that limits the sovereignty of conscience.

Expositing the thirteenth chapter of the Epistle to the Romans early in his career, Calvin declared that the proper jurisdiction of a well-ordered government is exclusively that "part of the law that refers to human society," or the second table of the Decalogue whose basic principle is that "all individuals should preserve their rights." "There is no allusion at all," he asserts, "to the first table of the law, which deals with the worship of God." Because "the whole of [Paul's] discussion [only] concerns civil government," "those who bear rule over consciences attempt to establish their blasphemous tyranny... in vain."[111] In short, the subject matter of the first table is the province of conscience, which, except when it threatens to subvert the civil and economic rights of others, ought to be entirely free from state regulation.

In keeping with this line of thought, the church, for Calvin, is the locus of what he calls "liberated consciences." Its members comprehend more fully than non-Christians the "goal and rule of all laws" – the principle of equity (respect for the rights of all supplemented by special concern for the deprived and vulnerable) – and they are endowed with a new capacity to embrace and

---

[109] Calvin, *Commentary on the Psalms*, m.ccel.org/ccel/calin/calcomo8.titlepage.htimi, 82:3, 331–2.
[110] Robert M. Kingdon, "Social Welfare in Calvin's Geneva," in *Church and Society in Reformation Europe* (London: Variorum Reprints, 1985); and Jennine E. Olson, *Calvin and Social Welfare: Deacons and the Bourse francaise* (London: Associated University Presses, 1989).
[111] Calvin, *Epistles of Paul the Apostle to the Romans and to the Thessalonians*, 283–286.

act on its requirements by means of the "law of the spirit," *not* the "law of the sword." For this reason, Calvin is particularly emphatic about constitutionalizing the church, about carefully defining and separating the powers of church government so as to maximize the opportunity for voluntary participation by "the people," thereby protecting their fundamental rights – including, above all, their right to conduct their affairs free of state interference. It was, of course, regarding just such issues that Calvin was expelled from Geneva in 1538 by town fathers jealous of their authority over church life. That he was invited back in 1541 marked a certain concession on their part to his belief in an independent church.[112]

It should be stressed that this more liberal side of Calvin's thought presupposed the existence of a natural moral law that is universally both accessible and obligatory. Otherwise, it would not be possible to hold non-Christians accountable, and therefore legitimately subject to coercion, for violations of the restrictions on arbitrary power. It is clear Calvin held such a view, but he held it only some of the time.[113]

That brings us to the "other side" of Calvin's thought regarding the proper shape of constitutional government. Although, in my view, he was always ambivalent about the natural moral capability of human beings, he became increasingly skeptical toward the end of his life, somewhere, perhaps, around 1553 with the trial and execution of Michael Servetus, as Witte suggests.[114] It is after that event that he specifically reversed himself regarding limiting the jurisdiction of the state to the second table of the Decalogue, then calling on civil magistrates to enforce "the outward worship of God" as well as "sound doctrine of piety and the position of the Church."[115] Obviously, such prescriptions radically restricted the right to freedom of conscience and, by implication, to the exercise and enjoyment of other rights as well. To establish religion, to bring both tables of the Decalogue more directly under the control of the state, is to limit the opportunities of citizens not only religiously but also politically, civilly, and economically. Although Geneva during Calvin's career was never free of such regulation, it appears to have intensified after 1555 when Calvin reached his full powers of influence.

Calvin's growing skepticism about natural moral capabilities appears also to have colored his constitutional preferences in both church and state. While at

---

[112] Philip Benedict, *Christ's Churches Purely Reformed: A Social History of Calvinism* (New Haven, CT: Yale University Press, 2002), 7, 120.
[113] See David Little, "Calvin and Natural Rights," *Political Theology*, 10, 3 (2009).
[114] Witte, *The Reformation of Rights*, 67–70.
[115] Calvin, *Institutes*, bk. 4, ch. XX, para. 2, 1487.

pains to expand democratic participation in both places, he was undoubtedly biased, in the final analysis, toward the "aristocratic" side of his constitutional proposals. What he said about the administration of the church could also go for civil order: Special deference to officials is required in elections, as in the general conduct of affairs, "in order that the multitude may not go wrong either through fickleness, through evil intentions, or through disorder."[116] Moreover, his deepening suspicion of natural moral capabilities also strengthened in his mind the indispensability of the Reformed church as the locus of true righteousness, and therefore as the exclusive foundation of state authority and practice.

Although Calvin made considerable room theoretically for a "liberal" interpretation of constitutional government, based on an expansive understanding of the right to freedom of conscience, both inside and outside the church, he very much qualified that interpretation in practice – increasingly, in the latter years of his tenure in Geneva. It is this ambivalence on Calvin's part toward liberal nationalism, expressed in terms of irresolution and oscillation toward the scope of the constitutional protection of freedom of conscience, that is central to Calvin's legacy as it spread throughout northern Europe, and especially England and colonial New England, after Calvin's death. Calvinism was directly associated with severe political convulsions in Europe and the British Isles from the 1550s throughout much of the seventeenth century. They occurred in Holland beginning with the Dutch Protestant insurgency against the Catholic Hapsburgs in 1581, in France with the long-running civil war between the Huguenots and Catholics, in Scotland beginning with the Scottish Reformation of 1560, in England with the Puritan challenges to the Anglican establishment starting in the 1560s and leading up to Civil War and Interregnum, and in New England with the struggles over religious freedom within the Puritan community beginning in the 1630s. All of these contests concerned national constitutional reform, and especially the relations of state to religion. In all of them, Calvinist participants exhibited, in different ways and degrees, ambivalence over the meaning of the "rights of the people," particularly as they applied to religious freedom, but with significant consequences for the broader enjoyment of civil, political, and economic rights as well.[117]

---

[116] Ibid., bk. 4, ch. III, para. 15, 1066.

[117] See Witte, *The Reformation of Rights*, chs. 2, 3, and 4, on Theodore Beza, Johannes Althusius, and John Milton, respectively. These chapters discuss the evolving thoughts on constitutionalism, the protection of rights, and church-state relations of the three figures in relation to the violent struggles over national reform in France (Beza), the Netherlands (Althusius), and England (Milton) in the sixteenth and seventeenth centuries.

The most striking example of the tension between liberal and illiberal nationalism implicit in the Calvinist tradition is the case of colonial New England. Although they by no means agreed on everything, American Puritans, "in their covenanted towns and congregations," as David Hall puts it, *were* of one mind that the "crucial feature of all covenants" is "a people's willing consent" and that a "covenant [is an] instrument and expression of popular decision-making."[118] That common conviction underlay their commitment to constitutional government and, in fact, explains their pioneering role in the rise of modern constitutionalism.

According to a leading authority, the Charter of Massachusetts Bay of 1629 "was not strictly a popular constitution, because it was in form and legal effect a royal grant, but in its practical operation after the transfer, it approximated a popular constitution more closely than any other instrument of government in actual use up to that time in America or elsewhere in modern times."[119] Moreover, Massachusetts Bay authorities went well beyond the original wording, claiming that their charter permitted an astounding degree of political independence. As early as 1641, they refused help from the English Parliament because the colony might "then be subject to all such laws as [the Parliament] should make or at least such as [it] might impose upon us."[120] When in 1646 the authorities were criticized for considering themselves "rather a free state than a colony or corporation of England," they agreed! Parliament might have authority in England, but "the highest authority here is in [our legislature], *both by our charter and by our own positive laws.... [O]ur allegiance binds us not to the laws of England any longer than we live in England.*"[121] This same interpretation applied to the charters of the other colonies as well. Though American Puritans were slow to admit it, it was not a large step to the eventual replacement of the authority of the English Crown, as well as of Parliament, with the will of "the people" who inhabited the colonies.[122]

Of greatest importance was the impulse in Massachusetts Bay and other colonies to adopt declarations of rights as an important feature of their early constitutions. The Body of Liberties was adopted by the Massachusetts Bay legislature in 1641 and amounted to an exceptionally lengthy list of fundamental

---

[118] David D. Hall, *A Reforming People: Puritanism and the Transformation of Public Life* (New York: Alfred A. Knopf, 2011), 157.
[119] C. H. McIlwain, *Constitutionalism and Its Changing World* (Cambridge: Cambridge University Press, 1939), 241.
[120] From *Winthrop's Journal* cited in McIlwain, *Constitutionalism and Its Changing World*, 234.
[121] Ibid., 235, emphasis added.
[122] Donald S. Lutz, *Origins of American Constitutionalism* (Baton Rouge: Louisiana State University Press, 1988), 37.

rights.[123] Though it incorporated provisions from English statutes and precedents, it went well beyond them. It redefined and restructured the traditional rights of English subjects in the light of Puritan Christianity, adding modified portions of biblical law and some "daring rights proposals"[124] from left-wing English Puritan pamphleteers.

The document opens, significantly, by referring to "such liberties, immunities, and privileges" that "humanity, civility, and Christianity call for as due to every man in his place and proportion without impeachment or infringement," highlighting the several grounds, religious *and* natural, on which rights were believed to rest.[125] In the first article, the document goes on to enumerate certain fundamental protections against taking life or property, or imposing penalties and burdens, "unless it be by some virtue or equity of some express law... established by the [legislature] and sufficiently published."[126] David Hall makes much of the idea of equity in Puritan New England, echoing what it meant for Calvin – respect for the rights of all supplemented by a special concern for the deprived and vulnerable. Equity "may best be understood," he says, "as expressing strong hopes for even-handedness in a world where 'unrighteousness and iniquity were visibly present in the workings of English politics, civil society, ecclesiastical governance, and the law, each of which was aligned with structures of privilege and power.'"[127] He mentions several kinds of legal reform present in the Body of Liberties aimed at creating a more "equitable society."

One was "a cluster of rights and privileges for plaintiffs and defendants with virtually no equivalent in English law," including a "more impartial method of selecting juries than was the norm in England."[128] Another was significantly limiting capital punishment and abolishing what the code calls "revolting barbarities of the English law." Still other legal reforms were the abolition of monopolies, which in England had been arbitrarily dispensed to favorites of the Crown, as well of the practice of primogeniture. In its place was established (though not always observed) a more equitable system of inheritance, including provisions for female children. In that way and others,

---

[123] Edmund S. Morgan, *Puritan Political Ideas, 1558–1794* (Indianapolis: Bobbs-Merrill Co., 1965), 171–197.
[124] Witte, *The Reformation of Rights*, 280.
[125] Morgan, *Puritan Political Ideas*, 172–173. I have modernized and here and there "translated" some of the archaic words and forms of speech in the Body of Liberties, and in some of the subsequent citations from Puritan writings.
[126] Ibid., 173.
[127] Hall, *A Reforming People*, 147.
[128] Ibid., 150.

according to Hall, "the colonists eliminated all but a few traces of the social privileges that pervaded the English system and remade justice into a matter of equal treatment before the law."[129] Incidentally, in respect to the distribution of wealth, Hall stresses that Puritan rhetoric was fervently and repeatedly addressed to the obligations of the affluent toward the indigent, accompanied by efforts to make tax policy more equitable than was the case in England[130] and in places to guarantee "each adult male" "some land, free and clear."[131]

There was, however, one part of the Body of Liberties that generated a particularly strong division of opinion: the rights pertaining to religious belief and practice, namely, Section 95, Articles 1 through 11, identified as "A Declaration of the Liberties the Lord Jesus hath given to the Churches." According to these articles, all members of the colony have "full liberty" to practice religion according to conscience, though only so long as they "be orthodox in judgment"; in addition, "every church has full liberty to elect church officers," "provided they be able, pious and orthodox."

This was, of course, the basis of what John Cotton, a prominent clergyman in the colony, referred to as the "theocratic" character of Massachusetts Bay, namely, a state governed by officials regarded as divinely guided.[132] It is true, that Cotton and other leaders believed that church and state should not be "confounded," so that magistrates were precluded from holding church office, and church officials from holding civil office. At the same time, he and his associates affirmed with equal resolution that only church members might vote in civil elections, that churches and clergymen should receive direct public support through taxes and other donations, and that religious beliefs and practices should be extensively and severely regulated by laws covering blasphemy, irreverence, profanity, idolatry, and "schismatic" activity.

Although this position was widely shared, by no means did all Puritans agree with the official Massachusetts Bay policy concerning the meaning of "full liberty" of religious belief and practice or with the commitment to established religion. Roger Williams, a controversial figure from the time he set foot in the New World in 1631, and himself evicted from the colony for unorthodox beliefs five years later, strongly opposed the Massachusetts Bay establishment and, from his new-found perch in Rhode Island, took up the case against it in a lengthy and heated dispute in print with none other than John Cotton himself.

[129] Ibid., 152.
[130] Ibid., 67–70.
[131] Ibid., 64–65.
[132] Cotton actually uses the term to describe what in his mind is "the best form of government in the commonwealth, as well as the church," in Morgan, *Puritan Political Ideas*, 163.

In essence, the conflict between Cotton and Williams personified dramatically the two sides of the Calvinist background. Both figures were staunch constitutionalists, favoring limited government and most of the protections enunciated in the Body of Liberties – though they differed, of course, on the *degree* of limits and the *range* of protections. Both were committed to Reformed doctrine and the use of scripture in guiding faith and morals, though Williams, it is true, was increasingly skeptical, as Cotton was not, of Reformed ecclesiology. Williams seemed to take to extremes the motto, "the church reformed, always reforming."[133]

What divided them most fundamentally was the right to the freedom of conscience and the implications of that difference for the organization of church-state relations and the enjoyment of civil and political rights. Williams put the issue between them as sharply as possible quoting passages that pitted

---

[133] It is this aspect of Williams's views that Hamburger devotes exclusive attention to in expositing Williams's thinking on church-state relations (*Separation of Church and State*, 38–53). Hamburger refers to Williams's insistence on purifying the church of all worldly influence, including his radical anticlericalism, as favoring "a sort of separation" (484), a position Hamburger regards as idiosyncratic, if not just plain weird. On Hamburger's construction, this obsession with church purification, leading Williams eventually to abandon membership in any congregation and to oppose all existing forms of church organization, caused him to turn his back on the state and all "worldly activities" (42), and thereby to embrace, if circuitously, his highly peculiar view of church-state separation. Clearly, Hamburger's objective is to marginalize Williams's contribution. However, this is a seriously distorted interpretation of Williams's position. For one thing, it ignores several other prominent lines of argument employed by Williams in favor of separating church and state (alluded to in the text) that are quite consistent both with (liberal) Calvinist thinking and with subsequent eighteenth-century approaches to the subject. For another, Williams's convictions concerning the purification of the church have little bearing on his broader theory of church-state relations, which explicitly leaves the matter of religious belief and practice, including religious organization, entirely up to the consciences of others. Williams nowhere demands adherence on the part of others to his anticlerical or anti-ecclesiastical views.

It is distressing that Hamburger's characterization of Williams continues to be highly influential on reputable historians and legal scholars alike. See, for example, Gordon S. Wood's comments on a recent book on Williams in a review entitled, "Radical, Pure, Roger Williams," *New York Review of Books* (May 10, 2012), 45–46. "Williams's beliefs were too extreme, too eccentric, too individualistic to have much relevance today." As with Hamburger, Wood's argument for Williams's alleged irrelevance is that he was gradually disillusioned with all forms of organized Christianity and isolated himself from any corporate religious experience. Hamburger's misrepresentations of Williams's views replicate in many ways the similarly mistaken but widely echoed claims of Mark DeWolfe Howe, *The Garden and the Wilderness* (Chicago: University of Chicago Press, 1965). One particularly distressing example of Howe's distorting influence on the understanding of Williams is in the otherwise compelling and insightful writings on law and religious liberty by Douglas Laycock, *Religious Liberty: Overviews and History* (Grand Rapids, MI: Eerdmans Publishing Co., 2011), I, 68. Citing Howe, Laycock says that for Williams "religion is sacred and the state corrupt, so that separation of church and state is necessary to protect religion from corruption by the state."

Calvin against himself. When Calvin declared that Romans 13 restricts the jurisdiction of the state exclusively to the second table, he was an "excellent servant of God," as Williams writes in *The Bloody Tenent of Persecution*, published in 1644.[134] But when Calvin assigned "Christ's ordinances and administrations of worship... to a civil state, town or city, as [in] the instance of Geneva," Williams rejected that practice unconditionally as a contradiction of Calvinist principles.[135]

---

[134] Roger Williams, "A Bloody Tenent of Persecution," in *Complete Writings of Roger Williams*, 7 vols. (New York: Russell & Russell, 1963), III, 153.

[135] Ibid., III, 225. A key implication of Williams's critique of Calvin here is that legal protection of the rights of conscience is an indispensable means of limiting the state from exercising arbitrary power, an insight Calvin himself appreciated and asserted early in his career, even if he went back on it later. Ironically, Williams's central conviction is well expressed by Winifred Sullivan, a putative critic of freedom of religion, rule of law, and human rights. (See the critique of Sullivan's views in Chapter 6.) Her claim that "to be religious is not to be free, but to be faithful" (156) is true in regard to conscience, but *not* in regard to the state. That is the whole point: Being subject to the one means being free, at least in part, from the other.

The problem is Sullivan's concessions here deeply compromise her recurring attacks and those of her colleagues against what they consider to be the perverse influence of "protestant" "hyper-privatization" on questions of religious freedom. On the one hand, Sullivan's formulation – completely consistent with Williams's ideas – presupposes an irreducible individualism (what I have called elsewhere "conscientious individualism"). Despite the indispensable influence of social experience, it is, finally, *individuals who have consciences*, which, according to the implication of Sullivan's formulation, are to be protected *as such* by a well-ordered state against undue coercion or restraint. On the other hand, there is no reason to assume, as Sullivan and associates seem to do, that the protection of conscience is hopelessly wedded to a preoccupation with "private belief" understood as unrelated to behavior, group membership, or public life in general. Williams respected "free exercise" or practice as well as belief, and he also respected the "non-protestant" groups many people at the time identified with, such as Jews, "Mohammedans," and Native Americans, so long as they complied, as many of them did on his account, with "second table standards" and allowed, in one way or another, for the "right of the individual" "to life outside the state," a principle Sullivan herself endorses. As to the public aspect of freedom of conscience, Williams never tired of arguing that protecting individual rights of conscience enabled the state to do its true job, namely to ensure to all citizens *impartially and equally* the *public goods* of peace, safety, and civic welfare. Continuing to consider, in accord with due process, "challenges of conscience" to the state's jurisdiction performs a critically public function of calling the state to account in this regard.

Sullivan also seems sympathetic to an idea Williams favored, namely extending freedom of conscience to those, in Williams's words, "who turn atheistical and irreligious" (*Complete Writings of Roger Williams*, 7, 181), although she disregards the fact that human rights standards follow Williams by enshrining that very idea (see *Impossibility of Religious Freedom*, 157). In "The Conscience of Contemporary Man," Sullivan affirms the Supreme Court's extension of the right of conscience to nonreligious people (as in *U.S. v. Seeger*), but then, inexplicably, goes on to render such a development "outdated" by invoking a number of recent anthropological studies without making clear what bearing they have on the issue of conscience and state. A similar criticism might be leveled against her interpretation of the ruling in *Warner v. Boca Raton*, the central focus of her argument throughout *Impossibility of Religious Freedom*. It is hard to follow why, *on Sullivan's own assumptions*, she would not favor a ruling that, on grounds

Williams proceeded to develop his case against Massachusetts Bay very much within the framework of Calvin's "liberal" side. There is the same reliance on the distinction between the "inward" and the "outward" forum, and the accompanying distinction between "spirit" and "sword" and between the two tables of the Decalogue that Calvin presupposed. There is the same belief that human beings are, within limits, naturally capable of recognizing violations of "second table crimes" prior to and independent of special religious enlightenment, and insofar as they do not violate those prohibitions, they may – and should – be left free to determine their religious convictions as their consciences dictate. It is important to emphasize that in constructing his position, Williams (like Calvin) invoked several separate arguments: some based explicitly on reason and experience, others derived from scripture and doctrine. To his mind, these arguments all worked together, suggesting a constructive relation between the two tables of the Decalogue, properly implemented.[136] In particular, he repeatedly emphasized that the persecution of conscience "fills the streams and rivers with blood," in keeping with the findings of Grim and Finke, mentioned earlier.[137]

It is, of course, on these grounds, taken together, that Williams opposed so fervently all forms of established or what he called "National" religion

of conscience inclusively understood, extended the right to erect upright gravestones in an area otherwise legally limited to flat gravestones. She here and there toys with such a conclusion, but nowhere forthrightly embraces it (see, e.g., 136–137). Cf. Kent Greenawalt, *Religion and the Constitution*, 2: *Establishment and Fairness* (Princeton, NJ: Princeton University Press, 2008), 330–331, for a related criticism.

[136] Williams writes: "I affirm that state policy and state necessity, which (for the peace of the state and the preventing of rivers of civil blood) [safeguards] the consciences of men, will be found to agree most punctually with the rules of the best politician that ever the world saw, the King of kings and Lord of lords." He speaks of the civil protection of conscience as an "absolute rule of this great politician for the peace of the field, which is the world, and for the good and peace of the saints, who must have a civil being in the world" (*Complete Writings of Roger Williams*, III, 178–179). The point is that the teachings and life of Jesus, based on appeals to conscience, not coercion, match and flourish in a civil order that protects conscience and make a critical contribution to civil or "worldly" peace for which Jesus's true followers, "the saints," have a singular responsibility. At the same time, there is nothing compulsory about the convergence; Williams's view of Christianity, though compelling for him, is by no means an "official requirement" for a constitutional system to work, as he makes clear more than once. In fact, he believed most Christians of his time and place, by turns predatory and overbearing, had much to learn about the authentic Christian message by respecting the equal rights of Native Americans and interacting with them sympathetically. (See Nussbaum's moving discussion of Williams's contribution to the ideals of "respect and sympathetic imagination" as exemplified by his attitudes toward the Narragansett Indians whom he befriended (*The New Religious Intolerance*, 149–158).)

[137] See fn. 8.

so prevalent at his time. He was very clear: Given forms of political "power, might or authority [are] not religious, Christian, etc., but natural, humane, and civil."[138] The purpose of the "wall of separation" between church and state Williams favored was not to protect the church from an invariably corrupt state, as is so frequently asserted, but to protect church and state equally from what he called the "wilderness of National religion," a condition that utterly confuses the proper roles of *both* institutions.[139] Along with religious warrants, his commitment to the principle of nonestablishment was based on a belief in an independent natural moral law accessible to and obligatory on all people, and it led to a remarkable expansion not only of the rights, of conscience but also of civil, political, and economic rights, as expressed in the Rhode Island Civil Code of 1647 and the Rhode Island Charter of 1663.

Martha Nussbaum has demonstrated convincingly in her book, *Liberty of Conscience*,[140] that it is Roger Williams, not John Locke, Thomas Jefferson, or James Madison, who provided the intellectual foundations for the expansive constitutional protection of conscience, that, she believes, Jefferson and Madison also intended. The only shortcoming in Nussbaum's otherwise excellent book is the failure to appreciate the Calvinist background or at least one side of it. She mistakenly invokes the Stoics as the basis for Williams's approach, thereby neglecting the tradition of constitutionalism and natural rights that Calvin and many of his followers so clearly, if sometimes so ambivalently, represented.

Of course, the contribution of the Williams-Jefferson-Madison lineage to the ideals of liberal nationalism has constituted only one part of the American experience. That lineage has had to contend persistently with strong tendencies in the opposite direction, tendencies that have promoted one or another form of religious establishment at both state and national levels – or more recently, the preservation of "Anglo-Protestant Culture," something Samuel P. Huntington has considered an indispensable expression of American national identity that to him is at present under severe threat.[141] These tendencies reflect the illiberal side of the Calvinist background, and they are

---

[138] *Complete Writings of Roger Williams*, III, 398.
[139] See Chapter 9 for an elaboration of this critical point.
[140] Martha C. Nussbaum, *Liberty of Conscience: In Defense of America's Tradition of Religious Equality* (New York: Basic Books, 2008).
[141] Huntington, *Who Are We?*, ch. 4. See David Little, "Culture, Religion, and National Identity in a Postmodern World," *Anuario del Derecho Eclesiastico del Estado*, XXII (2006), for a critique of Huntington's argument.

reflected in other ways as well. Despite the fact that Rhode Island adopted one of the first American antislavery laws in 1652 and that Roger Williams had an impressive record of deep respect and equal regard for Native Americans, he assisted in rounding them up and selling them into slavery after King Philip's War of 1675–1676, probably as the result of an uncharacteristic flash of vengefulness over the destruction done. Williams's ambivalence toward slavery set the tone for similar ambivalence on the part of Jefferson and Madison, though, in their case, with even more baleful consequences for the ideals of liberal nationalism.

A concluding and very significant example of reformist attitudes toward early nationalism is the work of Alberico Gentili (1552–1608), an Italian-born Calvinist[142] who taught international law at Oxford around the turn of the seventeenth century. "As the precursor of [Hugo] Grotius, and the one who substantially and effectively prepared the way for him, Gentili is [arguably] the real 'father' of the modern law of nations."[143] In sum, "the pioneer work of Gentili was in harmony with the larger movement of the sixteenth century which witnessed a transformation of society, the establishment of a new spirit and wider outlook, the decline of theocracy, and the rise of the modern State."[144] Central to the idea of the modern law of nations, already incipient in the earlier thinking of the conciliarists and Catholic theorists such as Victoria and Suarez, is the extension of the norms of constitutionalism, including, especially, the universal protection of rights, to a new international order made up of a multiplicity of independent national states. That meant establishing general laws and practices able to restrain arbitrary power, not only *within* the new nations but also *among* them, particularly in regard to the use of force.

Calvin did not comment at length on the law of nations, but he did support the idea against those who wanted to make universal "the political system of Moses."[145] Whatever the variations in detail and degrees of punishment among the law codes of the world, all nations, he said, enforce second-table rights and may be called to account in respect to them. These rights are expressions of natural law and equity, which, in turn, underlie the law of

---

[142] In her definitive study of Gentili, Gezina H. J. van der Molen, *Alberico Gentili and the Development of International Law* (Amsterdam: H. J. Paris, 1937), makes a strong case for Gentili's Calvinism, both theologically (249–256), and politically (201–221).
[143] Coleman Phillipson, "Introduction," in Alberico Gentili, *De Iure Belli Libri Tres*, translation of the 1612 edition by John C. Rolfe (Oxford: Clarendon Press, 1933), 18a.
[144] Ibid., 25a.
[145] Calvin, *Institutes*, bk 4, ch. XX, sect. 14, 1502.

nations.[146] In that connection, he also devoted some attention to the "right of the government to wage war"[147] and its duty to observe "restraint and humanity in war,"[148] briefly invoking some of the standards of the just-war tradition, albeit ambivalently.[149]

Gentili elaborated on the law of nations and the law of war at much greater length and with more serious study and expertise than Calvin. However, he shared Calvin's general perspective, as well as some of the deep ambivalence in Calvin's thought, at times developing certain liberal themes, and at other times veering toward more illiberal ones.

An important part of Gentili's theory of force accords with Calvin's views, particularly his "early" thinking. Like Calvin, Gentili distinguished sharply between the two tables of the Decalogue: the laws of religion "are divine, that is between God and man; they are not human, namely between man and man."[150] "Religion is a matter of the mind and ... will, which is always accompanied by freedom."[151] "Therefore, no man's rights are violated by a difference in religion, nor is it lawful to make war because of religion."[152] "Force in connexion with religion is unjust."[153] Gentili registered strong support for religious freedom and pluralism, both among and, more surprisingly, *within* states, thereby challenging the principle of religiously uniform states authorized by the Peace of Augsburg and Westphalia.[154]

Accordingly, human laws alone – second-table rights – are the proper domain of earthly government, in both domestic and international relations. "Now this is a just cause [for the use of force, if] our own rights have been interfered with.... Everyone is justified in maintaining his rights."[155] The only

---

[146] Ibid., sect. 16, 1502.
[147] Ibid., sect. 11, 1499.
[148] Ibid., sect 12, 1500.
[149] Ibid., sect 16, 1505: "There are countries which unless they deal cruelly with murderers by way horrible examples, must immediately perish from slaughters and robberies. There are ages that demand increasingly harsh penalties."
[150] Gentili, *De Iure Belli*, bk. 1, ch. IX, 41.
[151] Ibid., 39.
[152] Ibid., 41.
[153] Ibid., 38.
[154] Ibid., bk. 1, ch X, 43–46: "Violence should not be employed against subjects who have embraced another religion than that of the ruler ... with the reservation, 'unless the state suffer some harm in consequence' [such as disturbance of the peace – a fully modern limitation].... I for my part hear of battles and wars where no place is given to religion. I do not hear of them where there is room for different religions." In this regard, Gentili was considerably more liberal than Grotius, who favored religious pluralism and freedom internationally but *not* domestically.
[155] Gentili, *On the Laws of War*, Book I, ch. I, 8.

truly just cause for using force, inside or outside national borders, is the protection of the legitimate temporal and material rights of nation-states and their citizens. Excluding religion as a cause for war, whether civil or international, and expanding the society of states to include infidel and even barbarian nations that are independent and politically organized,[156] are indispensable conditions of peace. By developing his approach to international law in this way, Gentili advanced the secularization and liberalization of international law.[157]

Like other sixteenth-century Calvinist authors, Gentili supported constitutional restrictions on political power and authority, including a right of rebellion in extreme cases. However, he occasionally equivocated on the subject, exemplifying the ambivalence about these matters characteristic of reformist thinking. On the one hand, rulers who betray their subjects by failing to defend them or by breaking agreements with them may be replaced, and, in fact, rebellions may be assisted licitly by outside powers, as in the case of the support given to the Dutch Revolt of 1581 by Queen Elizabeth of England.[158] On the other hand, Gentili temporized at times. He worried that things might go too far and concluded that because anarchy is worse than tyranny,[159] considerable indulgence is owed earthly rulers. Now and again, he suggested that they have overriding authority that must be submitted to, appearing at times to disregard the authority of "constituted lesser magistrates" to stand up to a deviant ruler that was countenanced even by Calvin himself.[160] For example, Gentili stated that rulers may not be put on trial by their people, and that although they are not entitled to deprive their people of property without just cause, a ruler has the final say in determining whether a just cause exists![161]

Gentili's thoughts on international obligations during wartime also reveal some ambivalence. Along with respect for religious diversity, he strongly emphasized protection of noncombatants, restraints against cruelty to prisoners, moderation of vengeance against a conquered enemy, and conservation of religious buildings and other architectural and artistic treasures. At the same time, he countenanced the enslavement of conquered peoples, the right of booty, the sacking of cities, and the use of reprisals.[162]

---

[156] Phillipson, "Introduction," in Gentili, *De Iure Belli*, 25a.
[157] Van der Molen, *Alberico Gentili*, 214ff.
[158] Ibid., 237.
[159] Ibid., 236.
[160] Ibid., 239.
[161] Ibid., 133, 136.
[162] Ibid., 244.

CONCLUSION

Following the advocates of "the liberal peace," I have assumed that "liberal nationalism," consisting of the orderly and properly sequenced development of constitutional democracy, including provisions for economic prosperity, is a critical condition of national and international peace, whereas the presence of illiberal institutions – namely those that are seriously fractured religiously, ethnically, economically, and in other ways – promise a high probability of violence. At the same time, I have paid attention to some of the challenges to those assumptions represented by adherents of the new idea of "justpeace," such as the neglect of religion, questionable neoliberal convictions about economic justice, an exclusive devotion to the merits of retributive justice, and the benefits of state-centered solutions to violent conflict. In addition, I have acknowledged the inescapable dilemmas of nationalism, such as the intermixture of liberal and illiberal elements and the abiding tension between national and international obligations, as well as the complications of attempting to administer a system of equal rights fairly and equitably.

Accordingly, I reexamined the historical origins of nationalism and offered a fresh account that does two things: First, it reveals the saliency of religion by establishing the centrality of the Protestant Reformation and the complexity of its influence on the rise of nationalism. The three types of attitude toward a new understanding of nation- or peoplehood – accommodationism, renovationism, and reformism – give clear evidence of the conflicting tendencies between liberalism and illiberalism that have become central to the study of nationalism, and they help explain why the conflicts are so deep-seated and so persistent. Second, it reveals some significant intellectual resources for reevaluating and correcting our understanding of the liberal peace and that bring it more closely into line with the ideals of the advocates of justpeace.

By demonstrating that religion was "present at creation," this account shows why religion and nationalism have up until now been so closely associated, as well as why the dilemmas of nationalism, both domestic and international, are not likely to go away. It also reveals, especially where reformists – mainly liberal Calvinists – give prominence to renovationist ideas, how the concept of the liberal peace can be improved. In particular, the Calvinist notion of equity, drawing as it does on the Anabaptist impulse to modify both economic inequality and the severity of retributive law, contributes to adjustments in approaches to peacemaking that seem abundantly confirmed by experience. That is also true of the liberal Calvinist emphasis, again adapted from central Anabaptist convictions, on limiting the state and expanding the sphere of conscientious belief and action, religious and otherwise. That development makes way for supplementing state-centered peacemaking policies with a broad array of nongovernmental innovation.

For all these reasons, it is imperative to take a new look at the origins of nationalism.

9

Roger Williams and the Puritan Background of the Establishment Clause

INTRODUCTION

Just over a hundred years ago, the Austrian legal scholar, Georg Jellinek, published a small, but important book on the American colonial origins of declarations of rights and their place in modern constitutional history.[1] The book contains two arresting conclusions. One is that "the idea of legally establishing inalienable, inherent and sacred rights of the individual is not of political but religious origin. What has been held to be a work of the [French] Revolution was in reality a fruit of the Reformation and its struggles."[2]

The second conclusion is even more daring. The "first apostle" of this radical rights doctrine, particularly as applied to the freedom of conscience, was not an eighteenth-century Frenchman, such as Lafayette, ardent supporter of the American Revolution and the French Declaration of the Rights of Man and Citizen. It was an earlier, more improbable person: the seventeenth-century Puritan outcast and founder of the Rhode Island colony, Roger Williams (1603–1683?). "Driven by powerful and deep religious enthusiasm," says Jellinek, Williams "went into the wilderness in order to found a government of religious liberty."[3]

As to the first conclusion, Jellinek draws attention to seventeenth-century New England Puritans,[4] heirs of the Calvinist branch of the Protestant

---

[1] Georg Jellinek, *The Declaration of the Rights of Man and of Citizens: A Contribution to Constitutional History* (Westport, CN: Hyperion Press, 1979), first published in German in 1895. Available online at http://files.libertyfund.org/files/1176/Jellinek_0162_EBk_v5.pdf. Jellinek's work was translated into English by Max Farrand in 1901. Farrand later compiled the standard reference work on the drafting of the U.S. Constitution: *The Records of the Federal Convention of 1787*.
[2] Ibid., 77.
[3] Ibid.
[4] Although Jellinek does not specifically include the founders of the Plymouth colony (1620), known as "Pilgrims," in his account, it is important to do so. Technically, Pilgrims were not

243

Reformation, and their "Plantation Covenants" or early constitutions that were imitated throughout the colonies.⁵ A prominent feature, initiated by the New Englanders, was the inclusion of declarations of rights as part of a colony's founding document. Although there remained differences among them, eleven of the thirteen original states adopted constitutions between 1776 and 1789 that included declarations of rights; the other two retained their original colonial charters. Connecticut's dated from 1662 and Rhode Island's from 1663, making these two documents, according to Jellinek, "the oldest written constitutions in the modern sense."⁶

Jellinek contends that it is the Puritan background that was decisive in the rise of modern constitutionalism in both the American and French cases. The U.S. Constitution, along with the Bill of Rights, was a direct consequence of

---

Puritans, because they wished to separate themselves entirely from the Church of England, whereas Puritans, often very reluctantly, remained within the church the better to reform it. Still, the Pilgrims and Puritans shared a common theological and political outlook, and after the Massachusetts Bay colony was established in 1629, "very rapidly the distinction between the Massachusetts Puritans and the Plymouth Separatists lost its meaning, and the story of Plymouth became in large part that of Puritan New England," Francis J. Bremer, *The Puritan Experiment: New England Society from Bradford to Edwards* (Hanover, NH: University Press of New England, 1995), 36. Moreover, Williams himself argued "that there has hardly ever been a conscientious Separatist who was not first a Puritan." *On Religious Liberty: Selections from the Works of Roger Williams*, James Calvin Davis, ed. (Cambridge, MA: Harvard University Press, 2008), 65.

5 Jellinek, *Declaration of the Rights of Man and Citizens*, 64ff. Jellinek does not claim the Puritans acted all on their own. He singles out the crucial contribution to the American experience of a radical English Puritan sect known as the Levellers. In the late 1640s toward the end of the Puritan Revolution (1642–1649), the Levellers drafted a series of new constitutions for England that they sought, without success, to lay before the entire population for acceptance. Such "remarkable" document, writes Jellinek, limited the powers of the legislature "in a manner similar to that later adopted by the Americans," and marked out certain matters that "in future should not lie within the legislative power of the people's representatives," limitations that would take on central significance in the deliberations over the American constitution. Principal among these was a guarantee of freedom of conscience, "reckoned among the inherent rights, the 'native rights,' which [the drafters] firmly resolved to maintain with their utmost strength against all attacks." Along with parallels to the religion clauses of the First Amendment to the U.S. Constitution, there are other intriguing similarities between the two documents: for example, to Article 6 of the U.S. Constitution, prohibiting religious tests for public office, and to four other amendments: the Fifth (against self-incrimination), Sixth (procedural right to a speedy trial), Eighth (against cruel and unusual punishment); and Sixteenth (right of government to collect taxes, although the Leveller document stipulates that taxes may only be imposed "by an equal rate, [proportional] to men's real or personal estates," and mostly exempting "persons not worth above thirty pound."). See A.S.P. Woodhouse, ed., *Puritanism and Liberty* (Chicago: University of Chicago Press, 1974), 357–367.

6 Jellinek, *Declaration of the Rights of Man and of Citizens*, 22. See fn. 10.

the colonial experience,[7] and the French Declaration of the Rights of Man and Citizen was not, as hinted earlier, the product of the French Revolution or of Lafayette, Rousseau, or other French Enlightenment figures, but was also drawn, often word for word, from the declarations of rights of the American colonies.[8]

Above all, Jellinek contends that the early American documents were remarkable innovations. Although they selectively incorporated aspects of English common law, they were anything but carbon copies. "A deep cleft separates the American declarations from ... English enactments," such as the Magna Carta (1215) and the Petition of Right (1628):

> The English statutes are far removed from any purpose to recognize general rights of man, and they have neither the power nor the intention to restrict the legislative agents or to establish principles for further legislation. According to English law, Parliament is omnipotent and all statutes enacted or confirmed by it are of equal value.... The American declarations, on the other hand, contain precepts which stand higher than the ordinary lawmaker. In the Union, as well as in the individual states, there are separate [arrangements] for ordinary and for constitutional legislation, and the judge watches over the observance of the constitutional limitations by the ordinary legislative power.... The declarations of rights even at the present day are interpreted by the Americans as practical protections of the minority.[9]

Subsequent scholarship has confirmed and expanded on Jellinek's first conclusion. According to a leading authority, the Charter of Massachussets Bay of 1629 "was not strictly a popular constitution, because it was in form and legal effect a royal grant, but in its practical operation after the transfer, it approximated a popular constitution more closely than any other instrument

---

[7] Ibid., 85–89.
[8] Ibid., ch. II, "Rousseau's 'Contrat Social' was not the Source of the [French] Declaration," and ch. V, "Comparison of the French and American Declarations." It ought to be added that certain wording in the French Declaration does bear Rousseau's stamp, wording that, significantly, is not to be found in any of the colonial declarations: Article 6, "Law is the expression of the general will; all citizens have the right to concur personally, or through their representatives in its formation." Some colonial Puritans – though certainly not all of them – did extensively restrict individual rights, particularly rights of conscience, on the basis of majority rule. However, none of them shared Rousseau's extreme collectivist views, epitomized by the phrase, "general will," which stipulated "the complete alienation by each associate member to the community of *all his rights*" (J.-J. Rousseau, "The Social Contract," in *Social Contract*, ed. by Ernest Barker (New York: Oxford University Press, 1960), bk. I, sect. 6, 180; original italics). See Jellinek, *Declaration of the Rights of Man and of Citizens*, 9. Colonial Puritans would have found Rousseau's views quite mysterious.
[9] Ibid., 46–47.

of government in actual use up to that time in America or elsewhere in modern times."[10]

To be sure, the process by which Puritan colonial thought and practice came to embrace the terms of modern constitutionalism was gradual and complex.[11] None of the founding documents of seventeenth-century Puritan New England manifested all of the characteristics of modern constitutionalism: a written code understood as fundamental law antecedent to the government and based on a "self-conscious," "direct and express" act by "the people" whom the government is taken to represent; attribution of political and legal authority, including limits on and division of power, such that any act of government outside the enumerated limits is an exercise of "power without right" and properly subject, if need be, to coercive restraint; an independent judiciary responsible to interpret statutory law and to evaluate its constitutionality; and the codification of a set of inalienable individual rights, whose enforcement is regarded as a critical condition of legitimate government.[12] On the other hand, some of these characteristics were present early on, at least incipiently, and their number expanded and they grew more pronounced as time went by. The pattern of their development is important for understanding what came later. "[By adopting the U.S. Constitution] in the summer of 1787, Americans brought to completion the tradition of constitutional design they had begun more than a century and a half earlier."[13]

Central to that pattern of development were the religious and political predispositions the Puritans brought to the task of interpreting and implementing royal charters and other instruments that authorized their "errand to the wilderness." Like other colonial charters, the Massachusetts Bay charter granted the proprietors a certain amount of discretion in designing the form of government

---

[10] C. H. McIlwain, *Constitutionalism and Its Changing World* (Cambridge: Cambridge University Press, 1939), 241. It is to be noted that whereas Jellinek thought the constitutions of Connecticut and Rhode Island to be "the oldest written constitutions in the modern sense," McIlwain gives Massachusetts Bay that honor. Another scholar favors the Plymouth colony (see Bailyn, *Ideological Origin Ideological Origins of the American Revolution* (Cambridge, MA: Harvard University Press, 1967), fn. 32, 190). Although Lutz does not say which colony had the earliest constitution, he does say that "the Connecticut Charter of 1662 and the Rhode Island Charter [of 1663] served effectively as colonial constitutions, and as proper state constitutions as well." Donald S. Lutz, *The Origins of American Constitutionalism* (Baton Rouge: Louisiana State University Press, 1988), 49. For our purposes, all of the rivals for having adopted the earliest approximations of a modern constitution were *Puritan* colonies. See the later discussion.

[11] See Lutz, *Origins of American Constitutionalism*.

[12] Charles Howard McIlwain, *Constitutionalism: Ancient and Modern* (Ithaca: Cornell University Press, 1966), 9, 14, 21, 76, 81, 117, 139–140.

[13] Lutz, *Origins of American Constitutionalism*, 5.

according to which their assigned territory would be administered.[14] However, Governor John Winthrop and the General Court[15] went well beyond the original wording, asserting that their charter permitted an astounding degree of political independence. As early as 1641, Massachusetts authorities refused help from the English Parliament because the colony might "then be subject to all such laws as [the Parliament] should make or at least such as [it] might impose upon us."[16] When in 1646 the authorities were criticized for considering themselves "rather a free state than a colony or corporation of England," they appeared to agree! Parliament might have authority in England, but "the highest authority here is in the general court, *both by our charter and by our own positive laws.... [O]ur allegiance binds us not to the laws of England any longer than we live in England.*"[17] Though the Puritans were slow to admit it, it was not a large step to the eventual replacement of the authority of the English Crown, as well as of Parliament, with that of "the people" who inhabited the colonies.[18]

Something called the "Agreement of the Massachusetts Bay Company at Cambridge, England" (Cambridge Agreement), adopted on August 26, 1629, by the stockholders or "freemen" of the company before they sailed, helps clarify the burgeoning commitments to constitutional self-government. The document served in effect to modify the Charter of Massachusetts Bay by transferring the government and the control of the charter to the colony. Moreover, it is a statement by the participants declaring their intention to establish a colony in accordance with principles they themselves consent to, and it emphasizes not the commercial purposes highlighted in the charter, but their mutual dedication to work for "Gods glory and the churches good."

The reactions of the Massachusetts Bay authorities and the sentiments contained in the Cambridge Agreement reflect a broader system of what one scholar calls "Puritan teachings on liberties of covenant and covenants of liberty [that] were one fertile seedbed out of which later American constitutionalism grew. Many of the basic constitutional ideas and institutions developed by the Puritans in the seventeenth century remained in place in the eighteenth century."[19] Some of the key ideas are well represented in the Mayflower

---

[14] Ibid., 36.
[15] The "General Court" is the traditional name for the Massachusetts legislature, a designation that has continued into the twenty-first century.
[16] From *Winthrop's Journal* cited in McIlwain, *Constitutionalism and Its Changing World*, 234.
[17] Ibid., 235, emphasis added.
[18] Lutz, *Origins of American Constitutionalism*, 37.
[19] John Witte, Jr., *The Reformation of Rights: Law, Religion, and Human Rights in Early Modern Calvinism* (Cambridge: Cambridge University Press, 2007), 318.

Compact of 1620, adopted by the original Plymouth Pilgrims. Aspiring, they say, to "plant" a colony to the glory of God, the advancement of the Christian faith, and the honor of king and country, they "solemnly and mutually in the presence of God and one another, covenant, and combine ourselves together into a civil body politic, for our better ordering and preservation, and... to enact, constitute, and frame just and equal laws, ordinances, acts, constitutions, offices from time to time, as shall be thought most meet and convenient for the general good of the colony."[20]

The Pilgrim Code of Laws, adopted a few years later, is another example. Having acknowledged the authority of the English king, the code declares the right of Plymouth colonists to "ordain, constitute, and enact" in such a way "that no act, imposition, law, or ordinance be made or imposed upon us at present, or to come but such as shall be imposed by consent of the body of associates and their representatives assembled, according to the free liberties of England."[21] Similarly, the Fundamental Orders of Connecticut of 1639 exhibits a strong sense of self-government based on a covenantal agreement. It lays out the institutions of government and lawmaking authority and provides for popular sovereignty expressed through majority rule, and the Connecticut Charter of 1662 described at length the governing institutions, thereby strongly resembling a modern constitution. "The charter looked very much like a constitution because that is what it was."[22]

In particular, a strong Puritan disposition in favor of legal codes and publicly recorded statutes, aimed at preventing magistrates from proceeding "according to their discretion," prevailed against staunch opposition by some leaders.[23] What is more, Puritans stood for a federal structure of government in which both church and state, however closely combined, were divided into semiautonomous sub-bodies, each with its own internal, plural, and formally regulated structure, and all undergirded by a commitment to a set of fundamental individual rights. The state consisted of town governments, each with its own separate executive, legislative, and judicial authority, and all of them confederated into a broader colonial, and eventually state government.[24] Finally, it was the colonists' specific experience with declarations of rights and their unshakeable loyalty to them that comprised a major reason for the eventual incorporation of the Bill of Rights into the U.S. Constitution in 1791. Although

---

[20] The Mayflower Compact, in Williston Walker, *The Creeds and Platforms of Congregationalism* (Boston: Pilgrim Press, 1960), 92.
[21] Cited in Lutz, *Origins of American Constitutionalism*, 40.
[22] Ibid., 48.
[23] Witte, *Reformation of Rights*, 316.
[24] Ibid., 317.

originally opposed to the addition of a declaration of rights, James Madison and other drafters changed their minds after they came to understand why the Constitution was at first resisted across the colonies. It was, said Madsion, because "the great mass of people who opposed it, disliked it because it did not contain effectual provisions against the encroachment on particular rights, and those safeguards which they have been long accustomed to have interposed between them and the magistrate who exercises the sovereign power."[25] "Americans," says Jellinek, "could calmly [append a bill of rights to] their plan of government..., because that government and the controlling laws had already long existed."[26]

There is also growing support for Jellinek's second conclusion – that a seventeenth-century American Puritan, rather than figures of the eighteenth century, whether French or American, provided the decisive inspiration for a doctrine of "inalienable, inherent and sacred rights of the individual" and, most especially, of a right to liberty of conscience.[27] In particular, Williams's fervently held belief in the right to liberty of conscience has led one scholar to assert that "the Nonestablishment Principle is a keystone of [Williams's] political career and is amply demonstrated in his writings."[28]

It is, indeed, the issue of the establishment of religion – whether or not the government might enforce by law one or more religions – that most divided Williams from other New England Puritans. Although many in the colonies believed that natural rights, including a right to "full liberty" of conscience, and a certain degree of separation of church and state, were central features of constitutional government, Williams's unconventional interpretations set him at odds with his fellows. The distinction between conscience and coercion

---

[25] Cited in Robert Allen Rutland, *The Birth of the Bill of Rights, 1776–1791* (Chapel Hill: University of North Carolina, 1955), 201.

[26] Jellinek, *Declaration of the Rights of Man*, 89.

[27] Several scholars have recently moved toward confirming Jellinek's original insights about Williams: Timothy Hall, *Separation of Church and State: Roger Williams and Religious Liberty* (Urbana: University of Illinois Press, 1998); Isaac Kranmick and R. Laurence Moore, *The Godless Constitution: A Moral Defense of the Secular State* (New York: Norton & Co., 1996, 2005); Martha C. Nussbaum, *Liberty of Conscience: In Defense of America's Tradition of Religious Equality* (New York: Basic Books, 2008); Sumner B. Twiss, "Roger Williams and Freedom of Conscience and Religion as a Natural Right," forthcoming in Sumner B. Twiss, Marian Gh. Simion, and Rodney L. Petersen, eds., *Religion and Public Policy: Human Rights, Conflict, and Ethics* (New York: Cambridge University Press, 2015). Although the first three publications, especially Hall's and Nussbaum's, make especially valuable contributions to understanding the importance of Williams's thought in the American tradition, only Twiss's paper explicitly and systematically connects Williams's doctrine of liberty of conscience to the broader idea of natural rights, a connection Jellinek perceptively identified.

[28] Nussbaum, *Liberty of Conscience*, 69.

entailed in his mind very radical consequences for the relations of church and state. For him, state power in matters of conscience ought to be much more restricted, and efforts to "establish by law" conscientiously held beliefs and practices to be much more suspiciously regarded than anywhere else in the colonies. Moreover, Williams propounded a more elaborate doctrine of the right to the liberty of conscience, including well-developed arguments from both religious and nonreligious premises,[29] than could be found anywhere else in the colonies.[30]

Finally, it has also become ever clearer, as Jellinek saw so acutely, that Williams's ideas laid the foundations for much of the thinking behind the adoption of the "religion clauses" of the First Amendment to the U.S. Constitution, and especially (for our purposes) of the Establishment Clause: "Congress shall make no law respecting an establishment of religion." For example, James Madison, a principal architect of the clause, advanced arguments against the establishment of religion strongly following Williams's lead, focusing on related questions of the greatest concern to Williams. One was guarding conscience by protecting minorities from majorities, as in allowing exemptions for conscience from generally applicable laws.[31] Another was finding grounds for the liberty of conscience that are independent of religion in order to assure equal treatment of all citizens regardless of religious affiliation or belief.[32]

---

[29] By describing Williams as a man who founded a government of religious liberty because "he was driven by powerful and deep religious enthusiasm" (*Declaration of Rights of Man*, 77), Jellinek obscures Williams's distinctly bifocal approach to justifying the right to religious liberty, according to which he supplied grounds that are *both* religious (scriptural/doctrinal) *and* nonreligious (rational/experiential). See the later discussion.

[30] That includes William Penn and the establishment of his "holy experiment" in Pennsylvania in the 1680s. See David Little, "Constitutional Protection of the Freedom of Conscience in Colonial America: The Rhode Island and Pennsylvania Experiments," forthcoming. Williams, of course, did not invent his approach to rights, including the rights of conscience, whether scripturally or naturally understood. He draws on several traditions. One of them went back to Calvin, and to the medieval and conciliar thinking on which Calvin drew. Another stemmed from sixteenth- and seventeenth-century Anabaptists and other "free-church" sectarians.

[31] "I observe with particular pleasure," Madison wrote, "the view you have taken of the immunity of Religion from civil jurisdiction, in every case where it does not trespass on private rights or the public peace." Madison to Edward Livingston, July 10, 1822, cited in Robert S. Alley, ed., *James Madison on Religious Liberty* (Buffalo, NY: Prometheus Books, 1985), 82.

[32] Madison states, "If [as the Virginia Declaration of Rights says] 'all men are by nature free and independent,' all men are to be considered as entering into Society on equal conditions; as relinquishing no more, and therefore retaining no less, one than another, of their *natural rights* [emphasis added]. Above all they are to be considered as retaining an 'equal title to the free exercise of Religion according to the dictates of Conscience.'" He continues, "whilst we assert for ourselves a freedom to embrace, to profess and to observe the Religion which we believe to be of divine origin, we cannot deny an equal freedom to those whose minds have not

THE PURITAN SETTING: RIGHTS AND RELIGION

Though the governing ideals and rules expressed in the Massachusetts Bay charter and the Cambridge Agreement took time to evolve from corporation to commonwealth, and when completed amounted more to oligarchy than democracy – given the fear on the part of some of untrammeled popular control[33] – the Puritan authorities nevertheless "left out of their foundations two principles of government, the feudal and the hereditary, upon which democracy had always found it difficult to [develop]." Beyond that, the apprehensions about democracy of some leaders were partially counterbalanced by other leaders who affirmed the merits of elections as a necessary restraint on arbitrary government.[34] Also of the greatest importance was the impulse in Massachusetts Bay and fellow colonies to adopt declarations of rights. Among other things, this impulse bespoke significant movement toward drawing a distinction between the judicial and legislative aspects of lawmaking, and of confining the judicial function to the interpretation and enforcement of "a relatively stable corpus of statutory written law,"[35] including the bills of rights that for the inhabitants took on some of the characteristics of a constitution.[36]

The Massachusetts Body of Liberties (or "Liberties of the Massachusetts Colony in New England") was adopted into law by the General Court in 1641; it amounted to an exceptionally lengthy list of fundamental rights.[37] Though its author, Nathanial Ward (1578–1652), a prominent pastor and lawyer, incorporated provisions drawn from English statutes and precedents, the Body of Liberties went well beyond those antecedents. The new code redefined and restructured the traditional rights of English subjects in the light of Puritan Christianity, adding modified portions of biblical law and some "daring rights proposals"[38] from left-wing English Puritan pamphleteers.

---

yet yielded to the evidence which has convinced us " "Memorial and Remonstrance," in Alley, *James Madison on Religious Liberty*, 57.

[33] As one leader, John Cotton, put it, "If the people be governors, who shall be governed?" "A Letter from Mr. Cotton to Lord Say and Seal" (1636), Edmund S. Morgan, ed., *Puritan Political Ideas, 1558–1794* (Indianapolis: Bobbs-Merrill Co., 1965), 163. Cf. John Winthrop's opposition to democracy, cited in Francis J. Bremer, *John Winthrop, America's Forgotten Founding Father* (Oxford: Oxford University Press, 2003), 355.

[34] See Witte, *Reformation of Rights*, 317.

[35] George L. Haskins, *Law and Authority in Early Massachusetts* (New York, Macmillan, 1960), 119–120.

[36] One such declaration of rights, the Body of Liberties, adopted in 1641, " was intended to serve as a constitutional bill of rights for the Massachusetts Bay Colony, and studies of later colonial case law make clear that it was so used – although inevitably, like every law in action, it was also blatantly breached, especially in the hands of some early leaders with oligarchic and theocratic pretensions." Witte, *Reformation of Rights*, 287. See the later discussion.

[37] Morgan, *Puritan Political Ideas*, 171–197.

[38] Witte, *Reformation of Rights*, 280.

The document opens, significantly, by referring to "such liberties, immunities, and privileges" that "humanity, civility, and Christianity call for as due to every man in his place and proportion without impeachment or infringement," highlighting the several grounds, religious *and* natural, on which rights were believed to rest.[39] The author, Ward, makes the same point in a pamphlet written four years later, claiming that the enumerated rights are founded on a combination of "God's rule," experience, public deliberation, and the "light of nature." Underlying all these references, he says, is a universal set of moral "essentials," where, beyond local differences and variations in the form of government, "rule and reason will be found all one."[40] The tradition, originated by Massachusetts Bay, was particularly important in the proliferation of written rights guarantees in all the colonies by 1701, as well as in the elaboration of colonial declarations of rights in the 1770s and 1780s.[41]

There was, however, one part of the Body of Liberties that generated a particularly strong division of opinion: the rights pertaining to religious belief and practice, namely, Section 95, Articles 1 through 11, identified as "A Declaration of the Liberties the Lord Jesus hath given to the Churches." According to these articles, all members of the colony have "full liberty" to practice religion according to conscience, though only so long as they "be orthodox in judgment," and, "every church has full liberty to elect church officers," "provided they be able, pious and orthodox."

The special conditions on religious rights – permitting free exercise but only in conformity with orthodox scriptural and doctrinal interpretation – points to what John Cotton himself called the "theocratic" character of the Massachusetts Bay Colony, namely, a state governed by officials regarded as divinely guided.[42] This attitude led officials of the colony, such as John Winthrop, John Cotton, and Nathaniel Ward, to oppose ideas of religious toleration and liberty of conscience, ideas that had the effect, as Ward put it, of hanging the Bible on the Devil's girdle and, consequently, of undermining social order.[43]

---

[39] Morgan, *Puritan Political Ideas*, 172–173. I have modernized and here and there "translated" some of the archaic words and forms of speech in the Body of Liberties and in some of the subsequent citations from Puritan writings.

[40] Nathanial Ward, "The Simple Cobler of Aggawam" (1645; first published in 1647), in Perry Miller and Thomas H. Johnson, eds., *The Puritans: A Sourcebook of Their Writings* (New York: Harper Torchbook, 1963), vol. 1, 236.

[41] Jellinek, *Declaration of the Rights of Man*, 24ff.

[42] Cotton actually uses the term to describe what in his mind is "the best form of government in the commonwealth, as well as the church," in Morgan, ed., *Puritan Political Ideas*, 163.

[43] Miller and Johnson, eds., *The Puritans*, vol. 1, 230.

Although leaders such as Cotton argued that church and state should not be "confounded," because they serve different ends and jurisdictions,[44] the two spheres should nevertheless be "close and compact and co-ordinate one to another,"[45] precisely so as to prevent the kind of heterodoxy in thought and practice and the consequent disruption of social order that Nathanial Ward warned of. As one contemporary divine put it, "the interest of righteousness in the commonwealth and holiness in the churches are inseparable. The prosperity of church and commonwealth are twisted together. Break one cord, you weaken the other also."[46]

"Twisted together" church and state most certainly were. Although magistrates were precluded from holding church office, and church officials from holding civil office, only church members were allowed to vote in civil elections. In addition, churches and clergymen received direct public support through taxes and other donations, and religious beliefs and practices were extensively and harshly regulated by laws covering blasphemy, irreverence, profanity, idolatry and "schismatic" activity. Ministers were regularly called on to provide instruction on the pertinence of God's law to new legislation.[47]

It should be emphasized that governmental support for religion, as practiced by Massachusetts Bay, remained a significant factor in several states during and after the drafting and adoption of the U.S. Constitution. Vermont did not relinquish its system of establishment until 1807, Connecticut until 1818, New Hampshire until 1819, and Massachusetts until 1833. Numerous other states, including Pennsylvania and Delaware, imposed religious tests for public office, which often excluded Catholics, Jews, and atheists.[48] For example, all appointed and elected officials in Delaware were required to profess "faith in God the Father, and in Jesus Christ His only son, and in the Holy Ghost, one God blessed forever."[49] States also frequently enforced religiously preferential laws, following the Massachusetts model of mandating exposure to Calvinist doctrine public schools and of outlawing theater-going, blasphemy, and disturbing the Sabbath.[50]

---

[44] Morgan, ed., *Puritan Political Ideas*, 162–163, 164–165.
[45] Ibid., 163.
[46] A statement by Urian Oakes, pastor and president of Harvard, cited by Witte, *Reformation of Rights*, 310.
[47] I am drawing here on Witte's excellent summary of the church-state arrangement in the Bay colony; see ibid., 310–312.
[48] Nussbaum, *Liberty of Conscience*, 84–85.
[49] Kramnick and Moore, *Godless Constitution*, 30.
[50] Kramnick and Moore, *The Godless Constitution*, 119–120.

ROGER WILLIAMS AND THE NONESTABLISHMENT PRINCIPLE

Although it was widely shared throughout the colonies, by no means all Puritans agreed with the official Massachusetts Bay interpretation of the right of "full liberty" concerning religious belief and practice or with the preference apparent in many of the colonies for one version or another of established religion. The task of articulating and mobilizing a staunchly opposing view fell principally to Roger Williams, who was in trouble with the Bay authorities almost from the time he first set foot in New England in 1631. Although Williams was widely reviled in seventeenth-century America, he was the first person on American soil to articulate fully the principles that ultimately would be embodied in the Constitution of 1787 ("no religious test" for public office) and the First Amendment to the Bill of Rights (forbidding Congress from enacting laws "respecting an establishment of religion" or interfering with the "free exercise of religion").

After being forced to move from one church to another because of his controversial views, Williams was indicted for continuing to oppose laws enforcing religion, as well as other official beliefs and practices he found offensive, including the assumption that colonial lands belonged to the English monarch and not, as he thought, to the Native Americans; or that the English flag was legitimate even though it prominently displayed a Christian cross at its center, thereby, in Williams's view, hopelessly confusing civil and spiritual spheres; or that public oaths should be required of unbelievers, who would thereby be compelled to hypocrisy. Predictably, Williams was found guilty as charged and condemned to return to England for punishment. However, he eluded the authorities and, with the help of Narragansett Indians he had befriended earlier, found his way in 1636 to the territory that, under his leadership, would ultimately become the Rhode Island and Providence Plantation.

In 1643 Williams acquired a minimal patent for the towns of Providence, Portsmouth, and Newport from Parliament, which by 1647 was expanded into a fuller constitutional document that "gives us power to govern ourselves and such others as come among us, and [to establish] such a form of civil government as by the voluntary consent, etc., shall be found most suitable to our estate and condition." In words less hesitant than the sentiments found in Massachusetts Bay, the document specifies without apology or reservation that the form of government will be "democraticall," which is to say "a government held by the free and voluntary consent of all, or the greater part of the free inhabitants," assuring "each man's peaceable and quiet enjoyment of his lawful right and liberty." Then it continues in language largely reminiscent of the 1629 Charter of Massachusetts Bay and the 1641 Body of Liberties to outline a representative political system together with legal institutions carefully regulated by due process, including extensive rights and liberties against arbitrary injury, trial, imprisonment, loss of property, and so on.[51]

Where the Rhode Island and Providence colony differed most sharply from Massachusetts Bay and the other colonies was in the treatment of religion, a point articulated most eloquently in the Rhode Island and Providence Plantation Charter of 1663 – promulgated thirty years after Williams first moved to Rhode Island – that Williams and his associate, John Clarke, were able to acquire from King Charles II. It is this document, says Lutz, that "served effectively as [a] colonial constitution and as [a] state constitution as well"[52] The charter commends the aspirations of the colonists "to hold forth a lively experiment,that a most flourishing civil state may stand and best be maintained... with the full liberty in religious concernments... and... in the free exercise and enjoyment of all... civil and religious rights." In a radical departure from Massachusetts Bay's traditional and circumscribed understanding of "full liberty," it then expresses a radically modern conception articulated in language that anticipates not only Jefferson's Statute of Religious Freedom of 1786 but also the U.S. Constitution:

> No person within said colony, at any time hereafter, shall be [in] any wise molested, punished, disquieted, or called into question, for any difference of opinion in matters of religion, and do not actually disturb the civil peace,... but that all and every person and persons may... freely and fully have and enjoy... their own judgments and consciences in matters of religious concernments,... they behaving themselves peaceably and quietly.[53]

Williams's entire approach can be summarized as a sustained and unrelenting assault on the idea of the legal establishment of religion, whether in its multiple historical guises; or in the form it took in England before, during, or after the Puritan Revolution; or in the various colonial versions Williams knew firsthand. For Williams, "freedom of religion" and "no establishment of religion" were concepts that were inextricably connected, and these concepts, which he shared with Madison, ultimately would become hallmarks of the U.S. Constitution. Both men agreed that a state "establishment of religion" is a violation of freedom of conscience and of the freedom of religion. Although states have the *power* to establish a religion, they have no *right* to do so.

---

[51] See http://oll.libertyfund.org/index.php?option=com_content&task=view&id=1040S&Itemid =264, p. 7.
[52] Lutz, *Origins of American Constitutionalism*, 49. See fn. 10.
[53] See http://avalon.law.yale,edu/17th_century/rio4.asp, p. 1.

The titles of Williams's two best-known works, *The Bloody Tenent* (1644) and *The Bloody Tenent Yet More Bloody* (1652), epitomize what is for him the essential problem. The legal enforcement of religion, according to which people are punished for their conscientious convictions, opposes all that is right and holy and, into the bargain, gives rise to violence and bloodshed. Williams supported this conclusion by several different arguments, though all of them were based on an age-old supposition about the difference between conscience and government that lay deep within the Christian tradition and was developed in various directions by the Calvinist heritage in which he squarely stood.[54]

To be sure, Williams was a peculiar Calvinist in one respect. Like many of his fellow Puritans at the time, and quite unlike Calvin,[55] he embraced strong millenarian views.[56] Millenarians typically expected the imminent return of Christ and the establishment of a "new millennium" of divine rule, though there were differences among them as how the new order would look and be administered. However, the important point is that, Williams's views on the imminence of the millennium changed over time. Beginning in the early 1640s, with the onset of the Puritan rebellion against Charles I, he, like many of his Puritan confreres, believed the millennium was at hand.[57] But as the disappointments and shortcomings associated with Cromwell's rule appeared, Williams "revised his millennial timetable," projecting "his hope for... renewal... into a more distant future."[58]

Some scholars have interpreted this development to mean that Williams was becoming more and more indifferent to and disaffected from the world, and therefore was increasingly motivated in a "relentless quest for religious purity" to fence off religious belief and practice from the corruptions of the world, including the state.[59] That would explain, among other things, his strong convictions concerning "separation of church and state," for which he is famous. The problem is Williams was not indifferent to the world, and

---

[54] Though Perry Miller did not always get Williams right, he is correct on this point: "[Williams] remained to the end a stalwart Calvinist, believing firmly in predestination, reprobation, irresistible grace, and, above all, the perseverance of the saints." *Roger Williams: His Contribution to the American Tradition* (New York: Atheneum, 1953), 28.

[55] Along with one or two other books of the Bible, Calvin refrained from writing a commentary on the Book of Revelations, a primary source for those with millenarian views.

[56] See Clark W. Gilpin, *The Millenarian Piety of Roger Williams* (Chicago: University of Chicago Press, 1979).

[57] Ibid., 57.

[58] Ibid., 165.

[59] Philip Hamburger, *Separation of Church and State*, 51.

certainly not to the state. His indefatigable efforts in establishing the Rhode Island colony, in serving as a government official at considerable financial loss and as the recipient of interminable abuse from antagonists inside and outside the colony, in helping to acquire a charter for the colony and imploring citizens to abide by it, and in publishing tome after tome justifying the new experiment, all make that unmistakably clear.

In Williams's case, it was just because Christ's reign was deferred indefinitely that he thought it necessary to attend – in the interim – to the importance of the natural and the temporal, to creating well-ordered political and legal institutions necessary to guaranteeing the equal rights of all, a subject of intense concern to the Calvinist tradition. In short, by modifying his millenarian beliefs, he made room for his Calvinist leanings.

Drawing on Augustine, Thomas Aquinas, and others, John Calvin (1509–1564) previously had called attention to a sharp distinction between two forums or tribunals: the "internal forum" (conscience) and the "external forum" (civil authority).[60] The first concerns personal, inward deliberation regarding fundamental belief and practice that is regulated by "spiritual power," and the second concerns "external" or public deliberation regarding "outward behavior" – the needs of "the present life," such as food, clothing, and the laws of social cooperation – that is regulated by the "power of the sword."[61] Calvin sometimes speaks of these as "two worlds," over which different kings and different laws have authority, requiring that they "always be examined separately."[62] The "outward" sphere of social order, underwritten by the threat of force, is clearly set apart from the sphere of conscience and, as such, is delimited by it.

Calvin says as much in his commentary on the thirteenth chapter of the Letter to the Romans. The proper jurisdiction of a well-ordered government is defined exclusively by the "part of the law that refers to human society," or the second table of the Decalogue whose basic principle, according to Calvin, is that "all individuals should preserve their rights." "There is no allusion at all [in Paul's discussion of political order] to the first table of the law, which deals with the worship of God,"[63] and Calvin stresses the same point elsewhere: Because "the whole of [Paul's] discussion concerns civil government[, those] who bear

---

[60] Calvin, *Institutes of the Christian Religion*, ed. John T. McNeill, trans. Ford Battles, 2 vols. (Philadelphia: Westminster Press, 1960, bk. 3, ch. XIX, para. 15, 847–848; bk. 4, ch. X, para. 5, 1183.
[61] Ibid., bk. 3, ch. XIX, para. 15, 847.
[62] Ibid.
[63] Calvin, *Epistles of Paul the Apostle to the Romans and to the Thessalonians*, trans. Ross Mackenzie (Grand Rapids, MI: Eerdmans, 1976, ch. 13, v. 10, 286.

rule over . . . consciences attempt to establish their blasphemous tyranny . . . in vain."[64]

This, of course, was not *all* Calvin said. He occasionally contradicts himself: "No government," he says elsewhere, "can be happily established unless piety is the first concern; and those laws are preposterous which neglect God's right and provide only for men."[65] He solemnly pronounces that "civil government has as its appointed end, so long as we live [in the world], to cherish and protect the outward worship of God, to defend sound doctrine of piety and the position of the church,"[66] a principle he heartily favored in sixteenth-century Geneva.

As much as anything, this antinomy in Calvin's thought over the legal establishment of religion came to signify the basic division between Williams and many of his fellow colonists. Williams embraced the first part, the liberal side, of Calvin's thought, and wholeheartedly rejected the second, whereas Massachusetts Bay affirmed and implemented the second part by playing down, if not entirely discarding, the first.

For Williams, there could be no two ways about it. Experience, reason, and religion all ultimately point the same way: The law of the sword – the indispensable instrument of the "external forum" – is not all powerful. It must defer to and protect the law of the spirit – the law of reason, will, and affection that governs the "internal forum."

When this rule is not observed, the historical lessons are clear. In Williams's words,

> A most lamentably true experience of all the ages [is] that persecution for the cause of conscience has always proved pernicious. . . . He that reads the records of truth and time with an impartial eye shall find this to be the lance that has pierced the veins of kings and kingdoms, of saints and sinners, and filled the streams and rivers with their blood.[67]

> A breach of civil peace [does not arise from] false and idolatrous practices [themselves, but from] the wrong and preposterous way of suppressing, preventing, and extinguishing such doctrines or practices by weapons of wrath and blood, whips, stocks, and imprisonment, banishment, and death by which men are commonly persuaded to convert heretics.[68]

---

[64] Ibid., 283.
[65] *Institutes*, bk. 4, ch. XX, para. 9.
[66] Ibid., bk. 4, ch. XX, para. 2.
[67] Roger Williams, *A Bloody Tenent of Persecution*, in *Complete Writings of Roger Williams* (New York: Russell & Russell, 1963) III, 182. Citations from Williams are modernized for easier understanding.
[68] Ibid., III, 80.

Attempting to coerce conscience is to make a grievous mistake about how the mind works. For one thing, many of those who persecute conscience, including the Massachusetts Bay leaders, displayed an unseemly inconsistency by failing to apply to themselves charges that they freely leveled against others. Ready to "cry out against persecution when they are under the hatches," such people are nevertheless ready "to persecute when they sit at the helm."[69] This tendency "to gross partiality," which "denies the principles of common justice" prompting people "to weigh out to the consciences of others what [is judged] not right to be weighed out to their own," is nothing more than "Machiavellianism," which makes a religion "but a cloak or stalking horse to [self-serving] policy and private ends."[70]

But a greater shortcoming would be to neglect the conceptual distinction between physical force and conscience. If one is attempting to regulate what Calvin called the "outward behavior" of human beings – to prevent them from taking what does not belong to them, or maiming or killing others to their own advantage – "cannons, ... bullets, powder, muskets, swords, [and] pikes ... are weapons effectual and [proportionate]." Such weapons are appropriate because without them physical harm or injury would occur. They are required for and capable of restraining action considered morally and legally illicit, and they may, if necessary, be effectively applied without or against the consent of the offender. It is precisely because the behavior in question is "outward" that it is under the jurisdiction of the "external forum," whose essential function is the regulation of legitimately administered physical force.

But things are different with the internal forum:

> To [try to] batter down [the strongholds of] false worship, heresy, schism, [spiritual] blindness or hardness [of heart] [and drive them] out of the soul and spirit, it is vain, improper, and unsuitable to bring those weapons which are used by persecutors – stocks, whips, prisons, swords, gibbets, stakes[.] ([W]here these seem to prevail with some cities and kingdoms, a stronger force sets up again what a weaker pulled down[.]) ... [They are] never able to effect anything in the soul ... [B]ut against these spiritual strongholds in the souls of men, spiritual artillery and weapons are proper.[71]

---

[69] From Williams, *A Bloody Tenent*, cited in Miller, *Roger Williams*, 140.
[70] Williams, *Bloody Tenent Yet More Bloody*, *Complete Writings*, III, 498.
[71] Williams, *Bloody Tenent*, *Complete Writings*, III, 148–149. I have omitted passing references Williams makes to God's role in changing consciences because they are incidental to the more general conceptual point Williams affirms here and elsewhere concerning the implied distinction between reasons and causes I call attention to in the text.

According to the tradition in which Williams stood, the heart of the conscience is inward consent based on a conviction of truth and right. That is something that physical force, in and of itself, is incapable of producing. As a logical matter, force cannot compel belief because belief depends on reasons consisting of arguments and evidence. The threat of force, as in a case of robbery or rape, is not a reason in the proper sense because it lacks a valid justification. Thus, the only "weapons" suitably employed in the internal forum are "spiritual," namely, appeals and arguments subject to commonly understood normative standards, whose object is consensual or heartfelt agreement.

Accordingly, Williams's statement that physical weapons are unable to have any effect on the soul is basically a normative claim. He frequently asserts that "forcing of the conscience of any person" is equivalent to "spiritual" or "soul rape,"[72] implying that while attempts to force conscience do in fact have consequences, those consequences are invariably grave. Such attempts degrade or deform the conscience by inducing hypocrisy, narrow-mindedness, or self-betrayal precisely because they defy so completely the proper rules and procedures appropriate to the conduct of the internal forum. In a word, the use of force against conscience is a fundamental violation because of the nature of conscience itself.

This distinction is so powerful that it is understood, however dimly, even by highly disreputable people. "Do not even the most bloody popes and cardinals... put a difference between the crimes of murder, treason and adultery (for which although the offender repent, yet he suffers punishment) and the crimes of heresy, blasphemy, etc., which upon recantation and confession, are frequently remitted?"[73]

In short, the idea is that the conscience – the internal forum, designed, as it is, to operate according to "the laws of the spirit" – must be respected as a special preserve free of direct forcible regulation, and any effort by the external forum to "invade" the internal forum is an atrocity against what Williams calls "the natural conscience and reason of all men."[74] This is the primary explanation, to his mind, of why "rivers of blood" predictably follow such "invasions." Wherever they "seem to prevail with some cities and kingdoms," it is because superior force succeeds temporarily in quieting opposition, though not in eliciting inward consent nor eliminating potential resistance.

Along with references to experience and reason, Williams adds extensive appeals to Christian scripture, doctrine, and history. In one place, he writes

---

[72] Williams, *Bloody Tenent Yet More Bloody*, *Complete Writings*, IV, 325,
[73] Ibid., 443.
[74] Ibid., 443.

that in shedding "the blood of so many hundred thousand of poor servants [of Jesus] by the civil powers of the world, pretending [thereby] to suppress blasphemies, heresies, idolatries, superstition, etc.," the persecutors of conscience are "lamentably guilty" of spilling the "most precious blood" of Jesus himself.[75] The decisive transgression took place

> when Constantine broke the bounds of this his own and God's edict, and [drew] the sword of civil power in suppressing other consciences for the [sake of] establishing the Christian [church.] [T]hen began the great mystery of the churches' sleep, [by which] the gardens of Christ's churches turned into the wilderness of National Religion, and the world (under Constantine's dominion) into the most unchristian Christendom. . . . There never was any National Religion good in this world but one [namely, ancient Israel], and since the desolation of that nation, there shall never be any National Religion good again.[76]

This passage makes clear that Williams's famous image of the "wall of separation" between "the garden" and "the wilderness" does not mean, as Mark deWolfe Howe has claimed,[77] that the wilderness is the civil state from which "the gardens of Christ's churches" must be walled off pure and undefiled and with which the churches must have nothing whatsoever to do. Howe asserts erroneously that Williams favored a wall between the garden and the wilderness "not because he was fearful that without such a barrier the arm of the church would extend its reach. It was, rather, the dread of worldly corruptions which might consume the churches if sturdy fences against the wilderness [of the civil state] were not maintained."[78]

On the contrary, the wilderness Williams fears is the condition of an established religion where *both* church *and* state are mutually degraded and corrupted by failing to observe the critical distinction between the inward and outward forums. A state where there is no establishment – where conscience is free to exercise itself as it should – is, to be sure, a place in which "the gardens of Christ's churches" can exist as intended, but it is also a place in which the state can perform its duties as intended as well. It is such circumstances that

---

[75] Ibid., 494.
[76] Ibid., IV, 442. The reference to "ancient Israel" as the one exception to the Nonestablishment Principle underscores Williams's belief that the close interconnection of the religious and civil communities evident in the Old Testament was provisionally authorized by God "until Christ came." That arrangement was, as Williams says often, "a Nonesuch," or something never to be repeated.
[77] *The Garden and the Wilderness* (Chicago: University of Chicago Press, 1965).
[78] Ibid., 6.

exhibit the desirable degree of consonance and harmony between religious and civil organizations, thereby fulfilling the proper vocations of each.

Williams is simply reiterating – now in theological terms – the distinction between the inward and outward tribunals, directed by their different laws and sanctions and tied to the key difference between the First and the Second Tables of the Decalogue, all of which Calvin emphasized. Indeed, Williams introduces his own discussion of the difference between the two tables, and its importance for governing, by referring enthusiastically to "that excellent servant of God, Calvin" and then by citing Calvin's comment limiting the jurisdiction of the civil government to the Second Table. At the same time, Williams is equally resolute in rejecting the "other side" of Calvin. That there is any value to the proposal that "Christ's ordinances and administrations of worship [should be] appointed... to a civil state, town or city, as [in] the instance of Geneva," "I confidently deny," writes Williams.[79]

Williams's notion of the details of the difference and the relations between church and state, as well as the theological interpretation of those details, is somewhat complicated, though he never strays very far from his nonestablishment position. He occasionally argues that scripture and history prove that "although the ... church and the civil kingdom or government [properly understood] be not inconsistent, but ... may stand together, yet they are independent,"[80] such that a political order may exist peacefully either without the presence of the church or alongside churches that are divided from each other, so long as those divisions do not take control of the affairs of state.

Williams is frequently quite explicit in echoing one side of Calvin's thought to the effect that church and state are "two worlds" over which different kings and different laws have authority, requiring that they "always be examined separately":

> The civil nature of the magistrate we have proved to receive no addition of power from the magistrate's being Christian, no more than it receives diminution from his not being a Christian; even as the commonweal is a true commonweal although it have not heard of Christianity, and Christianity professed in it... makes it no more a commonweal, and Christianity taken away... makes it none the less a commonweal.[81]

Williams is confident that the ingredients for "civility," for a common life among people of different creeds, origins, and identities, are there ready to

---

[79] Ibid., III, 225.
[80] Ibid., III, 224–225.
[81] Ibid., III, 355.

be put to use under the right conditions. A civil order based on what has been called a "thin approach" to government, where citizens are able, singly or in groups, to pursue their own notions of the good so long as common rights and interests are not compromised, is largely compatible with Williams's view:

> Frequent experience in all parts of the world tells us that many thousands [of people] are far more peaceable subjects, more loving and helpful neighbors, and more true and fair dealers in civil interaction than many who account themselves to be the only religious people in the world.[82]

Utterances of this kind might lead us to think that for Williams church and state have, after all, very little to do with each other and are indeed "two worlds" that must "always be examined separately." In fact, Williams does speak in one place of "divers sorts of goodness" wherein a subject or magistrate "may be a good subject, a good magistrate, in respect of civil or moral goodness," and wherever such virtue exists, "it is commendable and beautiful, though Godliness, which is infinitely more beautiful, be wanting."[83]

This way of putting things is certainly part of Williams's outlook, but it is by no means all there is. He also strongly favors a creative and constructive affinity between a civil authority liberated from religious control and what he believes to be the true message of the Christian Gospel. Although it is undoubtedly possible for secular regimes to organize themselves in peace and prosperity without Christian assistance, the proper Christian approach adds a significant layer of support and encouragement for a modern constitutional order, including the disestablishment of religion and the protection of the rights of free conscience. In short, the world needs all the help it can get in disabusing itself of the distortions of "national religion," and in thereby recovering its preexisting capacities for common civil and moral goodness. The Christian message, properly preached and practiced, may be of considerable auxiliary assistance. How else may we interpret the following passages?

> There is a sword of civil justice, being of a material nature [designed] for the defense of persons, estates, families, liberties of a city or civil state, and the suppressing of uncivil or injurious persons or actions, which cannot, *now that it is under Christ, when all nations are merely civil*, extend to matters of the spirit and soul.[84]

---

[82] Williams, *Bloody Tenent Yet More Bloody, Complete Writings*, IV, 238.
[83] Ibid., IV, 246.
[84] *Bloody Tenent*, cited in Miller, *Roger Williams*, 133 (italics added). I confess I have reconstructed this statement, thereby (I hope) sharpening its meaning.

I affirm that state policy and state necessity, which (for the peace of the state and the preventing of rivers of civil blood) [safeguards] the consciences of men, will be found to agree most punctually with the rules of the best politician that ever the world saw, the King of kings and Lord of lords.[85]

It would be impossible to read Williams's complete writings without appreciating his deep conviction, expressed repeatedly, that Christian scripture (properly interpreted) provides overwhelming evidence of the consonance between the Christian message and the legal disestablishment of religion.[86]

Beyond these reflections on the nonestablishment principle, Williams commented on two other related matters that came to exercise the thinking of Madison and other drafters of the U.S. Constitution a century later.

One was the tension at the heart of modern constitutionalism over accommodating the interests of the majority with those of dissenting individuals and minorities. Williams was a political contractualist and therefore embraced the idea that "the will of the people is the supreme law," an idea fundamental to Calvinist constitutionalism. Such thinking underlay the several Rhode Island charters he obtained, or helped to obtain, first from the Parliament during the Interregnum and later from Charles II after the Restoration.

> The sovereign, original, and foundation of civil power lies in the people (who are the civil power as distinct from the government). If so, a people may erect and establish what form of government seems to them most meet for their civil condition. It is evident that such governments as are by them erected and established have no more power, nor for any longer time, than the civil power or people, consenting and agreeing, shall entrust them with. This is clear not only in reason, but in the experience of all commonweals, where the people are not deprived of their natural freedom by the power of tyrants.[87]

---

[85] Ibid., III, 179. In several places, Williams suggests a somewhat more positive role for the magistrate in regard to supporting the Christian church. Once he says that a magistrate ought to "cherish (as a foster father) the Lord Jesus in his truth [and] in his saints, . . . and to countenance them even to the death," without clarifying what he means. He also refers to the obligation to protect Christians from civil violence and injury, but that would presumably apply to all religious groups (ibid., III, 129). In another place, he speaks of countenancing and encouraging the church without explaining further, though he adds, again, a reference to protection from violence (which is a general obligation of the magistrate), and he immediately proceeds to condemn magistrates who encourage and protect only those religious groups "which they judge to be true and approve of, not permitting other consciences than their own" (ibid., III, 280).

[86] See, for example, James P. Byrd, Jr., *The Challenges of Roger Williams: Religious Liberty, Violent Persecution and the Bible* (Macon, GA: Mercer University Press, 2002).

[87] Williams, *The Bloody Tenent, Complete Writings*, III, 249–250.

He goes on to emphasize, again in the spirit of (liberal) Calvinism, not only that "the very nature and essence of a civil magistrate" derives from "the people's choice and free consent" but also that it has as its *exclusive* purpose "the common-weal or safety of [the] people in their bodies and goods,"[88] or the adoption of "such civil laws [as] concern [their] common rights, peace, and safety,"[89] elsewhere characterized as "material civil nature"[90] or Second-Table concerns.

Basic to Williams's approach is the protection of individual rights, including most prominently individual (and minority) rights of conscience. However important the people's will may be, whether expressed unanimously or by majority rule, a legitimate government – one not deprived of "natural freedom by the power of tyrants" – has an irreducible obligation to safeguard "any civil right or privilege" due a citizen simply as a human being ("as a man," in Williams's words),[91] or what he calls in another place the "natural and civil rights and liberties" of all citizens.[92]

Although these fundamental rights apply to matters of property, political participation, and legal protection (as they did in Calvin's thought, as well as in Massachusetts Bay, Rhode Island, and other colonies), Williams's preoccupation, as we would expect, is with the special protection of the right of religious freedom or freedom of conscience. Williams denies to the state any authority "to govern the spiritual and Christian commonweal, the flock and church of Christ, to pull down or set up religion, to judge, determine, or punish in spiritual controversies,"[93] thereby insisting on a constitutional restriction on civil power and a protected space for the free exercise of conscience.

Once the principle of nonestablishment is accepted, the key remaining question, of course, is just where to draw the proper line between the state and conscience. Williams is clear that in the face of a conflict between conscience and compelling state interest, such as public safety, peace, and common rights, conscience is expected to yield. For example, in all cases "wherein civility is wronged in [regard to] the bodies and goods of any," as in recorded instances of religiously sanctioned human sacrifice, "the civil sword is God's sword" "for suppressing such practices and appearances," including "the very principles" on which they rest.[94]

[88] Ibid., III, 354.
[89] Ibid., III, 366.
[90] Ibid., III, 160.
[91] Williams, *Bloody Tenent Yet More Bloody, Complete Works*, IV, 414.
[92] Ibid., IV, 365.
[93] Ibid., III, 366.
[94] Williams, "The Examiner Defended," *Complete Writings*, VII, 243.

When the vital interests of the state are not at issue, Williams occasionally condones special exemptions from general laws for religious individuals and groups, even though he is not always entirely clear or consistent in the way he arrives at his conclusions. With some plausibility, he implies that because taxation pertains only to "outward" bodies and goods, religious activities and appurtenances, as something beyond the "merely civil," may be granted "immunity and freedom from tax and toll," perhaps endorsing, in keeping with subsequent American jurisprudence, a fitting limit on the civil control of religious affairs. Not too much can be made of the point, however, because Williams leaves the matter to the discretion of the civil authority.[95]

As to the question of the "seeming incivility" of Mary's virgin birth outside wedlock, he makes an impassioned plea for special exemption, in part, interestingly enough, on the basis of the principles of the administration of civil authority. He claims that it is beyond question that even "the most civil and the severest judge, upon due examination of the whole matter, might rationally and judiciously . . . have found [any] violence of civility, [or any] wrong to the bodies or goods of any."[96] Such reasoning opens the door, at least, to a claim Madison would later make in favor of religious exemptions from general laws unless the rights of others are violated or there is a substantial threat to public safety.[97]

At the same time, several of Williams's other judgments are harder to follow. In interpreting the aborted sacrifice of Isaac by Abraham, his claim that this, too, is a case of only "seeming incivility" is much less convincing, because a direct threat to bodily injury is obviously at stake.[98] Moreover, his assertions that practicing offensive patterns of dress and speech by certain religious groups, such as "the monstrous hair of women up[on] the heads of some men" or the use by Quakers of the familiar and, to Williams, contemptuous "thou" in addressing superiors, represented significant threats to public order and safety and, therefore, should be outlawed are controversial, at best.[99]

There is another example of special interest. It concerns Williams's response to the objection of some members of the Providence Plantation to a

---

[95] Williams, *Bloody Tenent, Complete Writings,* III, 252. See Nussbaum, *Liberty of Conscience,* 60, for confirmation of such an interpretation, though she criticizes him for not stipulating that tax exemption "should be given to all religions on the basis of some fair principle; here he sells his own ideas grievously short."
[96] Williams, "The Examiner Defended," *Complete Writings,* VII, 245.
[97] See fn. 37.
[98] Ibid.
[99] See Edmund S. Morgan, *Roger Williams: The Church and the State* (New York: Harcourt, Brace & World, 1967, 134–135.

requirement of compulsory military service. Williams answers by employing a metaphor concerning the role and responsibility of a ship's captain. Under normal conditions, the captain has no right to tell the crew and passengers how or whether they should worship or how they should determine other matters of conscience. However, if the ship comes under attack, the captain is within his authority to command all hands to rally to the ship's defense. This is, it would appear, a simple matter of the necessary protection of the outward bodies and goods of the people on board and is thus a consistent application of the basic principles of constitutional authority.[100] Williams's argument, unlike that of Madison a century later, does not make allowance for a constitutionally protected exemption of conscientious objection to military service. It is possible that those whom Williams was addressing were opposed not just to conscription but also to the legitimacy of civil authority itself, in which case he was simply putting forward a general defense of civil government. However, it is also possible that in cases of conflict between an individual's conscientious objection to fighting and the "people's" compelling need to defend their common interest, Williams decided in favor of the latter. If so, Madison and Williams are simply at odds on this matter.

However, it is hard to be sure about Williams's settled position. In another place, where he again employs the metaphor of the role and responsibility of ship officials – this time, "the master and pilot," as he refers to them – Williams comes to a different conclusion with different implications for the constitutional division of powers and the exercise of conscience.[101] The special focus of the lengthy disquisition is on whether a prince, who happens to be on board, or the master and pilot of the ship are finally responsible for the ship's welfare. Williams answers that it is the master and pilot who have final authority, so that in a case where the prince commands one thing about how the ship shall be run or which course to take, and the ship's officials another, sailors "may lawfully disobey the prince, and obey the governor of the ship in the actions of the ship."

But Williams goes further. Should the officials "out of base fear and cowardice, or covetous desire of reward," acquiesce to the command of the prince "contrary to the rules of art and experience," and "the ship come in danger and perish, and the prince with it," the officials would be guilty of malfeasance and rightfully subject to punishment. The suggestion here is that the

---

[100] Hall, *Separation of Church and State*, 109, discussing Roger Williams to the Town of Providence, ca. Jan. 1654/55, in *The Correspondence of Roger Williams*, ed. Glenn W. LaFantasie (Hanover and London: Brown University Press/University Press of New England, 1988), 2:423–24.

[101] Williams, *Bloody Tenent, Complete Writings*, III, 376–380.

ship officials forfeited their authority by failing in their duty. Indeed, Williams states explicitly that the officials should be obeyed unless the commands "be in manifest error, wherein it is granted [that] *any passenger* may reprove" the officials (italics added). Williams's underlying point favors the right of groups *or individuals* to hold the actions of established authorities to account and to express (and apparently to act on) conscientious disagreement with their decisions, according to commonly accessible "rules of art and experience." Obviously, this line of thinking favors a quite expansive sphere of protection for individual conscience over against governmental authority.

A last question related to the establishment of religion concerns the grounds of the "fundamental law" of a constitutional system. As was safeguarding individual and minority rights in face of "the will of the people," this issue was of intense concern to Williams.[102] If a particular religious point of view is the foundation of civil law, on what basis might nonbelievers be held accountable? It is true that Williams's fellow Puritans in Massachusetts Bay and elsewhere, had, like Calvin before them, invoked "humanity" and "civility," interpreted "in the light of nature," as providing grounds for their declarations of rights. As with Calvin, this was important for establishing universal liability; all human beings might justly be held to account for transgressing the law of their own nature, whether they had heard of and accepted Christianity or not.

The problem for Williams was that Calvin and many of his spiritual descendants went well beyond this standard. When they proceeded to claim that their version of "orthodox" Christianity was indispensable to the security and prosperity of the state and that, therefore, citizens could legitimately be punished not just for violating a moral code commonly accessible to human beings as such but also for transgressing what they thought were the clear teachings of the "Lord Jesus," they caused a catastrophe for both religious and civil communities.

---

[102] This point has consistently been overlooked in part, I believe, because scholars either have underplayed the importance of the natural rights idea in Calvin's thought, which is such an important foundation of Williams's political outlook, or have failed to connect Williams to that tradition. For example, Brian Tierney, in an article on natural rights and religious freedom, claims incorrectly that Williams never used rights language ("Religious Rights: An Historical Perspective" in John Witte, Jr. and Johan D. Van der Vyver, eds., *Religious Human Rights in Global Perspective: Religious Perspectives* (The Hague: Martinus Nijhof, 1996), 42); John Witte in *Reformation of Rights* totally ignores Williams; and Martha Nussbaum, in her otherwise forceful study of liberty of conscience in the American tradition and of Williams's central place in that tradition, entirely overlooks the natural rights side of Williams's thought. Instead, she mistakenly traces the grounds of Williams's extrareligious appeals to Stoic thought. There is not the slightest evidence in Williams's writings that he paid any attention to the Stoics or other classical sources. His political thought is (liberal) Calvinist through and through. See Little, "Calvin and Natural Rights," *Political Theology* vol. 10, no. 3 (2009), 411–430.

For Williams, the central tenet of the natural rights tradition was all important: "[F]rom the beginning, the subjective idea of natural rights was not derived specifically from Christian revelation," "but from an understanding of human nature itself as rational, self-aware, and morally responsible."[103] That understanding lies behind the Rhode Island Charter of 1663, which Williams helped design and obtain, when it assures citizens of "the free exercise and enjoyment of all their civil and religious rights," or of "their just rights and liberties." It also underlies Williams's own references to the "common rights" of citizens or to "any civil right or privilege" due a person simply as a human being, or when he implies that these follow from what he calls a law "simply moral, civil, and natural." All such references suggest a well-developed belief in a natural right to conscience, taken to be antecedent to the government, and to warrant special protection in face of "the will of the people," that rests on foundations independent of Christian revelation, or any other religious principle.[104] He underscores this commitment in one of his most ringing declarations concerning the nonreligious basis of civil authority. Political "power, might, or authority," he says, "is not religious, Christian, etc. but natural, humane and civil."[105]

> There is a moral virtue, a moral fidelity, ability and honesty, which other men (beside church members) are, by good nature and education, by good laws and good examples nourished and trained up in, that civil places of trust and credit need not be monopolized into the hands of church members (who sometimes are not fitted for them) and all others deprived and despoiled of their natural and civil rights and liberties.[106]

Williams registers these same sentiments in an early book he published on the language and ways of the Narragansett Indians whom he befriended in the process of settling Rhode Island[107]:

> Boast not, proud English, of thy birth and blood,
> Thy brother Indian is by birth as good.
> Of one blood God made him and thee and all,
> As wise, as fair, as strong, as personal.[108]

---

[103] Tierney, *Idea of Natural Rights*, 76.
[104] Sumner Twiss has elaborately and convincingly elucidated Williams's doctrine of natural rights in his brilliant paper, "Roger Williams and Freedom of Conscience and Religion as a Natural Right." See fn. 27.
[105] Williams, *Bloody Tenent, Complete Writings*, III, 398.
[106] Williams, *Bloody Tenent Yet More Bloody, Compete Writings*, IV, 365.
[107] Williams, *A Key into the Language of America*. 1644. Reprint, Bedford, MA: Applewood Books, 1997. Portions reproduced in Perry Miller, ed., *Roger Williams: His Contribution to the American Tradition*.
[108] Ibid., 64.

This, despite some very harsh comments Williams makes about the religious beliefs and practices of the Narragansetts and other Native Americans he was able to observe. Indeed, what is especially interesting about his comments on the manners and morals of the Narragansetts is how much his assessment of them, and even of their final spiritual destiny, is affected by their degree of compliance, to Williams's mind, with the law that is "simply civil, moral, and natural."

> I have known them leave their house and mat
> To lodge a friend or stranger,
> When Jews and Christians oft have sent
> Christ Jesus to the manger.
>
> If nature's sons both wild and tame
> Humane and courteous be,
> How ill becomes its sons of God
> To want humanity.
>
> By nature, wrath's his portion, thine no more,
> Till grace his soul and thine in Christ restore.
> Make sure thy second birth, else thou shalt see
> Heaven ope to Indians wild, but shut to thee.[109]

CONCLUSION

With the help of recent scholarship, I have confirmed two important conclusions drawn a century ago by the Austrian legal scholar, Georg Jellinek, that provide historical and conceptual background for the protection of religious freedom guaranteed by the Establishment Clause of the First Amendment to the U.S. Constitution.

The first conclusion – that the doctrine of legally enforceable individual rights taken to be essential to modern constitutions "is not of political but religious origin" – has been verified with reference to the contributions of the Puritans of colonial New England. Drawing on their Calvinist heritage and its commitment to the constitutional protection of civil rights and liberties, they expended considerable energy designing and implementing declarations of rights as an indispensable part of their civil covenants. Antedating by many years the French Declaration or the U.S. Bill of Rights, these declarations prepared the groundwork for the later documents.

[109] Ibid., 62–64.

Jellinek's second conclusion – related to the first – has also been corroborated by examining Williams's writings in the light of fresh scholarship. It is not to eighteenth-century figures, whether French or American, that we must look to find the distinctive source of this radical rights doctrine, but to a colonial Puritan, Roger Williams. The principal difference between Williams and his fellows is conveniently summarized in reference to his opposition to the establishment of religion. He strenuously objected to the various forms of "National Religion" found not only in England and Europe at the time but also in the other colonies, arguing that case because he believed those arrangements profoundly misconstrued both the teachings of Christianity and of the "the light of nature." Only by recovering the proper balance between the inward and outward forums jointly prescribed by nature and the Christian tradition can truth and right prevail.

PART IV

Public Policy and the Restraint of Force

10

Terrorism, Public Emergency, and International Order

The U.S. Example, 2001–2014

PROLOGUE

About a year after the terrorist attacks against the United States on September 11, 2001, I completed an initial essay on terrorism and public emergency, whose special focus was the impact of the U.S. response to the attacks on the existing international order.[1] International order was taken to mean the system of collective security defined by the United Nations Charter, together with the body of universal human rights, established in 1948 and developed over the years, mostly under the auspices of the UN, as well as the system of humanitarian law codified in the 1949 Geneva Conventions – all of which, of course, were products of the post–World War II era. The essay summarized and criticized the early record of the Bush administration through 2002.

I updated the record through 2006 in an unpublished lecture delivered that year at the law faculty of the Technical University of Dresden, Germany. It summarized the argument of the earlier essay and expanded on its conclusions, paying special attention to acts of the U.S. Congress and rulings of the U.S. Supreme Court between 2003 and 2006 in response to the antiterrorism polices of the Bush administration. The gist of the evaluation was, on balance, strongly critical.

In 2012, I composed a third essay on the subject, "National Security Policy: Obama vs. Bush and Romney," which appeared on a website favoring the candidacy of Barack Obama for president.[2] It completed the review of all

---

[1] The chapter was later published as "Terrorism, Public Emergency, and International Order: The U.S. Example," in *Human Rights, Democracy, and Religion*, ed. by Lars Binderup and Tim Jensen (Odense, Denmark: University of Southern Denmark, 2005), 127–155.
[2] Savvyvoters.com.

eight years of the two Bush administrations, also drawing attention to continuities in personnel and ideas with the Romney presidential candidacy of that year. In addition, it expanded the overall evaluation of U.S. policy to include Obama's first term, drawing some comparisons and contrasts among the three men. The comparisons and contrasts, although generally more favorable to Obama than to Bush and Romney, did not altogether spare the president. As to Obama's second term, it seemed important, at the last minute, to add both a concluding note concerning President Obama's revised policy on surveillance and national security, given the strong controversies surrounding that subject, and also a few remarks on the release of the extensive study of CIA detention and interrogation practices during the Bush administration.

In what follows, I recast these three efforts into a single composite essay, covering the period from September 11, 2001 to 2014, and the middle of the second Obama administration. In the light of my dedication to the subject of universal human rights as a definitive framework for the legitimate organization of political order, both internationally and nationally, I have had a long-standing interest in the subject of public emergency. In my opinion, the entire human rights movement, together with much of the support for modern humanitarian law and even for the UN Charter, was originally prompted as a reaction to the nefarious consequences of Hitler's massive abuse of an appeal to public emergency, beginning in the early 1930s. At that time, the Weimar Constitution was suspended on the strength of Article 48, the emergency provision, and that occurrence eventually enabled Hitler to arrogate total power to himself and to give new, previously unimagined latitude to the idea of a "unitary executive authority." Moreover, appeals to emergency continue right up to the present to pose a dire threat to the cause of human rights and to the preservation of an international order designed to restrain arbitrary force. That is so because the degree of public fear naturally associated with emergencies, particularly in wartime and in other times of violent threat to national security, tempts governments to overreact by unduly suppressing ordinary rights and freedoms.[3]

There are several reasons for paying special attention to the United States. Its enormous and virtually unchallenged military and economic might, together with the widespread belief that the United States is exempt from ordinary rules and regulations by dint of "American exceptionalism," undoubtedly sharpens the temptation, under emergency conditions, to overreact and transgress the bounds of moral and legal propriety. With apologies to Lord Acton and to

---

[3] Geoffrey R. Stone, *War and Liberty: An American Dilemma: 1790 to the Present* (New York: W.W. Norton & Co., 2007), 168ff.

the English language,[4] if power tends to corrupt, super power tends to "super corrupt."

Furthermore, the United States does not have a particularly distinguished record of coping with national emergencies, as Geoffrey Stone has conclusively shown in a recent study, *War and Liberty*.[5] James Madison eloquently foresaw the problem in 1798: "Perhaps it is a universal truth," he said, "that the loss of liberty at home is to be charged to provisions against danger, real or pretended, from abroad."[6] Because the United States has regularly failed to heed that warning in the past, the country needs to be especially vigilant at present. Finally, because of its unrivaled position, the United States has a golden opportunity to set a good example for the rest of a world promiscuously inclined to take advantage of the threat of terrorism for malicious purposes.

The degree of success can be measured by tracking the U.S. record of compliance during times of national emergency with international obligations, including those imposed by human rights and humanitarian law, as well as with obligations enumerated in the U.S. Constitution. The task of identifying points of continuity and overlap between international and national legal standards is a natural part of the exercise.

As a party to a number of international treaties, the United States has assumed varying degrees of obligation. In the first place, the United States, as a party to the United Nations Charter (1945), is a full-fledged member of the UN and is, accordingly, bound by the responsibilities of membership. Beyond that, in *Hamdan* v. *Rumsfeld*, the Supreme Court held that the Geneva Conventions (GCs) (ratified in 1955) are enforceable U.S. law, including due process protection provided for in the 1977 Protocol I to the conventions. Although the United States has never ratified the protocols, the Court ruled that provision to be "indisputably part of the customary international law."

On ratification (1992), the International Covenant on Civil and Political Rights (ICCPR) became the "supreme law of the land" under the Supremacy Clause of the U.S. Constitution, ascribing to treaties the status of federal law. The United States is obligated to comply with the treaty as with any other law, including a requirement to submit a report of compliance every four years

---

[4] For splitting an infinitive, a practice that, though widespread, can and should be avoided in many cases.
[5] Ibid., 166: "The United States has a long and unfortunate history of overreacting to the dangers of wartime. Time and again, we have allowed fear to get the better of us." Stone's conclusion is based on a penetrating review of the U.S. responses to the near war with France in the 1790s, the Civil War, World Wars I and II, the Cold War, the Vietnam War, and the "War on Terrorism" in recent years.
[6] James Madison, May 13, 1798.

to the Human Rights Committee, which was established to monitor implementation of the treaty. U.S. responsibility is subject to certain reservations, understandings, and declarations announced at the time of ratification, as, for example, that the treaty is not self-executing. That means that, without specific enabling legislation, litigants are unable to sue in court for direct enforcement of the treaty.

Although in the U.S. case, the Convention against Torture, and Other Cruel, Inhuman, and Degrading Treatment or Punishment (CAT) (ratified in 1994) is also not self-executing and is subject to several other reservations, the United States has in fact passed legislation bringing its criminal code into conformity with parts of the convention (18 U.S.C 2340–2340A). Moreover, by issuing an executive order (Jan. 22, 2009) prohibiting any interrogation practice not authorized by the Army Field Manual, President Obama has, in effect, done the same for military law. These four examples show why it is fully appropriate to scrutinize U.S. law and policy in reference to its international obligations under the UN and under human rights and humanitarian law.

Finally, my concern with the relation of religion to human rights, apparent in many of the other chapters in this volume, is also pertinent here because the terrorist attacks that occasioned the public emergency in the United States were justified by the attackers in explicitly religious terms. The attacks were launched in retaliation against what were taken to be aggressive acts by the United States and its allies that desecrated Muslim lands and holy places to such an extent that they were believed to imperil the very heart of Islamic faith. Such aggression was said to constitute a desperate emergency for Muslims, warranting extraordinary action in response. Consequently, the complexities of the fateful interaction between the United States and its terrorist enemies, initiated on September 11, 2001, greatly complicated the challenges of balancing human rights and public emergencies by adding religion to the equation.

TERRORISM AND PUBLIC EMERGENCY

Initial and subsequent efforts by the United States to justify special protections at home and abroad against terrorist threats to national security are an example of a general appeal to public emergency. Such appeals go to the heart of the existing system of international order, including human rights and humanitarian law, as well as the supporting rules and institutions associated with the United Nations Charter.

The attacks of September 11 constituted for the United States a "public emergency which threaten[ed] the life of the nation," in the words of Article 4 of the ICCPR. That conviction shaped much of the subsequent activity of the Congress and the Bush administration. The Congress reacted by liberally increasing expenditures, including defense spending, for counterterrorism. It also passed special legislation designed to protect national security in time of emergency, such as the USA Patriot Act, which suspended certain civil rights and rule-of-law protections and which the Justice Department began administering aggressively in various controversial ways after the law was signed on October 26, 2001.

On December 4, 2002, the Bush administration announced that although the government could afford to provide, in some cases, large end-of-the year bonuses to political appointees, it would nevertheless be compelled to reduce the standard salary adjustment for civil servants from 4.1 to 3.1 percent because of the cost of the "national emergency" caused by the September 11 attacks.[7] Earlier, the president established special military commissions to prosecute alleged terrorists and ordered the detention of several thousand combatants in Afghanistan, some 300 of whom were transferred to Camp X-Ray at Guantanamo Bay. These prisoners were apprehended under conditions that the government claimed were exempt from the standards of international humanitarian law. In addition, the president authorized targeted killings of alleged terrorists by the CIA, such as took place in Yemen in early November 2002. That action raised questions whether President Bush was violating Executive Order 12333, which prohibited government sponsored assassinations appeared to override a long-standing executive prohibition on such actions.

At behest of the president, the Congress created an immense new government agency, the Department of Homeland Security, to regulate the domestic response to terrorism, though the range of its new powers was yet to evolve. For its part, the Defense Department began "constructing a computer system that could create a vast electronic dragnet, searching for personal information as part of the hunt for terrorists around the globe – including the United States."[8]

On September 17, 2002, the Bush administration released a document titled "The National Security Strategy of the United States," which summarized, among other things, the administration's response to terrorism. One observer called it "the most sweeping shift in U.S. grand strategy since the beginning of the Cold War."[9] According to the document, the United States promised to sustain global dominance such that "our forces will be strong enough to dissuade potential adversaries from pursuing a military buildup in hopes of surpassing, or equaling, the power of the United States." Consistent with the

---

[7] "White House Defends Return to Appointees' Cash Bonuses," *New York Times* (December, 5, 2002), A29.
[8] "Pentagon Plans a Computer System That Would Peek at Personal Data of Americans," *New York Times* (Nov. 9, 2002), A10.
[9] John Lewis Gaddis, "A Grand Strategy of Transformation," *Foreign Policy* (Nov.–Dec. 2002), 50.

theme of military predominance was the declared intention that, whenever and wherever it may so decide, the United States would determine, apparently without regard to the international system of rules and regulations, what constituted an imminent threat to national security and what should be done about it. "While the United States will constantly strive to enlist the support of the international community, *we will not hesitate to act alone, if necessary, to exercise our right of self-defense by acting pre-emptively.*"[10] The language strongly suggests that, in the last analysis, it is exclusively and totally up to the United States to decide what constitutes national self-defense and when and where it may initiate a premptive attack.

On October 10, 2002, the president received official congressional Authorization for the Use of Military Force against Iraq (AUMF) as part of the "war on terrorism" by votes of 296–133 in the House and 77–23 in the Senate. Even though the final language of the resolution was more restrictive than the language originally proposed by the administration, and even though congressional inquiry and debate exposed a number of reservations and apprehensions about the Bush administration's Iraq policy, in the end the resolution provided the president with wide discretion to "(1) defend the national security of the United States against the continuing threat posed by Iraq; and (2) to enforce all relevant United Nations Security Council resolutions."

On November 6, 2002, the UN Security Council finally adopted by a vote of 15–0 Resolution 1441, authorizing an intrusive weapons inspections program in Iraq to verify how far Saddam Hussein had yet to go in complying with long-standing Security Council demands that he eliminate entirely all weapons of mass destruction (WMD). The Bush administration believed that unless Saddam Hussein was thoroughly disarmed, he represented, among other things, an imminent threat to the United States as a potential supplier to terrorists of biological, chemical, or nuclear weapons.

The three months of debate in the Security Council over the language of the resolution were difficult and contentious, and the final version constituted a substantial compromise between strong impulses within the Bush administration and opposing concerns on the part of several members of the UN Security Council. As such, the resolution represented a provisional, and only partial, vindication of the principle of collective security.[11]

The Bush administration originally sought to circumvent the United Nations altogether and to justify independent military action with the intent of

---

[10] "The National Security Strategy of the United States, 2002," 6. Available at http://www.state.gov/documents/organization/63562.pdf.

[11] See the revealing account of James Taub, "Who Needs the U.N. Security Council?" *New York Times Magazine* (November 17, 2002), 46ff.

overthrowing Saddam Hussein. When it agreed to submit to UN authority, it hoped that the resolution would include authorization for an immediate and automatic resort to force, should Saddam fail to comply with UN demands. However, as the result of tough bargaining, particularly on the part of the French, the final resolution focused exclusively on disarmament, rather than "regime change," and contained no warrant for an automatic resort to force.[12]

Terms and phrases, such as "self-defense," "imminent threat," "preemption," "necessity," "if necessary," and "by all necessary means," which abound in the proposals, documents, and policies developed by the U.S. government and others in reaction to the attacks of September 11, are all-important code words in the vocabulary of public emergency. They coalesce around the idea of an imminent, undeniable threat to national security that is believed to justify extraordinary and highly exceptional government action.

To evaluate these appeals to public emergency in the light of the standards and institutions of international order, we first need some general orientation.

PUBLIC EMERGENCY AND INTERNATIONAL ORDER: THE NAZI BACKGROUND

It is not going too far to suggest that the entire system of international rules and institutions, including the United Nations Charter and human rights and humanitarian law – all, to a large extent, the product of World War II – constituted a concerted and definitive response to a massive abuse of an appeal to public emergency.

It was Article 48 of the Weimar Constitution – the emergency article – that facilitated Adolf Hitler's rise to power in Germany and thereafter provided him with the opportunity to bring an end to the Weimar Republic and to replace it with the Third Reich. Article 48 provided "an unprecedentedly broad basis for the exercise of emergency authority,"[13] by which the chief executive could suspend civil rights, including the opportunity for judicial review, "with almost no limit." On the strength of executive discretion alone, the article permitted extensive censorship, widespread searches and seizures, secret and unlimited detentions, and the establishment of irregular tribunals to prosecute individuals suspected of threatening national security. In the words of one contemporary observer, "the power of article 48 goes very far. But when we consider the events of these days, we shall find that this power is born out

---

[12] See 298–302, for an elaboration of this conclusion.
[13] Frederick Mundell Watkins, *Failure of Constitutional Emergency Powers under the German Republic* (Cambridge, MA: Harvard University Press, 1939), 15.

by the necessity of our time. It gives to the President a strong weapon which we cannot renounce under any circumstances."[14]

On the basis of Article 48, Hitler's immediate predecessors accommodated him by relaxing restraints on the use of strong-arm methods and intimidation, policies that facilitated Hitler's acquisition of power. By the time he was appointed chancellor in January 1933, he was able with relative ease to act on his claim that Germany was confronted with a permanent emergency, a view he had outlined in the last chapter of *Mein Kampf*, titled "Necessity [or Emergency] Defense as Right."[15]

When a nation is mortally threatened by enemies within and without, as Hitler believed Germany was in the early 1930s, the nation's only recourse, he thought, was to turn to the old adage: "necessity knows no law." Consequently, Article 48 conformed perfectly to his basic philosophy, which was, in effect, that anything and everything is justified when the life of the nation is at fundamental risk. The right of national self-defense trumps every other right, without qualification.

Hitler's trademark "Fuehrer principle," according to which all authority flows from the "leader" down, is but an adaptation of a military model that, Hitler believed, is the only appropriate pattern of organization in time of public emergency. When a nation is under imminent attack, there is no time for the niceties of democratic deliberation or the protection of individual rights and freedoms. These must all be eagerly sacrificed in a wider, more compelling cause. Hitler reinforced his thoughts on public emergency with a collectivist theory regarding the supremacy of what he called *das Volk* (the people). "National Socialism," he said, "takes as the starting point... neither the individual nor humanity... [but] *das Volk*.... The individual is transitory, the Volk is permanent.... National Socialism... desires to safeguard the Volk, even at the expense of the individual."[16]

These ideas all converged in Hitler's grand geopolitical vision that Germany could only successfully protect its national security – could only properly defend itself under conditions of emergency – by dominating other countries. As he put it, "the right to possess soil can become a duty if without extension

---

[14] Cited in Clinton Rossiter, *Constitutional Dictatorship: Crisis Government in the Modern Democracies* (Princeton, NJ: Princeton University Press, 1948), 33–34.
[15] Adolf Hitler, *Mein Kampf*, trans. by Ralph Manheim (Boston: Houghton Mifflin Co., 1971), ch. 15. Though the translation I offer changes the title of the chapter in the English version ("The Right of Emergency Defense"), my translation is more in accord with the original German: "Notwehr als Recht."
[16] Hitler, Speech at the Nazi Harvest Thanksgiving Celebration at Buckeburg, October 7, 1933; cited in Bullock, *Hitler*, 401.

of its soil a great nation seems doomed to destruction.... Germany will either be a world power or there will be no Germany."[17] So understood, preemptive invasions of neighboring countries such as France, Poland, and Norway are nothing but exercises in the "right of self-defense" against "imminent threats," because the continued existence of such countries as sovereign entities is itself taken to imperil mortally Germany's national security.

All this, of course, provided a rationale for what might well be called Hitler's Reign of Terror in the 1930s and 1940s, both inside Germany and abroad, or for the record of what the Preamble to the Universal Declaration of Human Rights calls "barbarous acts which shocked the conscience of mankind." And that record, in turn, constituted the frame of reference for developing, after World War II, the rules and institutions of international order, including the United Nations Charter and human rights and humanitarian law.

"HITLER'S EPITAPH"

Louis Henkin has aptly referred to the UN Charter as "Hitler's epitaph,"[18] but it seems appropriate to expand the reference to include human rights and humanitarian law as well. In one way or another, all these instruments and the institutions that support them were designed to redefine forever the permissible limits of, and reasons for, the use of force, so that what Hitler had wrought in the mid-twentieth century, or anything close to it, might never again occur.

The Preamble to the UN Charter makes clear the determination "to save succeeding generations from the scourge of war, which twice in our lifetime has brought untold sorrow to mankind;... [and] to ensure, by the acceptance of principles and the institution of methods, that armed force shall not be used, save in the common interest." Accordingly, the fundamental purposes of the UN include the maintenance of "international peace and security, and to that end, [taking] effective collective measures for the prevention and removal of threats to the peace and for the suppression of acts of aggression or other breaches of the peace, and [bringing] about by peaceful means, and in conformity with the principles of justice and international law, adjustment or settlement of international disputes or situations which might lead to a breach of the peace."

---

[17] Cited in William Ebenstein, *Man and the State* (New York: Reinhart & Co., 1948), 591–592.
[18] Louis Henkin, "Use of Force: Law and U.S. Policy," in Louis Henkin et al., eds., *Right v. Might: International Law and Use of Force* (New York: Council on Foreign Relations, 1989), 62.

In the light of the history of the Nazi experiment, a primary objective of the postwar international order was to prohibit the arbitrary use of force among nations, by coordinating all decisions involving force with "*collective measures for the prevention and removal of threats to the peace and for the suppression of acts of aggression or other breaches of the peace*" (emphasis added). The point is particularly clear in reference to appeals to the right of national self-defense and to determining what constitutes a bona fide threat to national security, limits, as we saw, that were systematically and grossly violated by Hitler.

Article 51 of the UN Charter, which clearly acknowledges "the inherent right of individual or collective [national] self-defense" in response to "an armed attack," nevertheless explicitly subordinates that right to the authority of the UN Security Council. Any state invoking the right to use force in self-defense must immediately report such action to the Security Council and may proceed as it sees fit only "*until the Security Council has taken measures necessary to maintain international peace and security.*" Moreover, Article 39 expressly ascribes to the Security Council the ultimate authority to "determine the existence of any threat to the peace, breach of the peace, or act of aggression, and shall make recommendations, or decide what measures shall be taken."

In making sure that "armed force shall not be used, save in the common interest," these provisions unmistakably "internationalize" the whole idea of national self-defense. They represent, therefore, nothing less than a conceptual revolution in the vocabulary of public emergency, which preeminently encompasses appeals to national self-defense. Henceforth, *nations do not, in theory, retain ultimate or absolute authority over what constitutes a threat to their national security or over how far they may go in responding to it*. Appeals to emergency in international relations are once and for all limited by the rules and institutions of the new international order that was established after 1945. Unquestionably, there lurks behind these radical innovations a spirit of profound apprehension about the "dark side" – the vast potential for abuse – that inevitably accompanies appeals to public emergency.

If the UN Charter focuses primarily on the use of force *outside* a country's borders, international human rights law, consisting of what is by now an expansive array of instruments mandated under the auspices of the United Nations, focuses on a state's use of force *inside* its borders. Human rights instruments are, at bottom, designed to provide limits concerning the domestic use of coercion – to restrict, that is, how far states may legitimately go in prosecuting, confining, and punishing citizens and resident aliens, as well as in inhibiting and controlling the economic, political, religious, and other interests of people living within their borders. As in the case of the UN Charter, the Nazi record stands as the decisive "negative model," in reaction to which the provisions set out in the UN Declaration of Human Rights – the definitive document for all subsequent UN human rights instruments – were self-consciously formulated.[19]

Of special pertinence is the "emergency clause," Article 4 of the International Covenant of Civil and Political Rights (ICCPR), mentioned earlier. It states (in part),

1. In time of public emergency which threatens the life of a nation and the existence of which is officially proclaimed, the States Parties to the present Covenant may take measures derogating from their obligations under the present Covenant to the extent strictly required by the exigencies of the situation, provided that such measures are not inconsistent with their other obligations under international law and do not involve discrimination solely on the grounds of race, color, language, religion, or social origin.
2. No derogation [among others] from articles 6. [prohibition of arbitrary life-taking], 7. [prohibition of the use of torture, cruel, unusual or degrading treatment or punishment], 8. [prohibition of enslavement], and 18 [protection of freedom of thought, conscience, religion or belief] may be made under this provision.
3. Any State Party to the present Covenant availing itself of the right of derogation shall immediately inform the other States Parties to the present Covenant, through the intermediary of the Secretary General of the United Nations, of the provisions from which it has derogated and of the reasons why it was actuated. A further communication shall be made, through the same intermediary, on the date on which it terminates such derogation.

If there is any suspicion that the subject of public emergency is unimportant from the perspective of human rights law, or that a strong concern to reduce the potential for abusing emergency appeals is absent from the law, Article 4 should remove such suspicion once and for all. It is specifically designed to illustrate how human rights law can prevent several of the most egregious forms of offense and violation associated with Hitler's record. One was his contempt for international public scrutiny of his allegations concerning the state of emergency that Germany faced. Another was his willful failure to disclose (and justify) which of Germany's laws were being suspended and why. Last and most abhorrent was his practice of flagrantly disregarding the "laws of humanity," which indubitably, if at the time imperfectly, prohibited certain elemental forms of human mistreatment. In response, Article 4 was formulated to require *public accountability, full disclosure,* and *the observance of basic standards of*

---

[19] See the Introduction and Chapter 1.

human decency in the face of a public emergency. Paragraph 2, conceding, as it does, the need to suspend some rights (outside of those that are "nonderogable" or unabridgeable), provides for substantial flexibility in regard to state action during emergencies. It thus acknowledges the peculiar difficulties that states confront in such circumstances and thereby displays a significant degree of "realism." At the same time, the principles of public accountability, full disclosure, and observance of basic standards of human decency, embedded in the article, place a huge burden of proof on governments so as to inhibit the nearly uncontrollable urge to exceed the bounds of propriety and decency in times of exceptional threat.

Finally, humanitarian law is itself but a special form of emergency law and is, accordingly, an important supplement to human rights law. As it developed, from the late nineteenth century up through the post–World War II period, humanitarian law has come to define the standards of permissible treatment of both combatants and noncombatants under the "exceptional circumstances" created by armed combat.

> [Humanitarian law and human rights law] are mutually complementary, and admirably so.... [They have] the same historic and philosophical origin[:]... to protect the human person against [menacing] hostile forces.... This common origin gave rise to two distinct efforts: to limit the evils of war and to defend [human beings] against arbitrary treatment. In the course of centuries these two efforts have developed along parallel lines.
>
> It is recognized that human rights represent the most general principles, whereas *humanitarian law has a particular and exceptional character, since it enters into force at the precise moment when war intervenes to prevent or limit the exercise of human rights.*
>
> The two juridical systems are different. Whereas humanitarian law takes effect only in the event of armed conflict, the law of human rights is of practical application most of all in peacetime and its instruments have clauses providing for derogations in the event of war. In addition, human rights pertain essentially to relations between the State and its own citizens, while humanitarian law pertains to the relations between the State and the citizens of its adversary.[20]

Indeed, the substitution of the term "humanitarian law" in the 1950s for what were known previously as the "laws of war" demonstrates the influence of the idea of human rights.[21] For one thing, the Geneva Conventions of 1949 speak

---

[20] Jean Pictet, *Development and Principles of International Humanitarian Law* (Dordrecht: Martinus Nijhoff Publishers, 1985), 3 (emphasis added).
[21] See Dietrich Schindler, "Human Rights and Humanitarian Law: The Interrelationship of the Laws," www.wcl.american.edu/journal/lawrev/31/schindler.pdf, 935.

explicitly of the "rights of protected persons," whereas earlier formulations of the laws of war had alluded "merely to the obligations of the contracting [state] parties."[22] The link between human rights and humanitarian law was made official in 1968 when the UN adopted a resolution calling the laws applicable in time of war, significantly, "Human Rights in Armed Conflict."[23]

Moreover, the Geneva Conventions, particularly the Fourth Convention, dramatically expand protection of the rights of civilians affected by armed combat in a territory either under attack or under belligerent occupation. Article 3, common to all four Geneva Conventions, is particularly important in applying certain fundamental human rights to "persons taking no part in the hostilities, including members of armed forces who have laid down their arms and those placed [outside of combat] by sickness, wounds, detention, or any other cause." Such persons shall be absolutely protected against extrajudicial killing and "violence to life and person, in particular murder, mutilation, cruel treatment and torture."

Of special relevance to the subjects of "terrorism" and "acts of terror" are two passages from the body of humanitarian law: one that is common to the two 1977 Additional Protocols to Geneva Conventions and one at Article 33 of the Fourth Geneva Convention, which prohibits collective punishments. These passages are, of course, simply specifications of Common Article 3, just mentioned. Articles 51 of Protocol I and 13 of Protocol II state, "The civilian population as such, as well as individual civilians, shall not be the object of attack. Acts or threats of violence, the primary purpose of which is to *spread terror* among the civilian population are prohibited."[24] [Such acts in reprisal are also prohibited.] Article 33 of the Fourth Geneva Convention states, "Collective penalties and likewise all measures of intimidation or of *terrorism* are prohibited."[25] It is obvious that, again, the infamous record of Hitler's campaign of terror during World War II, particularly of his military, provides the background against which these provisions were formulated.

Although the definition of "terrorism" is ordinarily confined to attacks "carried out by . . . a non-state group, operating clandestinely, and without uniform or insignia,"[26] these passages make clear that "acts of terror" and, indeed, the word "terrorism" itself – namely, *direct and deliberate attacks against defenseless civilians (as well as combatants "outside combat") that are intended to intimidate and thus to compel acquiescence or support* – can apply to members

---

[22] Ibid.
[23] Final Act of International Conference on Human Rights, UN Doc. A/CONF. 32/41 (1968).
[24] www.icre/inl/INTRO 470.
[25] www.icre.org/inl/INTRO 380.
[26] Adam Roberts, "Defining Terrorism," p. 2, unpublished ms. which he kindly shared with me.

of the armed forces as well. "[I]f committed by a belligerent in a war, [such acts] would constitute violations of the laws of war."[27]

Acts of that kind perpetrated by nonstate, clandestine actors, although technically not covered by humanitarian law,[28] nevertheless might be classified as violations of international law. The 1948 Genocide Treaty, particularly article IV extends liability to "private individuals," and the 1998 Rome Statute of the International Criminal Court, particularly article 7, designates acts such as murder or extermination as "crimes against humanity," insofar as they are "committed as part of a widespread or systematic attack directed against any civilian population, with knowledge of the attack."[29]

RELIGION, TERRORISM, AND THE EMERGENCY APPEAL

It is of the greatest interest that Osama bin Laden and his followers provided, in effect, a religious version of an emergency appeal, connected in a circuitous

---

[27] Ibid., 3.
[28] The Geneva Conventions apply only to state actors, and the Additional Protocols pertain to states and "organized armed groups" engaged in "sustained and concerted military operations."
[29] The Rome Statute of the International Criminal Court (http://www.Un.org/law/icc/statute/99_corr/l.htm). Cf. Roberts, "Defining Terrorism," 3. There is some ambiguity regarding the applicability of the Rome Statute to the attacks of September 11. In his article, "Staying the Course with the International Criminal Court," *Cornell International Law Journal* Vol. 35 (Nov. 2001–Feb. 2002), David Scheffer remarks on 83 (sect. 6) that "nothing in the ICC Treaty requires the inclusion of crimes of terrorism." The United States resisted inclusion of terrorism as a crime in the Statute of Rome, speculating that investigation of such crimes would be too demanding for the ICC and therefore should better be left to national courts and enforcement agencies (fn. 7, 50). The issue, he says, need only come up at the seven-year review conference if States Parties desire to take it up then. He goes on to say (on 84) that the 9/11 attacks "*may make* discussion of the crime of terrorism as a new crime for the ICC more plausible in the future" (emphasis added).

However, on 49, Scheffer asserts that the 9/11 attacks "were crimes against humanity that *probably would have fallen within the jurisdiction of the ICC had the Court existed on that date*" (emphasis added). And on fn. 6 (on 49), he says, the 9/11 attacks "*would appear to meet the criteria for crimes against humanity*" (emphasis added), as seems clear from the text of the statute (see esp. Art. 7). Moreover, it is clear that UN officials, such as former High Commissioner of Human Rights, Mary Robinson, have so understood the Rome Statute, as Scheffer himself acknowledges (fn. 6, 49) (see the later discussion). As to U.S. doubts at the time of drafting the statute concerning the infeasibility of the ICC's successfully managing the investigation and litigation of terrorist suspects, Scheffer has second thoughts in *All the Missing Souls: A Personal History of the War Crimes Tribunals* (Princeton, NJ: Princeton University Press, 2012). On 170, he suggests "the U.S. position may have been a mistake, ... regarding international terrorism." After 9/11, "the Bush administration's disastrous mangling of the rule of law in how terrorist suspects were detained and interrogated, and then how some were prosecuted before flawed military commissions, demonstrated some of the risks involved in national-only prosecutions."

way to national security, in defense of attacks such as occurred on September 11 and as are threatened to recur in the future.[30] In his *fatwa* (authoritative declaration), "Jihad against Jews and Crusaders," issued on February 23, 1998, bin Laden and his associates spoke of the "grave situation" that Muslims confront, caused by such activities as the following:

> First, for over seven years the United States has been occupying the lands of Islam in the holiest of places, the Arabian peninsula, plundering its riches, dictating to its rulers, humiliating its people, terrorizing its neighbors, and turning its bases in the Peninsula into a spearhead through which to fight the neighboring Muslim peoples.
>
> If some people have in the past argued about the fact of the occupation, all the people of the Peninsula have now acknowledged it. The best proof of this is the Americans' continuing aggression against the Iraqi people using the Peninsula as a staging post, even though all its rulers are against their territories being use to that end, but they are helpless.
>
> If the Americans' aims behind these wars are religious and economic, the aim is also to serve the Jews' petty state and divert attention from its occupation of Jerusalem and murder of Muslims there. The best proof of this is their eagerness to destroy Iraq, the strongest neighboring Arab state, and their endeavor to fragment all the states in the region such as Iraq, Saudi Arabia, Eqypt and Sudan into paper statelets and through their disunion and weakness to guarantee Israel's survival and the continuation of the brutal crusade occupation of the Peninsula.
>
> All these crimes and sins committed by the Americans are a clear declaration of war on Allah, his messenger, and Muslims....
>
> [Consequently, the] ruling to kill the Americans and their allies – civilians and military – is an individual duty for every Muslim who can do it in any country in which it is possible to do it.[31]

In his "Declaration of Jihad against the Americans Occupying the Land of the Two Holiest Sites," announced in 1996, Osama bin Laden had stated, "Terrorizing you, while you are carrying arms on our land, is legitimate, reasonable and [a] morally demanded duty. It is also a rightful act well known to all humans and all creatures."[32]

---

[30] See John Kelsay, "Bin Laden's Reasons," *Christian Century* (February 26–March 6, 2002), 26–29.
[31] Ibid., 28–29.
[32] "Bin Laden' Fatwa" (*A Declaration of War against the Americans*, August 1996), www.pbs.org/newshour/updates/military-july-dec96-fatwa-1996, August 23, 1996.

According to this line of argument, the "war on Allah, his messenger, and Muslims" being perpetrated by the United States and its allies is understood to constitute an overwhelming threat to the national security of Muslim states, whose sacred responsibility it is to defend the faith and the holy sites and territory of Islam. It is, by implication, such an extreme emergency, such an inescapable case of "necessity" – "known to all humans and creatures" – that justifies what, from an Islamic point of view, is an extraordinary prescription to launch deliberate and direct attacks against civilians.

Similar reasoning exists in the al-Qaeda operations manual, "Military Studies in the Jihad against the Tyrants." The manual poses this question: How can a Muslim spy live among enemies while failing openly to practice duties to God and to acknowledge Islamic identity? The manual's answer is that if "a Muslim is in a combat or godless area, he is not obligated to have a different appearance from those around him. Resembling the polytheist in religious appearance is [allowed because] 'necessity permits the forbidden,' even though [forbidden acts] are basically prohibited."[33]

Other examples from the literature of Islamic extremism make the same point. A text called *The Neglected Duty*, composed by the Islamic Jihad, which was responsible for the assassination of the president of Egypt, Anwar Sadat, in 1981, and the charter of Hamas, the militant Palestinian organization, both contend that standard prohibitions ordinarily covering the protection of unarmed civilians must be suspended or "stretched" under conditions of necessity.[34]

It is important to emphasize that suspending the protection of civilians in the name of necessity is by no means uniformly accepted among Muslims or Muslim authorities. Countless Muslim leaders and scholars of Islam have categorically denied "that crisis situations facing Muslims have [ever] been considered sufficient reason to override the provision against direct targeting of noncombatants."[35] A purported saying of Mohammed is frequently quoted in this connection: "Whenever [Mohammed] sent forth an [armed] detachment, he said to them, 'Do not cheat, or commit treachery, nor should you mutilate or kill children, women, or old men.'" The blanket prohibition of "treachery" is interesting, especially when compared with the excuses the al Qaeda manual gives for deceiving an enemy. Furthermore, Islamic scholars have also challenged the authority of someone like bin Laden to utter a *fatwa* in the first place.[36]

---

[33] See wednesdayreport.com/twr/gulfwar/terroristmanual.htm.
[34] See John Kelsay, *Islam and War: A Study in Comparative Ethics* (Louisville, Kentucky: Westminster/John Knox Press, 1993), 107.
[35] Kelsay, "Bin Laden's Reasons," 29.
[36] There is an additional problem with bin Laden's emergency appeal, from a human rights point of view. The ideal Islamic nation, whose security he believes to be so profoundly imperiled and

But, however sharp the divisions within the Islamic community are over attitudes toward the September 11 attacks, there remain among Muslims some unresolved controversies associated with the broader aspects of terrorism that are, as a matter of fact, also applicable well outside the Islamic community. The principal controversy, focused in the debates over current instances of Palestinian terrorism, is whether terrorism is ever excusable.

One response, which claims that direct and intentional attacks on defenseless civilians may be so excused if they have a just cause, a reasonable probability of success, and are undertaken as a last resort, is complicated by the fact that similar arguments have been employed in defense of direct and intentional attacks against civilians carried out as official military policy, such as occurred toward the end of World War II in the allied fire bombings of Dresden, Germany, or, as is often claimed, in the atomic-bombing of Japan by the U.S. Air Force.[37]

If, as I noted earlier, state actors (state officials and military personnel) are equally liable as nonstate actors (irregular, nonuniformed, clandestine

---

in defense of which the acts of September 11 were apparently performed, is best signified by the two regimes he specifically identified with, provided substantial financial support for, and received sanctuary from: the National Islamic Front government of Sudan and the Taliban government of Afghanistan. Among the regimes of the world most severely in violation of the rule of law, democracy, and human rights, these two regimes, during Bin Laden's time of residence, would indisputably stand out.

[37] In *Enola Gay and the Court of History* (New York: Peter Lang, 2004), Robert P. Newman states that in 1945, toward the end of the war with the Japanese, U.S. saturation bombing of Japan "had no effect on the Japanese generals and admirals. They were still determined to fight to the bitter end, but the spectacular atom, and the threat of many more, shortened a war that the best evidence shows would have gone on into 1946 without the new and frightening weapon. There *can* be justified terror, as there can be just wars" (xiv–xv; original italics). Cf. Michael Walzer, ch. 16, "Supreme Emergency," *Just and Unjust Wars: A Moral Argument with Historical Illustrations* (New York: Basic Books, 1977) for a similar argument in regard to some forms of indiscriminate bombing of Germany to force a Nazi surrender. For that Walzer would be willing to "accept the burdens of criminality here and now," acknowledging that the direct and intentional "destruction of the innocent, whatever its purposes, is a kind of blasphemy against our deepest moral commitments" (261). It is a sheer case of doing the lesser of two stupendous evils – attacking the innocent to prevent a Nazi victory. At the same time, Walzer condemns what he considers to be the excessive and unnecessary firebombing of Dresden (261–262), and, contrary to Newman, condemns the atomic bombing of Japan because in his view it was possible, without using the bomb, to find an acceptable conclusion to the war short of the unconditional surrender of the Japanese (263–268).

Whatever the moral status of a "necessity defense," it imposes, it should be noted, a highly stringent burden of proof, which is what distinguishes it from an act of gross arbitrariness (e.g., killing for the pleasure of it or for other self-serving reasons that are indifferent to the welfare of the victim and to the circumstances in which the victim is harmed). A bona fide act of necessity depends on verifying that all "necessitous circumstances" do in fact exist, namely, a truly imminent threat to an indisputably vital interest that can be avoided in absolutely no other way than by harming an innocent person.

persons) under international law prohibiting "crimes against humanity," then it is clear that reasons believed to mitigate responsibility in one case also have to be considered in the other. Insofar as it is regarded as excusable for an army to attack civilians in circumstances believed to offer no other feasible defense, then there seems no good reason to deny that this argument should be available to nonstate actors in what appear to be similar circumstances.[38]

This perplexity is one of the important "loose ends" of the discussion over terrorism and public emergency. It urgently invites further moral and religious reflection by Muslims, to be sure, but also by other religious groups and concerned citizens as well.

THE U.S. EXAMPLE: THE BUSH RECORD

"Fear and Anxiety Were Exploited by Zealots and Fools"[39]

Although deeply distressing overall, the Bush record is not completely negative. Nine days after the attacks, President Bush correctly stated that the campaign against terrorism is "not just America's fight. And what is at stake is not just America's freedom. This is the world's fight."[40]

Furthermore, President Bush and Secretary Powell on several occasions explicitly acknowledged the relevance of the United Nations. On November 10, 2001, in a speech before the UN, the president reiterated that "every nation has a stake in this cause," and he called for the broadening of the international coalition to fight terrorism. He also stated that "the most basic obligations of this new conflict have already been defined by the UN," including the responsibility to share intelligence and coordinate law enforcement efforts. "When we find terrorists," said the president, "we must work together to bring them to justice." In addition, after the NATO invasion of Afghanistan on

---

[38] I put forward here a composite argument constructed out of animated discussions of the meaning of terrorism in which I participated at a United Nations consultation in 2001. Of course, it must be emphasized that giving consideration to the idea of "justifiable terror" is still not completely open-ended. Proponents of such an idea have, it is true, surrendered what is understandably regarded as the essential condition of all morality, the absolute protection of noncombatant immunity – the violation of which amounts, in Walzer's words (fn. 34), to "blasphemy against our deepest moral commitments." Nevertheless, the remaining just-war standards of legitimacy – just cause, peaceful intent, last resort, reasonable probability of success, and proportionality – still apply.

[39] Philip Zelikow, aide to Secretary of State Condoleezza Rice and executive director of the 9/11 Commission. Cited in Jane Mayer, *Dark Side: The Inside Story of How the War on Terror Turned into a War on American Ideals* (New York: Doubleday, 2008), 335.

[40] Speech before for a joint session of Congress, September 20, 2001.

October 7, 2001 – itself an example of collective security – he committed the United States to "work with the UN to support a post-Taliban government that represents all of the Afghan people" (in accord with Security Council Resolution 1378).

Secretary Powell gave a similar speech at the UN the following day, adding this important thought: "No greater threat to international peace and security exists in the world today [than terrorism]. And, through this body, we have established and are establishing the tools to build a more robust defense." On the eve of the fifty-third anniversary of the Universal Declaration of Human Rights, President Bush issued the following statement: "The terrible tragedies of September 11 served as a grievous reminder that the enemies of freedom do not respect or value individual human rights. Their brutal attacks were an attack on these very rights." The president called on "the people of the United States to honor the legacy of human rights passed down to us from previous generations and to resolve that such liberties will prevail in our nation and throughout the world as we move into the 21st century."[41]

In issuing the U.S. State Department's Country Reports on Human Rights Practices on March 4, 2002, Secretary Powell remarked that "[t]oday, as America stands firm against terrorism with countries all around the world, we also affirm what our nation has stood for since its earliest days; for human rights, for democracy and for the rule of law. The worldwide promotion of human rights is in keeping with America's most deeply held values.... The Bush administration is working in cooperation with governments, intergovernmental organizations, non-governmental groups and individuals to help bring human rights into compliance with international norms.... [W]e will not relax our commitment to advancing the cause of human rights."[42]

On February 20, 2002, U.S. ambassador-at-large for war crimes, Pierre-Richard Prosper, announced U.S. policy in regard to the detainees in U.S. custody who were apprehended during the fighting in Afghanistan: "In bringing these abusers to justice the United States will continue to honor and uphold the rule of law and work within the norms of the global community in answering the challenge that faces us all. In so doing we will continue to uphold relevant legal standards of treatment with respect to the detainees in our custody." The policy was reaffirmed by U.S. military authorities at

---

[41] *President Proclaims Human Rights Day & Bill of Rights Week*, December 9, 2001. Cited in "USA: Treatment of Prisoners in Afghanistan and Guantanamo Bay Undermines Human Rights. International Memorandum to the US Government," Amnesty International Online, May 4, 2002 (www.amnesty.org), 4.

[42] Ibid., 5.

Guantanamo Bay on February 28: "The detainees will continue to be treated fairly but firmly in accordance with international conventions."[43]

These solemn utterances by the Bush administration concerning the relevance of human rights and humanitarian law to the campaign against terrorism – and particularly the president's statement that the strikes of September 11 "were an attack on these very rights" – are fully consonant with the judgment of former UN High Commissioner of Human Rights, Mary Robinson: "In the aftermath of the catastrophe of 11 September the human rights voice must be heard. The thousands of civilians who died in this atrocity lost the most precious of rights, the right to life. Those responsible for these cruel deaths must be made individually accountable for *the crimes against humanity* they perpetrated."[44]

Moreover, the United States has, up to a point, complied with its responsibilities as a member of the UN. On October 7, 2001, the United States duly informed the Security Council of its intention to respond to the attacks of September 11 by employing armed force against "Al Qaeda terrorist training camps and military installations of the Taliban regime in Afghanistan" in order "to prevent and deter further attacks on the US." The United States cited Article 51 of the UN Charter, authorizing "the inherent right of individual or collective self-defense if an armed attack occurs against a Member of the UN, until the Security Council has taken measures necessary to maintain international peace and security."[45]

Significantly, the United States received conclusive UN authorization for its use of armed force against the Taliban government of Afghanistan in response to the attacks of September 11.[46] On September 12, the Security Council had adopted Resolution 1368, which did several things: It implied "broad support" for the idea that the events of September 11 constituted an "armed attack" under the UN Charter. As such, the resolution "implicitly recognized that there existed a 'Chapter VII situation' thereby opening up the possibility of

---

[43] Ibid., 5.
[44] Statement at the International Conference on Human Rights and Democratization, at http://www.unhchr.ch/huricane/huricane.nsf/viewo1/Oct 8, 2001; cited in Scheffer, "Staying the Course with the International Criminal Court," fn. 6, 49 (emphasis added).
[45] "Negroponte Letter to the UNSC President," U.S. Department of State International Information Programs (Oct. 7, 2001). usinfo.state.gove/topical/pol/terror/01100813.htm. 2001).
[46] See Eric P.J. Meyer and Nigel D. White, "The Twin Towers Attack: An Unlimited Right to Self-Defence?" *Journal of Conflict and Security Law* Vol. 7 No. 1 (2002), 5–17 for a discussion of the legality of acts of self-defense undertaken by the United States in response to the attacks of September 11. Although the authors concede that the UN Security Council authorized armed response against the Taliban, they express concern regarding the failure of the Security Council to place limits around the doctrine of self-defense as employed by the United States. (See fn. 71.)

taking mandatory measures including, if necessary, the use of force."[47] It acknowledged the United States' "inherent right of self-defense," stressing "for the first time in UN history" that a terrorist attack is "a threat to international peace and security."[48] Finally, it called on "the international community to redouble their efforts to prevent and suppress terrorist acts" and "to work together urgently to bring to justice the perpetrators, organizers, and sponsors of these attacks."[49]

Two weeks later, the Security Council followed with a second antiterrorism resolution (1373), which enjoined all states to "prevent and suppress the financing of terrorism, as well as criminalize the willful provision or collection of funds for such acts."[50] Still later, the Security Council ratified the outcome of the military action in Afghanistan by adopting Resolution 1378, which committed the UN to support "the efforts of the Afghan people to replace the Taliban regime...."[51] On several occasions, UN Secretary-General Kofi Annan reaffirmed UN authorization for the military action in Afghanistan by publicly citing and commending these resolutions.[52] President Bush's September 12, 2002, speech to the UN, strongly supported by Secretary Powell and announcing his decision to work with the Security Council toward disarming Iraq of its weapons of mass destruction, was a significant example of international collaboration.

Finally, during President Bush's two terms in office, "there have been no direct federal criminal prosecutions of any individuals for antiwar dissent. This is a far cry from our past experience. It shows ... how far we have come. American values, politics, and law have now reached a point where such prosecutions seem almost unthinkable."[53]

---

[47] Ibid., 8, 5–6.
[48] Statement by Jean-David Levitte, French Ambassador to the UN, who was president of the Security Council when Resolution 1368 was adopted. James Traub, "Who Needs the U.N. Security Council?," 47–48. See, also, "UN Resolution Gives U.S. Right to Use Force, Envoy Says," International Information Programs (September 24, 2001). www.usinfo.stat.gov/topical/pol/terror/01092422.htm, p. 1.
[49] "UN Security Council Condemns Terrorist Attacks on U.S.," International Information Programs (September 12, 2001), www.usinfo.stat.gov/topical/pol/terror/01091221.htm, p. 1.
[50] "UN Security Council Anti-Terrorism Resolution," International Information Programs (September 28, 2001), www.usinfo.stat.gov/topical/pol/terror/1092902.htm.
[51] "UN Security Council Resolution 1378 on Afghanistan," International Information Programs (November 14, 2001) www.usinfo.stat.gov/topical/pol/terror/01111505.htm, p. 1.
[52] "U.N. Secretary-General Affirms U.S. Right to Self-Defense," International Information Programs (October 8, 2001) www.usinfo.state.gov/topical/pol/usandun/01100903/htm.
[53] Stone, *War and Liberty*, 128. At the same time, even this achievement, like most aspects of the Bush administration, has a dark side. "Members of the Bush administration have gone out of their way to tar their political opponents as 'disloyal.' Shortly after September 11, President Bush warned, in a phrase strikingly reminiscent of Adams, Wilson, and Nixon, 'You are either with us or with the terrorists.' Attorney General John Ashcroft went even further, castigating those

This history of compliance and engagement with the international order makes all the more glaring a contradictory pattern of obstinacy and recalcitrance that, if anything, worked to eclipse the positive picture. That pattern typically consisted of an initial disregard or defiance of international institutions and norms, sometimes followed, under pressure, by reluctant, even grudging, acquiescence. Such behavior suggests that the Bush administration did not clearly or consistently understand or care about a fundamental objective of the existing international order – to restrain the abuse of power under conditions of emergency. Nor did it go very far toward exemplifying the wisdom and sensitivity on the part of the U.S. government that are called for under "worldwide emergency conditions" generated by terrorism.

Indeed, the underlying unilateralist predispositions of the Bush administration are by now beyond dispute.[54] "Legitimacy, for at least most members of the Bush foreign-policy team, [arose] from a clearheaded assessment of [U.S.] national interest; little could be expected from the UN, a moralistic body squeamish about the exercise of power and largely hostile to American interests."[55] In January 2003, Defense Secretary Rumsfeld exemplified that attitude when he called on the UN to follow the U.S. lead and endorse the use of force against Iraq for the purpose of disarming Saddam. If it did not, he said, the UN would suffer "a loss of credibility and possible collapse." As noted earlier, the administration's own definitive grand plan, the "National Security Strategy of the United States," unflinchingly characterized the U.S. government as the ultimate arbiter and guarantor of international order.[56] Such, apparently, had for some time been the conviction of individuals like Paul Wolfowitz and Richard Perle, long associated with Cheney and Rumsfeld and then highly influential in the Bush administration.[57]

---

who challenged the necessity or constitutionality of the government's demand for restrictions on civil liberties. 'To those who scare peace-loving people with phantoms of lost liberty, my message is this: Your tactics only aid terrorists – for they erode our national unity and diminish our resolve. They give ammunition to America's enemies'" (129).

54   See, for example, Michael Hirsh, "Bush and the World," and John Ikenberry, "The Lures of Preemption," in *Foreign Affairs* (September/October 2002).
55   Traub, "Who Needs the U.N. Security Council?," 49.
56   Though the National Security Strategy was largely the product of National Security advisor Condoleezza Rice and her associates, Philip Zelikow and Stephen Hadley, it reflected the ideas of Vice President Cheney, Secretary Rumsfeld, Paul Wolfowitz, and other like-minded members of the administration. (James Mann, *Rise of the Vulcans: The History of the Bush's War Cabinet* (New York: Penguin Books, 2004), 331.
57   See Anatol Lieven's perceptive and disturbing analysis of the present Bush foreign policy, "The Push for War," *London Review of Books* (Oct. 3, 2002), available at www.MiddleEast .Org, p. 4. According to James Mann, the debate over limits on U.S. power abroad went all the way back to the 1970s and the Nixon-Ford years, pitting the likes of Cheney, Wolfowitz, and

Even Secretary Powell, usually pictured as the lone defender of multilateralism within the administration, was ultimately loyal to what might be called a doctrine of preemptory unilateralism. Commenting on a possible breach by Iraq of Security Council Resolution 1441, which authorized an intrusive weapons inspections regime in Iraq, Secretary Powell stated that, whatever the Security Council may decide, the United States "will reserve our option of acting" and will *"not necessarily be bound by what the Security Council might decide on that point."*[58] The internal debate between the rest of the administration and Powell appeared to be limited to differences over how prudent it was or was not in a given case "to enlist the support of the international community." All sides in the administration agreed that such counsel, provisionally mentioned in the national security strategy document, was entirely a matter of discretion on the part of the United States. There was no division of opinion over the "right" to ultimate unilateral U.S. authority.[59]

In two of his most definitive speeches regarding America's response to terrorism – an address to a joint session of Congress on September 20, 2001, and the State of the Union message on January 2, 2002 – President Bush demonstrated his own commitment to the doctrine of preemptory unilateralism. He *never once* in either speech mentioned the United Nations or United States' obligations under human rights or humanitarian law. In addition, apart from occasional references by Secretary Powell and Ambassador Prosper, mentioned earlier, the importance of the international order was not a prominent theme in the public statements of the chief foreign policy officials of the administration.[60]

Indeed, in the case of U.S. policy toward Iraq, Secretary Rumsfeld and Vice President Cheney, supplemented by a number of statements from the president and the National Security advisor, Condoleezza Rice, set the tone with uncompromising observations about why the United States must solve the problem of Iraq quite on its own, if need be, and on terms, including

---

Rumsfeld – "the Vulcans," as they called themselves – against more traditional foreign policy hands like Brent Scowcroft, James Baker, and Lawrence Eagleburger. The latter consistently favored seeking UN authorization for any military initiatives in places such as Iraq, whereas the former resisted such concerns. Mann, *Rise of the Vulcans* ch. 21, "Toward War with Iraq."

[58] Quoted in Michael J. Glennon, "How War Left the Law Behind," *New York Times* (Nov. 21, 2002), emphasis added.

[59] "In fact, Powell had never been the dove that he was assumed to be ... He did not possess any sweeping vision for America's role in the world that would have served as an alternative to the Wolfowitz team's notion of America as an unchallenged superpower. Nor did he put forward any substitute for [Condoleezza] Rice's National Security Strategy with its doctrine of preemption" (Mann, *Rise of the Vulcans*, 350–351).

[60] See David Little, "The World's Fight," *Christian Century* (February 27–March 6, 2002), 23.

"regime change," that it should dictate. The original formulations explicitly evaded the need for new congressional or Security Council authority.

Such unbending unilateralism was, of course, not well received at home or abroad, and the Bush administration, true to pattern, reluctantly acquiesced to a more collaborative mode of operation. It finally agreed to submit its case to Congress and to the Security Council, while still recommending language in both instances that preserved for the United States wider discretionary authority than either body was initially happy with. In Congress, a process of adjustment and compromise eventually produced a resolution somewhat improved for having tied the president's action more closely to the UN Security Council process than the administration originally favored.[61]

At the same time, the congressional resolution was still very open-ended, thanks in large part to the continuing influence of the advocates of unilateralism within the administration. Its language did not, as it should have, linked the right of national self-defense against Iraq to the United States' continuing obligation, under Article 51 of the UN Charter, to seek Security Council confirmation for *any* use of force. Nor did it sufficiently acknowledge the continuing, overriding authority of the Security Council, under Article 39, to determine "any threat to the peace."

In fact, the administration's dealings with the UN Security Council from November 2002 until March 2003 over the use of force in Iraq exemplified beyond doubt its overriding unilateralist predispositions. Basically as an effort in public relations, Powell entered into negotiations with Security Council partners, especially a reluctant France, to try to obtain authorization for the use of force in Iraq. On November 8, 2002, Resolution 1441, a compromise, was adopted by the Security Council.

While stating that "Iraq has been and remains in material breach of its obligations under relevant resolutions, . . . in particular through Iraq's failure to cooperate with [weapons inspectors]" [para. 1], the resolution nevertheless extends "a final opportunity to comply with its disarmament obligations under relevant resolutions of the Council; and accordingly decides to set up an enhanced inspection regime with the aim of bringing to full and verified completion the disarmament process established by [various] resolutions of

---

[61] Cf. "Resolution that Congress Approved on the Right to Use Force in Iraq," *New York Times* (October 12, 2002), A10, with "Authorization for War: What the White House Would Like Congress to Say," *New York Times* (September 27, 2002), A12. In contrast to the White House proposal, the final language incorporates into the binding portions of the resolution congressional support for efforts by the president "to strictly enforce *through the United Nations Security Council* all relevant . . . resolutions applicable to Iraq" and "to obtain prompt and decisive action *by the Security Council* to ensure that Iraq abandon its strategy of delay, evasion and non-compliance and strictly complies with all relevant . . . resolutions" (emphasis added).

the Council" [para. 2]. Crucially, the resolution goes on to call for status reports by the weapons inspectors [para. 11] *"in order to consider the situation and the need for full compliance with all of the relevant Council resolutions in order to secure international peace and security"* [para. 12; emphasis added].

Clearly, Resolution 1441 did not authorize states to make their own judgments as to whether to "use all necessary means" toward implementing its requirements. Rather, it ensured that the Security Council should first have the opportunity to appraise the state of affairs in Iraq with respect to the existence of weapons of mass destruction and then, on that basis, to make a final determination regarding the use of force. In short, 1441 foresaw the need for a second resolution.

The problem was that when Mohamed Elbaredi, head of the International Atomic Energy Agency (IAEA) responsible for nuclear inspections, and Hans Blix, head of the International Monitoring, Verification, and Inspection Commission (UNMOVIC) responsible for finding chemical and biological weapons, offered their initial report on January 27, 2003, they had found no proof of the existence of WMD. This was an embarrassing outcome for the United States and its supporter, the United Kingdom, which alleged that their combined intelligence had shown Iraq failing to disarm and still flagrantly violating Security Council resolutions. In addition, by mid-February the United States had already deployed more than 200,000 troops to the Gulf and was itching to attack before summer.

During January and February, Elbaredi kept emphasizing that Saddam Hussein neither possessed nuclear weapons nor had the ability to revive his program. In fact, it began to appear that Iraq's facilities were "in even more of a shambles than they had been in 1997 when the IAEA had concluded that the nuclear program was finished."[62] Blix also reported no evidence of chemical and biological weapons, though he harbored suspicions that they might eventually be found. In his report in January he expressed exasperation with Saddam Hussein's lack of cooperation, but was shocked by what he thought to be the Bush administration's unwarranted inference that further inspections were pointless. In subsequent reports he underscored the importance of continuing inspections and, by implication, the need before going to war for cautious and extended deliberation by the Security Council of the evidence for WMD in Iraq.

However, the Bush administration was losing patience. They feared that inspections might drag on indefinitely, and, in any case that the opportunity to achieve what was emerging as their main objective – regime change in Iraq –

---

[62] James Traub, *Best Intentions: Kofi Annan and the UN in the Era of American World Power* (New York: Farraer, Straus and Giroux, 2006), 180.

might be frustrated. On February 6, Powell exhibited evidence before the Council that the United States said it found convincing for holding Saddam Hussein in violation of Resolution 1441, evidence that in hindsight was much less secure than Powell let on at the time.[63] His claims had little effect on the opposition, at best leading dissenting members to redouble their support for extending weapons inspections. Neither did his bickering with the French representative before the vote help, nor his subsequent statement that the United States could go ahead with an invasion despite a divided Security Council.[64] True to form, Cheney was unfazed and continued to resist seeking any additional UN authorization, holding that the United States should simply declare it was time to move based on its own interpretation of the facts. Rumsfeld supported him, referring disparagingly to French and German opposition as an example of "old Europe."[65] Stephen Hadley, Rice's deputy, agreed that no additional authorization was needed, but urged successfully that an attempt be made, because Tony Blair, the UK prime minister and the United States' only major ally on the Security Council, was convinced it was important to try.[66]

As is well known, the attempt to secure UN authorization for an invasion of Iraq failed because the great majority of states on the Council concluded that circumstances of such uncertainty warranted nothing more than further inspections – and anything but a precipitous resort to force. Small, weak states such as Guinea, Cameroon, and Angola and middle-sized states like Chile and Mexico – all members at the time of the Council – stood resolutely with France, Germany, and Russia against incredible pressure exerted by the United States and the United Kingdom to persuade them to vote in favor of

---

[63] In light of illuminating retrospective studies, such as James Risen, *State of War: Secret History of the CIA and the Bush Administration* (New York: Free Press, 2006), and Thomas E. Ricks, *Fiasco: The American Military Adventure in Iraq* (New York: Penguin Press, 2006), it is now clear that prewar intelligence was much less reliable than the Bush administration claimed and that a clear "rush to war" sentiment existed among people such as Cheney, Rumsfeld, Wolfowitz, Rice, and others. In *State of War*, Risen refers to the now famous Downing Street Memo, providing a British assessment of the Bush administration's war plans after a secret meeting between the CIA and British intelligence in July 2002: "[M]ilitary action was now seen as inevitable. Bush wanted to remove Saddam, through military action, justified by the conjunction of terrorism and WMD. *But the intelligence and facts were being fixed around the policy*" (113). Also, as Ricks shows in *Fiasco*, the administration irresponsibly disregarded warnings about the aftermath of the war from leading military figures like Gen. Anthony Zinni, former chief, U.S. Central Command; Gen. Eric Shinseki, former Chief of Staff, U.S. Army; and others (68–81).

[64] Mann, *Rise of the Vulcans*, 356.
[65] Ibid., 340, 354.
[66] Traub, *Best Intentions*, 183.

a second resolution. Eventually, the United States and the United Kingdom recognized they were beaten, and rather than suffer a humiliating defeat by permitting the resolution to come to a vote, they withdrew it. On March 19, 2003, the United States invaded Iraq without UN authorization, producing results that, more than ten years later, are at best controversial and at worst nowhere near worth the cost.[67]

> Given the widespread fear of crossing the U.S., the failure to win a second resolution came to be seen as proof of the bullying clumsiness of American diplomacy. "If you're publicly threatened with the consequences if you don't go along," says Kieran Prendergast, Anan's head of political affairs, "then if you're a self-respecting country, you can't go along." The Bush administration had dissipated the good-will that came with the terrorist attacks by its rhetorical bellicosity, [and] its unwillingness to acknowledge that other nations might have legitimate interests of their own.[68]

In light of the fact that after the invasion no WMD were found, Council members who opposed a second resolution "were right and the U.S. and the U.K. were wrong," declares Philippe Sands. "It could be said that the UN system worked."[69] Sands is certainly correct, at least up to a point. One key benefit of collective security assumed in the UN Charter was powerfully vindicated, namely, that subjecting all proposals for the international use of force to *collective* scrutiny, deliberation, and authorization is an effective way to detect rashness and disingenuousness. Also vindicated was the ability of collective procedures to identify courses of action short of force that, if followed, could prevent needless death and destruction. To that extent, the UN system performed as it was intended to by providing legal obstacles to the exercise of arbitrary force.[70] At the same time, of course, the system did not

---

[67] See "Afterword: Betting against History," in Ricks, *Fiasco*, 430–439, which begins: "History will determine if President Bush was correct in asserting that the invasion of Iraq 'made our country more secure.' But the indications at this point [mid-2006] aren't good" (430). By 2013, they are even worse: a total cost to the U.S. treasury of around a trillion dollars that helped deepen the 2008 recession; 4,487 U.S. troops killed, 32,223 wounded, 20% of whom have serious brain or spinal injuries; more than 100,000 Iraqi casualties; and an increasingly authoritarian Iraqi political system, ethnically fragmented and allied with the governments of Syria and Iran, both of which are the source of enormous mischief in the region.

[68] Traub, *Best Intentions*, 184.

[69] Philippe Sands, *Lawless World: America and the Making of Global Rules from FDR's Atlantic Charter to George W. Bush's Illegal War* (New York: Viking, 2005), 202.

[70] The president of the American Society of International Law estimated that some 80% of international lawyers hold the invasion of Iraq to be illegal, but other experts have estimated a higher number than that. See Jutta Brunnee and Stephen J. Toope, *Legitimacy and Legality* (Cambridge: Cambridge University Press, 2010), 246.

work perfectly because, in the end, it failed to prevent such an exercise from being carried out.

To be sure, the Bush administration's attitude of "reluctant engagement" with and ultimate defiance of the UN was consistent with the doctrine of preemptory unilateralism stated in its National Security Strategy, according to which international institutions are of nothing more than instrumental value: They are to be used and worked with so far as they are useful to U.S. interests. At bottom, that doctrine, amply manifest in the way the United States handled Security Council Resolution 1441, represents a deep and radical challenge to the very foundations of the UN Charter.

Some observers have gone so far as to argue that the record of violation of UN Charter provisions regarding the use of force, such as occurred in the case of Iraq, has sharply eroded, if not destroyed, Charter authority and that, as a matter of law, states may now arguably use force as they see fit.[71] In fact, however, the case of Iraq teaches the opposite. The reason for resisting such a conclusion and for reaffirming Charter authority is the same reason that undergirded the creation of the post–World War II UN Charter system in the first place. That is the compelling concern, in reaction to the Nazi record, to inhibit and restrain states from defining "imminent threats" and "rights to self-defense," let alone rights to occupy and reconstruct countries by force, solely on their own authority.

In respect to compliance with human rights and humanitarian law, the Bush administration exhibited the same mixture of defiance, ambivalence,

---

[71] See Glennon, "How War Left the Law Behind." Cf. a longer version of the article, "The Fog of Law: Self-Defense, Inherence, and Incoherence in Article 51 of the United Nations Charter," 25 *Harvard Journal of Law and Public Policy* 539 (2002). Apart from the handling of SCR 1441, the record, especially recently, appears to be considerably more ambiguous than Glennon acknowledges. Although NATO military action in Kosovo in spring 1999 was not authorized by the Security Council, efforts by the Russians to rally the Security Council to censor the action were explicitly rejected. Moreover, the action was significantly collective, was actively supported by most of the Balkan neighbors, and was informally upheld by none other than the UN Secretary-General, Kofi Annan, based on his repeated appeals to expand Charter authorization so as to permit armed humanitarian intervention. See David Little, "Force and Humanitarian Intervention: The Case of Kosovo," in William Joseph Buckley, ed., *Kosovo: Contending Voices on Balkan Interventions*(Grand Rapids, MI: Eerdmans Publishing Co., 2000), 356–359. None of these conditions applied to unilateral U.S. military action in Iraq. Furthermore, as I mentioned earlier, Security Council resolutions in support of U.S. armed action in Afghanistan in response to the attacks of September 11 represented an important reassertion of Security Council authority in respect to the campaign against terrorism, even if the Council may not have gone far enough in exercising continuing supervisory authority. See Eric P. J. Meyer and Nigel D. White, "The Twin Towers Attack: An Unlimited Right to Self-Defence?," 16.

and inconstancy, along with some of the same grudging acquiescence, that was apparent in its dealings with the UN. Although, as I noted, President Bush, Secretary Powell, and other officials on occasion paid their respects to human rights and humanitarian law, the Bush administration was anything but a model of steadfastness in honoring its obligations.

To begin with, the United States failed, inexplicably, to comply with its responsibilities as an adherent to the International Covenant on Civil and Political Rights by acting "immediately [to] inform the other States Parties to the present Covenant, through the intermediary of the Secretary-General of the United Nations, of the provisions from which it has derogated and of the reasons by which it was actuated" (Art. 4.3). As we saw, the requirements of international public accountability and full disclosure concerning the suspension of any and all civil protections under emergency conditions lie at the heart of an international system designed to prevent anything close to a recurrence of the gross abuses associated with the Nazi record.

The following implied reprimand to the Bush administration from a respected, bipartisan commission reaffirms the same urgent concern that underlies the relevant provisions of the International Covenant on Civil and Political Rights: "[T]he United States should forthrightly address, rather than avoid, the policy tensions that arise when the imperatives of war against terrorism compete with human rights and democratic principles."[72] As is now well established, public accountability and full disclosure are not virtues the Bush administration had, in general, much use for.[73]

Shortly after the attacks of 9/11, Bush administration lawyers, such as John Yoo, David Addington, William Haynes, and Alberto Gonzales, began crafting a highly expansive interpretation of the doctrine of "unitary executive authority." In their hands, the doctrine effectively declared that "the President not only had power to defend the nation as he saw fit in ways that were not limited by any laws, he also had the power to override existing laws that Congress had specifically designed to curb him."[74] Compared to earlier infringements of civil liberties during times of emergency, as in the Civil War or World Wars I and II, the practical consequences of the doctrine were less grave. Nevertheless, the constitutional arguments and their implications were extremely ominous. David Addington, influential legal counsel to the vice

---

[72] *Enhancing U.S. Leadership at the United Nations; Report of an Independent Task Force Sponsored by the Council of Foreign Relations and Freedom House*, David Dreier and Lee H. Hamilton, co-chairs (New York: Council on Foreign Relations, 2002), 21.
[73] Linda Greenhouse, "A Penchant for Secrecy," *New York Times, Week in Review* (May 5, 2002).
[74] Mayer, *Dark Side*, 46–47.

president, was particularly aggressive in arguing that the president could only succeed against an enemy so persistent, inventive, and terrifying "by eliminating all hurdles to the exercise of his power," thereby allowing the United States the freedom to act unilaterally in a way that is "naturally hostile to international restrictions on its power."[75] The president himself reflected that attitude on several occasions: "International law? I better call my lawyer.... I don't know what you're talking about by international law."[76] Or, "I don't care what the international lawyer says, we are going to kick some ass [in Iraq]."[77]

The detention, prosecution, interrogation, and surveillance of terrorist suspects were four areas especially affected by the impulse of the administration to relax the protection of civil rights in face of the emergency brought on by the 9/11 attacks. Critical findings of the courts and others to the Bush record between 2001 and 2009 substantiate an increasingly profligate pattern.

Detention

Under the USA Patriot Act,[78] the centerpiece of the government's "emergency legislation," aliens may be held secretly, and virtually indefinitely, not for what they have done, nor on the basis of evidence supporting probable cause that they are a risk to public order and safety, but typically for trivial offenses and because they are regarded by the Attorney General for some undisclosed reason as "a danger to national security." As a result of this legislation, Ronald Dworkin reported in early 2002 that

> our country now jails large numbers of people not for what they have done, nor even with case-by-case evidence that it would be dangerous to leave them at liberty, but only because they fall within a vaguely defined class, of which some members might pose danger.[79]

---

[75] Jack Goldsmith, *Terror Presidency: Law and Judgment inside the Bush Administration* (New York: Norton, 2007), 126.

[76] Global research, Ca, December 2003.

[77] Cited in Sands, *Lawless World*, 174.

[78] Its full (less than felicitous) title is "The Uniting and Strengthening America by Providing Appropriate Tools Required to Intercept and Obstruct Terrorism Act of 2001." The Patriot Act was renewed by Congress in 2006 and 2011 with only modest changes.

[79] Ronald Dworkin, "The Threat to Patriotism," *New York Review of Books* (Feb. 29, 2002), 44–49, 44. Dworkin elaborates: "If the Attorney General declares that he has 'reasonable grounds' for suspecting any alien of terrorism or of aiding terrorism in the broad sense that is defined, then he may detain that alien for seven days with no charge. If the alien is then charged with any, even a wholly unrelated crime, and the attorney general finds that 'the release of the alien will threaten the national security of the United States or the safety of the community or any person,' he may be detained for six months and then for additional six-month periods so long

In addition to the expanded opportunities for detention of terrorist suspects on U.S. soil under the Patriot Act, the Bush administration also moved quickly to create a capacious detention center at the American military base outside the United States at Guantanamo, Cuba, for suspects apprehended abroad. Rather quickly, some 650 detainees were assembled there from around forty countries. Administration lawyers believed this location was beyond the reach of both American and international law, thus creating what has become known as a "legal black hole." Accordingly, detainees

> would have no legal representation. They could have no right of access to any court or tribunal. They could be held until the end of the "war on terrorism" without charge, indefinitely and forever if necessary [lacking the protection of habeas corpus, or the right to hear charges]. They would be interrogated. They might face the possibility of truncated military proceedings before tribunals which could apply the death penalty. And they would have no rights under any of the rules of international law which Roosevelt and Churchill had championed in the 1940s. In particular, they would have no rights under the Geneva Conventions of 1949, intended to protect combatants and civilians from the excesses of war and armed conflict....[80] [Furthermore,] the U.S. solicitor general could not have put it more bluntly...: the International Covenant on Civil and Political Rights "is inapplicable to conduct by the U.S. outside its sovereign territory."[81]... It follows that the U.S. is free to treat them entirely as it wishes.[82]

Though there was some resistance from Powell and his lawyers at the State Department, Rumsfeld, supported by Cheney and the legal team of Addington, Yoo, and Gonzales, sent an order on January 18, 2002, to the Joint Chiefs of Staff of the U.S. military that they were henceforth to disregard the Geneva Conventions in dealing with all members of al Qaeda and the Taliban who had been apprehended.[83]

The waiving of one particular protection guaranteed by the Geneva Conventions was of special consequence for detainees. It was Article 5, Geneva Convention III, covering the treatment of prisoners of war, which stated that

> as the attorney general continues to declare that his release would threaten national security or anyone's safety. The Justice Department has now detained several hundred aliens, some of them in solitary confinement for twenty-three hours a day. None of them has been convicted of anything at all, and many of them have been charged with only minor immigration offenses that would not by themselves remotely justify detention. It has refused repeated efforts on the part of the ACLU, and other groups even to identify these detainees" (44).

[80] Sands, *Lawless World*, 144.
[81] Ibid., 145.
[82] Ibid., 146.
[83] Mayer, *Dark Side*, 123.

"should any doubt arise as to whether persons, having committed a belligerent act and having fallen into the hands of the enemy [should qualify as prisoners of war, under the preceding Art. 4], such persons shall enjoy the protections of the present Convention until such time as their status has been determined by a competent tribunal." Of the greatest importance, this provision was reaffirmed and expanded on in Article 75 of Protocol I to the Geneva Conventions, adopted in 1977. It states that no penalty may be inflicted on a person found guilty of an offense related to armed conflict "except pursuant to a conviction pronounced by an impartial and regularly constituted court respecting the generally recognized principles of regular judicial proceedings," including the right of habeas corpus, "all necessary rights and means of defense," protection against self-incrimination, and the right to cross-examine witnesses.

In addition to denying the right to a hearing, there were, from a detainee point of view, other ominous implications of the administration's total rejection of international humanitarian law. Article 75 is not only about due process. It also recalls Common Article 3 found in all four of the Geneva Conventions, which, in similar language, prohibits "at any time and in any place whatsoever, whether committed by civilian or military agents" such things as murder, "torture of all kinds, whether physical or mental," corporal punishment, mutilation, "outrages upon personal dignity, in particular humiliating and degrading treatment, enforced prostitution or any form of indecent assault." Although the United States has never ratified the Protocol, parts of it are widely recognized as customary international law, and the U.S. Army's *Operational Law Handbook* explicitly accepts the applicability of Article 75.[84]

By the spring of 2004, when the scandal surrounding the gross mistreatment of detainees at Abu Ghraib prison in Baghdad broke, the consequences of ignoring international human rights and humanitarian law began to register with a vengeance. These consequences were especially telling in regard to the permissive interrogation techniques the administration had condoned (see the later section). But they also began to take hold in regard to legal due process, as reflected in two Supreme Court cases decided later in 2004. In *Rasul v. Bush*,[85] U.S. courts were judged to have habeas corpus jurisdiction over Guantanamo Bay detainees. Contrary to the arguments of the Bush administration, detainees were granted legal recourse to challenge the government as to whether their status as enemy combatants had been determined according to an "impartial and regularly constituted court respecting the generally recognized principles of regular judicial proceedings."

---

[84] I am relying here on Sand's illuminating discussion, *Lawless World*, 147–153.
[85] 542 U.S. 466 (2004).

In *Hamdi v. Rumsfeld*,[86] the Court reinforced the point by rejecting Bush administration claims they could, at their own discretion, classify Yaser Hamdi, an American citizen, as an enemy combatant and then detain him indefinitely without counsel or formal accusation. In a ringing opinion, Justice O'Connor pronounced that

> a state of war is not a blank check for the President when it comes to the rights of the Nation's citizens.... It would turn our system of checks and balances on its head to suggest that a citizen could not make his way to court with a challenge to the factual basis for his detention by his government, simply because the Executive opposes making available such a challenge.... An interrogation by one's captor... hardly constitutes a constitutionally adequate fact-finding before a neutral decisionmaker.

Even Justice Scalia came to a similar conclusion: "Indefinite imprisonment at the will of the Executive" attacks "the very core of liberty."

Jack Goldsmith, head of the Justice Department's Office of Legal Council from fall 2003 until July 2004, characterized these rulings as mere "slaps on the wrist" of the administration. But they were more than that, at least symbolically, because by Goldsmith's own reckoning the decisions expressed "changes in context and culture" as to what degree rights might be sacrificed in dealing with emergencies.[87] The general attitude of permissiveness across the country that the administration had enjoyed immediately after 9/11 was beginning to disappear.

Prosecution

Resistance to the administration's way of balancing national security and civil rights was particularly intense in regard to the special military commissions created by executive order on November 13, 2001. These irregular tribunals were designed to try noncitizens apprehended in connection with the campaign against terrorism and were summarily characterized by one conservative columnist, normally sympathetic to the Bush administration, as "kangaroo courts."[88]

A 2013 book, *Terror Courts: Rough Justice at Guantanamo Bay*, by Jess Bravin, is reported to lay out in extensive detail "how a small group of Bush-era appointees managed to develop a parallel justice system designed to ensure

---

[86] 542 U.S. 507 (2004).
[87] Goldsmith, *Terror Presidency*, 134–135.
[88] William Safire, "Kangaroo Courts," *New York Times* (Nov. 26, 2001); cf. Safire, "Seizing Dicatorial Power," *New York Times* (Nov. 11, 2001).

a specific outcome."[89] Some of the features of that system are described as follows:

> Strip the defendants of rights. Have an administrator who is both judge and jury. Be selective about military-commission history on which the system is based... and then make sure to exclude the military's lawyers so that their fealty to the Uniform Code of Military Justice (UCMJ) doesn't get in the way of their mission.[90]

In fact, the Pentagon's general counsel, William Haynes, who was responsible for the military commissions, instructed those drafting commission rules "to avoid using the word rights – except to state, as the document did, that the order conferred none." Moreover, the administration endeavored to transfer prosecutions of terror suspects from civilian courts, under the jurisdiction of the Justice Department, to military commissions that were controlled by the Defense Department, with dubious results.[91] Since 9/11 federal prosecutors have won sixty-seven terrorist convictions in civilian courts, a large number of which yielded important information, whereas there have been only seven convictions in military commissions, two of which were overturned on appeal.[92]

Specifically, the procedures authorized by the 2001 executive order departed in important ways from the UCMJ: Classified information, not disclosed to defendant or counsel, could be used, along with coerced confessions and hearsay evidence. This was all required, according to the order, by the emergency conditions generated by the war on terrorism.[93]

On January 4, 2002, the American Bar Association Task Force on Terrorism and the Law issued a prestigious legal critique of Bush's military commissions. It displayed special sensitivity to the need for such courts to be guided by the International Covenant on Civil and Political Rights, which, at Article 14, requires that all tribunals be "independent and impartial," "with the proceedings open to the press and public, except for specific and compelling reasons, and [with] the following rights for the defendant: a presumption of innocence; prompt notice of charges, and adequate time and facilities to prepare a defense; trial without undue delay."[94]

---

[89] (New Haven: Yale University Press, 2013), reviewed by Dina Temple-Raston, "Lifting the Veil on Guantanamo Justice," *Washington Post*, March 31, 2013, B7.
[90] Ibid.
[91] Ibid.
[92] "Somali's Case a Template for U.S.: Terror Suspects in Federal Courts," *Washington Post*, March 31, 2013, A1, A9.
[93] Stone, *War and Liberty*, 136.
[94] American Bar Association Task Force on Terrorism and the Law; Report and Recommendations on Military Commissions (Jan. 4, 2002), 16–17; cf. 12–13.

In response to the avalanche of criticism, the Bush administration made some efforts to bring military commission procedures more in line with due process requirements, but the efforts were far from sufficient for the Supreme Court. In the spring of 2006, the Court decided *Hamdan v. Rumsfeld*, ruling that criminal prosecutions of suspected terrorists or anyone else may only take place either in federal courts or in accord with the UCMJ, as Congress had authorized.[95] Salim Ahmed Hamdan was a Yemeni citizen and Osama bin Laden's driver, who had been captured in Afghanistan and turned over to the U.S. military. However dangerous he might be, the Supreme Court held that the president, in subjecting him to prosecution, "cannot simply make up the rules as he goes along, but must 'comply with the Rule of Law.'"[96]

Unlike the decisions in *Rasul* and *Hamdi*, Justice Stevens's majority ruling in *Hamdan* explicitly states that "the procedures adopted to try Hamdan ... violate the Geneva Conventions." Consequently, all individuals prosecuted by the United States are protected by Common Article 3, requiring, among other things, that Hamdan be tried by a "regularly constituted court affording all the judicial guarantees which are recognized as indispensable by civilized peoples." The opinion continues,

> While the term "regularly constituted court" is not specifically defined in either Common Article 3 or its accompanying commentary, other sources disclose its core meaning. The commentary accompanying a provision of the Fourth Geneva Convention, for example, defines "regularly constituted" " tribunals to include "ordinary military courts" and "definitely exclud[e] all special tribunals." And one of the Red Cross' own treatises defines "regularly constituted court" as used in Common Article 3 to mean "established and organized in accordance with the laws and procedures already in force in a country."

> Inextricably intertwined with the question of regular constitution is the evaluation of the procedures governing the tribunal and whether they afford "all the judicial guarantees which are recognized as indispensable by civilized peoples." Like the phrase "regularly constituted court," this phrase is not defined in the text of the Geneva Conventions. But it must be understood to incorporate at least the barest of those trial protections that have been recognized by customary international law. Many of these are described in Article 75 of Protocol I to the Geneva Conventions of 1949, adopted in 1977. Although the United States declined to ratify Protocol I, its objections were not to Article 75 thereof. Indeed, it appears that the Government "regard[s]

---

[95] 128 S.Ct. 2749 (2006), discussed by Stone, *War and Liberty*, 137.
[96] Stone, *War and Liberty*, 137.

the provisions of Article 75 as an articulation of safeguards to which all persons in the hands of an enemy are entitled."

Even Jack Goldsmith, looking back after leaving the Office of Legal Counsel in the Bush administration, admitted that "this time the Court's decision seemed to have more bite."[97] To hold that Common Article 3 of the Geneva Conventions "applied in the war against al Qaeda and its affiliates... as a treaty obligation... was hugely consequential."[98] As a result, the 1996 U.S. War Crimes Act was applicable to government officials, bringing "CIA worries about retroactive discipline to new highs."[99]

In response to the tremors caused by *Hamdan*, the Bush administration attempted to recoup its losses by inducing Congress to pass the Military Commissions Act of 2006, which in its original form would have restored things to the way they were before *Hamdan*. After strenuous resistance by most congressional Democrats and a few Republicans, a somewhat altered bill was adopted, though one that still permitted substantial deviations from several judicial guarantees "recognized as indispensable by civilized peoples." For one thing, it unduly limited the application of Common Article 3 of the Geneva Conventions to the War Crimes Act[100] and, at the same time, unduly expanded the discretionary authority of the president to interpret the Geneva Conventions.[101] It set aside the right against self-incrimination and allowed use of hearsay evidence, which violates the defendant's right to confront accusers. It also set aside the right of habeas corpus, though that exclusion was rendered unconstitutional by the Supreme Court in *Boumediene v. Bush* in 2008.[102]

Moreover, Congress did all these things without the slightest attempt to defend such actions or provide evidence that the stakes involved were even

---

[97] Goldsmith, *Terror Presidency*, 136.
[98] Ibid., though it is hard to imagine on what basis Goldsmith believes this conclusion is "legally erroneous" (136), because Common Article 3 of the Geneva Conventions, to which the U.S. is a party, is understood to apply to all persons "who, at a given moment and in any manner whatsoever, find themselves, in case of a conflict or occupation, in the hands of a Party to the conflict or Occupying Power of which they are not nationals conflict." Even a "person detained as a spy or saboteur, or as a person under definite suspicion of activity hostile to the security of the Occupying Power... shall nevertheless be treated with humanity... [as defined in Article 3]." (Geneva Convention IV, Articles 4 and 5).
[99] Ibid., 137.
[100] "The MCA's limitation of the War Crimes Act to the grave breaches' [of Common Article 3] it defines is too narrow and may be read to permit conduct that plainly violates Common Article 3." "Report on Executive Detention, Habeas Corpus, and the Military Commissions Act of 2006," New York City Bar Association (May 2006), 44. http://nysba.org.
[101] Ibid. "[U]nder our constitutional system, it is the judicial branch that has the authority to interpret treaties" (47).
[102] 553 U.S. 723 (2008).

understood. Rather than face up to "the tensions that arise when the imperatives of war against terrorism compete with human rights and democratic principles," the Republican House leadership responded characteristically: They called all opponents of the bill "dangerous" and charged them with ignoring national security in favor of what they disparagingly called the "rights of terrorists."[103]

Interrogation

The degree of panic with which the Bush administration met the 9/11 attacks may have been understandable, as perhaps was their desperate need for information to help prevent any recurrence, along with the resulting temptation to go to any lengths to obtain that intelligence. However, there are two reasons for questioning their reaction. First, had they more carefully heeded early warning signals of imminent threat, they might have had cooler heads and been better prepared when the attacks occurred.[104] Second, high-ranking members of the administration, such as Cheney, Rumsfeld, and Wolfowitz, had long nursed deep frustrations over the proliferation of legal restraints, both national and international, on the authority of the president.[105] Did the attacks occasion due vigilance, or were they simply an excuse for realizing, at last, long-standing ambitions?

What is not in doubt is that the administration seized the conditions of emergency caused by the attacks to initiate a completely unprecedented policy of "enhanced interrogation," one that deliberately defied existing international and national legal standards and produced untold unaccountable suffering.

In *The Dark Side*, which presents a comprehensive, if distressing, account of Bush interrogation policies, Jane Mayer points out that sixty years after the rulings of the Nuremberg war crimes tribunal, which laid down a seemingly "immutable principle, that legalisms and technicalities could not substitute for individual moral choice and conscience, America became the first nation ever to authorize violations of the Geneva Conventions." It did that despite the fact that the United States "had long played a special role as the world's most ardent champion of these fundamental rights," "not just as a signatory but also as the custodian of the Geneva Conventions, the original signed copies of

---

[103] Stone, *War and Liberty*, 140.
[104] Mayer, *Dark Side*. Except for Richard Clarke, "terrorism hadn't ranked anywhere near the top of the new administration's national security concerns. . . . Frozen in a Cold War-era mind-set, [the administration] overlooked threats posed not by great armed nation-states, but by small, lithe rogue groups waging 'asymmetric' warfare" (6).
[105] Ibid., 7.

which reside... in a vault at the State Department."[106] Especially notable was the untroubled, matter-of-fact way in which Vice President Cheney, a few days after the 9/11 attacks, announced the administration's readiness to disregard the entire system of procedural and humanitarian protections codified by the Geneva Conventions that had been designed precisely for such occasions: "We've got to spend time in the shadows in the intelligence world. A lot of what needs to be done here will have to be done quietly, without any discussion... And... it's going to be vital for us to use any means at our disposal... to achieve our objectives."[107]

The story begins with a White House beside itself to obtain actionable intelligence in the fight against terrorism. Faced with large numbers of detainees who were believed to be brimming with valuable information, government officials, particularly the CIA staff, consulted with experienced interrogators in places such as Jordan, Saudi Arabia, and Egypt who had long spent time "in the shadows of the intelligence world," "doing things quietly and without any discussion" and routinely using "any means at their disposal." These contacts yielded many innovative suggestions as to how to "enhance" interrogation techniques, including some from Israeli sources – despite the fact that in 1999 the Israeli Supreme Court had famously distinguished itself by explicitly outlawing torture and other coercive interrogation techniques in response to extensive abuse by the Israeli General Security Service. In the memorable conclusion to its decision, the Israel Supreme Court said that it is "the destiny of democracy [that] not all means are acceptable to it, and not all practices employed by its enemies are open before it. Although a democracy must often fight with one hand tied behind its back, it nonetheless has the upper hand."[108] The ruling was, of course, particularly compelling because Israel, unlike the United States, has faced a continuing threat of terrorism throughout its existence.

In a memo by Alberto Gonzales, legal counsel to the president, written on January 25, 2002, the administration began to build its case for a conclusion directly opposite to that of the Israeli Supreme Court. The memo argued that the Third Geneva Convention on prisoners of war (POW) does not apply to members of the Taliban or al Qaeda, thereby precluding "any need for case-by-case determinations of POW status."[109] It described a "new paradigm" requiring "the ability to quickly obtain information from captured terrorists

---

[106] Ibid., 9.
[107] Ibid., 10.
[108] Sanford Levinson, ed., *Torture: A Collection* (New York: Oxford University Press, 2004), 180–181.
[109] Mark Danner, *Torture and Truth: America, Abu Ghraib, and the War on Terror* (New York: New York Review Books, 2004), 83–87.

and their sponsors in order to avoid further atrocities against American civilians," one that "renders obsolete Geneva's strict limitations on questioning enemy prisoners and renders quaint some of its provisions requiring the captured enemy be afforded [certain privileges]."[110] The memo was challenged by Colin Powell, but upheld by the president a few days later, who reaffirmed the existence of a "new paradigm" requiring "new thinking on the law of war."[111] Such thinking, said the president, should be "consistent with the principles of Geneva," a loose formulation that allowed the administration virtually unlimited discretion in applying those principles.

The next critical step in building the case was taken on August 1, 2002, when another memo, this one written mainly by John Yoo of the Office of Legal Counsel and signed by Assistant Attorney General Jay Bybee, was circulated, effectively negating the legal force of the Convention against Torture (CAT) and the enabling U.S. legislation (USC 2340A).

It did that, in the first place, by extensively narrowing the meaning of "torture" from that defined by the CAT and by the U.S. legislation. Rather than accepting the broader definition, which the United States had *not* qualified in the statement of reservations, understandings, and declarations issued on its ratification of the CAT,[112] the Bybee memo limited the meaning to physical pain "equivalent in intensity to the pain accompanying serious physical injury, such as organ failure, impairment of bodily function, or even death," and to mental pain or suffering that amounts to "significant psychological harm of significant duration, e.g., lasting for months or even years,"[113] thereby exempting a wide range of intensely painful methods conventionally described as torture. Moreover, it specified that "the infliction of pain as such must be the [interrogator's] precise objective,"[114] suggesting that if the objective of an interrogation is to acquire information, the interrogator would not be liable to a charge of torture.

In the second place, the memo articulated an extremely broad understanding of "unitary executive authority":

> Even if an interrogation method arguably were to violate Section 2340A, the statute would be unconstitutional if it impermissibly encroached on the President's constitutional power to conduct a military campaign. As Commander-in-Chief, the President has the constitutional authority to order interrogations

---

[110] Ibid., 84.
[111] February 7, 2002, ibid., 105–106.
[112] See www.unhchr.ch/html/menu2/6/cat/treaties/convention-reserv.htm.
[113] Danner, *Torture and Truth*, 115.
[114] Ibid., 117.

of enemy combatants to gain intelligence information concerning the military plans of the enemy.[115]

The memo provided legal authorization for practices that had been officially condoned earlier and would be so subsequently. These included such techniques as "hooding," "exploitation of phobias," "stress positions," "deprivation of light and auditory stimuli,"[116] as well as the "removal of clothing," "use of scenarios designed to convince the detainee that death or severely painful consequences are imminent for him and/or his family," "exposure to cold weather or water," and "use of wet towel and dripping water to induce the misperception of suffocation" (water-boarding).[117] All these techniques were forbidden by the *Army Field Manual*, but many of them (and more) were used in Abu Ghraib. In addition, such methods were apparently lavishly employed in "black sites," or clandestine CIA prisons in Eastern Europe and elsewhere, established by the administration for the purpose of "intelligence gathering" in a way that most assuredly could be "done quietly, without any discussion," as the vice president had put it.[118]

It is important to emphasize that there was consistent and forthright opposition to such policies right from the start; for example, by Gen. Alberto Mora, General Counsel of the U.S. Navy, as well as by a whole host of military lawyers and by some lawyers in the State Department, who made themselves quite unpopular with the administration. What turned out to be the most consequential opposition came from Jack Goldsmith who, as a new member of the Office of Legal Counsel, had decided in December 2003, before the Abu Ghraib scandal broke, that the earlier legal opinions regarding interrogation "must be withdrawn, corrected, and replaced" because they were "legally flawed, tendentious in substance and tone, and overbroad."[119] Unfortunately, Goldsmith then weakened the force of his worthy decision by suggesting, against considerable evidence to the contrary, that the Military Commissions Act was an important step toward "putting counterterrorism policy on a more secure and sensible foundation."[120]

---

[115] Ibid., 142.
[116] Mayer, *Dark Side*, 220.
[117] Ltc. Jerald Phifer, letter to Joint Task Force, Guantanamo Bay, October 11, 2001. Phifer was deputy to General Geoffrey Miller, commanding officer of the U.S. detention facilities at Guantanamo and in Iraq. Danner, *Torture and Truth*, 167–168. See 170–214 for Department of Defense memos detailing the government's highly permissive attitude toward interrogation techniques.
[118] See Mayer, *Dark Side*, ch. 7, "Inside the Black Sites," for an account.
[119] Goldsmith, *Terror Presidency*, 146 and 151.
[120] Ibid., 140.

Particularly chilling examples of the early attitudes of Bush administration officials toward interrogation were reported in a 2003 news account on the practice of "rendering," or outsourcing terror suspects to other countries for questioning typically conducted in a coercive manner. All the national security officials interviewed for the story "defended the use of violence against captives as just and necessary.... 'If you don't violate someone's human rights some of the time, you probably aren't doing your job,'" said one. Cofer Black, formerly head of the CIA Counterterrorist Center, exulted in the new "operational flexibility" introduced for dealing with terror suspects. "All you need to know [is]: After 9/11, the gloves came off." According to another official, "We don't kick the [expletive] out of them. We send them to other countries so *they* can kick the [expletive] out of them." Still another spoke evasively of "knowing" whether or not a suspect had been tortured by non-American officials: "If we're not there in the room, who is to say?" One official, when asked if the United States worried about the probable use of torture on suspects passed along to Egypt, replied: "You can be sure we are not spending a lot of time on that now."[121]

In 2004, Mark Danner accurately summarized the Bush record on interrogation:

> Behind the exotic brutality so painstakingly recorded in Abu Ghraib... lies a simple truth...: that since the attacks of September 11, 2001, officials of the United States, at various locations around the world, from Bagram in Afghanistan to Guantanamo in Cuba to Abu Ghraib in Iraq, have been torturing prisoners.
>
> They did this, in the felicitous phrasing of General Taguba's report, in order to "exploit [them] for actionable intelligence" and they did it, insofar as this is possible, with the institutional approval of the United States government, complete with memoranda from the President's counsel and officially promulgated decisions, in the case of Afghanistan and Guantanamo, about the nonapplicability of the Geneva Conventions, and, in the case of Iraq, about at least three different sets of interrogation policies, two of them modeled on earlier practice in Afghanistan and Cuba.[122]

The record of the two Bush terms as summarized by Danner has generated extensive debate over the moral and legal permissibility of torture as a means of interrogation.[123] Aside from moral and legal questions, the debate has included

---

[121] "U.S. Decries abuse but Defends Interrogations," *Washington Post* (Dec. 26, 2002), A15.
[122] Danner, *Torture and Truth*, 10–11.
[123] See, for example, Levinson, *Torture: A Collection*; David Luban, "Liberalism, Torture, and the Ticking Bomb," *Virginia Law Review* 91.6 (October 2005), 1425–1461; Jeremy Waldron,

extensive differences of opinion over the practical efficacy of torture, with strong arguments against its usefulness under any circumstances.[124] But even among those who would allow for the provisional use of torture or for less severe measures sometimes called "torture lite,"[125] it is difficult to find anyone (except some former administration officials) willing to justify the officially condoned practices of the Bush administration for much of its time in office. There is general agreement that even if, at times, coercive interrogation is excusable, it must be conducted under the most stringently restricted and carefully defined conditions, lest its readily authorized use, evident during the Bush years, produce "untold unaccountable suffering."

Surveillance

During the Ford administration, it became unlawful for the government to spy on religious and political activities without probable cause.[126] Attorney General John Ashcroft relaxed that restriction in the spring, of 2002, authorizing surveillance without suspicion of guilt. The new, permissive policy was consistent with sections of the Patriot Act that allowed the government to investigate the private records of citizens, also without probable cause, whether they pertained to business, library use, health care, higher education, or other activities. There were considerable objections to the policy, but it remained more or less intact after the Patriot Act was renewed in 2006.

Of related concern was the decision of the Bush administration, after 9/11, to wiretap international telephone calls and e-mails. In the 1970s, President Nixon had argued that, to protect national security, the executive must be permitted to wiretap without a warrant. However, the Supreme Court ruled against the argument, holding that showing probable cause and obtaining a warrant, as required by the Fourth Amendment, apply to all such surveillance.[127]

"Torture and Positive Law: Jurisprudence for the White House' (unpublished paper, 2005); and Jordan J. Praust, "Executive Plans and Authorization to Violate International Law Concerning Treatment and Interrogation of Detainees," 43 *Columbia Journal of Transnational Law* 811–863 (2005).

[124] See Ali Soufan, *Black Banners: Inside Story of 9/11 and the War against Al Qaeda* (New York: W.W. Norton, 2011).

[125] See Amos N. Guiora, *Constitutional Limits on Coercive Interrogation* (New York: Oxford University Press, 2008); Alan Dershowitz, "Tortured Reasoning," and Richard A. Posner, "Torture, Terrorism, and Interrogation," both in Levinson, *Torture: A Collection*.

[126] I am relying here on the excellent account of the expansion of government surveillance during the Bush administration by Stone, *War and Liberty*, 140–165.

[127] *United States v. United States District Court* (Keith) 407 U.S. 297 (1972).

Congress, troubled by warrantless wiretapping that took place during the Vietnam era, passed the Foreign Intelligence Surveillance Act (FISA) in 1978, establishing a special FISA court to authorize foreign intelligence surveillance in exceptional circumstances. It thereby attempted to strike a reasonable balance between the protection of rights and the need for special executive prerogatives during emergencies.

However, shortly after the 9/11 attacks, the Bush administration, true to form, disregarded existing restrictions on executive power and secretly gave the National Security Agency authority to monitor electronically the foreign communications of Americans without probable cause or warrant. It is estimated that by 2006, the government was eavesdropping on the communications of hundreds of American citizens and had access to the conversations of millions more.[128]

In justification of this surveillances, administration lawyers provided a series of secret legal opinions similar to those that supported enhanced interrogation techniques, save that the opinions regarding surveillance remained secret. It may be inferred that the lawyers posited two grounds for the administration's case. First, congressional authorization for the use of "all necessary and reasonable force" – Authorization for the Use of Military Force (AUMF), passed by Congress on September 14, 2001 – was taken to provide a reason for ignoring FISA. Second, a Justice Department brief claimed that, consistent with the expanded notion of unitary executive authority, the Constitution entitles the president "to conduct warrantless intelligence surveillance (electronic or otherwise) of powers and their agents, and Congress cannot by statute extinguish that [right]."[129]

The argument based on AUMF is unconvincing. In the event of a declaration of war, FISA legislation explicitly limits to fifteen days the right of the president to authorize surveillance without probable causes and a warrant.[130] His only alternative would appear to be to change the legislation. The constitutional argument is equally unconvincing, because "the suggestion that the Constitution makes the president the supreme ruler in matters of national defense is simply false."[131]

Jack Goldsmith shared some of the Bush administration's frustrations with the FISA process, but "deplored the way the White House went about fixing the problem."[132] Bush administrative officials dealt with FISA "the way they

[128] Risen, *State of War*, 44.
[129] Ibid., 44–45.
[130] Stone, *War and Liberty*, 147.
[131] Ibid., 148.
[132] Goldsmith, *Terror Presidency*, 181.

dealt with other laws they didn't like: they blew through them in secret based on flimsy legal opinions that they guarded closely so no one could question the legal basis of the operations." Goldsmith wrote that he had attempted to work with FISA in order to give the president more flexibility in apprehending terrorists. "From the beginning the administration could have taken these and other steps to ramp up terrorist surveillance in indisputably lawful ways, ... [b]ut only if it had been willing to work with the FISA court or Congress. The White House had found it much easier to go it alone, in secret."[133]

THE U.S. EXAMPLE: THE OBAMA RECORD

According to one assessment, "President Obama has in fact decisively broken from the Bush approach. While he has continued to employ tactics traditionally employed in war – military detention, killing and war crimes trials – he has sought to reconcile those practices with the rule of law Bush rejected."[134] On his first day in office, the president repudiated by executive order the worst features of the Bush antiterrorism program, terminating both CIA overseas secret prisons and any further use of coercive interrogation methods. In addition, he pledged, against strong continuing resistance, to close the Guantanamo Bay Center. Later, he released previously secret torture memos, directed military commissions to be reformed in closer conformity with due process, and imposed new substantive and procedural standards for detention in Afghanistan.

In these ways, President Obama has moved to bring U.S. antiterror policy considerably more in line with the international order than under President Bush. Also, he has gone further than Bush in facing up, in theory at least, to the tension between constitutional rights and national security. On March 21, 2009, in a speech at the National Archives, he laid out a thoughtful framework for balancing security and values. The key guidelines are as follows:

- Safety is a high priority, but governmental efforts to achieve it must always be constitutionally constrained by the rule of law and due process.
- However indispensable the "state's secret" privilege may be for protecting intelligence gathering and surveillance, invoking the privilege must always be subject to oversight by Congress and the courts. Transparency is an abiding virtue.

---

[133] Ibid., 182.
[134] David Cole, "Obama and Terror: The Hovering Questions," *New York Review of Books* (July 12, 2012), 32.

- "Enhanced interrogation techniques," such as waterboarding, are absolutely impermissible.
- "Wherever feasible," the United States "will try those who have violated criminal laws in the federal courts – courts provided by the US Constitution." Other detainees will be released or, where release is not feasible, indefinitely detained or tried by reformed military commissions.
- The prison camp at Guantanamo Bay will be closed.

Although these guidelines set standards to which the Obama administration must be held accountable, they have not, in some respects, been observed. This failure is partly due to the calculated intransigence of congressional Republicans, here and there abetted by Democrats, based on promoting the "politics of fear." Sometimes this failure has been the result of a decision to avoid risking policies of higher priority. But other examples of discrepancy between principles and practice are not so easily explained or justified. While Obama is, in some respects, preferable to Bush on the subject of human rights and national security, there is reason for continuing concern and vigilance in assessing Obama's performance in a second term.

Five policy areas are the subject of sharp dispute: closing Guantanamo Bay Detention Camp, terrorist trials, military commissions versus civilian courts, military detention without charge, terrorists and the use of force, and intelligence gathering and surveillance.

Closing Guantanamo Bay Detention Camp

President Obama's pledge to close Guantanamo was based on a strong and widely held conviction that the camp had become a serious moral and legal liability to the reputation of the United States. In 2004, the Red Cross sharply criticized conditions there, charging that the American military had intentionally employed psychological and sometimes physical coercion "tantamount to torture." The status of the camp as a "legal black hole," deliberately designed by the Bush administration to stand beyond the reach of both U.S. and international law, added appreciably to its disreputable image, even though the U.S. Supreme Court eventually upheld the rule of law in *Rasul v. Bush* and *Hamdan v. Rumsfeld*, extending the rights of legal access to all detainees.

The primary obstacle to closing Guantanamo has been finding a way to transfer the remaining 160 detainees to other locations. The failure of the Obama administration to transfer those detainees is primarily the responsibility of Congress, which has played on the irrational apprehensions of American citizens. When the government attempted to resettle in Virginia a group of Chinese Muslims, judged to have been wrongfully detained and harmless, Rep. Frank Wolf (R. VA) and Senate Majority Leader Mitch McConnell, abetted by Senate Minority Leader Harry Reid, encouraged "a fear-induced insurrection in Congress that threatened one of the president's most high-profile campaign promises. On terrorism, it was becoming increasingly clear, the politics of fear were as strong as ever."[135]

The same readiness to trade on fear also animated congressional reaction to administration efforts to locate a maximum security facility in the United States to accommodate the fifty or so prisoners too dangerous to release and ineligible for prosecution because evidence against them had been obtained by torture. Several possibilities were explored, including in Michigan and Illinois. But with "Congress and Cheney stirring up fear, there were not a lot of communities offering themselves as Gitmo North," and "it made no difference that there were already half a dozen convicted terrorists as dangerous as anybody at Guantanamo locked up for life in various supermax prisons" in the United States.[136]

Given that Guantanamo will remain open for the foreseeable future, there is one aspect of Obama administration policy there that has been criticized by the courts: the decision, selectively and at government discretion, to deny legal access to prisoners at Guantanamo regarding appeals for habeas corpus. On Thursday, September 6, 2012, a federal judge rebuked the administration for that decision in the strongest terms, describing it as an "illegitimate exercise of executive power." The judge claimed that, when asked, the government did not explain why the existing policy of open access, which is working well, should have been altered.[137] Clearly, the administration ought to show in what way the denial of legal access better satisfies the president's own principles of ensuring that policies are "always subject to oversight by Congress and the courts" and are "constitutionally constrained by the rule of law and due process." The failure to do that is an example of a recurring deficiency on the part of the administration to defend itself responsibly in public. Absent such a defense, the policy appears to deviate substantially from the administration's own announced principles.

---

[135] Daniel Klaidman, *Kill or Capture: The War on Terror and the Soul of the Obama Presidency* (Boston: Houghton, Mifflin, Harcourt, 2012), 109.
[136] Ibid., 137.
[137] CNN, "Security Clearance" (Sept. 6, 2012) (internet).

Terrorist Trials: Civilian Courts versus Military Commissions

The Obama administration came to office strongly favoring the trial of terrorists in civilian courts. In support of Attorney General Eric Holder, Harold Koh, the top State Department legal counsel, argued early on that Khalid Sheik Mohammed (KSM), chief architect of the 9/11 attacks, should be tried in a civilian court rather than a military commission both to prove U.S. commitment to the rule of law and to deny KSM the satisfaction of being pictured "as a fearsome person and great military leader, when in fact he is just a common criminal."[138] There were other reasons to try him in a civilian court. The military commissions, created in November 2001 by the Bush administration were regarded as a scandal until the Supreme Court ruled them illegal according to the standards of the Geneva Conventions and the Military Code of Justice.

What is more, since 9/11 more than two hundred terrorists, including Zacarias Moussaoui and the "shoe bomber," Richard Reid, had been convicted in civilian courts with little conservative opposition. Federal judges and prosecutors had a record of considerable accomplishment and experience in conducting such trials, and Mayor Bloomberg was initially confident such a trial could be held safely in New York City. Most important, the chances that KSM would be acquitted were infinitesimal. Many hours of prison yard conversations amounting to admissions of guilt had been secretly recorded, and they meant that KSM had effectively convicted himself. He had provided evidence that was in no way tainted, as was all the previous evidence against him that had been obtained by harsh interrogation instigated soon after his arrest in 2003, including 183 waterboarding sessions.

As the result of a combination of factors, however, KSM was eventually tried not in a civilian court but in a military commission. There was the strong opposition of Sen. Lindsay Graham (R. SC), backed up, predictably, by congressional Republicans; Obama' chief of staff, Rahm Emanuel, along with assorted congressional Democrats also were strongly opposed.[139] There was also the failure of Attorney General Holder to prepare the way with politicians and law enforcement officials in New York City by briefing them, with the Congress by means of effective testimony, and with the public at large through extensive media appearances (opportunities for which were largely thwarted by Rahm Emanuel). However, the major responsibility for the failure to try

---

[138] Klaidman, *Kill or Capture*, 7.
[139] Though they frequently acquiesced on such matters, Senate Democrats did not always do so. Encouraged by the White House, they defeated a bill sponsored by Sen. Graham to prevent KSM and other 9/11 defendants from being tried in a civilian court (ibid., 163–164).

KSM in a civilian court ultimately rested with President Obama himself. With members of his staff deeply divided over this issue, he decided not to fight for the cause, taking what appears to have been the line of least resistance. He was loath to risk support for his domestic agenda on an issue some of the American public cared little about and which others were aroused by the "politics of fear" to oppose at all costs.

A second more successful example in regard to trying alleged terrorists in civilian courts, is the case of Ahmed Abdulkadir Warsame – the principal liaison between Shabad, a Somali extremist group, and AQAP, a Yemeni al-Qaeda affiliate – who was captured by U.S. Navy Seals in April 2011 while crossing the Gulf of Aden. He was not sent to Guantanamo, but, in accord with the laws of war, was detained for two months on a U.S. ship for questioning, having been charged with providing material support to foreign terrorist organizations. The interrogation proceeded with complete propriety, and Warsame, fully cooperative, yielded valuable intelligence concerning the work of AQAP in Yemen, as well as evidence that could serve effectively in his own civilian trial. He was soon transferred to a New York prison and is awaiting trial in a New York federal court. So far, Sen. McConnell's predictable efforts to scare the public by warning that a terrorist has been "purposefully imported into the U.S." have not succeeded.

Despite criticism from both left and right, authoritative opinion regards this case as "a welcome and long-overdue step." The administration "has firmly embraced the American legal system and its courts as a viable tool in its arsenal against captured terrorism suspects." It has begun "to create a post-Guantanamo world. Warsame was not brought to Gitmo; he was not hidden in a prison in Afghanistan." Since Guantanamo opened in January 2002, "Warsame is essentially the first high-value foreign terror suspect to be rounded up abroad and brought [directly] into U.S. custody."[140]

Arguably, the Warsame case substantiates the commitment of the Obama administration to uphold the rule of law in national security cases. The KSM case, too, showed considerable effort in that direction, even if it was finally sacrificed to a prudential calculation concerning policy priorities. Even where the Obama administration has agreed to resort to military commissions, as in the KSM case, its record is an improvement over that of President Bush:

---

[140] Karen Greenberg, "Obama's Gitmo Breakthrough," *Daily Beast* (July 6, 2011). Greenberg is executive director of the Center on Law and Security at New York University. Of this case, Klaidman remarks, "For Obama the reflexive criticism from both ends of the political spectrum suggested he had gotten Warsame exactly right. Yet as was so often the case in his presidency, he got no credit for slicing a path through the sensible center" (*Kill or Capture*, 260).

Bush grudgingly sought authorization from Congress for military commissions only after the Supreme Court declared his unilaterally created commissions unlawful; Obama went to Congress of his own accord in 2009 to make the tribunals more fair (by, for example, prohibiting coerced testimony and restricting hearsay). And when a panel of the US Court of Appeals for the DC Circuit ruled that his military detention authority was not limited by the laws of war, President Obama took the extraordinary step of telling the court that it granted him too much power, insisting that his authority to detain is limited by the laws of war....

It is true that, much to the dismay of many human rights groups, President Obama has continued military detention without charge and military commissions. But these are not "Bush policies"; they both have a well-established place in wartime that extends far back at least to the nation's founding. Even most human rights and civil liberties organizations acknowledge that an armed conflict exists in Afghanistan with al-Qaeda and the Taliban. Wars routinely involve detention of the enemy without charge, and often involve military trials for war crimes....

Obama has unequivocally repudiated [Bush] practices, and has sought instead to conform his counterterrorism policy to law. This is an important and welcome change.[141]

Military Detention without Charge

As the extract ending the previous section indicates, the assessment of Obama's policies is more complicated than many critics of the Obama administration, particularly on the left, understand. The laws of war do not altogether prohibit military detention without charge, as in the case of prisoners of war. Moreover, there is evidence of conscientious effort on the part of the administration to find reasonable solutions to some of the complications, including the possibilities for abuse that detaining without charge creates. At the same time, there is also evidence that the administration has not, as in other aspects of national security policy, satisfactorily explained and justified its policies.

Important intelligence had been obtained from terrorist suspects such as Warsame and Faisal Shazad, the would-be Times Square bomber, by delaying informing them of their Miranda rights. Because of that, the administration favored legislation loosening the Miranda requirement, as well as extending the amount of time until a court hearing is required to permit lengthier interrogations, settling on four rather than seven days after considerable debate.

[141] Cole, "Obama and Terror," 33.

These changes were particularly urgent because it was doubtful that suspects like Warsame and Shazad could correctly be classified as prisoners of war.

However, congressional Republicans had no patience for these niceties and undertook to pass "far more draconian measures" that had "police-state overtones."[142] These mandated that all terror suspects, even ones captured in the United States, be placed immediately in military custody and be automatically stripped of U.S. citizenship. In May 2012 the House passed by a vote of 238–182 a defense authorization bill endorsing the indefinite detention of terrorist suspects without trial, even for U.S. citizens captured in the United States. Earlier, in a signing statement, President Obama had declared, "My administration will not authorize the indefinite military detention without trial of American citizens. Indeed, I believe that doing so would break with our most important traditions and values as a nation." In February 2012, the administration outlined seven new rules as to when the FBI, not the military, could retain custody of al-Qaeda terrorist suspects who are not U.S. citizens but are arrested by federal officers.[143]

Although these steps constitute a welcome move away from the grossly permissive provisions in the House defense authorization bill, it is, again, important for the administration to explain to the public exactly what its present detention policies are and how they are "always subject to oversight by Congress and the courts" and "constitutionally constrained by the rule of law and due process," principles the president laid out in his National Archives speech.

Drones and Terrorists

The U.S. drone attack on September 30, 2011, which killed Anwar al-Awlaki, an American-born Muslim cleric and leader of the Yemeni terrorist al-Quaeda affiliate, AQAP, brought into focus a nest of complicated moral and legal problems surrounding the use of force in pursuing terrorists, especially those who are U.S. citizens. With justification, even sympathetic critics of the Obama administration have wondered whether we should "be satisfied with a wholly executive process that involves no adversarial testing" and whether, time permitting, there should not be a more established and impartial form of judicial review in such matters, similar to the FISA courts.[144] Here is another point at

---

[142] Klaidman, *Kill or Capture*, 191.
[143] "House OKs Indefinite Detention of Terror Suspects," *Newsmax* (May 18, 2012).
[144] Cole, "Obama and Terror," 34. FISA courts are courts established under the Foreign Intelligence Surveillance Act of 1978.

which the Obama administration seems obligated to explain itself by showing how its practices match the principles eloquently enunciated in the National Archives speech.

But there are broader questions at stake, such as whether drones (unmanned aerial vehicles) are themselves at present lawfully employed in the fight against terrorism. The Obama administration has greatly expanded their use.

> In Pakistan, the number of suspected U.S. drone strikes rose from four in 2007 to peak at 122 in 2010, declining to 48 strikes in 2012. In Yemen, suspected drone strikes rose from three to four in 2010 to peak in 2012 [, ... amounting to] at least 26..., and possibly as many as 87. The U.S. has also carried out a smaller number of strikes in Somalia, and there are unconfirmed rumors of ... strikes in Mali and the Philippines as well. All told, U.S. drone strikes have killed an estimated 4,000 people in Pakistan, Yemen and Somalia. The percentage of civilian deaths is unknown, and existing estimates are all controversial.[145]

The administration claims drones are a legitimate weapon of war in accord with both the Authorization of the Use of Military Force (AUMF) passed by Congress in September 2001 and the right of self-defense. The claim appears warranted when the weapon is employed against al-Quaeda operatives, their affiliates, or the Taliban on a recognized battlefield such as Afghanistan. Moreover, complaints that drones cause excessive collateral damage are convincingly refuted by statistical comparisons with conventional weapons showing that drones typically cause much less damage and are many times more discriminating in locating their target than conventional weapons.[146] In addition, claims that continuing use of drones by the U.S. will likely encourage the expansion of such use by terrorists and others in retaliation are unfounded. Weaponized drones are readily vulnerable to air defense systems, and require sophisticated support and take-off and landing facilities, not typically available to terrorists.[147]

However, serious moral, legal, and political questions arise when drones are directed, in "targeted killing" operations, against individuals who may not clearly be part of al Quaeda, its affiliates, or the Taliban or are located outside a recognized battlefield or in a nonbelligerent country, such as Pakistan or

---

[145] Rosa Brooks, "Drones and the International Rule of Law," Georgetown Law Center, http://scholarship.law.georgetown.edu/facpub/1287, 10–11. I am indebted to Professor Brooks for what I consider to be one of the most insightful treatments of the subject I have read.
[146] Michael W. Lewis and Emily Crawford, "Drones and Distinctions: How IHL Encouraged the Rise of Drones," *Georgetown Journal of International Law* vol. 44 (2013), 1156, citing several reliable sources.
[147] Ibid., 1163.

Yemen. A "kill test" has been developed applicable under such circumstances, and there is evidence it is taken very seriously by the Obama administration, right up to the president who signs off on any decision to strike. A legitimate target would have to be a senior member of al Quaeda or, it is assumed, of its affiliates or the Taliban; one who is "externally focused" or deliberately determined to attack the United States or its assets; one who represents a "continuing and imminent threat" or is actively engaged in putting into practice an act of destruction; and, lastly, one who is "infeasible" for capture.

To be sure, the Obama administration's approach has provoked widespread criticism nationally and internationally. The problem is that in applying its drones policy the U.S. is "sole arbiter of its own actions: with zero transparency, it determines what law to apply and it comes up with its own interpretation of core concepts."[148] The administration bases at least part of its legal case on the doctrine of self-defense, but that involves substantially reinterpreting, for example, the key idea of "imminent threat." According to the leaked 2011 Justice Department White Paper, the U.S. does not consider itself required to provide "clear evidence that a specific attack on U.S. persons and interests will take place in the immediate future," contrary to the conventional understanding. Reinterpretation is justified since terrorist opponents of the U.S. are "continually plotting attacks" and "would engage in such attacks regularly [if] they were able to do so," and the U.S. "may not be aware of all ... plots they are developing and thus cannot be confident that none is about to occur."[149] Moreover, the use of force in self-defense entails complying with the principles of necessity and proportionality, but if decision-makers lack specific evidence regarding the character and timing of future attacks, it is impossible to determine whether drone strikes meet those requirements. Accordingly, it is also impossible to determine whether non-lethal means, such as disrupting terrorist financing and communications, would be sufficient to prevent attacks,[150] or whether suspected terrorists are or are not able to be captured rather than killed.

As to disregarding state sovereignty in the process of combating terrorism, the U.S. practice of relying on the consent of states where terrorists take refuge, or of deciding when a state is "unwilling or unable" to "prevent and suppress terrorist acts" and consequently has no right to resist counterterrorist strikes, raises further questions. What is to be made of circumstances in which consent is at best ambiguous? In Pakistan, for example, the executive reportedly gives

[148] Brooks, "Drones and the International Rule of Law," 24.
[149] Cited at ibid., 19.
[150] Ibid., 20.

consent in private, but, in league with the legislature and judiciary, denies it publicly. As a matter of fact, however, the question of consent is irrelevant, since the U.S. reserves to itself the overriding authority to decide when a given state is unwilling or unable to combat terrorist acts, and when it is therefore properly liable to counterterrorist strikes whether the state has consented or not.

All these alleged violations of international law by the Obama administration raise a still deeper difficulty: that the characteristics of terrorism – its shadowy and elusive nature, its irregular hit-and-run tactics, and especially its tendency to seek safe refuge across borders from which to direct continuing military operations – challenge key concepts of the international legal order, suggesting that "this is not so much an issue of law-breaking, [as] of [the] law's brokenness."[151] Though its guidance is anything but clear and definitive, UN Security Council Resolution 1373, issued on September 21, 2001, provides some degree of authority for the Obama administration's drone policy. Declaring that acts of international terrorism "constitute a threat to international peace and security," and make applicable "the inherent right of individual or collective self-defense" under Article 51 of the UN Charter, the resolution enjoins member states to "work together to prevent and suppress terrorist acts" and "take necessary steps to prevent the commission of terrorist acts," instructions specifically issued in reference to Chapter VII, authorizing the use of force.

It is true, of course, that Article 51 permits wide latitude in defining self-defense only until such time as "the Security Council has taken measures necessary to maintain international peace and security." However, what happens when the Security Council does not take action, "paralyzed," is it is, "by anachronistic voting rules that are themselves arguably inconsistent with rule of law norms"? Under those circumstances, what rightfully prevents a state from continuing to define self-defense as it sees fit? Furthermore, while it is "easy to point out the absurdity of the U.S. definition of 'imminent threat'," "the U.S. is not wholly wrong to argue that traditional definitions of imminence are inadequate in the context of today's [terrorist] threats." Similarly, it is "easy to lambast circular U.S. arguments about sovereignty, but here again, the U.S. is not entirely wrong to argue that when many lives may be at stake, sovereignty cannot be an absolute bar to intervention."[152]

There is no question that the liminal state in which the international law against terrorism at present finds itself winds up allowing for an impermissible degree of arbitrariness on the part of states like the U.S. What that proves above

---

[151] Ibid., 25.
[152] Ibid., 26.

all, though, is the urgent need for international law reform. President Obama has on occasion called for such reform, as has his recently retired chief legal counsel, Harold Koh,[153] but, to its discredit, the administration has not yet produced any concrete proposals to that end.

Intelligence Gathering and Surveillance

This final area is one in which the administration's obligation to defend its policies would appear to be particularly acute.[154] Here are some examples:

- Without explaining itself, the Obama administration supported and acted on a provision in the Patriot Act under which the government may confiscate the assets of a group it designates as having terrorist ties without showing probable cause of wrongdoing, in apparent violation of the Fourth Amendment.
- As a candidate, Obama called for strict limitations on National Security Letters, provided for in the Patriot Act as a means of secretly subpoenaing

---

[153] Harold Hongju Koh, "How To End the Forever War," Oxford Union, Oxford, UK, May 7, 2013. http://www.lawfareblog.com/wp-content/uploads/2013/05/2013-5-7-corrected-koh-oxford-union-speech-as-delivered.pdf.

[154] Although as of April 2014 – well into the second Obama administration, the complaints that follow continue to represent serious failures to reconcile principle and practice, there is reason to believe that one much-maligned aspect of intelligence gathering and surveillance, the National Security Agency's telephone metadata program, is on the way to being corrected. Geoffrey R. Stone, a member of the faculty of the University of Chicago Law School and a member of the five-person Review Group, appointed in August 2013 by President Obama to evaluate the NSA program, is, he says, "delighted to report" that the legislation proposed by the president to reform the program "tracks almost perfectly the Review Group's recommendations" (*The Daily Beast*, March 27, 2014). "First, the NSA will no longer itself hold the vast store of telephone metadata. This is essential because one of the most serious concerns about this program is that, in the wrong hands, access to this information can wreak havoc on the privacy and civil liberties of Americans." "Second, when the government wants to access the metadata, the proposed legislation would require the NSA to obtain an order from the Foreign Intelligence Surveillance Court, rather than being able to access the information whenever the NSA decide that a RAS [reasonable, articulable suspicion] exists." To protect against governmental bias, "it is essential for a neutral and detached judge to make the decision whether any particular query is warranted." "Third, instead of requiring the metadata to be retained for five years, the president's proposed legislation would compel the telephone companies to hold the data for only 18 months." This provision limits greatly the "risks of abuse." "The president should be applauded for supporting these reforms. I can say that it was not at all obvious or inevitable that the White House would come to this point. During the course of the Review Group's deliberations with the White House, serious opposition was raised to these recommendations." Residual complaints are still heard: Shouldn't the president move on his own, without waiting for legislation, to institute some of these reforms? In addition to FISA Court rulings, shouldn't an adversarial process be included further to assure impartiality? Still, Stone's testimony is extremely encouraging.

allegedly suspicious private documents, and absolutely silencing recipients. But as president he asked Congress to expand their scope, and retain the gag rule, even though in 2010 the Inspector General cast severe doubt on the utility of the letters in apprehending terrorists.

- Obama lawyers have aggressively and expansively defended the "state's secrets" privilege involving documents obtained by means of warrantless wiretapping. This line of argument puts document owners in an untenable position, should they want to challenge the government. Standing to sue the government is possible only if the document in question can be produced, and that is impossible as the result of the "state's secret" privilege![155]

It should be stressed that, despite a troubling hesitancy to reconcile principle and practice in regard to some aspects of national security policy, the Obama administration represents, overall, a far more reassuring approach than that of the Bush administration. President Obama has renounced many of the worst features of his predecessor's record and has gone some distance toward rectifying them and bringing national security policy into closer conformity with international and constitutional standards. That he has not succeeded to the degree desirable is the result partly of an obstructionist opposition, partly of weak support in his own administration and party, partly of having to make hard choices among policy priorities, and partly from his own failure to explain and justify discrepancies between policies and ideals. But however preferable Obama's record is, particularly the last set of complaints is cause for continuing concern.

POSTSCRIPT CONCERNING THE SENATE INTELLIGENCE COMMITTEE'S REPORT ON THE CIA'S DETENTION AND INTERROGATION PROGRAM (2001–2009)

President Obama was right to support the release of the report, which, whatever the controversies over method and detail, places an enormous burden of proof on those who deny that between 2001 and 2009 the U.S. government extensively violated the standards of international human rights and humanitarian law with regard to detention and interrogation.

What is unfortunate, as critics have long argued, is that the president himself did not initiate a similar investigation early in his administration. The idea that

---

[155] Taken from an important book, *Taking Liberties: The War on Terror and the Erosion of American Democracy* by Susan N. Herman (New York: Oxford University Press, 2011).

such a study would have generated Republican antipathy and intransigence and made governing all the harder has little merit since it is difficult to imagine higher levels of Republican antipathy and intransigence than those evident from the very start.

A prompt, presidentially-authorized inquiry would have smartly demonstrated America's willingness to hold itself accountable to the international standards it so readily applies to others. It would also have reminded the world of the conditions in which human rights and humanitarian norms emerged, conditions associated with fascist appeals to emergency before and during World War II. Those conditions are important to remember, particularly in the light of debates now engulfing the Intelligence Committee Report.

1) It is precisely in face of emergencies that special caution and restraint is mandated, lest the victimized become the victimizers.
2) Resort to torture, as one means of responding to an emergency, is inherently liable to arbitrary use. That is one reason a general proscription against torture is justified, as we contended in Chapter 1 (52–53). Whether or not torture can occasionally be said to "work" – a much disputed point, it does so only in the most exceptional circumstances, a fact implying stringent regulation and monitoring, lest the scandals occurring at Abu Ghraib and likely elsewhere be repeated. And even in those rare circumstances, it is virtually impossible to work out meaningful, nonarbitrary limits on the duration and intensity of the pain inflicted.
3) Legal authorization for engaging in practices like torture is itself subject to challenge. Were the authorizing opinions themselves legal? Is domestic legal authorization in compliance with international standards? These are urgent questions clearly posed by the report.

The Senate Intelligence Committee Report belatedly reminds us of these considerations. It is a pity we did not face them earlier.

CONCLUSION

The present international order, prominently including the United Nations Charter and institutions, together with the system of human rights and humanitarian norms, rests, as I have argued, on a fundamental aversion to the dark temptations and dangers that invariably accompany appeals to public emergency. That worldwide aversion was generated by Hitler's sustained and systematic abuse of such appeals.

The moral of the story is that governments that are party to "Hitler's Epitaph" – the UN Charter and the various human rights and humanitarian law instruments – have a primary responsibility to endeavor to support and comply resolutely with the provisions and standards of the international order, both to prove they are not themselves succumbing to the dark temptations and dangers associated with emergencies and to help other governments do the same. That is especially true, as I have suggested, of the "world's number-one superpower," the United States, confronted, as it is, with an ongoing emergency created by international terrorism. Because of its unrivalled military and economic prowess, the United States is uniquely positioned to help "make or break" the international order.

So far, the achievements of the U.S. government provide no cause for rejoicing. On balance, the Bush record was deeply distressing, seriously failing to acknowledge the tensions between security and rights, or "war and liberty," and to find, accordingly, a reasonable balance between them. "The U.S. Example" under Bush is largely a cautionary tale. It shows how easy it is to lose track of the entire rationale for the post–World War II international order. Thanks mainly to outside pressure, national and international, and to the U.S. Supreme Court, a semblance of sanity was eventually restored during the Bush years.

So far, the Obama record is somewhat better, though even there, there is reason for concern. Despite strong subversive tendencies to the contrary, evidence exists in the records of both administrations that the imperatives of the international order are not without effect. May the impact of those imperatives be strengthened.

11

The Role of the Academic in Times of War[*]

VIETNAM BACKGROUND

The unavoidable starting point for a discussion of the role of the American academic in times of war is the armed conflict that occurred in Vietnam during the 1960s and early 1970s.

In those "explosive years," as one observer puts it, "both faculty and students crystallized opposition to the Vietnam War."[1] American colleges and universities constituted the center of public reflection on the war and, generally speaking, of agitation against it. As a young man, I witnessed all this at close range. I began my teaching career at Yale Divinity School in 1963 and stayed there through a very tumultuous period until 1971. For reasons soon to be explained, I had occasion during 1968 to broaden my awareness by visiting other college campuses as well.

Since the conclusion of the Vietnam conflict in 1975, we have not seen anything approaching the degree of academic energy devoted to the subject of war. That is true even though the United States continues, as we speak, to be involved in a very costly and increasingly unpopular and controversial war in Iraq, not to mention earlier conflicts – a substantial one in the Persian Gulf in 1990–91, and smaller ones in Bosnia in 1994–95, and Kosovo in 1999, among others.

The singularity of the Vietnam experience raises two critical questions: (1) How can we explain the difference between those "explosive years" and what came after as far as the academic preoccupation with war goes? (2) How should academics, standing where we do now and looking back, regard the Vietnam experience? Should it represent a kind of model for us? Should we

---

[*] A lecture delivered at St. Olaf College, Northfield, MI on Sept. 27, 2007.
[1] David D. Newsom, *The Public Dimension of Foreign Policy* (Bloomington: Indiana University Press, 1996), 121.

try to emulate it, or at least some parts of it, to the degree possible? Or, was the Vietnam experience an aberration? Did it represent a breakdown of academic propriety, a violation of the academic vocation?

Though I want to spend most of my time on Question (2) – on what we academics now should make of Vietnam – several obvious factors help explain the huge gap between that time and ours. Paramount among them, surely, was the existence of a military draft. If students in this audience want to understand something of "how it was in those days," they should imagine themselves faced with the prospect of having to fight in Iraq. There is no better way to focus the mind, both personally and institutionally. That is particularly true because the Vietnam War was, like the Iraq war, so contentious.

Beyond that, the war came to symbolize regressive policies characteristic of a time of society-wide revolutionary change against entrenched injustice. The spirit of reform expressed itself in campaigns for civil rights, gender equality, new patterns of sexual behavior and substance use, concern for the environment, participatory politics, and grassroots community action. Moreover, Vietnam also symbolized a worldwide period of "decolonialization" or what we now call "postcolonialism." If you were not there, it is hard to appreciate how profound a time of world transformation it was, with many countries, particularly in Asia Africa, and the Middle East, struggling to gain their independence.

Vietnam was one example. Having become a French colony in the mid-nineteenth century, it achieved its independence temporarily in 1945 after ejecting the Japanese at the end of World War II. France then reasserted its colonial control, quite brutally, in 1946, only later to be defeated by Vietnamese nationalist forces in 1954 at the famous battle of Dien Bien Phu. In the same year, Vietnam was temporarily and provisionally divided by a controversial agreement known as the Geneva Accords. The North, under the leadership of Ho Chi Minh, was communist, and the South was noncommunist, supported by the United States. According to critics of the war, the United States thereby became a neocolonial power, swimming against the current of history by illicitly interfering in a nationalist civil war.

As I say, I want to devote special attention to Question (2) – to what we should make of the Vietnam experience so far as the connection between academic life and the study of war goes. But before doing that, I need to provide a fuller account of what was going on during that period, as I saw it.

PERSONAL REFLECTIONS

I was hired by Yale Divinity School in 1963 to teach ethics and sociology of religion. I came to the job with a strong interest in international affairs and

American foreign policy, together with a certain set of predispositions about those subjects, because I had spent my high school years in the Philippine Islands in the late 1940s and early 1950s. In 1946, the United States granted independence to the Philippines, an event that was accompanied by the emergence of a vigorous communist insurgency, something perceived at the time to represent a significant threat. What is more, the Korean War broke out in 1950, while I was still in the Philippines. That event was widely regarded as having ominous implications for the whole of South Asia, especially when viewed against the backdrop of a newly reconstituted Communist China and the strong belief that China was sponsoring insurgencies in places such as Malaya, Thailand, and Indonesia.

In the light of this background, I confess I was surprised by the tenor of the criticisms of U.S. Vietnam policy, which appeared in a series of "Teach-Ins" on the war conducted on campuses across the country, beginning in 1965, and in less formal discussions among students and faculty that took place earlier in places like Yale. The criticisms seemed simplistic and only partially informed. They appeared to me to disregard the perilous state of affairs that I believed existed in Southeast Asia at the time.

For example, critics began citing a book that would become famous, *The Making of a Quagmire*,[2] first published in 1965 by David Halberstam, who was then a *New York Times* reporter. Both the author and the book were recently in the news upon notice of Halberstam's untimely death in April 2007. (Of late, the book has been linked by some to the situation in Iraq, which is similarly characterized as a "quagmire.") Critics took that book to be an unqualified attack on U.S. Vietnam policy, as the title might imply. But while he did an excellent job of describing the huge difficulties the United States had gotten itself into in Indochina, Halberstam neither underrated the threat North Vietnam represented, nor did he call for immediate withdrawal of U.S. support. Toward the end of the book, he made a strong argument for continued U.S. commitment to South Vietnam. To do otherwise, he said, would "mean a drab, lifeless and controlled society for a people who deserve better."[3] Turning our backs on the large majority of South Vietnamese who unquestionably opposed communism would also mean that "U.S. prestige will be lowered throughout the world, and it means that the pressure of Communism on the rest of Southeast Asia will intensify."[4] Halberstam concluded that forsaking our responsibilities "means that throughout the world the enemies of the

---

[2] David Halberstam, *The Making of a Quagmire: America and Vietnam during the Kennedy Era*, Revised edition (New York: Alfred A. Knopf, 1988).
[3] Ibid., 177.
[4] Ibid.

West will be encouraged to try insurgencies like the one in Vietnam. Just as our commitment in Korea in 1950 has served to discourage overt Communist border crossing ever since, an anti-Communist victory in Vietnam would serve to discourage all so-called wars of liberation."[5] I have not read Halberstam's recent book on the Korean war[6] – published posthumously – but it does not appear from reviews that his present assessment of that war was quite as positive as it was in 1965.

To be sure, Halberstam went on to warn eloquently of the dire consequences of Americanizing the war, a step, he said, that would alienate the very people we were trying to save and therefore put victory well beyond reach. Still, as of 1965, Halberstam could write, "Just conceivably," the dissenting forces in the country might still unite, providing "a strong enough base for a viable military approach to the situation," which was, to his mind at that time, the only basis for responsible negotiations.[7]

This example came to focus three lasting conclusions of mine:

1. From a moral and policy point of view, the situation in Vietnam *was more complex* than many campus critics were admitting, and my perception of things, born of my high school experience in the Philippines, was not completely misguided. (Vietnam *really was* a quagmire, and there were good reasons why it was difficult to get out.)
2. Too many academics, in the heat of the moment, *were guilty of violating some fundamental norms of scholarship* – particularly, scrupulous use of sources and evidence, including honest and forthcoming admission of countervailing facts and considerations. As in the case of Halberstam's *The Making of a Quagmire*, critics too often failed to display conscientiously all aspects of the arguments of one author or another, or to give due recognition to inconvenient facts or arguments here and there put forward. As a matter of fact, Halberstam himself faltered in this regard on at least one occasion.[8] Incidentally, these deficiencies were true of

---

[5] Ibid.
[6] David Halberstam, *The Coldest Winter: America and the Korean War* (New York: Hyperion, 2007).
[7] Halberstam, *Making of a Quagmire*, 178.
[8] In his later book, *The Best and the Brightest* (Greenwich, CT: Fawcett Publications, 1972) in which he blamed many of the policy makers associated with the Kennedy and Johnson administrations for what he came to think of as the serious misadventure in Vietnam, Halberstam was not as forthcoming as he should have been about the similarity of some of his own early views, cited earlier, to the convictions of the people he criticized. In this respect, he may himself be accused of the failure to live up to scholarly standards that I found in so many other observers. In particular, the account of his earlier views contained in *The Best and the Brightest* is very misleading. He admits that in *The Making of a Quagmire*, "written in 1964 and published in

participants on all sides, not just the critics. I was especially sensitive to the critics because they were in the ascendancy at Yale and elsewhere.
3. In stressing the moral and political complexity of the situation in Vietnam, I eventually came to believe that I myself was guilty of some of the same failings I accused my colleagues of. In the name of scrupulousness and even-handedness, I wound up overemphasizing Halberstam's reasons for supporting U.S. policy, while playing down unrealistically his reasons for skepticism. I finally corrected what I thought were my mistakes and turned against the war, although much too late, I now believe.

In the interest of defending scholarly norms, as I understood them, I undertook, with no little temerity, to become an active participant in the academic discussions taking place at Yale and at other campuses and to begin publishing on the subject. I engaged in public debates around the university and local community with William Sloane Coffin, then chaplain of Yale and a leader of the antiwar effort across the country. Rather on the order of Daniel in the lions' den, I confronted none other than Noam Chomsky before a packed auditorium at the Yale Law School at the time of the Tet Offensive in February 1968. Later in the same year, I took time off from Yale, and went to work in Washington, DC, as part of the presidential campaign of Hubert Humphrey. To do that was to take up the cudgels on behalf of Humphrey's Vietnam position, which, however at odds with Lyndon Johnson's policy, was still too close for comfort for many critics at the time. It was in that connection that I traveled to numerous college campuses around the country where I encountered the antagonism and derision typically visited on supporters of "The Hump," as Humphrey was disparagingly known, mainly because of his Vietnam stand.

In 1969, I published a small book, *American Foreign Policy and Moral Rhetoric: The Example of Vietnam*,[9] in which I represented myself as "a critic of critics." Rather doggedly, I tracked out and called to account the arguments of many of the critics of U.S. policy. I did that on the pattern of my response to the use made of Halberstam's book, always coming back to the need for scholarly responsibility. At the same time, there is considerable agonizing on my part

---

April 1965," he had said, "we owed it to the Vietnamese to stay little longer" – presumably for the reasons I cite in the text (though they are not mentioned!). However, he also states that "*in the fall of 1963 I came to the conclusion that* [our involvement in Vietnam] *was doomed and that we were on the wrong side of history*" (*Best and the Brightest*, 814, emphasis added).

[9] David Little, *American Foreign Policy and Moral Rhetoric: The Example of Vietnam* (New York: Council on Religion and International Affairs, 1969).

in that book, especially over the question of Halberstam's greatest perplexity: *whether in fact successful military and political policies could be found, at reasonable overall cost in the lives and treasure of Americans, Vietnamese, and neighboring peoples.* Indeed, it was these concerns that soon became for me the basis for recanting my support of U.S. policy and for joining the critics. Inching closer to that position, I concluded my book by saying that officials charged with responsibility for Vietnam were more to be pitied than censured.

JUST-WAR APPROACH

In an effort to sort out and clarify the complexity of the debate over Vietnam in a scholarly way, I endeavored in several articles[10] and talks to organize the debate and express my evolving opinions about it, in keeping with what is called just-war doctrine.[11]

That doctrine is a set of secular rational standards for appraising the use of force that developed out of Western Christianity and eventually influenced the modern law of armed combat. I studied the doctrine in graduate school and came to believe that the eight standards represent indispensable reference points for appraising the justifiability of lethal force in given circumstances. Six of the standards apply to considerations bearing on the decision to use force, or *jus ad bellum*. Such a decision is licit if it is made by a *legitimate authority* on the basis of a *just cause* and is undertaken in keeping with four conditions: *just intent, last resort, a reasonable probability of success,* and the *general proportionality* of costs to benefits. The two remaining standards apply to the way force is used, or *jus in bello*. Force is licitly administered if it respects *noncombatant immunity* and *military proportionality*, or avoiding excessive indirect and unintentional injury or destruction. The whole point of the doctrine is to try to provide assurance that force is being used for "good reason," and not arbitrarily. The intention is to avoid at all costs what I have called the "pathology of force," or that state of affairs in which force takes on a life of its own and readily spirals out of control.

Working my way through the various just-war standards in regard to Vietnam policy, I argued that the conclusions of many of the critics were not as clearly supported as they thought, and with some reservations, I advocated extending

---

[10] See David Little, "Is the War in Vietnam Just?" *Reflection* 64, 1 (1966), 1–5; and "A Just War or Just a War?" *Reflection* 64, 3 (1967), 6–10. For a later retrospective analysis, see David Little, "Just-War Doctrine and United States Policy in Indochina," in Stuart Albert and Edward C. Luck, eds. *On the Ending of Wars* (New York: Kennikat Press, 1980), 157–171.

[11] Professor Edmund Santurri invoked this doctrine in an excellent talk he delivered earlier in September 2007 as an introduction to the series of which this lecture is a part.

a certain benefit of the doubt to the Johnson administration. However, as time wore on I became increasingly unconvinced by certain features of the policies of the Johnson and later, the Nixon administrations, and I belatedly turned against those policies.

Because there is no space to cover all aspects of the war, I shall simply give a few examples of my various judgments in regard to the applicability of some of the just-war standards.

Legitimate Authority and Just Cause. On balance, the South Vietnamese government did have a certain legal legitimacy, and thus U.S. military assistance was permitted. Recent scholarship supports this point, in my view.[12] The Gulf of Tonkin Resolution was passed overwhelmingly by Congress in August 1964, giving the president extensive discretion with respect to U.S. military assistance to South Vietnam (House, 414–0; Senate, 88–2). Whether the alleged North Vietnamese gunboat attacks on a U.S. warship in the Gulf of Tonkin occurred or not, they were mentioned in the resolution only in passing. A much greater emphasis was placed on the wider "deliberate and systematic campaign of aggression" by North Vietnam, whereby the North Vietnamese were directing and fully supporting an insurgency in the South.[13] As Halberstam implied, such a campaign constituted a valid *casus belli* under the circumstances.

Reasonable Probability of Success. As I hinted earlier, this is one of the points at which my mind changed profoundly during the course of the war, though I, like Halberstam, was uncertain about it at the beginning. In all my public statements, I regularly agonized over this question, and finally came to agree with one observer that success in Vietnam was increasingly unlikely because

---

[12] On balance, I side with Moore and Turner against Mendlovitz and Velvel in a debate over the legal issues in the U.S. commitment to Vietnam, described as follows: "Resolved: That the Basic U.S. Commitment to Defend South Vietnam Was Lawful under Both International and Constitutional Law"; John Norton Moore and Robert F. Turner, affirmative; Saul Menlovitz and Lawrence R. Velvel, negative. In John Norton Moore and Robert F. Turner, eds., *The Real Lessons of the Vietnam War: Reflections Twenty-five Years after the Fall of Saigon* (Durham, NC: Carolina Academic Press, 2002), 99–146.

[13] Although the *Pentagon Papers* state that "the war began largely as a rebellion in the South against the increasingly oppressive and corrupt regime of Ngo Dinh Diem," "the study also disputes many critics of American policy in Vietnam who have contended that North Vietnam became involved in the South only after 1965 in response to large-scale American intervention." "It is equally clear that North Vietnamese Communists operated some form of subordinate apparatus in the South in the years 1954–60." "In 1959, ... Hanoi made a clear decision to assert its control over the growing insurgency and to increase its infiltration of trained cadres from the North. Thereafter, ... Hanoi's involvement in the developing strife became evident," Neil Sheehan et al., eds., *The Pentagon Papers* (New York: New York Times, 1971), 67–69. Cf. Douglas Pike's authoritative study (*Viet Cong: The Organization and Techniques of the National Liberation Front of South Vietnam*. Cambridge, MA: MIT Press, 1966), 79.

we had such "a lousy client" and such a "determined adversary." The rampant corruption and ineptitude of the South Vietnamese government and military simultaneously encouraged the Americanization of the war and increased the incapacity and dependency of the South Vietnamese, making the chances of long-term resistance to the North less and less likely.[14] I must add that insofar as "ought implies can," as Immanuel Kant taught us, the standard of Reasonable Probability of Success took on for me a special saliency. What cannot be achieved cannot be obligatory.

General Proportionality. There were two sets of costs and benefits to be assessed in regard to the prosecution of the war: (1) the lives and treasure of the Vietnamese, their neighbors, and the United States and (2) U.S. strategic interests. Regarding lives and treasure, the calculation had to be made in relation to other just-war standards, especially Reasonable Probability of Success. As the benefits of success became less and less attainable, the costs of continuing the war became less and less bearable. In judging whether the United States should have agreed to negotiate for peace and withdraw, it was of course necessary to take account of the "unfavorable aftereffects," particularly the costs to South Vietnamese and neighbors like Cambodia and Laos, once the North gained control. There were likely to be huge costs (as there were), which was one reason for trying to "limit defeat." On the other hand, was it rational to pursue a futile policy – with all the continuing cost in lives and treasure that that involved – to prevent such an outcome?[15]

---

[14] Together with Jeffrey Record, "Approaching the 'Lessons' of the Vietnam War through the Lens of Current Military Behavior," in Moore and Turner, *The Real Lessons of the Vietnam War*, 27–49, see Record, *The Wrong War: Why We Lost in Vietnam* (Annapolis, MD: Naval Institute Press, 1998) for what is in my view a convincing refutation of many of the revisionist historical arguments about the "winnability" of the Vietnam War contained in *The Real Lessons of the Vietnam War*, and Ross A. Fisher, John Norton Moore, and Robert F. Turner, eds., *To Oppose Any Foe: The Legacy of U.S. Intervention in Vietnam* (Durham, NC: Carolina Academic Press, 2006). In support of Record's views, see Neil Sheehan, *The Bright Shining Lie: John Paul Vann and America in Vietnam* (New York: Random House, 1988). For a more recent assessment that raises questions for the revisionists, see William R. Polk, *Violent Politics: A History of Insurgency, Terrorism and Guerrilla War, from the American Revolution to Iraq* (New York: HarperCollins Publishers, 2007), chs. 9–10.

[15] There is no denying the harsh consequences for many South Vietnamese citizens of the eventual U.S. withdrawal after the Paris settlement in January 1973. Thousands lost their lives or suffered as a result of the victory of the North Vietnamese. However, a final reckoning regarding this outcome hangs on one's decision regarding "winnability". The effects of U.S. involvement in Vietnam on Cambodia are much more complicated, as shown in Sheehan, *Bright Shining Lie*, 745–746, Michael Charles Rakower, "The Khmer Rouge: An Analysis of One of the World's Most Brutal Regimes," in *To Oppose Any Foe*, 210 makes clear that U.S. and South Vietnamese incursions into Cambodia in 1970 indirectly facilitated the rise to power of the Khmer Rouge, led by Pol Pot. Moreover, it was, ironically, the North Vietnamese

Regarding U.S. strategic interests, Halberstam had stressed the importance of the implications of a loss in South Vietnam for Asia and the rest of the world. I agreed with him at the time. In the early 1960s, communism seemed to be on the march in China, Indonesia, the Philippines, Thailand, and elsewhere – though I now admit that all that began to change in 1965, just the year, ironically, when Johnson began to Americanize the war. In the Philippines and Malaysia, there had been successful counterinsurgency operations, and in Indonesia the communist movement was rejected, albeit in a brutal and bloody way. Most important of all, China gave up its expansionary program by turning inward in 1964 as a consequence of the Cultural Revolution. By 1970, under the leadership of Zhou Enlai and his protégé and successor, Deng Xiaping, China moved to improve relations with the United States, developments that led to the famous "Nixon opening" in 1972. Though I did not appreciate it at the time, I now think that these developments moved things toward a more favorable balance of interests in Asia from a U.S. point of view.[16] That translated into a change in the ratio of costs to benefits and, accordingly, weakened the strategic rationale for pursuing the war in Vietnam.[17]

---

who in 1979 ended the genocidal rule of the Khmer Rouge and opened the door to eventual improvements in the Cambodian political system (ibid., 233).

[16] John Mueller, *Retreat from Doomsday: The Obsolescence of Major War* (New York: Basic Books, 1988), 182–183.

[17] It is puzzling, though by no means inexplicable, why Kissinger and Nixon, both so involved in the new opening to China in 1972, came so late to make the necessary adjustments in respect to Vietnam policy. In his memoirs, Kissinger admits that "if we had offered at one dramatic moment all the concessions we eventually made in three years of war, and if the military actions we took with steadily declining forces over 1970, 1971, and 1972, in Cambodia, Laos, North Vietnam (even without the last bombing assault), had been undertaken all together in early 1970, the war might well have been appreciably shortened – though it is hard to tell at this remove whether Saigon would have been ready to carry the burden of going it alone after a settlement. In the face of the domestic turmoil and the divisions in the Administration I did not fight for my theoretical analysis" (Henry Kissinger, *White House Years* (Boston: Little, Brown & Co. 1979), 308). This is an astounding admission in several respects. For one thing, as events turned out, Saigon was not much better able to sustain itself after the Paris settlement three years later than it would have been earlier. For another, we learn from Kenneth Haldeman in the *Haldeman Diaries: Inside the Nixon Whitehouse* (New York: G.P. Putnam's Sons, 1994), 221, that most likely the real reason Kissinger resisted pushing for an earlier settlement and U.S. withdrawal was because an "adverse reaction to it could set in well before the '72 elections."

For views that are, on balance, at variance with mine regarding the geopolitical benefits and costs of the U.S. experience in Vietnam, see Peter Rodman, "The 'Geopolitical' Costs of Vietnam," in Moore and Turner, *The Real Lessons of the Vietnam War*, 15–24; Michael Lind, "Was the Vietnam War Necessary? in Moore and Turner, *The Real Lessons of the Vietnam War*, 423–446; and Michael A. McCann, "A War Worth Fighting: How the United States Military Presence in Indochina from 1965 to 1975 Preserved Global Democratic Security," in Fisher, Moore, and Turner, *To Oppose Any Foe*, 77–158.

By explaining how I have thought about Vietnam in reference to just-war doctrine over the years, I am trying to demonstrate the doctrine's utility in providing a rational framework for attending to the relevant aspects of the complicated task of evaluating the use of force. Making a comprehensive judgment about a policy of force involves not only bearing all eight standards in mind but also weighing one or another particular judgment against the others. This in itself, as you will understand, makes for considerable "complexity." But whether or not one agrees with my particular judgments, this kind of framework is, I am suggesting, what academics (among others) need to employ in order to "do justice," as they say, to the complicated character of justifying force.

THE ACADEMIC COMMUNITY AND THE STUDY OF WAR

A central conclusion based on my experience in the Vietnam debate is that the academic community is a very fitting place in which to discuss the subject of war. To a certain extent, at least, the academic debate over Vietnam has been for me a kind of model of what ought to be taking place.

One reason is that the debate provided a strong example – too often a negative one, in my view – as to how important scholarly norms regarding the use of evidence and argument are in such a discussion, as well as how indispensable it is to have an eye for moral and political complexity. Not only had many academic critics failed to arrive at careful judgments in relation to this or that just-war standard but they had often also failed to bear in mind and attend in a comprehensive way to the variety of considerations that are captured by all the just-war standards taken together.

The norms requiring conscientious attention to detail and to honest and self-critical evaluation of evidence are so urgently relevant, partly because they are so seriously at risk when academics take on the role of public critic. It is precisely when academics enter the public sphere that they need to bend over backward in the scrupulous practice of their trade, for, like everyone else, they are going to feel the pressures and passions of the policy arena. If they have problems applying the norms of their profession in such settings, think of the difficulties politicians and policy makers face who are rarely rewarded for scrupulous care and judiciousness, or for attention to complexity. I hasten to add that taking unpopular positions is frequently not cost-free. One Yale colleague recently described me as "a rather lonely figure" during that period forty years ago.

My own experience in the Vietnam period also testifies to just how hard it is to stand by scholarly norms in the heat of debate. In adopting unpopular, minority positions, it is easy to confuse conscientiousness with stubbornness.

Holding fast to complexity, to "how complicated things are," can under some conditions blind one to new realities and the need for new thinking. It can lead to what used to be called "the paralysis of analysis," the same thing that caused Harry Truman to long for a one-armed economist unable to give advice "first on the one hand and then on the other."

But be that as it may, I must now say something more forthright than I have so far about why I believe the evaluation of war is an appropriate subject for the academy. There are two aspects to my position: a general comment about ethics and scholarship and some specific thoughts on the academic study of war.

ETHICS AND SCHOLARSHIP[18]

If I take the position, as I have, that the moral (and other) appraisal of policies of force, such as took place in colleges and universities during the Vietnam period, is an appropriate activity in the academy, what is to be said about the supposed "gap" between "facts and values," between "description" and "evaluation," which is thought to be at the heart of the academic enterprise? What business do academics have taking part in the moral critique of public policy?

Hilary Putnam, the retired Harvard philosopher, takes the correct approach by arguing that the academic enterprise is, steeped in values.[19] He makes two critical points. First, contrary to the idea that "facts" are one thing and "values" another, Putnam claims that what I have called "scholarly norms" – rules of evidence, logic, and mathematics – themselves constitute a set of values, according to which we judge "facts" and determine "good and bad scholarship."

Second, there is a difference, which we all assume, between "scholarly values" (or what Putnam calls "epistemic values") and "ethical (or moral) values," but the two sets of value are deeply and unavoidably intertwined with one another. For one thing, committing oneself to observe scholarly values is itself an ethical decision, just as deciding which field of study to pursue and which particular subjects to examine depends on a "personal" and usually "ethical" decision.

For another, the very terms one uses in social scientific scholarship are, as Putnam puts it, "invariably ethically colored." You can see the salience of

---

[18] See Appendix by the same name.
[19] Hilary Putnam, *The Collapse of the Fact/Value Dichotomy and Other Essays* (Cambridge, MA: Harvard University Press, 2002).

Putnam's point in a field I am very involved in, the social scientific study of ethnic and religious conflict. It is obvious from this vast and ever-expanding literature that the scholars involved are "ethically disturbed" by the existence of serious ethnonational tension or violence in the societies they take up. They are interested not only in the "neutral study" of the causes and character of ethnic tension and violence but also in indicating or implying ways to reduce tension and violence.

Moreover, scholarly categories such as "ethnocracy" (the political domination of a society by one ethnic group, of which Myanmar is a good example) are associated causally with the incidence of violence. The clear "ethical implication" of studies employing terms like these is that ethnocracy is something that ought to be avoided or minimized.

In the first instance, then, I have tried to show that ethical values are anything but irrelevant or out of place in the academic environment. Indeed, with Putnam, I think they are unavoidable. It is as important to keep in mind the distinctions between them as it is to appreciate their interdependence.

THE STUDY OF WAR

But these comments get us only partway. We still need to know why the specific study of war and, more precisely, of policies related to the use of force have a special place in the academic environment, as they did in the Vietnam period.

My key reason is what I would call the extraordinary ethical or moral valence of the use of force. Force or violence – understood as the infliction of death, impairment, suffering/injury, or confinement – requires an extremely strong justification, wherever it occurs, for two principal reasons: the obvious adverse consequences that result from using it and the strong temptation in human affairs to use it arbitrarily. The fact that the use of force, wherever it appears, inescapably carries with it a "warning label" means that people who are its victims, and very often its agents, demand to be given "good reasons" of a very exacting kind for its use.

I believe this has something to do with the way the human mind works, that human beings are so constituted that certain kinds of reasons – for example, egoistic reasons such as "I'm hitting you in the face because I want to," could not imaginably be an acceptable excuse for using force "in anybody's language." Human beings are in the business, you might say, of demanding very special kinds of reasons for using force and of constantly testing those reasons, constantly holding them to account, according to *public* standards. I think this understanding helps explain why societies typically impose all sorts of institutional checks and restraints on the use of force – for instance, of a legal or medical kind – and why just-war standards and their codification in international law have become so indispensable in evaluating force.

Although there are no doubt many different reasons for using force in different cultures, there are certain extreme negative examples that we expect everyone to acknowledge, such as Hitler's use of force during World War II. That has become the indisputable model of unjustified or arbitrary force, of which we have recently been reminded by Ken Burns's PBS series *The War*. Any country or group shown to be using force in a way that approximates Hitler's use *must now stand as universally condemned*.

One way to grasp just how arbitrary Hitler's policies were is to hold them up to the just-war standards I introduced earlier, standards designed, as I said, to root out arbitrary force. Hitler's policies fail, and fail systematically, on every one of the eight standards. Of special interest in regard to Hitler's "reasons" for using force was the notorious wholesale violation of scholarly norms – a preposterous racial theory and blatant factual misrepresentations of the threat to Germany posed by neighbors such as Poland, Denmark, and Norway. In addition, Hitler consistently subverted the idea of independent scholarship. According to the Civil Service Restoration Act, passed two months after he attained power, all Jews and opponents of the National Socialist regime were forced to retire from university service, and many professors fled for their lives. By 1936, German universities had been brought completely into line with the policies and objectives of the National Socialist government.[20]

If I am right, then, we can see why the evaluation and criticism of the use of force warrant concerted attention in the academic community. Since scholarship is intertwined with ethics, since scrutinizing the use of force has strong ethical priority, and since the application of scholarly norms represents one important "institutional check" on the misuse of force, the home of scholars – the academic community – is a crucially important place to take up the subject.

CONCLUSION

Had we time, we might now take up the Iraq War, but I must leave that to you. As for myself, I have been actively involved in discussions of Iraq since they began several years ago, and, in fact, I gave a talk opposing the invasion of Iraq at this very institution shortly before it happened. In part because of second

---

[20] Max Weinreich, *Hitler's Professors: The Part of Scholarship in Germany's Crimes against the Jewish People* (New Haven, CT: Yale University Press, 1999).

thoughts about Vietnam, I was, and have remained, much more sensitive to the possible abuses of just-war reasoning than I was forty years ago. I am now sadder but wiser about policies of force. As was eventually true in the Vietnam case, my major objections to the occupation of Iraq have to do with Reasonable Probability of Success and General Proportionality, though there are serious problems, in my view, in applying some of the other standards as well. I do, however, admit that there are abiding "complexities" about our policy there – both going in and coming out – that sensitive observers must acknowledge and contend with.

Although I believe, as I hope you now understand, that the use of force is a particularly compelling subject for academic study, I do not suggest that it is the only significant subject that might be considered. I do not propose rechristening this institution "St. Olaf War College." If there is a difference, as I posit, between "ethical" and "academic values" – however intertwined they may be – then academics must surely be given the right to decide for themselves what issues they shall take up and, within scholarly limits, how they shall go about it.

My main concern is that whatever public issues are taken up, including, I hope, the subject of war, academics will go about considering them in a self-consciously academic way. Let them endeavor as a consequence of their calling to exemplify to society at large what it means to think about public questions according to a conscientious and self-critical application of scholarly norms.

12

Obama and Niebuhr

Religion and American Foreign Policy*

The connection between President Barack Obama and the Protestant theologian Reinhold Niebuhr is well worth discussing because Niebuhr's perspective on religion and politics (which I came to appreciate as a student of his in the late 1950s) does cast light on Obama's approach, both as to where the two men agree and where they occasionally differ. I emphasize that I am here restricting my consideration of Niebuhr's relevance to certain aspects of current American foreign policy. Others may carry the comparison further, including its pertinence to domestic matters. It is just that I am subject to the limits of time and space.

I am hardly the first person to consider the connection. Numerous commentators have discussed it.[1] In fact, all the attention highlights a growing resurgence of interest in Niebuhr, thanks in part to Obama's public acknowledgment of his influence. Obama's words of praise appear on the cover of a new 2008 edition of Niebuhr's *Irony of American History* – first published

---

* Versions of this talk were delivered at the U.S. State Department, April 5, 2010, in Charlemont, MA, July 22, 2010, and at the American Academy of Religion, Atlanta, GA, Oct. 31, 2010. This is an expanded and updated version and includes additional footnotes.
  The talk given in Charlemont is of special interest because the Niebuhr family had a summer residence nearby in Heath from 1933 to 1955. The events surrounding their experiences there are the subject of *Serenity Prayer* (New York: Norton, 2003), written by Niebuhr's daughter, Elizabeth Sifton. In the book, she states that Niebuhr composed and first uttered that famous prayer for a worship service at the Heath Union Church in 1943. The prayer speaks of needing serenity to accept things that cannot be changed, courage to change what can and should be changed, and wisdom to know the difference. Controversy over the composition of the prayer continues (Richard Fox, *Reinhold Niebuhr* (New York: Harper & Row, 1958), 290–291), though Sifton strongly defends Niebuhr's authorship (*Serenity Prayer*, 9–14).

[1] See, for example, R.Ward Holder and Peter B. Josephson, *The Irony of Barack Obama: Barack Obama, Reinhold Niebuhr and the Problem of Christian Statecraft* (Farnham, Surrey: Ashgate, 2012).

in 1952 – with an introduction by Andrew Bacevich, professor of history and international affairs at Boston University. Bacevich calls it "the most important book ever written on American foreign policy."[2]

NIEBUHR AND IRONY

In tracking the connection between Niebuhr and Obama, it is worth starting with Obama's brilliant off-the-cuff summary of *Irony of American History*:

> I take away [from the book] the compelling idea that there is serious evil in the world, and hardship and pain. And we should be humble and modest in our belief we can eliminate those things. But we shouldn't use that as an excuse for cynicism and inaction. I take away [that we must] make ... efforts knowing they are hard, and not swinging from naïve idealism to bitter realism.[3]

For Niebuhr, human beings, particularly in political life, can neither escape nor can they easily resolve the conflict between good and evil, between right and wrong. The problem is they are strongly tempted to try both things – to avoid morality altogether or, conversely, to exaggerate their capacity for righteousness – when yielding to either temptation only makes matters worse. If people try to bracket moral questions as not important in politics, they become "bitter realists," whose "cynicism and inaction" amount to nothing more than moral irresponsibility. But if they represent themselves as exemplars of the good and the right, able to subdue evil and right wrongs simply by exertion and good intentions, they become "naïve idealists," blind to their own mixed motives and to the harm that typically accompanies moral crusades.

The best corrective for either affliction is to employ the idea of "irony" – hence, the title of Niebuhr's book. For Niebuhr, irony describes a state of affairs perversely contrary to expectations, as when frenzied efforts to securitize loans bring the whole practice of lending almost to a halt. To see the irony in something is to perceive the "perverse incongruities" between what is expected and what occurs in a way that the parties involved do not see because of some flaw or other. As Niebuhr puts it, "if virtue becomes vice through some hidden defect in the virtue; if strength becomes weakness because of the vanity to which strength may prompt the mighty man or nation; ... if wisdom becomes

---

[2] Reinhold Niebuhr, *Irony of American History* (Chicago: University of Chicago Press, 2008), with a new introduction by Andrew J. Bacevich, ix. Unfortunately, Bacevich is not a reliable interpreter of Niebuhr, because he exaggerates the "realist" side of Niebuhr's thought (the centrality of vital material national interests in making foreign policy) to the exclusion of his "idealist" side (the importance of moral ideals and values). See the later discussion.
[3] Printed on the back cover of the 2008 edition of *Irony of American History*.

folly because it does not know its own limits – in all such cases the situation is ironic."[4] That in World War I President Woodrow Wilson set out idealistically to make the world safe for democracy, and wound up in reality agreeing to a postwar German settlement that gave rise to one of the most antidemocratic regimes in history is, for Niebuhr, the height of irony.

Looking at American history through the eyes of irony reveals, in Niebuhr's view, a long record of naïve idealism, accompanied by recurring outbursts of bitter realism. Occasionally, even rarely, some leader, like James Madison or Abraham Lincoln, manages to avoid the extremes and find a middle way. By means of extraordinary insight into themselves and their fellows, they grasp the irony of American history. They recognize the self-righteousness of the virtuous, as well as the moral callousness of the worldly wise, but they yield to neither. Rather, they promote institutions and policies that correct for both kinds of failure. In a word, they *pursue ideals in a realistic way*.

It is *combining* realism and idealism, becoming a "realistic idealist," that is the heart of Reinhold Niebuhr's approach to morality and politics, including his emphasis on irony. President Obama gets Niebuhr's position exactly right: There is indeed for Niebuhr "serious evil in the world," evil that human beings are inescapably obligated to try to combat. At the same time, resisting evil and pursuing good are in reality very "hard," as Obama puts it. Individuals and groups readily mistake their own interests for other people's interests, or they too easily discount or minimize the often mind-boggling complexity of trying to balance competing interests and ideals.

No wonder human beings so frequently oversimplify the moral task or, alternatively, give up on it altogether and opt for simply serving their own naked individual or collective self-interest. Like it or not, human beings live under a moral demand they can neither disregard nor fully achieve. To understand the human predicament that way is to see the irony of it, to see the inevitable gap between what is expected and what occurs.

For Niebuhr, this approach calls for a strong *religious sensitivity*. Although he never suggests that only religious people can see the world ironically – in fact, it is very often they who do not! – he does assert that, rightly understood, religious sensitivity is of great value. "Christian faith," he says, "tends to make the ironic view of human evil in history the normative one."[5] Because their ultimate faith is not in themselves, not in their capacity for righteousness, but in God, Christians may honestly confess their own complicity in the complex historical entanglements of vice and virtue, vanity and power, and

[4] Ibid., xxiv.
[5] Ibid., 155.

wisdom and folly without giving up on virtue, power, and wisdom. They are at once humbled and hopeful, contrite and emboldened. They are inspired, with Niebuhr, to pray for serenity to accept the things that cannot be changed, for courage to change what can and should be changed, and, above all, for wisdom to know the difference.

Niebuhr's religious sensitivity enabled him, among other things, to discern the importance of religion in history, both as cause and effect and as a source of benefit and harm. He showed the importance of religion at a time when social scientists were busy reporting the decline of religion as the result of the worldwide "secularization" of modern society. Niebuhr's approach has in part been vindicated by the upsurge in the study of religion and politics following the collapse of the Soviet Union, as it pertains particularly to nationalist conflicts and extremist movements.

His acuity in discerning the connections between religious ideals and worldly realities was at times astounding. In 1932, he anticipated the contribution that "religious imagination" might make to developing nonviolence as an effective technique for overcoming racial injustice in America. In a setting where whites massively outnumbered blacks but still paid lip service, however hypocritically, to the "insights of the Christian religion," blacks, Niebuhr thought, might dramatically redeploy those insights in the form of a strategy that could, on the one hand, avoid the catastrophic consequences of armed revolt, and, on the other, exert necessary pressure. Certainly, he believed that whites would not yield ground unless pushed. It was that very message that Martin Luther King famously and effectively embraced in the late 1950s, claiming Niebuhr as his primary influence and considering nonviolence to be essentially "a Niebuhrian strategy of power."[6]

Set in the midst of the Cold War, *Irony of American History* is devoted to analyzing the "perverse incongruities" of both communism and democratic capitalism, especially the American brand. For Niebuhr, each side saw the mote in the other's eye without acknowledging the beam in its own.

There *was*, he thought, painful truth in communist criticisms of the United States, centered in some of the "contradictions of capitalism," originally espoused by Karl Marx. Niebuhr's principal indictment was the abject failure of an unregulated, "free" market to satisfy, in his words, "minimal standards of 'welfare' in housing, social security, and [note well] health services."[7] Niebuhr believed that it was the toxic alliance of American religion with virulent

---

[6] Fox, *Reinhold Niebuhr*, 282–283, and Niebuhr, *Moral Man and Immoral Society* (New York: Scribners & Sons, 1960), 252–256.
[7] Niebuhr, *Irony of American History*, 32.

anticommunism[8] and doctrinaire opposition to an active federal government that so severely oversimplified the real moral task confronting the United States at that time.

However, there was also profound truth in the charges against communism. More than American ideals, communist aspirations were disastrously illusory and self-defeating. Given the failure to limit authoritarian control, the communist dream turned inevitably and catastrophically into a nightmare.[9]

In *Irony of American History*, Niebuhr sided with the United States and its allies against the communist alternative, and that conviction grew firmer still throughout the 1950s and 1960s. He came strongly to favor American constitutional democracy, especially as seen through Madison's eyes, because it proved to restrain, fairly effectively and equitably, multiple conflicts of power and interest.

All the same, he was a pragmatic rather than a dogmatic liberal. He advocated a foreign policy constrained by an abiding sense of the limits of American power and virtue. In particular, he was suspicious of declarations of rights intended to apply universally. He associated such proposals with Thomas Jefferson and Woodrow Wilson, both naive idealists in his mind. He was only slightly less critical of the prospects for the Universal Declaration of Human Rights, adopted after World War II, because he doubted it would do much good.[10] He was also pessimistic that rights schemes and constitutional "contrivances" could find much traction outside the West.[11]

In contrast, Niebuhr eventually did support the United Nations because it represented a step forward by doing what it could and not promising too much.

---

[8] While rejecting the anticommunist tactics of Senator Joseph McCarthy and the House Un-American Activities Committee – himself being a target at times of McCarthy-inspired anticommunist investigations, Niebuhr occasionally adopted a simple-minded version of anticommunism. In 1953 he wrote "Why Is Communism So Evil?" which his biographer, Richard Fox, correctly calls "an egregiously shallow analysis." In 1961 he published an essay proposing the sorely short-sighted thesis, later to be made famous in the Reagan years by Jeane Kirkpatrick, that once in power communist regimes, unlike authoritarian dictatorships, are "irrevocable" (see Fox, *Reinhold Niebuhr*, 252–256 and 274–275).

[9] Niebuhr, *Irony of American History*, 15.

[10] Writing in 1945 just after the adoption of the UN Charter, and anticipating the drafting of the Universal Declaration, which would be accepted by the UN in 1948, Niebuhr expressed considerable pessimism. The effort to craft and adopt "an international bill of rights" "has been lauded by all international idealists, despite the fact that there is no international sovereignty that could enforce its provisions upon any constituent states." He said that it "deserves all the praise that the hopeful have bestowed upon it, provided you do not look too much beneath the surface... [where] the political realities are such as to give little assurance for the future." "The San Francisco Conference," in D. B. Robertson, ed., *Love and Justice* (New York: Meridian Books, 1957), 213.

[11] Niebuhr, *Irony of American History*, 136.

Though it would be unable to solve the East-West conflict, the UN could at least serve to bring the policies of "even the most powerful of the democratic nations [guess who?] under the scrutiny of world public opinion."[12]

Niebuhr repeatedly exemplified his way of bringing together moral ideals and political realities in books like *Irony of American History*, but he did not generalize much about his method. Speaking for him, we may at least say this: To make decisions according to a "Niebuhrian method" is to accept responsibility for acknowledging and disclosing how complex and precarious such decisions are. They are complex because morality and power find it as hard to live with as without each other. They are precarious because determining the right combination, especially in the thick of politics, is usually frustrating, arduous, and controversial. Acknowledging and disclosing means to explain and defend, clearly and carefully, the "ideal" purposes at stake and the "real" costs and obstacles to pursuing them, all in a spirit of due contrition because of the predictable failure of human beings to practice what they preach.

THE OBAMA CONNECTION

Judging from his three key foreign policy speeches – at Oslo, Cairo, and West Point – and from other writings and reports (especially his book, *Audacity of Hope*), Obama has been strongly influenced by Niebuhr, and particularly by the notion of realistic idealism and its connection to irony and religious sensitivity. There are, at the same time, also some points of difference.

Obama does not explicitly apply the ideas of "divine judgment" and "sin" to national life as much as Niebuhr did, though here and there he makes the same point. He emphasizes the fallibility of human beings and their susceptibility, even with the best intentions, "to the temptations of pride, and power, and sometimes evil."[13] He speaks eloquently of the experience of the black church and its impact on him, underscoring "the intimate knowledge of hardship" and "the grounding of faith in struggle." "Out of necessity," he says, "the black church rarely had the luxury of separating individual ... and collective salvation" or drawing sharp "lines between ... sinner and ... saved." Sin is shared, it is public, and redemption is inescapably social. It involves feeding the hungry, clothing the naked, caring for the sick, and challenging the powers and principalities.[14] These are all profoundly Niebuhrian sentiments.

---

[12] Ibid., 136.
[13] Barack Obama, "Oslo Speech": "Remarks at the Acceptance of the 2009 Nobel Peace Prize."
[14] Barack Obama, *Audacity of Hope: Thoughts on Reclaiming the American Dream* (New York: Crown Publishers, 2006), 206–207.

On the subject of religion and public life, Obama builds on Niebuhr and, in some ways in my opinion, improves on him. Very few presidents, except Jefferson, Madison, Lincoln, and possibly Kennedy, have been as thoughtful as Obama on the matter. On the one hand, he pointedly challenges liberals and secularists to learn to tolerate actively religious expression in the public square, however much they disagree with it. "Scrub language of all religious content," he writes, "and we forfeit the imagery and terminology through which millions of Americans understand both their personal morality and social justice." "Imagine Lincoln's Second Inaugural Address without references to 'the judgments of the Lord,' or King's 'I Have a Dream' speech without reference to 'all God's children'."[15] There is room for government officials such as Obama to express in public, without apology and where appropriate, their own religious sentiments.

On the other hand, no president has gone so far as Obama in clarifying what it means *to think publicly* about religion and to spell out the obligations for religious people. For one thing, it means to treat members of the public truly inclusively and equally when it comes to religion. "Whatever we once were, we are no longer just a Christian nation," Obama writes. "We are also a Jewish nation, a Muslim nation, a Buddhist nation, a Hindu nation, and a nation of nonbelievers."[16]

For another thing, it means religious people (and others) must learn to adapt to the demands of what has been called "public reason." When it comes to passing laws and designing policies that have the force of law, "the religiously motivated [must learn to] translate their concerns into universal, rather than religion-specific, values." "Their proposals must be subject to argument and amenable to reason."[17] Obama speaks here of a common language of deliberation that all members of the public may be expected to share, one that rests on "universal values," identified as "the Golden Rule [and] the need to battle cruelty in all its forms,"[18] as well as the rule of law and human rights.[19] The implication is that if we do not adopt such a language, we face two serious problems: We are in danger of going back on an obligation to equal inclusiveness, thereby becoming a sectarian nation after all. Second, it is patently unfair to hold dissenters and unbelievers accountable to laws grounded in principles they cannot be expected to share. This means, presumably, that even the most

---

[15] Ibid., 214.
[16] Ibid., 218.
[17] Ibid., 219.
[18] Ibid., 224.
[19] Cairo and Oslo speeches.

fervent religious statements by government officials, when offered in support of a law or policy, must finally be testable by public reason. If not, we might encounter the case, say, of a president who ultimately bases a decision to go to war on an alleged private revelation from God.

All of this is simply commentary on Obama's strong commitment to the separation of church and state protected, as he believes, by the U.S. Constitution. And it is a commitment, he emphasizes, that was resolutely supported not just by Deists and free-thinkers influenced by the Enlightenment but also by devoted Christians and others in the eighteenth century and, he might have added, in the seventeenth century, as well. His point here illustrates his persistent disposition to look for the progressive, as well as regressive, influences of religion on American ideals.[20]

Although Obama, like Niebuhr, does not favor imposing the U.S. Constitution on other countries, the two men do not see all aspects of this question in the same way. More than Niebuhr, Obama espouses, as I mentioned, the worldwide applicability of the broad principles of the rule of law. He not only affirms the value of the UN, as did Niebuhr, but he is also more emphatic about the importance of international law in regulating the use of force. And he gives much more weight to the idea of universal rights. Such rights, he says "are not just American ideas. They are human rights, and that is why we will support them everywhere."[21] Incidentally, whether the ideals of Obama's human rights policy match the practice cannot be taken up here.[22]

For now, let me summarize the way Obama's religious sensitivity affects his attitude regarding American policy toward the Muslim world. Like Niebuhr, Obama is exceptionally attuned to the bearing of religion on world politics, both as cause and effect and as source of benefit and harm.

In addressing "the great tension between the United States and Muslims around the world," Obama gives expression to the daunting complexity of the connections between religion and global politics. He understands that Islam, like any religion, is a storehouse of different, even divergent ideas and impulses, susceptible of multiple interpretations and subject to nonreligious influences. He mentions colonialism, the Cold War, and "the sweeping change brought by modernity and globalization" as critical influences on Muslim hostility and resentment toward the West and as affecting the inclination of a "small but potent minority of Muslims" to turn to indiscriminate violence.

---

[20] Obama, *Audacity of Hope*, 216–218.
[21] Cairo speech.
[22] See "Postscript: The Problem of Human Rights" at the end of this chapter.

He goes on to imply that Muslim hostility and resentment, as well as the resort to indiscriminate violence, will only begin to be reduced when on-the-ground conflicts, as between Israel and the Palestinians, are mitigated and when significant improvements are made in the areas of rule of law, human rights, and economic and educational development.

One point he emphasizes is that religious attitudes – in this case, those of Muslims – are affected by nonreligious causes and must be so understood. It will not do simply to blame the religion of Islam for anti-Western attitudes or terrorism or to believe that a change in religious outlook will make all the difference in overcoming these things.

But Obama makes another point, which serves as a counterweight: It concerns the positive significance of religion in addressing enmity and indiscriminate violence. Obama spends considerable time detailing the civilizing effects of Islam, highlighting Qur'anic and other resources within the tradition for opposing religious intolerance and indiscriminate violence and for affirming the rule of law and human rights. Obama is on firm ground here. He has the support of numerous contemporary scholars of Islam who come to similar conclusions.

In the Cairo speech, Obama mentions, in passing, U.S. policy toward Afghanistan and Pakistan as one of the possible impediments to improved relations between the United States and the Muslim world. It is a subject, of course, that he takes up in much greater detail in his Oslo and West Point speeches, and this brings me to some final reflections on a central – and controversial – aspect of current American foreign policy. The major point I want to make is how compellingly *the way* Obama goes about defending his policy illustrates his commitment to realistic idealism, though he does it in a fashion somewhat different from Niebuhr.

There are, to be sure, strong Niebuhrian accents in both the Oslo and West Point speeches touching on the severe moral and other complexities and risks that attend decision making in complicated circumstances. However, by emphasizing as much as he does the importance of *a just-war framework* for thinking about the use of force in Afghanistan and Pakistan and by employing that framework to defend his policy, Obama moves beyond Niebuhr. He agrees with Niebuhr that force must sometimes be used in a fallen world. However, Niebuhr did not write much about a just-war approach, claiming that, although moral and legal distinctions are needed for limiting force, "finiteness and sin" inevitably imperil the approach's practical usefulness. For him, it smacked too much of naïve idealism.

Obama's attitude is different. Without discounting the potential for abuse, he has more confidence in the just-war framework. The fact that it includes eight different standards that must be considered in deciding whether force in a given circumstance is justified or not appears to reflect his sense of the severe moral and factual complexity of making decisions about force. Far from oversimplifying the task of limiting force, a just-war framework, Obama seems to say, *expands and complicates* a policy maker's scope of moral responsibility, of the things he or she may be held accountable for in arriving at a particular decision. If such an approach is applied conscientiously, it exemplifies a form of idealism that is not naïve, but highly realistic.[23]

According to just-war teaching, a decision to use force is strongly justified if it satisfies all eight standards: (1) that it be initiated under *legitimate authority* (in the case of Afghanistan and Pakistan, under the charters of the UN and NATO, and the U.S. Constitution); (2) that it serve a *just cause* (such as "self-defense" or "international peace and security," in the words of the UN Charter); (3) that it exhibit a *peaceful intent* (no imperial designs); (4) that it be undertaken only as a *last resort* (after exhausting all reasonable nonviolent means of resolution); and that there be; (5) a *reasonable probability of success*; and (6) a *favorable overall balance of benefit to cost*. Two additional standards apply to the conduct of armed conflict: (7) *noncombatant immunity* (meaning no direct, intentional attack on defenseless people) and (8) *military proportionality* (avoiding excessive indirect and unintentional injury or destruction).

Mind you, there is nothing automatic about applying this framework. A moment's reflection will show that judging the facts against each standard, let alone weighing all the judgments together and then coming to an overall verdict, is a complicated matter. Maybe a military campaign has proper authority, protects against serious regional and international threats to peace and security, intends peace, is undertaken as a last resort; yet, does it have a reasonable probability of success, or do overall costs outweigh benefits, or is the campaign conducted in accord with noncombatant immunity and military proportionality? Trying to reconcile conflicting judgments concerning the different standards perfectly illustrates the deep perplexity of adjusting ideals and reality in the context of something like Af/Pak policy. In my view, for what it is worth, that is exactly the sort of moral and policy complexity and perplexity President Obama has been faced with since he took office.

---

[23] Though Obama mentions only four of the just-war standards in his Oslo speech, he winds up touching on all eight when the Oslo and the West Point speeches are considered together. I concede that my account makes the just-war framework more explicit and systematic than Obama does, but that he introduces and employs the framework is a fact of the greatest importance. As I say later, it is a pity Obama does not persevere in applying the just-war framework to the evolving changes in Af/Pak policy.

But however each of us comes out on whether or not, all things considered, the Af/Pak campaign is justifiable, it is important to bear in mind two specific ways the just-war framework fits into President Obama's version of realistic idealism.

First, it highlights some of his key moral ideals, as well as the means he accepts as necessary for promoting them. While his Oslo speech is suffused with an "acute sense of the cost of armed conflict," the speech also reflects his abhorrence of *arbitrary force* – of resorting to armed conflict, that is, without meeting some or all of the eight tests of the just-war framework. He condemns terrorism and torture, which are, of course, examples of inflicting severe suffering directly and intentionally on defenseless people, in direct violation of just-war standards.

One may infer that for Obama arbitrary force is one of the forms of cruelty that are universally wrong and that ought so to be prohibited. He acknowledges the power of the nonviolent message represented by King and Gandhi and partly agrees that military force is not sufficient to achieve the desired objectives in places such as Afghanistan and Pakistan. Nevertheless, he (like Niebuhr) also holds that, in the real world, force, regrettably, is sometimes necessary in the pursuit of justice and peace.

Second, the just-war framework provides a religiously neutral set of universal moral and legal standards for assessing the use of force. As such, it is consistent with Obama's emphasis on "public reason" that is at once religiously neutral and carefully limited and that everyone, regardless of religious identity, may be expected to embrace.

In this respect, Obama's approach is profoundly different from the approach to religion and foreign policy of George W. Bush, who frequently invoked religious reasons in the lead-up to the war in Iraq. At the first anniversary of the terrorist attacks, Bush attributed to America and its ideals a messianic role, rewriting the opening verses of the Gospel of John by substituting America for the Word of God as the "light that shines in darkness."[24] Immediately after 9/11, he declared that America's "responsibility to history is already clear: to answer these attacks and rid the world of evil."[25]

Obama and Niebuhr would regard such utterances as examples of the most blatant and harmful form of naïve idealism, suggesting both a total failure to appreciate the limits of American power and virtue and a distressing misunderstanding of the place of religion in American foreign policy.

---

[24] George W. Bush, Remarks at Ellis Island on the first anniversary of the 2001 terrorist attacks.
[25] Remarks at National Day of Prayer and Remembrance, National Cathedral, September 14, 2001.

It is important to add some comments on the Af/Pak policy in the light both of Bob Woodward's book, *Obama's Wars*, published in 2010,[26] and of decisions made by the Obama administration since then. During the drafting of the West Point speech, Woodward quotes Obama as saying, "The American people are idealists, but they want their leaders to be realistic. The speech ought to convey that."[27] *Obama's Wars* is very much the account of a president struggling conscientiously and insistently to find a policy that reconciles ideals with the hard realities of Afghanistan and Pakistan and that does it against the background of the standards set by the just-war framework.

The tone of the book is radically different from *State of Denial*,[28] Woodward's final assessment of the war policies of the Bush presidency. The two books represent a poignant contrast between one president – subservient to the military and his Secretary of Defense, incurious, evasive, indifferent to detail, inattentive to discrepancies in policy – and another, who was persistently engaged, an aggressive, almost prosecutorial, questioner, committed to "evidence-based reasoning," doubtful of military self-assurance, and deeply troubled by the costs of war and by the risks and uncertainties of the present course of action. According to Steve Coll in his *New Yorker* review of Woodward's book, Woodward reveals "much of what Obama promised voters when he sought the White House: realism and intelligence." He describes a president "who has taken responsibility for the most fateful decisions he can be called upon to make.... He has ... shouldered his burdens."[29]

Not surprisingly, the just-war requirement of a "reasonable probability of success" received by far the most extensive and anguished attention throughout the book, followed closely by an abiding concern for the "favorable overall balance of benefit to cost" in respect to the blood and treasure of all concerned. On the one hand, there was within the administration much more dissent and skepticism concerning the feasibility of the policy than had previously been divulged, which could not help but lower its level of confidence that the United States was on the right course. On the other hand, there was simultaneously widespread agreement regarding the urgent importance of stability in the region that was directly linked to a reduction of the extremist threat. In short, the welter of conflicting opinions and conditions described by Woodward only intensified the perplexity Obama faced at the time in trying to relate ideals and reality in Afghanistan and Pakistan.

---

[26] Bob Woodward, *Obama's Wars* (New York: Simon & Schuster, 2010).
[27] Ibid., 307.
[28] Bob Woodward, *State of Denial: Bush at War, III* (New York: Simon & Schuster, 2006).
[29] Steve Coll, *New Yorker* (Oct. 11, 2010), 36.

Since 2010, however, Obama does not seem as conflicted. As announced on January 11, 2013, he is firmly committed to a policy of withdrawing by 2014, and perhaps sooner, most NATO personnel from Afghanistan, down to a small residual force. Based on a recent "series of meetings to redefine the American mission in Afghanistan, known informally as 'Afghan Good Enough,'"[30] he has apparently concluded that the prospects for stabilizing the region at a reasonable cost are no longer favorable enough to warrant continuing U.S. and NATO military involvement at any where near the present level. If, in reality, it is impossible or highly unlikely to realize the desired ideal, then it is irrational (and immoral) to continue trying.

The earlier objective of "disrupting, dismantling, and defeating" the Taliban and other extremists in Afghanistan and Pakistan appears to have been substantially cut back. The implication is that it is better, on balance, to provide severely diminished support to the locals – however uncertain and improbable their chances – than for outsiders to continue to pay the high price of endeavoring by present means to remove deeply entrenched and widespread political and social obstacles to eliminating extremism.

This policy is clearly in line with national (and international) attitudes, resulting from growing public fatigue and indifference, manifest in the 2012 U.S. presidential election, as well as from successful counterterrorist operations by the Obama administration, including killing Osama bin Laden on May 2, 2011 and continuing effective, if controversial, antiterrorist drone attacks in Pakistan, Yemen, and elsewhere.

But however politically agreeable the policy, what is lacking, from the perspective of the "Niebuhrian method," is any recent effort by the president to acknowledge and disclose – explain and defend – how the present policy combines ideals and realities in a way consistent with the whole range of considerations identified by the just-war framework, something he introduced in 2009. We may infer from his general announcement in January 2013 that, if he ever did, the president no longer sees for Af/Pak policy a "reasonable probability of success" at a "favorable overall balance of benefit to cost." The earlier uncertainties surrounding those two just-war standards have, it appears, been dispelled. However, this judgment still leaves other standards, such as "just cause," unaccounted for. Has the threat of extremism to "international peace and security" in the region been reduced, particularly in regard to the security of Pakistan's nuclear weapons and to the prospects for violent conflict between Pakistan and India? If not, are there perhaps alternative policies that

---

[30] "Obama Pledges to Name Close Aide on National Security as Chief of Staff," *New York Times* (Jan. 17, 2013), A15.

hold promise for lessening those threats once NATO forces are withdrawn? If so, what might they be? More broadly, what are the key ideals and purposes to be pursued in the region after the withdrawal, and how will the salient costs and obstacles be addressed?

Finally, what may be said in retrospect about how ideals and realities have been combined in the ten-plus years NATO has been involved in Afghanistan and Pakistan? To what degree have the eight standards of the just-war framework been met? It is particularly important for the president to provide that assessment of the performance of his own administration. For example, was the 2009 surge in U.S. forces justified? Or, knowing what we now know about the situation, should we have commenced withdrawing at that time? Only when questions of this sort have been answered can it be said that the president has fully embraced the obligations of realistic idealism.

CONCLUSION

Obama and Niebuhr do not see everything the same way, but they have much in common. They are both realistic idealists. They both feel the force of a moral demand that can neither be disregarded nor fully achieved. Both have a sense of irony – of the "perverse incongruities" between what is expected and what occurs, resulting partly from the deep-seated defects of human nature – and both are religiously sensitive as a way of living with irony.

When it comes to foreign policy, as exemplified by the U.S. approach to Afghanistan and Pakistan, Obama, like Niebuhr, accepts the use of force in the service of justice and peace; yet, again, like Niebuhr, he understands how complex and precarious are all decisions surrounding its use. For Obama, the just-war framework provides a common, religiously neutral set of standards that account for the variety of moral imperatives and real-world considerations relevant to the use of force, as well as for the challenges involved in trying to balance all such matters licitly and effectively. Though Niebuhr saw the need for moral and legal restraint, he had less confidence than Obama that the just-war framework could be employed with sufficient dispassion and impartiality.

Despite Niebuhr's reservations, however, the benefit of the just-war framework to the cause of realistic idealism is that it identifies standards of accountability, which are morally and practically sensitive to the realities of combat, for the public assessment of policies involving force. Such an approach is a particularly apposite example of the "Niebuhrian method," which, I suggested, involves explaining and defending, clearly and carefully, the "ideal" purposes at stake and the "real" costs and obstacles to pursuing them, always in a spirit of humility because of the limitations of making decisions under such conditions.

Given the welter of conflicting opinions and conditions confronting Obama as he took charge of Af/Pak policy in 2009, he did reasonably well in living up to the demands of the Niebuhrian method. As Steve Coll put it, he "shouldered his burdens" "with realism and intelligence," in dramatic contrast to his predecessor. However, he has not been as constant in explaining himself as the policy evolved. He has delivered no Oslo or West Point speeches as follow-up, and citizens are left to infer on their own what Af/Pak policy amounts to at present.

Still, whatever the differences and disagreements over the details of American foreign policy, and however disheartening Obama's failure to continue "acknowledging and disclosing" how particular policies combine ideals and realities, he shares with Niebuhr, in general, a degree of thoughtfulness and conscientiousness in respect to the difficult issues of religion, morality, and politics of which we have great need.

POSTSCRIPT: THE PROBLEM OF HUMAN RIGHTS

It is frequently argued that in regard to human rights policy the Obama administration has not lived up to the standards of realistic idealism. The administration is charged with one-sidedly sacrificing human rights ideals in its effort to accommodate to domestic and international political realities.

Kenneth Roth, director of Human Rights Watch, published a provocative article in the Spring 2010 issue of *Foreign Affairs*, "Empty Promises? Obama's Hesitant Embrace of Human Rights," which provides a helpful catalogue of some of the alleged shortcomings of the administration. These include failure to investigate persistently and comprehensively possible human rights violations on the part of the previous administration, extended detention of terrorist suspects without trial, and sharp discrepancies between a commitment to human rights and generous support for governments that appear not to share that commitment.

There is no time to assess these charges. What can fairly be said is that, as yet, the president has not made a very conscientious effort to give a general account of his human rights strategy, of how particular policies match broader guidelines, and what principles govern those guidelines.[31] Few presidents are

---

[31] Secretary of State Hillary Clinton gave a speech on human rights policy at Georgetown University on Dec. 14, 2009, but the speech did not address acute points of tension between ideals and realities, such as the challenge of balancing human rights objectives with U.S. strategic interests in places such as Uzbekistan and Turkmenistan.

as good as President Obama in doing that sort of thing. Why has he not done it in this case?

Lacking that, we have no defined standards of accountability – such as are supplied by the just-war framework – according to which the public is prompted, as honestly and impartially as possible, to evaluate administration performance.

It would be especially distressing if preaching and practice in an area of such importance turned out to be significantly inconsistent. It would betray the president's own impressive efforts elsewhere to honor the imperatives of realistic idealism, and it would betray Reinhold Niebuhr's insistent campaign to temper the "perverse incongruities" of American foreign policy. It would, in a word, be doubly ironic.

Afterword

Ethics, Religion, and Human Consciousness

FURTHER REFLECTIONS ON A "TWO-TIERED" APPROACH TO JUSTIFICATION

In taking up the question of the conditions of comprehensive justifications of human rights language, and especially those justifications that are religious, I begin by recalling the "two-tiered" approach to justification I discussed in the Introduction and Chapter 1. The first tier, I said, concerns a secular (or religiously neutral) appeal taken to be moral and universal in character and one that is limited to the specific rights enumerated in the Declaration and its progeny. It entitles every human being "to all the rights and freedoms set forth in the Declaration, without distinction of any kind, such as...religion." The second tier concerns appeals that may be specifically religious in character (though they need not be religious). Such appeals are protected by Article 18 of the Declaration, guaranteeing the right to "freedom of conscience and religion or belief." That right invites individuals and groups, as desired, to develop and embrace, according to conscience, their own religious (or nonreligious) justifications for human rights and, of course, for much else.

I also want to recall two other subjects I dealt with here and there in this book and that are, to my mind, closely tied to my two-tiered approach: the ideas of natural rights and of conscience. There is little doubt that the Western natural rights tradition, purely in historical terms, significantly influenced the formulation of human rights language, though as I suggested in Chapters 1 and 2, following Morsink's emphasis on the importance of the fascist experience as background to human rights language, it was not only the attraction of that tradition that explains the widespread appeal of human rights language. Similarly, the long-standing tradition of Western Christian cogitation on conscience unquestionably colored the understanding of the word, "conscience," as it appears in the human rights documents, although, again, that influence hardly exhausts the reasons for the appeal or interpretation of the term, either at the time the Declaration was drafted or subsequently.

In the discussions of both ideas, a distinction is drawn between what we might call "natural" and "extranatural" appeals. Natural appeals concern those aspects of experience that are taken to apply uniformly to all mature human beings, individual capacities permitting.[1] They represent ideal conditions, universally binding, for human belief and action. Thus, "natural rights" are understood to be minimal[2] and enforceable moral entitlements that are universally obligatory and that assume common human rational and psychological capabilities. Competent human beings are "naturally" expected to know enough about the world around them and about the conditions of moral responsibility to be held everywhere accountable to such minimal moral standards. The same goes for the idea of conscience, understood as a "private monitor" or *forum internum* – a center or seat of moral and religious authority and deliberation ideally inherent in every human being that calls for special deference and protection from the *forum externum* (the civil authority).

At the same time, the ideas of both natural rights and conscience allow for, indeed entail, "extranatural appeals," appeals to "higher" authoritative standards or beings that are taken to transcend the "natural world" in some way and that assume a sacred character. As such, the "higher" notion of sacred authority is understood to provide the "ultimate warrant" for the minimal moral standards supported by the natural appeals, as well as to authorize an extensive set of comprehensive beliefs and actions typically believed to govern a "whole way of life."

A critical feature of the distinction between the two tiers is that first-tier standards are assumed to be enforceable, by physical coercion, if necessary, whereas second-tier standards are not. Accordingly, the Puritan theorist, Roger Williams (taken up particularly in Chapter 9), represents one very important position in the traditional understanding of natural rights and conscience by contending emphatically that, whereas the Second Table of the Decalogue (the minimal "moral" commandments regulating interhuman relations, such as prohibitions of murder, theft, etc.) is enforceable by the *forum externum*, or civil authority, the First Table (the "religious" commandments regulating divine-human relations, such as worship, religious utterance, respect for holy days, etc.) is not.

[1] See Chapter 1, 39–40.
[2] See Introduction, fn. 2.

The challenge before us, then, is to sketch the outlines, at least, of a convincing philosophical account that supports and elaborates this two-tiered picture of the process of justification in human moral and religious life.

THE STUDY OF HUMAN CONSCIOUSNESS

The best place to start, though not to end (as I shall argue), is with the arguments of three contemporary philosophers, John Searle, Colin McGinn, and Thomas Nagel, concerning the status of human consciousness.[3] The common heart of their arguments – somewhat differently presented and nuanced by each and thus suggesting different implications for our subject – is to me thoroughly compelling. It is that there exists a virtually[4] irreducible distinction between the kind of knowledge that is associated with human consciousness and the kind of knowledge that is associated with determining "the workings of the physical [or natural] world," in a phrase of McGinn's.

As a way of understanding the distinctiveness of consciousness, Searle draws an initial distinction between "subjective" and "objective ontology." In his words,

> an entity has an objective ontology if its existence does not depend on being experienced by a human or animal subject; otherwise it is subjective. For example, mountains, molecules, and tectonic plates are ontologically objective. Their existence does not depend on being experienced by anybody. But pains, tickles, and itches only exist when experienced by a human or animal subject. They are ontologically subjective.[5]

---

[3] In pursuing these thoughts, I am drawing on the work of Thomas Nagel, *Other Minds: Critical Essays, 1969–1994* (New York: Oxford University Press, 1995), and *Mind and Cosmos: Why the Materialist Neo-Darwinian Conception of Nature Is Almost Certainly False* (New York: Oxford University Press, 2012); John R. Searle, *Rediscovery of the Mind* (Cambridge: MIT Press, 1992), and Colin McGinn, *The Mysterious Flame: Conscious Minds in a Material World* (New York: Basic Books, 1999), as well as the frequent reviews by all three in the *New York Review of Books* of recent studies of the theory of consciousness. Nagel, Searle, and McGinn all in their various ways repeatedly undertake to refute versions of materialism and naturalism that reduce consciousness to nonsubjective factors.

[4] While Searle argues strenuously that at present the mind-body connection remains totally beyond human comprehension, he believes the mystery will likely someday be solved, thus presumably eliminating the irreducibility of the distinction. McGinn and Nagel are much more skeptical that the problem can ever be solved. See fn. 10.

[5] Searle, "The Mystery of Consciousness Continues," *New York Review of Books* (June 9, 2011), 50. Given the proposed irreducibility of this difference, one famous philosophical conundrum would appear to be solved. It concerns the question of whether, if a tree falls in the forest, there

According to Searle, this ontological distinction is not the same as an epistemological distinction, though they appear to be related. A statement is epistemically objective, he says, "if its truth or falsity can be settled as a matter of fact independently of anybody's attitudes, feelings or evaluations; it is subjective if it cannot."[6] So long as the evidence is available, anyone can know whether or not a certain person died, but not anyone can have access to what the deceased "truly meant" to a particular relative unless the relative chooses to reveal that knowledge. Objective knowledge is one thing; subjective another.

Still, even though subjective knowledge remains inaccessible to the outsider, it is possible for anyone to recognize objectively the difference between the two kinds of knowledge and to identify their contrasting characteristics. As Searle says, "a science of consciousness" is possible.[7] Because one can "know about" another's consciousness without experiencing it for oneself, it is clear that ontology and epistemology in this regard are not the same thing. Yet, they are surely connected. Searle's ontological point about the existence of "pains, tickles, and itches" being dependent on whether they are experienced by a human (or animal) subject is itself only "knowable" because of the developing understanding of what it means to be a human subject with privileged access to consciousness.[8]

The distinction between objective and subjective knowledge needs to be sharpened further. Although we may follow Searle, as well as McGinn and Nagel, in construing the distinction in one critically important way they all agree on, there are, I believe, some notable refinements to be added, which McGinn and Nagel introduce and which represent deviations from Searle's position.

The critically important way of distinguishing objective and subjective knowledge common to all three philosophers is as follows: Objective knowledge is "third-person" or "transsubjective" knowledge – knowledge similarly

---

is a sound. The answer is, only if a human or animal subject is present to hear it. Because the concept, "sound," is defined as some form of disturbance in the natural environment "capable of being detected by the organs of hearing" (*American Heritage Dictionary*, 1234), there could be no sound unless existing human or animal subjects experience it. Whatever the necessary (objective) conditions in the natural world for stimulating the organs of hearing, sounds as such are, it seems clear, irreducibly part of subjective ontology. One simple way to "prove" this conclusion is to imagine a tree falling in a place where every living creature "within ear shot" is stone deaf.

[6] Ibid.
[7] Ibid.
[8] Up to a point, it is also possible to infer from animal behavior a comparable distinction between objective and subjective knowledge. A key difference, however, between humans and higher animals would appear to be the capacity for developed "self-consciousness."

accessible to *anyone* – of the sort pursued by the scientific method. Accordingly, the scientific method is a procedure (or set of procedures – observation, description, measurement, prediction, etc.) for determining the workings of the physical or natural world. Special attention is accorded to discovering *causal connections* among objects in that world.

In contrast, subjective knowledge, the knowledge of consciousness, is personal and subjective in that it is an "inner, first-person, qualitative phenomenon"[9] that cannot be reduced to "objective" (or external) conditions (i.e., the physical structure and dynamics of the neurons of the brain). It is in that respect an "emergent property" in an expanded sense[10] because it is

---

[9] John Searle, "The Mystery of Consciousness," *New York Review of Books* (November 2, 1995), 60.

[10] Searle, in *Rediscovery of the Mind*, 111–112, defines an "emergent property" in both a minimal and in an expanded way. The minimal understanding ("emergent 1") holds that some features of a system "cannot be figured out just from the composition of the [system's] elements and environmental relations, but have to be explained in terms of the causal interactions among the elements." The expanded sense ("emergent 2") suggests that the new property is more than simply the product of causal interaction; rather, it takes on "a life of its own" independent of the prior causal conditions on which it initially depended. Because Searle continues to hold out the hope that a satisfactory "materialistic" account of the causal relation between body and mind can be given, he does not accept "emergent 2" as applicable to consciousness. However, in my opinion, he is inconsistent in refusing to do so. This expanded sense is, it would seem, precisely what it means to speak of consciousness as "irreducible" – namely that it is capable of "caus[ing] things that could not be explained by [objective causal conditions]."

In *The Mysterious Flame: Conscious Minds in a Material World*, Colin McGinn comes close to embracing this expanded sense of emergent property. Like Searle, McGinn discusses the subject of brain-mind connection in terms of "emergent properties" (100). Although he does not introduce Searle's notion of "emergent 2," his extensive discussion of what he calls "an *irreducible duality* in the faculties through which we come to know about mind and brain" (47; italics added) would seem to presuppose the expanded usage. McGinn writes, "When you have an experience of yellow your conscious state does indeed depend for its existence upon what is happening in your neurons in the visual area of your cortex. But it is not true that your experience has such neural processes as its *constituents*. It is not *made up* of the processes that constitute its neural correlate. The conscious state does not have an internal structure that is *defined* by its physical underpinnings.... *[This is] because conscious states do not have neural parts*" (58; emphasis added).

McGinn goes on: "It follows that physics, construed as the general science of matter, is incomplete, because the general properties of matter that the brain exploits to produce consciousness are currently unknown. It also follows that neurophysiology, the special study of the brain, is also incomplete, because the specific feature of the brain that permits it alone to generate consciousness is currently unknown" (101). Indeed, for McGinn, such knowledge may well lie "outside the possible scope of human comprehension" (i.e., the relation between body and mind will remain forever "mysterious").

In "Searle: Why We Are Not Computers," in *Other Minds*, 96–110, Nagel makes the same point against Searle about the high probability that the distinction between objective and subjective knowledge is ultimately incomprehensible in scientific terms (esp. 104–105). In analyzing an "emergent" as opposed to a "reductive" account of consciousness in *Mind and*

necessarily perceived as causing things that cannot be explained by objective causal conditions of the sort considered by the scientific method. In short, the idea of "subjective agency," implying the notions of "intentionality" and "self-determination" ("self-causation"), is constitutive of the experience and understanding of consciousness.[11]

Related to the idea of consciousness as subjective agency, including intentionality and self-determination, is a certain set of values, roughly "ethical values," making up a sphere of reflection and action conventionally characterized as "practical reason." Consciousness is inescapably experienced and organized in relation to emotions, desires, and interests that are, in turn, decided on, authorized, and pursued on the basis of certain "higher" values – superior and authoritative or "ethical" values, having to do with the concepts

---

Cosmos, Nagel goes further in calling for "a form of understanding that enables us to see ourselves and other conscious organisms as specific expressions of the physical and mental character of the universe" (69; see 54ff.). This conclusion leads him to contemplate – rather radically and unfashionably – an account of human evolution that considers consciousness (together with its constitutive ideas of purposefulness and intentionality) as neither reducible to physical causes nor as an accidental and largely inexplicable side effect (as proposed by Elliott Sober, see the later discussion), but as somehow "there all along."

[11] McGinn emphasizes the connection of subjective knowledge to the idea of "subjective agency," which Searle also stresses. "The question of consciousness and the question of the self are intimately related" (157). Just as consciousness is not reducible to the laws of brain function, neither is the idea of the self reducible to those laws. Hence, we are necessarily faced, according to McGinn, with two quite distinct and independent notions of causation: "The causation of behavior by mental states is nothing like the kind of mechanical causation of which physics treats. When billiard balls collide, they impart energy in the form of momentum to each other, and there are laws that govern this type of interaction. But beliefs and desires don't make contact with action, and there are no comparable laws governing how behavior will evolve in the causal circumstances. We simply have no general theoretical grasp how mental states cause behavior. . . . Free will is mental causation in action, the mysterious interface between mind and action" (167–168).

In a similar vein, Nagel speaks of mental phenomena as *sui generis* in that they are "not analyzable in terms of behavior or anything else about the body," even though they are in some important sense "connected with the body" (*Other Minds*, 95). In *Mind and Cosmos*, Nagel puts it this way: "What has to be explained is not just the lacing of organic life with a tincture of qualia but the coming into existence of subjective individual points of view – a type of existence logically distinct from anything describable by the physical sciences alone" (44). Whatever valid problems they may raise about Nagel's book, critical reviews by Elliott Sober ("Remarkable Facts: Ending Science as We Know It," bostonreview.com (November/December 2012) and Brian Leiter and Michael Weisberg, "Do You Only Have a Brain?" thenation.com (October 2012) fail to deal with this central point. To assume a "subjective individual point of view" – that is, to be a self-conscious agent in the way human beings think of themselves – is to take up a perspective that, on pain of self-contradiction (!), can never be reduced completely to a nonsubjective causal account. Otherwise, who is it exactly that is providing the nonsubjective account?

of good and bad, right and wrong.[12] The higher values are "first-person" (or "subjective") in two ways: They are "self-involving" in the sense of being the object of *subjective commitment*, and they are taken to constitute the highest court of appeal according to which the self justifies its own actions and the actions of others. In addition, the patterns of action certified by the values may be deviated from and variably complied with, depending on the "strength or weakness of will" of the subject in question. In a word, the higher values provide the final reasons as to why consciousness for each person is organized and directed as it is, and, accordingly, authorize the standards for the self-evaluation and criticism of the subject's own beliefs and behavior. Incidentally, it is particularly in these ways that subjective knowledge is tied to the traditional understanding of the idea of conscience, a point to be commented on later.

Let us continue to edge our way toward a fuller understanding by means of some comments on mind-body relations. According to what Nagel calls a "dual aspect theory," the mind and body are at once critically interconnected and irreducibly distinct.[13] Clearly, a body can be looked at "scientifically" – in accord with discovering causal relations among objects of the physical world, including by the person whose body it is. *Up to a point*, there are causal connections between the body and subjective consciousness of a sort typically studied by the scientific method. Under uniform conditions that are objectively knowable, neural reactions of the body predictably cause, for example, a conscious experience of physical pain. If a tooth is drilled without anesthesia, a subjective sensation of sharp pain will invariably result. We can say

---

[12] The specific place of emotions, including "moral emotions," in human practical experience is a large and important subject I cannot take up at length here. Let me simply say, that on my interpretation, emotions, including moral emotions, have a "cognitive core." That means they are inescapably tied to patterns of good and bad reasons. Accordingly, however insusceptible emotions are to direct rational control, they are finally evaluated as "appropriate" or "inappropriate," depending on their compatibility with what is adjudged "right or wrong," "rational or irrational," about practical decisions in given circumstances. A failure to "be deeply moved" by violations of the logic of pain would be a seriously deficient expression of emotions.

[13] In "Searle: Why We Are Not Computers," Nagel refers to the term, "dual aspect theory" as "somewhat less unacceptable than the other unacceptable theories currently on offer. "I share," he says, "Searle's aversion to both dualism and materialism, and believe a solution to the mind-body problem is nowhere in sight" (*Other Minds*, 105, fn. 6). In *Mind and Cosmos*, Nagel does not use the term, "dual aspect," but he describes it well: We human beings "ourselves are large-scale, complex [interacting] instances of something both objectively physical from outside and subjectively mental from inside. Perhaps the basis for this [dual] identity pervades the world" (42).

that the neural effects of such an action constitute objective causes in that they externally (or "objectively") affect the quality of the consciousness of the recipient. Not only does a certain kind of subjective sensation of pain predictably occur but that experience will also prima facie be strongly unwanted by the individual whose tooth is drilled. Thus are body and mind "critically interconnected."

But however interconnected are body and mind, consciousness nevertheless remains "irreducibly distinct" from the neural effects of such actions in three ways: (1) The subjective experience of pain is something altogether different from the neural processes of the body; "conscious states do not have neural parts," as McGinn puts it; (2) only the person in question, *and no one else*, can have the particular experience of pain referred to in the example – literally speaking, an outsider cannot *know* another's pain (contrary to Bill Clinton's famous comment), but can only "know about" that pain; and, most importantly; (3) the particular quality of the experience – what is made of it, how it is interpreted – varies up to a point, at least, according to the distinctly subjective or first-person predispositions and ethical commitments of the individual involved.

The third feature is especially important and calls for some elucidation. Although, predictably, the experience of pain caused by drilling a tooth will be thought of as best avoided if possible, it might, if it occurs, be adjudged "to be worth it" and even welcomed were it the result of an emergency dental procedure designed to prevent a life-threatening condition. In this case, the infliction of pain is justified because it is the result of what is deemed, all things considered, to be a "good" or "right" act. On the other hand, if the act of drilling is unnecessary, or is performed negligently or, worse yet, from a desire to cause suffering as an end in itself, the act causing the pain will predictably be regarded as unjustified and thought of as "bad" or "wrong."

The process of assessment taking place in these examples is irreducibly subjective in three ways. First, it is *sui generis*; it is *self*-directed in that it is prompted in accord with the emotions, desires, interests, and beliefs dear to the subject, thereby being a matter of "subjective agency." It is decisively *not* the product of external, nonsubjective causes. As such, the assessment is carried out in accord with a standard of good and bad reasons consistent with the ethical beliefs embraced by the subject. Second, particular assessments will vary, within limits, according to the subjective dispositions of the individual in question. One person's acceptable level or kind of pain is not necessarily another's. Third, ethical standards can be disobeyed – depending on the strength or weakness of will of the subject – whereas causal conditions cannot be. Deviations from accepted causal laws disprove the law; deviations from ethical standards do not disprove the standards.[14]

We now come to a crucial juncture in the argument, still related to my claim, introduced earlier, that the particular quality of consciousness – what is made of it, how it is interpreted – varies *up to a point, at least*, according to the distinctly subjective or first-person ethical commitments of the individual in question. It is the words, "up to a point, at least," that need attention. The underlying issue is illustrated by another important difference of opinion between Searle and Nagel.[15]

In characterizing subjective knowledge, Searle seems to include all evaluative judgments of a nonscientific sort, and he leaves it at that. "The claim that Van Gogh died in France is epistemically objective. But the claim that Van Gogh was a better painter than Gauguin is, as they say, a matter of subjective opinion. It is epistemically subjective."[16] In part, of course, he is correct. I also have contended that judgments, opinions, and the like associated with consciousness are irreducibly subjective. They are different from the kinds of assessment scientists make in determining "the workings of the physical [or natural] world."

But are we to go on to agree, as Searle's comment suggests, that there are *no* standards whatsoever that might be called "objective" – in some peculiar sense consistent with all that has been said so far – in regard to value judgments of an aesthetic or ethical kind? Nagel thinks not. In disagreeing with a point similar to Searle's made by Bernard Williams, Nagel proposes that ethical standards might plausibly be thought of as "objective," *albeit in a very special sense*:

> Admittedly, objectivity here would have to be *sui generis* and nothing like scientific objectivity, but that doesn't prevent us from telling a story about practical reason that is at least structurally analogous. Our initial judgments about what to do and how to live are, on this interpretation, not merely subjective but implicitly, perhaps inchoately, objective in intention. That would be so if an external view of ourselves, which is after all one of the

---

[14] Sigmund Freud once powerfully refuted a claim by anthropologist Eduard Westermarck that a stringent taboo against incest exists because incest is so unappealing and deviations from the taboo so infrequent. Freud convincingly argued the opposite: It is just because incest is so appealing and the temptation to deviation so strong that the taboo against it is so stringent!

[15] The following difference is an elaboration of the dispute between Nagel and Searle (McGinn is closer to Nagel) over the ultimate irreducibility of subjective and objective knowledge; see fn. 10.

[16] John R. Searle, "Mystery of Consciousness Continues," *New York Review of Books* (June 7, 2011), 50.

essential features of rational humanity, were involved in practical judgments from the start – so that a judgment about what I should do was also, at least implicitly, a judgment about what the person who I am should do. This is entirely compatible with the recognition that the *I* who reflects is also the *I* who desires and acts. Practical deliberation can be simultaneously first and third-personal.[17]

The idea here is that subjective knowledge associated with consciousness presupposes "from the start" its own special objective viewpoint – an ethically ideal standard potentially applicable to anyone – from which the self can view and assess itself (and others), but in a way that "is nothing like scientific objectivity." Such would appear to be the meaning of Nagel's words, "practical deliberation can be simultaneously first and third-personal."

The objectivity in question is nothing like scientific objectivity[18] because it incorporates as essential the two features of subjective knowledge: (1) a "self-involving" commitment to a set of ethical values taken to provide the highest court of appeal according to which the self justifies its own actions and the actions of others, and (2) an understanding that the values may be deviated from and variably complied with, depending on the strength or weakness of will of the subject in question. At the same time, the notion of nonscientific or ethical objectivity implies that there are transsubjective standards of practical justification, of good and bad reasons for action, that impose critical (ethical) limits on the "subjective agency" – the organization and direction of consciousness – of anyone. Consequently, these standards provide a reference point for "an external view of ourselves" in accord with which the "I" scrutinizes and

---

[17] Nagel, "Williams: Resisting Ethical Theory" in *Other Minds*, 180. See Nagel, *Mind and Cosmos*, 72, for an elaboration of the idea of practical deliberation as "simultaneously first and third-personal," or what Nagel describes as the self's "capacity to transcend subjectivity and to discover what is objectively the case that presents the problem. Thought and reasoning are correct or incorrect in virtue of something independent of the thinker's beliefs, and even independent of the community of thinkers to which he belongs."

[18] At first blush, there is one way in which ethical objectivity and scientific objectivity appear, contrary to Nagel's claim, to be "something like" each other. But the appearance is only superficial. The issue concerns the fact that scientific endeavor itself implicitly requires a "commitment of fidelity" to the method. Having adopted the scientific method, a scientist may be held accountable to that method and may be ethically criticized for culpably failing to comply with it. Isn't such an implied commitment after all "subjective" in character? Isn't it a "first-person" matter? It most certainly is, showing that the characteristics and purposes of the scientific method are irreducibly different from a personal commitment to take them up. In a word, the (first-person) commitment of a given scientist to "live by" the scientific method cannot itself be explained by use of the scientific method! If a scientist claims to be (objectively) constrained to do science in order to "serve truth," or some such, *that is an ethical, not a scientific, claim.* Such an argument is an example of simultaneous, though still distinct, first- and third-person deliberation.

evaluates itself – calls itself to account – thereby engaging simultaneously in first- and third-person deliberation, in Nagel's formulation.

ETHICAL OBJECTIVITY

Something along those lines is, of course, what I tried to establish in my discussion of the "logic of pain" in Chapter 1. The basic argument, now expanded on in the light of all I have been saying, is this: Given that human consciousness is inescapably organized and directed in accord with ethical values, including standards of good and bad reasons, and given what subjects know of having a conscious experience of severe pain, only certain "good" reasons could possibly "make sense" of that experience, could possibly make it "sufferable." Only if pain is inflicted with the purpose of avoiding or relieving greater pain, of assuring survival or preventing unwarranted pain, and only if it is inflicted with "due caution" (necessity, proportionality, and effectiveness) could acts causing severe pain be justified. In contrast, if pain is caused for certain "bad" reasons, the experience "makes no sense" and is distinctly "insufferable." If pain is inflicted for exclusively self-serving reasons (on the part of the inflictor), or for reasons that are manifestly unfounded, or if it is avoidably inflicted without "due caution," the act causing the experience cannot be justified. In ordinary speech, such action is typically censored as "senseless violence." Because it cannot be "understood," "comprehended," or "made sense of" *in moral terms*, it cannot, as a moral matter, be tolerated.

In short, if the cause of the experience of severe pain is under someone's control, the experience *simply must be stopped* unless a very, very good reason can be given why it should not be. If there is no good reason, and particularly if the reason given by the inflictor of pain is exclusively self-serving or manifestly unfounded, the act causing the pain has to be assessed as ethically "wrong" and the person responsible, as ethically "bad." The act *has* to be adjudged an "atrocity."[19]

As I suggested in Chapter 1, it is this sort of analysis that warrants the reaction of the drafters of the UDHR to what they regarded as "barbarous acts" committed at the hands of the Hitler government and the other fascist regimes of the period. Such acts consisted of the massive infliction of pain and

---

[19] Such action can, of course, be "made sense of" in scientific terms: The causal connections in the imagined case between the way pain is inflicted and the resulting consequences are readily understandable and fully predictable. What cannot be understood, and why it is that the action must be classified as grossly and culpably "senseless" or incomprehensible, is the knowing failure of the inflictor of pain to comply with the moral standard of good reasons demanded in such cases.

other strongly aversive experiences for unmistakably self-serving and knowingly unfounded reasons. Moreover, people who commit such acts, no matter who or where they are, are understood to be legitimately liable to enforceable restraint and punishment.

Assuming, therefore, that such acts are in an ethical sense objectively "bad" and "wrong" and that ethical objectivity is *sui generis* – namely, systematically distinguishable from scientific objectivity – the question arises as to how such acts are to be theorized comprehensively. How do they fit in with the self-contained patterns of practical justification tied to the "higher" ethical values that play a constitutive role in the organization and direction of subjective experience? One thing is clear: Prohibitions against violations of the logic of pain are only one small part of practical life. Ethical values apply to the whole of subjective experience, thereby signifying a comprehensive system of practical guidance. A critical task of ethical reasoning is to show how the different parts of the system relate to one another.

Still, logic-of-pain prohibitions occupy a special place in ethical reasoning. They constitute *fixed outer limits* or *outside constraints* on any comprehensive system and in some critical ways "set the tone" for ethical reasoning in general. Above all, they establish the distinctive objectivity of ethical reasoning: standards of good and bad reasons for action that are simultaneously first- and third-person. They apply to anyone, but concomitantly require the subjective commitment of every subject. They make up one part of what might be called 'a universal constitution of human consciousness,' according to which each "I" calls itself and everyone else to account.

THE PLACE OF "THE SACRED" AND THE LIMITS OF SCIENTIFIC OBJECTIVITY

A crucial aspect of ethical objectivity so understood is that the prohibitions in question amount to "sacred" prohibitions or to what are sometimes called "taboos." That means they are in the fullest sense "given"; as with divine standards in general, they are not to be challenged or tampered with, and they are absolutely "unrevisable" or *a priori*, in philosophical lingo.[20] Indeed,

---

[20] In *Mind and Cosmos*, Nagel argues for an "objective" or "mind-independent" theory of "ethical" or "value realism" (98ff.), a view for which I have strong sympathy. In passing, he even exemplifies his theory with reference to "avoid[ing] grievous harm to a sentient creature" (102) and coming to think of pleasure and pain not just as matters of subjective likes and dislikes but also as values related to what is "good" and "bad" understood transsubjectively, values that play a central role in practical justification (110ff.). However, I am unclear whether he would agree that some basic "absolute" rights against certain kinds of arbitrary infliction of pain exist.

such prohibitions may be said to take on a quality of "numinousness," to borrow a term from the history of religions. Such an interpretation helps clarify what is distinctly hinted at in the famous words of the Preamble to the UDHR: "disregard and contempt for human rights have resulted in barbaric acts which have outraged the conscience of [human]kind."

It is the purported sacredness of logic-of-pain prohibitions that suggests why the human mind is disposed to move from the first tier to the second tier in the terms of our framework. As implied by the natural rights tradition, it suggests why the human mind invariably directs its attention from natural to extranatural appeals.

Let me make the central idea here as sharp as possible. I have argued throughout that human beings are bound "naturally" to concede the ethical force of the logic of pain; that is, they may be held accountable on the basis, simply, of what we know "naturally" about pain and about the character of human consciousness. That point is crucial to our reappraisal of human rights language. However, the idea that certain important ethical directives – certain prohibitions – are sacred (objectively unrevisable) obviously begs further questions about the ultimate grounds of such beliefs, as well as how those beliefs cohere with beliefs about many other aspects of human experience.

This is where second-tier, extranatural comprehensive appeals, including religious appeals, come in. Comprehensive doctrines must do at least two things: They must give a metaphysical account of the sacred aspect of certain ethical directives,[21] and they must connect that account to a broadly inclusive

> In an earlier article, he rejects the claim that "rights are natural in Locke's religious sense or in anything near it," though he also says that the "recognition of rights is a moral and social practice, but it answers to a need deeply rooted in human nature." Also, having hinted that rights are best justified on rule-utilitarian grounds, he proceeds to state that "there are some deontological restrictions on how people may treat one another [against being murdered, tortured, or enslaved], that do not rest on a rule-consequentialist foundation," and may be defended on Kantian grounds. Nagel, "Rights" in *Equality and Partiality* (New York: Oxford University Press, 1991), 140, 141, and 145. On the matter of whether rights against the arbitrary infliction of pain are best justified on rule-utilitarian grounds, I agree with Judith Thomson: "I cannot bring myself to believe that what makes it wrong to torture babies to death for fun (for example) is that doing this 'would be disallowed by any system of rules for the general regulation of behavior which no one could reasonably reject a a basis for informed, unforced general agreement' (as argued by T. M Scanlon, "Contractualism and Utilitarianism," in Amartya Sen and Bernard Williams, eds., *Utilitarianism and Beyond* (Cambridge: Cambridge University Press, 1982). My impression is that explanation goes in the opposite direction – that it is the patent wrongfulness of the conduct that explains why there should be general agreement to disallow it." Thomson, *Realm of Rights*, 20, fn. 15 and 30, fn. 19.
> [21] I agree with Nagel in *Mind and Cosmos* that, although ethical realism does not require "a metaphysical postulation of extra entities and properties" (105), because, as I have argued, it is in certain respects self-evident, it does finally require a metaphysical defense against reductionist

(comprehensive) understanding of the practical and theoretical aspects of human experience. Such undertakings are, of course, what are protected under Article 18 of the UDHR (and its progeny).

In line with the proposals of many natural rights proponents, human rights language protects the development and defense of second-tier, extranatural comprehensive doctrines as a *subjective* affair – dependent, that is, on individual conscientious discretion and not as something that may be coercively imposed by the state[22] or anybody else. As such, comprehensive doctrines, religious or otherwise, are protected. Taking one stand or another as to the "ultimate grounds" of sacredness is finally a matter of subjective disposition.

I would only add that the sacredness of logic-of-pain prohibitions makes plausible the consideration of religious appeals. For one thing, prominent secular philosophers, such as Ronald Dworkin and Thomas Nagel, have of late taken a new interest in the "religious temperament," as Nagel calls it,[23] something that can be connected in both cases to a belief in ethical

---

accounts, including Darwinian explanations of a certain kind (115 and 111). Without such a defense, "the realist interpretation would be refuted" (111). If there are good reasons to believe in ethical realism (or ethical objectivity), as I have argued, then there are good reasons to resist any account that undermines it, as some forms of Darwinian explanation surely do. They do that by contending that there are no mind-independent normative or evaluative standards because belief in such standards is the accidental result of natural selection and might well be overturned in future by new survival needs. A fitting metaphysical defense would attempt to provide reasons for believing in mind-independent ethical standards that are ultimately "extranatural," precisely in not being reducible to naturalistic or materialistic phenomena.

Interestingly, Darwin himself leaves the door open to such a belief in a remarkable passage in *Origin of Species and Descent of Man* (New York: Modern Library). Having claimed that moral sentiments, including sympathy and altruism, are the product of natural selection by giving groups that develop them a competitive edge, he admits that such virtues are also maladaptive in important ways. Eliminating "the weak in body and mind" is good for survival, yet "we civilized men ... do our utmost to check the process of elimination; we build asylums for the imbecile, the maimed and the sick. ... There is reason to believe that vaccination has preserved thousands, who from weak constitution would formerly have succumbed to small-pox. Thus the weak members of civilized societies propagate their kind. No one who has attended to the breeding of domestic animals will doubt that this must be highly injurious to the race of man. ... The aid which we feel impelled to give to the helpless is mainly an incidental result of the instinct of sympathy, which was originally acquired as part of the social instincts, but subsequently rendered ... more tender and more widely diffused. *Nor could we check our sympathy, even at the urging of hard reason, without deterioration in the noblest part of our nature*" (501–502; italics added).

[22] See Chapter 1, fn. 54, on both the permissibility of and strict limits on "state religion."
[23] Thomas Nagel, *Secular Philosophy and Religious Temperament: Essays 2002–2008* (New York: Oxford University Press, 2010); Ronald Dworkin, *Religion without God* (Cambridge, MA: Harvard University Press, 2013). Jürgen Habermas, in *Between Religion and Naturalism: Philosophical Essays* (Cambridge: Polity Press, 2012), is another example, though, it would appear, that the position he defends is not that of an ethical realist or objectivist.

objectivity. Earlier, Ronald Dworkin had argued for a secular understanding of "the sacred" along the lines of the awe-filled respect that everyone, religious or not, ought to feel in the face of great art, architecture, or the "wonders of nature,"[24] and he had compellingly characterized the universal legal prohibition against torture as a proper taboo ("sacred prohibition").[25] However, in *Religion without God*, which he was barely able to complete before his untimely death, he went considerably further. He offered an "endorsement of the supernatural," "something beyond nature that cannot be grasped even by finally understanding the most fundamental of physical laws"[26] and that includes a belief in "the full, independent reality of value" or "the objective truth ... about value."[27] Still a nontheist, Dworkin, was nevertheless becoming more and more sensitive to the dimension of the sacred in aesthetic and ethical experience.

For it is religious appeals, presupposing as they do beliefs in a sacred authority taken in one way or another to be "extranatural," that are particularly apposite. That is because, by specializing in the sacred, religious appeals provide a consistently *sui generis* account of ethical authority, thereby expressing the self-contained character of human consciousness. If, *ex hypothesi*, the ethical grounds of consciousness cannot be reduced to (explained by) "scientifically objective" causal sequences in the material world (however "interconnected" with them they may be), then it will be necessary to give an account that is systematically distinct from such causal explanations. This distinctive account will have to attend consistently to the grounds and conditions of "subjective agency," of "self-causation," including the features of "self-involving commitment" and variations in "the strength and weakness of the will," that go together to make up our understanding of consciousness. These issues are the standard stuff of religious reflection.[28]

---

[24] Based on a discussion of Dworkin's argument in Michael J. Perry, *The Idea of Human Rights: Four Inquiries* (New York: Oxford University Press, 1991), 25ff.
[25] Ronald Dworkin, "Report from Hell," *New York Review of Books* (July 17, 1986), 16.
[26] Dworkin, *Religion without God*, 6.
[27] Ibid., 10.
[28] Interestingly, though both are atheists, McGinn (*Mysterious Flame*, 77–95) and Nagel (*Mind and Cosmos*, e.g., 21–26, 94–95) give serious and respectful attention to religion. This is surely not accidental. Both reject Darwinian and other reductionist accounts of the occurrence of consciousness and therefore are bound to consider alternative explanations, which include religious ones. McGinn even considers the plausibility of an argument for the existence of God – the Argument from Sentience. "Sentience cannot be explained by means of Darwinian principles plus physics, because it needs to be possible to make mind from matter if natural selection is to explain how sentience arises by means of natural selection operating on material things. In other words, a Darwinian explanation of consciousness works only if materialism about consciousness is true. But we have already seen that it is not true." Therefore, "the cause

The implication, we must remind ourselves, is that in these matters explanations associated with "scientific objectivity" are incomplete. However pertinent they may be, sociobiology, neurophysiology, or evolutionary psychology can never give a complete account because ontologically and epistemologically their methods are capable of understanding only "one aspect" of human knowledge. We appear to be stuck with a world that as Nagel and Kant agree must ever be viewed, in Kant's words, from "two standpoints."[29]

To be clear, there is a role for scientific reasoning in these affairs, but it is a secondary or supportive role. As we saw, the neural effects of certain stimuli on the human (or animal) body have causally predictable results on subjective experience. Drilling a tooth without anesthesia produces a predictable sensation of pain. But, as we also saw, consciousness, depending on how it is subjectively organized and directed, has the final say as to the way that sensation and the act causing it shall be interpreted and responded to. There remains an ineliminable subjectivity to the response that cannot be explained by the scientific method. Hence, the incompleteness of the scientific approach to the topic and the need for an account that "does justice" to the character of conscious experience.

---

of sentience must be another sentience." McGinn finally rejects such an argument, but it "cannot," he says, "be dismissed as mere confusion" (82–84).

Nagel devotes less sustained attention to the subject, and although he rejects the arguments of supporters of intelligent design, he credits them with raising some important questions (10–12), as he does in the case of the religious philosopher, Alvin Plantinga (27, 94n). Nagel himself provides an arresting characterization of the religious temperament: "It is the idea that there is some kind of all-encompassing mind or spiritual principle in addition to the minds of individual human beings and other creatures – and that this mind or spirit is the foundation of the existence of the universe, of the natural order, of value, and of our existence, nature, and purpose. The aspect of religious belief I am talking about is belief in such a conception of the universe, and the incorporation of that belief into one's conception of oneself and one's life" (4–5).

See Chapter 7 in this volume for an account of my own attempt to defend a set of religious beliefs.

[29] Even if it is possible to demonstrate scientifically that evolution has shaped the "moral sense" of human beings in particular ways (e.g., Marc Houser in *Moral Minds: How Nature Designed Our Universal Sense of Right and Wrong* (New York: Ecco, 2006)), it is still an open question how that knowledge shall be interpreted and applied subjectively. That is the inescapable relevance of the "naturalistic fallacy" to all attempts to explain ethical thought and practice exclusively from an "objectively scientific" perspective. Attempts to derive an "ought" from an "is" exemplify that fallacy. Although Hauser takes up this issue at the beginning of his book, he does not appear to understand the force of the challenge it represents to his own work. Apart from these philosophical issues, the empirical validity of the claims of evolutionary psychologists in regard to ethics has been sharply challenged and remains highly controversial. See Hilary Rose and Steven Rose, eds., *Alas, Poor Darwin: Arguments against Evolutionary Psychology* (London: Jonathan Cape, 2000). See also, Hilary and Steven Rose, "The Changing Face of Human Nature," *Daedalus* (Summer, 2009).

THE TWO TIERS AND THE ROLE OF FORCE

I am now in a position to explain what I spoke of earlier as a "critical feature" of the distinction between the two tiers, namely, that first-tier standards are coercively enforceable and second-tier standards are not. As I pointed out, this aspect of the distinction is a consistent and central theme in natural rights thinking, as well as in traditional reflection on the conscience, as it is, in human rights language. The idea is that there is something about extranatural appeals and, similarly, something about appeals to conscience that, up to a point, entails exemption from direct forcible regulation.

That "something" is related to our observations about the mind-body relationship – a relationship in which human consciousness is at once "critically interrelated" with the causal workings of the physical world and "irreducibly distinct" from them. I concluded that viewed from "one aspect," an individual human being, as owner of a body, is subject to certain invariable causal laws that decisively affect the quality of consciousness. My example was the predictable and severely unappealing sensation of excruciating pain induced by drilling a tooth without anesthesia.

However, viewed from a "second aspect," the inescapable neural effects of the drilling do not have the last word. They must still be processed and interpreted in regard to the emotions, interests, desires, and beliefs as subjectively organized and directed. As such, they must still be evaluated as justified (or not) in reference to a set of good and bad reasons consistent with the fundamental values of the subject. Is the act generating those effects "right" or "wrong"? Is the agent responsible for the act "good" or "bad"? It is these judgments, inextricably part of subjective consciousness, that mark the "irreducible distinctiveness" of the subject's experience.

Because the process of reason-giving, of justification, is *sui generis*, to try to "cause" a change in someone's beliefs by inflicting pain is to misunderstand the relationship between causes and reasons. The whole point is that beliefs depend on subjective or first-person reasons, and such reasons are, in the process of deliberation, independent of and prior to causes. As philosophers say, reasons are supervenient on causes, which is another way of saying that reasons trump causes.

Given that force (in a military or legal sense) involves *causing* pain (among other unwanted causal effects), it is now clear why using force to try to "compel belief" is inappropriate. Ethical, religious, and other beliefs, according to which human consciousness is organized and directed, operate in line with patterns and standards that are completely unlike the causal laws (including neural effects on the human body) that characterize the physical or natural world. Causes "wait on" reasons, not the other way around. Thus, the irreducible distinction drawn in the natural rights tradition between the "law of the spirit" and the "law of the sword" makes eminent sense.

The point to be remembered is that attempts to compel belief amount to violations because they manifest a profound mistake. The age-old canard, "might makes right," illustrates the mistake. Any use of force, causing pain or other unfavorable effects, necessarily begs justification. *Authoritative* reasons are required, and they must do more than state a causal proposition that failure to comply with a demand will be met with unwanted consequences. *Why* ought the thing demanded be done? *By what right* may the threat enforcing it be issued? An old Western movie captures the point eloquently. In one scene a cattle rancher insists that a homesteader vacate his homestead, and the homesteader asks for a reason. The cattle rancher, a sinister smile on his face, draws his pistol and utters what both parties understand to be a cruel play on words: "I've got six good reasons right here." Threats of that kind amount to a cruel joke because they have nothing whatsoever to do with good (or justifying) reasons and simply beg the original question all over again.

To be sure, threats do have a significant indirect impact on a subject's beliefs; otherwise, the threat would be pointless. They undoubtedly influence the degree to which the person threatened will act as belief dictates. Practical beliefs naturally entail actions, and coercively impeding or frustrating actions consistent with belief frequently does *curtail belief*, as we might put it. People are regularly prevented from acting as they think they should by an intervening use or threat of force.

At the same time, curtailing belief in that way exacts a high cost; it frequently induces severe distress, which regularly leads, as natural rights proponents such as Williams, Locke, Jefferson, and Madison keep reiterating, to resentment, evasion, hypocrisy, and, in extreme cases, to sedition and rebellion.[30] The explanation, on our account, is that efforts to compel belief by forcibly

---

[30] It is, of course, possible that coercion might dispose someone to consider a belief favorably and, as an outcome, to decide eventually to embrace the belief. Two points in response: (1) Whether that is the case or not is an empirical question, because it is obvious from the history of dissent and deviance in various religious and cultural traditions that coerced belief is clearly not a guarantee of adherence. (2) Giving coercion as a "reason" for embracing a belief might be an explanation, but never a justification. People often say, for example, that they hold certain moral beliefs because "they were brought up that way." By that they appear to mean they acquiesced to parental instruction that was presumably "imposed" on them by various forms of "conditioning," possibly including coercion. In growing up, did they, however, acquiesce to *everything* their parents told them? Did they not rather pick and choose, and question at least some of the things their parents believed, including moral and religious beliefs? If so, they thereby presupposed certain "reasons of their own" for justifying the selection, reasons that are necessarily separate from "having been brought up that way." The key question is, what *those reasons* are.

constraining or threatening to constrain action consistent with belief disregards the essential characteristics of human consciousness: Human beings are self-causing or self-determining agents – *actors* – whose emotions, interests, desires, and beliefs are organized and directed in accord with standards of good and bad reasons resting on subjective, first-person commitment. To ignore these characteristics by trying to *cause* belief, rather than to convince by giving reasons, inverts the proper normative relation between reasons and causes. As with the example of the cattle rancher, it is the height of arbitrariness.

The obvious implication favors a strong presumption against using force or threatening it where belief is concerned, including coercively restraining actions consistent with belief. This conclusion explains why second-tier or extranatural appeals of the sort connected with comprehensive doctrines and the actions that follow from them are specially protected as they are in much of the natural rights tradition and in the human rights instruments.

But, of course, that is not the whole story. There are still the first-tier standards that *do* permit coercive restraint of action and thus curtailment of belief under certain circumstances. Those circumstances concern uses or threats of force undertaken for "bad reasons," beginning with purely self-serving or manifestly unfounded "reasons." Hitler's fascist policies were described as "barbaric acts which have outraged the conscience of mankind" because they systematically disregarded the elements of what it takes to justify (give good reasons for) a use or threat of force: a disciplined consideration of the fundamental moral interests – the survival and welfare, understood in secular terms – of those affected. As we have seen, the human rights system was erected precisely to provide equal protection of the secularly defined moral interests of all human beings, by the use, where required and duly measured, of counterforce.

Consequently, fascist beliefs, and all similar beliefs, might legitimately be curtailed insofar as they prompt or (in human rights language) "incite to" action that violates first-tier standards. This understanding is completely consistent with the underlying commitment to protect the proper normative relation between (good) reasons and causes.

To elaborate, first-tier standards, designed to protect equally the secularly defined moral interests of all human beings, are summarized as a set of critical "public goods": order, safety, health, morals, and the fundamental rights and freedoms of everyone.[31] It is assumed that all human beings share a common interest in the protection of these public goods and that the state, understood as a body of officials possessing an effective monopoly of the legitimate use of force

---

[31] I understand the set of economic, social, and cultural goods enumerated in the ICESCR and other human rights instruments to be an elaboration of the "public goods" for which the state is responsible.

over the inhabitants of a given territory, is strictly confined to the regulation and administration of the public goods. In short, the state's jurisdiction is restricted to the implementation of first-tier standards. Comprehensive beliefs and accompanying actions that do not conflict with first-tier standards are exempt from state jurisdiction. As I suggested in Chapters 3 and 4, first-tier standards define the sphere of "public reason" according to which the human rights system is properly administered. In Chapter 4 I examined how that works in practice.

THE SIGNIFICANCE OF CONSCIENCE

In 1980, Timothy Potts pointed out in a book titled *Conscience in Medieval Philosophy*[32] that "conscience has been much neglected by philosophers." "Indeed," he continued,

> there has been a tendency of late towards a gap between the philosophy of mind and ethics, even to the extent that one group of philosophers has concentrated upon philosophical logic and the philosophy of mind, while a different group has concentrated upon ethics and political and social philosophy. Conscience lies within this gap; it is not obvious, off-hand, whether it is a topic in the philosophy of mind or an ethical topic, so reflection upon it may serve ... to bring together again what has been sundered.[33]

Things have not greatly changed since then.[34] Although Thomas Nagel, for example, creatively combines work on the philosophy of mind and ethics, he does not couch his discussion in terms of conscience.

The neglect of the idea is unfortunate, because the deep interconnection between ethics and the study of human consciousness, particularly in Nagel's work, cries out for a consideration of conscience. The etymological root of the idea, the Greek term, *syneidesis* (Latin: *conscientia*), which appears in the New Testament, contains a range of meanings. Interestingly, one of them, where the prefix, *syn-* or *con-* (= "with") does not modify the attached noun (*eidesis* = "knowledge"), is simply "consciousness,"[35] or "subjective knowledge." However, where the prefix does modify the attached noun, the word means "knowledge with," which, in turn, can be understood in two different ways: "knowing something in company with others" and "knowing something with oneself." This second meaning has specific reference to an individual's

---

[32] (Cambridge: Cambridge University Press, 1980).
[33] Ibid., 1.
[34] There is only one incidental reference to "conscience" in Nagel's *Other Minds*, and *not one* reference to the idea in either Searle's *Rediscovery of the Mind* or McGinn's *Mysterious Flame*.
[35] Potts, *Conscience in Medieval Philosophy*, 2.

being a "witness" or a "judge" for or against oneself in regard to "actions or omissions as right or wrong in the circumstances," evaluations that are determined "by measuring [the actions or omissions] against [the individual's] standards of behavior."[36]

Given this array of meanings, it seems reasonable to conclude that the idea of conscience has evolved to mean a special form of subjective consciousness focusing particularly on moral evaluation in respect either to a subject's own behavior or to the behavior of others. As such, the idea epitomizes perfectly my account of the deep interrelations of human consciousness and ethics.

Four things about the connection between the idea of conscience and our account bear special emphasis:

1. *Conscience as the focus of first- and third-person deliberation.* The notion that conscience is a context or setting for self-critical deliberation and assessment is fundamental to the traditional understanding of the term. Going back to the New Testament, conscience is conceived of as an "internal forum" or "tribunal," in which the subject considers thoughts that "bear witness," "now accusing, now even defending" the subject in reference to whether actions or omissions, performed or contemplated, do or do not comply with "the requirements of the law written on [the] heart."[37] On this conception, the "first person" in question commits to a "third-person" perspective in accord with which, and after due process has taken place, a judgment concerning the guilt or innocence of the subject is rendered by the subject itself.

2. *Conscience as moral knowledge "with others."* The "third-person perspective," assumed in what has just been described, is taken to apply to others and not just to the subject. Conscience is traditionally linked to the idea of "natural law" as an expression of "ethical objectivity," a version of which I have advocated. Thus, there are certain common virtues such as nonmaleficence, veracity, prudence, justice, and benevolence that are accessible to and incumbent on all human beings regardless of religious, cultural, or ethnic identity. This understanding helps make sense of the phrase, "conscience of mankind," which appears in the Preamble to the UDHR, and to which I have consistently called attention throughout these pages. It also helps make sense of the statement in Article 1 of the UDHR: "All human beings are . . . endowed with reason and conscience and should act toward one another in a spirit of brotherhood."

3. *Conscience as the protected preserve of every subject.* The notion of the "sovereignty of conscience," always implicit and often explicit in

[36] Ibid., 3–4.
[37] Romans 2:14–15.

traditional reflection on the idea, is connected to the understanding of conscience as the locus of commitment to and deliberation about a set of authoritative values regarding the organization and direction of the emotions, interests, desires, and beliefs of a subject. The understanding is that each individual is ultimately responsible for determining and applying those values. Accordingly, the *forum internum* of every person is, up to a point, sacrosanct from the perspective of the *forum externum*, the civil authority. All that I wrote about force and justification in the last section applies here as well. The idea that "reasons trump causes" is at the heart of the relations between the conscience and the state.

At the same time, there are the very same limits or constraints on conscience and actions consistent with it as I elaborated on in the last section. If the conscience of a given individual dictates actions that violate the sovereignty of another's conscience – arbitrarily forcing a person to act against conscience or for reasons otherwise adjudged to conflict with the "public goods" enumerated in the last section – the state has the right to restrict such actions and thereby curtail the associated beliefs.

Consistent with this conclusion, traditional reflection on the conscience came to incorporate the familiar (two-tier) distinction between natural and extranatural appeals, generally holding that the former may be coercively regulated and the latter not. In particular, extranatural appeals were believed to be protected by the notion of "erroneous conscience," which held that in matters of belief people "had a right to their error," unless, of course, their beliefs led to actions that violated basic natural rights. This line of thinking provided an important foundation for the emergence of a belief in freedom of conscience.

4. *Conscience as the locus for reflection about sacred authority.* In traditional cogitation, it is typically assumed that the grounds of conscience – the ultimate authoritative beliefs – are to be regarded as in some sense "sacred" – that is, "objective," "given," "not to be tampered with," "unrevisable," and so on. For this reason, the idea of conscience is traditionally associated with religious belief, and accordingly, it features importantly in medieval and post medieval theological discussions, for example, in the Reformed Protestant tradition. To be sure, these discussions were deeply ambivalent over the range of permissible freedom, but in keeping with the underlying idea of subjective agency emphasized earlier, the right to freedom of conscience was gradually extended to a wide variety of beliefs, religious and nonreligious, while still resting on the conviction that conscience is in some way inseparable from a notion of sacredness.

That conviction has been challenged and rejected on the supposition that the whole idea of sacredness promotes religious and ethical absolutism, something that underlies the evils of authoritarianism. However, it is interesting how difficult it is to discuss the grounds of conscience without referring – albeit negatively – to religious belief. The labels, "*a*-theist," "*a*-gnostic," "*non*-believer," "nihilist," and now "nones" ("not-religious" in recent social science literature[38]) are all negative derivatives, as we might call them. We cannot make sense of the terms without recalling what they *oppose*. The implication is that these terms are all conceived of in reaction to religiously colored notions of sacredness central to the idea of conscience. Therefore, they may fairly be described as implying *reflections on sacredness*, however negative their conclusions.

But this is more than a logical point. When it comes to protecting the right to freedom of conscience of the atheist, agnostic, nonbeliever, nihilist, or one of the "nones," as is resolutely supported by many natural rights proponents and by human rights language, such people must do more than deny the concept of sacredness. To be eligible for this protection, it will be necessary for them to identify the "functional equivalent" of a sacred ground in their comprehensive beliefs comparable to the notions of religious believers. Without providing in some way for the "sacrosanctity" of the *forum internum*, it is hard to understand, from their point of view, on what basis the doctrine of the freedom of conscience might cover them.

Moreover, as a practical matter, it seems clear that such people must still provide, on their terms, a satisfactory account of what are hard to deny as "sacred prohibitions" against practices such as recreational torture and genocide. Such prohibitions are reasonably thought of as "absolute" offenses against the "conscience of mankind" and will need to be theorized accordingly.

A CONCLUDING NOTE ON MAX WEBER

Though Weber's name has been mentioned in passing in several chapters in this book, I have not until now referred to him in this Afterword. For those familiar with Weber, the omission will seem peculiar because so much of what

---

[38] Robert D. Putnam and David E. Campbell describe the growing number of people in American society who reject all religious identification as "nones," another "negative derivative" to be added to our list. *American Grace: How Religion Divides and Unites Us* (New York: Simon & Schuster, 2010), 120ff.

I have been arguing is reminiscent of Weber's philosophy of social science. That is especially true of his emphasis on "value-freedom" (*Wertfreiheit*), which conveys a sharp separation between ethics and science – something I have defended – and on "value-relevance" (*Wertbeziehung*), which conveys, in reverse, an interdependence between ethics and science – something I have also defended.[39]

Despite the unquestionable pertinence of Weber's approach to my argument (as well as to his long-standing, general influence on my thinking), I have not mentioned him for two reasons. I did not want to encumber or overcomplicate things by making my presentation, even in part, a commentary on Weber's work. I wanted to let my position stand or fall simply on the strength (or not) of the evidence and the argument, as presented, I hope, freshly and with some originality. The second reason is related. I deviate from Weber in one important respect, and it would have been a great distraction to go into that as I was making my case.

The point of difference has to do with ethical objectivity. In my view, Weber was unclear about the subject; he forswore any allegiance to ethical relativism and sometimes even avowed (though never defended) adherence to a belief in natural rights.[40] Still, if he was an ethical objectivist, it was a curious form of objectivism. Weber occasionally affirmed, quite strenuously, a morally pluralistic universe in the face of which he seemed to call for a kind of ethical decisionism. One heroically affirms an ethical stance for which it is impossible to give objective reasons of any kind.[41] It should be clear that that is not the position defended in this book.

Still, there are several ways I am deeply indebted to Weber in this Afterword, as well as in several of the chapters and the Appendix of this book. Apart

---

[39] See Appendix, "Ethics and Scholarship," for an attempt to defend, enlarge on, and apply, a version of Weber's theory of the relation of values and science as developed in Max Weber, *Methodology of the Social Sciences*, Edward Shils and Henry A. Finch, eds. and translators (New York: Free Press, 1949).

[40] "Afterall, it is a gross self-deception to believe that without the achievements of the Rights of Man any one of us, including the most conservative, can go on living his life." From Max Weber, "Parliament and Government in a Reconstructed Germany" (1917) in *Economy and Society: An Outline of Interpretive Sociology* (New York: Bedminster Press, 1968), 3 vols., vol. 3, 1403.

[41] According to Weber's wife, Marianne Weber, in *Max Weber: A Biography* (New Brunswick: Transaction Publishers, 1995), his version of "value pluralism" was nevertheless not relativistic. For him, "there can be different and equally justified opinions about the nature of moral obligations, but for him it was an indubitable inner certainty that only the choice and recognition of ideals, tasks, and duties gave meaning and dignity to human existence." Human beings cannot derive meaning and value from empirical study but he believed "we must be able to create this meaning for ourselves" (325).

from meta-ethical questions, I share much of his commitment to a "dual aspect" theory of human knowledge, namely, the simultaneous difference and interconnection of subjective and scientific knowledge. In the last analysis, I have simply tried to shore up and improve on that theory in the light of recent developments in the philosophy of mind. In many other connections, as in this matter, Weber turns out again and again to be right.

Because of his support for a dual-aspect theory of the sort I have defended, Weber's empirical work, premised on that theory, was consistently fruitful, if not always accurate in detail. The fruitfulness is particularly true in regard to appreciating and understanding the role of religious and ethical values in social life. To grasp, as he did so powerfully, that reasons and causes in human experience are at once "irreducibly distinct" and "critically interrelated" was in its own way a kind of "Copernican revolution" in the social sciences, a revolution that is still very much at work. In this volume, especially Chapter 8, "Religion, Peace, and the Origins of Nationalism" and Chapter 9, "Roger Williams and the Puritan Background of the Establishment Clause" – which accord independent importance to religious influences – are inconceivable without the influence of Max Weber.

APPENDIX

Ethics and Scholarship

Within the precincts of Harvard University, it is still possible to hear an ardent defense of the venerable distinction between "facts" and "values" or, as it is sometimes put, between "description" and "evaluation." Arguments over this distinction go to the heart of the relation of ethics to scholarship, as was vividly illustrated recently by a controversy in this university concerning a doctoral dissertation proposal in "ethnonational studies." Among other things, the proposal, which envisioned an examination and critique of ideas of citizenship as they bear on a contemporary case of ethnonational conflict, was criticized for being more a piece of advocacy, more the subject for an op-ed article, than serious scholarship. The possible consequences were portentous. If the case against the proposal had stood, the candidate would, in effect, *have had no right as a scholar* to pursue such a line of inquiry in the way proposed.

As the controversy unfolded, it became evident that on all sides opinions were not thoroughly thought out. If, as suspected, confusion and uncertainty on this issue are widespread, a general effort at clarification may be of use, especially if the stakes, personal and professional, are as high as they appear to be. Seen in that way, the controversy perhaps serves a good purpose. It prompts members of the university community to confront a problem with broad and profound importance both inside the academy and elsewhere.

There are two fundamental points of concern. The first and most general has to do with the present status of the conventional and much-disputed distinction between "descriptive" and "normative" statements, sometimes referred to as the "fact/value dichotomy," classically associated by Max Weber with the principle of *Wertfreiheit* ("value neutrality"),[1] or as the well-known

---

[1] "The Meaning of 'Ethical Neutrality' [*Wertfreiheit*] in Sociology and Economics," in Max Weber, *The Methodology of the Social Sciences*, Edward A. Shils and Henry A. Finch, eds. (Glenco, Ill.: Free Press, 1949), 1–47.

Humean distinction between "is" and "ought" statements.[2] Defenders of the "dichotomy" who are of interest to us believe that works of scholarship should be purely "descriptive" in character, and not "normative" or "advocative."[3]

The second concern has to do with the character and objectives of ethnonational studies, that rapidly growing area of investigation devoted to understanding the sources and prospects of conflicts prominently involving issues of ethnic and national identity. Rather than confine our attention solely to the more abstract theoretical questions raised by our first concern, it will also be helpful to examine the actual practice of scholars engaged in a specific area of study to see how the more theoretical conclusions work out on the ground. This example is selected both because of its connection to the particular case before us and because, as we shall see, it represents an interesting test of the proposition that scholarship should be "purely descriptive" and "in no way normative." Beyond that, what is learned from one specific area of study will, it is hoped, be applicable elsewhere.

THE STATUS OF THE FACT/VALUE DICHOTOMY

The initial, more general concern, about the acceptability of the "descriptive/normative" distinction has been dealt with thoughtfully by Hilary Putnam in his 2002 book, *The Collapse of the Fact/Value Dichotomy and Other Essays*.[4] Putnam makes four important points.

First, the very distinction between descriptive and normative statements, taken to be synonymous with the fact/value dichotomy, is misleading in a quite rudimentary way. The act of describing or "stating facts" is itself already a normative activity. Necessarily presupposed in the endeavor are norms (or canons) of evidential verifiability and logic (and sometimes mathematics). Putnam calls these "epistemic values," which are necessarily assumed in descriptive judgments of "proof," "coherence," "plausibility," and "reasonableness," or, in C.S. Peirce's words, of "what ought to be" in regard to reasoning.[5] Accordingly, we conventionally distinguish between "good and bad description" or "good and bad fact-stating," sometimes loosely identified as "good and

---

[2] David Hume, *A Treatise of Human Nature*, L. A. Selby-Bigge, ed. (Oxford: Clarendon Press), 469–470.
[3] For purposes of this discussion, it shall be assumed that "advocacy" constitutes a strong, specially focused kind of "normative" utterance – "urging public support for a particular policy or cause," from the Latin, "to call to one's side," presumably in a conflict or contest (*Concise Oxford English Dictionary*).
[4] (Cambridge: Harvard University Press, 2002).
[5] Ibid., 31.

bad science." So it must be that any valid distinction we wish to draw is in reality between *different kinds* of norms (or values or oughts), and *not* between norms (or values or oughts) and something else. (We already witness some erosion of the famous dichotomy.)

Second, Putnam correctly emphasizes that there are, in fact, "differences between epistemic and ethical values."[6] It does make sense to speak of "description" and "evaluation," but only so long as we know what we are doing and are sufficiently sensitive to conceptual complications and to the complex ways the two systems of value interact.

One problem with the distinction between epistemic and ethical values is what to call the broad class of "personal" norms or values that includes ethical commitments along with religious, aesthetic, and other nonepistemic commitments – designations that notoriously beg their own special problems of definition. This is a difficult matter for which I have no ready solution. We may simply assume, with Putnam, that we do indeed presuppose such a distinct class and, for purposes of our discussion, continue to refer to it under the rubric of ethical norms or values.

Putnam is not entirely clear as to what the basic distinction between epistemic and ethical values is. As a pragmatist, he resists the idea that there is any "objective" (metaphysical) distinction and assumes instead some kind of "working distinction." I am not so sure about that, but we need not settle this complicated matter here. For our purposes, *that we do assume such a distinction is the important point.* It seems true that in some significant way ethical (and other "personal" religious or aesthetic) claims involve beliefs and commitments that are consistently distinguishable from "fact-stating," "descriptive" claims (e.g., the difference between statements such as "the cat is on the mat" and "it is right and good that the cat is on the mat").

At the same time, if the distinction between two sorts of value is important, it is equally important that they interact and overlap in various ways. One way pertains to ethically value-laden terms, such as "cruelty," which represent an admixture of epistemic and ethical values. Certain factually verifiable features (deliberate infliction/ of /severe suffering/ an /innocent party/) are singled out as being ethically wrong. The statement, "slapping the infant because it cries is cruel," entails both proving that the defining features are in fact present and asserting the ethical wrongness of the combination of features. Another way that they interact is by applying certain epistemic values (say, the rules of logic and a certain use of the rules of evidence) "constructively" to ethical (or religious or aesthetic) subject matter, thereby arguing that ethics (or religion,

[6] Ibid.

etc.) is a "form of knowledge," subject in certain ways to epistemic values. A third way is studying ethical (or religious or aesthetic) values descriptively (according to the epistemic rules of evidence, coherence, etc.) while reserving ethical judgment as to the worth of the values studied. However, even there, such studies are by no means ethically irrelevant, because they are typically defended as being "fairer," "more balanced," "more honest," or as having some other virtue in greater measure than studies with an apologetic slant.

Third, Putnam points out some deeper complexities in the connections between description and evaluation that very much complicate the picture. On the one hand, he agrees with Weber (and certain unorthodox economists such as Amartya Sen) that "the decision as to what question the social scientist investigates *is and has to be one that involves ethical values*."[7] As a matter of fact, Putnam could have made more of this point by emphasizing its relation to a broader theme of great importance to Weber, namely that a commitment to the scientific method (epistemic values) itself rests on a prior ethical decision. "Whether," as Weber says, "science is a worthwhile 'vocation' for somebody, and whether science itself [is] an objectively valuable 'vocation' are [matters of personal value judgment]."[8] On the other hand, Putnam states, again in agreement with Weber, that "once the choice is made, ascertaining the answer to the scientist's question *is not to be dictated by the scientist's [ethical] value system*," but rather by proceeding according to the full array of epistemic standards.[9]

In the light of these two points, then, ethical values are both indispensable to the scientific enterprise and distinguishable from it. Acknowledging *both* the relevance of the two sets of value to each other *and* the distinction between them *would seem to be part of the scientist's ethical commitment*. That is, having chosen (on ethical grounds) what it is "right and good" to study, it is also assumed to be "right and good" (in an ethical sense) to embrace and live up to epistemic values in investigating the question selected for study.

---

[7] Ibid., 63; emphasis and tense altered. Weber famously characterized the unavoidable role that a scientist's personal values play in "determin[ing] the selection and formulation of the objective of empirical investigation" (my translation) as "value-relevance" (*Wertbeziehung*). "The Meaning of 'Ethical Neutrality,'" 21–22.

[8] Max Weber, "Science as a Vocation," in *From Max Weber: Essays in Sociology* (New York: Oxford University Press, 1958), 152.

[9] Putnam, *The Collapse of the Fact/Value Dichotomy*, 63 (emphasis and tense altered). In Weber's words, "one can only demand of the teacher that he have the intellectual integrity to see that it is one thing to state facts, to determine mathematical or logical relations or the internal structure of cultural values, while it is another thing to answer questions of the value of culture and its individual contents and the question on how one should act in the cultural community and in political associations." Weber, "Science as a Vocation," 146.

Fourth, Putnam takes things one step further by calling attention to a *second point* at which ethical and epistemic values overlap. He appreciatively invokes Sen (specifically, Sen's value-laden "capabilities approach" to the study of economics) against Weber by pointing out Weber's failure to acknowledge that "the terms one uses even in *description* in history and sociology and other social sciences are invariably ethically colored; this is nowhere more true than in the case of the terms Weber used to describe his 'ideal types.'"[10] Though there is some ambiguity, and perhaps confusion, in Weber's writings on this point,[11] Weber does say that an ideal type in his sense of the term "has no connection at all with value-judgments."[12] As Putnam implies, this conviction seems to blind him to the fact that, for example, his famous ideal-typical category, "charisma," is "ethically colored" in a very important way. That charisma is described by him as essentially counterrational and anarchic in character is undoubtedly connected to Weber's own particular ethical theory of the nature of "ultimate values," which for him are similarly counterrational and anarchic, or radically nonepistemic in character.[13]

These two points – the "ultimate ethical orientation" of science and the "ethical coloring" of the categories of scientific analysis – lead Putnam to speak convincingly of the "interdependence" or the "entanglement" of "valuation" and "description."[14]

FACTS, VALUES, AND ETHNONATIONAL STUDIES

As I mentioned, the growing body of ethnonational literature is essentially aimed at examining the causes and prospects of conflicts prominently involving issues of ethnic and national identity. Examples are general books on

---

[10] Putnam, *Collapse of the Fact/Value Dichotomy*, 63; author's emphasis.
[11] In discussing the study of culture, which, he believes, is the central focus of social science, Weber asserts that the "concept of culture is a value-concept" and that "empirical reality becomes 'culture' to us because and insofar as we relate it to value ideas." "It includes those segments and only those segments of reality that have become significant to us because of this value-relevance." Weber, "'Objectivity' in Social Science and Social Policy," *Methodology of the Social Sciences*, 76. This line of thinking suggests that the basic orientation of the scientific study of culture, including, one would have thought, the very categories of analysis, are predetermined, so to speak, by their "value-relevance." If this interpretation is right, then at least part of Weber's thinking is in line with Putnam's position, and it suggests that he should not have been surprised if his ideal types could be shown to be ethically colored.
[12] Ibid., 98.
[13] See, for example, "Meaning of 'Ethical Neutrality,'" 18–19: "There is no rational or empirical scientific procedure of any kind whatsoever that can provide us with a decision" regarding the validity of ultimate meaning and values.
[14] Putnam, *Collapse of the Fact/Value Dichotomy*, 62–63.

the subject such as *Faith in Nation: Exclusionary Origins of Nationalism* by Anthony Marx,[15] *Peoples versus States: Minorities at Risk in the New Century, Ethnic Conflict and World Politics* by Ted Robert Gurr and associates,[16] *From Voting to Violence: Democratization and Nationalist Conflict* by Jack Snyder,[17] and *Electing to Fight: Why Democracies Go to War* by Edward D. Mansfield and Jack Snyder.[18] There are books on South Asia such as *Sri Lanka: Ethnic Fratricide and the Dismantling of Democracy, Buddhism Betrayed? Religion, Politics, and Violence in Sri Lanka,* and *Leveling Crowds: Ethnonationalist Conflicts and Collective Violence in South Asia,* all by Stanley Tambiah;[19] *The Work of Kings: New Buddhism in Sri Lanka* by H. L. Seneviratne;[20] *Managing Ethnic Tensions in Multiethnic Societies, Sri Lanka, 1880–1985* by K. M. de Silva;[21] and *Religious Nationalism: Hindus and Muslims in India* by Peter van der Veer.[22] Several books describe the Former Yugoslavia such as *The Bridge Betrayed: Religion and Genocide in Bosnia* by Michael Sells[23] and *Yugoslav Inferno: Ethnoreligious Warfare in the Balkans* by Paul Mojzes,[24] or are on Sudan such as *War of Visions, Conflict of Identities in the Sudan* by Francis Deng,[25] or are on the United States, such as *America Right or Wrong: An Anatomy of American Nationalism* by Anatol Lieven.[26]

Putnam's two critical points just elaborated – the ultimate ethical orientation of science and the ethical coloring of the categories of scientific analysis – are profoundly relevant to ethnonational studies.

All of the books cited (and many more that could be cited) unequivocally illustrate Putnam's first point. It is safe to say that all of the authors mentioned are, in their various ways, "ethically disturbed" by the existence of serious ethnonational tension and violence in the cases they take up. They are interested not only in studying the causes and character of ethnic tension and violence but also in indicating or implying ways to reduce them.

H. L. Seneviratne's extraordinary book on Sinhala Buddhist monks in modern Sri Lanka is an excellent example. "The rise of new nation-states upon the

---

[15] (New York: Oxford University Press, 2004).
[16] (Washington, DC: United States Institute of Peace Press, 2000); (Boulder: Westview Press, 2004).
[17] (New York: W.W. Norton, 2000).
[18] (Cambridge, MA: MIT Press, 2005).
[19] (Chicago: University of Chicago Press, 1986); (Chicago: University of Chicago Press, 1992); (Berkeley: University of California Press, 1996).
[20] (Chicago: University of Chicago Press, 1999).
[21] (Lanham, MD: University Press of America, 1986).
[22] (Berkeley: University of California Press, 1994).
[23] (Berkeley: University of California Press, 1996).
[24] (New York: Continuum Publishing, 1994).
[25] (Washington, DC: Brookings Institution, 1995).
[26] (New York: Oxford University Press, 2004).

eclipse of empires," he writes, "has given rise to new nationalisms which have developed hegemonies over ethnic and other minorities that are no less oppressive than colonial hegemony.... [Widespread social problems] demand the anthropologist's involvement, not merely as allegedly objective and impartial analyst of culture, but as a participant in unraveling social ills with a view to contributing towards their amelioration. The anthropologist's role has changed from participant observer to observing participant."[27] And he goes on to state as his central thesis that "the definition of a new role for the Buddhist monk, which was one aspect of the movement to modernize Sri Lankan Theravada Buddhism in the twentieth century, has been detrimental to the happiness and well-being of the people of Sri Lanka."[28]

Let it be emphasized that this is a serious scholarly book, carefully documented and reasoned, one that appears to be fully in accord (in the judgment of highly competent scholars of Sri Lanka) with the epistemic requirements of sound description. It would not be true to say that Seneviratne's conclusions are "dictated" (in Putnam's word) by his ethical position, in the sense of doctoring evidence to prove his preconceived ethical convictions.

Seneviratne demonstrates conclusively (among other things) that an important group of monks did indeed hold the views and have the influence he finds so objectionable, and he makes a strong case regarding the deleterious effects of these people on "the happiness and well-being of the people of Sri Lanka." "Related to the monkhood's lack of broad social and human concern is the warmongering propaganda of the elite monks and the theory that a military victory alone would solve Sri Lanka's ethnic problem when it is perfectly clear that, *had the monkhood taken a firm stand for peace, the question would have been easily solved.*"[29] This is a book dedicated to understanding, in a "scientifically reliable way," the effects on ethnic tension and violence of a formidable Sri Lankan religious body. But it is also a book with a strongly "normative" starting point – one might even say, a strongly "advocative" starting point.

The question is whether Seneviratne's "ethical predisposition" is somehow inappropriate, somehow damaging to the investigation he undertakes. It is, frankly, difficult to see how it would be. Of course, ethnonational – or any other – studies may legitimately be undertaken "more neutrally" or more noncommittally, from an ethical point of view. But three points need to be made in regard to Seneviratne's volume. First, conducting his study in the way Seneviratne does by no means invalidates its "epistemic" worth; second,

---

[27] Seneviratne, *Work of Kings*, 6.
[28] Ibid., 7.
[29] Ibid., 324; emphasis added.

adopting an "ethically neutral" stance is itself an ethical choice; and third, finding literature in the field of ethnonational studies that exemplifies such a posture is next to impossible, most likely because there is something ethically odd about assuming an attitude of ethical indifference toward the study of group antagonism and violence.

Two of the central categories of analysis contained in a book such as Jack Snyder's *From Voting to Violence: Democratization and Nationalist Conflict* are, it seems clear, "ethically colored" in an important sense. This example confirms Putnam's second point. In studying the relation of forms of democracy to violence, Snyder, one may safely assume, has an "ethical disposition" toward peace. He wants to understand the connection of political organization to violence, the better to reduce violence and encourage peace. Were that not so, he would not spend so much time toward the end of his book *prescribing* "ways to avert nationalist conflict in an age of democratization," as the title of his lengthy concluding chapter reads.[30]

Snyder's central categories, "civic" and "ethnic nationalism," are more than simply purely descriptive in character. They are evaluatively compared in relation to their respective tendencies to encourage violence. Ethnodemocracy (democracy based on ethnic nationalism), he says, is a "threat to democratic peace." "Any movement away from civic democracy [democracy based on civic nationalism] would undermine the democratic peace because it would deactivate the mechanisms that keep relations between democracies peaceful."[31] He continues,

> Civic nationalisms, like those of the British, the United States, and for the most part the French, base their appeals on loyalty to a set of political ideas and institutions that are perceived as just and effective. Inclusion in the group depends primarily on birth [*jus soli*] or long-term residence with the nation's territory, though sufficient knowledge of the nation's language and institutions to participate in the nation's civil life may be a criterion for the naturalization of resident aliens.... Ethnic nationalisms, like those of the Germans and the Serbs, base their legitimacy on common culture, language, religion, shared historical experience, and/or the myth of shared kinship, and they use these criteria to include or exclude membership from the national group.[32]

Snyder's book is one grand (and in my view successful) argument (carefully documented, carefully argued) in favor of civic democracy and in opposition

---

[30] Snyder, *From Voting to Violence*, 313–353.
[31] Ibid., 352–353.
[32] Ibid., 24.

to ethnodemocracy.[33] Again, one might even say that the book "advocates" civic as opposed to ethnic democracy. It is, however, hard to see how such an "ethically colored" argument invalidates the work. Snyder's book is highly regarded in the study of the politics of ethnonationalism.

In my opinion, the real "father" of modern ethnonational studies is Gunnar Myrdal in his classic work, *An American Dilemma: The Negro Problem and Modern Democracy*[34] (first published in 1944), which by itself "changed American life," according to a review by Harvard historian, Oscar Handlin.[35] By 1963 the book was in its twenty-sixth printing, and according to Handlin, "its recommendations have helped shape the strategy of every organization interested in legislation and in judicial interpretations. It was cited in the Supreme Court decision of 1954 that ended segregation in the public schools and killed the doctrine of separate but equal."[36] It is worth quoting a memorable statement from the author's preface, because "changing American life" was exactly what Myrdal had in mind: "When looking back over the long manuscript [1483 pages!], one main conclusion – which should be stressed here since it cannot be reiterated through the whole book – is this: *that not since Reconstruction has there been more reason to anticipate fundamental changes in American race relations, changes which will involve a development [away from racism and] toward the American ideals.*"[37] Myrdal famously identified these ideals as what he called "the American creed," understood as "the essential dignity of the individual human being, of the fundamental equality of all men, and of certain inalienable rights to freedom, justice, and a fair opportunity [that] represent to the American people the essential meaning of the nation's early struggle for independence."[38]

Although indisputably and unapologetically a work of social and political advocacy, based on unmistakable ethical passion,[39] *An American Dilemma* was

---

[33] His study has been further refined and expanded in his well-reviewed book with Edward Mansfield, *Electing to Fight: Why Democracies Go to War*.
[34] (New York: Harper & Bros. Publishers, 1944).
[35] Handlin, "A Book that Changed American Life," *New York Times Book Review*, April 21, 1963, 1, 27,29.
[36] Ibid., 1
[37] Ibid., xix; author's emphasis.
[38] Ibid., 4.
[39] Myrdal concludes *An American Dilemma* with the following words: "To find the practical formulas for [the] never-ending reconstruction of society is the supreme task of social science. The world catastrophe places tremendous difficulties in our way and may shake our confidence to the depths. Yet we have today in social science a greater trust in the improvability of man and society than we have ever had since the Enlightenment" (1024).
   I must express my deepest appreciation to Sissela Bok, Myrdal's daughter, for kindly sending me a copy of *The Essential Gunnar Myrdal*, edited with commentary by Orjan Appelquist

at the same time, a work of impeccable and innovative scholarship, which has generated all sorts of further studies, including, no doubt, numerous doctoral dissertations. Here is Handlin again: Myrdal's book "drew upon a significant body of sociological, historical and psychological research that specialists had been assembling for two decades. Myrdal was able to incorporate into his own synthesis a valuable fund of information gathered in investigations not previously known."[40]

On the basis, then, of both logical analysis and scholarly practice I have tried to refute any attempt at a radical divorce of ethics from scholarship. But if the basic terms and commitments of both practices are intimately entangled, they are by no means completely indistinguishable. As much rides on accurately marking and maintaining the boundaries between "ethical" and "epistemic values" as it does on appreciating their interdependence.

---

and Stellan Andersson, trans. by Richard Litell, Sonia Wichmann, and others (New York: New Press, 2005). In her illuminating introduction, Sissela Bok calls attention to the concluding words to *An American Dilemma* as an illustration of her father's dedication to wide-ranging social reform (xxiiff.). Additionally, one section of the book is titled "On Evaluation in Research," wherein Myrdal is quoted as indicating "how my conception of the valuation problem has changed.... [Earlier,] I thought there was valuation-free economic theory.... Now, after continued study in many areas, I know that this conception is wrong and that value premises are necessary in order to scientifically observe reality" (54). Elsewhere in the volume, the following words of his, echoing Weber and Putnam, are reproduced: "[S]ocial facts or the behaviour of their quantitative characteristics do not organize themselves into a scientifically analysable system merely by being observed and recorded. A viewpoint, indeed a correlated complex of concepts, is needed, which constitutes a theory. Prior to answers there must be questions, and the questions we raise stem from our interest in the matter, from our valuations. Indeed, our theories and all our scientific knowledge are necessarily pervaded by valuations" (19).

[40] Handlin, "A Book that Changed American Life," 1.

Index

Abdullahi An-Na'im, 83, 84, 85, 86, 87, 88, 89, 90, 91, 93, 94, 95, 97, 99, 100, 102, 103, 106, 107, 108, 111
Abu Ghraib, 52, 306, 312, 314, 315
accommodationism, 212, 215, 219, 220, 223, 241
al Qaeda, 290, 310, 312, 323, 324, 325, 326
American Bar Association, 59, 72, 74, 308
American conservatism, 72, 73
Anabaptists, 160, 201, 206, 220, 221, 222, 223, 224, 227, 241, 250
Anglicanism, 216
anticolonialism, 28, 61, 62, 63, 77, 79
Aquinas, Thomas, 257
Asad, Talal, 27, 28, 93, 94, 95, 96, 97, 98, 100, 101, 102, 103, 104, 108, 226
Augustine, 257
authoritarian secularism, 88
Authorization of the Military Use of Force (AUMF), 317, 325

Bible, the, 95, 192, 196, 252, 256, 264
Bill of Rights, 244, 248, 249, 254, 270, 293
bin Laden, Osama, 288, 289, 290, 309, 358
Buddhism, 88, 394, 395
Bush administration, 102, 275, 276, 278, 279, 280, 293, 294, 296, 298, 299, 301, 302, 303, 305, 306, 307, 309, 310, 311, 315, 316, 317, 319, 321, 329
Bush, George W., 97, 292, 293, 295, 297, 301, 303, 318, 356

C. v. United Kingdom, 130
Calvin, John, 178, 180, 181, 182, 183, 184, 185, 186, 187, 195, 196, 223, 224, 225, 226, 227, 228, 229, 230, 232, 235, 236, 237, 238, 239, 240, 256, 257, 258, 259, 262, 265, 268
Calvinism, 110, 178, 179, 180, 182, 183, 184, 185, 186, 187, 189, 195, 196, 208, 223, 230, 231, 234, 235, 237, 238, 240, 241, 243, 253, 256, 257, 264, 265, 270
Cambridge Agreement, 247, 251
Carroll, James, 161, 162, 163, 164, 168
Carter, Jimmy, 63, 77, 148, 149, 156
Catholics, Catholicism, 60, 88, 102, 108, 161, 182, 209, 210, 212, 214, 215, 216, 217, 230, 238
Cheney, Dick, 296, 297, 300, 305, 311, 312, 320
Chomsky, Noam, 336
Civil Rights Act, 76
Clinton, Bill, 101, 370
Cold War, 59, 61, 72, 73, 207, 277, 279, 311, 349, 353
collective liberation, 61, 62, 66, 76, 77
communism, 60, 73, 334, 340, 349, 350
conciliarism, 210, 211, 212, 215, 216, 219, 224, 226, 227, 238
Conference on Security and Cooperation in Europe, 62
Confucianism, 88
constitutional essentials, 115, 116, 118, 119, 122, 123, 125, 126, 140, 141, 142
contractualism, 29
Convention on the Elimination of All Forms of Racial Discrimination, 139, 147
Cotton, John, 188, 233, 234, 251, 252, 253
Cromwell, Oliver, 69, 185, 256

399

Dahlab v. Switzerland, 133
Dalai Lama, 154, 158
Darby v. Sweden, 130
Decalogue, 110, 183, 194, 225, 228, 229, 236, 239, 257, 262, 364
democratic society, 36, 66, 118, 125, 133, 134, 135
dignity, 31, 32, 34, 123, 190, 196, 306, 386, 397
Du Bois, W. E. B., 75, 76
Dworkin, Ronald, 30, 304, 376

Efstatiou v. Greece, 128
Elizabeth, Queen of England, 27, 216, 217, 240, 346
Emanuel, Rahm, 321
English Civil War, 69
Enlightenment, the, 103, 188, 189, 190, 206, 245, 353, 397
ethnonational studies, 389, 390, 394, 396, 397
ethnoreligious nationalism, 144, 202
European Convention for the Protection of Human Rights (ECHR), 113, 126, 132, 134, 135
Evans, Malcolm, 112, 137
extranatural appeals, 364, 375, 376, 377, 379, 381, 384

fact/value dichotomy, 389, 390
fascism, 25, 38, 42, 47, 53, 60, 98, 144, 169, 192
Fish, Stanley, 149
Foreign Intelligence Surveillance Act (FISA), 317, 318, 324, 328
forum externum, 364, 384
forum internum, 128, 129, 130, 131, 132, 133, 135, 141, 364, 384, 385
freedom of religion or belief, 35, 40, 54, 55, 93, 99, 111, 112, 113, 114, 118, 119, 123, 124, 125, 126, 127, 128, 134, 137, 138, 142, 155, 170, 171, 172, 173, 183, 186, 188, 190, 204, 207, 230, 243, 255
French Declaration of the Rights of Man and Citizen, 58, 243, 245
Freud, Sigmund, 193, 371
fundamental human welfare, 34, 46

Geneva Conventions, 275, 277, 286, 287, 288, 305, 306, 309, 310, 311, 312, 315, 321
Genocide Convention, 34, 64, 75

Gentili, Alberico, 238, 239, 240
Gerson, Jean, 67, 209, 211, 212, 214, 215
Graham, Billy, 73, 75
Grotius, Hugo, 28, 58, 67, 68, 69, 238

Halberstam, David, 334, 335, 336, 337, 338, 340
Hamdan v. Rumsfeld, 277, 309, 310, 319
Hamilton, Alexander, 58
Hamilton, Marci, 170, 171, 172, 173, 175, 176, 303
Hasan and Chaush v. Bulgaria, 135
Hawthorne, Nathaniel, 180
Hinduism, 87, 88
Hitler, Adolf, 38, 42, 48, 49, 50, 51, 53, 55, 56, 92, 98, 124, 276, 281, 282, 283, 284, 285, 287, 330, 344, 373, 381
Hobbes, Thomas, 58, 67, 68, 208
Hoffmann, Stanley, 59
Holocaust, 38, 42, 58, 64, 65, 66, 191
Hooker, Richard, 213, 215, 216, 217, 218, 219
Human Rights Commission, 75, 76, 115
Human Rights Committee, 105, 107, 114, 115, 119, 121, 126, 127, 129, 135, 136, 142, 148, 278
human rights revolution, 144, 192
Hume, David, 43
Hussein, Saddam, 280, 281, 299, 300

International Atomic Energy Agency (IAEA), 299
International Bill of Rights, 32
International Covenant on Civil and Political Rights (ICCPR), 32, 33, 35, 36, 37, 54, 77, 78, 105, 106, 113, 115, 118, 119, 121, 124, 126, 129, 132, 135, 138, 140, 143, 146, 147, 148, 151, 155, 277, 278, 285
International Covenant on Economic, Social and Cultural Rights (ICESCR), 32, 37, 146, 155, 159
International Criminal Court, 101, 288, 294
international human rights law, 30
Iraq War, 333, 344
Islam, 27, 31, 32, 83, 86, 87, 88, 89, 90, 91, 93, 98, 102, 108, 111, 161, 164, 165, 166, 289, 290, 353, 354

Jahangir, Asma, 114, 138, 142
Jefferson, Thomas, 153, 172, 237, 238, 255, 350, 352, 380

Index

Jellinek, George, 71, 72, 243, 244, 245, 249, 250, 270, 271
jihad, 289, 290
Johnson, Lyndon, 340
Judaism, 31, 89, 98, 103, 109, 111, 163, 166
jus ad bellum, 337
jus cogens, 34, 100
just war, 337, 338, 339, 341, 344, 345, 354, 355, 356, 357, 359, 361
justpeace, 205, 207, 241

Kant, Immanuel, 117, 196, 339, 378
Karaduman v. Turkey, 133
Khalid Sheik Mohammed, 321, 322
King, Martin Luther, 76, 349

League of Nations, 33
Leibowitz, Yeshayahu, 103, 104, 109
Leiter, Brian, 170, 171, 173, 174, 175, 176, 368
Lemkin, Raphael, 64, 65
Levellers, 69, 70, 71, 186, 187, 189, 244
liberal peace, 202, 203, 204, 205, 206, 207, 241
Lincoln, Abraham, 348, 352
Locke, John, 67, 68, 69, 70, 189, 190, 237, 380
logic of pain, 48, 51, 53, 54, 55, 92, 124, 369, 373, 374, 375, 376
Lord Acton, 184, 276
Luther, Martin, 76, 178, 213, 349

MacIntyre, Alasdair, 26
Madison, James, 172, 237, 238, 249, 250, 255, 264, 266, 267, 277, 348, 350, 352, 380
Malik, Charles, 39, 59, 120
manifestation of religion or belief, 107, 133, 139, 141
Margalit, Avishai, 149, 160
Maritain, Jacques, 29, 60
Martha Minow, 149, 150, 151
Marx, Karl, 349
Massachusetts Bay Colony, 231, 233, 236, 246, 247, 251, 252, 253, 254, 255, 258, 259, 265, 268
McCarthyism, 73
McGinn, Colin, 365, 366, 367, 368, 370, 371, 377, 378, 382
Metropolitan Church of Bessarabia and others v. Moldova, 134
Mill, John Stuart, 154, 156, 157, 158, 161, 174

modernity, 93, 353
moral apriori, 48, 50
Morgenthau, Hans, 59
Morsink, Johannes, 33, 38, 39, 66, 100, 363
Moyn, Samuel, 28, 57, 58, 60, 61, 62, 63, 64, 65, 66, 67, 68, 69, 70, 71, 72, 76, 77, 79
Muentzer, Thomas, 220
Mussolini, 48
Myrdal, Gunnar, 397, 398

NAACP, 75, 76
Nagel, Thomas, 365, 366, 369, 371, 372, 373, 376, 378, 382
Napoleon, 48, 202
National Council of Churches, 73
National Socialism, 282, 344
Nazism, 48, 49, 65, 66, 77, 101, 138, 140, 193, 281, 282, 284, 291, 302, 303
Nicholas of Cusa, 211
Niebuhr, Reinhold, 59, 346, 347, 348, 349, 350, 351, 352, 353, 354, 356, 359, 360, 361
Niebuhrian method, 351, 358, 359, 360
Nietzsche, Friedrich, 193
Novak, David, 31
Nussbaum, Martha, 28, 55, 237

Obama, Barack, 275, 276, 278, 318, 319, 320, 321, 322, 323, 324, 325, 328, 329, 331, 346, 347, 348, 351, 352, 353, 354, 355, 356, 357, 358, 359, 360, 361

Patriot Act, 279, 304, 305, 316, 328
political constructivism, 117, 124
Powell, Colin, 292, 293, 295, 297, 298, 300, 303, 305, 313
predestination, 178, 182, 187, 256
Presbyterianism, 153, 177, 178, 179
Prophet Muhammad, 87
Protestantism, 59, 88, 219
 Ecumenical, 60, 73, 74
 Evangelical, 73, 74, 75
public good, 119, 126, 173
public reason, 85, 116, 117, 121, 140, 141
Puritans, Puritanism, 69, 71, 72, 109, 178, 179, 180, 186, 187, 217, 218, 230, 232, 233, 243, 244, 246, 247, 248, 249, 251, 255, 256, 271, 364, 387
Putnam, Hilary, 342, 343, 390, 391, 392, 393, 394, 395, 396

Qur'an, 86, 181

Rasul v. Bush, 306, 309, 319
rational competence, 40, 55
Rawls, John, 29, 30, 85, 115, 116, 117, 118, 119, 120, 121, 122, 123, 126, 174
Reagan, Ronald, 63
Reformation, the, 71, 164, 207, 208, 209, 210, 212, 213, 216, 218, 219, 223, 224, 230, 241, 243, 244
Reformed Christianity, 177, 178, 179, 182, 192, 194, 195, 208, 216, 217, 229, 230, 234, 384
reformism, 212, 223, 241
religious nationalism, 201, 216
religious pluralism, 32, 83, 88, 107, 108, 116, 128, 135, 239
Renaissance Humanism, 210, 224
renovationism, 212, 219, 223, 241
rights
  basic, 116, 118, 119, 122, 123, 125, 126, 140, 141, 194, 225, 226
  civil, 75, 100, 186, 265, 269, 270, 279, 281, 304, 307, 333
  derogable, 37, 53, 77, 118
  human rights language, 25, 26, 27, 28, 29, 30, 32, 39, 40, 55, 59, 60, 62, 64, 65, 72, 76, 78, 79, 92, 121, 162, 169, 363
  individual, 28, 47, 48, 61, 62, 66, 77, 78, 79, 246, 248, 265, 270, 282
  inherent, 30, 244
  morally grounded, 37
  natural, 58, 61, 67, 68, 69, 70, 71, 76, 77, 185, 189, 211, 225, 237, 249, 269, 363, 364, 375, 376, 379, 380, 381, 384, 385, 386
  nonderogable, 37, 40, 51, 53, 77, 286
  political, 37, 40, 54, 104, 234
  right simpliciter, 46
Rome Statute, 123, 288
Roosevelt, Eleanor, 75, 78
Rorty, Richard, 26, 149, 153, 160
Rousseau, Jacques, 245
Rumsfeld, Donald, 277, 296, 297, 300, 305, 307, 309, 311, 319

Sachedina, Abdulaziz, 31, 32, 88, 102, 108
Sahin v. Turkey, 134
Salvador Allende, 62
Searle, John, 365, 366, 367, 368, 369, 371, 382

secular moral foundationalism, 32
secular state, 83, 84, 85, 89, 93, 97, 98, 109, 111
Seligman, Adam, 161, 162, 166, 167, 168
Seneviratne, H. L., 394, 395
September 26, 275, 276, 278, 279, 281, 289, 291, 293, 294, 303, 304, 307, 308, 311, 312, 315, 316, 317, 321, 341, 356
Servetus, Michael, 181, 182, 229
Shari'a, 83, 86, 87, 90, 91, 108
Skinner, Quentin, 215
Socialism, 38, 62, 77, 282
Soroush, Abdolkarim, 89, 102, 161, 162, 164, 165, 166, 168
sovereignty of conscience, 130, 172, 182, 184, 187, 190, 191, 197, 228, 383
St. Paul, 110, 163, 192, 214
Stalin, Joseph, 48
state of nature, 47, 212
States Parties, 33, 34, 96, 100, 285, 288, 303
Stout, Jeffrey, 28, 185
Sullivan, Winifred, 170, 171, 172, 175, 176
Supreme Court, the, 43, 235, 275, 277, 306, 309, 310, 312, 316, 319, 321, 323, 331, 397

Talal Asad, 27, 93
Taylor, Paul, 127, 128, 129, 135, 136
The Immanent Frame, 27
Thlimmenos v. Greece, 131
Thomist, 39, 120, 212
Tierney, Brian, 67, 68, 102, 103, 161, 162, 164, 168
two-tiered approach to justification, 36, 92, 98, 123, 363, 365

UN Charter, 33, 74, 75, 276, 283, 284, 294, 301, 302, 330, 350, 355
UN Declaration of Human Rights, 284
UN Declaration of the Rights of Indigenous Peoples, 78
UN Declaration on the Elimination of All Forms of Intolerance and Discrimination (DEID), 113, 114, 137, 145, 155
UN Special Rapporteur on Freedom of Religion or Belief, 113, 114, 115, 118, 121, 127, 135, 136, 137, 138, 140, 142
UNESCO, 29
United Nations Charter, 97, 275, 277, 278, 281, 283, 302, 330

United States Constitution, 243, 244, 246, 248, 250, 253, 255, 264, 270, 277, 353
Universal Declaration of Human Rights (UDHR), 25, 28, 30, 32, 34, 35, 36, 37, 38, 39, 40, 42, 47, 48, 51, 54, 60, 61, 64, 65, 66, 74, 76, 78, 79, 91, 113, 118, 119, 120, 121, 123, 124, 125, 129, 133, 140, 190, 283, 293, 350, 373, 375, 376, 383
utopianism, 61, 62, 63, 64, 65, 66, 77, 79

V. v. The Netherlands, 128
Valsamis v. Greece, 128
Vietnam War, 317, 332, 333, 334, 335, 336, 337, 338, 340, 341, 342, 343, 345

Ward, Nathaniel, 251, 252, 253, 346
Watergate, 63

weapons of mass destruction (WMD), 280, 299, 300, 301
Weber, Max, 179, 184, 385, 386, 387, 389, 392, 393, 398
Weimar Constitution, 48, 276, 281
Whitgift, John, 213, 215, 216, 217, 218
Williams, Roger, 72, 109, 110, 172, 187, 188, 195, 197, 233, 234, 235, 236, 237, 238, 243, 249, 250, 254, 255, 256, 257, 258, 260, 261, 262, 263, 264, 265, 266, 267, 268, 269, 270, 271, 364, 371, 380, 387
Wilson, Woodrow, 348, 350
Winthrop, John, 188, 231, 247, 251, 252
Wittgenstein, Ludwig, 51
Wolterstorff, Nicholas, 30, 31
World War II, 25, 28, 60, 64, 66, 72, 76, 77, 98, 99, 114, 141, 144, 281, 283, 287, 291, 333, 344, 350

Lightning Source UK Ltd.
Milton Keynes UK
UKOW06n0054150515

251563UK00003B/67/P